SNOW FLOWERS

SNOW FLOWERS

Hungarian Jewish Women in an Airplane Factory, Markkleeberg, Germany.

Zahava Szász Stessel

Madison • Teaneck
Fairleigh Dickinson University Press

Associated University Presses
2010 Eastpark Boulevard
Cranbury, NJ 08512

The paper used in this publication meets the requirements of the American National Standard for Permanence of Paper for Printed Library Materials Z39.48-1984.

Library of Congress Cataloging-in-Publication Data

Stessel, Zahava Szász, 1930–
Snow flowers : Hungarian Jewish women in an airplane factory, Markkleeberg, Germany / Zahava Szász Stessel.
p. cm.
Includes bibliographical references and index.
ISBN 978-0-8386-4178-1 (alk. paper)
1. Markkleeberg (Concentration camp) 2. Holocaust, Jewish (1939–1945)—Germany—Markkleeberg. 3. World War, 1939–1945—Concentration camps—Germany—Markkleeberg. 4. World War, 1939–1945—Prisoners and prisons, German. 5. World War, 1939–1945—Conscript labor—Germany—Markkleeberg. 6. Jews, Hungarian—Germany—Markkleeberg—History—20th century. I. Title.
D805.5.M37S74 2009
940.53′18134—dc22

2008022599

PRINTED IN THE UNITED STATES OF AMERICA

I dedicate this book as a memorial to the babies that were never born to Markkleeberg camp survivors.

Contents

Foreword 9

Acknowledgments 11

Introduction 13

1. Establishment of the Camp 25
2. Origin of the Prisoners and Their Road to Markkleeberg 40
3. Arrivals, Housing, and Work in the Quarry 58
4. Life in the Camp 79
5. Prisoner Officials, Sick Room, and the Babies Born in Markkleeberg 103
6. Finance and Work at Junkers 123
7. The Camp's Informal Structure and Our State of Mind 143
8. The Commandant and His Staff 160
9. Cultural Activities and Holidays 176
10. Human Relations with the Factory Workforce and French Political Prisoners 194
11. Smaller Factories, the Final Days and Evacuation of the Camp 215

12. The Death March 246

13. Liberation 272

14. Life of a Survivor 289

15. Return to Markkleeberg 320

Appendix A. Markkleeberg Prisoners' List 334

Appendix B. List of Arrivals at Theresienstadt 371

Appendix C. The Songs in Their Original Text 386

Appendix D. Photographs 394

Notes 411

Bibliography 424

Index 433

Foreword

PERHAPS NO OTHER EVENT IN WORLD HISTORY HAS BEEN AS THOROUGHLY documented as the Holocaust. More than 5,000 independent and periodical references pertain to the destruction of Hungarian Jewry alone. The pace of the investigations and publications has been accelerated by the systemic changes of 1989–90 that followed the collapse of the communist system in Central Eastern Europe. The opening of the archives of the former Soviet bloc nations made it possible for researchers in all fields of the social sciences to gain new insights into many hitherto overlooked aspects of the Holocaust.

This new book by Zahava Szász Stessel is a case in point. Dr. Stessel offers a well-documented, autobiographical, scholarly account of the trials and tribulations of Hungarian Jewish women who had been transferred from the death camp of Auschwitz to Markkleeberg, Germany. Her study focuses on the daily life of approximately 1,300 female forced laborers deployed in the Junkers aircraft manufacturing plant in Markkleeberg between August 1944 and early spring 1945. Among these women were the author and her teenage sister. The slave laborers were exploited to the limit with the speedy mass production of the Ju 87 Stuka dive-bombers essential for the German military, which was confronted with the rapid advance of the Allied forces.

The women slave laborers were leased by the SS and they were under control of the SS. After work the prisoners returned under SS escort back to the concentration camp, situated near the factory. As Stessel vividly describes, the women tried to cope with their harsh life in the camp and the exhausting factory labor by composing and singing songs and establishing a support system of camp-sisters and camp-families. Their upbringings and the background of strong family ties characteristic of Hungarian Jewish life played a crucial part in their survival. Back in the camp after a hard day's work, the women also had to endure the cruelties of the SS and *Aufseherinen,* the women overseers in military uniform, who were often just as cruel as their male counterparts.

In contrast to the SS, some of the civilian German workers in the factory, as Stessel reveals, were quite humane. The occasional friendly smile of a civilian worker or the treasure of an imperceptibly passed small sandwich was enough to lift the spirits of the women. Stessel recalls the humane behavior of a German civilian worker who whispered them the good news about the expected imminent end of the war. This worker empathized with the suffering of the women, because he too was in pain: his two sons in the Wehrmacht had been reported as "missing."

The ordeal of the slave laborers continued during the death marches that followed the evacuation of Markkleeberg in April 1945. Some of the prisoners managed to escape, only to encounter Germans with different reactions to their ordeal. They met ordinary Germans who would not believe their stories about Auschwitz and the other camps. Some of these Germans were so hostile, Stessel reveals, that they chased the survivors out of their towns. Others, however, were more sympathetic. Many of these were in mourning themselves, having lost friends and family members in battles or in the wake of the massive Allied bombings. These Germans and the surviving Jewish women had something in common: they shared the great human tragedies that the Nazies had caused by their foolhardy attempt to build a New Order in Europe. The Third Reich, which was envisioned to last a thousand years, will forever remain the darkest chapter in the history of Germany—a stark reminder of the evil consequences of racism and anti-Semitism.

The story of *Snow Flowers* is gripping and authentic—a "must" read for all those interested in combating the evils of discrimination and racism and in advancing the cause of toleration and pluralism.

Randolph L. Braham
Distinguished Professor Emeritus
Graduate Center/CUNY

Acknowledgments

THE BOOK *SNOW FLOWERS* WAS BORN AT A VISIT TO BUCHENWALD. There in the archives I found the Transport Lists of Markkleeberg prisoners. Looking carefully at the old and dusty document, I saw the names of my fellow inmates emerge. They were there—the girls and women—with whom I had shared life in the camp. I heard their voices and I knew I had to let them speak.

Writing is a solitary activity, yet it doesn't mean that one writes entirely alone. I was privileged at the beginning of my research to find some of the older women of the camp and factory still alive. Their extended memory, keen perception, and insightful comments added rich details to the story of *Snow Flowers*. The names of my fellow survivors and their testimonies are recorded individually in the references and bibliography.

One of those camp sisters whose memory didn't fade with the transport list of Markkleeberg was my friend Hava Hartmann Kleinberg. Hava was instrumental in establishing a memorial at the campsite. With her energy and humor she brightened our visit to Germany. Hava accompanied me several times to Markkleeberg. We planned to return once more after this book was published. Unfortunately, on April 27, 2007 Hava suddenly passed away. May *Snow Flowers* be a memorial to her devoted spirit.

My thanks also go to Kathy Zelmanovitz Goldstein, another of my Markkleeberg camp sisters. Kathy came with me from New York. In Markkleeberg we joined Hava Hartmann Kleinberg and rekindled that old feeling of camaraderie that nourished us in the camp.

The closest of my camp sisters is still my real sister, Erzsike, or Hava Szász Ginsburg. As we remained alone, when teenagers in Auschwitz, we became substitute parents to each other. I know I would not have survived without her. Hava helped me to recall events from the camps in vivid descriptions.

In Germany, my very special thanks go to Dr. Bernd Klose, Lord Mayor of Markkleeberg. Dr. Klose supported the memorial and invited us for visits. When we arrived we were given a warm welcome and a fine reception. My gratitude is extended also to his lovely wife and the opening of their home to us.

My appreciation is given to Ms. Evelin Müller, who with her kind ways made our visit a pleasant one. I am also grateful to Mr. Andrew Höhn, the local historian, for showing us around the town of Markkleeberg, which we had never seen while in the camp. Mr. Höhn also retraced with us the route of the Death March.

My special thanks to Dr. Irmgard Seidel, Senior Executive at the Buchenwald Memorial. Her compassion and empathy is felt by each survivor who meets her. Dr. Seidel, a writer and researcher, generously provided help and assistance. I extend my thanks also to Rosemarie Hoffman, librarian at the Buchenwald Memorial.

My greatest depth and gratitude is to my daughter Miriam (or Miri) who knows my way of thinking and understands the meaning even beyond my unexpressed thoughts. Miri faithfully read the manuscript and gave me her thoughtful and valuable comments. When in doubt she turned to her husband Dr. Oded Shenkar, who himself is the author of several books. Oded was also encouraging when work on the book was a bit too overwhelming.

Joining in emotional support was my younger daughter Yonit Levy. With her quiet assurance Yonit was at my side in years of writing and researching.

The best relief came from the company of my children and grandchildren. After ten years of childlessness and several miscarriages I regard my daughters as miracle children and my grandchildren as the continuation of the miracle. Since the publication of my first book, in addition to the children living in Israel, Dov Israel Levy and Ella-Tzofia Levy, and in the United States, Keshet and Joshua Shenkar, there is Rakefet (Riki) Shenkar who likes to write mystery stories and Yarin Levy who loves to dance. It is good to spend time in their world.

To Meier, my husband of fifty-nine years and fellow Auschwitz survivor, I am grateful for his quiet appreciation. The snacks he placed silently on the table next to my computer sweetened the harshness of the memories I was writing about. Meier's love, understanding, and support extend beyond the finest words I could express.

My utmost gratitude and greatest debt is to my parents Miriam-Margit and Sándor Szász and grandparents Róza-Rachel and Nathan Szász. They showed me the way to fairness and loyalty that still governs my actions. Their cruel deaths in Auschwitz continue to haunt me as they were never registered—a tragedy beyond the pages of history.

SNOW FLOWERS

Introduction

ON THE OUTSKIRTS OF TOWNS AND CITIES IN GERMANY, THE MEMORY OF World War II turns up in unexpected places. Walking along in a lively neighborhood in an idyllic-looking town, one is suddenly confronted with a reminder of the town's unpleasant past. A small memorial plaque in Markkleeberg, just such a town, recalls a camp under the Third Reich. For me, that place continues to keep me its prisoner for life.

Actually, I was out of that prison for a time while I was finding my way back to the community of free people. I married, completed my education, and worked as a librarian. Then in 1996, a letter from a Ms. Clajus, a German schoolteacher, made me think again about the camp in Markkleeberg. The letter came to me through a friend and former inmate at the camp, Hava Hartmann Kleinberg. Ms. Kleinberg had corresponded with the town of Markkleeberg concerning a memorial at the site of the camp, and Ms. Clajus's query reached her in that way.

In her letter, Mrs. Clajus described that how in 1971, while walking in Wolfswinkel, a section of Markkleeberg, she came across the remnants of barbed wire and barracks. Since she had moved to town only in 1952, after the war, she wanted to know details about the place. People in town could provide limited information. Many did not know, and those who had been involved were reluctant to speak. Ms. Clajus wondered what kind of people had been imprisoned there, where they came from, what they did, and what their treatment was in the camp. She believed that the knowledge would be educational for her students.

Touched by the teacher's interest, I wanted to tell her that the camp had housed prisoners for forced labor in a factory producing aircraft engines for the German war industry. The factory belonged to Junkers, and the majority of the laborers who stood twelve hours per shift, day or night, by the machines or who cut heavy logs of iron bars were fragile Jewish girls from Hungary. Two of them—Katalin and Erzsébet (Erzsike) Szász, age fourteen and thirteen—were from Abaújszántó. We were brought there, my younger sister and I, from Auschwitz-Birkenau by way of Bergen-Belsen to work, even though we could hardly reach the machines.

I wanted to tell her that the winter of 1944–45, especially cold, was harsh as we walked in wooden shoes with no socks, or stood for hours in the snow. We were cold, hungry, and so scared. Those German women overseers, whom we called *Aufseherins* in German, must have been chosen for the job by being the cruelest, most heartless of women. Finally, I wrote a letter to Ms. Clajus, saying that I was moved by her interest and I would like to provide my testimony. The letter remained unanswered. Ms. Clajus, by then, was no longer living in Markkleeberg. Later, the question about the camp surfaced again. This time I was requested to fill out a questionnaire prepared by Dr. Imgard Seidel, from the Buchenwald memorial museum. Dr. Seidel was researching the histories of Buchenwald's women sub-camps, such as Markkleeberg. By answering the questionnaire, I established contact; and in the spring of 1998, when a new memorial tablet was placed on the former campsite in Markkleeberg, my sister and I were among the few invited guests of the city. In my speech at the dedication ceremony, I explained how hard it was to return to Markkleeberg, the place from which I had always wanted to flee. Details about the monument and the dedication ceremony are found in chapter 15.

Being there among the German population who came to the dedication and were eager to hear our story made me a bit more at ease. By their sympathy and their apologetic questions, my prison walls became a bit thinner. Learning that they knew so little about the camp, of which there is almost no physical evidence today, I decided to write down our story. By retelling it, I hope to populate the campsite, projecting images of the past into the present void.

Our Background and Culture

The German occupation created a violent, destructive, and unpredictable realm in which most conventional, traditional, and cultural values eventually lost their effectiveness. For Jews in particular, life was gradually reduced to the most fundamental aspects of human existence. In this situation, our background and upbringing played a crucial part in our survival.

In Markkleeberg, all the Jewish women prisoners were first in Auschwitz-Birkenau. Although born in different parts of Hungary, the culture we shared was common to us all. It rested on principles of humanity and fairness known to all civilized persons. The new rules were as cruelly incomprehensible as the commanding German language that we hardly understood.

Keeping a word or a promise, in my parents' world, overrode all other considerations, as is shown by the following episode. There were two sisters, separated on arrival from their mother by Dr. Josef Mengele, the chief doctor at Auschwitz-Birkenau, where he selected incoming Jews for either labor or extermination. The girls were already among those chosen for work, when suddenly their mother, Mrs. Ethel Herskovitz, who was still relatively young, rushed after them with a bag of homemade cookies. Mrs. Herskovitz, who knew German, implored Dr. Mengele to permit her to give them the cookies, which she had kept in her purse the whole trip. Mengele, probably in a minute of softness or mockery, told the mother okay. Mrs. Herskovitz rushed after her daughters and happily gave them the cookies. No one was watching; the mother could have stayed with the girls. Yet it never entered their minds to take advantage of the situation. Mrs. Herskovitz hurried back to keep her word given to Dr. Mengele. The sisters, mourning their mother, struggled with the question of "what if" for the rest of their lives.[1]

The Nazi racial ideology and practice of persecution was aimed not only at the individual, but also at the specific culture and civilization embodied in each person.[2] My research strengthened the idea that what we had learned at home and the impact of our city or small town of origin governed our mental lives and behavior. As our possessions, clothing, and all vestiges of human identity were gradually taken from us, we retained only what remained in our minds and souls. With this, we entered and—at least some of us—left the camps. "When traditions and conventions are stripped away, Nechama Tac writes, "we are confronted with an uncluttered view of the human condition. The study of the Holocaust provides a unique opportunity to gain a better understanding of life in extremis."[3] The volume offers valuable information about how women reacted in extreme situations. The struggle of two teenaged sisters, Erzsike and myself, and the devotion we shared will be the guiding theme in the book.

The Nazi universe destroyed the families and community, but not the interpersonal relationship of its victims. Self-help and close friendship were important means to survive and existed in a number of different frameworks. A girl who was separated or lost her family attached herself to a group or to another girl and formed a new relationship that became a source of mutual assistance and strength. Some became "camp-sisters" and supported each other. If they remained alone or isolated and had no one to encourage them, to give them help and company, they perished faster than the others. Details about camp-sisters and camp-families can be found in chapter 7.

The most prevalent form of escape from everyday life in the camp was in the songs that were written by the inmates. They raised our spirits and means of resistance. Songs were the only frame in which we could exercise some freedom of speech. The fact that we were all Hungarians, having the common traditions, helped us to act in ways that were familiar and provided emotional support.

The literary creations, mostly in Hungarian, included songs of longing, satire, or rhymes about people and happenings of the camp and the factory. The majority of the songs spread orally, and their composers remain unknown. Many songs were lost, but a few that could be salvaged are translated by the author. They are found in chapters 7 and 9 and integrated into various other chapters.

The Camp and Its Inhabitants

We have to consider that there was a great difference between the German labor camp and the Eastern European extermination center. Markkleeberg was a labor camp (*Arbeitslager*), rather than an extermination camp (*Vernichtungslager*). Our work was needed to manufacture for the war. This must be understood if we are to appreciate how prisoners were able to undertake the activities that we are examining in this book.

To look better, the girls in Markkleeberg put their overalls under the mattress at night. It took out the creases and pressed the edges. The most frequent punishment girls received in Markkleeberg was for washing part of their clothing in the factory's soapy water. Seeing the approach of the commandant SS *Oberscharführer,* Alois Knittel (the *Ober,* as we called him) did not help, as the girl quickly put on the shirt she had just washed. Her number was taken, and after her night's shift, she had to stand hours, for discipline, in front of the SS offices. The SS were an elite military unit of the National Socialist German Workers, or Nazi Party. The initials SS stood for *Schutzstaffel* (Defense Echelon). Despite the severe punishment, girls would take the risk and try again. I will discuss our survivor skills in chapter 4, "Life in the Camp."

Junkers, a firm known for aircraft production, had factories and camps in different places in Germany. The SS "hired out" its prisoners to companies that needed to replace workers serving in the military. No law protected the worker. The Red Cross was not allowed to intervene. The SS received payment for each Jewish worker. The company took full advantage both of the slave and the forced labor. Today the factory, as well as the Junkers Company, does not exist.

Civilians from all over the conquered territories worked for the German war industry. In Markkleeberg, in addition to the Jewish slave laborers producing ammunition for German aviation, there were civilians conscripted for labor from the conquered territories of Europe. They came from Italy, Belgium, France, and the Ukraine, showing the extent of Germany's plan of enslaving the world for its benefit. There were also German civilian workers and men unfit for the army who had to work in the factory.

Seeing the girls work so hard, some German workers and supervisors felt pity for them, as did the foreign technicians and workers. It was forbidden—on pain of death—to establish contact with the Jewish prisoners, but when the SS guards were not nearby, the German workers asked questions, and slowly a network of human relationships developed. There were workers who gave the Jewish women some food during unobserved moments. Fearing the SS, or just not wanting to show his soft side, a German engineer, while adjusting my sister Erzsike's machine, put down a small paper bag and hinted that it was for her. Erzsike looked in and saw a small jam sandwich inside. She was elated; and as she tried to thank him, the elderly man averted his eyes and moved on to the next machine. We shared the sandwich and never forgot the kindness. I mentioned it even in my speech at Markkleeberg at the dedication of the monument by the camp.

The foreign workers, who themselves suffered under the Germans, were sympathetic to the Jewish prisoners. They made our life a bit brighter by giving us a smile or an encouraging word and by bringing news from the front. Details about the relationship of the forced laborers as well as the German civilian workers are covered in chapter 10.

Besides the 1,300 Jewish slave laborers in the camp, there were 250 French women who were political prisoners, living in a separate barrack next to us, inside the barbed wires. They arrived in Markkleeberg in February 1945. The French women were accused of sabotage at Abteroda, where they worked in the factory of BMW. They were brought to Markkleeberg as punishment. The French political prisoners were under the protection of the Red Cross. Their treatment was slightly better. The French women did not work in the factory. Details can be found in chapter 10.

The Death March and Liberation

The camp in Markkleeberg existed from August 31, 1944, until April 13, 1945. Then, as the Allied forces were near and freedom was close, the Germans drove the inmates on a death march. This evacuation was considered the last organized criminal act of the Nazi reign. In Markkleeberg, 1,500 women were sent on the march without food or appropriate clothing. Frightened and hungry, we again found ourselves on the way to the unknown. Details of the death march and our encounter with the German populace are described in chapters 12 and 13.

Liberation meant going home. The idea of going home, with its warm and sweet connotation of the word, kept our spirits up in the camps. At home, reality descended on us with merciless wings of truth: we had no parents, no home, and no belongings. Starting anew, we passed many stations and barriers, both physical and emotional. Our backgrounds and upbringing again served us a bit to go on, just as in the camps. This period will be covered in chapter 14, which will deal also with issues of restitution and Holocaust denial.

The major camps, such as Auschwitz and Buchenwald, were each linked to a dozen or more satellite camps or *Aussenkommando* (outside unit). The camp in Markkleeberg, located in Buchenwald's geographic proximity, was placed under its command. These smaller, nearby operations were built to increase the capacity of the camp system and to provide additional work sites. The story of Markkleeberg offers a glimpse of the hundreds of sub-camps throughout Nazi territory, a part of Holocaust history that still needs substantial investigation.[4]

Methodology and Documentation

The sources employed in this study are of two types:

1. German documents directly related to the history of the camp, including archival materials, transport list, register of arrivals to Theresienstadt on April 29, 1945, and court records
2. Material written by the prisoners themselves, of two kinds:
   a. Sources written in the camp, such as poems and diaries
   b. Autobiographical memoirs published after the war, testimonies of Yad Vashem, and recorded interviews by the researcher

The Transport List

In the closing stages of the war, the SS in Markkleeberg destroyed virtually its entire holding of official records, leaving gaps in our knowledge. With the barbed wire around the camp removed, the few remaining buildings have been converted today to private industry. The factory disappeared like a straw in the storm. Yet seeing the site did not touch me as much as reading the transport list of prisoners brought to the camp. The register contains the names of 1,300 Hungarian Jewish women, who worked in the factory as slave laborers and 250 French women political prisoners.[5] The names listed were those of my comrades, sharing the train ride, the living quarters, the work, the death march. They were the girls with whom I stood in a five-person line in *Appels* (roll calls). I see them and I see myself with short hair and gray uniforms, standing with no coats, barefoot in wooden sandals in the snow.

The transport list is a lifeless document, a dust-collecting inventory, until a name is identified. Then it miraculously becomes real, the people alive, their stories unfolding. The list provides the name, age, place of birth, profession, and prisoner number. The transport list is a fading trace of Hungarian Jewish history. Cities and towns listed as birthplaces of the inmates document the locations where Jews lived in Hungary before the Holocaust. Today there is no Jewish community in most of the provinces mentioned.

The family names in the transport list relate to the memory of our parents, who went directly to the gas chambers; little account remains of their existence. As the survivors of the camp in Markkleeberg married, they changed their last names, leaving the transport list a slim record of their Hungarian past.

To locate survivors from the list, I availed myself of the services of the U.S. Holocaust Memorial Museum in Washington, D.C. I also placed ads in Canadian, Hungarian, and Israeli newspapers and attended national survivors' gatherings. My best sources were always the personal contact of one survivor to another. For many it was the first and the only interview.

We talked, recalling events together. It was a special experience, for both of us, to speak with another who had been there. The survivors talked with me freely, appreciating the idea of having a written history of the camp. I followed each interview with a written communication, sending a photo of the memorial and some pictures from my visit in Markkleeberg. In consequent correspondence, I also sent copies of some Hungarian poems that we knew from home.

I conducted interviews over a period of eight years, between 1998 and 2006. Different versions of the same event, described by several individuals, enriched the testimony. The conversations lasted anywhere from an hour to an hour and a half. Some respondents I met personally and, with others, I talked and recorded on the phone. We spoke several times after the initial interview. I used a set of core questions as a guideline; but in general, I encouraged my respondents to tell their deeper, personal stories. Being one of the camp inmates, I could center on details, which made the topic clearer for both of us.

Speaking Hungarian, our mother tongue, enabled me to interview survivors living in Hungary, Israel, Brazil, Germany, Canada, and the United States. There were a few who spoke in Hebrew or English. Survivors, especially if they are older, often communicate on a deeper level in their first language. In our conversations, we exploited the nuances and the emotion behind the words.

I transcribed each taped interview and translated it into English. The story that emerged is both unique and typical of the persecution of Hungarian Jewish women in Nazi Germany.

Personal Aspects and Motivation

There was tenderness and love among the victims inside the camps. This feeling of communal unity in the face of adversity that we knew from home, surrounded by non-Jews, was recreated in the camp. As I interviewed the survivors, I was temporarily back in that world of camaraderie and fellowship that existed among us, facing the danger and uncertainty of our prison life. Talking about the camps in the security of our homes, we felt a bit of the triumph and joy of liberation that we had never fully experienced before. After almost every interview, I felt that we had touched each others' lives. Listening to my former camp mates, I recovered also some of my forgotten memories about how we lived and the things we dreamed of.

Many of my respondents had reached their eightieth birthdays, which they were happy to relate to me. Some survivors, such as Klára Roth Oren, are less fortunate. At 76, Klára, a resourceful and talented woman, is suffering from cancer. When I first called her, she was in the early stages of her treatment. We could not talk much, but she asked me to call her back. I hesitated at first, but I wanted to keep my promise. Klára, hearing my voice, was so happy. She right away called me by my Hungarian first name, Katalin (or Katika, in the endearing form). As we started to talk, we discovered that I knew some of the verses Klára had composed in Markkleeberg. I knew the songs, but, as in camp life, did not know who the author was. We started to hum together. Gradually, each time I called, Klára filled in forgotten words. Finally, we reconstructed about three verses that she had written in the camp. One of the songs was especially close to Klára's heart. About suffering and hope, singing it gave her comfort even in her current condition.

> The days are passing, so are the weeks and the months;
> And we are still in the camp.
> Since then, we have worked a lot.
> And have been in many camps,
> First Auschwitz, then Krakow.
> Today we are in Leipzig,
> And who knows where we will be tomorrow.
> One thing heartens us:
> That it will not always be like that.
> All will end one day,
> As God comes to our aid.[6]

Every historian must deal with the problem of relative credibility of testimony with regard to a variety of facts and figures such as names, dates, and numbers. My concern in every interview was the trustworthiness of the respondent's account, especially after such a lapse of time. One way to validate was to compare with other sources. I also retrieved testimonies previously given to Yad Vashem by my interviewee. If I felt some doubt about something, I asked other survivors. I required at least two witnesses saying the same to use the information obtained. Existing German documents made it possible to correct certain inaccuracies. In other cases, the consistency of information over a number of testimonies served as evidence of its validity.

Although the history of World War II is well researched, hundreds of slave-labor camps such as Markkleeberg have remained a blank page in the annals of the Third Reich. The lack of scholarly interest in the subject stemmed from a dearth of German documentary sources, which had either been lost or deliberately destroyed, and the language difficulties. The testimonies of former prisoners were recorded in several languages and never translated into English. Adding to the lack of information is the fact that, in small camps, the management was interested in hiding the degree of its involvement and so destroyed the documents. Thus, many details and the extent of the profit made from the slave labor will never be fully known.

I feel fortunate that, in almost our final hours, I still had the chance to salvage the narrative from our collective memory. When there are no more survivors, then perhaps future archivists will obtain access to certain papers that today are still unavailable, but they will lack the principal source. They will not have the living memory of the witnesses to convey, in their own language, to a fellow camp mate and survivor.

Acts of inhumanity and heights of human greatness shed light on both our way of life and our way of death in the camps. Research into the Holocaust, as this book shows, deals not only with a study of human evil, but also with human courage, thus holding seeds of hope.

The book records our collective experience and our personal stories: how we struggled, what we went through. Yet the truth was much worse. It can never really be told. We cannot tell our deepest humiliation. We cannot even face it ourselves. Being survivors near the end of our lives, we are more eager to tell our stories. We salvage memories for the future as much as for the past, to memorialize our parents and the world we knew. What makes me write, above all, are the silences I want to break: the silence of the barracks; the silence of the transport list; the silence of the SS; the silence of my lost parents, grandparents, and the other victims. I want to make them speak; I want them to be heard.

As we look at the empty place where the World Trade Center once stood, we do not want to accept that emptiness, the eternal silence. We want to bring back a little of the sparkle and the traces of the lives that it once held.

Recounting our life in the camp, which was still close to the spirit of the world of our fathers, I give tribute to my parents and our heritage. Thanks to them and their teaching, we acted as human beings, even in the most trying conditions.

Describing life and our interpersonal relationships in the camp, I want to show appreciation to the values of the pre-Holocaust Jewish world and Jewish life. The ethics, traditions, and image of those days were still with us and governed our actions in Markkleeberg.

I am grateful for the years given to us. At thirteen, as a child unfit to work, Erzsike, my sister, would have been condemned by the Germans to death. The miracle that we left alive, probably because we looked like twins, makes me humble all my life. Erzsike is the youngest returnee to our town. Although I had a few classmates, Erzsike had no one from her class who survived Auschwitz.

May this volume serve as—an ancient Jewish memorial medium—words on paper. For me it will also be an inscription that I have been composing the last sixty years on the nonexistent tombstones of my parents, grandparents, and the other Hungarian victims of the Holocaust.

1

Establishment of the Camp

LOCATED IN THE STATE OF SAXONY, ABOUT FOUR MILES SOUTH OF LEIPzig, Markkleeberg is a picturesque town amid rolling hills and rivers, with acacia trees, colorful flowers, and large open places. The population in 1939 was 18,109; today it is about 24,000. According to Ingeborg Weinberger, a former Jewish resident of Markkleeberg, and Andreas Höhn, a local historian, there were between fifty and sixty Jewish families in Markkleeberg before the war. For religious services, they had to go to Leipzig because no synagogue existed in Markkleeberg. Ironically, some of the Jews lived in Gautzschen, close to the concentration camp in Markkleeberg West.[1]

JUNKERS

Leipzig was an important center for the German air force in World War II. The company Junkers Flugzeug und Motorenwerke A.G. (Junkers Aircraft and Engine Works A.G.) had a large workplace close to the airport of Leipzig-Mockau. Parts of the JU 88, the dive-bomber, were built and mounted there.[2] Junkers JU 87 Stuka dive-bomber was one of Luftwaffe's (German air force) most effective aerial weapons and an integral part of Blitzkrieg (lightning war) strategy. When German Nazi leader Rudolf Hess created an international sensation by secretly parachuting into Scotland on an abortive mission to negotiate peace between Britain and Germany, his airplane was built by Junkers.

Traveling in the region today, one can see signs designating former camps. The plaques are from the time of Russian occupation and do not mention the fact that the prisoners were mostly Jewish.

As the war continued and the need for production of warplanes increased, the Junkers Flugzeug und Motorenwerke A.G., with the main office at Dessau, decided to open a new plant. Realizing the hazard of Allied bombing, the firm was looking for safer locations. Markkleeberg was a good site. So, in 1943, the Junkers firm rented production spaces from Stoehr & Company, a weaving plant located at 1 Stöhrstasse, in the

Gautzschen section of Markkleeberg.[3] The area was quite secluded, in a town with a relatively small population. There were good rail connections to Leipzig and other locations.

In September 1943, Junkers sent a letter to the city administration advising it of the plan and preparations for an ammunition factory. The branch in Markkleeberg was called Junkers Flugzeug und Motorenwerke A.G. Motorenbau Zweigwerk Markkleeberg. Special permits for the expansion of the armaments industry were granted speedily because of the situation at the front and continuing air attacks by Allied bombers. A few representatives from the town of Markkleeberg tried to object that an armaments factory built in the middle of a residential settlement would potentially make their town an Allied target, but their objections were unheeded. The plant began its operation in October 1943.[4] At first, the same workers were employed who had worked in the spinning and weaving factory, among them a considerable number of women. Junkers' original employees were the engineers and supervisors, professional German workers excused from the army, but there was a shortage of low-level personnel. As the war continued, the number of German women and men available for work did not suffice. Forced labor soon followed.

The Workforce

The Nazi program of forced labor began with compulsory work decrees inside Germany. At first, both conscripted and volunteer labor forces from the area were used. Then these were extended to the occupied territories. During 1939 and 1940, thousands of men and women came voluntarily to work in German agriculture, industry, or domestic service. As the need for manpower increased in mining, building, and war production, voluntary recruitment was replaced by coercion and terror. Forced laborers could be experts or assistants in the weapons industry, as well as domestic personnel in the homes of the National Socialist leaders.[5]

Military setbacks, particularly in Russia, forced Germany to intensify the system and fully mobilize its economy for war. Labor, especially that of foreigners, was systematically exploited. More and more Belgian, French, Dutch, Italian, Yugoslav, Polish, Slovak, Czech, and Ukrainian laborers were used in the armament industry. Forced-labor camps were constructed to accommodate the workers, first in Eastern Europe and later in Germany itself.

In Markkleeberg, the Junkers factory employed forced laborers in addition to the German civilian workers. They were the so-called "free-willing," some of whom were volunteers and some were forced to come from the German-occupied territories. The foreign workers volunteered at first because they were promised good pay and good food. When the number of volunteers was not enough, workers were obtained by conscription. Civilians all over the conquered territories of Europe were conscripted for labor.

The working camps reflected the policy of the Third Reich to use the workforce of the conquered or annexed countries for the benefit of Germany. They were made up of three levels:

1. The population of the occupied country, on which compulsory labor for the Reich was imposed
2. Forced laborers, including prisoners of war, who were brought to work camps within Germany itself, either as voluntary recruits or as the victims of terror tactics
3. Prisoners of large concentration camps hired out to private employers and controlled by the SS

The Nazis' primary instrument of terror, the SS, oversaw the building of the concentration camps and served as staff members and executioners in them.[6]

German corporations exploited millions of non-Jewish forced laborers, although on terms somewhat different from those faced by the Jewish slave workers. Early in the war, for example, foreign "guest workers" from France, Belgium, Italy, and other countries were actually paid small amounts for their work. By late 1943, however, the large majority of these foreign workers had been imprisoned, in effect, by the companies that "employed" them. Most were forbidden to return home, and the salaries supposedly sent home to their families ended up in German government hands. Those caught attempting to escape corporate concentration camps faced death through hard labor at the hands of the SS.[7]

The Wannsee Conference

On January 20, 1942, sixteen high-ranking SS officers met in an elegant villa in a suburb of Berlin to plan the "final solution to the Jewish question." It was attended by Nazi senior bureaucrats led by Reinhard Heydrich, head of the SS and Gestapo, and it included Adolf Eichmann, chief of Jewish affairs for the Reich Central Security Office. The meeting took ninety minutes. This is all the time they needed to approve the rounding up of all Jews throughout Europe to transport them eastward. The final protocol of the Wannsee Conference did not explicitly mention extermination; but within a few months after the meeting, the first gas chambers were installed at Auschwitz and Treblinka. After the Wannsee Conference, Jews from all over occupied Europe were systematically evacuated to concentration and extermination camps, where they were either killed or forced into slave labor.

Responding to pressures from the Ministry of Defense to enable industries achieve their prescribed production quotas, the SS agreed to provide German defense industries with slave labor drawn from the inmate population.[8] The camps were transformed from detention centers to slave-labor operations. Their primary purpose was no longer political, but economic. After the Wannsee Conference, the principal inmates of the concentration camps, instead of political enemies and prisoners of war, were Jews. Although these developments were at first limited to the territories in the east, with the military failure of the German Sixth army at Stalingrad in 1943, the flow of foreign prisoners to the labor pool slowed. After that, more and more concentration camp prisoners were used in weapons' production within the old borders of Germany. There is no doubt of the economic strength of the Third Reich and the benefits to the German population derived from unpaid work of the millions of starved prisoners that were locked in hundreds of anonymous camps in Europe.

The Forced-Labor Camp in Markkleeberg

In the beginning, the forced laborers in the Junkers factory at Markkleeberg were from France, Belgium, Italy, Holland, Poland, Russia, and Yugoslavia. They were young and, except for a small minority, unmarried. The forced laborers were allowed freedom of movement, but they had to report for work daily and were under supervision. They also received a small wage. The hostelries of Schloss Rheinsberg, Damhirsch, Sonne-Kantine, Friedrichsheim in Connewitz, and the Waldschenke were converted to mass housings.

Later, on Eintracht 04, the former athletic ground at 270 Equipagenweg, Markkleeberg, seven barracks were built for 768 persons. With German efficiency, seventeen points prescribed how doors, toilets, and sleeping quarters had to look. The blueprint shows a camp for 768 men.[9] Some changes were made during execution of the plan; and the camp eventually housed 1,539 prisoners. The camp was in western Markkleeberg, in the section called Wolfswinkel. The city council was concerned with the complaints of Markkleeberg's Wolfswinkel section residents who were unhappy about foreigners in the area and the changes to their suburban community. The foreigners walked around the neighborhood during their free time, and, according to residents, they stole fruit from the gardens and behaved in ways that required extended police activity.[10] The inhabitants of Wolfswinkel were unhappy with the changing character of the community. A few Markkleebergers tried to object to the fact that an armaments factory was built in the middle of a residential settlement.[11]

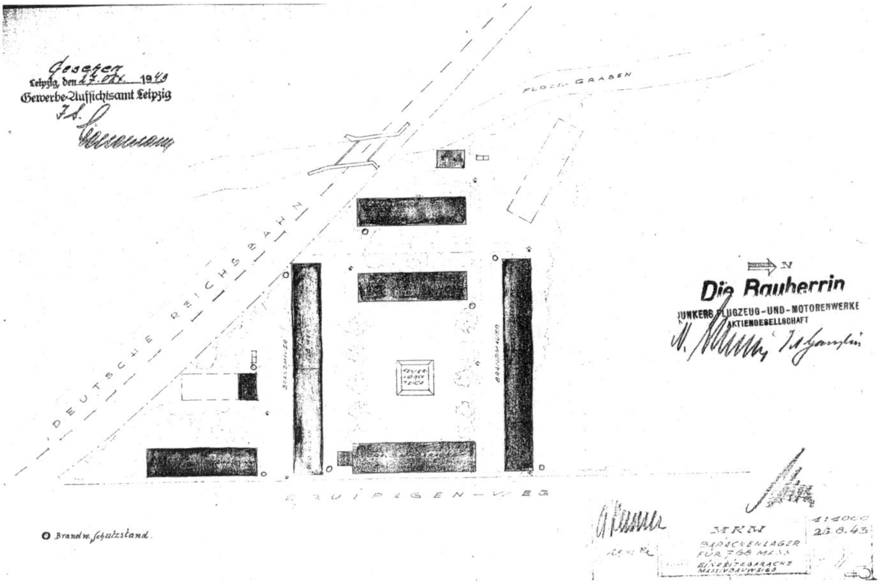

Blueprint of the camp in Markkleeberg.

Markkleeberg was a small part of a massive economic empire operated by the SS. Aircraft companies, like Junkers, were major consumers of the concentration camp.[12] The running of this huge system required the labor of millions of men and women. It was a money-making endeavor, and its considerable profits went in several directions. The Reich got a share; the SS as an institution became fabulously wealthy; and private interests—German companies, banks, as well as individual civilian and SS entrepreneurs—had the opportunity to "get rich quick," and many of them did.[13]

The foundation of this economic empire and the reason for its immense profitability was the widespread use of slave labor. The early goal of the concentration camps, "preventive detention," was replaced by the newer goals of removing undesirables from society and exploiting their labor. These goals were brought together in the "extermination through work" (*Vernichtung durch Arbeit*) program that characterized SS labor policies until the end of the war. The purpose of the camps, instead of detention, was forced labor. The ultimate fate of inmates, instead of eventual release, was usually death.

On February 1, 1942, a single new agency, the Economic and Administrative Main Office (WVHA) was created within the SS. Based in Berlin, the WVHA supervised the Nazi concentration camp system and coordinated the economic exploitation of the inmate labor force. This organization was a huge corporate enterprise with extensive power.[14]

Under the guidance of General Oswald Pohl, chief of the WVHA, the SS directed efforts to carry out a more "rational" exploitation of inmate labor in the interest of raising productivity. General Pohl described the shift necessitated by the Russian campaign: "The mobilization of the labor power of internees, primarily for war tasks (increase of armaments) must take precedence."[15] At the same time, the camps continued to fill their original ideological role as a place for the torture and physical elimination of political opponents and racial enemies of the Third Reich.[16]

The WVHA not only exploited 500,000 to 600,000 slave laborers, but it also rented out and transferred the prisoners for use as slave labor by German corporations. With the severe labor shortage in Germany, one of the few places to "recruit" additional workers was from the concentration camps.

There were twenty major concentration camps and 165 sub-camps under the control of the WVHA, which was also responsible for concentration camp construction and all booty stolen from camp inmates. The industrialists suffering from manpower shortages besieged the SS with applications for slave labor. The aircraft companies Messerschmitt, Junkers, and Heinkel were among them.[17]

Requests for workers came from thousands of German firms engaged in war production that needed help to meet their own work schedules. The demand was larger than the supply. Those companies with the highest priority or the best connections were given preference. Concentration camp prisoners were sent to companies only after the companies made a request. In their letters, the companies had to state in detail what measures they had taken to guard the laborers. Then they waited for approval before inmates were transferred. SS Standartenführer Gerhard Maurer headed the work assignment department (WVHA-AMT D II) that processed German corporate requests for concentration camp labor. Each company using labor from a camp was given a secret code number that the camp commanders were directed to use in all correspondence relating to that company.[18]

The joint SS–private sector concentration camp system became, in most instances, an opportunistic form of what was viewed at the time as clever entrepreneurship. By the end of the war, virtually all surviving concentration camp inmates had spent at least part of their captivity "leased out" by the SS to private German companies.[19]

Hungarian Jewish Labor

The year 1944 was crucial in the lives of Hungarian Jews. The March 1944 military decision of Nazi Germany to conquer its own ally shattered the hopes of Hungarian Jewry. The Jews of Hungary had been confident that, unlike the Jewish communities in neighboring states, they would survive.

Until 1944, Hungary was the only European country with its Jewish community almost intact.

Hitler ordered 100,000 Hungarian Jews to be brought to Germany as a labor force. One of Germany's plans was to expand aircraft production with the aid of Hungarian manpower and industrial resources. Horthy's consent in May 1944 to deliver the necessary Jewish workers was one of the foundations of Eichmann's deportation program.[20]

The military setbacks in 1944 raised the question for the German leadership of what to do with the Jews, including the Hungarian ones in eastern Poland. The decision to transport Hungarian Jewish prisoners to camps inside Germany postponed their death and saved hundreds of thousands from the fate of the millions who were killed.

1944

Nineteen forty-four was a disaster for the German military. In the west, the Allies had successfully launched their cross-Channel invasion and were beginning the process of liberating areas of Western Europe from Nazi control. By the year's end, they stood ready to march into Germany itself. In the east, the Soviet forces had gained momentum, and by late 1944 they controlled the areas east of a line drawn roughly from the Baltic Sea through Warsaw and Budapest. In Germany, there was a general mobilization for the maximum war effort. The few Germans who had thus far stayed home because of disability were now assigned to the war industry. The armament factories had to increase their production at the same time that they relieved workers for the army. In 1944, arms production was mainly in the hands of slave laborers.

For many inmates, the "final solution" of "the Jewish question" was delayed as long as their physical and mental condition still brought profit to the armaments industry. Inmates were housed at the factory sites in specially adapted camps designated as work camps or *Arbeitslager*. The number of prisoners varied with each firm, but no allocations were made unless the firm could use at least 500 concentration camp inmates.[21] The Jewish inmates were given hard and dangerous work. Yet they were eager to leave the concentration camp to go to the work camps. Lives of many of the prisoners in Markkleeberg, among them my sister and I, were indirectly saved because we were employed in vital war work. Had Germany won the war, our fate would have been sealed.

The inmates working at Junkers' factory in Markkleeberg were all women. According to the data in the International Tracing Service (ITS), Bad Arolsen, the large-scale procurement of women for the munitions industry, began only in mid-August 1944. Women adjusted to all kinds of automated work that did not need a lot of physical strength. Some women were assigned to specific tasks such as delicate handwork in the factory. The Nazis believed that they could do these jobs better than men because the women had smaller hands, more dexterous for certain types of factory work. Women were not spared from hard-working conditions just because they were female, however. Some were forced to do the most arduous physical labor, such as paving roads, loading bricks, digging ditches, and felling trees. They suffered job-related injuries and cruel treatment by guards and *Aufseherins* (German women overseers in military uniform). The work and the mistreatment were overwhelming, sometimes to the point of death. The private companies paid the SS less for the female laborers they "leased" because they were considered unskilled workers. The prisoners received no pay and were in no position to make demands.

In August 1944, next to the already existing work camp for foreign forced laborers in Markkleeberg, a section was put at the disposal of the SS to house female concentration camp prisoners. It was prepared as a sub-camp of Buchenwald under the guards of the SS.[22] The designation *sub-camp* was of purely administrative significance. Women on the transports were registered through Buchenwald and provided with consecutive new numbers. With few exceptions, women without detour to Buchenwald were taken directly to the various sub-camps in freight trains. Buchenwald, which was a camp for men, in March 1945 administered twenty-six women's sub-camps with a total of 26,000 prisoners.

Ehemalige Außenkommandos des KZ Buchenwald

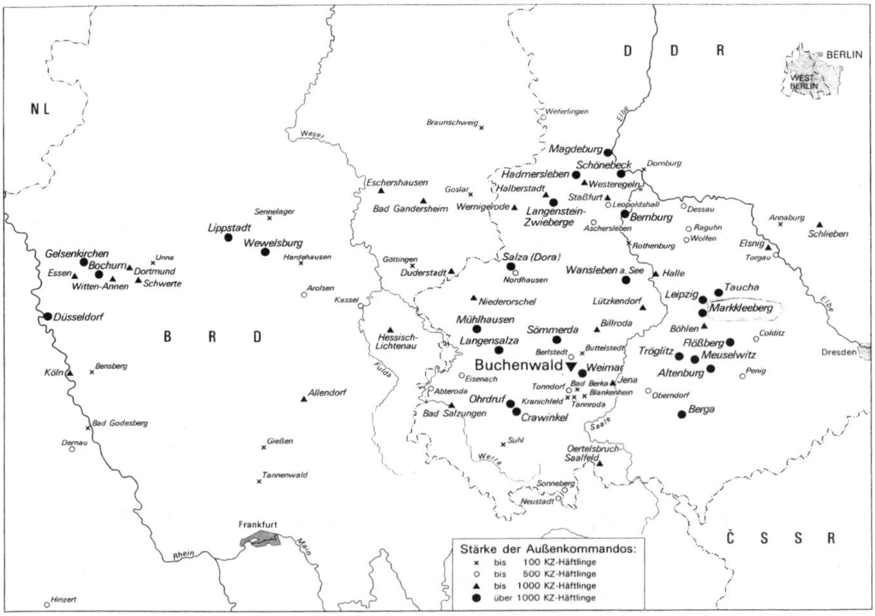

The sub-camps of Buchenwald.

The area in Markkleeberg had the advantages of a favorable transportation network and a railway artery. The region had forests and an energy supply due to the nearby coal mines. The first transport of Hungarian woman arrived on August 31, 1944 brought directly from Auschwitz. In the camp and around the barracks, additional high-voltage electrified barbed-wire fences were set up, and watchtowers were raised and manned with guards who were armed with machine guns. The chain-link, barbed-wire fence had lights for better guarding at night.

The Camp in Markkleeberg

The camp that was prepared for the Hungarian Jewish women slave laborers was located in a beautiful scenic area. The entrance to the camp territory was a paved sidewalk from the street. Across the street from the camp were small houses, and the rows of single-family homes are still there on Wolfswinkel and Equipagenweg Streets. The local historian, Mr. Andreas Höhn, said in 2000 that the area had not changed much.

The trees and forest camouflaged the campsites in Markkleeberg. There were trees all around. Even when I was in Germany in 2001, just seeing the trees conjured up images of the camps. There were watchtowers in three corners of the fence and large searchlights. Barbed wires with electricity

The intersection of Wolfswinkel and Equipagenweg Streets, across from the Markkleeberg's camp entrance. Photo taken in 2000 by the author.

Standing by the Markkleeberg camp's water basin in 2000. Left to right: Hava Hartmann Kleinberg, Kathy Zelmanovitz Goldstein, and the author, Zahava Szász Stessel.

surrounded the camp. In the middle of the camp was a basin of water, the remains of the swimming pool of the former sports club of Eintracht 04. Living quarters for the inmates were neatly set about this central area, which had a high flagpole flying the SS flag. In front of the water basin was the *Appelplatz* or the central plaza for roll calls. On Christmas, a lighted Christmas tree was placed there.

As the girls arrived, Erzsébet Frank was excited to see the swimming pool. "The scenery was beautiful, and the air was good," she recorded.[23]

The *Aufseherins* had a separate barracks outside of the electric fence, behind barracks number six. They had nice rooms with white furniture, books, radios, and flowers. Inmates were assigned to clean the rooms of the *Aufseherins*. Some *Aufseherins* also lived in town and came to work in the camp each day.

Deep underneath the ground was an air-raid shelter, also called the bunker. It had a strong roof made of cement topped by a layer of earth covered with grass. From the outside only the vents for air could be seen, and these were also protected from shells. Inside, the shelter looked like a long winding corridor lined with benches.

From the water basin and block number two, we could see a small train running early in the morning and at night. The train was a bit elevated; the travelers could see us and we could see them if we were doing road work by the factory or standing waiting to go to work.[24] Fifty girls who worked at a small branch of Junkers in the nearby town of Zwenkau took the train every morning, Lilly Waldman among them. Although they were kept in a separate compartment, Lilly was aware of the curious glances toward them from the other passengers.

The SS personnel arrived with the Hungarian Jewish women prisoners. The SS command, responsible for the internal security of the munitions plants, supervised guarding procedures. According to German orders of August 17, 1944, the women prisoners had to be attached to a group of soldiers when outside and to a number of SS supervisors when inside the camp. Commandant of the Jewish women camp was the *Oberscharführer* (chief guard) Alois Knittel.[25] He had a wife who stayed with him in the camp.

The prisoners were controlled by *Aufseherins.* While the guards were older men unfit for military duty, the overseers were overwhelmingly young German women. The *Aufseherins* were taught how to detect sabotage or work slowdowns and how to punish prisoners within the camp regulations. The *Aufseherins* dressed in tight-skirted gray army suits and army hats. They carried no guns, but a rubber whip or horsewhip. Even if they did not use it, they were holding the whip in a threatening manner. Prisoners were instructed to address them as "*Frau Aufseherin*" ("Madame Overseer") without using a last name that we did not know. We gave them nicknames or just called them "SS Women." In the factory, the *Aufseherins* as well as the *Oberscharführer* had to consider the presence of civilians; but inside the camp, far from the eyes of criticism, their rein was unchecked.

In carving a place for itself, the camp quickly asserted its dominance. Its tasks included gaining superiority over existing public authorities; securing the material and logistical assistance of local contractors, suppliers, and laborers; and winning the compliance of the local population. This was not accomplished without a measure of challenges and tension. In the face of the camp's superior power, however, the camp easily brushed them aside.[26]

The Camp for Foreign Workers

The foreign workers in Markkleeberg lived in the large area near the camp prepared for the Jewish women prisoners. They had a fence, but not an electrified barbed-wire fence as we did; and they were not escorted by armed guards. The difference between the treatment of the Jews and the non-Jews was that the non-Jews were not worked to death. The SS *Untersturmführer* Wiegand was the commandant of both camps.

The Junkers Factory

Leipzig and the surroundings area came more and more frequently under attack by the Allied air forces. The Junkers factories were especially targeted for intensive bombardment.[27] In February 1944, the temporary barracks of the foreign workers and some of its inhabitants fell victim to one of these attacks in Markkleeberg.[28]

Employment in the aviation industry originally carried elite status. Anyone allowed to work for the great German air force was especially conscientious and proud. The aviation worker was granted, besides modern installations to work in, many benefits. Before the war drained the industry of manpower, it was unimaginable that foreign laborers or concentration camp prisoners might work there.

Surviving documents provide only a sketchy account of the use of Jewish slave labor by major German firms during the war. Among the hundreds of corporations to which nearly one-half million camp or ghetto inmates were sent by the end of 1944, the greatest offenders were the munitions and arms makers in the narrowest sense: Dynamit Nobel, Rheinmetall-Borsing, Krupp, Messerschmitt, Heinkel, and Junkers.[29]

Until 1934, the Junkers Company was a purely private capitalistic enterprise. Its founder, Hugo Junkers, was a businessman and a scientist. Between 1932 and 1939, his JU 52 was the most widely used transport airplane in the world. In World War II, it was a standard transport airplane seen in Nazi airports. Through multiple transactions, the Nazis changed the private enterprise of Junkers into a government-controlled one. In 1936, the name was changed to Junkers Flugzeug und Motorenwerke A.G. (Junkers Aircraft und Engine Works A.G.). Its main business was the development and production of aircraft and aircraft engines. On May 1, 1939, the factory in Dessau and the branch in Halberstad were decorated as “Nazi Model Factories.” This change of a private industry to a government-controlled one was typical of the governmental monopoly that evolved. As Christa Naumann points out in her dissertation, the fascist takeover of the Junkers organization was a typical example, in several regards, of the forced government monopoly of German factories important for the prosecution of the war.[30]

In 1944, plants were appealing for workers wherever they could be found, mostly for construction projects at first, and then for assembly-line service. In the use of prisoners, Junkers and Messerschmitt were granted first choice.[31]

Selection of Workers from the Jewish Prisoners

The representatives of the German armaments industry were sent to select the workers. Standing next to the SS officers, Junkers representatives were given the opportunity to pick prisoners with both intelligence and physical endurance. The Junkers' delegation of civilian engineers and managers came to Auschwitz and Bergen-Belsen. Wearing their gray civilian business suits they inspected the rows of prospective slave laborers and picked out the women they considered most suitable for factory work. During this process, we all had to disrobe and walk naked, one by one, holding our clothing in our left hands and raising our right hands. Whenever a girl raised suspicions of trying to hide a sore or a pimple with her clothing or her hand, she was asked to uncover herself and they examined her even more carefully. The civilians in business suits laughed and talked as we passed. The process was both degrading and humiliating, but the terror and fear for our lives surmounted our natural instinct for modesty and eliminated the full impact of the sense of shame. In my eyes, the SS were not men, not human beings, but a kind of life-menacing, pain-inducing monstrous machine. They were part of that reprehensible other world that crushed all that was human and civilized.

Parading naked in front of German SS guards engendered strong emotions; but, in an absurd and ironic way, men in business suits represented civilized society with all its rules, morals, and obligations. Being nude, shaved all over, and observed by these men in civilian outfits with their watchful eyes was especially disturbing for us young teenage girls from sheltered, small-town environments. Personal modesty had been ingrained into Jewish women from childhood. To undress in front of strange men was unthinkable and caused a dreadful, disorienting shock and threat to our personal integrity. In my shamed and scary imagination, once it seemed that a civilian spoke Hungarian. But perhaps it was not imagination: Elisabeth Stein Székely, who had come in the first transport, also remembered hearing a selecting officer speak Hungarian. It made it worse to hear our own language, the reminder of home and civilization. My feeling of shame became even more real, more humiliating, juxtaposed beyond that insane world of the Nazis.

A civilian representative of Junkers who was present during the selection in Auschwitz was recognized by Frida Kaller Roth in an encounter later in the Markkleeberg factory. The tall, good-looking gentleman with blond hair and blue eyes, wearing britches-style pants, as Frida remembered him so well, probably worked in Dessau, the main office of Junkers. One day he visited Markkleeberg. Frida, who was doing quality control at the large factory, was sitting in a central location of the Middle Hall. She was surprised to see the officer again. She stood up and saluted the man who had selected her in Auschwitz. Frida, a lovely, vivacious girl—who is still pretty even at the age of eighty—asked if the Junkers representative remembered her from Auschwitz. There, during selection, Frida had raised her hand and said she would be a good worker. As not too many inmates dared to speak, much less make a request, the Junkers' representative remembered her well. He asked Frida to go with him. She got scared about what would happen, but the officer meant well—he wanted to put her to work in an office. Frida thanked him, but she preferred her job with the rest of the girls.

Besides being humiliated during selections, we were trembling from the fear of separation. Everything—my breath, even my heart—stopped in those minutes that we passed the inspection panel. Erzsike, my sister, who is younger than I, went first and I was to follow her. As we were similarly unfit for work, they had always rejected us together. Based on our physical conditions and our small bodies, we thought we had no chance of being accepted for work and escape Auschwitz. The progress of the Russian army and the German plan to move the able-bodied inmates out of Auschwitz worked in our favor. We were selected and taken to Bergen-Belsen, which was a collection center, for further action.

The Transports

According to the records, there were four transports. By December 1944, a total of 1,293 Hungarian Jewish women worked in Markkleeberg. The transports were registered through the political branch of Buchenwald. Numbers between 49,001 and 51,000 were assigned to the Jewish women in Markkleeberg.[32]

For the first transport of 500 girls to arrive, the conditions in the camp, being less crowded, were more favorable. The group received towels and kerchiefs. As more transports arrived, the situation became harsher.

Now that we are familiar with the setting, the next chapter will introduce the prisoners themselves. We will travel their road from law-abiding citizens to slave laborers.

Table 1. List of Arrivals and Departures of Prisoners in Markkleeberg.[33]

Date of Arrivals	Number of Women	Departed or Died	Transported to or from	Date of Registration	Total in the Camp
8.31.44	500		Auschwitz	9.21.44	500
10.15.44	200		Auschwitz		700
10.25.44	300		Bergen-Belsen	10.31.44	1,000
11.19.44		1	#31882 Meskowitz		999
11.28.44		1	#31764 Raab		998
12.8.44	300		Bergen-Belsen	12.17.44	1,298
1.21.45		4	Bergen-Belsen	1.30.45	1,294
2.3.45		1	#049485 WilhelmLea		1,293
2.28.45		1	#49144 GroszHelena		1,293
3.10.45		1	#50169 Lowy		1,291
3.15.45		1	#49102 Freund		1,290
French Women Political Prisoners					
2.12.45	125		Akdo, Abterode	2.21.45	1,415
2.26.45	124		Akdo, Abterode	3.6.45	1,539

2
Origins of the Prisoners and Their Road to Markkleeberg

Hungary

THE EMANCIPATION OF 1867 GRANTED CITIZENSHIP AND EQUALITY TO the Jews of Hungary. In the years that followed, they participated fully in Hungarian life, serving as professionals, businessmen, and artisans. Urban Jews were highly acculturated, even assimilated, while Jews in rural communities led more traditional lifestyles. Although they had legal equality, Hungary's Jews were still the targets of anti-Semitism. They were blamed for Hungary's territorial losses in World War I and for the economic difficulties that followed. Beginning in 1938, Jews were subjected to further anti-Semitic measures.

Hungarian domestic and foreign policy between the two world wars was dominated by a desire to revise the Treaty of Trianon. This peace treaty between Hungary and the Allied countries, signed on June 4, 1920, had deprived Hungary of nearly three-fourths of her prewar territory. The vision of a greater Hungary and the "rectification" of the nation's "dismemberment" became a major national issue. There was much satisfaction when, on November 2, 1938, Czechoslovakia returned to Hungary the upper province of Felvidék. Among the territories that were returned then was Kosice ("Kassa" in Hungarian). Kosice was close to the border and to my hometown, Abaújszántó, which had always been in Hungarian territory.[1]

We were so happy when Kosice was returned to Hungary. My mother's two sisters Hanni Geiger and Rózsi Klein were living there with their families. We soon were able to visit them, and I was delighted to see my cousins—especially Lili Klein, who was close to my age. As the food shortage worsened in the cities, we started bringing them goose and duck meat and goose liver that they liked very much.

With the return of the Upper Province, Hungary enacted the first anti-Jewish law in 1938, which was designed to force the Jews out of the economy. The second, and more severe, law passed in 1939 curtailed the civil rights of Jews, including those in the newly acquired territories. The new law limited Jewish participation in the economy, declared Jews unfit for military service, and discharged those on active duty. In place of military service, Jews were conscripted into special "Labor Service" units under military control.

TRANSYLVANIA

An integral part of greater Hungary, Transylvania was allotted to Romania at the end of the First World War under the Treaty of Trianon (1920). By the terms of the so-called Second Vienna Award, arbitrarily imposed by Nazi Germany and Fascist Italy, Transylvania was split: Hungary was allowed the northern half, which she annexed in September 1940 and which had a population of 2.5 million. Of these, more than 164,000 were Jews.

The third anti-Jewish law in 1940 was to "protect the purity" of the Aryan race. In the following years, anti-Semitism became the official policy of the Hungarian government. The road was open for Hungary to join Hitler's project for the "Final Solution."

A secret order issued by Hitler explained the need to invade Hungary. The Hungarian Regent Miklós Horthy was invited for a meeting to be held on March 18, 1944, outside of Salzburg. Even before Horthy returned to Budapest, on March 19, 1944, a Sunday, the German forces had invaded Hungary without firing a shot. The special operational commando unit known as "Hungary," previously organized by Adolf Eichmann in the Mauthausen concentration camp, arrived in Budapest on the same day to implement the deportation of Hungary's 725,000 Jews. After the Germans installed a collaborationist government in Hungary that March, the fate of the Hungarian Jews was sealed. On March 31, an order was issued that Hungarian Jews had to wear yellow badges.

Although we knew the seriousness, we did not fully grasp the peril of the situation. Young people still composed songs such as the following one of resilience and resistance. The lyricist is unknown, and it was written to the tune of a popular hit song of the time.

> The Jew is proud wearing the yellow star;
> He is not gloomy; this is not his type.
> He carries the yoke waiting for a better tomorrow.
>
> The time will come when there will be no yellow star.
> Those who gave it to us will comprehend,
> Those who gave it to us will realize
> That they cannot do without the Jew.[2]

The relocation of the Jews of northeastern Hungary began on April 16, 1944. It started in rural districts, where Jews were collected in designated locations; from there they were taken to the cities, usually county seats. By June 1944, with terrible efficiency, Hungary was emptied of its rural Jewish population, and 95 percent of these Jews were killed.

Deportation from Abaújszántó

It was early in the morning on Sunday, April 16, 1944, when the village drummer in Abaújszántó announced that the Jews of our town were not allowed to leave their homes.[3] Soon after that, my sister and I watched our father and grandfather feverishly raise one of the wood floorboards in a stable where we had horses. My father placed there in the ground some of our valuables, such as gold and diamond jewelry.[4] When we were discovered watching, my sister and I were sent away; as children were not trusted in matters of that kind. My parents may also have given some of our precious possessions to our Christian neighbors for safekeeping, but if so, they did not tell us.

We did not have much time for preparations, because we had to be ready to leave in two hours. We organized a small suitcase and a duffel bag for the limited amount we were allowed to take on the road. We looked for important papers and photographs. My father took our citizenship papers, birth certificates, his trade license, and other precious legal documents. I had some stories that I had written to take with me. We dressed in our holiday clothing: My sister wore her orange angora coat that was new for Passover, and I put on my stylish new platform shoes. I was still packing when two civil service employees, who held the previously prepared list of deportee names and addresses, came and called the names of my seventy-five-year-old grandfather, seventy-one-year-old grandmother, my father, mother, thirteen-year-old sister, and myself—fourteen at that time. Representatives of the Jewish community had prepared the list. The police and the two civilian government officials made us join the procession of Jewish families already waiting outside.[5]

In Abaújszántó, as we walked toward the public school building, our collection center, I suddenly realized that our cat, Mici, might have been left locked in the house. I even heard its thin voice of "meow." I started to cry, but there was no way of going back. I continued walking and worrying about my kitten, who might die without food in the house. My preoccupation with Mici dulled the pain of leaving our home and postponed my realization that we might never come back. People reassured me that the cat would not be alone too long because officials would enter the house shortly after we left, but this gave me no comfort.

Townspeople were gathered on the street that Sunday afternoon. Most who lined the street, young and old, watched us passively. Some had

The author's parents Miriam-Mariska and Sándor Szász in 1940.

smiles on their faces; others, with their arms folded, looked on with bemused curiosity.

In the school yard where we were taken, we met all our friends from school and other girls from the neighborhood. I ran to Márta Krausz, my best friend and classmate. I would meet Márta again later in Bergen-Belsen. We greeted each other, but we had to remain with our own families. Later Márta came over as I was wiping my eyes after the harsh removal of the gold earrings that I had worn from birth. Márta had just had the same experience.

Not far from us stood Márta Weisz Paran with her family. Márta would be one of the slave laborers with us in Markkleeberg. Waiting to be processed was Ilona Roth, also destined for Markkleeberg. Ilona was older, but we knew her from the synagogue and the shoe store her parents owned on the main street of the town. Elza Reich Szamosi, a cheerful girl, would become a good friend to us in Markkleeberg.

My sister Erzsike said hello to her friend Judith Rosenberg, there with her older sister Eva Rosenberg Eichler, and their mother. Judith, a lovely child pampered by her older sister and brother, lived not far from us. Erzsike and Judith used to visit and play with each other often. Sadly, Judith and her mother were not to pass the selection in Auschwitz, as we would learn when we met the older sister Eva in Markkleeberg.

In Abaújszántó, we spent the night at the public school building. Early on the morning of the next day, April 17, 1944, half of the two hundred Jewish families of Abaújszántó were taken by train to the nearby city of Kosice. My family was among that first group. On the way to the railway station, we passed our house, where I was born and had spent all the years of my life.

Still worrying about the fate of Mici, I looked at our cherished residence. In the front were my father's clothing shop and grandfather's meat store. Through the gate to the yard I could see the flower garden that my grandmother nurtured with so much love and care. We lived in separate apartments: my grandparents in the front of the long yard and my family in the back, close to the large vegetable garden and fruit orchards.

My father, an only child, had made my sister and me our grandmother's pride; she gave us her full love and attention. Our good-natured grandfather, with his long pipe and big moustache, dutifully fulfilled my grandmother's requests. One day grandfather appeared in my first-grade class, bringing my unfinished breakfast. The memory of the embarrassment I felt then in front of my classmates turned out to be my grandchildren's favorite bedtime story.

Our lives in the small town had been steady and secure. Residents depended on and trusted one another. We knew almost every member of the Jewish community; people had worked throughout their lives in the same place and at the same professions. Except for short two-week visits with my mother to our maternal grandmother's house in the nearby city of Sátoraljaujhely, we had never left our home. Children in the countryside did not go then to summer camp.

Our faithful maid of forty-six years was Boriska. She escorted my father to school and carried me to kindergarten and to first grade. By the time of the anti-Jewish laws, Boriska was old and could not work anymore. She had a sister whose health problems depleted Boriska's savings. When her sister finally passed away, Boriska, old and frail, with no family and without Social Security or welfare, depended on us for help. We supported her, even throughout the final years when our economic conditions were difficult because of the anti-Jewish laws. Boriska's abandonment, her loss and grief, was one of the genuine expressions of sorrow we received at the time of our deportation.

Continuing toward the railway station, I gave a last look through the faint rays of early dawn at the disappearing traces of my home. I felt pity and compassion for the solitary structure. Like a family member who was left behind, the building stood there lonely and deserted. Later, after all the upheavals in my life and the distances fate had led me, I always returned to have another look at my old home. I was there last with my daughter Yonit and my three grandchildren in 2000. I do not think I ever got over that first of my many separations.

The author's daughter, Yonit Levy, and granddaughter, Yarin, in front of the former family home in Abaújszántó in 2000.

The Ghettoes

To facilitate the process of destruction, the Nazis created ghettoes, thus accelerating Jewish isolation. The formation of the Hungarian ghettoes soon led to Auschwitz and to the catastrophe that befell Hungarian Jewry there.

Kosice had one of the largest Jewish communities in Hungary. Its three major "Jewish streets" were designated as "Jewish houses" and were isolated from the rest of the city by a fence. Escape at this point was still possible, however.[6]

In 1943, my cousin, Lili, from Kosice had spent two weeks of summer vacation with us. The atmosphere was tense, but we could still enjoy the company of our city cousin. We learned from her a few of the latest hit songs. Later, in the camp of Markkleeberg, girls were singing the songs Lili taught us. In Kosice, only our Aunt Hanni dared to visit us in the Jewish houses. She brought with her papers for our escape. They consisted of non-Jewish identification documents for a woman and two girls. For the men, Hanni had not been able to obtain false documents. Accepting the offer would have meant my mother would have to leave my father and her parents behind. My mother, without hesitation, decided against the escape. It was a choice that cost her life. Hanni, Lili, and her mother Rózsi survived the war in hiding.

Kosice was one of the first Hungarian deportation zones. On April 28, 1944, the trucks arrived and transferred the Jews of Abaújszántó from the Jewish homes to a sealed brickyard on Kosice's outskirts. That was the official ghetto. Escape from there was almost impossible. Anyone nearing the fence was to be shot without warning. The ghetto served as a convenient point for the inconspicuous and efficient deportation of the Jews.

The Jewish populace from other rural communities in Abaúj-Torna County surrounding Kosice was also concentrated in the Kosice ghetto. There we met families from the nearby villages, including girls I knew from middle school in Abaújszántó. We greeted each other and took comfort in meeting friends. Having others in the same situation made our prison seem a bit less threatening. Hava Hartmann Kleinberg and her sister Miriam Hartmann Carmi waved to us as they were greeting their good friend Márta Weisz Paran.

Soon they were joined by Margit Lang Stein, Márta's classmate from Göncz, a town not far from Abaújszántó. Margit, who was older than us, was friendly and talked to us. Agnes Glück Rabinovics and Klára Spitz Snitzler from Encs were also in the ghetto. Klára Spitz Snitzler was talking to us with her older sister and her mother, a friendly and pleasant lady. They all looked elegant in their stylish outfits. We admired Klára, who was close to my age. I looked for her later on, but things in the ghetto were so hectic that I lost trace of her. None of us then guessed the sad fate and separation that was ahead of us in Auschwitz. I met Klára again when we arrived in Markkleeberg. All these girls from Abaújszántó and the surrounding area who reached Markkleeberg would become part of our family of *Landsmanshaft,*[7] people from the same town or community who knew each other before the war and formed a substitute family.

Days were hard in the ghetto. Our emotions were driven by rumors, bad ones and good ones. Then a group of additional Hungarian policemen arrived. They would assist, we were told, in our resettlement for work in Kenyérmező.

Kosice was the site where Hungary handed over the Jews to the Germans. By July 9, 1944, the number of Jews who had been deported reached 438,000. Of all these, less than twenty percent were selected as "fit for labor." Implementation of the "Final Solution," which required four-and-a-half years in Poland, took only three months in Hungary. These steps were carried out quite openly in view of the local population and of the entire world.

Although the Jews of southern Transylvania, like the Jews of Romania, survived the war almost intact, the Jews of Magyar-ruled Northern Transylvania ended up in Auschwitz. Many of those girls were among us, slave laborers in Markkleeberg.

Auschwitz

From the Kosice ghetto, the Jews of Abaújszántó, together with others from the area, were divided into three groups and sent to Auschwitz between May 14 and June 7, 1944. They were among the first of the mass deportation from Hungary.[8]

We were in the second transport, which left in late afternoon on Friday, May 19, 1944. The police were hurrying us while my mother helped grandmother up the high steps of the freight train and father was supporting grandfather. As we advanced, my mother looked back for a second to check if we were following. Suddenly, a policeman hit her on the shoulder with his rubber stick. It must have hurt my mother very much; I saw the pain in her face, but she tried to smile, reassuring us that it was nothing. My brave mother. I still have her painful smile with me. The scene and the hurt return each time I see a picture showing deportation and people boarding the trains.

We all entered the same cattle car or cattle wagon and tried to find some space close to one another. I was scared and hugged my mother with all my strength as she was standing. She let me sit on her feet for a bit of rest.[9] We thought that our situation would improve; we had never heard the name of the place before.

Although Hungarian Jews had lived in the shadow of Auschwitz for several years, they had no specific knowledge of the gas chambers and the mass murders that were being committed there. We had not known, but the Jewish leaders in Hungary were aware of Auschwitz. It is a painful chapter of Hungarian Jewish history. Had the leaders shared that knowledge, some lives might possibly have been saved.[10]

The Language of Death

In the sanitized vocabulary that pervaded the Third Reich, the process of choosing who would die immediately and who would die later was called "selection." The executions were referred to as special "treatment," "delousing," "disinfecting," or "special action." The euphemism concealed for a time the grisly truth from the victims and thus made enforcement easier. People entered resettlement transports and shower rooms with much less coercion when they did not realize what awaited them there. The less offensive words perhaps also permitted the executioners, somehow, to delude themselves into lessening the severity of their deeds in their own minds. The evasive terminology in some way "detoxified" killing and aided the guards in making it routine.

Arrival in Auschwitz-Birkenau

It was early dawn when our train arrived on Monday morning, May 22, 1944. People were motionless, half asleep. I probably woke up when the train stopped. I looked out through the small window, laced with metal bars, and I saw in the distance bald men with striped-pajama uniforms waiting for the arrivals. My grandmother stood next to me and stroked my hair. I still feel the softness of her fingers. Then she hugged me, my little grandmother. Anticipating what might happen next, she tried to make it easier to bear. Knowing that I was proud of my long blonde braids, she said that if they cut my hair, I should not worry—it would grow back. My honest, trusting grandmother, who all her life had tried to do the right thing, could not imagine the full horror before us, the coming minutes that would mark or steal our lives forever.

Auschwitz-Birkenau was the point where it all began and ended. There a German officer whom we later knew as Dr. Josef Mengele, the "angel of death," would render an instant death sentence, deciding whether one lived temporarily or died immediately: the "selection."

We were barely conscious after the long night's ride, but as the door of the train car flew open, I recall some strange people in uniform entering and throwing our belongings to the platform. There was no time to think; everything happened so fast. As we stepped out of the cattle cars, a lineup of storm troopers, wearing shiny black boots and carrying whips, was waiting for us alongside snarling German shepherds. The SS officers shouting of "*Loss, loss, aussteigen, aussteigen!*" ("Hurry, hurry, get out, get out!") became mixed with the screams of people looking for their family members. The wagons disgorged thousands of people onto the platform. The SS guards pushed people with their rifle butts from both sides, and the crowd surged forward.

My father and grandfather were separated from us first. They had to join the men's group. It went so fast that I just remember my father's confused, throbbing expression. Around us, people pushed and shoved in fear and bewilderment. I only saw my father and grandfather one more time before the crowd swallowed them completely.

Where we stood, a column formed itself. There were constant shouts to hurry up; we were ordered to walk five in a line. Dr. Josef Mengele, whom I knew by his high, polished boots, gave a sign, and the camp prisoners started pulling people out and sending them in different directions; they all went where they were told very quickly. My sister and I walked next to mother as my grandmother was holding on to my mother's arm. Suddenly Erzsike and I were pointed to go to the side, while my mother and grandmother continued to walk. It all happened so fast that we were surprised; we did not expect to be separated. We cried when the guards forcibly pulled us away. We wept and begged to go with our mother and grandmother, but to no avail. My mother's last look of despair and my grandmother's helplessness as her little frame disappeared in the distance froze in my heart and accompany me all of my life.

Later, my sister Erzsike and I were asked whether we were twins. Erzsike, who was only thirteen years old, was probably saved by the assumption that we were twins because, as twins, Dr. Mengele would want us for his genetic experiments.

As we review in our minds those terrible last moments, each one of us is haunted by questions of what if, or what could have been. I always think of the ways in which my mother might have been selected to survive with us.

Barbara Klein Stark, who possesses an excellent memory and provided much information about the camp in Markkleeberg, walked with her mother and her seventeen-year-old sister. When Dr. Mengele signaled to separate them, the mother beseeched and begged tearfully that she could not stay alone. Dr. Mengele, in one of his sinister acts, left the younger girl to please the mother. Barbara remained alone. Aiding her survival was her friend and *lager* sister, Magda Schön Hilf. I will return to them later in the following chapters.

All the Hungarian girls in Markkleeberg, even those who arrived from Bergen-Belsen, were first in Auschwitz-Birkenau. Our fate was sealed there, as we passed the selection and the ordeal of separation. Each one had her special ill fortune and painful experience. Every one of us lost close members of our families, such as mothers, sisters, and little brothers.

Looking for My Father

When men came to do work in the women's camp in Auschwitz, they always called out the name of the town they came from. They wanted to know if anyone was from their home. When I heard the name of even a familiar place, I listened with excitement. Then when I saw how bad the men looked, how disgraced and degraded they were, I was almost afraid that I would recognize my father in them.

Although I did not meet my father as a prisoner, my sister and I had an encounter with a lady who knew my father as a young man. We were there the second week after our arrival, suffering from shock and separation. Lost and lonely, Erzsike and I were holding onto each other.

One morning, we were waiting outside, as usual, in the area between two barracks. The sun was strong on our shaven heads, and there were few shaded places around. Not knowing what to do, we just stood there, when a lady approached us. She was a slender woman, about forty, with a gentle face and a congenial smile. She asked us where we came from. When we said Abaújszántó, she smiled and pointed confidently at my sister. "You are the daughter of Sándor Szász; you have his eyes and expression."

We were stunned and shaken just from the mention of our father's name. "My name is Szerén," she continued. "I knew your father very well. I almost married him." As she talked, with a slight twitch in her face, I recalled a story grandmother told me when, as a young teenager, I was eager to hear about my father's boyhood adventures. My father, Sándor Szász, was an only child under grandmother's strong scrutiny and protection. The task was not easy: Sándor was a fun-loving bachelor of a well-to-do family. The girls liked his company, and Sándor had difficulties saying no without hurting the girls' feelings. Among his friends was Szerén, for whom Sándor sincerely cared. She was a good-looking, delicate girl from a nearby town. Szerén received grandmother's full approval, until one day she noticed a tremor in Szerén's face. The slight tic was indiscernible by anyone else, but for grandmother it was a serious concern. The struggle that ensued between mother and son, grandmother did not tell me, but she was satisfied when Szerén's visits subsided.

Szerén encouraged us to be brave and to trust that the war would soon be over and the world would be a better place. We talked about the good times and the delicious food at home. Szerén said she had a son who had gone with his father. He would be perfect for Erzsike when we got home, she said. Szerén's friendship eased much of the hardship of our life at the beginning in Auschwitz. As we grew to cherish and respect her, we painfully noticed that Szerén's health was deteriorating. To hide her worsening tic, we placed Szerén in the middle of the five-person line. It obscured her for awhile, but eventually there was no escape from the penetrating eyes of the SS. The day Szerén was pointed at, to step forward, was one of the darkest in our camp life.[11]

Medical Experiences

In our barrack, which was designated as an experimental one, we were under surveillance. We knew that we were checked for signs of fever, but only later did I learn that sufferers of typhus and scarlet fever had been housed in our barrack before. Assigning us to that barrack, the Germans experimented to see how many would develop typhus or scarlet fever during twenty-one days of exposure. A medical committee visited from time to time, checking and eliminating those who contracted the disease. Our fellow inmates warned us that anyone who felt sick should hide, and those who had a fever should not disclose it.

I became sick with a high temperature. I could hardly keep my head up on that early morning *Zehlappel.* To my sister's heartbreaking plea, I stood up, supported by her and a friend. Szerén was no longer with us; and, outside, Erzsike begged other girls to let me stay in the middle of the line and hide from SS scrutiny. Luckily, there was no special inspection that day. I slowly recovered, and by the next time, I could stand on *Appel* with no support. In a few days, our quarantine ended.[12]

Leaving Auschwitz

Eventually, after many rejections and with the camp population greatly reduced, there was a selection for which we did not have to undress. Dr. Mengele was not there, and the SS looked only at our eyes. We were to be sent to Bergen-Belsen, which was only a transfer station. Leaving Auschwitz, we had a chance to see the other places in the camp. Up until then, we were only allowed to be in or around our own block. When I returned in 1994 to visit Auschwitz, I had a special feeling of freedom to know the area.

We received clean dresses that were taken from other prisoners or from those who had died at the crematorium. These dresses remained with us during our time in camp. Our shoes were exchanged for wooden ones. We also received half of a small loaf of bread and a bit of salami for the road. It was the first time in the last few months that we felt a bit of excitement. We did not even know how lucky we were to leave Auschwitz alive. We hoped somehow that they had taken our parents somewhere else too.

On the way to Bergen-Belsen, the German guard allowed the heavy sliding door of the freight car to be kept open, and we could watch the changing scenery in our two-day trip by Poland into Germany. During daylight hours, as the train passed through agricultural land, we could see cows and workers doing their jobs. We stared, not believing that the earth had continued its regular orbit and the world sustained its normalcy while we were in Auschwitz. At night, the train passed by towns and cities with lighted windows. We were thinking of the people behind the lights—that they were free and lived their usual lives. Only we were the outcasts, our world destroyed. Somehow my prisoner status just dawned on me then—something I had never fully comprehended. I thought a prisoner or an inmate had to *do* something bad to be punished: This was our education from home. We had trusted the law of the state and world order—we had believed that everyone had been forced into labor camps because of the war. We also thought that only criminals were placed in jail. Suddenly understanding the nature of the injustice that had imprisoned us made it hurt even more. Although we were prisoners, at night our minds were free to roam. The train in my imagination became a star-driven carriage in the sky that took me home to better times.

Bergen-Belsen

Bergen-Belsen, near Hanover in northwestern Germany, was established in 1943, originally as a prisoner-of-war camp. Designed to contain 10,000 soldiers, it was used later as a provisional or transit camp to house civilians who were to be exchanged for German prisoners of war. In 1944, SS Major Josef Kramer, later known as "the beast of Belsen," began accepting inmates from other camps. The population increased by thousands of new Jewish prisoners. By early 1945, Bergen-Belsen held 41,000 inmates.

Our Arrival at Bergen-Belsen

When we arrived at the end of September, the same guards who were with us in the train led us on a walk lasting several hours to reach the camp. Shortly after our arrival, registrars filled out cards with our personal data. Somehow many things were erased in my mind, but the registration at the tables that stood outside the tents I remember very clearly. Maybe it impressed me that people wanted to know about us. They asked our names, ages, parents' names, and places of birth. I received the number 5420 and Erzsike became number 5419.

The fear of separation and death continued to haunt us in Bergen-Belsen. In one of the early days of our stay there, we were called for a special *Appel* in the middle of the day. We did not know then what had happened, but we found out later that someone had cut a piece from the tent we were living in to make an article of clothing. Over the loudspeakers, the Germans called those who cut the tent to come forward. "If nobody will take responsibility, every tenth person will be shot," were the terrifying words that poured out from the loudspeaker with a Hungarian translation.

We continued to stand there petrified, in the most frightfully dramatic hours of our camp life. What if Erzsike would be the tenth on line? They would not let us change, so I would not be able to take her place. Without Erzsike, my last ray of hope, the final connection to my past, to our home, and the only link to the world I knew would be lost. It would be unbearable. Probably the same thoughts troubled Erzsike as we clutched each other's hand. No, we will not let them chase us away as they did with mother and grandmother, I thought. We will have the same fate; they will have to shoot us both.

From the distance, we heard the sound of the cart bringing our meal. The carriage reached us and turned back, without distributing the food. The hunger and the disappointment were great. The uncertainty continued and minutes seemed like days. The hours were eternity as we stood there waiting for the execution to begin. The loudspeakers continued to shriek, this time only in German, angrier and angrier; words that we did not fully understand. After hours standing at attention, inmates started to collapse, but no one was allowed to help the fallen. I looked at Erzsike, fearing that I would be the next to faint, when suddenly it was quiet. We did not dare to breathe in the eerie silence. At the front, high-ranking German officers consulted one another. In my nightmarish fear, I even saw the machine guns taking position. Then, with no explanation, the order was given to disperse. Staggering back to our barracks with the newly gained experience in terror, we were petrified that, at the next *Appel,* the torture would continue. This was only one of the many chilling incidents to which we were exposed. Each one of the girls who came to Markkleeberg carried a backlog of frightening memories.

In Bergen-Belsen we made friends with the Lörinch sisters, Margit and Isabella. They were a bit older: Isabella was three years my senior, and Margit even more, but we got along well.

The tuberculosis in Bergen-Belsen was the greater menace, silently taking people's health and affecting their lives. As the situation worsened, girls died on the floor around us. In the mornings, the dead were collected from the floor and placed in front of the tents. Later, prisoners with a cart took them away. At first, we were very shocked and scared. I pulled Erzsike away and asked her not to look at the bodies. We listened with empathy to the mourning of family members. Some cried loudly, others silently. We felt better if we did not know them. A girl sleeping not far from us did not wake up. Her heartbroken sister, Ica, could not accept the fact. "She was well yesterday," she cried. "Maybe she will get better!" But they took her sister away quickly as Ica lamented. We moved next to Ica, and both Isabella and Margit came to talk to her. Ica was about my age and her sister had been two years older. Erzsike and I had the terrible thoughts, but we did not share them. Between crying and resting, Ica told us about the good times she and her sister had had at home. What would she tell her father, she worried. At that time, we still believed that our parents were alive and would come home after the war. When Ica started to sob uncontrollably, gazing at the place her sister used to be, we asked her to come outside with us. She agreed, and luckily, she met girls from her hometown there. They took her to their tent and convinced a girl to change places with her. We saw Ica maybe once after that—she started crying as soon as she saw us—and then we lost each other. I hope she survived.

We had one pleasant moment that lonely and forlorn autumn when we learned that Erzsébet Markovics Dicker, my cousin, was alive and stayed in one of the barracks. The daughter of my mother's sister, Erzsébet or Bözsi, as we nicknamed her, was much older and had lived in another city; but I had a special closeness with her. We stood out in the family for having the same blonde hair. How good it would be to meet Bözsi. We could recover together a bit of the feelings and happy memories from home. Bözsi was so close and yet so unattainable. With all our attempts and the help of other inmates, we could not find her. I imagine how much she was also looking for us, but we will never know because Bözsi died in Bergen-Belsen shortly after liberation.[13]

Meeting My Best Friend from Home

Going to the latrine one day, I heard a familiar voice calling me from the other end. Pulling Erzsike with me and following the sound, we reached Márta Krausz, my childhood friend and classmate. Márta was always full of life, and that made me so happy to be her friend. We had lived close by, shared our teenage secrets and, having no telephones, visited each other at all hours of the day. From the ghetto, we were taken in different transports to Auschwitz and lost contact with one another. By the time we met in Bergen-Belsen, Márta was disheveled; Erzsike described her later as sickly looking, but I did not see it. I looked at her brown eyes, still expressing the childhood faith and optimism that I liked so much about her. Márta and her sister Vera, two years her senior, had arrived in Bergen-Belsen later than we did, after working in a factory and surviving a death march. They had also been separated from their mother and grandmother. We hugged each other, and tears just began to cloud our eyes when Márta's group had to leave. Deeply affected by the meeting, I was thinking how seeing Márta gave me both pain and some happy feelings of reconnection to that old world that was so far away from us. How nice it would be if the four of us could be together. We would almost have the five-person line completed in *Appel.* I started to visit the latrine every time I could, taking Erzsike with me. We stayed in the latrine as long as it was possible, but I never met Márta. One of those days shortly after that, as I was again in line with Erzsike for the latrine in search of Márta, we were told that there would be an *Appel* for selection to work.

We were all excited, but I still insisted on going to the latrine, hoping that maybe Márta would be there. Erzsike was worried, but she came with me, only to be disappointed again. We hurried back and started to get ready for the *Appel.*

Selection

It was at the beginning of December. Isabella quickly gave me a comb she had borrowed, and both Erzsike and I combed our hair. Margit admired my blonde hair, which looked good since growing out a bit. Margit's compliments gave me some confidence. We stood in line to wash our hands and faces from water in the pipe outside. We were told that we would not have to undress for the selection. Erzsike, who was more resourceful than I was, obtained a piece of cloth for me to put on as a belt for my dress, which was far too wide on me. This way it looked better. We smoothed out our dresses and prayed that they would not separate us. As we stood on *Appel* in the muddy field, the selection process began. Our hearts hardened with fear as we passed the committee. To our luck and advantage, there was a shortage of prisoners and slave workers, so the SS was more lenient in selection. They passed the two of us, and the Lörinch sisters together. We blessed our fortune; and even today, as I am writing these lines, I am grateful to God that we were assigned to the fourth and the last transport to Markkleeberg.

I had no way to let Márta know about my departure. With all the fear and excitement of leaving, I still thought of Márta's loving face. How long did she continue looking and hoping to find me? Would she realize, knowing the unpredictability of camp life, that it was not my fault? Thinking of our magical games and childhood play, I was sending her my mental note of love and friendship forever. Trusting that Márta had received my message on its miraculous wings of childhood magic, I felt a bit better.

Had I known then Márta's tragic fate and that I would never see her again, my pain would have been even stronger. After the war, I was told by Gizella Sternberger, a girl from Abaújszántó who was with them, that Márta and Vera were housed in the same barracks as Anne Frank in

Class picture from 1942. Márta Krausz, the author's classmate, is second from the left in the third row. Zahava Szász Stessel is before her in the row. (Only half of her face is visible.)

Bergen-Belsen. Suffering from typhus, Vera died a day before liberation and Márta survived only a few days longer.[14]

Of all the events in the camp, the memory of meeting Márta is one that never fades. When I see those terrible photographs of skeletons awaiting burial from Bergen-Belsen, I see my friend Márta's sad face among them.

Leaving Bergen-Belsen

As we walked five in a line to the train station, the rain falling on our bare feet in wooden shoes turned to snow. At the gate, the guard let us out: 300 women. We walked for ten kilometers, and we stumbled constantly on the pebbles of the unpaved road. Finally we reached the trains. We were happy to sit down and nurse the blisters on our feet. I cut a piece of my belt and gave it to Erzsike to bandage her foot. After we had been traveling for some time, suddenly bombing and explosions shook our train. It stopped and then started to move again very fast. When we looked out after a while, we saw a building with a tower. Someone recognized it as a Napoleon memorial of Leipzig. The train traveled another half an hour and we arrived at a small station. We could still see Leipzig in the distance.

Population of the Camp at Markkleeberg

The inmates in Markkleeberg were all from Hungary and annexed Hungarian territories.[15] The Jews of Transylvania and the upper province of Felvidek in Czechoslovakia shared the pro-Magyar attitude of Hungarian Jewry, both culturally and linguistically. They felt an integral part of greater Hungary.

Some of the Jewish prisoners in Markkleeberg were American citizens. Erzsebet Biro was born in Zalaegerszeg on October 22, 1910, and lived in New York. She returned to Hungary and was deported with the rest of the Jewish population. Ms. Biro's prisoner number was 49511; she is on the list of those who reached Theresienstadt.

The first two of the four transports came directly from Auschwitz-Birkenau. The other two brought women who were also in Bergen-Belsen. The first group from Auschwitz, arriving in Markkleeberg on August 31, 1944, was previously in Plaszow, near Krakow in Poland. The movie *Schindler's List* related happenings in Plaszow, and it was actually filmed in the camp.

In Auschwitz, the women could not always tell which group was "the good one." Ilana Sajovits Breiner was very anxious after the selection. She wanted to try going to the other side. As she stood there with her sister and cousin, a Czech girl told her, "Do not worry you are going to a good place!" Then Ilana relaxed a little.

3

Arrivals, Housing, and Work in the Quarry

The First Transport

On the last day of August 1944, the first group of Hungarian Jewish women, most in their twenties, arrived from Auschwitz. The SS had requested 500 workers; they were shipped in freight trains. The trip took three days.

At the railroad station, the girls and women were met by the commandant. The *Aufseherins* directed their disembarkation and accompanied them to the camp. It seemed to the girls that they had arrived in a forest. Only the tall factory chimney could be seen from a distance. One of the *Aufseherin* asked about the girls' luggage; she was surprised that they had no personal belongings.

The women had been sent to Krakow Plaszow first, and when they returned to Auschwitz, their hair was cut again. In Markkleeberg, they arrived completely bald, and *Oberscharführer* Alois Knittel asked if their hair was cut because they had lice.

When the girls arrived at the camp, they were directed to assemble by the former pool or water basin. Then Knittel told them, "You have come here to work. If you will work well and be good I will be your father instead of your real father." The head of the *Aufseherins,* who was standing next to him, said, "I will be your mother instead of your mothers." It was a good beginning.

The girls were housed in the factory camp. Each received a towel, toothbrush, soap, kerchief, and a dish for meals. The area was so beautiful that the girls felt as if they were in heaven—especially after Auschwitz. The *Aufseherins,* new to their jobs then, were pleasant, inexperienced. The girls' joy lasted only a few days.[1]

Each camp had its own style of clothing. In some places, the inmates wore regular civilian outfits. In Markkleeberg, we received prison uniforms consisting of dark gray cotton overalls made from hard, thin, canvaslike materials, and a shirt to wear underneath. The shirt had sleeves with buttons that could be detached and removed to shorten them. The overall looked like an apron in the front, with shoulder straps that we crossed in the back. The legs of the overalls were long and tied with black string at the ankle. On the side of the pants was a red stripe, and a large red X was painted in oil across the back of the blouse. Prisoners actually painted the red X and the stripes on the overalls. The marks were used to identify us as prisoners and to discourage escape. No one ever tried to escape from the Markkleeberg camp. During the Death March, however, our prison uniforms gave us difficulties: We knew we could not go far without being identified by the population.

After a week of quarantine and administrative matters, the Markkleeberg camp with the first 500 Jewish prisoners was established. The women began to work in the factory on September 7, 1944.[2]

Second Transport

With the second transport in October 15, 1944, there were only 200 Hungarian Jewish women. Markkleeberg was their first camp after leaving Auschwitz. They had traveled three days.

The Third Transport

The third transport of 300 girls arrived from Bergen-Belsen in October 25, 1944. Knittel, by that time, had gained experience. His welcoming speech was short. Among those in that transport were my friends Elza Reich Szamosi, Hava Hartmann Kleinberg and her sister Miriam Hartmann Carmi, Márta Weisz Paran, Eva Rosenberg Eichler, and Klára Spitz Snitzler. They would greet us later when Erzsike and I arrived.

The Fourth and Final Transport of Jewish Women

I have more complete details of the fourth transport to Markkleeberg, since Erzsike and I were among the 300 who arrived on Friday, December 8, 1944.[3] We got off the train, organized in lines of five, and started to walk. The station was a short distance from the camp. As we walked inside the camp, girls called to us in Hungarian. When we answered back, they were all excited. Each one hoped to find or at least hear about family members from whom they were separated. As we continued, we were pleasantly surprised by what we found. The barracks were built of cement with glass windows, and they had electricity!

I remember feeling relieved when they led us to our living quarters, and the girls around us shouted, "You've arrived at a good place! Here we are

One of the barracks in the camp of Markkleeberg in 1944. The original is in the Heinetmuseum in Markkleeberg.

treated as workers." It was encouraging that we were no longer in an annihilation camp. The women in the barracks next to ours came from various cities and towns all over Hungary. They asked us, as new arrivals, many questions about the world of concentration camps and about Auschwitz and Bergen-Belsen, where they had been before.

We had ten three-tiered bunk beds in our room. On every bed was a mattress made of jute cotton filled with straw and an army blanket. We were all Hungarian except two girls, Hanka and her friend, who were from Poland. We could hardly sleep that night, despite the fact that it was the first time in our camp life that we each had a separate bed. We were so excited to be in the new place, which was, of all the camps, the most bearable. Later, as we became adjusted, however, we found that, for prisoners, life even in Markkleeberg was not easy.

Our First Days in Markkleeberg

The next day was Saturday, and we assembled in a large square. In the center stood a group of German soldiers and *Aufseherins.* Knittel made a speech, saying, "I hope you will be satisfied here. We will give you fair treatment, but we want to be pleased with your work." Zsuzsanna Csanyi, the official translator, translated his words. Knittel tried to appear friendly by smiling at us, but somehow I noticed only his shiny boots, the SS uniform, and his fierce eyes.

We were dismissed, and girls came to visit us later in the afternoon. They called the names of towns from Hungary and its annexed territories. As we listened, suddenly we heard the name of Abaújszántó. Erzsike looked at me and we jumped forward. It was only the two of us, out of the new arrivals, who were from Abaújszántó. The girls from our small village were dispersed, after Auschwitz, among the many camps in Germany.

Calling the name of Abaújszántó was Elza Reich Szamosi, whom we knew well from home. Elza had lived in a section near the railway station called Marcinfalva. Going to the center of the town or to the synagogue, she would pass our house, and we always talked a bit. Elza, some years my senior, was a resourceful and vivacious girl. Seeing her and having her hug us with real delight gave me a warm feeling, a reminder of home and of personal identity.

Despite her puzzled expression at first, seeing us so different than at home, Elza assured us that we looked good. Elza especially praised Erzsike, who was always pretty even as a child. After asking many questions about girls from Abaújszántó, Elza remembered that she had to go back to her barracks. She returned later with Márta Weisz Paran, another girl from Abaújszántó. Márta, older than Elza, was an exceptionally fine person whose father owned the large courtyard called the "*Zsidó udvar*" (the "Jewish yard"), with its many tenants. As was proper for visitors in our culture, Elza brought a gift—a bit of cane sugar that she had saved from her meal the day before. Both Márta and Elza assured us than our new residence was much better than Bergen-Belsen.

On Sunday they woke us a bit later because the German staff wanted to sleep longer. The factory was closed on Sundays and the girls from the whole camp were in the barracks. The *Appel* lasted longer that Sunday. There stood Bella Spitz, the *Lagerälteste,* looking well fed and warmly dressed. With her were Mrs. Erzsébet Iczkovits, her helper and work organizer, and Zsuzsanna Csanyi, the translator and office worker who spoke perfect German, French, and English. The *Aufseherins,* in their gray army skirts and jackets, were well groomed and perfumed. Some had teased blonde hair. As they watched the arriving group of soldiers, some of these women flirted openly with them. Then the head of the *Aufseherins,* the *Oberin,* stood in front of Knittel and recited the following standard opening text: "*Arbeit lager Markkleeberg, Ausen-commando Buchenwald.*" She then read the total numbers of those present and those sick.

The faces of many of the soldiers around were familiar to us because they were *Volksdeutsche,* ethnic Germans from Hungarian territories, and we knew their type well. With the arrival of Knittel, the entire staff was on the *Appelplatz* (assembly place). There was complete silence as we were counted three times over.

Later, the girls standing next to us hummed the following song. We quickly learned it.

> In Markkleeberg every daybreak, we head for the *Appel* place.
> We stand there for hours, our hands and feet chilled to the bone.
> We fall into lines of five, headed by the *Blockälteste.*
> Then the *Stuben* counts us over, God forbid if you are missing.
> The crowd thrusts you left and right. You better stand at attention right away.
> Whether it rains or the wind blows, you are a Jew so don't be disheartened.
> Everything will pass one day and all will come to an end.
> Every December holds the promise of a new May.[4]

Finally we were allowed to the blocks, and the girls from our town and the surrounding area came to visit again. Márta Weisz Paran brought with her Margit Lang Stein, who was born in the nearby small town of Gönc. We asked Margit about the Reinitz family, our relatives in Gönc; but she did not know their whereabouts. Margit was a classmate of Márta Weisz Paran while attending middle school in Abaújszántó. Both Margit and Márta were alone after the selection in Auschwitz—Márta lost her parents and a brother; while Margit's parents and younger sister also died in Auschwitz.

Márta and Margit worked in the large factory, while Elza was assigned to the smaller former chocolate factory. The factories, as we knew, were managed by Junkers Flugzeug und Motorenwerke A.G. Motorenbau Zweigwerk Markkleeberg for producing airplane parts.

The news of our arrival spread among the girls in the camp. Klára Spitz Snitzler, whom we met in the ghetto, came to see us later. Klára's mother and sister were sent to the other line when Klára was placed in the group for Markkleeberg. Klára was happy to see us, even though we had no news about her mother and sister. Klára's good friend was Eva Rosenberg Eichler. Eva's younger sister Judith had been Erzsike's playmate in Abaújszántó. Judith had been sent with her mother to the side of "no return" in Auschwitz. Since they were alone in Markkleeberg, Klára Spitz Snitzler and Eva Rosenberg Eichler also became *lager* sisters. They survived together and continued their lifelong sisterhood. Later we met the Hartmann sisters also—Hava Hartmann Kleinberg and Miriam Hartmann Carmi. They were born in Abaújszántó, but later left for the nearby town of Szikszó. The sisters had stayed together with girls from Abaújszántó and its neighboring area.

"What do you think of Bella, the *Lagerälteste?*" Elza asked.

"Bella is a heavy smoker," she told me, "and the girls who receive cigarettes from the foreign workers or from the German foremen sell them to Bella. For each cigarette, Bella gives two plates of thick soup, which she takes from our portions. Others, such as the *Blockältestes,* also steal from our meals," said Elza.

"What do you know about Knittel?" I asked Elza.

"We are all afraid of him," she answered. "He is a strange, mean person with scary, penetrating eyes. In the workplace, we never know when he will appear. The biggest sin was when someone spoke with a German civilian worker or forced laborer."

Elza and the other visiting girls looked orderly. It seemed as if their overalls were ironed, with a crease in the front. They looked at us in our wrinkled dirty clothing and large wooden shoes sorrowfully.

Our transport, the fourth and the last one of Jewish prisoners, was called "the group with the coats." Elza told us to take out the linings and the collars from the coats or they would be taken away from us anyhow, but we were afraid.

The girls visiting us were surprised that the Germans brought us still in December. They felt that the work in the factory was less at that point due to lack of raw material.[5] The Germans were also retreating, and the end of the war seemed near. As usual, we did not understand the SS plans or actions. Knowing today about the secret German plan for their offensive at the Battle of the Bulge (December 16, 1944–January 25, 1945), we can understand their optimism a bit.[6] We just felt enormously fortunate that somehow, always at the edge, our lives hanging on the thinnest thread, we were saved.

We had Saturday and Sunday to get oriented. We calculated the time by watching the changing of the guards. On Sunday afternoon, we had a bit more time to observe the camp and the barracks around us. Like other new arrivals, we were pleased with our improved accommodations. We had some concern about the work in the factory—whether we would be able to do it—but we did not want think about it.

Sunday night there was no *Appel.* We ate supper and waited for the next day. On Monday morning, we were called to the *Appelplatz.* There were no Germans at first; only Bella and some *Blockältestes* were present. Then the *Oberin* and the *Aufseherins* appeared. We stood there almost two hours. It was already light outside when we noticed Knittel. He was angry, and his frightful eyes flashed toward us. "*Hergott szakramentum!*" He screamed because some girls did not stand at attention. He passed our lines, cursing. Afraid even to look at his face, I just noticed his tall and shiny black patent leather boots and his firm steps.

By that time, each *Blockälteste* had taken her place at the head of her block. As we were waiting, Knittel told us, "Check how the girls who came before you march; you will have to do the same." Bella, standing next to Knittel, commanded in a loud singing voice, "*Links, zwei, drei, vier . . . Links . . . Links . . . Links.*" The girls, all in overalls, marched to the rhythm like soldiers. With them went some guards and *Aufseherins.* We watched them as they left by the gate and disappeared in two directions.

Our group was directed to the warehouse. We had to hand in our coats and each one received an overall. We were happy because we thought that we would be working in the factory with the overalls, but we had to pass the test of endurance for that. As we were waiting, one of the *Aufseherins* told us, "You have been brought here to work, and if someone will not work well, she will be sent to another camp."

We returned to the barracks and then again we were summoned to an *Appel.* Knittel watched as white ribbons with numbers were given out to each of us. My number was 50,226; Erzsike's was 50,225. We also received needles and thread to sew the white strip with the numbers onto the left arm of the overall sleeve.

The next day it seemed that we had just fallen asleep when suddenly the light came on in our room and someone screamed "Get up! *Appel!*" right in my ear. I jumped up, and soon the lines of shivering girls began forming. Then came Láju or Lajcsu, our *Blockälteste,* to count us. The *Lagerälteste* arrived next. The guards were already standing at the side, while the *Aufseherins* walked around to inspect whether the girls stood in line according to order. We knew our place was at the front; the taller girls stood in the back. The line next to us did not keep the order, and the *Aufseherin* nastily reprimanded them. We were relieved when she passed us by. Meanwhile, the girls from the other blocks, who already knew the morning ritual, stood erect with army discipline. All the prisoners from the blocks assembled in the yard not far from the water basin, forming a rectangle. The camp grew silent in anticipation. Knittel arrived with military stride. He stood directly in front of our group and gave a short speech, saying, "I hope you will be content here. Your work has to be good, to our satisfaction, and we will treat you well. Now, pay attention to how the other girls came before you. You will have to walk the same way. I like military order and discipline!"

Then the inmates organized in groups, according to their place of work. Each group was a *commando* or work group. The *Lagerälteste* began her usual singing: "*Links . . . zwei . . . drei . . . vier . . . Links . . . zwei . . . drei . . . vier . . . Links . . . Links . . . Links . . . .*" The line of girls in uniform overalls started to march in rhythm, accompanied by the guards and the *Aufseherins.* They left by the gate and disappeared.

The rest of us remained standing, and finally we all returned to the barracks, where we received breakfast: a cup of brown water that they called coffee! It was a cloudy raw day, and our unheated room gave little protection from the December chill. Wrapped in our blankets, we slowly drank the warm, dark liquid. It would have been good if we had saved some of our bread from the previous night, but we were afraid that it would be stolen, something that had happened to us before.

Suddenly we heard noises, and Mrs. Iczkovits, the work organizer, and Zsuzsanna Csanyi, the translator and secretary, stood at the door of our room complaining that we could not take such a long time for breakfast. Then suddenly Mrs. Iczkovits noticed the blankets on us. "How dare you use the blanket in daytime? Don't you know that it has to be spread nicely on the bed at all times!?" She scolded us angrily. I rushed to cover the beds, and we ran out fearfully.

Outside, with icy efficiency they counted us again and assigned us to different work groups. We could not work in the factory with German civilians and foreign workers until we passed the quarantine period to be sure we brought no communicable diseases with us. We were assigned instead to work crews outside of the camps. Some of the girls were added to existing commandos. Twenty girls were assigned to woodcutting; twenty to the carpentry shop; others to tailoring; some to the shoemaker's shop; twelve to collect garbage; twenty for gardening; twenty for road repair; and eight for coal shoveling.[7] The rest of us, a large group of sixty girls, Erzsike and I among them, were assigned to work in the quarry as our initiation to Markkleeberg.

Shortly, as we were standing and waiting to leave, an SS soldier of the lowest rank appeared. He led us out of the camp. At the gate, they counted us, and from the storage area we picked up shovels, pickaxes, and spades to carry to the quarry.

The Stone Quarry

The work in these squads of prisoners was among the hardest physical torment we had to endure. The rock quarry was a notorious place, designed for special uninterrupted ill-treatment by the SS. The women toiled in the bitter cold without protective clothing. Some axed out the stone, others crushed it to load onto carts or wheelbarrows and move it, using primitive methods, to other parts of the camp where they had to pile it up. The work was not only physically grueling, but also dangerous. It was the kind of December weather with dry cold and heavy winds. With each breath, our lungs filled with bitter cold air. Our hands froze as we walked, carrying the heavy shovels on our shoulders to the quarry. Some of the girls wrapped their feet in pieces of cloth they had taken from the lining of their coats. We were afraid to do it, so our bare feet became icy in the wooden shoes.

The quarry was not far from the blocks, over the road. It was in the form of a cavity deep in the ground. The elderly SS who led us to the quarry explained something angrily that no one understood. We could not imagine why he was so angry. Later we found out that he was a *Volksdeutsche,* an ethnic German from the territories who had volunteered for the SS. We referred to him as "Lófogú" or "Horse-teeth" because of his large extruding teeth. Lófogú always seemed to have a sarcastic smile. He was the most vicious of the SS guards.

Giving up his attempt to explain the job, Lófogú counted out thirty girls to put down into the two-meter-deep pit. Erzsike and I, who always stayed next to each other from a constant fear of losing one another, were among them. We were required to produce gravel for the road to beautify the camp. We all knew that it was not necessary, and the only purpose of it was to keep us working to torture us.

Lófogú came down into the pit shortly and stood next to us. While talking, he demonstrated the process we were expected to follow. First, those with the pickaxes, such as Erzsike, had to cut into the soil as the first step in producing the gravel. He showed how to push pickax into the hard wall of sand and gravel. Even he had difficulties doing it because the soil was all frozen. Then those with the spades had to dig deep into the loosened soil. The resulting gravel had to be shoveled and lifted up over the top of the two-meter-deep pit.

The soil was so frozen that only with tremendous effort with the pickax and spade could the girls produce a small amount of gravel. Lófogú was angry. He expected us to work like strong men. I watched Erzsike as she tried with all her strength to cut into the frozen wall of earth and stone. Then those of us with the shovels also had trouble scooping and throwing the stones to the surface of the pit. The earth and stones on the shovel were very heavy and they tumbled right back. I could hardly move the shovel once the stones were on it, and Lófogú complained that we did not raise the shovels high enough. To make us better understand his German orders and his threats, Lófogú asked for a volunteer translator. At the beginning, we did not know Lófogú's background, did not know that he came from southern Hungary and that he spoke the language well. We only discovered it later when he was a bit tipsy and cursed a girl in Hungarian. That first day, a woman volunteered, and she translated Lófogú's instructions to work faster and faster. The translator, a lawyer by profession, dared to tell him that we never did such work before and we were in weakened physical condition. For that, Lófogú kicked the woman so hard that she limped for weeks after that.

Lófogú continued angrily to push, curse, and hit anyone nearby. When he moved close to Erzsike, I was petrified of what would happen. Lófogú raised his whip, and I heard the girl next to Erzsike cry. Lófogú continued to strike her so hard that she fell down. Then he kicked her as she lay on the ground. Having enough, Lófogú left and went up to harass the second group of girls above the pit. I ran to my sister as she was kneeling down to comfort the unfortunate victim, whose name was Judit. On our way to Markkleeberg, Judit had been sitting next to us in the boxcar, and she was very friendly. She was the young wife of a well-to-do estate owner, and she was liked and respected by the other women of her town. Hearing our sympathy and heeding the pleas of those next to us, Judit slowly stood up and assessed the damage to her body.

Pulling the Heavy Carriage

On top of the pit was a huge sieve to sift the gravel or sand. After sifting, the girls put the gravel on a four-wheel carriage. Pulled by the girls, this transported the gravel to the group who worked in road maintenance. They spread the gravel and straightened the road and the *Appelplatz.*

Lófogú screamed at the girls on top of the pit to fill the carriage higher. Finally satisfied, he assigned the thirty girls to be the horses. Seven stood at each side of the carriage, the rest standing at the front and the back. In addition to his whip, Lófogú picked up a big tree branch to hit the girls. The group tried to pull the heavy load with the crushed rock and gravel, but they could not move it. In desperation, the girls accused one another of not pulling hard enough. As they were maneuvering, the unstable carriage laden with its heavy cargo derailed, striking those who failed to get out of the way in time.

Replacing the stones and gravel on the collapsed cart, the girls started anew to pull. Down in the pit we could rest a bit as Lófogú tortured the others above. We watched, petrified, how the veins bulged on the necks of those who pulled the carriage in front, their heads bent and one foot forward. We were afraid that they might tear themselves in half as they unsuccessfully pulled and pushed the heavy cargo. Lófogú started to scream and curse, raising his whip high to come down in force and bludgeon his victims; then as if by a miracle, the carriage started to roll.

We kept silent, knowing that our turn would come again soon. Trembling from fear and cold, we leaned on our shovels and pickaxes to rest a bit. Lófogú ran back, but luckily we noticed in time that he was coming down, and we started to work. Lófogú did not like our work and began to strike out in all directions. I felt the edge of the whip on my back, which hurt a lot, but I ignored it so Erzsike would not worry.

In the meantime, we noticed a group of girls from the *Eskommando* carrying our soup. Stopping his blows and curses, Lófogú gestured that it was lunch break. He counted us, and we returned to our barracks in camp.

Sitting exhausted on the beds in our frosty room, we waited for the meal.

The door opened and we could see a big container. From it, we received a plate of warm soup. We ate it slowly, keeping it in our mouths to last longer and enjoying every drop of it. Then, from beyond our door we heard voices shouting, "Don't eat so slowly! Line up outside quickly." We knew that it was Mrs. Iczkovits. We gobbled the reminder of our soup and, with some still in our mouths, we ran outside. There we organized in five-person lines and waited.

Lófogú arrived, and we marched back to the quarry and continued to produce the gravel. Our tears and sighs mixed with the dust. My back still aching from the morning, I was in constant tension, fearing Lófogú's presence. Probably tired and more agitated in the afternoon, Lófogú indiscriminately hit everyone around him. How would we take it four more hours, until five o' clock, not to mention tomorrow and all the other days? No one had an answer. Meanwhile, even for Lófogú, the cold was a bit too much. He took a break, and another guard came to relieve him. With the new guard, the time passed faster, and eventually we found ourselves on the evening *Appel,* trembling and aching in every part of our bodies.

At night, we hardly had strength to take off our wooden shoes as we fell into bed. It seemed that we did not even close our eyes before we were back at the morning *Appel.* Freezing and shivering in the biting cold, we could hardly stand straight. After the usual counting and recounting, the groups started to depart. Those who worked in the factory at Zwenkau left first. By the time our turn came, the night shift had arrived back from work. Girls from the night shift could sleep until five o'clock in the afternoon if there were no air raids that forced them into the air-raid shelter or bunker. The night shift began at 6:00 PM.

That second day, instead of tossing gravel with the shovel over the top of the pit, we collected the stones and gravel in baskets and carried them up by hand. The task would have been easier if not for the big wooden clogs I was wearing. My back was still aching from the day before, and the bruises on my hand from the heavy shovel and my neck from Lófogú's whip had turned into painful sores, which made it harder to climb and carry the stones up to the top of the pit. The ordeal of mining gravel from the frozen walls continued with no letup. The spades were heavy, and to the weakened girls, were hard even to hold. The soil was like ice. I felt so sorry for Erzsike that I offered to change places with her, but she refused and continued to dig fearfully, relentlessly, and unsuccessfully. Luckily, two strong girls next to her worked extra hard, hoping also to warm up by moving; and they produced enough stones and gravel to cover Erzsike's failure.

Changes in winter weather and the falling of heavy snow added to our misfortune. Every two hours, the guards were relieved because of the bitter cold, even though they wore warm boots, sweaters, and heavy winter coats. We found a bit of relief from our stress and predicament in poems that the girls composed to the tunes of popular Hungarian songs. Although we could not voice our complaints or pain, the songs expressed our hopes and wishes for revenge.

Three girls are up on the ditch pondering a bad shovel;
Hey, it is hard to push that bursting wheelbarrow!
You should pull and push that jam-packed dump-cart,
Even if you are weary of dragging the yoke!
Whoever ordered this, God should strike,
Hey, with iron nails onto his ugly face![8]

We sang this song cursing the SS with gusto whenever we had a few minutes when the Germans were at a distance.

Our friends from home came to see us, mostly on Sundays. We were still afraid to leave the area of our barracks. Klára Spitz Snitzler brought news from the world, while Márta Weisz Paran with her quiet manner tried to comfort and reassure us that the factory gates would soon open for us. Working there would shield us against the fury of the winter winds and against Lófogú's violence. It was a nice aspiration, but in the meantime, each workday was a nightmare repeating itself. I woke up with fear of what the day would bring. I was worried and scared, especially for Erzsike. On *Appel,* I stood in front of the line, before Erzsike, so that she would not notice the uncontrollable tears flowing down my face. Our peril was not only the heavy work, but the danger of Lófogú's rages.

The Translators

Translators at work were targets for the anger of the SS. Either they were accused of being too slow in translating or—if the reaction of the girls was not exactly what the SS expected—of not translating well. Lófogú had a special reason to be angry. He knew Hungarian and understood what we were saying. On one occasion, Lófogú made a girl translate to us, among other insults, that we did not know how to do physical work because we had been too busy collecting usury from the Christians. Our reaction, expressed in Hungarian, may not have pleased him.

Then Lófogú went on his break. During this time, he consumed some quantity of liquor to get warm. When he returned, he moved toward the translator, and, without any cause or provocation, he slapped her face with such force that she fell backward. Lófogú probably did not like the comment the girl had added earlier. Unfortunately, the girl fell into a wheelbarrow and hurt her rib. She fainted and was taken to the *Revier* (Camp Infirmary). There she came to herself as the nurse washed the blood off her face and gave her a warm glass of tea and encouraging words. She never wanted to translate again after that.

Lófogú was given a new translator who spoke perfect German, but even she did not understand sometimes what Lófogú was saying. Being *Volksdeutsche,* Lófogú spoke with an accent and a special dialect. The translator asked him to repeat his commands, which brought the old SS man into a rage; he started to curse and slapped her face.

Desperation

A girl named Zsuzsi was one of our partners in the five-person line. She was suffering from frostbite, bladder problems, and low spirits, as were so many of us. Zsuzsi told us of her thoughts about touching the electrified wire. Suicide, which was the only means of escape from the camp and its agony, entered the minds of many of the prisoners. We had contemplated it in Auschwitz, but only a few could really go through with it. There was one dark, stormy, snowy morning in Markkleeberg when we were on our way to the quarry, and suddenly we noticed a body hanging on the camp's electric fence. It was someone who had touched the electric wire. The sight was so horrible, so frightening! The victim was a woman wearing an overall like ours. Her corpse was held to the fence by the power of the electric current. I turned quickly away and told Erzsike not to look. Zsuzsi continued to stare, however. She kept silent the rest of the way. We never heard the word suicide from her again. The unfortunate woman who took that desperate action was called Eva, as we learned later. She grieved for her eight-year-old daughter whose birthday would have been that day. The little girl had walked with her grandmother and that way they were separated—the grandmother and child sent to die in Auschwitz.

A New Temporary Assignment

One morning when the work in the quarry had been temporarily cancelled, Mrs. Iczkovits counted out fifteen girls from the quarry work group, Erzsike and I among them, to join another work group. There we saw Isabella Lörinch Szilás and her sister Margit Lörinch Hamburg. They waved, as they stood there with three cousins. We knew them from Bergen-Belsen, where we had been together in the same barracks.

In addition to the quarry, the Germans invented other special tasks to occupy the members of our transport. They made the women dig holes in rocky terrain and carry the earth, with the stones, to several locations. Then, in a few days, the whole thing had to be brought back. The work was a senseless and useless doing and undoing. We were assigned to pick up wheelbarrows, spades, and shovels. Erzsike had the shovel and I was given a spade that time. Isabella and her cousin pulled a wheelbarrow. Even carrying the large, wet shovel and the heavy spade was an effort in our run-down condition. Finally we reached a field where the ground was ice-covered from the bitter cold. We had to dig up and transfer the earth and gravel to another location.

My hands, with no gloves, were so frozen that my nails were aching. I could not even move the spade. Erzsike looked worried, but she had her own struggle to dig into the soggy ground with the heavy wet shovel. Lófogú, who seemed to be supervising everywhere outside, stepped aside for a while. Erzsike quickly offered to put my hand under her arm. That way I could warm it a bit while still moving the spade in my other hand. While hoping not to be noticed as we all worked close to one another, I suddenly felt a strong slash on my back. It was Lófogú's whip again. The pain brought me close to fainting, but somehow I collected all my strength and started to work. Luckily it was not the same place that I was hit before. I was scared that if I stopped moving that meanest man on earth would continue to beat and kill me. It seemed like a miraculous rescue when Lófogú's attention was drawn to a wheelbarrow turning over, pouring out its contents. He rushed over and vented his full fury on the girls who were working with the wheelbarrow.

I tried to push the spade, while my tears turned to ice on my frozen overall. Suddenly Margit, Isabella's sister, came near and hurriedly dug out a large amount of soil in front of me to impress Lófogú if he returned. Fortunately, Lófogú was no longer interested and left me alone, but Margit's compassion touched my heart. In the evening I shared with Erzsike her portion of bread so I could take mine to Margit. The bread was my only thing of worth by which I could express my gratitude. Margit, hungry as she was, hugged me and returned the gift.

The heavy snowstorms in December gave us a few days of rest, then the work resumed—back to the quarry again. The quarry was full of snow, and Lófogú forced us down the hole to shovel out the snow from the inside. The snow reached our waists, and we became thoroughly wet. Shivering all over, we listened to Lófogú shouting, cursing, and torturing a girl, Piri, his latest victim.

Lófogú Exposed

Assigned to our group that day was an *Aufseherin* instead of the regular guard. She watched Lófogú's sadism with horror. The *Aufseherin* was trained to be brutal, but even for her it was too much. At that time, Lófogú was screaming at Piri for failing to understand his commands in German. Piri was in her mid-thirties and was very run-down physically. Lófogú started to beat her with the shovel until the handle broke on the poor woman's body. Piri fainted and mercifully stopped feeling the blows; but Lófogú, like a madman, continued to beat her with the shovel's broken handle as she lay on the ground. As we could only cry in desperation, we did not even notice when the *Aufseherin* left. Shortly she returned with Knittel who talked to Lófogú and the two left together. Freezing from the cold in wet clothing, and shivering from Lófogú's cruelty, we did not believe our luck as we were led back to the barracks. Piri, still unconscious, was taken to the *Revier.* She never recovered fully, though, and she died during the Death March.

The Musician

The following morning, the winter, still in its rage, made us even more fearful to start another day with Lófogú in the quarry. The warmly dressed *Lagerälteste,* Bella Spitz, who later would be working in the quarry herself, and Mrs. Iczkovits arrived. Our cries sounded everywhere: "I can't take it!" "We will all be killed by Lófogú!" Seeing the guards approaching, I started to tremble. Erzsike noticed, and not wanting to admit my fear, I said that I was shivering with cold. The guard who came to our group was not Lófogú, however, but one whom the girls called "the Musician." He was more tolerant, and we were relieved. The Musician established a congenial atmosphere, and he was only as strict as necessary. Then we heard that Lófogú had been transferred back to Buchenwald.

We were always happy when the Musician worked with us. He was a *Wehrmacht* soldier (regular German army) short of build and previously had been a conductor of the orchestra in Berlin.[9] He seemed sympathetic to us and let us rest. Only when he noticed Knittel coming, he hinted with his hand, and we would get back to work. The Musician especially liked Erzsike, the youngest of all of us.

One morning that was even colder than the day before, the Musician asked if we knew some Hungarian songs. The girls started to sing, and some spirited ones even danced the csàrdàs, a lovely Hungarian national dance. The Musician enjoyed it, as he kept an eye out for Knittel's sudden appearance.

Punishment of Barracks Six

Finally it was lunchtime that day. Sitting in our room with hands still frozen from the piercing cold, every minute we could stay inside counted.

To please the Germans, Erzsébet Iczkovits, the work organizer, arranged for us to be ready and wait outside after lunch. Usually we obeyed, but that day it seemed to us that she wanted to chase us out even earlier than usual. With the winds shrieking around, some girls who worked in the quarry were a bit slow returning to *Appel* after lunch. They were understandably reluctant to stand in the below-zero weather for a long time before the guards arrived. Mrs. Iczkovits ran for Bella Spitz who was very angry. To make sure that it would not happen again, Bella declared that the next day we would have no lunch. Then the two of them chased everyone out into the windstorm.[10]

At night, after that hard day, block six had to stand for punishment as Bella complained to Knittel about us. We stood on *Appel* late into the night. Erzsike hugged me as soon as the *Aufseherin* passed us by. We were shivering from the cold. Girls fainted, and one collapsed next to me. Then, finally, the group was allowed back into the barracks. The next day at lunch time we were waiting for the soup, but it did not come. Instead, Bella arrived. "You are being punished for your behavior yesterday, you rotten girls. I told you that you will not be given food as punishment."

"Aunt Bella, please help us! We are so hungry, we will not be able to work in the afternoon," beseeched some young girls. Bella was unmoved. We went back to work without food, shaking and almost dizzy from hunger. It would be four more hours until we would receive our evening bread. It was very hard; even the next day, we felt the missed calories.

Workers for the Internal Operation of the Camp

The tasks inside the camp that involved feeding, housing, and minding the inmates were run by the prisoners themselves. Separate work crews performed them. The workers, as camp personnel, did not stand on *Appel,* and they received their midday meal at the workplace.

Storeroom Workers

The storage and sewing room was part of the long barracks containing the laundry, shoemaker, carpentry shop, and storage. It was in the southern end of the camp. The train tracks were not far from there. The storeroom was a large space containing wooden shelves where the girls had to store and organize the clothing taken from the prisoners, such as coats and underwear. There were also blankets and garments sent from other camps stored there. Miriam Porat worked in the storeroom with a helper, while others did the sewing and mending. The *Aufseherins* visited quite often to select things for themselves, and their visits caused extra tensions for the workers. An SS guard that we called Tischler (carpenter) was in charge. He came to check on them from time to time; when he was not there, he locked the girls in from the outside. Hearing the lock click always gave them a creepy feeling.

The girls working in the storeroom prepared tickets and prisoners' card numbers to list the clothing of each prisoner. It was a large assignment. The cards listed our names and the clothing each had. We stood, dead tired after a day of hard work at the quarry, and waited on an endless line for our turn. Two typists wrote down our prisoner numbers, followed by name, birth date, profession, country of origin, and the articles of clothing. The cards had no practical use because we all had almost the same outfits. After all our misery, no one ever looked at the cards, which were, like many other documents in the camp, destroyed at the end of the war.[11]

The Hairdresser

Irene Keisler Schnur, a vivacious young girl, was working in the stone quarry with her sister, Klára Keisler. Being almost at the end of their endurance, they looked for some way out. As with all societies, networking—knowing someone or having personal connections—was useful even in the camps. Irene knew Mandi, who was in charge of the laundry. When Knittel looked for a hairdresser for his wife, who had just had a permanent wave and did not know how to care for it, Mandi recommended Irene. Irene not only knew her trade, but she also had a good knowledge of German.

During roll call, Irene heard her name called and got very scared. Knittel inquired where she had studied and asked Irene for a demonstration. He warned her that if she was not really a hairdresser she would be punished severely. He then watched as Irene set his wife's hair. Passing this test satisfactorily, Irene was assigned to the job. Every night, she set Mrs. Knittel's hair and combed it out in the morning. Irene also began grooming the hair of the *Aufseherins* who lived in the camp. Just as for Knittel's wife, she set their hair at night and combed it in the morning. She also applied color and other treatments. When Irene was not busy with hairdressing, she had to help the girls clean the rooms of the *Aufseherins*. The work power had to be fully utilized![12]

The Barracks

Cleaning outside was a good way to learn the layout of the camp and the different barracks. The barracks were also called "blocks"—a block referred to a place as well as to its residents. There were about six of these elongated brick buildings in a rectangular or U-shape, with room for roll call in the middle. The barracks were built from stone because of the frequent bombing and danger of fire. They were unheated, cold, and damp; but we did have rooms with windows, washrooms, and relatively normal indoor flush toilets. No maps or charts are left of the actual campsite. A plan was drawn by Rosalia Lazar, one of the survivors who gave testimony on March 25, 1971, to the Federal Justice Bureau for the clarification of Nazi crimes. Her drawing comes close to the arrangement of the camp.[13]

According to the plan drawn by Lazar and by my recollection, the camp had a rectangular form. Some of the barracks used for the officers and housing the SS personnel were outside the fence. There were also barracks for storage and workshops inside the barbed wire. A strong iron gate ensured that the prisoners could not escape. There was a post or guard's room with doors at both sides of the entrance and two guards stationed at each side. In the winter, the post rooms were heated. The SS flag was flying at the entrance.

Before entering the camp on the left, outside the fence, was the office of Knittel, the *Obersharführer,* or camp commander. From his office, Knittel could look inside to the camp. The home of Knittel and his wife was next to his office.

There was a long barracks containing workshops for shoe repair, carpentry, the two laundries, and also a storage room for clothing and sewing.

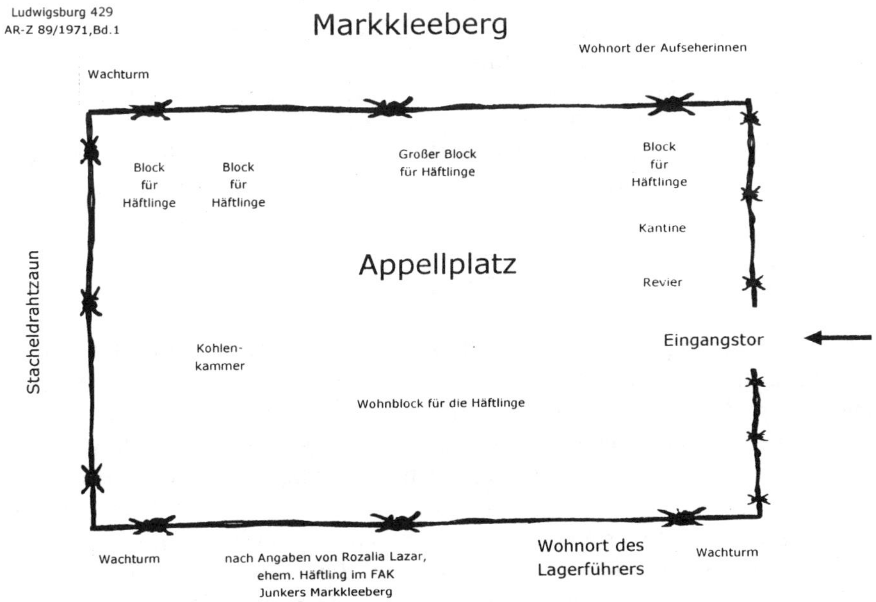

Map of the Markkleeberg camp by survivor Rosalia Lazar.

Some of the guards lived in town with their families. Others had their home in the camp. The rooms of the guards were plain, with simple iron-framed beds and uniform-colored bedding.[14]

On the right side entering the camp was barracks number one. The *Revier* and the canteen were part of that barracks. There were also some rooms for inmates. The entrance to that barracks was on the other side, so when we entered the camp and passed by, we saw only the windows. Márta Maget Leitmann was the *Blockälteste* in barracks number one. Later she moved to barracks number three.

Barracks number two was a long one that was at our back during *Appel.* The air-raid shelter was in the corner of barracks two, and the train ran beyond the fence there.

Barracks number three was a long barracks not far from barracks two. The welders who worked in the Westhalle of the large factory stayed in room twenty-two of barracks three. Erzsebet Frank wrote a poem about the welders in barracks three.

Before they emptied barracks number four for the arrival of the French women resistance fighters, girls from the first and second transport were housed there. Behind barracks number four was the electric fence. When the French political prisoners lived there, a Red Cross sign was put on the barracks.

Opposite to barracks four and three, at the corner close to the fence, was barracks number five. Wide and long, it could be seen from the entrance and from barracks number one. Erzsébet Iczkovits and the *Lagerälteste* Bella Spitz stayed in block number five.

Barracks number six was our barracks when we arrived. All 300 of us were housed there. Laju (or Oecillia) Friedman was the *Blockälteste.* Laju, who was from Halm, stayed with her sister, Olga Friedman, in room number one. Laju was a good person and got along well with us.

Our Living Quarters

The barracks, made of stone, contained individual rooms. Long corridors ran throughout the length of the hallway. The rooms had stone floors, and every room had two windows. With the first transport, there were ten girls in each room. The beds were two-tiered bunk beds made of widely spaced narrow strips of wood.[15] Each had a bare straw sack for a mattress. As more transports arrived, the crowding increased and the beds became three-tiered. There was a ladder to climb to the upper bed. Later there were between twenty and thirty girls in the room. Our room was full, with beds left, right, and in the middle, including ten triple bunk beds. We had to keep any possessions with us, except the blankets, because the other inmates might covet even the smallest item.

The small stoves that each room had were made of black metal. At the beginning, girls from the first transports even received portions of coal and were permitted to light the stove. As the coal supply grew smaller, the German staff in the camp decided to keep all the coal for themselves. Our rooms remained unheated even in the coldest weather of minus ten or fifteen degrees. Some girls were able to steal cooks (square pieces of coal) to heat the room. Having a bit of warmth and the possibility of washing one's hair was a pleasure that women later recalled vividly from their memories of the camp. It also brought heavy punishment if someone was caught.

Washrooms and Toilets

There was a washroom inside each barracks. The water—only cold —flowed from faucets in a round basin. We had to let the water run a little because the pipe was often frozen, and icicles hung from the faucets in winter. The water was so cold that our bodies steamed as we washed in the icy water.

Erzsike and I made it a point to wake up early in the morning, because later it would be very busy around the faucets. Half asleep, we stood and washed ourselves with no soap in the cold water and went directly to *Appel.* Today I do not know how we could stand it.

Not far from the washroom was the toilet area. There were four toilets with normal "Niagara flushing," but we had no toilet paper. The doors, at least, could be closed from the inside.

"Free" Time

There was no restriction on visiting other barracks, except when it was "blocksperre" (barracks curfew). Then it was forbidden to leave one's place. Even with no restrictions, though, we were so busy with all kinds of *Appel* and special activities in the camp that we were always under time pressure when we visited the other barracks.

At 8:30 in the evening, the lights were turned off, and the barracks were locked for the night. Reflectors around the fence lit up the area of the camp. Wooden shades with locks were on the windows. It was a bad feeling to be locked in our barracks and know that, in case of fire, we would be unable to escape. Later, when the bombing increased, the guards told some of the girls in Hungarian that the shades were not locked and that we could get out in the event of a fire, but I did not know that at the time.[16]

In the morning, the *Aufseherin* came and opened the door. By then, the *Blockälteste* was already up and was running to wake the girls. The

Aufseherin, as she came in, also shouted, “Get up!” We were given five minutes to get ready.

Soon We Will Be Factory Workers

As the days became a bit warmer, advancing toward spring, it was not so bad to work outside. Lófogú was no longer with us, and there was a more relaxed atmosphere. Then, as if to ensure that we could never have certainty in camp life, came a surprise. On a nice sunny morning around the middle of January, the factory representatives arrived and gave us news we had wished for all winter: Ninety percent of the girls from block six were assigned to factory work. A small group would work in the former chocolate factory, which was a smaller place, but Erzsike and I would be going to the large factory.

4

Life in the Camp

Overview of the Camp Environment

As members of the last-arriving group of Jewish Hungarian prisoners, Erzsike and I joined an already-established society created by the inmates. Opportunities to make prison life easier were present for those who were enterprising or had certain skills or knowledge of languages. Although we had no money, we had some bartering possibilities. Those more resourceful were a bit less hungry and sometimes even less cold. This was the so-called concentration-camp universe.

We knew, of course, that even in Markkleeberg our existence was precarious, that we were always at the edge. New orders effecting immediate changes in our lives could be given at any time. Yet to survive, we had to adapt to those constantly changing situations. The resilience and ability to cope we developed in the camp may have helped us in building new lives after the war.

The "internal history" of the camp reveals that each prisoner employed her own personal strategy in the struggle for survival. Those twenty to thirty years old had a better chance of standing up under the harsh conditions. Social status did not appear to be a significant factor, except that members of the lower middle class or petit bourgeoisie seemed to adapt to camp life better than the intellectuals or the well-to-do.[1] Only in exceptional cases, such as having a medical degree, did the prisoner's former education influence her place and adjustment. We, as young teenagers, were often slow to recognize opportunity and less daring than our elders. We followed the daily routine with a sense of resignation, having only some few moments of simple pleasure.

The Struggle to Be Clean and Groomed

The girls tried to keep clean by all means they could, risking heavy punishments to do so. The biggest discipline problem faced by SS *Oberscharführer* Alois Knittel in the factory was the challenge of preventing the girls from washing themselves and their clothes. The high value women traditionally place on personal appearance must be a natural inclination, for even the most disciplined inmate would risk punishment for a little bit of hygiene. We all associated neatness with better self-esteem, health, and survival. Through fright and peril, the inmates transgressed rules when it concerned their personal hygiene. Even talking about it today, some said they felt very lucky not to be caught. Many were.

To catch violators day and night, Knittel alerted the *Aufseherins* to watch for transgressors. Thus, in addition to Knittel, we had to worry about the female guards who circled around. One *Aufseherin* noticed that Klára Spitz Snitzler had wet hair. Klára, our friend from home who had always been neat and well dressed, had used the warm water near her machine. She did not have a towel or anything to dry her hair, so it was very wet for a long time. The *Aufseherin* wrote down her number. At night, after *Appel* and without receiving her portion of bread, Klára was taken to stand by the fence at Knittel's window. Klára had to gather all her strength not to fall forward on top of the electric fence that was so close. Keeping alert and away from the fence was a challenge in the cold after a long day of work in the factory. We all felt sorry for her; and our friend Elza Reich Szamosi came to collect little bits of bread from all of us who knew Klára from home. It was not until after the light was turned out at 8:30 that Klára was released, so we could not see her. Exhausted and hungry, she came to her bunk and found her bowl with morsels of bread on her bed. She knew right away from whom they came. The next day we all got warm hugs in return.

Erzsike and I, who were so afraid of going against the rules, found another way to keep a bit clean. We heard that girls in the washroom were willing to wash overalls for a day's portion of bread. It was a big sacrifice, but our overalls were hardened with dirt from months of wearing them. Even after showers, we had to put on the same dirty overalls. Although our survival instincts drove us to carry on, we were miserable to have only one set of clothing to wear, day and night.

It was springtime, bright and fresh, and we wanted to be a little bit of dirt free. After much consideration, we gave Erzsike's overalls to be cleaned. We worked at night, so when we slept in the day, the girls from the laundry took the overalls with them. We did not sleep well that day from worry that we would be called suddenly to *Appel* or have an air raid. Luckily, nothing happened, and the girls brought back the overalls late in the afternoon. When Erzsike put them on, the overalls were still damp. The next week I gave my overalls to be cleaned. We shared one portion of bread between us. It felt so good to look a bit human in the clean overalls. We thought about mother and grandmother and imagined how proud they would be. We just could not accept and refused even to think that they were no longer among the living. Looking back now, I think that it was an unconscious coping mechanism that we and other inmates developed.

Unfortunately, my delight with the clean overalls did not last long. A few days later, as the girls were pushing and pulling during mealtime, someone poured soup on me. I was so upset that Erzsike offered to give me her overall pants, but I would not accept. I cleaned the spill a bit with the morning "coffee," and we also obtained some emery from the factory. Other girls showed me how to use the emery, and it did not look so bad. If I was caught, I knew I would be punished; yet the conditions in the camp forced even scared young girls to go against the rules.

The dress we wore underneath the overalls we washed in cold water from the faucets in the barracks' water fountain. Then we put the dress under the mattress, and it dried at night from our body heat. Elza told us also to fold our overall pants by the seam and put them under the straw mattress: that straightened out the fabric and made lines or edges as if it had been ironed. We could hardly stand from tiredness and hunger, but we folded our overall pants. Keeping our clothing a bit decent improved our feelings of well-being. Sometimes, even with all our motivation, however, we were so terribly tired that we just fell on the bed with our clothing and even our shoes on. Then we looked at Hanka, a young Polish girl who took off her clothing every night thinking that would prevent her from getting lice. Even if the light was already off, she would carefully arrange her clothing. One night when we still worked in the quarry, we came in very late after a long punishment *Appel.* Everyone else just fell into bed, but Hanka sat like an obedient child from a good home, properly folding her few rags of clothing; and she still had the strength to sing a soft melody.

Hanka, whose last name we never knew, stayed in our room with her friend, another Polish girl. They were always together, and we thought that they were sisters. We communicated only by sign language, but Hanka's gentleness and intelligence were noticeable. Girls who could talk with Hanka in a bit of German told us that she had been separated from her mother at Auschwitz. Her father, a rich manufacturer, was among the first taken by the Gestapo.[2] Hanka was in Ghetto Lodz with her mother, and from there they were deported to Auschwitz. Somehow she ended up in Markkleeberg like us. Hanka met her friend, the other Polish girl, in Markkleeberg and they become close, like sisters. With her beautiful singing voice, Hanka was everyone's favorite.

In those days when we worked in the quarry and during the nights of terrible cold, Hanka would sing "My Jidishe Mame" (my Jewish mother) in the darkness of our room. We, who were so much absorbed in our Hungarian culture, did not know Yiddish and could not understand the words of that beautiful touching song of the devoted Jewish mother. We just listened to Hanka's soft, heartrending melody and the word *mame,* and that was enough to bring us to tears. Pouring out our pain while remembering the presence of our mother helped Erzsike and I face the next day's quarry work a bit more easily. The song also brought us closer to Hanka. We found a common language of longing as we spoke about the group of devoted women we called Jewish mothers.

Songs and cultural activities not only boosted the psychological well-being of the inmates, they also formed the bridge between different groups. The most important benefit was the return, even temporarily, to human virtues such as pity, brotherhood, and respect for others that the Nazis tried to stamp out. When we were a bit less stressed about the work outside, Hanka sang cheerful songs, which made us momentarily forget our troubles. With the changes in work schedules, Hanka and the other Polish girl were moved to another barracks. I would meet Hanka again in the Death March under very sad circumstances.

Showers

We usually cleaned ourselves daily in the washroom under the few faucets that were set up in circular fashion in each barracks. The water was ice cold, and sometimes the windows were broken, letting in the angry winter wind. Erzsike and I, fearing more lice, decided every evening to get up early the next morning to be first in the washroom, before the crowds took possession. But then, when morning came, we were so tired that it was hard to keep our plans.

Close to the offices of Knittel and the German staff was a small room with showers. Girls in the first and second transports each received a piece of soap and a small gray towel. They also used the towel as a kerchief or a hat. There were no guards in the showers; only the *Aufseherins* supervised the bathing. Girls from the second transport, who came directly from Auschwitz, were terrified when they were led to the showers, afraid that gas would come out instead of water. *Aufseherins* who probably did not know much about the death camps wondered what was the matter with them.

The shower room was very small, and only ten girls were allowed in at one time. We had no soap, and five girls received one towel to share, which we had to leave in the shower. The water was very hot. The one small towel (thirty by fifty centimeters) for five girls was sufficient only to wipe our faces. Surprisingly, we were all considerate to the others and really only wiped the water out of our eyes.

At the beginning, they heated the showers every weekend, and each time another group was taken for a shower. Our turn came about once a month.

In the final months, we had fewer showers and, when we did, we just changed back into our vermin-infested clothing.

Women who had larger-size breasts suffered greatly in the camps. In Auschwitz, for instance, when a girl received a dress much smaller than her size, especially at the breast, she was not only uncomfortable, but ashamed to be seen in such a small outfit all the time. In Markkleeberg girls cut a piece from the length of their dresses, under the overalls, and made themselves some kind of brassiere, either by sewing or tying together the pieces. Others who worked in the electro commando, for instance, made panties and bras from the rags they received to clean the electric outlets.[3] Those who knew to how to sew and could obtain some kind of cloth made bras for themselves and their friends. Wearing a brassiere gave them a feeling of neatness. It was also a good bartering item: Girls were ready to sacrifice their portion of bread for it.

Undressing for the showers and revealing the extra clothing under the overalls caused fear and anxiety. In the factory, a kind German civilian foreman, for instance, brought Gitta Susitzky Hönig a shirt with thread and needle and told her to go to the bathroom and sew the shirt under the overalls' blouse. When the *Aufseherins* were checking clothing during the showers, Gitta was terribly scared; but luckily, the illicit shirt was not found.

We came out all soaked from the hot showers and stood on *Appel* waiting for the others. Without any covering on our wet heads, we stood in the cold night as the snow was falling on us in large flakes, like silver stars. After thirty or forty minutes, this seemed an eternity; the guards came, counted, and took us back to the barracks. Markkleeberg residents who could observe the camp from a distance noted how prisoners were left outside, partly dressed after the shower, and had to stand there for an endless time.[4]

We obviously lacked basic everyday necessities in the camps. Items crucial to a normal life were unavailable. We did not receive combs or brushes, even though our hair had grown back two or three inches since it was shaved in Auschwitz. The majority of us did not have underclothes of any kind. There was no toilet paper. Paper was considered dangerous by the Germans because it could be a means of communication for sabotage or other underground activity. We could not cut our nails or brush our teeth. We could only bite off our fingernails. Probably due to malnutrition, our toenails grew very slowly.

Neither I nor the other survivors whom I asked remember how we coped with the lack of those daily essentials. It seems that our state of mind was so far from normality that we did not consider it even a problem. I remember only the more pressing concerns such as hunger, cold, and fear of selection.

It was dehumanizing for women to wear clothing that did not fit; for formerly elegant ladies who had never been seen in public without makeup, it was very hard psychologically. For some, makeup had not only covered blemishes, but also had concealed facial abnormalities. One young woman prisoner in Markkleeberg, Maca, who came on the second transport, was cleaning with us around the barracks. Maca was a quiet, pleasant woman in her late twenties. She sat with us and two other girls during lunchtimes and told us about her predicament. She was very conscious of being an albino. A pharmacist by profession, Maca was extremely sensitive about her pale eyebrows. Each selection was mental anguish for Maca because she was rejected while her friends were transported away to work. Maca searched desperately for some eye makeup to paint her eyebrows. One day, as if by a miracle, a girl who worked in sorting out the possessions of the arriving victims found an eyebrow pencil. She smuggled it out and bartered it to Maca for two days' portion of bread. Maca hid the pencil in her shoe and used it during selections. Coloring her eyebrows helped Maca relax, and she was finally selected for work in Markkleeberg. She used the eyebrow pencil sparingly when she worked in the factory. She even found a girl who could sharpen the pencil in her machine. Maca's luck had run out, she told us, two weeks earlier when an *Aufseherin* scolded her and beat her up for painting her eyebrows. Luckily, she did not look for the pencil. Maca was low in spirit when she told us her story. Soon, though, Maca was assigned back to factory work. The next time we met, she was smiling and had her eyebrows darkened. She told us happily that the *Aufseherin* who had been so mean to her was transferred away.

Shoes

Our shoes were the only remaining possession from home and from our former life. When we arrived in Auschwitz, they took away all our belongings except the shoes. We took our shoes with us to the showers. Having suitable shoes could spell the difference between life and death. Without socks, ill-fitting shoes broke the skin and created blisters that easily became infected. Many of the survivors had some emotional memories connected with their shoes.

In my mother's family, almost everyone had engaged in shoe retailing and shoe manufacturing, so shoes, for us, were our ancestors' trademarks. My grandparents had measured wealth in terms of shoes. We were always proud that grandfather was the first Jew in the city of Sátoraljaújhely who received a permit for boot making. Later, he opened a shoe store in the center of the city, and mother worked there before her marriage. Many of our relatives also had shoe stores in the same city of Sátoraljaújhely. After marrying my mother, father added shoes to his clothing store in Abaújszántó. In school, we always wore the nicest shoes. Erzsike, who was pretty and who liked to dress well, was especially proud of her attractive shoes. During deportation, when we had to leave home in a hurry and could take only a limited number of items, Erzsike had a hard decision to make regarding which pair of shoes she should take with her! Finally she decided on the dressy, wine-colored shoes that had a little heel.

When we got to our block in Auschwitz the first day, the *Blockälteste* said to Erzsike, "Take off your shoes, I will give you another pair." Anyone who was never a prisoner in Auschwitz could not know the power of the *Blockälteste.* To refuse her command would be one's death sentence. Erzsike, without daring to say a word, handed her the shoes. She received in return a much-worn pair in a size larger than her foot. I was sorry for Erzsike, whom I expected to be very upset and even cry; but the events of that day had taken us completely out of reality. The pain came later and was renewed each time Erzsike saw the *Blockälteste* wearing her pretty shoes. Tears clouded my little sister's eyes as she pointed the shoes out to me. I offered her my shoes, but she would not take them. Later, both of us received wooden shoes.

Erzsike and I came from Bergen-Belsen in large Dutch-style wooden clogs. We had a chance to have leather shoes, but they had high heels and we did not know how to walk in them. The wooden clogs we wore had black linen or canvas material on top. Not only was it difficult to walk in them, but they also rubbed and blistered our feet. The *Aufseherin* we called "*Kutyu*" (doggie), who was blonde and pleasant, showed us how to manage the wooden clogs so they would be more comfortable.

The shoes were always a problem because we walked five in a row and could not avoid the puddles or the mud on our way to work. Many shoes were lost or badly damaged that way. A few lucky girls, such as Elisabeth Stein Székely, had original shoes from home that lasted until they got back home to Hungary.

"Organize" was the term used in wartime and postwar Europe for pilfering something. As girls "organized" from the factory, so did some from their fellow prisoners. The rules of camp society may have been different, however, but they still existed. Stealing from a fellow prisoner—especially stealing bread—was an abomination. In some cases, human interaction in the camps descended to the level of "survival of the fittest," resulting in the abuse of the weaker by the stronger. This mostly happened in the extreme conditions of suffering, such as in Auschwitz or in Bergen-Belsen toward the end. Some individuals were capable of stealing bread from dying fellow prisoners. In my experience, though, and to the knowledge of other survivors I interviewed from Markkleeberg, in our camp the willingness to help outweighed the viciousness and ill will.

Crowding and Lack of Privacy

One of the great shocks of camp life for us was the crowd of people and the pushing and pulling we had to endure. Erzsike and I came from a small town with a population of only five thousand. We were accustomed to knowing our neighbors and of having a one-on-one relationship with all. To deal with a crowd of people, the seemingly endless queues and rows, was not part of our previous experience and was overwhelming for us. We were frightened, but we had to learn to manage if we did not want to be pushed aside. Holding hands, Erzsike and I kept our place in the crowd.

Today, I am still very apprehensive in the presence of a large group of people. With all the experience of camp life behind me, I am usually the last one to board a city bus or a train, if a group of people all wants to be first.

At the time of the Holocaust, women, especially Orthodox Jewish women, had been trained from childhood to be modest. Suddenly we were required to parade naked in front of each other, and worse, in front of male and female Nazi personnel. Periodically we could expect to be "controlled"—that is, subjected to shakedown inspections. It was a painfully upsetting experience. The inmates of a particular block were taken outside their barracks and made to undress in the presence of Knittel, the *Aufseherins,* and the German guards. The *Aufseherins* would then go through our clothing, item by item, checking for any unauthorized objects and things stolen from the warehouses or factory. Meanwhile, other *Aufseherins* did the same inside the barracks, searching under beds, in the mattresses, and under floorboards in certain rooms.

Graduates from the training school in Ravensbrück, the *Aufseherins* knew well what hurt the prisoners. They conducted surprise raids that we called "*razzia,*" searching our rooms when we were away. An *Aufseherin* who was like Satan in cruelty we nicknamed Lucifer. She was especially anxious to find more diamonds and jewelry that girls may have discovered in shoes or clothing given to them. The *Aufseherins* checked the blankets, turned over the mattresses, and threw everything on the floor. They confiscated any small items that made life for the prisoners a bit easier: a comb, a needle, sewing thread, a mirror, a pencil, or a piece of paper that the girls may have acquired. Coming to the barracks tired in the evening, we had an extended *Appel* when we were confronted with the forbidden items found in our room or bed. The welders, who worked only eight hours on different shifts, used to tell us the news about the searches when they came to work.[5]

Besides the room searches, they began checking us as we came back from the factory. After a whole night of work, we had to stand on *Appel* and be inspected to see whether we had brought home some little thing like a piece of emery or a scrap of rag. It was especially hard when it was snowing. As we were standing at attention in January's bitter cold, our tears mingled with the snow, turning into icicles on our faces. Yet, despite the scare of searches and punishment, the cold was so unbearable that girls still took chances to pilfer some emery or paper to pad their overalls.

The rooms and our beds were always temporary. Any time a new transport arrived, we had to squeeze and make room for the others. Sometimes returning from work, girls found newcomers assigned to their beds and learned they were being transferred to another barracks. There they had to contend with the resentful roommates crowding to make room for them.

The complete lack of privacy and the appalling accommodations were a constant ordeal in addition to the work and the food that our lives centered around. Nothing belonged to us anymore. The Germans took our clothes, our shoes, our hair, and our names. We were always hungry, sleepy, filthy, and tired beyond any normal human comparison. Most of the time, by any ordinary standards, we were seriously ill. "If we die," women used to say, "We will be ashes in the field, crossed out numbers in the registrar, leaving no trace in memory." Erzsébet Frank also wrote in her diary how sad it was to live between barbed wires, to wear one set of clothes summer and winter in the heat and in the freezing wind, to work twelve hours at the machine, and in between to wait always for liberation. We were girls once, but all that was once nice was forgotten and buried.[6]

Night Visits by Knittel or the *Aufseherins*

At night, while we were sleeping, there could be a sudden appearance by Knittel. Once he came and found half of the beds empty. Sisters, mother and daughter, or two girls from the same room shared bed and blankets to be a bit warmer. Some even placed the free mattress above them. Knittel, probably concerned with homosexuality, which was known to exist among the *Aufseherins,* was angry and demanded that each one should sleep in her own bed. To see if we obeyed the order, Knittel continued to conduct surprise visits in the middle of the night. Despite the warnings, girls slept two in one bed. In January, it was so cold that even Erzsike and I, who were so afraid to act against the rules, squeezed into one bed close to each other, using both our blankets. Being so terribly cold, we took chances and continued to sleep in one bed, but we were scared even in our dreams.

Our survival in general did not depend merely on correct or incorrect behavior. There were those collective punishments for actions of an individual in the block or in the room that all the rest were made to suffer. Erzsike and I seldom transgressed the rules and never volunteered, but people who dared and took chances were sometimes temporarily better off. It was not always predictable, however, because so little was under our control. We were like passengers on an airplane: one can fly better in the first-class section, but one cannot change the direction or the fate of the plane. Luck, more than any other factor, determined our survival in the camp.

Suffering from the Cold

It was so cold in the unheated room in January that puddles from our wooden shoes turned into ice. Our feet remained cold all through the night. Water seeped through the roof, and the ceilings in the rooms were covered with rime frost. Our roommate Vera had contracted tuberculosis and coughed all through the night.

In the morning, the girls who slept on the top bunks collected the frozen strings of ice on the ceiling. They were afraid that during the day the ice would melt and drip on their beds. Outside, the icicles hung from the trees in the below-zero temperature. The pipes in the barracks froze, and we had no water to wash or flush the toilets.

Working in the fields, pulling or pushing the carriages laden with stones, was unbearable without hats, gloves, or socks. We cried in desperation. I looked at Erzsike shivering in her wooden clogs, shaking, with her teeth clenched to keep them from chattering. Her face seemed to turn blue, as my nails changed color and ached from the bitter, penetrating cold. My feet swelled so that the shoes, which were two sizes too large, became tight on my bare toes. I feared the fate of those girls who, with the mighty swellings and inflammations, no longer wore shoes and finally ended up in the *Revier.* Fortunately that did not happen to me, but we had problems even walking in our wooden shoes; slipping and tripping, we felt we had no control over them. Nature's icy brutality went to our souls and bodies.

Outside the temperatures dropped to minus fifteen degrees centigrade at night, and a fierce wind swept through the barracks. Even the guards and the *Aufseherins* stayed inside their heated compartments. One day Sári, a girl in our room, was assigned to work in the wood storage. There she hid in her overall pants a few pieces of firewood. Part of it she bartered for a little coal. When she returned to the room, Sári and the girls lit the stove. They felt safe knowing that the guards were happy to be inside in that bitter cold. They would not go to look for smoke at night coming from some chimney. The storm, with its fierce wind, was blowing outside as we hurried to our room that night. Our surprise of seeing the fire in the stove was unimaginable. It was like a slice of life from home. We let down our guard and put the worries away as we watched the glowing embers. Sári warmed water in her bowl and washed her hair over the sink outside, pouring the warm water over it. Soon the lights were turned off in the barracks, and we watched the final glitters of the coal embers. Although cold quickly reclaimed its realm in our room, we still went to sleep with some sparkles in our hearts. That warm, magic moment with the fire in the stove remains strongly in my memory. Now when I am in my pleasant, heated room during winter storms, I often think how lucky I am.

The frosty winds were unrelenting and the *Aufseherins,* complaining of cold in their warm winter outfits, seemed to harass us even more. They demanded we move faster and faster, while walking became increasingly difficult because of the snow stuck to the wooden shoes. It was like moving on a ball in an ice-skating rink.

Food and Hunger

Food was always in our consideration. In the lowest points, when our minds were completely empty, the lone thought that remained was the desire for soup, bread, and sleep. Eating and working permeated all aspects of our existence. Both food and work were used by the Germans as segregation devices and murder weapons.

There are things that remain vivid in my memory, such as the selections and the cold we suffered, but somehow the hunger, that at the time drove all thoughts from our minds, did not leave an enduring memory. Only when I recall some episodes, such as the following ones, do I realize how hungry and thirsty we really were.

Once in the winter, as we worked outside in the yard in Markkleeberg, the guard left us for a few minutes. We noticed how the girls quickly made snowballs and ate them. At first we found it strange; but Erzsike, always thc practical one, said let's try it. We selected a spot where the snow was still clean and filled our mouths with a ball of snow. It was so delicious that we were sorry to stop when the guard returned. We may have tried it once more, but then gave up as the snow became muddy.

I was so hungry and desperate once that I placed myself in a strange situation with no way out. This happened when we were on our way from Bergen-Belsen to Markkleeberg. A German soldier guarded our compartment of the freight train. At early dawn, we arrived at a station where the train halted temporarily. We were sitting on the floor, eighty girls in a small space, warming each other with our body heat in the cold winds of December. The door opened and remained open for a while, when suddenly a loaf of bread came flying right into my lap. Before I could react, the girl next to me grabbed the bread and sat on it. The whole thing happened so fast that no one among the tired, sleepy girls noticed it. At that time, I was very frightened and shaken up. Erzsike just woke up when the soldier, our guard, argued with his friend about the bread he had not received. The other soldier, who divided and threw the bread to our place, was angry and asked if anyone had seen the bread. All said a loud “no.” I looked at my neighbor, a woman of about thirty, who was sitting on the bread and was afraid to confess. She was pale and shaking. The guard repeated his question with threats of severe punishment for those who knew and were unwilling to report. There was no going back after that. My neighbor looked at me with tremendous fear in her eyes. In the beginning, I had resented her audacity in taking the bread away from me. I could have had my revenge by exposing her, but it would have been out of character for me to do so. I also had deep fear of dealing in any way with the German soldiers. I gave the girl a reassuring glance, conveying an unspoken promise that I would not give her away. I was glad that Erzsike did not have to share my anxiety. While the two soldiers continued to argue, my neighbor and I were praying to get out of that tense situation safely. Finally, the signal sounded for the train to move. Our guard received his bread and the door closed. We, the prisoners, were given no food, and the train advanced toward Markkleeberg. As the door closed and the place grew dark again, most of the tired hungry girls fall back to sleep. Shortly the woman next to me placed two big pieces of bread in my lap. Without a sound, I pushed the bread to my sister’s mouth. She was silent as we stuffed ourselves with the forbidden food. Even today, I think Erzsike does not know the full story of that bread. My neighbor and I kept away from each other after that. Both of us were uncomfortable with our secret, which was the result of great hunger. As for the others in the wagon, I do not think that anyone really knew; otherwise they would have demanded to share.

Our daily food allotment in Markkleeberg consisted of a bowl containing about three quarters of a liter of watery soup. In it were sometimes small portions of real meat as well as pieces of cabbage, potato, or rutabaga, which otherwise was used as cattle fodder. The content depended on the person who divided the soup and whether she had stirred it well or just given from the top. We had no breakfast—just the warm brown liquid, or occasionally, ersatz coffee made from corn. In the evening, we were each given a piece of coarse bread, about seven ounces—not quite half a pound. With the bread, twice a week we received a “*Zulage*” addition: either a spoon of marmalade, a dab of margarine, or a sliver of salami. On Sundays, we were given three spoons of sugar in a small bag. We learned to mix the sugar with the margarine to spread it on the bread. The tea or ersatz coffee in the morning was warm, and we made it sweet with a bit of sugar.

A song that reminded us of the food we did not have was written for Lenke Schwarz Fine's birthday, which was February 27. The poet called "Iluci," which is the pet name of Ilona, wrote the following poem at the request of Lenke's sister, Blanka Schwarz Friedman. The authors of camp poems and songs were known sometimes only by a nickname as "Iluci" was.

> My dear Lenke, what should I wish for you?
> Something endearing, something nice,
> So you will feel how I love you with all my heart.
>
> I would have liked that you be at home
> And not have to eat thin broth, but the most delicious cake.
> All is not lost it's delayed, and camp life will come to its end.
>
> [Then a group of friends added their collective wishes as a chorus.]
> Now you are going to promise us
> That a year from today you will be a happy bride,
> And even if you will not invite us for your wedding
> You will think of us with love.[7]

This was written on a piece of paper and signed "Iluci." Blanka Schwarz Friedman gave it to her sister Lenke to express her appreciation. Blanka presented Iluci with a portion of her bread. At first, Iluci was reluctant to take it, but finally she accepted.[8] These young poets carried us on the wings of their imagination back to a better, earlier world. A sisterly love and a will to find an escape from our despondency were very strong in us.

At least the food in Markkleeberg was better than in Auschwitz or Bergen-Belsen. The diet, in good times, was about 800 calories a day. Toward the end, it deteriorated to 450 calories, just as our diet had worsened over time in Bergen-Belsen.[9] Protein, fat, vitamins, minerals—almost every building block of life had been stripped from the diet, leaving only traces of food value. With that we were compelled to work and fight for our survival.

Bread

The bread—even though sometimes made only from bran, rutabagas, or sawdust—was very important in camp life. It was also more easily transferable for bartering purposes than soup. The *Blockälteste* gave out the bread at the evening *Appel,* and we divided it in our room. We could choose whole or cut bread. The girls liked to cut it themselves, rather than receiving it cut, because they could divide it more equitably. Slices of equal thickness were not really equal, since the ends of the loaf were smaller than the middle. We measured the size of the bread, as if it were a precious stone. One girl who was trusted would be designated to cut the bread. We were efficient at dividing our bread and saving some for later. The women perhaps had it a bit easier than the men; with more homemaking experience, we knew how to ration the food.

There was no scale to measure the bread and there were few knives, but the girls had other ways to give everyone an even portion. Our partner was Rozsi, our roommate and *Appel*-line mate. Rozsi was a bit older than we were, and we trusted her fully. We had a piece of string on which we marked three equal parts. For slicing, Rozsi borrowed a knife that had been shaped from a piece of metal, which the girls had bartered for bread. Rozsi cut the bread according to the measured string. The middle of the bread was still a bit larger than on the edges, so girls took turns in choosing the largest part, meaning each girl in a group got a larger portion every third or fourth day.

The bread had to last us twenty-four hours. It was a dilemma whether to eat it all at once or to leave a little bit for the morning. With the hunger came the constant fear that we might not get food the next day. A natural instinct of saving for an uncertain future was in our character. Controlling hunger by saving for the next time was the only power we had. To make it last longer, we tried to cut the bread in thin slices so we could eat one portion in the evening and the other in the morning. Before Rozsi returned the knife, she let us use it. Once, as Erzsike was slicing, she accidentally cut her palm, and it bled profusely. Luckily it stopped without the need for her to go to the *Revier,* but it left a deep mark that Erzsike has worn all these years in memory of the bread and hunger in Markkleeberg.

Klára Spitz Snitzler and other girls like her, separated from their mothers or sisters in Auschwitz, had a little bread saved at all times, in case they might meet their relatives again. There was always that hope. When we arrived, Klára offered us some of her saved bread because we reminded her of home and family. We were grateful, but naturally we could not take it. According to our prewar custom, it was nice to offer, but the polite thing was not to accept. Given the enormous worth of a piece of bread in the camp, we really needed this inspiration from our parents' good manners to be able to adhere to our tradition.

Bread became worth more than diamonds in Markkleeberg. One day, as she was fixing a pair of shoes, Gabriella Klein Heimlich, who worked in shoe repair, found hidden inside the heels two beautiful gold rings and a pair of diamond earrings. Gabriella was stunned, and she hurriedly showed them to the other two girls. They all looked with awe at the jewelry shining at them. It gave them a feeling of connection to that other world at home.

They tried on the rings and even the earrings, while watching to make sure that the guards or the *Aufseherin* should not surprise them. The rings with diamond and ruby settings were a bit large on their skinny fingers; nevertheless, it gave them a warm feeling, as jewelry usually does to girls. Each girl recalled with longing the beautiful jewels she once had at home. With their joy of remembrance also came the sad realization of how all their treasures had been taken from them.

Knowing they would not be able to keep the newfound treasures, one of the girls then suggested they exchange them for food. They offered it to the *Blockälteste* in return for bread. Lacking the entrepreneurial spirit, the *Blockälteste* was not willing to make the exchange. She told them that, in the camp, bread *was* the gold. The girls, fearing inspection, hid the jewels among the shoe-repair tools. After a few days of worry, they decided it would just be safer to discard the jewelry by flushing it down the toilet.[10]

In February 1945, the portions of bread became smaller. The German population also had a shortage of bread because it was needed by the army at the front. For us, one loaf was divided among five instead of the three who had shared it previously. There were days we did not receive any at all.

Soup

The soup, our main meal, the night shift received at midnight; if we worked days, then lunch was at noon. We were fed either in the factory or, if we were working in the fields, in the barracks. The kitchen and the bakery were outside the camp, close to the large factory. Knittel had authority over the food and the kitchen. As Frank writes, "He deals and negotiates with the chef in the kitchen."[11]

On Sundays, the soup was brought to the door of each room. We ate crouching on the beds or sitting on the floor in the corridor. We had to eat quickly before roll call came again. As time went on and we had less bread, the soup became the highlight of our days. We were so hungry that we even dreamed of the soup. We liked Wednesdays best, because they cooked any leftover bread into it to thicken the soup. We also received barley, beet, or cabbage soup in the early days. Later the soup was made only of cabbage and rutabaga, with no meat or even fat.

Food Distribution

The food was brought for distribution by the five to eight members of the *Esskomando*s. They carried the heavy soup kettles from the kitchen to the factory, to the blocks, or to the *Revier* to be distributed. At night they transported the bread to the barracks. Members of the *Esskomando* received extra portions of food.

In the factory, we had a thirty-minute break, half of which we spent waiting in line when we reached the huge cauldron of soup. Doling out the soup was invariably accompanied by pushing and pulling, as starving prisoners crowded around, nearly knocking the cauldron over. Usually the girl who divided the soup gave the portions that might have a piece of potato or even meat in it to those with whom she had a personal connection. The meal had to be consumed quickly because, in no time, we were herded back to the machines. As the food distributors gave bigger and heavier portions to their family and friends, those who were pushed aside to the end were sometimes left without food.

The *Blockälteste* and her helpers handled the distribution of the food in the barracks. In block six, our barracks, Laju divided the food. As she wanted, she gave a ladle from the bottom or she gave from the top, which was mostly water. In our block, girls had only one minor complaint against Laju: She gave them soup from the top.

Toward the final days of the camp, our bodies were reaching their limits. We were ready to do anything for a little more food. We were even praying to get a bit more of the thick soup toward the bottom of the container. When it happened that Erzsike received the end and I got the beginning of a new container, Erzsike insisted we mix our two soups so each one of us should have some of the part containing potatoes and maybe some bread or rutabagas. Sometimes we even counted the pieces of potato to share it equally. On the rare occasion when we found a piece of meat, each of us urged the other to have it.

The girls from the *Esskommando* who divided the soup at the factory favored their family and friends. They not only gave them from the bottom of the container where the soup was thicker, but they also allowed their friends or relatives to go through the line two or three times, while telling others to leave the line. The Germans measured and gave out the soup by counting the exact number of portions. Thus, anyone going twice deprived someone else of having soup. Once when Erzsike and I were waiting, suddenly the girls who divided the soup told us to leave the line. We were complaining, but not only did no one listen, the soup dividers threatened to call the guards. Not knowing how to express ourselves in German, we did not want to risk punishment. Resigned to our bad luck, we remained starving as we had a few times before, while some others had double or even triple portions. On this occasion, however, we were luckier. A young woman named Flora Kaff Goldring, who was fluent in German and who worked in the office of the factory, noticed the injustice of our predicament. She called out in German, "Look at the children who are being left with no food!" Flora's words attracted the attention of the factory personnel. She explained to them the problem. We probably looked very pitiful, because the civilian workers brought us parts of their lunches, even an apple. Our tears blended with the most delicious food we had eaten in a long time. Flora, whom we had not known before, came and hugged us. A tall, impressive-looking lady, Flora had much empathy for us and anger at the others. When we thanked her, she replied that she had to uphold the virtues of fairness and decency that we knew from home. Flora turned down an offer to divide the soup for the prisoners, even though it would give her an extra portion. She did not want to benefit and deal with possible criticism.

Our mistreatment brought changes in the factory food distribution method. It was decided after that to close the line at the end, so that no one could deprive others by returning for second portions.

I could never forget Flora and her compassion. I wanted so much to thank and praise her again. She stood up for us, upholding our parents' teaching by risking punishment from the Germans and anger from the girls in the *Esskommando.* During research for this book, I asked everyone about Flora. Finally I found someone—Nelly Winkler Rochlitz—who had Flora's address and phone number. A deeply religious lady, Flora survived, as did her two sisters. She settled in the Boro Park section of Brooklyn, New York. A great-grandmother, Flora recalled how she had been touched by seeing us young girls pushed aside by the rest. She added that she had learned German from her mother; thanks to her, she was able to help us.[12]

As the food supply decreased, the soup became thin broth. The additions of salami, jam, and sugar were less frequent and finally stopped completely. We comforted ourselves that it meant we were nearing the end of the war and our imprisonment. This was our way to interpret and accept the increasing meanness of the SS toward us, too.

Food Bowls

I have forgotten many things from camp life, but the food bowl remains clearly in my mind. It was so precious and important that we guarded it with the greatest care. We put the bowls under our heads in Auschwitz or hugged them in our sleep. Without a bowl, we could not have food, and there would be no hope of living.

When we arrived in Markkleeberg, each one of us was given an enameled metal bowl, a cup, and a spoon. The bowl and the cup were all the same red color with white sprinkles scattered around. The girls who worked as welders drew a monogram with their initials on the red bowls. Each spoon had a hole, and both the bowl and the cup had handles that enabled us to put a string on them. Some girls wore them as a belt. Erzsike and I did not even have a string, so we each laced the bowl in the side of our overalls where they made noise when we walked.

On the Death March, the bowl was the most important thing among the little we possessed. Although we received food only once or twice in our bowls then, I used mine as protection against rain and air attacks. The bowl shielded my head as I lay in the ditch at the side of the road, seeking shelter from low-flying bombers.

Food Favor

Once in Auschwitz, as we were sitting hungry and dispirited, waiting for the next meal and *Appel,* a *Blockälteste* from the nearby barracks came to ask whether anyone there was from Abaújszántó. Hearing the name of our town, we jumped up and approached her.

"Was in your town a yeshiva? Did you give meals to students in the yeshiva?" she asked.

We remembered a young boy who used to eat by our grandmother on Sundays and with us on Thursdays. He was a tall, polite boy from Czechoslovakia who spoke Hungarian well, we told her.

"That was my brother!" said the *Blockälteste* excitedly. "He even wrote us that he had two days a week with a nice family." She took me and Erzsike to her room and gave each of us a big plate of thick soup. "I feel so good to be able to repay for my brother," she said.

Twice she brought us bread after that, but then we were transferred from the A to the C lager. We heard later that she had found some others from our town who had also helped her brother when he was hiding in Hungary. That *Blockälteste,* like other girls from Czechoslovakia, had already been in Auschwitz a year or more. They were all bitter and pessimistic about life and about our chances of remaining alive, yet she did her utmost in the way of benevolence. Doing kindness reinforced our sense of worth and of loyalty to family and their values. It also brought back memories of a better life in the past and strengthened our ideals for the future. We tried to stay human to the end.

Cigarettes Traded for Food

Cigarettes were important, especially for male prisoners. Their suffering was great when they could not smoke, and they would exchange their portion of bread for a cigarette. Renowned Auschwitz inmate Viktor Frankl reported that, when an ordinary prisoner, one without special privileges, would smoke, others would correctly assume that he had given up and decided to "enjoy" the last moments of his life.[13] Women smoked less at that time, but some were also deeply addicted to nicotine.

Inmates in Markkleeberg obtained some cigarettes from the German civilian or foreign workers in the factory which they either smoked or exchanged for food. Bella Spitz, our *Lagerälteste,* was a heavy smoker. To feed her habit, she took from the food of the prisoners and exchanged it for cigarettes. Bella paid two portions of soup for one cigarette. Her cigarette craving finally cost Bella her job and resulted in punishment in the bunker. Magda, a girl from Transylvania, knew about Bella's dealings. Working in the *Gartenkommando* (gardening crew), Magda would talk to the guards in Yiddish, which is close to German. They liked her because she was a simple, talkative girl who also sang them songs in Romanian, which the guards—especially one named Esele—enjoyed. On one occasion, as was his custom, Esele asked Magda to sing, but Magda answered, "Not today, I am not in the mood."

"I command you, and you have to listen to me!" shouted the guard.

"I am very hungry," Magda answered, "and it is hard to sing when one is starving. Because of the *Lagerälteste,* we had smaller portions of soup today. She had to pay for the cigarettes she bought."

"The *Lagerälteste* buys cigarettes with food?" the guard questioned.

"Last time, she didn't give lunch to the whole block six as a punishment."

"What happened to the meal? What did she do with it?"

"She gave it to the other block and those who were her favorites," answered Magda.

"You come right with me to Knittel," insisted Esele.

Knittel, after hearing the story, gave Magda a slap on her face for complaining. After that, Knittel quietly observed, until he surprised Bella as she was taking out the potatoes and meat from the food before dividing it for the inmates. Catching Bella red-handed, Knittel slapped and punished her with a three-day confinement in the bunker.[14] Placed in the cold bunker in only an overall, without her coat and sweater, Bella received a small piece of bread each day. The girls could hear her singing to keep herself company and so that the others would not feel sorry for her. Bella had a charismatic personality, and some girls felt pity and visited her in the bunker during lunchtime.

"I am well. I just need a match and a cigarette," Bella complained. Even with the danger of punishment, someone took her a cigarette or two. Bella looked very pitiful as she came out of the bunker. Yet she passed by Knittel with her head raised, wearing a smile. Knittel then sent her to work in the quarry.[15]

Illicit Possessions

One rainy day when the girls were tired and gloomy and even the wheelbarrows sank deep in the earth, Tereza Frankl noticed something in the mud. She picked it up with a feeling of anticipation. When she washed off the mud, the delicate stones of a short necklace became visible. She put it on and enjoyed feeling a bit feminine again. Tereza wore the necklace, giving us all feelings of nostalgia and connection with the world beyond our prison's gates. The inmates' delight and Tereza's good luck lasted only a few days, however, before Knittel's penetrating eyes spotted the ornament during *Appel.* He grew angry at seeing such an adornment and started to curse. He ordered Tereza to hand him the necklace. Then he threw it to the ground and crushed the delicate design with his boot. We looked on, horrified, feeling as if our dreams, hopes, and desires all lay under Knittel's high boots. We were also fearful for Tereza and her expected punishment; but it seems that by destroying the necklace, Knittel had vented his anger. He left Tereza and all of us with shattered feelings and gloom at the renewed reminder of the camp's harsh reality.

We had almost nothing, thus every little insignificant item was valued. We had arrived in Markkleeberg from Bergen-Belsen with coats, and the girls had advised us to take out the linings, because the coats would be taken away when we received our overalls. A pair of scissors circulated to help take off the padding, the fur collars, the pockets, and any other removable items. From the linings, the girls made stockings, vests, and bags to hold bread or sugar. Erzsike and I looked at our coats, tempted to do the same, but the fear of punishment outweighed the girls' advice.

After we decided against pillaging our coats, I had an odd experience. Erzsike noticed that the wool covering on one of the large buttons on my coat was worn out. As I checked it on my bed in the evening, the tear became larger and, to my astonishment, a shiny gold coin rolled into my hand. Instead of feeling joy at having something of value, I interpreted it as a sad message; and, in a way, I was scared. In their last-minute struggles to save their valuables, members of the European Jewish community had purchased gold coins or dollars to hide in different ways. Their only remaining assets could be found in the clothing and shoes that they took with them during deportation.

What should I do, I wondered, with that coin and the others that might be hidden still under the fabric of the coat? Trying to keep low profiles and just be average girls in the camp, we did not want anything unusual that might bring attention to us. That was survival instinct, personality, and our conscious strategy. Erzsike, who was a bit more daring, suggested that we try to barter the coin. Being young and not knowing how to trade, that was not so simple. I carried my forbidden treasure fearfully the next day, worrying all the while. We hoped to contact Elza or other friends in the evening and ask their advice or even give them the coin. Meanwhile, in the afternoon, a special *Appel* was suddenly called. Being new in Markkleeberg, we feared that every *Appel* meant some new danger, change, searches, or other trouble. So on the way to the *Appelplatz,* I hid the coin in the side of a snow pile, with the hope that I could recover it later. When we went back, however, the snow was disturbed and I could no longer recognize my coin's secret location. I searched again later with no success. The following day they collected the coats. Fearing punishment for missing buttons, I gave it back with the rest of the gold coins intact.

Today, I wonder who finally derived pleasure from the labor of that distressed Jewish family who originally owned the coat. It was a lovely orange coat with a fur collar. I can imagine that it belonged to a young person or somebody with a sunny disposition. She or her family may have long scrimped on buying everyday necessities to purchase the ill-fated coins hidden in the coat.

Valuables found in the camps provided Lucifer and the other *Aufseherins* incentives to search us. Bruno Eisert, in his report on Markkleeberg, mentioned the *Aufseherin* Helene Pöschel from Markkleeberg, whom we knew as Lucifer. "Pöschel enriched herself with jewelry that some of the women prisoners had succeeded, up until then, in hiding from the eyes of the SS."[16] A week or two after we returned the coats, the *Aufseherins* conducted special searches again. They may have found the gold coins and looked to locate the missing one or hoped for similar treasures. I do not think they found anything else of value, judging by the anger with which they treated the girls with the vests or extra pieces of clothing, which they discarded immediately in the garbage. For having extra clothing, the girls were taken to stand in punishment *Appel* in front of Knittel's office. There, after endless hours in the cold, the ice-covered inmates were happy to escape with their lives.

As the frozen land melted and our lives became easier, there were still rainstorms that could strike us on the way to work or during *Appel.* Already chilled to the bone marrow, we had the pricking rain knocking on our bare heads. There was no shelter or stopping, rain or snow; the schedule had to be maintained. Our clothing remained damp for days, and even at night, we could not warm up. When we were almost at the edge of endurance, the storms finally stopped, and the sun reflected a bit in the puddles of the camp road.

Bartering

The camp, with life of its own, had economic activities based on pilfering a variety of raw materials from the factory or the fields. Prisoners were forbidden to take anything from their work sites; even scraps of paper or small pieces of wood could get one charged with sabotage. Yet there was an active trade in all sorts of material illicitly obtained from the workplace.

The best bartering was done on the night shift. Enterprising girls used resources from the plant to produce other goods such as bags, clothes, and jewelry. Women used rags handed out at the factory to clean the machines to make underwear. Others in the quality-control room unraveled the gloves they were given and used the yarn to knit stockings or vests. From the emery cloth intended to clean the manufactured parts, women could also pull out threads, which were light blue or gray, to make vests to wear under the overalls.

Women who happened to have long dresses underneath their overalls could cut a piece off and make a bag for keeping the bread. That item was a good seller because part of the evening bread could be saved and protected until breakfast that way. Before handing in their coats, many girls took off the linings and the fur collars. These things were all good merchandise for barter. Erzsébet Frank, for instance, bought a valuable fur collar for one day's portion of bread. She wanted to give it to the German civilian foreman Johanes Walter, who was a good-hearted man, and Erzsébet Frank wanted to repay him in some way for his occasional help. The mores of basic human decency still existed in the camp. Erzsébet told him that the fur was for his wife. Walter brought back a needle, thread, a comb, and a red onion for Erzsébet. Fifty-seven years later, when I interviewed Erzsébet, she recalled how happy she was to recompense the actions of a good man.

Everything had a price calculated in units of bread rations. A unit was one prisoner's daily ration. Girls could buy a pair of stockings, for instance, for two portions of bread and margarine.

Coal was available from girls who worked at the factory shoveling coal to the machines. Choosing warmth over sustenance, some girls bought coal with their bread. The girls who could "buy" things by giving up the little bit of bread we received usually had some extra source of food. Some worked in the kitchen, others had a relative in a supervisory position at camp or had some other means of obtaining extra portions. It was to the inmate's advantage to eat the food allowed to her. Foregoing the daily portion of bread was hard, and it was rarely based on rational considerations.

Bartering always involved the risk of punishment. For Erzsike and me, two sheltered schoolgirls, the fear that the Germans would find us with gloves or stockings was stronger than the cold we suffered. Those who took the risk were daring; as with most entrepreneurs, they were the risk takers. One also had to know how to find the merchandise for buying and selling. We were not too good at it, which we clearly demonstrated by our experience with the gold coin I found on my coat.

When I did research for this book and talked to other survivors, I was surprised to learn about the thriving bartering business that had existed in Markkleeberg. I was unaware of its full extent while in the camp. The instinct for trading to make a living went on even at the most primitive level of society that the camp represented. Women who had learned their trading sense from home were especially skilled at it because they had worked previously in their family businesses. Some of them had experience managing stores, and they had good business sense. They were also alert and resourceful. The world of the camp was small, but one could possibly get a bit more food than the others by being bold and inventive or by having the right connections. Many survivors, however, were as ignorant as we were about the considerable bartering opportunities in the camp.

Burial Ground

After the war, with the number of deaths in the camp, people wondered where the cemetery was. As a labor camp, Markkleeberg did not have facilities for burial or cremation. The dying and the sick who were *verbraucht* (used up) were shipped back to Auschwitz to be gassed. They were then replaced by another shipment of workers. When it was not possible to transport them before they died, they were burned in a private crematory in Leipzig, which then billed the SS thirty-five Reichsmarks plus some fees.[17]

Table 2. Those Who Died in Markkleeberg[18]

Prisoner's Name	Date and Place of Birth	Prisoner Number	Date of Death
Adler, Sali	25.12.1925 Dombo	50004	January 1945
Freund, Magda	03.11.1927 Tany	49103	March 15, 1945
Grosz, Helena	26.12.1926 Rahonya	49144	February 28, 1945
Löwy, Margit	01.12.1904 Wien	50169	March 10, 1945
Wilhelm, Irma	24.09.1920 Udvard	49489	March 2, 1945

The following victims were cremated in Südfriedhof, Leipzig. They were given cremation numbers. In July 3, 1946, the urns were transferred to the Ostfriedhof cemetery in Leipzig, where again they were given numbers and the urns were placed in section No. 10. The cemetery is located in Ostrasse 119, Leipzig 04299.[19]

The camps did not have to submit reports on the causes of death. Jewish workers, as Benjamin B. Ferencz wrote, "were less than slaves. In our vocabulary there is no precise word to describe the lowest status of unpaid workers who were earmarked for destruction. Slave masters care for their human property and try to preserve it. The Nazi plan was that the Jews would be used up and then burned."[20]

The next chapter will discuss the Jewish functionalist. We will see how the Germans added to suffering with the aid of our own members.

Table 3. Prisoners Cremated at Südfriedhop

Prisoner's Name	Date and Place of Birth	Prisoner Number	Date of Death
Hoffmann, Aranka	10.3.1919 Unknown	93183	January 25, 1945 *
Cremation # 85004, Ostfriedhof cemetery # 2203, file #13, Location X 10 E 4 (Urn)			
Moskovitz, Ilona	16.02.1910 Gyulahaza	38062	November 10, 1944
Cremation # 83720, Ostfriedhof cemetery # 2218, file # 27, Location X 10 M 8 (Urn)			
Raab, Irene	12.08.1920 Ekel	30764	November 28, 1944
Cremation # 83938, Ostfriedhof cemetery # 3127, file # 0, Location X 10 M 2 (Urn)			
Weisz (newborn)	24.01.1945 Markkleeberg	49778	January 26, 1945
Cremation # 84920, Ostfriedhof cemetery # 2221, file # 42, Location X 10 D 2 (Urn)			
Weisz, Etel (mother)	15.07.1912 Rababogyoszlo	49778 **	

* Hoffmann, Aranka is not in the list of Markkleeberg prisoners. She was transported from Ravensbrück to Penig and then to Markkleeberg where she died, according to her death certificate. Unlike the other victims whose cause of death is not listed, Aranka Hoffman's death was due to tuberculosis.

** Fate is unknown. The baby had the same prisoner number as the mother.

5

Prisoner Officials, Sick Room, and the Babies Born in Markkleeberg

ALTHOUGH THE NAZIS SUCCEEDED IN ORGANIZING A WORKING SYSTEM of Jewish functionaries, in terms of the individual prisoners, the structure failed. Each one of us brought our knowledge and our own good and evil into the camp, even though all other links to the past had been severed. As all vestiges of our identities were stripped from us, we retained still what remained in our minds and souls. We fought against conditions designed to break our collective spirit. We had little influence on the material part of our lives, but we at least fought for our souls. Placed in a world we never knew before, we tried to hold on to as much as we could from our upbringing and traditions. We appreciated cultural activities and were ready to give our day's bread to the writer of a song that we liked. The Germans usually opposed artistic expression unless they could control it. Artistic creation, if discovered, would be severely punished.

THE JEWISH FUNCTIONARIES

Within the camp, the prisoner was subject to three authorities: (1) the German commander and his subordinates; (2) the *Aufseherins;* (3) the internal Jewish administration. Prisoners were assigned positions supervising their fellow inmates and working in the camp administration as block and camp elders. The woman or girl who was selected had to be representative and had to speak German.

The Lagerälteste

The first position of the internal Jewish administration was the *Lagerälteste.* She was a woman prisoner representing the inmates to the commando of the camp. The *Lagerälteste* was responsible for the day-to-day operation of the camp. It was her job to submit a daily report of the number of those who were fit for work, those who were ill, and the number who had died. She also had to translate into Hungarian the orders and other communications given by the Germans. The *Lagerälteste* was entitled to separate living quarters with her family. The first *Lagerälteste* in Markkleeberg was Bella Spitz. The girls called her Aunt Bella (Bella Néni). Born in Kosice (Kassa), Bella Spitz had lived in Sárospatak, an area that had always belonged to Hungary. She spoke German well, although with a Hungarian accent. Bella had two daughters with her.[1]

The *Lagerälteste* had also the job of making sure the inmates obeyed. As mentioned earlier, Bella Spitz burned herself into our memories on one of the coldest days in December when she denied us lunch. After work, we stood on punishment *Appel* late into the night, full of bitterness and bewilderment in our hearts.

It was a miracle that, despite the harsh weather, most of us never got a cold or even a runny nose. Without tissues or handkerchiefs, it would have been dreadful. Our good health did not last forever, as we will see later.

Some of the functionaries were a strange mixture of good and evil. Their actions under these harsh and bizarre circumstances cannot be judged by ordinary standards of today. Bella knew that her job—and maybe her life—depended how she could please the SS management. To maintain her position, the policy and the will of the SS needed to be carried out. According to Bella's daughter, Anna Spitz Gilbert, the price they paid for slightly better treatment was that Bella was first in line for Knittel's anger. Knittel could walk into their room at any time, check on what they were doing, ask questions and vent his anger.[2]

The *Lagerälteste* was in charge of general food distribution as well. This task got Bella Spitz in trouble and eventually caused her to lose her position. As mentioned in chapter 4, Bella was caught skimming the soup and bartering cigarettes for soup that was allocated to the prisoners. As part of her punishment, Bella was sent to work in the stone quarry. By that time, Erzsike and I had been assigned to other work, so we only heard how Bella was shivering like all the others in a thin overall.

Her addiction soon got Bella in trouble again. She begged for cigarettes from the civilian workers who came to do some work in the camp. Unfortunately for Bella, Knittel noticed it from his office window. By that time, everyone felt sorry for Bella.[3] After her punishment, Bella was placed in our barracks as one who worked day shifts outside. Bella behaved differently as she became one of us. With her amiable personality, she almost made us forget the hardship she had caused in the beginning of our stay in Markkleeberg. After the war, Bella Spitz left Hungary for Canada with her family and lived in Toronto. She died around 1995 at approximately ninety years old.

Bella Spitz was replaced by Erzsébet Méhes as the new *Lagerälteste.* Erzsébet Méhes, was born December 18, 1913, in Somogycsurgo (today

Slovakia). She was tall, good-looking, and younger than Bella. I know of no complaints against her. By that time, we all knew the rules. After the war, Erzsébet Méhes reached Terezin, and Klára Spitz Snitzler met her in Israel.

Under the camp senior was a carefully organized ladder of block leaders, a work organizer, a secretary-translator, and other administrative functionaries—all prisoners. These were the people who had direct and immediate control over the lives of their fellow inmates.

The Work Organizer

One of the *Lagerälteste*'s helpers was Erzsébet Iczkovits, who was born in 1910. In Markkleeberg, she worked closely with Bella Spitz, who was from the same hometown.

The responsibility of Mrs. Iczkovits was to make sure the girls would be ready on time for work. If someone was slow in eating in the morning before work, her meal was taken away and poured out.[4] Once that almost happened to us because I was arguing with Erzsike, who did not feel well, that she should have a bit more of the soup. Erzsike would not take any of mine, and meanwhile, Mrs. Iczkovits arrived. I almost choked, I gulped the soup so hastily, in fear that it would be taken away.

Inmates saw the Jewish functionaries as another means by which the Nazis inflicted their cruelties. By creating subtle division and privileges, the SS pitted the inmates against one another in a brutal struggle for survival.

Mrs. Iczkovits, as we called her, was in charge of the work crews, and she also took part in the counting of the prisoners. She was always seen with a pencil and a pad of paper. Mrs. Iczkovits and her daughter Agnes shared a room with Bella Spitz and her two daughters.[5]

For greater efficiency, Knittel and Iczkovits reorganized the women's living quarters, according to their work schedules. Those who worked on the night shift were moved into one barracks, daytime workers were in another, and those who alternately worked day and night shifts were put in a separate barracks. Iczkovits and Knittel did not take into account the hardship their plan created for families when members worked a different schedule. The system did not work very well, so later it was not strictly enforced. Erzsike and I were lucky that we always worked the same schedule.

Mrs. Iczkovits was a tough lady, and survivors recall many unpleasant experiences relating to her. Fifty girls, among them Nelly Winkler Rochlitz, worked in the small factory in town, along with civilians. To conceal the mistreatment in the camp, the inmates received winter coats to wear on their way to work. They were so happy and were the envy of the rest of the camp inmates. One winter morning, they were a minute late to *Appel,* when Knittel appeared. To avoid taking the blame herself, Mrs. Iczkovits told Knittel that the girls did not want to go to work because they did not get enough bread. It was a false statement, taken out of context: a girl had only mentioned casually that morning that she was so hungry she had no strength. Knittel grew angry and punished the fifty girls by taking away the coats that they wore to work in the city. This was a terrible loss in the middle of January.

The Translator and Schreiberin

The *Lagerälteste*'s other assistant was Zsuzsanna Csanyi, translating the orders from German to Hungarian.[6] Fluent in German, French, and English, Zsuzsanna Csanyi also worked at the office of the camp. She was responsible for keeping current the lists of the inmates, the number of sick workers, and deaths as well as records of transfer, the inmates' personal cards, and other clerical matters. Paperwork regarding our camp was regularly sent to the office in Buchenwald.

The Blockältestes

The camp in Markkleeberg was divided into blocks and rooms. Each barracks was headed by a female prisoner called the *Blockälteste,* or block elder. In Markkleeberg, the *Blockälteste* was in charge of keeping order and cleanliness in the barracks and the bathrooms.[7] It was also the task of the *Blockälteste* to wake up the inmates in the morning and get them out of the barracks for *Appel.* Once prisoners assembled, the block elder took the roll call and recorded it in her block book, which contained the names of the prisoners. She had to give an exact count of the prisoners and report to the *Aufseherin* how many were sick in the block and how many stayed in the *Revier* (camp infirmary or sick room). The *Blockälteste* was also authorized to make reports concerning any misbehavior of the inmates. Prisoners feared this because it would lead to punishment, including being sent to the bunker.

Block elders were responsible for getting the food from the kitchen to the barracks. The *Blockälteste* distributed the soup to those who remained in camp during the day. The *Blockälteste* had a helper called the Stubendienst, or room attendant—usually a family member. The *Blockälteste* wore an armband, and she communicated with the guards and other block elders. As with any comparable position, her power and influence were what she could make of it.

Most women supervisors of the barracks in Markkleeberg maintained tolerable relations with women prisoners and were not guilty of brutality.

The following are some of the *Blockältestes* in Markkleeberg. All came from territories annexed to Hungary.

MÁRTA. Márta Maget Leitmann was born in 1923 and lived in Kosice (today in Slovakia). She was the *Blockälteste* first in barracks one then in barracks three. Márta was with us on the Death March and reached Terezin. When I interviewed her a few times during 2003, Márta was happy to talk to me.[8]

FAJGI. A *Blockälteste* we knew only as Fajgi was from Harsfalva.[9] Fajgi was tall, young, and pretty. She earned a reputation of favoring too much her family and friends over others, however. When there was an opportunity to peel potatoes in the kitchen, Fajgi exchanged the girls on the kitchen detail with her relatives who worked in the quarry.[10]

PIRI. Piri, or Piroska Weisz Balek, was born in 1925 in Harsfalva, a territory annexed to Hungary. Piri was the *Blockälteste* first in block three and then in block five. Piri lives in Israel. I called her, but she was reluctant to talk about her time in the camp. She did not give any testimony. There were no special complaints about Piri by the survivors I interviewed. In fact, I felt sorry for Piri for feeling unable to tell her story because being a *Blockälteste* shadowed her past. Her children, if they find out—and usually they do—may have to deal with that fact. In their recollections, survivors often confuse Piri and Fajgi because both were young and pretty.

LAJU. The *Blockälteste* of barracks six was Oecjllia Friedman, born in 1922 in Halmi, a Hungarian annexed territory. We called her by her Hebrew name, Laju. When our transport arrived from Bergen-Belsen, we had to choose three inmates among us. The group selected Laju who, with Knittel's approval, became the *Blockälteste.* Her sister Olga, or Gila, and a cousin were her helpers. Laju spoke Yiddish, which is close enough to German that she could communicate with the German staff. Laju had her room with girls from her family right at the entrance to the barracks. We passed it as we entered. Laju, the daughter of the ritual slaughterer, was religious. To my knowledge, she never used her power to our disadvantage.[11]

Zahlappel (Roll Call)

The day began with lighting of the lights around the blocks. We were roused at four in the morning when the *Blockälteste* with her assistants walked around to shake all those tired, discontented, enslaved girls who wanted a bit more of the dream world, to escape the coming day and its events. Finally, the *Aufseherin* blew the whistle, for "aufstehen" (wake up). Shortly after, she raised her whip and screamed, "Schnell, schnell" (Fast, fast). We had to run to the bathroom, wash our faces a bit in the icy water, and make our beds in a militarily precise manner. We had to be as fast as we could to avoid the punishment for tardiness.

It was still totally dark when we assembled to line up in front of the barracks. Each block had a precise location, and every one of us knew her place in the formation of the lines.[12] We had *Appel* outdoors regardless of the weather, rain or shine, snow or hail. The stars slowly faded as the cold breeze battered our bodies through the thin overalls. Girls composed the following song that expressed fittingly our feelings about the *Appel.*

> In the morning, we wake to the whistle,
> And our Blockälteste's screaming "alles brics shön machen."
> Then comes the Zahlappel, to line up, aber schnell, so hurry up.
> You will get nothing, but a slam on the back there.
> Then comes the hard work and the smacks on your face,
> But we don't care, because we know that it will end.[13]

The "daily reports" of prisoners gave the number of women at the start and the end of the day. Attached to the report to the office of the SS were lists of the sick and the dead. Systematic recording of the prisoners became necessary to calculate the fees to be transferred to the SS authorities.

The *Blockälteste* counted us, followed by the *Lagerälteste.* A group of armed soldiers stood nearby. Finally, after almost an hour, as sometimes the snow was creaking under our feet. the *Aufseherins* appeared. They inspected us. If she was not pleased with something, Lucifer, for instance, would hit a girl with her leather-ended whip as well as her fist. The *Aufseherins* also counted us and accounted for those who were sick.

It was agonizing to stand at attention for hours at a time. Our legs were aching in the rigid and motionless assembly. For the sick, it could be life-threatening. Camp regulations forbade us to support or help one another in *Appel.* If an inmate fell over, she had to be left on the ground until roll call ended.

Eventually Knittel arrived, wearing his shiny, patent leather boots. With the first transport, Knittel did not know much about the *Appel,* but he learned fast. Like the *Aufseherins,* Knittel would use his stick to hit someone if he did not like the look of her overalls or did not approve of the way she stood. Knittel would also hit us if he thought we were too dirty. He might have been drinking before; he was known to be a bit drunk sometimes. Knittel wrote down the numbers of those unfortunate girls who did not pass his inspection. Some maybe looked disheveled because they already suffered from TB or other sicknesses that were not treatable in the *Revier.* After *Appel,* usually on Sundays, Knittel called these inmates and made them kneel on the snow. They had to stretch out their arms, holding a stone in their hands. After some time, the girls started to faint; some of them actually froze to death, according to witness Laura Lindenfeld, who testified to the Justice Department in Germany that investigated Knittel's activities in Markkleeberg.[14]

There were then high-rise apartment buildings in the vicinity that still stand today. They were on the other side of the camp, opposite the main entrance and not far from where we stood on *Appel.*

From their balconies, the residents could observe the camp. Ms. Erna Rötzscher testified after the war that she had seen the inmates every morning standing without socks in wooden shoes in the snow in front of the main building. Some women were beaten by the SS. Another witness was Ms. Jantzsech, a letter carrier from 1940 to 1945 in the Wolfswinkel section of Markkleeberg where the camp was located. She had to go into the camp often to receive signatures on registered mail. Ms. Jantzsech confirmed, too, that the women were left standing barefoot in the snow.[15]

In addition to overcoming the objections of local authorities, the SS sought the complicity of residents living in the immediate vicinity. After the first prisoners arrived, the camp personnel attempted to discourage residents from showing undue curiosity. However, they were unable to prevent citizens from noticing the mistreatment of prisoners. Inevitably, residents witnessed beatings and shootings. Those who lived close by were able to make out details of the inmates' conditions and appearance, their poor physical state, and the rough way they were handled.

We were often even worse off than we looked. Prisoners had to be careful to look normal; otherwise it would draw Knittel's attention. Afraid of being pale and not looking good, they tried to improve their appearance. A cream was available that served as both blush and lipstick. Girls prepared it from the powder of the pink chalk that was used to mark boxes and from machine oil from the factory. Irene Keisler Schnur, the hairdresser, worried that, because her sister Klára was so pale, they might be separated. She did not know about the chalk cream, but she made her own by obtaining a piece of red brick, which she broke into powder. She painted her sister's cheeks a bit with this and shared it with some other girls too. After liberation, the resourceful Irene became a beautician.[16]

To see the SS officers was very stressful. When they started to shout their orders, we were terrified, wondering what was next in our fragile existence. The fact that we knew so little German made the situation even more frightening. Until we got the translation, which took time—if the orders were translated at all—we helplessly tried to read the meaning from the expressions in our fellow inmates' eyes.

Roll calls generally went more quickly in the morning than at night to get the prisoners off to their workplaces. Evening roll call ended the day's

Apartment houses on Spinnereistrasse, Markkleeberg. Photo by the author in 1998.

labor. The exhausted, emaciated prisoners would stand rigid, motionless for another hour until everybody was accounted for. Once it was over, the siren sounded, indicating dismissal.

Punishment *Appels*

Additional *Appels* for punishment were called "*Strafappell.*" Sometimes certain blocks, or even the whole camp, might be given collective punishment. Stealing and talking back to a superior were considered major violations of camp regulations. The inmate being punished would either stand alone for hours in the courtyard or in front of Knittel's office, with no talking, moving, or eating. She might even be ordered to kneel on the gravel.

Guards and *Aufseherins* were rarely disciplined for abusing prisoners. Respect for human life was lost in the camps and so was adherence to legal frameworks, without which civilized living seemed tenuous at best.

Health Matters

The Revier

On the right side of the camp entrance, part of barracks number one was the camp infirmary. The *Revier* was not a hospital but merely a few rooms where the sick could be separated from the other inmates. At least it was heated, and the windows were covered with silk paper. The beds had mattresses without sheets as in the barracks.

Infirmary workers were classified as prisoner officials. They wore yellow armbands, giving them unrestricted movements inside the camp. Working with crude instruments and few supplies, prisoner doctors and nurses did what they could to help the sick. They were the only ones who treated the sick with any measure of human consideration. Sometimes, however, they were known for showing preferences. The doctors generally favored their own friends and others from their home territory.

One of the two physicians selected from the prisoners in Markkleeberg, Dr. Jozsa Adler was born on August 17, 1908, and was a pediatrician in practice.[17] She had served as a doctor in Auschwitz. The other physician was Dr. Szerén Elias, born on June 8, 1909, in Újpest, a traditional Hungarian territory.[18] She was a dentist by training. The doctors were housed in barracks number one, close to the *Revier.* Although some inmates had complaints about Dr. Adler, Dr. Elias was well liked by all the inmates. I specifically remember her kindness and sympathy to Erzsike when she was in the *Revier.* Dr. Adler survived the war, but Dr. Elias was not so fortunate. Márta Maget Leitmann, the *Blockälteste,* was with her when she passed away on the Death March.[19]

The doctors and nurses, with no medication at their disposal, had more than enough to do. They bandaged infected frostbite or other wounds and provided some yellow pills for dysentery. Unfortunately, against tuberculosis, which was taking many victims among us run-down prisoners in Markkleeberg, the *Revier* had no treatment. In March 3, 1945, there were thirty-seven sick reported by Knittel to Buchenwald in his daily account of prisoners.[20] Medical supplies and medications were provided by the factory owners. A nurse, escorted by an *Aufseherin,* brought the medicine from Leipzig.

A prisoner who felt sick would report in the morning before roll call to the *Blockälteste.* After that, she would join the long line at the infirmary. Women with a temperature of 102 degrees were admitted to the *Revier* unless the few beds there were already occupied by patients in more serious condition. Then they would be sent back to bed in the barracks. Some women, too exhausted to go to work, would prefer to stay and rest in the *Revier,* even though they knew the danger of sudden "selection" there. They resented it when Dr. Adler refused to admit them.

If patients in the *Revier* did not get better in a few weeks, they were taken in the small transports that ran about once a month to Auschwitz and later to Bergen-Belsen. In addition, the transports carried away the women who were selected during the roll call as unfit to work. Deemed useless, their numbers were written down, and they disappeared quietly with the monthly transport. In the camp, not being able to work was one's death sentence. To survive in Markkleeberg, one had to be productive. The fear of being sick and unable to work was greater in the camp than in normal life, where not working just meant insecurity and loss of income.

In general, most of the women avoided the sickroom whenever possible. Many were afraid to admit it when they were ill. Since the *Revier* offered almost no medication, it could be seen simply as a corridor to death. Yet, the comparative warmth and a few days' rest could help in some cases such as pneumonia or diarrhea, where the physician provided a coal tablet, water, and rest. Those with minor injuries were given first aid right in the factory. Others were admitted to the *Revier;* from there, the serious cases of injuries were taken to the hospital in Leipzig.[21]

Babies in Markkleeberg

Although the sick stayed in the *Revier,* the babies generally were born on dirty blankets in the barracks. I have data about four newborns, but the collective memory of survivors there were at least six babies born in Markkleeberg. The birth of a baby aroused deep emotions and mothering instincts in both the prisoners and their jailers. Except for monsters like Lucifer, the German staff felt sympathy for the innocent little creatures. Everyone was aware of the pitiless fate awaiting the infants, unless their captors intervened. Inmates fostered hopes that the babies would be protected. They formed legends that some infants were hidden and adopted by the Germans.

The first baby in the camp was born in October 1944. The child was a boy, and the mother gave birth in her room at one of the barracks. The original group of *Aufseherins* was still there at that time. Survivors remember how the *Oberin* held the baby in her arms as she was counting us during *Appel.* When the first *Aufseherins* left, the baby also disappeared, giving wings to tales that the *Oberin* took the baby and that the mother was sent back to Auschwitz.[22]

Early in November 1944, another baby boy was born in the barracks where Márta Maget Leitmann was the *Blockälteste.* In the morning, the mother-to-be reported that she was sick, and later she started labor pains. Márta was scared and called two other *Blockältestes.* They were present as Dr. Szerén Elias helped with the birth. It was a beautiful baby boy, to the delight of all the women, who commented, "How can they take him away to die?" The inmates were ready to risk their own safety to try to save the infant. The basic feeling of humanity was still there in the work camp. The girls decided to hide the baby in the barracks, which they could do only with cooperation from the German staff. They showed the baby to one of the *Aufseherin* who was checking the barracks that morning. She agreed to be silent. Dr. Elias admitted the mother to the *Revier.* After a week, the mother went back to work in the construction *commando,* and the *Blockälteste* watched the baby. The Musician, the former orchestra conductor, was the guard with the girls in the construction work group. They showed him the baby, and he also agreed to help in the rescue mission. The Musician not only let the mother leave work to nurse the baby, he even brought some milk for the mother and a baby bottle to give the infant water when the mother was away. Each one who helped was taking a risk and working as a team to save the baby. The *Blockälteste* gave the mother extra portions of food. Irena Lebovits Ehrenreich remembers how she and her sister, Jolan Lebovits, made a little shirt for the baby with a cloth for cleaning the machines in the factory.[23] A month passed by, and it was a miracle that they succeeded in keeping the infant healthy and growing. As the mother worked, Márta, the *Blockälteste* who was cleaning and was mostly in the barracks all day, watched the baby. Both the Musician and the *Aufseherin* came to visit and played with the cute baby boy who began to present his first smiles. Everyone was pleased to be part of the rescue mission.

Unfortunately, there were no fairy tale endings in the camps. One morning, after five weeks of secrecy, Lucifer appeared for her surprise search. Lucifer looked like a man in big boots; she had no sympathy for the baby. She flew into one of her rages when she found the infant and ordered him taken away to the *Revier*. The young, first-time mother was stunned when she returned from work and, instead of the baby, she found the sobbing girls and an order for her to report to the *Revier*. It was a sad day for everyone when the truck came and took the mother, baby, and some others from the *Revier* back to Auschwitz. Under the circumstances, Márta, the *Blockälteste,* was lucky that her only punishment was a beating by Lucifer and that she was allowed to keep her job.

According to Gabriella Klein Heimlich, another baby boy was born in the *Revier*. Rumors circulated that Knittel took the infant to a German family. The power of imagination probably worked to comfort the inmates; that Knittel would take such a risk, however, seems very unlikely. Other survivors also recalled that a baby was taken either by an *Aufseherin* or by Knittel. Even though it was close to the end of the war, it probably was not true; but who knows, maybe a Jewish child doomed to die did grow up hidden in the town of Markkleeberg.

There were two additional births that I was able to document in detail by interviewing Markkleeberg survivors of the camp. The drama of the birth of one baby girl unfolded right in front of the rest of the inmates in the barracks. The joy and tragedy of Lucy Sternberg and her newborn were related to me by former inmates, as well as by Lucy's older sister, Eva Székely Kulcsar, who resides today in São Paulo, Brazil.

On the night of January, 8, 1945, Lucy Sternberg returned from work to block two and started to have labor pains. It was only five days after her twentieth birthday.[24] Jolka Goldstein Grodan, who shared Lucy's room and slept next to her, described to me the evening and the following events.

The girls had returned tired from the day shift, and in the evening Lucy complained of a stomachache. They did not know what to do when Lucy's sobbing grew louder and louder. The girls were worried because the doors to the barracks and the window shutters were already locked for the night. After a stressful hour, the guard on his post finally heard Lucy crying and the *Blockälteste* calling for help. He alerted Knittel, who arrived very angry and said that Lucy probably had eaten too much of the rutabaga that was given out that day. Knittel blamed Dr. Adler for advising him to provide slices of rutabaga for the vitamin C. Lack of vitamins had, by that time, become a serious health problem for the inmates.

Lucy, in response to Knittel's anger, stopped crying in spite of her tremendous pain. It could not have been easy for her to hold back; Knittel's visit lasted for a while and her contractions must have been increasing. When Knittel finally left, Lucy started howling. Some older women, among them Bozsi, the wife of a physician from Kosice, finally interpreted Lucy's distress as labor pains.

Lucy continued to scream, and the *Blockälteste* again yelled for the guard. Knittel was summoned anew. During his cursing and yelling, a beautiful seven-pound baby girl was born. A Russian woman doctor from a nearby camp cut the umbilical cord. The baby was born on the dirty blanket of her mother. She came out by herself with no help. Jolka Goldstein Grodan remembers how the infant's skin gave off steam when they washed her in the cold water of the barrack. The baby was remarkably healthy and well formed, with a full head of hair. Mother and child were transferred to the *Revier,* where Lucy received clean bedding. In the morning, Knittel appeared with a wide smile and some fruit. He joked that Lucy was not clever enough; otherwise she would have had a son. The *Aufseherins* also came, and they called the baby Monika.[25]

Lucy had married Tibor Sternberg, her great love, in April 1944. Tibor was already in the forced-labor battalion of the Hungarian army. He had received four days vacation for the wedding. Lucy's father had been against the quick marriage, but people convinced him that it would prove beneficial if the Germans took them to work. We still had an idealized concept of German culture and civilization; we believed that married women would be protected. In our deteriorating situation in Hungary, people tried to foresee events to secure some safety. The concern that girls might fall prey to undisciplined German soldiers unless they were married explained several weddings in the ghetto.

Dr. Adler worried that she would be blamed for not discovering that Lucy was pregnant. She could not have known because almost none of us had our menstrual periods in Markkleeberg. We had skinny bodies and bloated stomachs due to malnutrition, disguising even pregnancy. In any case, we probably looked so strange in those baggy overalls that bodily changes were easily overlooked. Lucy herself probably did not realize she was pregnant. She was so surprised during the birth and had never said anything, even to her sister. Once, shortly before the birth, Eva, standing next to Lucy, asked her why she was moving so much. Neither of them thought that it might be a baby turning inside her.

Many Jewish women who did know they were pregnant would try to protect their unborn children. An expectant mother in Auschwitz, who somehow passed the first selection, was with us for a while. At night she was squeezed so tightly between us and the other girls that she cried and pleaded, "Please do not push me and hurt my baby!" We felt so sorry for her that Erzsike practically slept on top of me to provide additional space for her. All our efforts were futile, however: In a few days, the ill-fated lady was selected and taken away.

Other women poignantly tried to hide their pregnancies in the camp. Yet there was no mercy. Even after the painful childbirth, mother and child had equal death sentences. In Auschwitz, if the baby was disposed of, the mother had a chance of survival. Holocaust literature is full of those painful stories of mothers who were forced to abandon or starve their babies. They carried the anguish throughout their lives. In the working camps, both mother and baby were worthless together.

After Lucy gave birth, the girls in the barracks stayed awake with excitement, discussing the events of the night. Spontaneously, one of the participants began to compose the first stanza of a song. Someone else added the next sentence, and others followed. Finally, a satiric poem about the episode was created. The girls learned it by heart and passed it on orally to others.

With light spirit, ditties composed in camp painted the collective experiences, good or bad. The form in which most women composed was the couplet; short verses put to familiar melodies. Scores of anonymous humorous ballads were written in the camps in this way, mocking our captors. The intellectual content in the couplets was small and the rhyme sometimes vulgar. The Hungarian language that most of the women spoke was dominant in poetry and in our cultural activities.

The poem about the baby was composed to the tune of the wartime hit song (*slager*) "*Pannikam.*" At *Appel* the next day, we heard the girls humming it.[26]

Close to Leipzig is a small camp
Where strange things are happening.
At home they would appear, occasionally,
And fill the pages of comic books.

Turnip or *répafaszung* was given one evening,[27]
And it made a girl very sick.
We ran frantically
Calling the *Oberscharführer.*

"*Sacramentum,* damn it!" (yelled the *Oberscharführer*)
"You will get no more turnips
And you will not be gluttons any more!"
Whoever heard of such an affair!
Then the woman in her fright
Quickly gave birth to a little child.

There are different versions of the song with slight variations, due to the group participation in the creative process and the oral conveyance of it. The above is the version that I recall best.

Humor, as we know, provides us protection against despair. People laugh at themselves and their situations, and laughter has a positive influence on the immune system. Although the humor cannot change history's merciless ways, it can change feelings and the quality of life. There were also humorous verses about camp personalities and aspects of daily prisoner life. There was literary prose, songs of yearning, of protest or vengeance, and more. The great majority were passed by word of mouth, and their authors are now unknown.

One girl in our barracks, Manyi, had a good voice and knew many light songs with double meanings. On Saturday nights, before the lights were shut off, Manyi sang some of the songs, accompanied with a few dance steps that showed real talent. Sometimes Erzsike and I did not fully understand the double meanings of the jokes and the songs, but we liked the singing and the dancing. One Sunday morning, we were washing ourselves under the faucets in our barracks when Manyi started to sing and dance "*La Conga.*" This Cuban ballroom dance consists of three steps forward followed by a kick, and it is characteristically performed by a group following a leader in a single line. Some of the girls joined in, as we watched them with delight, not noticing that a skinny *Aufseherin* we called "*Kutyus*" ("Doggie," for her extruding teeth) stood at the door. When they saw her, the girls froze and we all became alarmed, anticipating punishment. To our surprise, the *Aufseherin* asked the girls to continue. Kutyus liked the dance, and a few other times she even asked Manyi and the girls to dance for her.

Cultural activities such as singing, dancing, and creating art were forms of spiritual resistance. Cultural activities could not carry us through every time and place, however. In our last month in Auschwitz, with the constant selections and low food supply, our strength was depleted and our spirits low. We could hardly think of anything but hunger. Even the most spirited girls were quiet. In Markkleeberg, too, we were sometimes too tired to sing after working in the factory. And silence presided totally during our Death March.

Shortly after Lucy gave birth, another baby was born in Markkleeberg. Lucy and the other mother in the *Revier* discussed the possibility of only one of them going back to the concentration camp with the two babies; the other would stay behind. The question was who would give up her baby, because they knew the babies would not be allowed to stay in Markkleeberg. The mothers had a difficult choice, if indeed it was their option to choose. Meanwhile, however, the Germans made the decision. On January 26, 1945, while we were at work, the mothers in the *Revier* had to get ready for departure. They received stockings and new clothing to replace their overalls. Anna Klein Weiss, who was standing by the electric fence for punishment, saw the mothers, babies, and two other women taken away. As the truck came, she recalled, one of the mothers wanted to give up her baby; but the Germans said no, you have to come too.[28]

Eva Székely Kulcsar always hoped to see her sister Lucy again. She carried with her a little bread, saved from her portion, in case she would someday find her only sister and her baby. Lucy, however, although surviving Bergen-Belsen until liberation, tragically succumbed to the typhus she contracted there. Her baby, Monika, had already died from starvation. Lucy's mother-in-law, Irena Sternberg, was also with us in Markkleeberg. She returned home, where she reunited with her two daughters and Tibor, Lucy's husband. Later, Tibor remarried and had children with his new wife.[29]

Born July 15, 1912, in Rababogyoszlo, Etel Weisz was another unfortunate mother whose baby was born in Markkleeberg. Her heartbreak is only known to us from the infant's death record. Etel had come to Markkleeberg from Bergen-Belsen with the first transport in October 1944. She succeeded in hiding her pregnancy of almost six months; otherwise she would not have been chosen for work in Markkleeberg. Her prisoner number was 49778. The baby born on January 24, 1945, lived only two days. The infant—I do not know if she had a boy or girl—carried the same inmate's number as the mother. Etel Weisz might have been one of the two women who were taken with Lucy's group on January 26, 1945, to Bergen-Belsen, although her baby was already dead by that time.

A Girl's Last Wish

Pity and compassion transcended our hunger pains. Women took risks to fulfill the request of a dying girl who suffered from diabetes and epileptic seizures. Her name was Sali Adler, and she was born in Dombo on December 25, 1925. Sali, who was also called Shima, came with our transport from Bergen-Belsen.[30] Sali's struggle for survival came to an end when she suffered a serious seizure. She was taken to the *Revier* where her cousins and friends visited her faithfully. Downhearted and sensing that her time was short, Sali reminisced about home and the taste of an apple. Being diabetic, she had always had to be careful with fruit. Sali mentioned her desire to Mandi, who had come to visit her. Although Sali did not actually ask for an apple, Mandi wanted to surprise her. We never received fresh fruit and obtaining an apple seemed out of the realm of possibility. Yet, with compassion and camaraderie, even miracles could be performed. Mandi, who was in charge of the laundry, knew Irene Keisler Schnur. Irene not only styled hair but also cleaned the rooms of the *Aufseherins.* Irene did not know Sali, but she wanted to help. After much reflection, Irene decided to take one of the apples she had seen in an *Aufseherin*'s room. While cleaning, Irene checked again that all the apples were still there, and then she took one. It was beautiful, red, and juicy. With trembling hands, she presented it to Mandi. Through the peril of sudden searches, Mandi had to hide the apple until she finished work. Then she hurried to Sali, who could scarcely believe they had managed this wonder. Sali begged Mandi to share it, but Mandi amassed all her willpower and refused. She watched with the greatest satisfaction as Sali savored every bit of the prized fruit.

Leaving the *Revier,* Mandi rushed to Irene and told her the details of her visit. They both enjoyed the reward of givers' satisfaction. A few days later, in early January 1945, Sali's cousin Lili Katz Yoskovitz went to visit her, but Sali was gone.[31] The *Aufseherin* never missed the apple, but Irene shook with fear for many days after she took it. Even during our interview, her voice trembled with anxiety and excitement.

The story of Sali and many other experiences in Markkleeberg challenge the view that morality was completely extinguished in the extreme circumstances of the camps. Certain individuals would not have passed an ethics test, but as a whole we still had a moral sense within us—at least in Markkleeberg, where life was a bit more tolerable than in the extermination camps. The need for human beings to find meaning in their lives was strong in the camp. Girls sought after some sort of goal beyond mere survival. This explains both the writing of Erzsébet Frank and the caring actions shown by the others. These were just some ways of coping that can throw light on the Holocaust experience and of life in extremis.

Sicknesses in the Barracks

Tuberculosis

Inadequate nutrition, overcrowding, poor sanitary conditions, and the constant strain of overwork made camp inhabitants susceptible to a chain of maladies. The most prevalent and fatal in Markkleeberg was tuberculosis. TB, an unmerciful disease in general, was even more deadly in the camp. The symptoms of weight loss, fever, fatigue, and lethargy were similar not only to many other illnesses, but also to the natural effects of our imprisonment. Therefore, the presence of TB was easily missed.

There was no hope for cure without medication, rest, and nourishment, so inmates suffering from tuberculosis were not expected to get better in the camp. Unless they were in the final stages of exhaustion, girls suffering from TB were not admitted to the *Revier.* The beds had to be vacated quickly because new transports and other patients who still had a chance for recovery arrived.

In Markkleeberg, the number suffering from TB increased steadily. The cold weather, lack of clothing and underwear, poor nutrition, and hours on *Appel* all contributed to the spread of TB among us. Girls arrived relatively healthy in the fall, but by the spring they were hopelessly ill. Many times, it seemed to strike the youngest and weakest first, and it was especially lethal for fragile teenage girls. It was so pitiful that, as the first signs of spring arrived, many of those sick young girls died after having already suffered through the harsh winter.[32]

Scabies

Inmates also suffered from scabies, or mange, a contagious skin disease caused by parasitic mites and characterized by itchy, scabby eruptions. Inmates suffering from scabies perished not only because of the physical suffering from a terrible itch that could get infected, but also because of the mental anguish of rejection and loneliness. A girl with scabies, Anna, came to a sad end during the Death March.

Vitamin Deficiencies

Lack of vitamins soon started to show strong effects in Markkleeberg. Deficiencies manifested themselves in different forms. Girls suffered from boils, pyorrhea, loosening of teeth, and bleeding gums. They also developed painfully infected sores on their tongues. The problem of furuncles in the camp is mentioned in the March 20, 1945, health report signed by Knittel.[33] They were aggravated by the dust from the machines. Medicine was not available, thus girls, when possible, turned to food remedies they knew from home. They would offer their bread to the French girls who worked in the fields in exchange for an onion.

"Oil Berries"

There was a problem with the factory machines: Some of them ran on oil and propelled hot bubbling oil onto the hands and faces of the inmates. All those who worked on these oil-splashing machines were covered with painful rashes and pimples that we called "*olajbogyo,*" oil berries. Even when the girls wore gloves, the hot oil went through and burned them. When the pimples became black and ulcerous, the girls went to the *Revier.*

Lice and Delousing

Wearing the same dirty clothes month after month with no possibility of washing them, we suffered from an unending plague of lice. Except for some lucky few who believed that the lice did not like their blood, everybody had the problem to one degree or another. We had no combs, so it was hard to deal with hair lice that itched all day.

The lice seemed to thrive especially on the weakened person. It was terrible to see, in the Death March, how much an unfortunate girl named Anna suffered both from mange and lice. Her body was almost consumed by sores and lice. On Sundays, when we had a bit of free time, I took Erzsike's head on my lap and searched for the minute bugs. We took turns, and Erzsike did the same for me. With care, tenderness, and a little free time, we recalled memories from home as we "groomed" one another. We missed our mother and grandmother terribly.

Those who had *lager* sisters or roommates did the same, hunting lice for each other. It was usually a slightly older girl who, like a big sister or a mother, looked for lice in the hair of her younger friends or roommates. They were performing not only a hygienic service, but also an act of nurturing and caring. Sometimes while delousing in small groups, someone would even tell a story.

Menstruation

Menstruation and its cessation (amenorrhea) were problems specific to women in concentration camps. We believed that a substance variously described as bromine or bromide was put as a birth control measure into the ersatz coffee, which made it smell funny. Elisabeth Stein Székely believed that it was in the soup too, because the broth looked black and unnatural. In Auschwitz, one young girl always felt sick and often threw up from the soup. There were SS guards in Auschwitz who would not eat the crusts of the bread because they believed it contained bromide.

The bromide rumor has remained part of "survivors' lore" that is nearly always mentioned in the memoirs of women. Most of the survivors are convinced that the camp authorities had mixed bromide or similar medication into the food to halt our menstrual periods.[34] How could it happen otherwise that, in such a relatively short time after arriving in Auschwitz, women prisoners stopped menstruating? Erzsike and I were only at the beginning of "becoming women," as grandmother told us lovingly the first time we received our periods. Erzsike had had her menstruation maybe once at home and never in the camp. I had twice before menstruated, but never in the camp. After liberation, like many former prisoners, I had difficulties regaining my normal menstrual cycle. Some girls at the age of puberty in the camps, such as my friend and classmate Katalin Schwartz, were thwarted in their development and remained infertile for life.

Bromine, survivors believe, not only stopped the period but also acted as a sedative. We could either dream more with the bromide or we could stop thinking of our sad situation. With sedation, the Germans also made us docile, without thoughts of rebellion.[35] There is no documented evidence that bromide was added to any food or liquid in the camps. It is generally believed that poor nourishment, mental shock, and the run-down state of the women's bodies were responsible for the change.[36] Malnutrition does cause the cessation of menses, which usually resumes when the body recovers and a normal proportion of body fat is attained. This, however, does not explain why it happened so quickly after we got to Auschwitz. The question of whether bromide was given to women to stop menstruation or whether malnutrition produced this result has not yet been satisfactorily resolved.[37]

In restitution payments by the Germans for the medical experimentation of the Nazis, those who claimed the cessation of menses as a cause of temporary sterilization were in fact compensated. In Markkleeberg, most of the women already had amenorrhea on arrival. Perhaps the trauma of separation from our families, the time spent in other concentration camps, and the general state of physical and often emotional exhaustion are enough to explain it. Although most of the girls had no period in Markkleeberg, some unfortunate ones, mostly from the first transport who had spent just a short time in Auschwitz, did have theirs. They had very little flow, however, and stopped after awhile.[38]

There were cotton rolls available in the *Revier* for those who knew to ask. Resourceful girls such as Erzsébet Roth, the sister of Klára Roth Oren, used cotton that she obtained from the *Revier* to line the vests she made for herself and her sisters to feel a bit warmer. Klára, who was a slim fifteen year old, also went with her sisters and was given cotton in the *Revier*. She succeeded once or twice, and then she had the bad luck of running into Lucifer there. She looked at little Klára and was sure that she was not telling the truth. Lucifer said to Klára, "Show me that you have your period!" Then she handed her a piece of cotton and put her behind a curtain. The others in the *Revier* watched as Lucifer triumphantly prepared the rubber truncheon that she always carried with her. Meanwhile, Klára, behind the curtain, knew what was waiting for her and started to pray. Terrified and desperate, Klára then had the idea to scratch her gums in the back of her mouth until she started to bleed. She wiped her gums with the cotton and fearfully showed Lucifer the resulting bloody cloth. Lucifer irritably said to the nurse in the *Revier*, "Give her one portion of cotton."

There is no record in Buchenwald of the shipment of any drugs to prevent menstrual periods. Some sanitary napkins were sent to the subcamps from Buchenwald, but they were not given out.[39] It is possible that the Germans destroyed documents on bromide because, during the Death March, not eating food from the camp, some girls did suddenly start having their periods—despite the fact that they were still terribly undernourished and run down![40] Some women worried that they would never be able to be mothers. The majority of them, however, were in no physical or psychological condition at that time even to care. It was our very last priority then. Our concerns, after hunger, were survival and the workplace where we spent most of our waking hours.

6

Finance and Work at Junkers

The Dresdner and the Deutsche Banks

With Hitler's rise to power, the Dresdner Bank became party to the "Aryanization" of the Berliner Bank owned by the Bechröder and Arnhold brothers. Aryanization was the Nazi (National Socialist) expropriation of Jewish property and businesses in Germany and occupied Europe. The authorities also deposited in the Dresdner Bank vaults precious metals stolen from the Jews.[1]

Not content with expanding German production facilities, the Dresdner Bank also undertook the financing of the expansion of the air forces of Nazi Germany's Axis allies. A contract in 1938 provided that the Dresdner Bank finance the construction of planes for the Hungarian War Ministry through a credit of RM (Reichsmarks) 27,500,000 to Heinkel, Junkers, Focke-Wulf, and twelve other firms.

Heinrich Koppenberg, general manager of Junkers from 1936 until 1941, was a member of the board of directors of the Dresden Bank. In 1937, Charles A. Lindbergh was allowed to enroll him in the Institute of Aeronautical Sciences. Koppenberg used this connection to approach American industries, such as Bendix, to bring American airplane designers to Germany to give Junkers the benefit of American experience and research.[2]

Koppenberg's interest in aluminum and oil arose because of their importance to the development of the superior plane demanded by Hermann Goering for the Luftwaffe. The research for it was carried out by Junkers.[3]

The Dresdner Bank made immense sums available to the giants of German industry, Junkers among them. In 1941 alone, the bank extended RM 32,000,000 to Junkers.[4] The nature of financial connections between Junkers and the leading German banks gives rise to many questions.

Loans extended by the Deutsche and Dresdner Banks in the field of rearmament in the air were in the millions of Reichsmarks. Junkers had loans of at least ten million RM in 1943.[5] One can wonder who Markkleeberg's forced and slave laborers were working for, besides the state.

The officials of the Nazi regime were well aware of the banks' hold on the German economy. In October 1943, the economic minister issued a directive to public companies demanding that they reduce the size of their boards of directors by removing agents of the banks.[6] Contrary to their postwar protestations that the German state or the National Socialists had forced their hand, the Deutsche Bank and Dresdner Bank clearly shared in the Aryanization, and thus in the theft of Jewish property. They gladly took the role of financing the joint SS–private sector concentration camp system. In most instances, "opportunities" formed from what was viewed, at the time, as clever entrepreneurship.

Layers of bureaucracy and foggy language were used to process and sanitize information to separate the "respectable people" of the bank's executive board from the "brutes" who packed people into gas chambers. In the case of gold looted from the mouths of the dead, the farther the gold got from the victims, the more the moral responsibility seemed to dissipate. The Deutsche Bank, for instance, entered the chain six or seven steps removed from the victim's body. Both the Deutsche and the Dresdner banks assigned their most senior officers to be liaisons with the SS and the Nazi party. It was an informal but effective network that coordinated policy on the private sector's exploitation of slave laborers.[7]

Junkers

The firm Junkers Flugzeug und Motorenwerke, A.G. was among those in the armament industry with the largest numbers of forced laborers in 1943. The branch in Markkleeberg produced engine transmissions (compact, enclosed units of gears, as in an automobile). Engineers and local workers were supplemented first by forced laborers and then by concentration camp prisoners. On July 4, 1944, anticipating the arrival of the Hungarian Jewish women, Junkers reported that, due to a rise in production, 600 additional machines would have to be procured.

In 1944, between September and December, the SS allocated 1,300 Hungarian Jewish women to the camp at Markkleeberg. On October 24, 1944, the mayor of Markkleeberg granted a permit for the construction of 300 additional machines. Separating walls or metal shields were erected between the machines to mitigate the damage of aerial attacks.[8]

The number of concentration camp inmates in Markkleeberg was very high in relation to the other workers. On November 30, 1944, for example, 530 out of a total of 654 workers in the large factory were slave laborers, which mean that 81 percent were inmates.[9] Junkers was one of the satellite enterprises of the Buchenwald concentration camp.

JUNKERS FLUGZEUG- UND MOTORENWERKE
AKTIENGESELLSCHAFT

MOTORENBAU
ZWEIGWERK MARKKLEEBERG

RB-Nr.: 0/0350/6596

85

JUNKERS FLUGZEUG- UND MOTORENWERKE AKTIENGESELLSCHAFT
Motorenbau Zweigwerk MARKKLEEBERG 1 · Postschließfach 23

Fernruf: Sa.-Nr. Leipzig 34281
Drahtwort: Jumo Markkleeberg
Fernschreiber: 05 1163
Postscheckkonto: Leipzig 285
Reichsbank-Girokonto: Leipzig 7/8363

An den Bürgermeister
der Stadt Markkleeberg
Baupolizeiamt,

Markkleeberg.

Abteilung: A. -Baub
Bearbeiter: Eberts
Hausruf: 15

Ihre Zeichen	Ihre Nachricht vom	Unsere Nachricht vom	Bei Antwort stets angeben Unser Zeichen	Tag
			Lu/Gö.	7.4.44.

Betreff:

Um die vom Reichsluftfahrtministerium angeforderte Produktionserhöhung erfüllen zu können, müssen in der Zeit vom 1.4.- 30.6. 1944 ca. 600 Maschinen neu - bez. umgestellt werden.

Wir bitten um die Bewilligung der erforderlichen Zementzuteilung.

Heil Hitler!

JUNKERS FLUGZEUG-UND MOTORENWERKE A.G.
MOTORENBAU ZWEIGWERK MARKKLEEBERG

i. A. [signature] i. A. [signature]

The letter of request for additional machines. Junkers' trademark, "the flying man," is at right corner. The original is at the Stadtverwaltung (city archive), Markkleeberg.

Wages and Profits

The Junkers company paid the SS "*Haftlingsentgelte*" a fixed amount for concentration camp prisoners per day. The inmates' so-called wages were transferred to the SS WVHA (Wirtschafts-und-Verwaltunghauptamt [Main Economic and Administrative Office of the SS]), under which all concentration camps stood. The companies took 40 percent for upkeep of the prisoners as an additional cost. Considering our poor nutrition, unheated and overcrowded barracks, and the surrounding fences in which the workers were caged, the charge of 40 percent was outlandish. For unskilled female laborers, plants paid the WVHA four Reichsmarks per day (about $1.60). After the deduction for upkeep, it was only 60 percent of that, however.[10] The prisoners themselves received nothing for their labor. No taxes or social insurance would be paid for them. Thus, private industry could not find cheaper labor than prisoners![11]

An elaborate accounting system was set up between the factory and the SS business administration to make certain that the companies paid for the labor and that the deduction for food provided by the companies did not exceed the maximum allowed. The inmates remained under the general control of the SS while being beneath the immediate supervision of the companies that used them.

The SS WVHA collected huge amounts for the sale of slave labor. In December 1944, Junkers paid 96,356 RM for 31,669 days' work of Markkleeberg prisoners. In February 1945, the payments were was for 34,116 days' work.[12]

Although the largest financial gain from the use of concentration camp prisoners in industry went to the SS, the employment of prisoners was also profitable for Junkers and its principal stockholders. The Holocaust was not just calculated genocide; it also included a plan for profiteering from the victims. No laws, of course, protected the Jewish prisoners. The SS placed almost no restrictions on employers concerning the safety or welfare of the workers. The result was that the companies did whatever they pleased. Their physical capital was greatly valued. The machinery was operated with care, oiled, greased, and allowed to rest. We prisoners, on the other hand, were like a bit of sandpaper that, rubbed a few times, becomes useless and is thrown away. When concentration camp prisoners died, the statements from Markkleeberg to Buchenwald listed the names but not the causes of death. The diminished number of inmates was reported only so that a new shipment of slave laborers would be sent.

In the SS policy of extermination through work (*Vernichtung durch Arbeit*), the concentration camp played a central role. The Jews were worked until they were no longer useful, and then they were pushed aside to die. The potentially useful would be cared for minimally. Those who were judged by the staff doctors (prisoner doctors were never involved in these decision) to be incapable of working were returned by subcamps back to the main camps of Auschwitz or Bergen-Belsen, to their deaths.

The owners of the factories were not innocent victims of Hitler. Many major German businesses voluntarily exploited the opportunities created by the Nazis. The factory manager's priority was not the political will of the state but to make the highest profit. The handful of corporate officials prosecuted in Nuremberg brought to light evidence of corporate complicity in the genocide. The Krupp and IG Farben trials revealed the extent of corporate involvement. German industry's exploitation of slave and forced labor in corporate-run concentration camps and the widespread looting of Jewish property are regarded by many as evidence of the criminal character of the alliance between the Nazi Party and the senior levels of Germany's economic power structure.[13]

Much documentation has been lost about the Junkers factory in Markkleeberg. It may never be possible to compile accurate details and statistics that would provide an overall view. The incomplete evidence sheds only dim light on who among the owners and sponsors of the Junkers factory derived large profits from our work.

The Factory

Hungarian Jewish women in Markkleeberg were included in the various operations of the factory. They performed not only dangerous work but physically heavy labor. The camp in Markkleeberg supplied slave laborers to three Junkers operations.

(1) The large factory in the former spinning mill where Erzsike and I were assigned—located on 1, Stöhrstrasse, Telephone: Leipzig 394 181—was the largest and the closest to the camp. The Junkers director in October 1944 was Giebler.[14] Girls liked to work there because the atmosphere was more relaxed than in the smaller places, which had tighter discipline.
(2) The former chocolate factory in Markkleeberg, which we called the small factory or the chocolate factory.
(3) The former beer factory in Zwenkau. The inmates commuted by train.

Once assigned to factory work, Erzsike and I waited anxiously to be in touch with the civilian world again. It had been almost a year since we were cut off from the human community. How exciting it would be to see civilian people, families, houses and stores! At that point, we did not even think about the danger of working in a municipal factory that might be a target of air attacks. We were unaware that there had been bombings already on July 7, 1943, and February 20, 1944, that had destroyed buildings and caused casualties.[15]

Roll call was over quickly in the morning, and soon we were in the midst of a huge column of women streaming out of the camp. A red "X" was painted on our overall backs and a red stripe on the pants. The way from the camp gate to the factory was about three to four kilometers, or a twenty-minute walk, along a footpath about two and a half meters wide. As we walked and shivered, we saw in the distance some of the high-rise buildings close to the camp. It was not yet six o'clock in the morning, people were just waking up, and no one seemed to be around. I tried to envision what lay behind those walls, to realize that people were living their normal lives. Guards with guns were on both sides of the column. Keeping tempo with the group was hard in the wooden clogs, and anyone who slowed down was pushed from behind. The *Aufseherins* walked both in the front and in the back with their whips. I was lucky not to be at the end of the line, where girls were most likely to be hit.

Finally, silence reigned on our first walk to the factory, except for the sound of the wooden shoes hitting the pavement. Then, among our monotone steps, the thin, melodic voice of a woman rose above the tramping. The sound moved our hearts as we recognized the familiar words of the Morning Prayer. Only those who were close, as we were, could hear the memory-laden, heartfelt plea and the gratitude of "*majde ani*" (or *modeh ani*): "I thank [God]."[16] It went straight to the deepest corner of our hearts. We listened with humility, remembering mornings at home that mother hurried to help father in the store while our Catholic maid, Boriska, stood with us to recite the prayer. Boriska watched that we pronounced every word clearly and properly. She had much experience because she had done the same with our father when he was as a child. We listened to the fading tune and silently added our own deep-felt supplications. We heard that beautiful melody on some other mornings, coming from a distance. It felt so good, filling us with hope for the new rising day.

Interviewing Ilana Sajovits Breiner, I was pleased to learn the identity of that gentle, pious lady who raised our spirits and lightened the burden on the way to the factory. The voice belonged to Olga Rosenberg, a forty-year-old mother whose twelve-year-old son had been separated from her in Auschwitz. Mrs. Rosenberg passed away a few years ago, but she left her mark on many of us Markkleeberg inmates with her unbending faith.

Forbidden to speak or to look to the side, we continued our march to the rhythm of "*Links! Links!*" (Left! Left!). Sometimes Ibolya Kail Gabori, our camp singer, began, and others followed her, singing Hungarian marching songs and popular hit tunes. The SS encouraged, sometimes even ordered, us to sing as we marched outside the camp. It created a rather benign impression for bystanders, as well as a diversion for the guards.

Singing and marching on the way, we met those from the night shift who had finished their work. Girls could exchange messages in the form of songs at this point. We learned about the meals we would have and the current events in the factory and the camp. Sometimes the singing message was about the punishment waiting in the camp because of room searches or other trouble.

As we came closer to the factory, we saw a huge red brick building with a high chimney that was heated by coal. Inside were the big halls (*halle*) surrounded by a number of smaller rooms.

We crossed the street and passed a garden with trees that belonged to the plant. Some girls told us that in September the place was striking, as trees laden with peaches bent the branches to the ground. They looked at the orchard as a beautiful but unreachable dream, a memory of that other world of home.

We entered the factory grounds at "The Jews Gate." The gateway opened for the inmates, but it was closed the rest of the time. We passed through five by five, in perfect order, under the guards' supervision. They called us to straighten our lines. The factory was unheated, but certain machines generated heat. A section separated by a glass wall for the office was heated. As we entered, we were set back by the loud noise. Hammering, sawing, and polishing—sounds that we were not used to hearing—assaulted our ears.

The work was technically demanding, and the workers needed to be proficient and alert. Both ability and knowledge were necessary. Inmates with intellect and skill were chosen for the specialized machines. The plant produced a variety of small parts, screws, and segments that needed accurate measurement.

On the transport list, our dates of birth had been changed by the Jewish inmates who registered us. They knew the danger for us of being too young for work, so they listed my sister as seven years older and me four years older, even though we had told them our correct ages. I do not know whether it was due to the transport list or whether Erzsike was given a job randomly on the automatic machine, while I was assigned to sweep around the machines. Even though my broom was a special heavy one made of strands of steel and I had to collect steel residues, my job was considered a good one. I was afraid that someone with connections, like the *Lager-* or *Blockälteste,* might recommend one of her family members for it. That would mean separation from Erzsike and probably working outside again. Fortunately, my fears did not materialize.

When the first transport arrived, the girls had time to study the different type of machines and what they did. They received two weeks' training in the factory. They also learned the measurements and the names of the machines.[17] Our group was given only a short hour of explanation. Although the talk was translated to Hungarian, there were many German technical words used. Being hungry, tired, and scared, we could hardly apply our minds to memorize the German terms concerning the work and the strange machines. Actually, it did not really matter because the majority of us attended only to automatic machines.

Despite our hopes and imagination, we had very little contact with the outside world. According to regulations, there was supposed to be no contact between the German civilian workers and the forced laborers.

The plant was directed by German civilians, and there were also German civilian women workers. We received our instructions from the German production manager and the forced-laborer technicians, or foremen. The girls were included in various operations of the factory, and we alternated day and night shifts with French, Belgian, Dutch, and Italian foreign workers.

The Machines

A number of machines were as huge as a room. The prisoners looked like dwarves beside them. The ear-splitting noise of the presses and the huge machinery seemed to define the space. Some machines looked like giant candelabras, others like a huge tulip or an upright piano. Instead of keys, there were grooves in which the worker placed the parts with which she worked.

Attending the automatic machines required the repetitive movement of the hands. The machine drilled automatically, but the material had to be placed and fastened in the machine. Then it had to be turned by hand one, two, three, or four times, depending on the different forms to be drilled. It was done first by the right hand, and then the same movement was repeated with the left hand. When the process was complete, it started again, the speed dictated by a specific quota to be met. All that work was performed under the crushing noise of other sawing, grinding, and drilling machines. Due to automation, prisoners worked on a single component and did not know what part of the airplane the element belonged to.

Production Halls

WESTHALLE. The plant had three large production halls: Westhalle, Mittelhalle, and Osthalle. In each hall there was a different type of operation. As we entered the factory, first was the Westhalle. There were many automatic machines, and the noise was deafening.

On two big machines in the Westhalle, Sarah Salamon Israel and others worked day shifts from 6:15 AM to 6:15 PM. From iron rods that the girls

The factory in 1994 before it was demolished to make room for residential housing.

fed to the machines, small screws and bolts were manufactured to precise millimeter measurements. This required delicate, exacting work and accurate measurements. Hindering their labor was the hot oil that the machines sprayed. Also in the Westhalle, in a central location opposite the bathroom, was the machine where poet Erzsébet Frank worked. Most of the girls could pass her on their way to the restroom.

Elisabeth Stein Székely's machine stood in the line behind Erzsébet Frank's. Elisabeth worked on the sharpening-polishing machine. Between two big cylinders, ring-shaped parts were run and sharpened to millimeter accuracy. Elisabeth and Erzsébet remained good friends after the war.

Next to Elisabeth Stein Székely was the automatic machine of Erzsébet Frank's sister, Katalin Frank Gallo. The sisters were petrified of being separated, so they were happy to work close to each other. Two lines behind Erzsébet Frank's machine were the *sweissers* (welders), a special group that inspired Erzsébet Frank to write a poem about them.

Because the welders engaged in a special type of work, they had to pass a test to show ability for both coordination and concentration. Good eyesight and attentiveness were crucial because they had to do three things simultaneously. The factory representative selected twelve girls for that task from the first arrivals to Markkleeberg. The twelve were housed in block three, room twenty-two. The welders' work site had a table set up permanently. On the table was an iron ring with a hole in the middle. To turn the ring, one had to step on a foot pedal and move the wheel, while holding in the left hand a rod made of some sort of acid and carbon. With the right hand, one had to apply the gas flame that melted the rod. There was a button by which the flame could be controlled. As the rod melted, dripping metal reached the middle of the ring and filled the empty place. The welder had to move the pedal as fast as the flow of the material required. She also had to watch that the melted rod flowed evenly and continuously to the exact place where it was intended. With the aid of special forceps, the completed ring was taken out and placed in a liquid of hot acid, and from there the finished product was placed in containers. The work demanded concentration and coordination of hands, feet, and eyes. The number of finished rings was counted to meet the daily quota.

The welders used goggles against the strong light and the splinters from the machines, but they lacked face masks or protective clothing. The special gas for welding was harmful for the lungs. The girls worked eight hours in daytime, in two shifts. One group of six girls started at 6:15 in the morning and the others started at 2:15 in the afternoon. I do not know whether the German engineers who tested and selected the girls were aware that there were three groups of sisters among the twelve girls. One of the sisters was Elizabeth Zucker Mermel, who carried the poem about the welders all the way home.[18]

A tall, skinny, elderly German civilian who spoke a bit of Hungarian was the supervisor of some machines in the Westhalle and the welders. He had studied once in Besztercebánya, Slovakia, and liked to talk to the women.[19] There was also a Flemish forced-laborer technician from Belgium who brought news of the happenings in the world. Thus, the Westhalle and the intelligent girls there became the center of information and activity.

Klára Spitz Snitzler, our friend from home, had a large, complicated-looking monster of a machine in the Westhalle that turned out copper pieces for the airplanes. Klára's job was to feed the machine with a strip of copper and to press a foot pedal at the right moment, so that she would get the desired product without wasting any copper. Klára complained that she had trouble reaching the foot pedal and was in constant fear of letting the cutting edge of the machine come down on her fingers. Gradually, Klára learned to master and even to like her machine.

Deeper in the large Westhalle was the machine of my sister. It was a large, noisy, automatic drilling machine. Erzsike had to drill round holes in the middle of a triangular-shaped piece of steel. The machine was moving up and down, and she needed to watch with full attention. Any little distraction could break the delicate drill, which might be interpreted as sabotage.

I came around Erzsike's machine with my broom and watched to make sure that she did not fall asleep. It was especially hard at night between 2 and 4 AM. Once I arrived and saw tears dropping from Erzsike's eyes as she attended the machine. She tried to smile among the tears, but then she admitted to being very tired and said that her back was hurting badly. With all her pain, Erzsike's greatest concern was that she would not be able to fill her quota for the night. The Dutch foreman-technician noticed her predicament, maybe even her tears; he sat down and completed the assigned work for her. Both he and the German civilian supervisor were compassionate toward the young girl struggling with a job beyond her capacity. After helping Erzsike, the foreman left, but he soon returned and put something in the drawer and indicated to Erzsike that it was for her. Erzsike peeked in and saw a small potato. She was so surprised she did not know what to do and kept repeating in a whisper, "*Danke*" (thank you). We were aware that the forced laborers did not have much food either.

Our joy at having the potato was great. We wanted to share it with our friend Klára Spitz Snitzler. Klára had always been so nice to us, and this was our chance to repay her a bit. Klára's machine was not far, but an *Aufseherin,* whom we called Rákoczi (because of her ponytailed hairstyle that reminded us of a Hungarian statesman) was always there chasing a handsome French foreman (technician) who worked by Klára's machine. I walked around, holding the potato and thinking how good it would taste and how pleased Klára would be. Unfortunately, the *Aufseherin* continued flirting. As the night shift drew toward an end, being reluctant to take the risk of a sudden inspection, we decided to consume our treasure. We had no knife, so Erzsike, hiding by the side of her machine, took two big bites from the raw potato. This was less than half, but she gave me the rest. It tasted as delicious as if it were from a Hungarian goulash. Erzsike, meanwhile, felt a bit better and was delighted to discover that we had only half an hour left in the shift. Erzsike usually waited eagerly for me to tell her the hour, because the clock was not visible from her machine. I always watched the slowness of the clock with disappointment. My frequent checking undoubtedly made time seem to move even more slowly.

The work was hard and tedious. We expressed our frustration in the only form we could, through song. Singing was not allowed in the factory, but we sang on the way to work or among ourselves in the barracks and the washroom. The women wrote poetry whether they were amateurs or literary professionals. One needed only a little bartering for paper and pencil. The finished product was easy to pass around verbally. Usually we did not know the author or composer. Interviewing Klára Roth Oren, I was pleased to discover that it was she who had written the following song that I remembered from Markkleeberg. Klára did not even need pencil and paper. She simply hummed to herself and, after she had all the words in her head, she passed them orally among us.

Everyone who works in the Junkers factory,
Twenty-one, twenty-two, twenty-three,
Could hardly wait for all the work to do.
Aufseherin, I have only one request:
Give us work nine days a week.
The labor is much, the food is little
But no one has stomach trouble.
At six in the evening we start toward the factory.[20]

Humor did not merely sketch a witty portrait of our suffering, but it provided us an outlet for emotional or mental rebellion against the Nazis. Although it did not save life, humor lessened the distress and changed our perspective on reality, thus helping us to cope.

Back in the factory, Erzsike learned to better focus her attention and to channel her efforts toward the machine. Still she had the constant fear that she might be sent out to work in the fields.

Inmates in the factory endured not only the hot oil blisters, but also scorching tools and iron splinters. Erzsike, in her desire to avoid trouble, was afraid even to ask for help when the spray of hot oil from the machine burned her neck and hand. The Dutch foreman gave her a piece of tissue paper to wipe off the hot oil, but it did not help much. The pimples became infected, yet Erzsike was still reluctant to go to the *Revier.* She tried to hide the sores, but the German civilian master noticed the abscesses and took her to the first-aid station in the factory. Erzsike was petrified, fearing she might be found unfit for factory work and sent back to Auschwitz or Bergen-Belsen. She relaxed a bit when, after putting on ointment and a bandage, she was allowed back to the machine. Meanwhile, her machine was tuned better and spread less of the hot oil.

The machine Erzsike worked on was one of the bigger ones in Westhalle. Although the Germans did not consider it exceptional, seeing a child next to that huge machine gave inspiration to one of the inmates working close by. Her name was Gizella, and she was a talented artist whose paintings had won first prizes in her Transylvania homeland. She made a few sketches while in the camp and might have been the one who did the illustration on the poem about the welders that we will see, but Erzsébet Frank did not remember for sure. One morning at the beginning of April 1945, Gizella surprised Erzsike with a beautiful drawing of her by her machine. About five by seven inches, the picture was a very good likeness. We looked at it again and again and then considered how we could save and protect the sketch. I found an old newspaper, and Erzsike had some emery cloth from cleaning the machine. We wrapped the picture carefully, first in the newspaper and then in the emery cloth. Erzsike carried it in her overalls. Luckily, this was toward the end of our stay in Markkleeberg, and the searches were both less thorough and less frequent. We continued to guard the drawing all the way home. It was always among the few precious things we had. As we left Hungary by illegally crossing the Austrian border, the picture in the suitcase, along with our few other precious belongings, was stolen from us. Even writing about it today, I have deep sorrow over that loss.

MIDDLEHALLE. The parts passed from one hall to another, undergoing the various stages of processing. Ilana Sajovits Breiner worked by a polishing machine and next to her, on the other line, worked her sister Sara. Not far from them was the machine of Klára Fisher Neuman, which produced small fixtures that had to be polished in a different section. Margit Susitzky Hönig was the last in a chain of an assembly line production. If she found something wrong, she was to return the part to the previous worker for correction. Some of the mistakes she could correct on her machine, too. Then Margit took the finished product to the control room where German civilians worked. Margit had a leather apron with a pocket. In the control room, a woman who was a German civilian worker occasionally put a piece of bread or an apple in her pocket. Margit ate the bread, but the apple she shared with the girls who worked close by.

OSTHALLE. The Osthalle was a big place divided into sections, with machines for cutting, grinding, and polishing. The girls had to watch the time set for each operation carefully. Barbara Klein Stark worked for a few months in the Osthalle, where her machine was in the first row. Elena Salamon Kaufman's machine sharpened and polished small parts. The Belgian foreman told her that her work required protective glasses, but they had none.

HÄRTEREI *(HARDENING SECTION).* In the *Härterai,* the iron was treated to be stronger, softer, or longer, according to specifications. There were iron rods that had to be put first in heat and then in cold, while being turned over in the process. The bars were so heavy that it took two or three girls to place them into the machine. Those who did it received a glass of milk for nourishment.

Twenty-nine girls and women worked in the *Härterai,* according to Rachel Janovics Mittelman. The job there was not only hard, but also hazardous. There were screws, coils, and other items that were baked and then dipped in an acid solution. The acid was boiling and splattering; it would injure the workers whenever it touched them. The gloves, if they had any, were inadequate for the blazing instruments. Many women still carry the burn marks they received from handling the hot items.

Hava Hartmann Kleinberg worked with her sister in the galvanizing section, and she also got blisters from dipping hot irons into cold water or oil. The steam and sparks that flew into the arms, face, and sometimes even the eyelids, were very painful.

Hans, the German foreman, consoled her by singing his favorite song:

Es geht alles vorüber,	Everything passes by
Es geht alles vorbei.	Everything passes away
Nach jedem Dezember	Following December
Kommt wieder der Mai.	Comes again May

It is a fragment of a German marching song dating probably from World War I.

Mistakes in Production

Being hungry, tired, and overworked, it was inevitable that we would make mistakes: *ausschuss* (waste in production). A certain number of errors—affecting two or three pieces—were allowed, and some could be covered by sympathetic foremen or other girls in the control room. Other misshapen parts the girls hid and discarded in the garbage or on the road back to the camp.

Although there was no deliberate or organized effort to produce waste, individual workers took advantage of the occasion to fritter away material if their machine broke or did not work properly. These personal acts of misuse in production had no influence on war manufacture in general. They may, however, have provided a psychological lift for the individual workers.

Sweepers

My task in the factory was to sweep and collect the falling debris (or the *anfall,* as it was called in German). The workers on each machine were responsible for keeping their area clean. I swept the pathways and the sections among the machines. My broom was made of wires, and it was harsh and quite heavy; but I was pleased because I had no pressure of a workload, and I could rest a bit and go to the bathroom whenever I wanted. Working with the broom, I could also visit friends. We could not talk too much, but even a nice smile or a juicy comment in Hungarian about the work and the supervisors lifted my spirit.

Although I was only concerned to be close to my sister, some resourceful girls knew the possibilities. They were eager to transport the garbage from the floors to the central gathering place because it enabled them to search for riches. The only "treasure" that I found was a broken knife. I hid it between the broom handle and my hand and took it excitedly to Erzsike. A knife like that was a precious commodity in our camp. I hid the knife under the machine by Erzsike. Then the rest of the night, we were weighing the risk mentally, in case they found it near us during a sudden inspection. As one would expect from two scared teenagers, we could not take the risk, so I returned the knife to the garbage pail where I had found it.

Having the broom as my shield and alibi, I could walk around a bit. One day as I was emptying my pail into the larger basket, a German civilian man was measuring the dimensions of the container. He might have been an outside contractor doing some work. He looked at me and my light blonde hair and asked how I got there. With my little bit of German, I could tell him only that I was Jewish. Then he said, "Don't work hard," and left. I was shaken by the attention and hurried away so as not to meet him again. With the freedom I had of moving from machine to machine, I was still very much scared of the German workers, guards, and *Aufseherins.*

Some other sweepers were older girls with whom I had little connection. Their activities, the potential profits that were available from my position, and the view of the garbage as a source of resources, I learned only after the war.

Working Conditions

We worked six days a week in twelve-hour shifts, from 6:15 AM to 6:15 PM or at night from 6:15 PM to 6:15 AM. As the day shift went to work after the roll call in the morning, the night workers returned. In some sections, the work was in three shifts: 6:15 AM to 2:15 PM, 2:15 PM to 10:15 PM, and 10:15 PM to 6:15 AM. On Sundays the factory was closed.

We received soup at twelve o' clock noon or midnight at the factory. We had half an hour for lunch and a ten-minute break. The girls generally used the short break for a quick nap. Those who worked at night were always sleep-deprived. We worked alternately day and night, shifting every two weeks. By the time we became accustomed to sleeping in the daytime, our schedules were altered.

The returnees from night shift theoretically could sleep from morning until five o' clock in the afternoon, but most of the time this was not really possible. The rooms had to be cleaned, and the day was filled with special *Appels,* air raids, and noise. Sundays, and sometimes weekdays, too, when we came home in the morning, we had to do extra work around the camp.

At 5:45, toward the end of the work shift, the machines were shut down and had to be cleaned. Each girl was responsible for her machine. She cleaned the residue that had fallen after the cutting and drilling, and she washed the floor around the machine. I cleaned and replaced my broom in the storage area. When all was ready, we stood in five-person lines to be counted, and, finally, the group left the factory. The road home was usually uneventful as we dragged ourselves down the familiar way toward the camp. On one occasion, we were surprised to see Knittel leading us. We went in a roundabout way that we did not understand. The guards and the *Aufseherins* all obeyed, and we walked an additional fifteen minutes. Later we learned that Knittel was drunk and his staff was reluctant to point out his mistake.

Coupons as Rewards for Good Work

There was an incentive system whereby workers could get a "premium," or coupon, for special productivity. The tickets were generally worth about one or two Reichsmarks. One Reichsmark equaled forty cents. On the coupon was written SS-Sandortkantine, Buchenwald Aussenkommando Wertmarke RM-1. It was given out by the factory management. The coupons could be spent in the camp canteen.[21]

In the early days, Sara Salamon Israel remembered how the girls could use the coupons to buy a toothbrush, toothpaste, a comb, a mirror, needle and thread, salt, cigarettes, shoelaces, and occasionally even a pair of fabric shoes with wooden soles, depending on the value of the coupon. The girls called it "Nazi money." Located in the same barracks as the *Revier,* the canteen was better at the beginning. Later, there was not much to buy with the coupons. By the time our transport arrived, there were no more coupons and the canteen was closed.

Work Hazards

In addition to the burnings and blisters cased by hot oil, acid, and chemicals, there were serious, life-threatening problems with the machines. Flora Kaff Goldring, who came to our aid when we were left without lunch, was still shaken fifty-five years later as she recalled her fright working on a faulty machine. A Ukrainian worker was severely injured when the machine malfunctioned while he was setting it up. The next day, Flora was assigned to the same machine. She was petrified, but the fear of being accused of sabotage if she refused was greater than the possible injury. With her excellent German, Flora gained the attention of a civilian engineer who was looking for help in the office. After two terrifying weeks on the dangerous machine, Flora was transferred to keep account of the office supplies. Another unfortunate inmate took her dangerous place. Wiping her eyes and holding back tears as she told the story, Flora said that no happiness in life after liberation could make up for what we had to go through in the camp.

Erzsike's polishing and grinding machine occasionally emitted splinters and sparks of dust. Once, a spark from the powdered metal went into Erzsike's eye. Luckily it did not pierce or injure her eye, but filled it with a thin dust of powder. The Dutch technician told Erzsike to get help at the *Revier,* but the girls warned her not to go because the rumors of a forthcoming selection. In the barracks, women gave all types of advice to Erzsike on how to treat her eyes. Elza Reich Szamosi, our friend from home, told Erzsike to pull up her eyelid and hold it a bit to make her eyes fill with tears to wash out the dust. Erzsike tried to do that even at night when she woke up from worry and discomfort. The steel dust irritated her eye and made it tear and itch painfully. The days while she was suffering seemed much longer, even to me, as I took the risk to visit her frequently with my broom. Luckily the Germans did not notice and Erzsike, with tears both real and dust-induced, continued her work without interruption.

There were numerous other work accidents, when girls' hair or fingers were cut in the machines. Many of the calamities happened at night when the girls were especially tired.

SS in the Factory

Adding to the civilian German engineers, foremen, and foreign laborer-technicians who watched over us, there were the *Aufseherins.* Knittel himself also appeared from time to time. We were not permitted to rest. In the production halls, the *Aufseherins* walked around and kept a watchful eye on us, out of concern for sabotage.

There were signs in the factory that forbade—on pain of death—civilian contact with the Jewish prisoners. Conversation was strictly forbidden, even among the inmates. Girls who were caught talking were punished. Knittel and his staff rarely hit the prisoners on the spot; they took down their numbers for later punishment back in the camp. Many of the individual *Appels* were connected with rule infractions in the factory. The unfortunate girl's prisoner number was called to summon her to reckoning.

Knittel, in his high, polished black boots, would often appear unexpectedly at night with his rubber whip and occasionally with his German shepherds. He went from machine to machine, from one hall to the other. It was unfortunate for the inmate if she was not next to her machine. Knittel walked down each line. Once he stopped next to Erzsike's machine. She still remembers the fear she felt. Luckily Knittel did not pay attention to her; it was an empty place by the next machine that had attracted his interest. If Knittel caught someone not working, talking to a forced laborer, or engaged in some other violation, the chances were that the girl's hair would be cut and she would have to stand on punishment *Appel* or spend time in the bunker. The inmates dreaded his visits. Word swiftly passed that the *öreg,* the old man, was there. When there was no time for verbal warnings, the girls used to give a signal like a hissing or a whirring sound. The forced laborers, even the civilians, learned to heed the warning when the girls called that the *öreg* was coming. The German civilian workers detested Knittel's visits.

Knittel would appear suddenly to crash down on the weak, tired, hungry, dehumanized girls. To ameliorate our pain, Klára Roth Oren composed a poem to the melody of a Hungarian hit song.

Everyone who works in the Junkers factory
Knows well what the old man does.
We fear him, ah so much,
I must admit it truthfully.
Markkleeberg is a factory,
But we hope it is not a factory of death.[22]

Completely lacking power against the strong German enemy, our cultural activities were the only actions left to us to aid ourselves and our fellow inmates. Comment on the horridness of the situation provided an avenue for the expression and communication of emotion.

Singing also documented the times, strengthened our hopes, and imbued life in the camp with some human qualities. Although many of the literary creations in Markkleeberg were lost during the Death March, I was fortunate to recover some for this work. They shed light on the rich cultural activity of the camp.

Factory work proceeded, in most part, without too much abuse or arbitrary punishment by the SS. Probably it was company policy that terrorizing the workers be kept under control. To have the slave and forced laborers work in tolerable circumstances undoubtedly maximized productivity. Although Knittel used his whip, especially at night, he generally acted the part of an army officer in the factory. When he noticed some transgression during the day shift, he usually only wrote down the inmate's number. Then in his own domain, he meted out the punishments. Every so often, Knittel or an *Aufseherin* would make a mistake in taking down a prisoner's number. As a result, some unfortunate inmate who had done nothing wrong was singled out during *Appel* with no idea why. She was scolded, beaten, and punished for an offense she knew nothing about. This happened to Irena Lebovits Ehrenreich, who despite her crying and protesting that it was an error, had to stand on punishment *Appel.* Finally, after hours in the bitter cold, when she was turning blue Knittel released her. In the morning, Irena was back at her machine with a perpetual fear that she would be held accountable again for someone else's wrongdoing.

The Ladies' Room in the Large Factory

Knittel's favorite place to catch inmates misbehaving was the ladies' room. During his frequent surprise visits, he often went directly to the restroom, especially at night. Then he waited for the girls to come out. As soon as a girl emerged, she received a big slap on her face or a box on the ear. We all knew what had happened from the victim's burning red face. Knittel was a large man, and when he hit someone, it left a mark.

In every hall was a bathroom with six toilets. In order to go to the ladies' room, the inmates had to ask permission, which was usually granted. When a worker went to the bathroom, her machine had to be shut down. The lavatory had an entrance door that stayed open, and there were no doors to the individual seats—nor was there toilet paper. An inmate was assigned to keep the bathroom clean. In the Westhalle, it was Marcsa whom we called "*vécés Marcsa*" (toilet Marcsa). She was a tall girl who urged the inmates to finish faster and leave. Poking the women with a stick, she hurried them along if they took longer than five or six minutes. When Knittel came, Marcsa had to report in detail how many were inside: "Six girls are sitting and ten are standing."

The inmates did not always listen to Marcsa, however. The girls devised special daily schedules, and visiting the ladies' room became an important part of life in the factory. Sitting on the toilets with no doors, women exchanged ideas and heard the latest news, called "the news from the latrine." The information was about the factory, the camp, and the world. If a girl had to go urgently, Marcsa forced the one who had been there the longest time to give up her seat.

Air Raids

Trips to the air raid shelter were a welcome break from work. The area was targeted for bombing because of its ammunition production. The German workers and the *Aufseherins* were very anxious during air attacks. They ran hurriedly to the shelter, which was underground in the factory. We girls, however, were relaxed, as if we had lost our survival instincts. We went slowly and happily deep inside the bunker, feeling a bit of satisfaction, a kind of sweet revenge, at seeing our feared oppressors in distress. Each attack raised our hopes that the war was coming to an end, bringing our salvation.

Toward the end of March 1945, the attacks grew more frequent, and the

Germans hurried even faster to the shelters. We especially enjoyed observing our guards who, unlike brave soldiers, were in an actual state of panic. We, who lived in terror anyhow, were not so afraid. At least we tried to convince ourselves we were not, but hearing the sirens and the threatening airplanes zooming above, our hearts did beat faster. I tried to stay close to Erzsike, since being together gave us some psychological sense of protection.

Living was hard both in the camp and in the factory. We had to get used to the new situation in order to stay alive. The next chapter will show some of our ways of coping and the support system we built.

7

The Camp's Informal Structure and Our State of Mind

One Resists with a Gun, Another with His Soul

In Markkleeberg, as in the other Nazi camps, there was terror for both mind and body. To survive, a prisoner thrust into this world had to compromise her inner values and discard some of the fundamental moral principles of normal society. We resisted this process and tried valiantly to hold onto our personalities, inner worth, and basic ethical standards.

We kept up our spirits and our humanity through cultural enrichment—singing, sharing recipes, creating and offering small gifts—and by helping one another to survive. We were united in common attitudes against the German tormentors, transforming them at times, with a joke or a song, from mighty killers to ordinary stupid creatures. The poems, especially the humorous ones that girls created about camp life, contributed to bonding and to expressions of a common fate. It was a comradeship that helped us morally, especially when we were not suffering physically and could feel a bit better about ourselves.

The selfish and cruel acts of Jewish camp supervisors and other pitiless individuals were balanced by the unforgettable gestures of selfless assistance and solidarity by other prisoners that we witnessed in our struggle for life. Research on the Holocaust entails the study of evil, but it also documents the manifestation of human courage, which opens a door of hope for mankind. This border line of malevolence and kindness, existing simultaneously, formed the basis of what is called "the concentration camp syndrome" described by both psychological experts and survivors.

Praying, singing, and other expressions of striving for hope and love were important group activities that worked against dehumanization. Social scientists presume that the more destructive an environment is the more survival depends on such mutual help and cooperation.[1] Nechama Tec concludes in her research that, "in times of upheaval, in the ruin of traditional society, cooperation and mutual protection rather than combativeness promote greater odds of survival."[2]

The Camp's Informal Structure — Bonding

The variety of social classes in the camp resulted in the formation of a heterogeneous society divided into a number of groups. These groups were created after the Nazi universe destroyed families and communities, but not the interpersonal relationships of its victims. Close friendships and relationships of mutual help existed in a number of different frameworks.

The trauma in the camp was both individual and collective, thus we looked for a support system in the form of a small group of comrades. The inmates in Markkleeberg, as in other camps, established mutually accommodating relationships. Social bonding—the formation of surrogate families for mutual aid and nurturance—served as an important coping mechanism. Just being together, partners in suffering, we managed to create a climate of freedom, dignity, and support.

The most important contribution of camp families was to supply mutual help. This answered a need for connectedness and provided emotional support in withstanding the hardship of the camps. In loneliness, there was no protection against violence and despair. As the days passed, we worked, rested, hoped, and despaired.

It was a truism of the concentration camp experience "that you could not survive alone." Most camps had informal support units, but not all prisoners had access to them. Some lacked the opportunity to join, others the will; still others lacked both. Those who kept themselves aloof due to shyness, lack of social skills, or for any other reason had a harder time withstanding camp pressures. Not having a friend, a confidante, or a supportive group to share one's grief and to lift one's spirit moved the person closer to despair. Many prisoners succumbed even with help, but without it they had little chance. After liberation, we all agreed that without the support networks provided by close friends or family—Erzsike in my case—few of us would have lived to see freedom.

Camp-Sisters and Camp-Families

The term *camp-sister* was coined by women in concentration camps. Girls who remained alone after selection looked for the support and company of others. They attached themselves to a group or to another girl, forming a relationship or camp-family that became the source of mutual assistance and strength. Eugen Kogon, a former inmate, pointed out that membership in such a group was perhaps the finest experience in a concentration camp.[3] Women left entirely alone tried to stay close to those who had something in common with them, such as people from the same town, city, or neighboring area. They formed a substitute family.

Camp-sisters or *lager*-sisters might have been classmates or had some other social affinity. Girls such as Barbara Klein Stark and Magda Schön Hilf, who came from the same area, both remained alone after selection and became faithful friends or camp-sisters. In the transient and unpredictable world of the concentration camp, friendship was the one thing one could count on. The friendship of Barbara and Magda, as with many of the camp-sisters, continues today. They both built their own families and have children and grandchildren, but their close relationship still serves as a substitute for an extended family of their own generation—which Holocaust survivors lack.

Many times, a girl alone joined with another to be *lager*-sisters simply on the basis of personal preferences. When you talked to someone, you could often sense she was compatible, your type of person. Women in the same barracks or work crew also formed friendships and bonded together for mutual help. They derived a measure of hope and comradeship from the human connection.

Larger mutual-aid units were molded on the traditional family component. The literature refers to these relationships as bonding groups or as camp- or surrogate families. Camp-families could be composed of as few as two girls or as many as seven or eight; but the norm seems to have been between three and five persons. Women from camp-families shared not only companionship, but also memories, hopes, and songs.

To establish friendships, the prisoners first looked for girls from their town or the surrounding area that, after parents, were the closest to them. Marie Politzer Kaufman arrived with girls from Papa, her hometown. They stood together on *Appel,* slept in the same room, and took every imaginable precaution against being separated. They protected and nursed one another when they became ill. Like many camp-families, they shared the benefits of their camaraderie with few outsiders.

The concentration camp environment basically erased most prewar social distinctions. Yet with women from the same town, "landsmen" who knew one another, respect for the person continued to exist. Belonging to a group of familiar girls was a source of strength that allowed the individual to retain a sense of her self-image as well as of her prewar identity.

From Abaújszántó, my hometown, girls also found friends among those from the area. Eva Rosenberg Eichler lost her mother and her sister during the first selection in Auschwitz. Then she met Klára Spitz Snitzler, who was also alone, and whom she knew from middle school. Eva and Klára supported each other, morally and physically, in their day-to-day existence. Their friendship extended throughout their lives in Israel.

Margit Lang Stein and Márta Weisz Paran also stayed together. In addition to being good friends, they belonged to the larger group of girls from our town and vicinity that supported one another. There were also Ilona

Roth and the Hartmann sisters, Hava Hartmann Kleinberg and Miriam Hartmann Carmi.[4] The closest to us were Klára Spitz Snitzler and Elza Reich Szamosi. They were our confidantes, whom we trusted and could depend on for help and counsel if needed.

Knowing one another prior to the camps made it possible for us to practice some of the warmth and hospitality we knew from home. In one wintry January 1945, for instance, as a miracle, Elza Reich Szamosi received an apple from a German civilian worker in the factory. It was an exceptional treat because we did not have fresh fruit during our stay in camp. Elza could just have eaten the precious gift by herself, but she saved it. Returning to the barracks, she collected all six of us from Abaújszántó. Borrowing a knife, Elza cut the apple into six thin slices so each of us had a portion. Before tasting it, Eva Rosenberg Eichler commented, "Let's say the prayer for fruit that we haven't had so long." Then we all added also the blessing "*Shehecheyanu*" giving thanks to God that we had reached that day. Our tears blended with the piece of apple, recalling times from home.

Mutual assistance was especially vital at times of sickness. Without friends to care and sometimes to cover up for you, an illness could be fatal in a world where one had the right to life only if she worked. *Lager*-sisters were created also by new acquaintances originating in the barracks, where we spent our little spare time and where we were less supervised by the SS. We also made friends by working and standing on line together. I felt a bit of that old camaraderie in 1998 when we returned to the camp in Markkleeberg for a memorial. We survivors were together again in our special situation. We had one aim: to be in unity as we were in the camp, and not in the competitive way. Later, at the airport, each one flew to a different destination, and we felt alone again in fresh circumstances and in new places.

Not all who were from the same location were close friends. Besides being a landsman, friendship still depended on previous social standing. Bella Spitz, the *Lagerälteste,* was from Sárospatak, but she had no special connection to Lenke Schwarz Fine, who was from the same town. Unlike Bella, Lenke belonged to the Orthodox congregation. Besides the religion, there was still the division of social standing. Bella's helper and good friend Erzsébet Iczkovits, also from Sárospatak, was the wife of a lawyer and had no relationship with Lenke either. Maybe if Lenke needed something, she might have had a bit easier time with Mrs. Iczkovits, simply because both were from the same town.

The Germans made us equal slaves, but we knew among ourselves who we were. We still respected former aristocrats and highly placed persons, provided that the individual was a decent human being and possessed an amiable personality. Erzsébet, the affluent wife of a physician from Kosice, and whom we called the "*Doktor néni*" (physician lady), was pleasant and supportive. She gave valuable advice and helped us to cope. Erzsébet was afraid to tell who she was at home because the Germans were especially cruel to the formerly well-to-do. Personality among us prisoners, regardless of former position and economic status, came out clearly in the camp. One could feel the home, the economic, and the educational level that a person came from.

Comradeship might also be established as the prisoners arrived in one transport or happened to be assigned to one room or close to one's bed. This somewhat informally established ties that set them off from other inmates.

Family Ties

We all had strong ties to our families. One could have other friends and acquaintances, but a person's primary orientation was to her family, as Erzsike was for me. She was ultimately who really mattered. Loyalty to and responsibility for family members are basic Jewish values. The strong family ties of our small European towns continued in the camp. They underlay the remarkable outpouring of caring and nurturing. There were some exceptions, but in the main, we cared for one another and remained true to our upbringing. The culture and education we had received stayed with us. "What you bring from home is what you are" women repeated throughout my interviews, and I knew it also from my own experience.

Family members would risk their own safety to take their sick relatives from the *Revier* to save them just before a selection. The love, warmth, and support we remembered from home helped us in the most difficult times. Even our desire to stay alive was connected with being together and the trust of reuniting the family.

The mutual help and the primacy of the family were important characteristics of the pre-Holocaust Jewish culture that gave support against the harsh outside environment, but it could also sometimes be an impediment. Loyalty to and responsibility for family members prevented many Jews from escaping to save their lives. This was the case in our family, when my mother refused the offer for escape.

Since our dreams of liberation were centered on homecoming and meeting family members, we were often in denial: We could not deal with the possibility that our parents may have died in Auschwitz. Our dreams of liberation centered on reuniting with them. Today, although fully aware of my parents' and grandparents' tragic fate, many of my actions are still governed by thoughts of pleasing them. Working on the history of Markkleeberg, I hope to present insight into the world of my parents, their values and traditions, as demonstrated by our actions in the camp.

Although I did not have the comfort of my mother, I had my sister Erzsike, who represented everything from my former life. We guarded and supported each other with all our remaining strength and immeasurable love. Having each other gave me a purpose in life and hope for the future. Our closeness also entailed some anguish. One day, before we were assigned to work in the factory, they needed a hundred girls for a certain job. Erzsike was number 100, and I was 101. There was nothing we could do to keep from being separated; the SS guard was standing there. I watched Erzsike being led away with the group. The *Blockälteste* and my friends reassured me that Erzsike would be back; but I knew that in the camp, one could never know where a group of people was being taken. It was difficult for me to pass the time that day. When Erzsike returned in the evening, life's meaning was given back to me.

Hunger, cold, and despicable camp conditions touched me less and left fewer emotional scars than the fear of separation and concern for the physical well-being of my sister. We were children from warm, protected family homes who suddenly found ourselves thrown into a strange and cruel world. We had to rely on one another to survive. After liberation, our neighbor, Mr. Rezsö Friedman in Abáujszántó, seeing how close we were, remarked, "Your parents had given you good provisions for the road." It felt so good hearing that. We survivors strongly believe that being together with friends or family members saved our lives in the camps. I am sure I would not have survived without my sister's unselfish devotion, optimistic outlook, and warm personality. This sisterly affection and emotional support continues between us today.

Fate and the selection process brought together relatives as a family unit. Sometimes a girl remained with her aunt or with her cousins. Lenke Schlesinger Rosenberg was with her two sisters and their two cousins, forming a unit of five. They stayed together in roll calls and supported one another by sharing their bread and their sorrows. Economics, social standing, and competition that might have distanced relatives before the war were factors that were replaced by personality traits and family devotion.

Birthdays in the Camp

A birthday was an emotional happening, a kind of remembrance of our former life. As the situation improved a bit in Markkleeberg, we slowly started to reconnect to our emotions. Birthdays at home, before the war, were modest compared to the parties and the presents we celebrate with today. The date of one's birth was more of a private family matter. We received a hug and a kiss from mother and grandmother, and maybe a pull on the ear as a distinction by a friend or a sister. In the camp, birthdays became a special expression of closeness. We remembered home, friendship, and family, which raised our spirits. For my birthday, Erzsike secretly hid her bread and carved a small doll from it. She used a bit of sugar to give the doll a face and an expression. My birthday, January 19, fell on a cold but sunny Friday in 1945. The weather matched the shine on Erzsike's face as she presented the doll to me that morning. I was so touched that I cried. On the way to work, we looked toward each other and knew that we were home on the wings of imagination, looking for the loving faces of our parents and grandparents. I remembered Mici, my cat, and I felt her purring and rubbing against my ankle. We kept the tiny bread doll until Friday night, when we celebrated by mixing sugar with margarine to make a special spread for the bread we received. It looked like a cream, and we ate everything including the doll, as if at a festive party. Now I recall the little bread doll in Markkleeberg each time I look at the birthday card and bouquet of flowers my sister sends me every year.

I was sorry that I could not do something for Erzsike's birthday on November 24, 1944. We were still in Bergen-Belsen then, and our spirits were so low that we did not even know the day as it passed by. The Germans were close to succeeding with their methods to annihilate the spirit and then the lives of their captives. Erzsike and I dragged ourselves to stand on the *Appels,* then either waited for the rain to end or for the next food distribution. During the first days in Auschwitz, the past was vividly with us, but by the time we got to Bergen-Belsen, we lived in the present. Our brains slowed in perception and memories dimmed. There were times when our souls stopped feeling any more. All that was human began to gradually disappear. Only the hunger, that strong drive, refused to be dulled. Starvation, with continuous fear, turned us into robotlike beings who could only wait and listen to the German orders. In Markkleeberg, Erzsike noticed the date of my birthday from the calendar at work.

Cultural Differences

The girls in Markkleeberg came from various places in Hungary—large cities and tiny villages—and had different family backgrounds. They were the children or wives of wealthy merchants, farm owners, lawyers, physicians, religious officials, craftsmen, small shopkeepers, or poor laborers. Some shared a conservative provincial character and a pious devotion to religion and tradition. Others were more modern. Differing in cultural background, education, and mentality, they included bohemians and converts to Christianity. Some already had a family; others were unmarried adults or young teenagers such as me and my sister. Most spoke Hungarian and were rooted in the Hungarian language and literature.

There were also girls among us from the borders of Hungary who had a strong background of Jewish folklore and tradition. Many lived in the area of Máramaros or Maramureş in the Carpathians, a mountain range extending from northern Slovakia to central Romania. It was a large, traditional Jewish population before World War II and was a center of Jewish religious life. The Carpathian Jews had a conservative culture, and many were followers of Hasidic rabbis. There was tension between those who lived in the area of Máramaros and those in central and western Hungary. Rachel Berkovics Zolf in her testimony to Yad Vashem mentioned that those from the original Hungarian territories did not like the women from the Carpathians.[5] Although there were some well-to-do Jews in the Máramaros section, numerous were poor, working the land. They had a reputation of being uneducated in Hungarian culture and of following dishonest business practices.

In the camp, we came face-to-face with the girls from Máramaros. They were considered to be arrogant, loud, and pushy. Those from inside Hungary found them strange or foreign, partly because they often did not speak Hungarian well and spoke Yiddish instead, which the Hungarians usually did not speak. Today in Israel, among the older Hungarians, if someone is overly forceful and untrustworthy, they might still say, "What do you expect? He is from Máramaros."

Using the name Máramaros was an expression of former prejudice based on economic, cultural, and religious differences. The writer Erzsébet Rab tried to understand why women from Máramaros seemed different from those of Hungary proper. "Maybe because they grew up in hard economic conditions," she reasoned, "they could withstand the hardship better than others."[6]

Many of the *Blockälteste* and their helpers, as well as members of the *Esskommandos* (those who carried the containers of food) and some kitchen workers, were from Máramaros.[7] The resourceful and daring girls from Máramaros looked down on the others and sarcastically called them *mamelandi* (from the mother country, the area that was always in Hungarian possession).

Although differences were noted in the camp, the prejudice was mild and was exercised only by some women. Interviewing survivors from both Máramaros and from inside Hungary, I found little bitterness and almost no mention of interpersonal prejudices as problems. The overcrowding, the despair, the hunger, the dying all around, and the fight for survival made some people in every group bitter, impatient, and domineering. In the majority, no matter what part of Hungary or its territories women came from, testimonies describe solidarity, mutual help, friendship, and sacrifice.

The World from Our Prison Walls

We were surprised that the world still existed while, for us, a personal earthquake destroyed all that was dear to us. We painfully discovered that, while we suffered so much without having done anything wrong, the earth continued in its orbit and people went on with their lives calmly and peacefully. Sometimes when the visibility improved, I looked across the entrance to the camp at the small red-roofed houses in the distance that resembled the home we once had. I envisioned the lucky people living their normal lives there. The sight of those remote private homes was my connection to the outside world and to the city of Markkleeberg. Further from these houses were the tall apartment buildings with windows and balconies that could be seen from the camp. On Friday nights, if I was not terribly tired standing on *Appel,* I looked at the illuminated windows of the German civilians' apartments. The lights reminded me of the Shabbat candles on Friday nights. I was envious of those families living in peace in their households, while we were the outcasts, kept among barbed wires with a constant fear of the SS and their next life-threatening orders.

Sometimes I closed my eyes and imagined that my parents were home worrying for us. It was very hard after the war to face reality and know that we had neither family nor home. Being barely more than children, we did not fully comprehend our situation. We were locked in barbed wires, but we did not consider ourselves prisoners. Prisoners, in our minds, were associated with criminals and those who acted against the laws, which we did not. Even now, writing about us as prisoners, I still have that uncomfortable and insulting connotation. In reality, we were treated worse than most prison inmates because they usually had rights and privileges.

Some of the more mature girls realized painfully our pitiful situation. Erzsébet Frank questioned if we would ever be free, ever again sleep in regular beds with fresh linen, ever have food besides the soup. Her tears frequently flowed as she watched the civilians in the factory going about their work freely and cheerfully.[8]

Different Ways of Coping

Many factors influenced survival, but only a few were under the control of the individual prisoner. A bit of alertness, determination, and lots of good luck came together to make one a survivor against the heavy odds of life in a concentration camp. The prisoner's personality, adaptive patterns, and coping mechanisms played some parts in camp life. These aptitudes were shaped by early life experiences, developmental histories, and emotional bonds within the family. What helped most of us to cope was the instinct of self-preservation that every human being possesses. We built a world of illusions that when the war was over, all would be as it was before. It was not logical, but our ability to deny reality helped us in the camp. When I closed my eyes, I could remove myself from my surroundings. I thought about the wonderful things that were, and that would be again after the war.

We used to play a game of letters in our free time to avert tense thoughts and hunger. One girl would say a letter and, from that, we built names of cities, mountains, actors, plays, or famous personalities. This mind-awakening verbal game helped us to concentrate and turn from the surrounding events.

Elizabeth Winkler Engel, who needed a reason for being, made it her task to mark the date of each passing day. It was important to her not to lose track of time. In the factory, there was a limited amount of paper, and she bartered a pencil for her bread. Elisabeth knew exactly the important dates when she had been transported out of Auschwitz and Bergen-Belsen; she also marked on her calendar every significant event in the camp. When she had to discard her notes during searches, she memorized the contents; then she started anew, somehow obtaining additional paper. It made her feel vital as a person. After liberation, Elizabeth had no problem recalling the dates of her life in the camp. Like Elizabeth Winkler Engel, there were others who kept some hold on their existence by knowing the date.

Sharing Recipes and Homemaking Skills

Food was always on our minds. Exhausted, cold, and hungry, we talked about the meals we longed for and about family dinnertimes we remembered. Former housewives described meal preparations, what they did and what they would be doing. Women cooked with words—to bring back memories of home, assuage their hunger, and provide their campmates, as Rochelle Saidel observed, "food for thought in the true sense of the expression."[9]

Married women imagined themselves back at home in their kitchens cooking for their families. For her husband who was somewhere in Ukraine, Elisabeth Stein Székely prepared chicken stewed with paprika, a favorite meal for all of us. Frida, another former homemaker, for her little daughter from whom she had been separated in Auschwitz, made an apple strudel *(almás rétes)* with apples from her pantry where she kept all that she preserved, looking ahead for the coming year. Others recalled how they prepared mushroom sauce with cream, or they debated the number of eggs preferred for a chocolate cake. Some explained the recipes for the tastiest heavy food, such as mousses, pancakes filled with walnuts *(dijos-palacsinta),* tortes, or fancy cakes—all topped with whipped cream or chocolate. Local variations in food preparation often reflected geographic areas. When women had similar memories of the way a dish was prepared and served, they were probably from near the same locale.

Talking about the preparation of special homemade food evoked for me the memory of my mother's hazelnut cake *(mogyoros torta).* I used to help her mix the ingredients with the prospect of having the residual batter from the bowl before cleaning. Mother was always generous, and in the camp, appetite sharpened by hunger, I could vividly remember that special sweet taste, sometimes even with a feeling of fulfillment or satisfaction.

The recipes discussed recalled the taste of Sabbath meals and followed the calendar of the Jewish holidays. For Shavuot, for instance, there was a conversation about flaky Hungarian strudel. Although I did not know how it was prepared, I knew how it tasted. I liked strudel filled with peppered fried cabbage, but Erzsike and the others preferred it sweet, with apples, cherries, or creamed cottage cheese. Sharing cooking techniques and memories of holiday meals helped us to cope better with hunger as well as with the longing for our parents, grandparents, and home. Finally, when our appetite for rich stuff slackened, we talked of the simple food: soups, meats, bread with butter, and the Hungarian yellow paprika that my mother used to prepare for our school lunches. These memories of simple meals sometimes fulfilled and satisfied us emotionally more than the elaborate cakes and heavy foods.

Even those who did not cook offered recipes for others. Sharing cooking techniques probably had a positive psychological effect because it reflected tradition, identity, and commitment to the future. Exchanging recipes also encouraged relationships based on shared memories. Mentioning the recipes of one's mother, aunt, or grandmother also connected one with the memories attached to the names—Aunt Anna's potato kugel (a baked casserole resembling a soufflé or pudding) or Grandmother Rachel's chicken soup. Sharing recipes helped the women retain a sense of "before" and a hope for "after" the war. Like giving gifts, it may have also helped them keep their sense of themselves as women. The discussion about cooking recalled our former lives when we had homes and status within our families and communities. When we were talking about food and cooking, we were sometimes dreaming of how things would be after the war and what dishes we would have. Klara Spitz Snitzler asked what she could serve us as a treat after liberation. I requested *dobos-torta* (a round, layered, fancy cake with a hard caramel top), while Erzsike dreamed of a napoleon (a pastry consisting of thin layers of puff pastry interlaid with cream or custard filling). Cooking by imagination became a form of resistance that kept up the spirit of groups of women in the concentration camp. Inmates exchanged recipes with the French women prisoners, too. Thinking of the rich and less familiar ingredients that the Frenchwomen described seemed to us like news from another globe.

Homemaking abilities, such as dividing the rations so they would last longer and sewing a pocket to save bread in, were life-sustaining survivor skills. Making a belt to adjust the clothing to look better, especially during selection, could be a life-saving adaptation in the camps.

Gender Differences in Coping

Historians researching the topic of coping and surviving in the camps had to read between the lines of survivors' testimonies to understand how gender considerations made the experiences of men and women different. Gender in this content refers to how the underlying social and economic structure imposed certain behavioral expectations and norms.

Although some gender restraints, such as submissiveness and modesty, resulted in undue mental and physical stress for women in pre-Holocaust society, their socialization skills helped them to survive. To relieve their pressures and to help one another, women were more practical and more verbal than the men. Women could and did go to other women and cry on their shoulders, opening up and pouring out their hearts to them. Friendly support was consistent, solid, and widespread in the women's camp.[10]

In their roles of homemaker and caregiver, women had developed skills that made them a bit better suited than men to withstand the privation and hardship of the concentration camp. Women also paid more attention to personal hygiene than men. In daily camp life, women were more successful than men in preserving the vestiges of the reality they had known in their former lives. Giving gifts and exchanging recipes, general nurturing and homemaking skills, were part of the gender roles that women were taught as they grew up.

Women's survival skills are a bit different than men's. Talking about food did not alleviate our hunger, but it distracted us. Food talk among men made them hungrier, so it was less useful as a coping mechanism. The men, on the other hand, had more experience with crafts and trades, which may have helped them to survive. Gender cannot be considered in a vacuum. Other factors such as social class, nationality, political affiliation, religious beliefs, age, health, and even luck influenced how women experienced the Holocaust.

Both sexes relied on the relief offered by joining or creating mutually supportive groups that improved the quality of their lives. Being part of these groups gave survivors a lifeline. I know from the recollections of my husband, who is also a survivor of Auschwitz and other camps, that there were men's mutual aid groups, too, although maybe not as intense as the women's. A member of one of those groups asked my husband to take his place when he was selected for a transport, away from his friends. My husband's work in the camp was very hard, and because he was there without any family, he agreed to change places.

The *Oberscharführer*'s Silver Wedding Anniversary

The Knittels had their silver wedding anniversary in November 1944. The girls found out about it and asked Erzsébet Frank to write something to greet Knittel. Erzsébet, who knew German, composed the following verse to the tune of a popular war song written to Lili-Marleen and sung by Marlene Dietrich.

Twenty-five years ago
In the middle of November
Our commandant wed.
We celebrate this holiday today,
And to God, our Lord, we pray
To bless him on this holiday,
To bless him, bless him still,
To bless him, bless him still.

He is our Leader, takes it seriously;
To his prisoners he is kind and has a good heart.
So may he live in happiness, in joy and comfort.
May he see his golden anniversary,
His golden anniversary.

Sincere are our wishes;
We stand here now on roll call
And so we ask, quite modestly,
A bit more food we would like, please.
So may he live in happiness,
In joy and comfort, may he see
His golden jubilee, a golden jubilee.

We now tell you all
What is in our hearts:
Less roll call and more often extra food please,
So may you live in happiness, in health and joy,
And may He bless your diamond jubilee,
Your diamond jubilee.[11]

Knittel's wedding anniversary was before our transport arrived in Markkleeberg, but Erzsébet Frank described how the girls stood on roll call and told Knittel that they wanted to sing for him. Ibolya Kail Gabori, who had an operatic voice, stepped out and sang solo while a few girls provided the orchestra. One was the drummer by knocking on her food dish. Another had a makeshift harmonica, and there were others who made music by buzzing and humming.

At the beginning, Knittel was generally friendly; therefore, Erzsébet Frank and the girls dared to talk with him. By being nice, they hoped to ease their lives a bit. In time, with the increased number of inmates, Knittel grew more brutal. Knittel was pleased with the song and the presentation, and the camp received a container of extra food that day. Erzsébet Frank holds the song, that indicator of our confused state of mind, as her most shameful memory from the camp.

Springtime

As flowers started to bloom in Markkleeberg, the spirit of spring touched us even in the camp. Marie Politzer Kaufman and her friends found a few violets among the pasture in the fields. They each put one in the buttonhole of their overalls to show the rest of us. As we were returning from the night shift, we met the girls with the violets on their overalls going out for the day shift. They announced jokingly that they were just coming from the Duna promenade in Budapest. We were young enough that their enchantment lifted our spirits.

Our State of Mind

We did not have the capacity for deep thoughts. In Markkleeberg, we probably were not given sedatives in our food, as in Auschwitz, yet we were in no shape for clearheaded contemplation—especially the last month when the bombing increased and our food supply diminished even further. We were like robots, driven by desperate hope and the instinct to survive. Girls often became forgetful, irritable, or apathetic. Our immediate needs were so great that we were governed by want and animal instincts. We were thinking only of when we would get food again, of having no punishment, and of being a bit warmer.

The horror of the camps was not just that the inmates were killed but that, before death, we were destroyed in stages. The so-called "Mussulman" was a prisoner in the process of termination. She was giving up and was also given up by her friends. We avoided looking at the unfortunate woman in that situation, fearing to see a preview of our own disintegration. Fear was our normal state of mind.

Survival in the camps was so precarious and beyond our control that girls looked for omens or different kinds of supernatural signs that they would survive. Many of us received some portent that gave us confidence and assurance that things would turn out all right. There were those who believed that God protected them through the intermediary of a parent, grandparent, or respected rabbi. Erzsike trusted that we would be saved because of grandmother's blessing. Grandmother, who was a profoundly religious lady, used to bless us each Friday after she lit the candles for Sabbath. Friday night in the train on our way to Auschwitz she still blessed us, as was her custom, even without having the candles to light.

I myself cherished the memory of the last Seder at home in 1944. My mother lit four candles, one candle for each of us, and my grandmother lit six, two for her and grandfather and four for us. My father was an only child, and we were our grandparents' sole grandchildren. As the lights shimmered in the newly polished silver candelabras in the middle of the large Seder table, I selected one candle as symbol for my survival. I hoped it would be among the last to burn out, and I watched with apprehension throughout the evening as the candles slowly smoldered away. I was relieved when my candle lasted until the very end. Thinking back on the miraculous ways we were saved from Auschwitz and Bergen-Belsen, and then sent to work in Markkleeberg with the last transport, I still see the light of that small candle shining over our lives.

Images of close family members often appeared to inmates, directing their actions. The shape of a respected, religious grandfather became visible in a dream to Lenke Schwarz Fine. He encouraged her to leave the Death March, which she would not dare to have done on her own. Lenke and her sister Blanka Schwarz Friedman escaped near Dresden and survived the war.[12]

The Holocaust did not have the same impact on all its victims. No event ever does. Age, faith, class, geography, nationality, and economic status were among the factors that differentiated one experience from another.

We had a nearly impenetrable emotional numbness. When they told us in Auschwitz that our parents were dead, we heard but could not comprehend. Although I had some moments of clear thinking that brought doubts to my mind about my mother's and grandmother's survival, yet in my heart I continued to nurture the elusive hope that all would be well. I just could not struggle for life physically and emotionally at the same time. Survivors' literature reflects this trust that we all would be united with our families.[13] We deluded ourselves into believing that, if we could just reach the end of the war, every thing would be well. Hope gave us the strength to survive. Being young, we believed strongly in happy endings, as the following song demonstrates.

> We will have our home again where we will return!
> Goodbye, barrack six!
> Mattock and turnip soup, we will forget you,
> When destiny leads us home,
> To our mothers, fathers, brothers, sisters, and husbands.
> Our home will be nice again, because we want to live and be alive.[14]

Information Sources

There was a variety of information sources for the inmates. The girls who found out about the Knittels' anniversary may have cleaned his apartment and overheard a conversation, or they may have been told by Mrs. Knittel, who was friendly with the girls. For the news of the world, there were the Wehrmacht radio broadcasts that girls cleaning the rooms of the

Aufseherins could sometimes hear. Understanding German only imperfectly, we gleaned mere hints of happenings, which we filled out with our hopeful imaginations. Sometimes, working around the camp, we could hear forced laborers call from a distance, "Hitler *kaput!* The war is ending!" Once, Rachel Janovics Mittelman and other girls emptied a container with ammunition that had been captured from the Russians. When they reached the bottom, they found a note in Yiddish saying, "Jews, keep up the faith, the redemption is near."

A civilian worker, Ms. Gertrud Holl, was accused by Wiegand, the commander of the camp, of transferring information to the prisoners. She allegedly made holes in the potatoes and hid notes in them. She was fined twenty-five Reichsmarks, and Wiegand threatened to lock her in the concentration camp herself. From the prisoners, Ms. Holl received handmade jewelry in gratitude, which she kept after the war; she was very proud of it.[15] Although I could not corroborate that specific fact from survivor testimonies, I know that girls such as Eva Czitter made rings, brooches, and pins from steel or copper available in the factory, which she exchanged for food. Girls who could afford to sacrifice their bread ration for handmade jewelry were those who were treated humanely by the German workers. They demonstrated their thankfulness and appreciation sometimes with a little present they bought or made themselves.

Newspapers that women obtained by different means were valid sources of information. Forced laborers secretly gave them the papers they received. The newspapers were censored, but they still contained relevant news items. Girls read and re-read them to understand and then disperse the news to others. Klára Spitz Snitzler asked her German civilian foreman for his newspaper after he had finished reading it. It was January 1945, but the foreman was still afraid of being reprimanded. He threw the paper into the wastebasket where Klára retrieved it. Risking punishment, Klára brought the paper to the barracks, showing us an article about the advancement of the Russian army. We learned that the area of Abaújszántó, our hometown, was already liberated. It brought us both sadness and hope. How unlucky we were to be still in the camp, we thought; but we trusted that eventually we would also be going home.

The days passed slowly in February and March while we waited for the rumored arrival of the Americans. We heard the sounds of war every day. Airplanes passed over our heads to bomb the cities of Germany. We heard from the forced laborers about the huge bombing of Dresden on February 13, 1945. Girls also continued to learn about the German retreat from Belgian newspapers. One was dated March 19, 1945, exactly a year after the Germans occupied Hungary and our nightmarish voyage commenced.

Leaflets were also thrown from the Allied airplanes. Once a leaflet fell next to an inmate who picked it up; but before she was able to read it, the

Aufseherin snatched it from her hand. Later, a Belgian technician who was a forced laborer told us that the leaflets came from the American army. They quoted Hitler, "Give me ten years and you will not recognize Germany." "He was right," the leaflet assured, listing the names of German cities that had been destroyed and conquered by the Allies.

We tried to imagine how it would be when the Americans arrived, how we would greet them happily, with our thanks, at the gate. How would the German staff behave? We were also thinking of the warm baths, clean clothing, and beds with sheets, meals, and freedom to walk anywhere we wanted.

During the second week of April, when the bombing had intensified and our yearning for news amplified, while I was sweeping around the machines, I noticed a German civilian worker disposing of a newspaper. Shaking in all my body, I pulled out the newspaper and quickly put it in my overalls; an act that I would not have dared before, I bravely did that day. I looked for Klára Spitz Snitzler, who knew some German, and I handed her the newspaper. Klára read it in the ladies' room and learned that President Franklin Delano Roosevelt had died on that day, which was April 12, 1945. The news made us downhearted, because we strongly believed that Roosevelt was our savior. I recalled my father's trust in Roosevelt and the risk he took by listening secretly to BBC broadcasts from England. He discussed it later with the other hopeful congregants after the morning service at the synagogue. Father had faith in Roosevelt and trusted that he would come to our aid. We only found out later that our hopes had no basis, in light of the disappointing actions (or lack thereof) by President Roosevelt on behalf of the Jews of Europe. The news of Roosevelt's death spread rapidly among us, even though most of our attention was on the reports of the camp evacuation. The reality of our departure from Markkleeberg turned out to be quite different from our hopes and dreams of an American liberation force.

8

The Commandant and His Staff

THE CAMP WAS RUN THROUGH THE EFFORTS OF AN SS AND A PRISONER hierarchy. At the top were the SS officials who directed the camps; below them were the surveillance officers and security guards. Then there were the prisoner "VIPs" as camp- and block-elders, work organizers, and infirmary supervisors. The real decision-making power was in the hands of the SS.

Research into Nazi terror emphasizes that the mass murders committed by the SS, led by intelligent and well-educated men, were undertaken in a manner intentionally devoid of human passion. Millions of Jews were murdered or gassed in cold blood: The term used by the Nazis was *eiskalt* (ice-cold blood). There was no passion in executing the Jews, just the engineering of death for ideological-political purposes. Or, at least, that was the attitude demanded of the murderer by the regime.[1]

The Nazis were not influenced by schooling, political affiliation, or religion in their conduct toward the prisoners. The architects of the Holocaust were doctors who supervised mass killings, judges who stripped citizens—especially Jews—of their rights, businessmen who bid on construction of the crematoriums, and men of science who seized on racial Darwinism to justify what they called genetic purification. Some were charming fellows who wore the SS uniforms that gave them license to kill.

As they wore their well-fitting uniforms, jackets buttoned up to their chins, the SS stood straight and tall, well built, lean, and muscular, slapping the officer's baton against their shiny leather boots. Some of them held German shepherds on leashes. The SS may have exhibited different types of behavior, but the separation of public and private could be found in all off them. They acted with the utmost brutality toward the inmates while continuing to lead private lives filled with love and protection. When Auschwitz commandant Rudolf Höss was asked whether he was "troubled" about killing children while his own lived at the camp, he responded, "I didn't personally murder anybody. I was just the director of the extermination program." Some of the SS had never seen a suffering face; all they did was manipulate large and odorless numbers in icy efficiency. Each concerned himself with only one small link in a vast chain and saw his task as a purely technical action. They always could shift their responsibility into the next link in the chain.

In the camp, this changed. Prisoners were exposed to the capricious moods of the SS who competed among themselves at tormenting and humiliating the helpless. Many of the guards were taken from the general *Waffen* (armed SS), or they were older military men or local policemen. They were not *eiskalt:* They, as well as the *Aufseherins,* behaved in a sadistic manner. The guards personally beat and clubbed victims or mercilessly shot stragglers during the Death March.

Camp Hierarchy

Wiegand

On the top of the Markkleeberg camp was the commander, *SS Obersturmführer Wiegand.* He came from Dora, one of the most terrifying slave labor camps. Wiegand, whose first name I was unable to discover, was the commandant of the entire working camp, including the forced laborers and political prisoners. We did not have much interaction with Wiegand. The survivors, including myself, do not recall him at all. Wiegand lived in the forest of Raschwitz before the entrance of the American army into Leipzig and Markkleeberg, and he eventually escaped to Nürnberg.[2]

Alois Knittel

In charge of the Jewish inmates was the *Lagerführer* and SS *Oberscharführer* Alois Knittel, whose rank was sergeant.[3] As *Oberscharführer* (chief guard), Knittel was the direct superior of the guards and the *Oberaufseherin* (female executive commander in charge of the *Aufseherins* in the camp). Knittel served, in principle, as an official of the factory. As commandant, Knittel was responsible for the overall operation of the Jewish slave labor camp. He oversaw the daily functioning of the camp, including the labor force. He was tall, wore an army uniform, and carried a stick. Sometimes he also walked with a German shepherd.

Alois Knittel was born June 6, 1897, in Oberneufnach. First, he lived in Friedberg, near Augsburg, at Kiesweg 3b. He died on December 30, 1962.[4] In civilian life, Knittel was a stonemason and bricklayer.[5] In 1944, at 47, Knittel was too old to fight on the Eastern front, so he had a perfect job. We named him the *öreg* (the old man), or *Oshsár* for short. When he was in a good mood, he called every girl Sara. Under Nazi rule, Sara was the designation of all Jewish females.

Survivors mostly agreed that, at the beginning, Knittel was more patient and less malicious, but with time and the increasing number of arriving prisoners, he had more responsibility. He realized fully that we were slaves, deprived of rights and basically condemned to death who, therefore, could be exposed to every insult. We had to stand hours, especially on Sundays, on *Appel* while he strode back and forth with rage. His specialty was delivering blows to the ears and nose. Terez Stern Hadnagy received a huge slap on her face just for looking at Knittel during *Appel.* Elegant like all SS men in his immaculate uniform and polished boots, he stalked the yard with an icy stare, ever on the hunt for a victim. I was frightened of Knittel and instinctively looked down or looked away, afraid to see his face. With a quick clandestine peek at him, I noticed his scary eyes. We were all very much afraid of him. "When he comes, he searches, hits, and punishes," noted Erzsébet Frank in her camp-written diary.[6] With the German political situation worsening at the front, Knittel became even crueler. He ordered stripes cut in the inmates' hair and sent women to the bunker with little cause. "My memories are washed out but alive in me the fear remained of the SS Oberscharfüehrer and the rest of the guards," writes Dr. Rachel Spielmann.[7]

KNITTEL AFTER THE WAR. A day or two after the Russians entered the camp at Terezin on May 9, 1945, Knittel was recognized by Anna Székely Shindler and some other girls as a prisoner of war among the German soldiers in Russian custody. Knittel's hands were tied behind his back. His wife was not with him.[8]

In Terezin former prisoners of the camp at Markkleeberg were asked about Knittel. They testified that Knittel was fair, and they appreciated that he brought them to Terezin. Rachel Berkovics Zolf in her testimony to Yad Vashem said he was "not a bad man."[9] In our state of mind at that time, if an SS soldier was relatively tolerant and did not harm us personally, he was decent. Inmates still had that prisoner mentality and awe of the SS soldiers. They were not strong enough to deal with issues of revenge and retribution. It seems that, in the hasty judgment of the first days of liberation, Knittel, with no charges of murder against him, was released and was able to move to West Germany.[10]

The Americans also questioned Knittel but they, too, let him go. He did not reveal his activities during the war, and on his identification card there was no mention of his duty as a former SS soldier. The first definitive testimony about Knittel in Markkleeberg was given by Veronika

Schiffmann in 1948. Veronica applied for German compensation, and she listed Knittel as the former *Obersharführer* of the camp.[11]

The records about Knittel mentioned his killings as commandant in Markkleeberg, but they had different dates of birth for him. There seemed to be two Knittels. One was listed as Alois Knittel and the other as Kurt Knittel. Both acted as SS *Lagerführer,* or commander. Kurt Knittel was listed as born on September 23, 1910. The two may have been related. To identify the commander from Markkleeberg, graphology experts were brought in to compare signatures, but that did not clear up the issue. Eventually the court in Ludwisberg indicted "Alois Knittel" for the following:

A) Crimes committed inside the camp:
   1. Killing prisoners on different occasions during the winter of 1944–45. The witnesses didn't know the victims' names.
   2. Causing the death of three young women by ordering the camp to stand on *Appel* naked after a shower. (It was a snowy winter evening as we stood outside waiting until everyone finished, and only then were we given back our clothing. The date was January 6, 1945, the first Saturday after New Year's Eve. I recall the event in detail in chapter 9.)
   3. Bringing about the death of women forced to kneel in the snow for a long time in the winter of 1944–45. (Knittel noticed that some prisoners did not stand straight or that their clothing was not in order to his liking. In chapter 5, I related the incident in detail.)

   The names of the six witnesses are Sara Breiner, Miriam Gross, Seren Rosenberg, Ella Czikk, Laura Lindenfeld, and Olga Eisdorfer.[12]

B) Knittel's crimes during the Death March involved shooting prisoners:
   1. Knittel and some SS guards whose names are not known shot prisoners who were exhausted and unable to march. According to the testimony of Sara Zeugin, between thirty and fifty women were shot.
   2. When starving Markkleeberg prisoners tried to pick up some potatoes or turnips from the ground, a guard noticed and started shooting. How many of the women were hit and died, as well as the names of the prisoners or the guard, the witnesses didn't know. Additional witnesses who testified to the Center of Federal Justice Bureau for the Clarification of Nazi Crimes were Irena Echrenreich, Emma Apai, Dora Kluska, and Olga Eisdorfer.

The process of indictment halted because Knittel, the perpetrator of the crimes in question, could not be positively identified.[13] Most of the former Markkleeberg inmates never knew Knittel's name, making the evidence against him circumstantial.

In 1960, Emma Winkler Apai, one of the eyewitnesses I interviewed, was called to the German consulate to testify in New York. Her name was taken from the list of those who received compensation from Germany. Ms. Apai was asked whether she would recognize Alois Knittel. Probably a face-to-face meeting was considered. Emma replied that she would. Alois Knittel died in 1962, and the proceedings stopped. He was never held accountable for his crimes. Knittel returned to civilian life unscarred. Maybe he was even granted a German pension for his military service.

MRS. KNITTEL. Knittel lived in the camp with his wife, a short, slim woman with brown hair and glasses. According to one of the prisoners, she was the daughter of a jeweler.[14] She was reserved and did not speak to the prisoners, but she was pleasant in her personal relations. Sara Sajovits swept the yard around the Knittels' home before she was assigned to the factory. Mrs. Knittel called Sara into her apartment and treated her with a piece of cake. Sara wanted to take it with her and share with her sister, Ilana Sajovits Breiner, but Mrs. Knittel told her that she had to eat it there. She wanted no one to know about her softness.[15] As the camp population grew, we heard less about Mrs. Knittel's actions. We knew that she accompanied her husband on the Death March.

SS Guards in Markkleeberg

In the camp at Markkleeberg there were twenty-two guards or soldiers. Among them, four were *Wehrmacht* (the German regular army) and the rest were *Volksdeutscher* (ethnic Germans born outside of Germany).[16] The *Volksdeutschers* with us were volunteers in the SS army, mainly from Hungarian territories. Some of them were more vicious than the German-born SS.

The guards acted as a backup force for the *Aufseherins*. They also watched the gate, patrolled the camp perimeter, and supervised and escorted prisoners on their way to and from work. Strong security was not actually needed. We were never allowed farther than the small area of our barracks.

The guards did not come inside the factory. Only Knittel and the *Aufseherins* walked around and watched us working. The younger guards or soldiers who were away from home longed for some light talk with people their own age. A good-looking SS *Volksdeutsche* who stood at the gate often spoke or joked with the girls. He also asked them to sing Hungarian songs.[17]

A tall, dark young guard warned Zsuzsanna Lengyel Urai and other prisoners who were carrying wood beyond the gate, "Girls, be careful; we are not the only ones who understand Hungarian!" Zsuzsanna, who was in the middle of a joke in Hungarian, stopped it speechless. Magda Schön Hilf also remembered how, one Sunday when we did not work, some of the young girls were singing love songs. The SS guards who knew Hungarian stayed and listened. There were other soldiers around the camp who did not speak Hungarian, but they liked to hear too.

BIRGEL. Birgel was the only one besides Knittel that the inmates of Markkleeberg saw who had been detained after the war. Birgel was a *Volksdeutscher.* He squinted, and his eyes were a bit crossed. Birgel may have been his true name, because the girls overheard someone calling him that. We also knew him as Bacskai, meaning someone who came from Bácska along the Yugoslavian border of Hungary. Lófogú, the cruelest among them, also came from Bácska. There were girls in the camp such as Erzsébet Weisz, born April 28, 1911, who were also from Bácska; but we do not know whether she recognized either Birgel or Lófogú from home. Even if she did, she would probably have been afraid to bring it to their attention. Even when the war was coming to an end, Birgel continued to be cruel and sadistic. He was the guard who shot the first prisoner, named Anna, during the Death March, as it is described in chapter 11. After liberation, Elisabeth Stein Székely and others saw Birgel among a group of prisoners led by the Russians. On Birgel's back was a big SS sign. Elisabeth gave Birgel's name to one of the Russian guards who marked it in his book.[18] The chances that Birgel or any of the German staff received serious punishment, however, are very slim; there is no documentation available.

The following are four Markkleeberg guards as they were listed at the Center of Federal Justice Bureau for the Clarification of Nazi Crimes.[19]

- Johann Reisensohn was born in Szabadka, Yugoslavia, on December 20, 1910. He died in 1957 or 1958 from an accident.
- Franz Wagner was born May 30, 1908, in Basszentiwan, Yugoslavia, and died on November 25, 1963, in Zweibrücken.
- "Josef" was an SS guard who came from Bácska. He might be the guard we called Birgel or Bácskai.
- Zimmermann—nothing else but this family name is given about him.

The Commandant's Team of Aufseherins (Female Overseers)

The *Aufseherins* were divided into two work groups. One group escorted the prisoners to work and watched them in the factory. The other had the responsibility inside the camp. They checked whether the prisoners stayed too long in the washroom, if they walked around too much in the corridors, and if they kept order in the rooms. The *Aufseherins* also supervised roll calls, meals, work crews, and other activities in and around the barracks.

In a study of 200 women overseers, it was shown that they came from all parts of German society. In general, they were of modest background and had little education.

There were three ways the *Aufseherin* were recruited:

- The women were selected from the munitions factory workers, through its personnel office. They were assigned to the job with the approval of the district workers' manager (*Arbeitsgau*).[20]
- Mayors of surrounding communities were contacted and requested to identify suitable female personnel and give a list to the SS. The women conscripted by the SS had no right to object.
- Women came as volunteers, attracted by the promise of "light physical work" and good pay.

They hoped to improve the conditions that they experienced in their previous place of work. The wages of the *Aufseherins* were dependent on their age, seniority, and family conditions. In 1944, the starting salary, for example, of a twenty-two-year-old unmarried *Aufseherin* was about 125 RM a month—one Reichsmark equaled forty cents—and if she was married, 135 RM. (An unskilled female textile worker at that time would have earned about 76 RM.) From the 125 RM, she had deductions for food, 37 RM; room, 15 RM; taxes, 7.60 RM; health insurance, 10 RM; payment for the German work front (*Deutsche Arbeitsfront—D.A.F.*), 2.40 RM; and clothing and entertainment, 33 RM. Expenses in total were 105 RM. The shoes and the uniforms she received free. Although the wages were modest, the women were promised good benefits when they retired.[21]

Technically, the *Aufseherins* were not bona fide members of the SS. They were employed by the SS, were paid, and wore a uniform, but they were not members of the SS itself. Some may have belonged to the Nazi Party, but the SS was an elite group for men only. Once drafted or recruited, the prospective overseer had to pass a short orientation and training course in the concentration camp Ravensbrück before her assignment. Some women under consideration to be overseers were deemed unsuitable, and they returned from Ravensbrück.[22] The rest—about 3,500 German women—passed the course in 1942–43. They were given instruction in the *Lagerordung,* the standardized regulations for all the concentration camps. The *Aufseherin* "studies," in general, consisted of training in deriding and exterminating human beings (*Schulung Menschenverachtung und Zerstörung*). The course lasted six weeks; when it was finished, the graduates were sent to their work at women's camps or the departments of women in mixed concentration camps.[23]

In 1966, the former *Aufseherin* Ulla Jürss was tried and sentenced to life in prison for her crimes against humanity. West German television (NDR) defined the school she had attended as a training ground for showing contempt to women and destroying them.[24]

The head of the *Aufseherins* was the *Oberaufseherin;* we called her *Oberin* for short. Officially, she was directly responsible to the camp commandant; it was her duty to oversee the other *Aufseherins* and to see that all those in detachments went to work precisely on time. She herself remained in camp and listed the prisoners who remained in camp because of illness. The first *Oberin,* was a short, pretty, blue-eyed woman who invited a different girl to clean her room each time. Then, instead of making her clean, she treated her with some food and asked about her family. When Gabriella Braver Kosinka was scheduled to clean the *Oberin*'s room, she was given a plate of soup and told to relax because the room was clean already. Then she was asked about her background and was told, "I am sorry for you girls." The *Oberin* was the only one among the *Aufseherins* who wanted to know about us. The rest of the SS personnel never asked.

The other early *Aufseherins* were not so vicious either. The girls called them *dadák* (nannies). They would sing with the girls on their way to work. Their favorite song was "Marienka, Ich liebe dich." They had flashlights to use in the dark as the girls walked to work. At the factory, the *Aufseherins* passed quietly through the place, not bothering anyone. Their job was to watch the inmates, not to converse with the workers. It seems that they were judged to be too nice, and the whole group was sent back to Ravensbrück for training. The new group of *Aufseherins* who arrived around October was much worse. They were well rehearsed in being heartless. Although there is no documentation, Ilana Sajovits Breiner believes that they came directly from Auschwitz.

The *Oberin* of the second group of *Aufseherins* was short, heavy, and wore glasses. The witness for the Center for Investigation, Ms. Blau, who referred to Oberin as Mrs. Andres or Anders, was mistaken and had her confused with Frau Anders, who was a supervisor in the small factory.[25] The *Oberin* had a separate room; other *Aufseherins* were two in a room.

The second *Oberin* was very mean. Once her boyfriend disappointed her by not coming to visit. In her anger, she scheduled a special *Appel* and hit anyone she could reach with her rubber club. Her boyfriend was a married man, as the *Oberin* confided to Márta Maget Leitmann, the *Blockälteste;* and it especially worried her when he did not appear. Márta tried to calm her by saying that she should not worry, he would come. The next day the *Oberin* was smiling and in a good mood as she told Márta, "You were right: he did come; only he was late."[26]

When the Allied forces were nearby, the *Oberin* told the women that we should not be looking forward to liberation. The Germans had enough ammunition to kill all the prisoners, she said, even at the last minute, they would not allow us to survive and tell our story.

Ironically, it was the *Oberin* who died at liberation. Markkleeberg survivors who came to the office of repatriation in Brune, near Prague in Czechoslovakia, where Gabriella Braver Kosinka worked, told her about the spiraling of events. American soldiers were guarding the main gate of the camp after they entered Markkleeberg. As the hated *Oberin* passed by in civilian clothing, one of the French former prisoners grabbed a gun from the American soldier who stood at the gate and shot her. We also learned that the Oberin had been pregnant.[27]

The *Aufseherins* in Markkleeberg hit us for the slightest cause—or even without any cause. They beat us even for looking at them or for not looking at them. They always found an unfortunate woman who attracted their attention. She might have been too pretty or too ugly, too tall or too short, or just something about her look made the girl the target of their rage and torment. For any little thing they did not like, they slapped us or copied down the numbers on our overalls to call us later for further punishment.

AN *AUFSEHERIN* RECOGNIZED AS A FORMER NANNY. One day on *Appel,* a girl called Zsuzsa, who was Ilana Sajovits Breiner's neighbor on line, suddenly recognized one of the *Aufseherin.* The woman in uniform was the girl who had once cared for Zsuzsa and her brother! Being a nanny in the early thirties, when the unemployment rate was high in Germany, was a good job for a young German woman. Well-to-do people in Hungary often engaged German women nannies as a status symbol, appreciating also that the children could learn German from them. Zsuzsa, from Budapest, was only about sixteen, and she could scarcely control her bewilderment. She told Ilana and the others next to her. The *Aufseherin* must have seen Zsuzsa, but she pretended not to notice. She probably did not want to reveal her own past. Zsuzsa, who was dealing with strong mixed emotions, did not know what to do. The *Aufseherin* continued to ignore her, and Zsuzsa fell quiet and never mentioned her again. Ilana did not know if the *Aufseherin* warned Zsuzsa to be quiet or whether Zsuzsa, seeing that unfriendly reaction from her former nanny, simply locked her wounded feelings inside her. Perhaps it was fortunate for both of them that the former nanny was transferred away with the rest of the first group of *Aufseherins.*

KUTYUS. Most of the *Aufseherin*s we knew only by the names we gave them. Nicknames were coined based on certain characteristics or behaviors of the individual *Aufseherin.*

One blonde *Aufseherin,* who had a head like a dog, the girls named *Kutyus* (doggy or puppy). She was skinny with protruding teeth and her behavior with us was relatively mild. Kutyus watched the girls working in the garden and did not mind if they rested; she just wanted to be careful when the guards walked around. Kutyus also guided the girls in the factory from one hall to the other. Once she escorted Gabriella Braver Kosinka, who spoke a few languages and could speak with many different people. Kutyus thought that Hungarian was the magic tongue. She asked Gabriella to teach her Hungarian so she could "speak with everybody like you do."

RÁKOCZI. One *Aufseherin* the inmates nicknamed Rákoczi because of her ponytail hairstyle that made her resemble a Hungarian nobleman and statesman by that name. She was tall, blonde, and well groomed with shiny long hair that attracted the attention and admiration of the guards. Her appearance and flirtatious manner brought out envy in the adolescent girl prisoners. It seemed to accentuate their pitiful state of having short hair, wooden shoes, and dirty overalls, at a time of life when personal appearance means so much to girls. As pretty as she was, one would not expect Rákoczi to be so mean. She would hit the inmates with her fists just because they were there.

LUCIFER. The *Aufseherin* who distinguished herself as a Satan for her cruelty received the nickname Lucifer. She had a few other names as well: *devil* or *witch,* for her evil spirit and demonic actions. Her real name was Helene Pöschel. A native of Markkleeberg, she came with experience from the infamous camp Dora. Pöschel arrived together with Commandant Wiegand, the head of the camp.[28] Pöschel knew her nickname and, when she came to wake us in the morning, she announced, "Get up, here is Lucifer!" She did not have to say it twice.

Although the civilian workers tried to avoid confrontation with the *Aufseherins,* occasionally they could not help from reacting to the maltreatment they witnessed. Paul Schulze, who worked as a locksmith, noticed how an *Aufseherin,* who might have been Lucifer, was hitting an inmate. He grew angry and reprimanded the cruel woman.[29]

Women have different memories of her appearance. Some recalled that Lucifer had dark hair, was slim, medium height, and a bit older than the other *Aufseherins.* For me and the majority of survivors, however, she seemed big and tall. I could never look at her face, but others said that she was ugly with a long witch's nose, a hunchback, and that she looked like a man.[30] We saw her that way perhaps because we hated her so much, but Lucifer may have looked a bit different. One way we all knew her was by her carrying a whip under her arm or holding it in her hand and moving her skirt with it as she walked. Lucifer always wore boots.

Lucifer's favorite game involved the raids she conducted in the barracks, as I described in chapter 4. Lucifer once found a needle in her search and pushed it inside her victim.

In spite of all our sufferings from the cruelty of human beings, we still tried to believe in people. Fairness and decency were the basis of our culture and upbringing. We embraced the rumor circulating around that Lucifer's mother had died during an air attack and her family home was destroyed. There is no evidence, and it almost certainly is not true; but it helped us to explain Lucifer's bitterness and vindictive behavior.

Lucifer had her "soft" moments too, however. On one occasion, Lucifer saw Miriam Liberman Kirsenbaum and others praying in the morning. They all worked in the night shift and that was their free time. Lucifer looked and left them alone.

If one trait of conduct could be called common to all the camp guards and *Aufseherins,* it would be their inconsistency. Compassion and brutality coexisted in the same person, despite all logic. In the course of the day, an individual could help one prisoner and send another to her death. All the camp personnel seemed subject to sudden shifts in attitude and temperament. Even the meanest guard or *Aufseherin* sometimes felt enough compassion to help a particular prisoner. Once during lunch, for instance, the Jewish inmate who was in charge of dividing the soup gave larger portions to her family or friends. Nelly Winkler Rochlitz was standing with her empty dish when Lucifer asked her why she did not eat. Nelly told her that there was no food left for her. "Come with me," Lucifer said. Nelly was quivering with fear as Lucifer took her to the kitchen, where she was given a special plate from the officers' meal. Lucifer then escorted Nelly back to the factory and sat next to her until she finished eating, so that no one would try to take it away. Nelly had mashed potatoes, meat with brine, and vegetables: a feast she never forgot. Lucifer watched her the next few days to make sure she received her portion of food.

After the war, Bruno Eisert, a former prisoner of Buchenwald, in his brief account of the camp in Markkleeberg, found that when the American army left the area in the summer of 1945, Helene Pöschel ran away with them to the West. Eisert mentions also that Pöschel was renowned for her cruelty.[31]

Gitta Susitzky Hönig saw Pöschel in Bucharest in 1946. There were a lot of refugees in Romania at that time. Gitta was on her way to Israel waiting for the ship when she noticed Lucifer dressed in ordinary peasant clothing. She could not believe her eyes. Gitta called out Lucifer's name to her friend. By the time Gitta recovered from her shock, Lucifer had disappeared. Gitta's response was more one of disbelief mixed with fear than it was of the thought of revenge. During our interview, Gitta was still analyzing that special sensation of seeing a former uniformed tormentor in a public place, dressed like an ordinary woman.

According to the records in Buchenwald, on September 23, 1944, there were ten *Aufseherins.* As more transports arrived, the number of *Aufse-*

herins increased. In March 20, 1945, there were twenty-seven *Aufseherins* in Markkleeberg.[32]

The following thirty-nine names are listed at the Center of Federal Justice Bureau for the Clarification of Nazi Crimes. It is not certain whether they were all in Markkleeberg or if some were in the other camp near Leipzig.

(1) Birnbaum, Elfriede
(2) Burchard, Johanna
(3) Brings, Luzie
(4) Deligha, Margarethe (bookkeeper)
(5) Döllmann, Katharina
(6) Feldner, Dorte
(7) Fischer, Hildegard
(8) Fuhrmeister, Margot
(9) Funke, Elfrieda
(10) Giesel, Elfriede
(11) Giskes, Sybille
(12) Grimm, Margarethe
(13) Grünert, Melanie
(14) Hauk, Irmgard
(15) Jahnke, Frieda
(16) Jung, Irmgard
(17) Kagelmann, geb. Opitz, Ilse
(18) Kaiser, Ursula
(19) Kaltofen, Elfrieda
(20) Kleine, geb. Günther, Annemarie
(21) Korfei, Luiese
(22) Krämer, Johanne
(23) Lerse, Luise
(24) Lorenz, Erna
(25) Meier, Elisabeth
(26) Michel (Swiderski), Charlotte
(27) Nitsche, Olga
(28) 0rtmann, Marianne
(29) Pösche1, Helene
(30) Täsch, Anny
(31) Rascher, Else
(32) Rehbein, Anni
(33) Rössler, Margarete
(34) Schmeer, Ursula (Elli)
(35) Uhndorf, Rosa
(36) Uhrmeister, Margot
(37) Weber, Irmintraut
(38) Wehr, Elisabeth
(39) Wunder, Gertraude[33]

Medical Personnel

According to the *Aussenkommando* records of January 31, 1945, which were compiled by the Waffen SS garrison doctor (*Der Standortarzt der Waffen-SS*), the medical personnel in Markkleeberg camp consisted of Dr. Dressler for the German staff members. Matters of health, in principle, were under the Buchenwald administration. For the inmates, there were two prisoner doctors and two nurses, as mentioned in chapter 5.[34]

The Bunker Prison Cell

The bunker was a cold cement cell in a small barracks. There were a few rooms for isolation. A plank bed with no mattress and a pail were all that was in the room. Sometimes the bed was even taken out. The room had a window, but it was tightly locked with a wooden shade. The sun could never touch the place. Once the door closed, the room was completely dark. When one walked near, one could usually hear crying inside.

Prisoners who were sent to the bunker for solitary confinement generally had been charged with the more serious offenses, but sometimes it depended on the mood of the SS personnel. One cannot say the inmates were guilty of any transgression because there were no legal proceedings to determine guilt or innocence. The mechanism, in theory, was that the *Aufseherin* made a report, perhaps on the recommendation of a prisoner officer, which was sent to the camp leader. He could hold an investigation and order incarceration in the bunker. Yet, there was no hearing before being sentenced to jail in the bunker. The evidence was whatever Knittel's personnel said had happened. They also decided the length of time of the confinement. It was usually from two to three days. Longer punishment required the approval of the commandant.

When a prisoner was placed in the bunker, the camp personnel were ready to act; they quickly found another girl for replacement at work. To make an example of her and to scare the rest of us, the inmate to be punished was escorted at lunchtime, when a big crowd could see and fear for their comrade. The prisoner sentenced to the bunker received soup, which she had to eat in a hurry, and then she was locked in that dungeon in complete isolation and darkness. We looked with compassion and trepidation at the unfortunate victim, knowing that it could easily be one of us next time.

The girl to be punished in the bunker could take her food dish with her and occasionally a blanket. At the entrance, they checked that she had nothing. The one blanket was not enough in winter to warm the trembling, freezing body of the unfortunate inmate in the unheated room. It was especially hard when she was lying down or sitting and was not able even to move in the darkness. The prisoner in the bunker heard no human voice night or day, when the rest of the girls were working. The time passed slowly, and one needed a strong character not to become desperate. After two days in the bunker, the pail started to smell. In the morning and at night, the prisoner received a glass of tea, and at lunchtime the soup, no bread. The food was placed in the room without a word. Some girls sang in the beginning, to keep up their morale, but after a few hours of solitude they generally broke down. Then they started to cry and yell from their loneliness and fear. Some called for their mothers, from whom they had been separated in Auschwitz. There were those who prayed and others who let out heartbreaking, wordless shrieks that could be heard from a distance.[35]

In 1975, Dr. Rachel Spielmann, a former Markkleeberg inmate, visited the camp. She met Irma Clajus, a schoolteacher, and in a letter to her, Dr. Spielmann described her experience and the reason for punishment in the bunker. Once, during a body search after the night shift, freshly laundered underwear that she had washed in the factory was found in her pocket. She was confined in the prison cell of the unheated bunker on a cold January day. There she stayed without food until the evening, when she was let out to join the night shift with rest of the workers.[36]

Punishment of the Kitchen Workers in the Bunker

The kitchen was housed in a separate building next to the factory. The main kitchen personnel, including the person in charge, were German civilian workers. They worked together with forced laborers, one of whom was a Dutch chef. They had compassion for the inmates and occasionally gave them extra portions. The German civilian in charge of the kitchen and his wife were especially nice.

Occasionally some of the kitchen workers received extra food from the forced laborers who worked there. The girls wanted to share it with their friends and family members, which sometimes got them in trouble. On January 23, 1945, during one of those searches at the gate as they were coming into camp, two girls had salami and a few potatoes with them. Realizing they were about to be searched, they quickly emptied their pockets; but an *Aufseherin* found the discarded food and demanded the guilty ones come forward. The girls were afraid to confess, and the others would not betray them. So the whole group, about ten, was placed in the bunker. There were no beds, and the women stood there all night in the dark, terrified. A fifteen-year-old girl kept crying and calling constantly for her mother. They passed a terrible, fearful night, and no one knew what the morning would bring. Thinking it over, the two girls decided to confess. They received the hated punishment of stripes, looking like a cross, shaved into their hair. The event was so shocking for Angyal Fischer Weisz that she fasted on January 23 for many years after liberation for surviving the terrible night in the bunker.

Sexual Matters

A woman, both as a Jew and female, was in double danger during the Holocaust. The Nazi racial laws that prohibited sex between "Aryans" and Jews should have protected Jewish women from being raped, but this was not always the case. A Nazi male could merely deny that he had raped a Jewish prisoner, and her testimony would not even be considered. There are no statistics and there is no way of proving how many rapes of Jewish inmates took place. Survivors are hesitant to talk about that part of their suffering.

In the camps, there was always the possibility that an SS soldier would select a Jewish girl to clean his room and then force her to submit sexually. Misfortunes of that nature were rare exceptions; in Markkleeberg, there were none that the survivors would recall. With all the other concerns and worries in the camps, we did not live in fear of being forcibly raped by our captors.

Lesbian Relations

I did not know of any lesbian relationships between prisoners in Markkleeberg. Most of the young women had been brought up in sheltered, puritanical homes and did not even know what a lesbian was. Survivors I interviewed all commented that they were too weak even to reflect on physical love. Being lesbian was not a problem that plagued the survivors in the camp or afterwards. The large majority married after the war and strived to establish a family.

Homosexuality did pose a problem for the German women. In Markkleeberg, there was a pretty prisoner whom an *Aufseherin* liked. Heidi (not her real name) knew some German and had had a fiancé before the war. The *Aufseherin* was not attractive; she had short hair and a peasantlike appearance. The girls called her *Csizmás Kandur* (booted tomcat) because she was always wearing boots. The *Aufseherin* brought Heidi food and cigarettes. When she came, the others left, and Heidi and the *Aufseherin* stayed alone in the room. Heidi's affair was common knowledge among the women in the camp.[37]

When Csizmás Kandur was transferred to Ravensbrück, she still came to visit Heidi on the weekends. Márta Maget Leitmann asked Heidi once what she was doing with the *Aufseherin.* Heidi cried and said, "What else can I do?!" She was hungry and the *Aufseherin* brought her food. If the affair had been discovered, Heidi would have received severe punishment because their act was against regulations. Heidi survived and married after the war. The attitude of the other prisoners was ambivalent. They recognized that Heidi was looking for a way to survive; yet there was, nevertheless, a note of reproof in their position. Although Heidi was condemned by some, she was also envied for having that extra food.

In the next chapter, I will describe our literary weapons against the German oppressors. We lost our homes and material possessions, but we still had the intellectual and spiritual provisions that our parents and teachers equipped us with for the road. They were hidden values that the searches of Lucifer could not seize and that Knittel's most severe punishment would not dim.

9

Cultural Activities and Holidays

IN OUR STATE OF HELPLESSNESS, FACING THE HIGHLY SOPHISTICATED AND powerful German enemy, prisoners used the only manners of resistance available to them: self-help, social activities, and cultural pastimes. A chat, a song, or a simple word of encouragement strengthened the inmate's hope and added a spark of humanity to her harsh existence. At such times, we could feel a sense of solidarity and shared destiny.

The prisoner who wanted to keep her sanity had to release the pain and sadness out of her heart from time to time. She did this with tears, with prayer, or with a song. Songs were our medicine. Our spiritual world was empty if we had no songs or poetry to recall. We tried to keep ourselves as human as possible. We had no books, we had no paper, but we had memories. Some intelligent and cultured women discussed literature, philosophy, music, and the world at large. They talked about travel, recited poetry, told stories, and described plays and movies. Each would give the group what she could.

Cultural activities such as singing, reciting poetry, and writing were a kind of coping that could be defined as resistance, because they lifted the spirit. I remember that, in Bergen-Belsen, we begged a woman with a beautiful voice to sing in the dark. I pulled Erzsike close to me as we were sitting on the floor in the large tent, and we listened as the place filled with musical resonances. The singer's soft voice carried me back home, to a similar but different tune: that of my mother's voice. I looked at Erzsike, who was half asleep, and gently helped her to lie down. I continued to listen and hear my mother's lullaby, rocking me into a sweet peaceful sleep, away from our dreary reality.

Despite the pain and humiliation, the young women's will to live was so strong that, through the pain, songs were born. Singing expressed the dream, the fantasy of escape. It served to submerge the individual into the group and thus lessen her sufferings. One needed only a little to barter for paper and pencil. The finished product was convenient to pass around. The singing began spontaneously, in Hungarian, the language most of us knew: One person would start, and then gradually voices from all corners of the barracks would join in. An infinite variety of songs was composed, their authors mostly unknown and forgotten over the years. They were written to the tunes of popular hit songs of the time, rendering a familiar melody with a new and relevant text.

Many of the authors created short simple songs or ditties. In a light spirit, the ditties commented on collective happenings, either good or bad. The ditties filled the place of the newspaper: covering daily events and criticizing the establishment. There were ditties that generated waves of laughter, like hymns to *Appels* and to lice. The anonymous lyrics passed from one prisoner to the next, giving expression to individual and collective emotional reactions to events, past and present, as well as to hopes for the future. The ditties constituted the only context in which the prisoners enjoyed freedom of expression, although we had to be careful not to provoke the authorities openly. Writing was prohibited by the SS, so the artists risked their lives. While documenting the atrocities in their creative ways, writers had seen a means to survive.

There were entertainers, singers, actors, and comedians who were lifesavers by simply being cheerful and keeping joy alive. Songs created an atmosphere in which we traveled on the wings of imagination into the better world we had known before. In our rest time, we listened to songs of the good life. They made us dream of delicacies and elegant clothes. We forgot for a few brief moments our bitter fate of starving and freezing.

The Author Erzsébet Frank

Erzsébet Frank was born in Mezőkeresztes, Hungary. She describes her initiation into camp life in her book *365 Nap: Vallomás a Pokolok Tüzéből* (365 Days: Testimony from Hell's Inferno), first published in 1946. Everything in the book is true, the author said. She believes that writing the book and describing the events lightened her suffering and saved her life. She carried the manuscript with her at all times in the camp. Erzsébet had never written a book before the war and has not written one since. The hard conditions and anguish in which she found herself brought out the poet and writer in her. Writing was a way to relieve her feelings of defenselessness and longing, and to fight for freedom and a sense of normalcy.

Erzsébet Frank kept her papers in the closet next to her machine at the factory. She wrote a few lines, put the manuscript away, and then wrote again later. Erzsébet would have an idea for a line or two at a time, therefore she wrote in poetry form. To write in secret, next to a noisy machine and under supervision, one could think only in two lines at a time, she explained. Erzsébet was ready to take the risk that she would be punished if caught. Her life was given purpose by writing. Besides her diary, she also wrote poems about things that inspired her, such as the poem about the welders. (See chapter 10.) When they returned from work, the girls might be greeted with a poem or a ditty in which Erzsébet put into rhyme the latest news, the people, and the events of life in the camp and factory. There were rhymes that immortalized various *Aufseherin*s, that conveyed information on perilous foremen, or that highlighted diverse social phenomena and even served as a gossip column. Her roommates cleaned the room on Sundays without Erzsébet's help, just so she could read to them from her latest compositions. By writing, Erzsébet not only got to express her emotions but also had the satisfaction of instant acknowledgment and respect. Erzsébet also had an illustrator, as is shown in the poem about the welders.

Erzsébet, who wrote the text, had a group of girls who presented the work. The singer, either Ibolya Kail Gabori or another inmate, was accompanied by an orchestra of four or five girls, each with a specific task to perform to produce a sound and provide the music. Tereza Frankl, the only one I could identify, did the whistling. Someone else would beat two pots together, another banged on a dish, and still another clapped her hands to the music. The audience participated by humming to the tune of any known melodies to which Erzsébet had written her lyrics.

Most of the poems she wrote did not survive the war. Still, some may be guarded by survivors somewhere because they were so much appreciated in the camp. Erzsébet never asked for anything, but the girls expressed their gratitude the only way they could: by sharing with her their portion of bread. It was an unbelievably huge sacrifice when we were always so hungry.

We found relief in sentimental Hungarian songs. Sometimes we just sang one or two lines from a poem, such as the following by the Hungarian poet Sándor Petöfi: *"Szülöföldem szép határa meglálak-e valahára?"* (My beautiful homeland, will I ever see you?) Regardless of how cruel people were to us, Hungary was our birthplace, the source of our culture and our way of life, and we had powerful ties to it.

My Mother's Song

Erzsike and I would not have dared to sing solo in public; but in those rare moments when our minds rose a bit above hunger and the daily struggle to stay alive, we sang quietly for ourselves. I remembered the songs that our mother used to sing. Most of them were from the First World War during

Mother's youth, and they were permeated with loss and longing. One of my favorite songs was about a family during the war. The little boy at home was playing with a map, marking the places his father traveled with the army in World War I. The child admired the map, with its many colors and symbols that enticed him to travel to exotic places. Then suddenly he remembered that his mother had stopped showing him his father's whereabouts. When he questioned her, the mother hugged him and answered, "There is no map from heaven, my child." The song has another stanza, but my mother used to sing us only the last one, which was close to our comprehension. I would hum it to myself and recall my mother's image by the ironing board at home.

How beautiful is the map, my dear mother!
I have never had such a nice toy.
So many colors and so many countries
I am longing to be there.
But for a long time you have not shown me
Father's travels somewhere, at the edge of the Russian border.
Embracing her child warmly:
"There is no map from heaven, my poor little one."[1]

Each prisoner sought solace in her own way. The songs of my mother gave me then, as they still do today, feelings of closeness and comfort. My children and grandchildren all know the tunes from their childhood lullabies.

Zionist Songs

The land of Israel was part of a Messianic dream that girls with Zionist education hoped would be realized at the end of the Holocaust. The following song expressed the Zionist longing for a country.

Israel is not forsaken;
It nourishes in us the hope that
What God has promised,
That land, He will return to us.[2]

Although we were listening to and singing Zionist songs, for us they did not have, at that time, deeper emotional roots. As children, Erzsike and I just wanted to go home and meet our family again. Only after the war, when we realized fully what had happened to us and our people, did we embrace the Zionist ideal of making Israel our country.

Fantasy and Storytelling

When one sings, one creates another world just like the storytelling, which was another form of cultural activity that was highly developed in the women's concentration camps. Prisoners were not permitted to keep books, even handwritten ones, but we would sometimes gather together and describe in some detail the contents of books we had read before our captivity. Some women were able to evoke whole plays from memory. After the narration, there were often discussions. Not infrequently, these sessions drifted into talk of recipes and of feasts of the past. Real or imaginary, it did not matter.

Fantasy and the ability to disassociate as a means of coping helped us mentally to disengage from the cruel reality. I was able to remove myself emotionally from the present because my memories from home were so recent and so warm. Dissociation was a lifesaver, especially during those endless roll calls. Many times in the morning, I was thinking of breakfast and imagining what mother and grandmother would prepare for us at home on such a chilly winter day. We also tried to keep some kind of conversation going among us. Besides envisioning what we would do once the Germans left, we were trying to recapture how life was before. Many of our strong memories of the past were associated with holidays.

The Jewish Holidays in Camp

One cannot comprehend the depth of the tragedy of the Jewish people unless one understands the culture that had permeated Jewish life for a thousand years. To obtain a prayer book, we were ready to sacrifice our bread. In Auschwitz-Birkenau once, when we had just received our awaited daily portion, Erzsike was thinking how best to divide it into smaller pieces so it would last longer, when two women approached us. They were collecting bread to barter for a prayer book and asked us to contribute. We looked at each other being really hungry, and then without a word, we gave away one portion of our bread. It was almost an automatic response. Just to hear the mention of the prayer book evoked in my mind the vision of my little grandmother on her way to Shabbat services carrying her prayer book. It felt so gracious to contribute for a religious purpose and for the sake of our parents and grandparents, for whom faith had meant so much. We felt their presence each time a noble idea or action occurred to us; even our throbbing hunger evaporated for a minute. We never had a chance to use the bartered prayer book because the following day we were transferred from the A to the C *lager*.

To remember the holidays, it was important to know the date. In Markkleeberg, some women had written diaries or just marked the days. Keeping track of the Jewish calendar, praying, and holding some services were vital parts of our spiritual life.

Sabbath

In the room next to us, one of the girls got a candle from a forced laborer. On Friday night, she asked a woman who was a mother to light the candle. The *Blockälteste* supplied the match. We joined in reciting the blessing, and all said "Amen." After a few minutes of reflection by the glow of the yellow flame, the girls blew the candle out to save it for the next week. Still not having learned that we could not save things in the camp, the slightly burned candle was soon apprehended and discarded in one of the room searches. Although we were sorry, we also felt lucky for the miracle that we did not get additional punishment, which would usually be given for having unauthorized articles in the rooms. Women tried to light candles any way they could. Angyal Fischer Weisz, who did not know the dates or the days, said she remembered Friday nights because she could see some faint light burning secretly in one of the rooms.

Tisha B'Av

Tisha B'Av, the day commemorating the destruction of the temple in Jerusalem, was on July 29–30 in 1944: Sabbath evening and Sunday. We had been in Auschwitz-Birkenau about six weeks. Erzsike and I would not have known the date, but religious girls were walking around and reminding us that the next day was the holiday. Most of the women were so rundown and apathetic, they did not even pay attention. We were sitting there dejected, also, waiting for the next meal or the next order. Hearing Tisha B'Av mentioned, my mind started to stir and come alive. I remembered how, each year, a group of elderly ladies had assembled in our backyard to listen to my grandmother's reading of Eicha, the scroll of Lamentation of Jeremiah. Wearing black kerchiefs, the pious ladies sat on a blanket in the grass next to our rose garden. I used to listen from a distance as my grandmother's voice carried in the darkness, while I watched the kerosene lamp under which she was reciting cast its mystical-seeming shadowy rays. Still under the spell of that scene, I told Erzsike that I would fast the next day. Erzsike, a bit hesitant, then said, "I will too."

On the day of Tisha B'Av, the soup at lunchtime was less watery than usual. We even noticed a few beans in it. It was very tempting, while others all around us were eating, but we hoped that because of our fasting, God would help us to see our parents and grandparents again. We carried our plates with the soup around for the next two hours. Then suddenly the

Blockälteste spotted us and started to scream, "You can't take the food with you like that all day! You have to finish it!" I told Erzsike that it would be enough if only I fasted: I was the oldest, and she should have the nutrition. Erzsike said no, I will fast and you should eat. Meanwhile, the *Blockälteste* returned and stood next to us threateningly. Fearfully, we noticed two young sisters that had been nice to us standing nearby. Quickly we gave them our soup, and they gratefully gobbled it up. Writing about it, it seems a simple story; but, in our situation, giving away food was an enormous sacrifice and one that showed immeasurable esteem and gratitude to our pious little grandmother.

In the evening, as the sun went down, we broke our fast with the slice of bread we received. We were sitting afterwards, still so very hungry, when suddenly one of the sisters to whom we had given our lunch surprised us with a portion of their bread. The two shared one piece and decided to give us the second. We were so grateful, it seemed like a miracle. We felt grandmother's spirit, carried by the scent of her rose garden, casting its fragrance and its mystic lantern rays on Auschwitz.

Rosh Hashanah

Rosh Hashanah (the Jewish New Year) was on Monday and Tuesday, the 18th and 19th of September 1944, or the Hebrew year of 5705. It was a date that somehow all of us knew even without a calendar. Those in Markkleeberg received carrots with their meal that day. It delighted the girls, especially the pious ones from Papa such as Rose Hoffmann Davis. They could fulfill the mitzvah of eating sweet for a sweet new year, as they remembered doing at Rosh Hashanah when they were home.

Erzsike and I were still in Auschwitz-Birkenau. There, on the first day of Rosh Hashanah, a group of women had a prayer book from which someone read in a low voice. Although it was hard for me to hear the words, my attention was focused on the book itself. I was thinking of my grandmother's ivory-covered High Holiday prayer book. There, in my mind's eye, was my skinny little grandmother in her black-satin synagogue dress with the white lace kerchief covering part of the brown wig that she wore mostly for religious occasions. Grandmother gave her full attention to devotional prayers from the beginning until the end of the services. We children, after saying some of the Morning Prayers to make grandmother happy, ran from her seat in the first row to my mother, a row behind. (Synagogue seats could be purchased permanently in our town, so my mother, who came later, had only been able to get a seat in the second row.) Together with her Mahzor (a Jewish prayer book designed for use on festivals and holy days), my mother had a small Hungarian booklet called "Miriam"—the same as my mother's name—containing devotional prayers for women. Looking again at the prayer book in Auschwitz at Rosh Hashanah, I found something concrete and visible from my parents' world and their faith. It gave me a bit of tranquility and the hope that things would improve in the New Year.

After the group concluded their prayers, we joined another small gathering in the corner of our long barracks. There girls were singing Zionist songs with bittersweet melodies. We knew only the following stanza of a longer poem:

> Balmy mountains from the distance are calling me.
> My exile will end; I will go home.
> At home in my lovely country, my soul will revive.
> The people of Israel alive, the people of Israel alive,
> Forever and ever and ever.[3]

The atmosphere was solemn, a time for reflection the way each of us knew best. Erzsike asked me, "Do you remember how you helped me to make peace with Ildiko before Rosh Hashanah? How you pulled us together to shake hands and forgive each other so that God should forgive us? How proud Anyuka (mother) was when we told her!"

Looking for spirituality the only way they knew, girls started to sing show tunes and arias from famous operas. Growing up in a small town, we had never seen an opera or anything like a Broadway show. Then a bit later we heard familiar Hungarian songs. We almost forgot for awhile where we were. Then the next morning, the second day of Rosh Hashanah, the *Appel* started at dawn and life in the camp continued with its selections, hunger, and uncertainties, as before.

Yom Kippur

Yom Kippur (Day of Atonement) fell on Wednesday, September 27, 1944. At sundown, we listened to a recitation of Kol Nidre, the opening of the evening service for Yom Kippur. One woman had a beautiful voice and transmitted the somber melody. We were moved, and when she finished, all begged her to say it again. She was in the middle of the second rendition when the *Blockälteste* entered, announcing the guards were walking around and we all had to be quiet. As we were laying in the dark that night, still under the strength of the moving melody, I reminded Erzsike in a whisper how, if we were at home, we would be standing in the crowded synagogue listening to the chazzan chanting of Kol Nidre. The rest of the scene, including the presence of our parents, we could only see in our individual visions; our neighbors demanded complete silence.

The next day, for Yizkor, the Jewish service for commemorating the dead, religious girls organized a small prayer group in our tent. A woman with a strong voice read the text from a sheet of paper that was circulating in the camp. It also had the Hebrew words in transliteration to make the reading and the pronunciation easier. The prayer of Yizkor was first said for the fathers, and each one had to say the name of her father. We listened but did not participate. Then the reader requested that, in order not to make the Germans suspicious of the large gathering, all those whose mothers were with them in the camp should leave. Those who wanted to pray for deceased mothers should stay. Erzsike left with me and with some other girls in our uncertain situation. In Bergen-Belsen, we still had the belief that our parents and grandparents were alive.

At lunch on Yom Kippur, we received our regular portion of soup. Erzsike and I were so weak and discouraged already by that time that we were happy to hear a Rebbetzin saying that, according to Jewish law, in extreme situations when fasting would be dangerous to our lives, we were allowed to eat. To keep some spirit of Yom Kippur, however, we decided to have only our soup and keep the bread for the next day.

Those in Markkleeberg were impressed that Knittel asked who wanted to fast and ordered them to be given lunch at night instead of in the daytime.[4] The girls found Knittel's act to be a fine gesture and remembered it to his credit after the war. In Markkleeberg, it was impossible to obtain a prayer book or even a page from one. The girls asked Sarah Salamon Israel, whose mother had passed away in 1942, to say Yizkor during their lunch break at the large factory. Sarah knew the prayer by heart, and the other women said it after her.

Terez Stern Hadnagy and ten other girls experienced a strange episode on Yom Kippur. They were assigned that day to pick apples in the garden next to the factory in Markkleeberg; this happened by chance and was not a deliberate torture plan by the Germans. The guard watching the women was quite lenient, and from time to time he left them alone. The inmates, who had not seen fruit in the camp, were placed in a real test of will and faith. Most of them took advantage of the occasion to hurriedly eat an apple each time the guard disappeared. Only two deeply religious girls, who would not eat the apples, risked hiding a few in their overalls. At night, after the fast, because they could not save their lunch, they appreciated having the apples with their portions of bread to break their fast, feeling good and thankful to God.

Sukkoth

Sukkoth, the harvest festival, began on Monday, October 2, in 1944. We were in Bergen-Belsen, weak and downhearted. Although we did not know the date, some girls may have been aware that it was Sukkoth, but there was no spirit to celebrate. Those who were in Markkleeberg at the time could not recall the observance of Sukkoth among them either.

Hanukkah

Hanukkah, the Jewish festival of lights that celebrates the rededication of the Temple by the Maccabees following their victory over the Syrians under Antiochus IV, is characterized by the lighting of the menorah. In 1944, it began on Monday, December 11, as we looked forward to an improvement in Markkleeberg, our new camp.

In the morning, we received the overalls and the numbers to sew on the sleeves. Late in the afternoon, women in our block reminded us that it was the first night of Hanukkah. Anna Szekely Shindler, who knew Rebbetzin Friedmann from Dombovár, asked her to compose something she could recite. Recalling the cultural evenings and the emotional celebrations at home, Rebbetzin Friedmann agreed. She just needed paper and a pencil. Anna went to look and hurried back with a red pencil she had borrowed from Laju, the *Blockälteste.* The pencil had to be returned shortly, otherwise Laju would not be able to mark in her *Appel* book the number of prisoners present from her block. Paper was the second problem, which the Rebbetzin solved by taking out one of the wooden planks from the bed. On the board she wrote a small poem.[5] Then in a piece of wood, Laju made eight small holes, in which she placed oil instead of candles. Erzsike called me to the room where girls sat on the beds and quickly filled the available places. Laju, a religious young woman, trembled as she lit the first light and said the blessing. Then we prayed "*Seheheyanu,*" expressing our thanks to God, king of the universe, who sustained and enabled us to survive so far. By then, we were all in tears. Choked by emotion, Erzsike whispered, "Do you remember how proud Grandpa was that we knew the blessings and sang the song '*Moaz zur*' with him?"

Anna Székely Shindler read aloud the poem that the Rebbetzin had written on the long board. It was so moving that everyone burst out crying again. To lighten the atmosphere, the three Schlesinger sisters from Kecskemét started to sing Hanukkah songs the way they used to do at home. Soon everyone joined them, creating a genuine holiday atmosphere. Lenke Schlesinger Rosenberg, one of the Schlesinger sisters I interviewed, reminded me of that emotional evening in the camp. Remembering the board with the poem, I hoped that maybe I would be able to locate it during my Markkleeberg visit in 1998. I received special permission to enter what was once barracks six; but by that time, it was altered and the beds removed. Who knows whether anyone wondered about the words on that board and the circumstances under which they were written? Probably it was simply discarded.

Purim

Purim, the Jewish festival commemorating the deliverance of the Jews in Persia from destruction by Haman, was on Tuesday, February 27, in 1945. Hanz, a short German civilian foreman who worked in the factory's *Härterai,* somehow knew that it was Purim. He brought a piece of cake to Rachel Janovics Mittelman, who worked with him. Talking was not allowed, thus Hans put it in the closet for Rachel and gave a sign of merriment; it was how Rachel herself learned it was Purim.

For Erzsike and me, Purim had been such a joyful day at home, with Mother preparing for days ahead by baking at least seven types of cake and cookies. This baking was Mother's pride. Then it was our turn to deliver her excellent creations to relatives and friends. In return, we enjoyed the attention and our messenger's reward of some pocket money, which we spent mostly in the candy or stationery store. In Markkleeberg, Purim passed us by without our even knowing.

Passover

March 29, 1945, was the first night of Passover. We knew this time from Elizabeth Winkler Engel and others who were marking the dates, and the pious girls counted it out after Purim and told everyone. Passover in Markkleeberg was remembered with faith, sacrifices, and loyalty to our upbringing. Resourceful women who had the opportunity exchanged their bread for potatoes. Flora Kaff Goldring, who worked in the office with German civilian workers giving out supplies, exchanged bread for potatoes with a young German girl who was a civilian office worker. Flora knew the language and, without the SS presence, the office workers dared to speak to her. Food shortages were felt also by the German population, so it was a fair exchange. The civilian worker put the potatoes in a white bag to keep them clean. Flora was able to give her a whole loaf of bread because she and her two sisters had saved it. When I interviewed Flora, she was still jubilant at the good fortune that allowed her to keep the commandment of not eating bread on Passover.

Márta Weisz Paran, from our town, traded her bread for soup from other inmates. She suggested we do the same, but there were only a few girls willing to make the exchange. Not being good at bartering, Erzsike and I decided that, at least the first two days for what would, at home, have been the Seder, the ceremonial dinner commemorating the Exodus from Egypt, we would not eat our bread. When I went to sleep hungry the first night, I recalled our last Passover and the time shortly after when we were ordered to leave our home. The day before, my sweet little grandmother was still explaining the Passover dishes to me, with special marking of the meat and milk plates. She wanted me to know, in case she was not able to show us the next year.

Back in the camp at lunchtime, we had no problem with the soup because we knew that we had to eat something to survive. Our consciences were concerned with the bread, the essence of observing the holiday. By the third day of consuming only the watery soup, we were very weak. Later we saw that one of the religious girls in our barracks, who also had not eaten the bread, fainted. We felt that that would happen to us, too, so we finished our bread with the feeling that, at least, we did keep the memory of Seder in Passover.

The Christian Holidays

Sunday

On Sundays, the only rest day, the roll calls lasted longer. The German crew appeared, including the *Aufseherin*s who smelled from perfume and looked alluringly toward the guards. The counting and recounting took longer than usual. As we stood there hour after hour, the girls started to recite poetry, one after the other. When they did not remember the lines, someone else always filled in the missing words. Sundays were also a favorite time for special room searches, work projects, and punishment *Appels*. In the factory, the brutality was under restraint a bit; but in the camp, Knittel and his staff did as they pleased. When the inspection was not a search for hidden items, it was to check for neatness and order. The blankets had to be kept folded precisely on the beds at all times. Next to the blanket, we each placed our plate for food, arranged in military order. Every prisoner had to stand at attention next to her bed while the *Aufseherin* passed by doing her inspection.

Work, with its exhausting day- and nighttime shifts, left us little energy or mood for "social life." Only on Sunday evenings, when we had finished most of the chores and eaten our bread, did we have an hour or two until the lights went out. We would meet in the corner of the barracks. The conversations then generated a sense of togetherness that was otherwise so lacking in the camp, where everyone pursued her own survival. There we reminisced about home, school days, and familiar tunes. Girls recited poetry, and the listeners had a chance to recall memories inspired by the poems. Sometimes the singer started in the middle, and then those in the audience completed the missing lines. Talented girls, even those without much education, placed words in rhymes and created songs about the life and hopes of the camp. With the poetry, women also exchanged recipes for cooking. Meanwhile, girls watched that the *Aufseherin* or the German guards would not surprise us. If they found us gathered together, depending on their mood, we might be punished.

The wardens grew more vicious as the Allies were closing in. One Sunday in February, the snow was falling steadily as we stood in roll call on the icy ground. We had been out since the morning. We stamped our feet to ward off frostbite, and only the sound of stifled sobs or laments now and then enlivened the rhythmic shivering and monotonous rhythm of thirteen hundred women standing in the cold.

"How long can we last?" we wondered. By noon we were all covered with the wet snow. Our feet froze and we had difficulty keeping our swollen, aching toes in the shoes. Erzsike was rubbing her toes together anxiously to reduce the swelling, but I made the mistake of taking off one shoe and could only replace my enlarged foot in the shoe with tears and great effort. I do not know what would have happened if the *Appel* lasted much longer. The blare of the air-raid siren, even though it brought other difficulties, came to our salvation.

Sunday's Air Raid

Hearing the alarm, everyone would run to the air-raid shelter. The noise was immense as the planes soared in groups overhead. The air-raid shelters were deep in the ground. On top of them was thick concrete, and above that was a layer of dirt covered with grass. From outside, one could only see the ventilation shafts that were also protected from the bombs. The shelters inside looked like long corridors. Guards stood on both ends. On Sundays, when everyone was in camp including the French women prisoners, there was not enough room in the shelter. Even with Lucifer and the guards hitting and pushing, it was hard to squeeze in 1,500 inmates. We were still on line when we heard a new squadron of planes arriving, making even the ground shake under us. We had no place to hide; our anxiety increased, listening to that ominous reverberation of engines above our heads. We even heard the shrieking whistle of the shells in the air and then the blast of detonation as they reached their targets. The echo of that explosion came so close that we felt the thrust of the air jolting us. Luckily we reached the entrance of the shelter, as the fearful crowd of inmates squeezed one another inside.

Although frightening outside, it was sometimes more chilling inside. During one Sunday air raid in March 1945, the bunker was full of water, and the tired, shivering girls had to squeeze in all the way. The planes were already above our heads as the *Aufseherins,* scared even more than we were, pushed and squeezed us in. It was hard to walk in the muddy, dark bunker, where water reached above our ankles as we pressed inside. We held each other tightly so as not to fall, be trampled, or lose one another in the crowd. There was just no place for everybody. We became panicky as Knittel arrived, and he kicked and pushed more and more girls into the dark wet bunker. Finally the doors were closed and the women, apprehensive about the shut doors, started to talk of a mass tragedy. We stood there for a long time then someone screamed, "There is no air to breathe! I am choking!" Girls fainted, falling one on the other, as the panic over lack of air continued. Erzsike and I looked at each other anxiously to see whether the other was still standing. Then, as in every darkness, some light appeared. A French girl started to sing in a beautiful, soothing voice. It was comforting to listen, even though we did not understand the words. Meanwhile, the oxygen really was getting low. Erzsike tightened her hold on my arm as the water covered our feet. "The American army were nearing, they may even be outside," said one of the women comfortingly. The crowd relaxed a bit, thinking of the prospect of freedom. Finally the door opened, and we were out in the light. Contrary to our hopes, the guards were all still there, herding us even more angrily.

During air raids that occurred at night, we stayed in the barracks. Usually we were not afraid of death—at any rate, not of *that* death—except on one occasion, when the barracks was shaking from the impact of the nearby bombing. It was totally dark, the girls started to cry, and I stayed close to Erzsike in her bed. Luckily, the camp was not hit. It was hard to run to the shelter when we worked at night and received no lunch in the daytime. On Sundays, when we alternated from day to night shifts, we had no lunch until midnight on Monday in the factory. It was a thirty-six-hour hunger, made even worse when we had to go to the shelter in the daytime on Monday. We did not eat and could not sleep.

Christmas

Christmas was about two weeks after our arrival. We looked forward to some good will to characterize the holiday. We even dreamed of extra food and a bit of rest, but Knittel and his team had different ideas.

In the large factory, a Belgian foreman called Freg brought Zsuzsanna Lengyel Urai and two other girls a pail of hot water as a Christmas present. The girls were grateful and hurried to wash their hair. Then Lucifer appeared. She struck the women with her whip and took down their numbers. The Christmas lights were burning all around as the three stood until midnight in front of Knittel's office in the heavy snow.[6]

On Christmas day, the temperature was still below zero. The snow turned to ice and lines of icicles hung from the trees nearby. We stood in that bone-chilling cold in our thin overalls, our bare feet in wooden shoes were completely frozen. Rubbing no longer helped. The *Aufseherin*s stamped their cold feet as they stood with fur-lined boots, coats, sweaters, and hats. Knittel, with his high boots and heavy winter coat, was too cold to stand in one place. He walked up and down, inspecting us with his photographic memory. Finally, they all had enough; but before dispersing us, the guards selected a group of thirty girls to clear snow. Unfortunately, Erzsike and I were among them. We looked at each other as the rest returned to the barracks. Already shivering in all parts of our bodies, we had to pick up shovels and a carriage for which we would be the horses transporting the snow.

Shoveling Snow on Christmas

The wind was so strong that if we did not hurry, it would blow the snow that we worked so hard to collect right out of the carriage. Our toes were so frozen that we could hardly stand. Shivering and rubbing our hands together to keep them from freezing, we did not know how we would be able to endure. We had to shovel the snow into piles, then fill up the carriage and pull it to a collection center in the camp. We did all that in wooden shoes, without gloves, hats, or stockings. The *Aufseherin*s wore high boots, fur hats, and heavy winter coats. Yet they were still freezing, and they vented their anger by whipping us like lazy horses to run faster. I remember looking at Erzsike as one of the lashes came close to her back, and every minute I expected to collapse. The snow, meanwhile, continued to fall steadily.

Mellowing a bit under our mutual adversary, the inclement weather, or maybe simply changing their strategy, the *Aufseherin*s told us that we only had to do half the job originally assigned to us. We were told that, as soon as we finished, we would be going inside. Electrified, the group moved even faster. With neither whip nor *Aufseherin*s on our backs, we worked as a unit to help one another to complete the job. The hardest thing was to hold the heavy shovel; twice it fell out of my frozen hands. Erzsike ran to help me pick it up. That time she was the stronger of the two of us.

I still wonder how we made it through that day. Either it was our destiny to survive or we had a very strong will to live that kept us alive. Today as I watch sometimes from my warm living room window the workers outside clearing the snow in heavy boots, fur hats, and winter coats, I think of the two emaciated teenaged girls in Markkleeberg. They could hardly move in the deep snow, pulling the heavy, snow-laden carriage through the gusty winds. I just do not know how I could have been one of them.

At night, in our room at the camp, we fell on the bed exhausted, but from time to time I woke up to shift my aching back, while listening to Vera's heavy coughing. Her bed was close to mine, and I feared becoming sick, so I turned away from her side as much as I could.

On Christmas, the soup was not special as we hoped it would be. There were no bonuses of extra portions. Instead, looking ahead, we now worried over any German holiday. Our concerns were well placed, as we will see.

New Year's Eve

The skies were dark, with a new snowstorm brewing, when the lights came on around the camp and we were called for an *Appel.* From the trees, long strips of icicles hung as we stood at attention. The guards locked the blocks so that we could not go in. Knittel ordered us to stand until they relieved us. A slow shiver began on the lines. The chill wind reached under our thin overalls and blew over every bit of our bare bodies. The five of us in our line moved close together so the cold could not take over the spaces between us. The wetness of the snow penetrated our shoes and froze our feet. The guards checked us every half hour from Knittel's office. We did not know why we were being punished. There were rumors that the *Appel* was called because the Germans suspected that forced laborers had hidden weapons in our barracks, but this was never substantiated. A German civilian worker, Anneiles Falkenberg, reported in her testimony that supposedly a Jewish woman prisoner was found resting in the daytime from lack of strength. As a punishment, all the prisoners were made to stand hours at night, barefoot, in the snow. The statement was confirmed by Ms. Janek, a Markkleeberg resident who lived in Spinnerei Strasse 23, close to the camp. She also worked in the factory.[7]

Finally, Knittel and his soldiers appeared. We straightened our lines and stood at attention. They started to count us again when suddenly, a girl who suffered from TB fainted. According to the roll-call rules, we should have left her on the ground until the end of *Appel,* but her sisters came to her aid. Knittel pushed everyone aside, saying that he knew how to administer first aid. He opened the girl's overall and noticed that she was wrapped in a blanket, despite his order that all blankets be left folded on the beds. Tipsy from the New Year's Eve celebrations, Knittel grew irate and, cursing, kicked the unconscious victim all over her body. Her two sisters began to scream and tried to protect their sister with their own bodies. The guards intervened and indiscriminately started hitting everyone nearby. Erzsike and I were a bit further away, so we escaped the beatings, but we were all shaken up. Finally Knittel had enough and permitted us to return to our barracks. The bleeding siblings carried their dazed sister, while other girls helped the injured bystanders and those who were close to fainting. The next day we had a bit of rest, except for those who waited by the *Revier.* The SS needed to recover from the previous night's celebration.[8]

The Shower after New Year

The first Saturday night after New Year, the inmates from the whole camp were taken for a shower and disinfection. We had to tie our garments in a bundle, which was numbered. After the shower, we were chased out naked and wet to wait outside in the snow until all the others joined us and our clothing was disinfected. It was unreal; the wintry cold was freezing our wet bodies. The water quickly turned to icicles in our hair and everywhere else. There was no means of protection from the burn of the relentless winter wind. Our teeth chattering, Erzsike pulled me closer for warmth. The situation fitted the remark of Imre Kertesz, Hungarian Holocaust survivor and Nobel Prize winner, when he returned after the war and people asked him, "Was it hell?" He answered, "I don't know hell, but I know concentration camps."[9] The snow melted under our bare feet. The flaked flurries of crystal snow were drifting in the air; those few that reached the ground turned to black slush around us. Still we continued to stand in the relentless, unbearable cold. Many girls sobbed aloud. Others whimpered, with teeth clenched, and some recited phrases they remembered from the Psalms. As we were on the edge of falling into the tranquility of death, our clothing arrived and we were allowed to go to the barracks. The next day, the *Revier* was crowded with women suffering from pneumonia, pleurisy, and infections of the urinary tract that troubled them for years to come.

The night of the shower was documented by survivors at the Center of Federal Justice Bureau for the Clarification of Nazi Crimes in Germany. The following was reported: "In the winter of 1944–45 (the exact date was not remembered), the women were not scheduled to work that night and were taken for a shower. Knittel then ordered the women to go out to the *Appelplatz* naked and wait there for all the others. He left them standing in the freezing cold from 8 until 11 at night. Three young women died as a result."[10]

Among those waiting on line in the *Revier* after the shower was Erzsike, my only bond to the past and the present. She was suffering from inflammation of the heart valve. It may have come from streptococcus in the throat that, in our run-down condition, attacked the valves in her heart. Erzsike was admitted to the *Revier*, and I was separated from her in the camp for the first time. I was petrified. The thought that she might not recover haunted me. My sister was the only remnant of the world that had been stolen from me, of my family and home. The possibility of losing her and, with her, part of my life, my happiness, my future was unbearable. I ran to visit her every minute of my free time. I felt that I had a knot in my heart each time I entered, for fear that I might not find her there. Days while she was there slid slowly, creating my most terrifying memories of

Markkleeberg. The two weeks that my sister was not standing with me at roll calls, was not giving me encouragement at work and faith at night for brighter days to come, was my hardest period in the camps. The miracle of her return lightened my murky days and warmed the cold of the winter sun. Luckily she was assigned back to her machine.

Among the many seriously sick girls after the shower was Irma Wilhelm, the roommate of Tereza Frankl. Irma was twenty-four years old. Her sister Adela, four years her junior, was with her in the camp. Irma suffered from pneumonia after the shower and died on February 3, 1945, in the *Revier.* The *Aufseherin* we called Kutyus, who was one of the milder ones, came to Tereza and asked her to tell Adela that her sister Irma had died. Tereza did not have the heart to be the bearer of that terrible message. The *Aufseherin* was angry, but seeing Adela later, Tereza knew that Kutyus had given her the news. Tereza and the other roommates consoled Adela as much as they could; all those who had a sister with her then felt, with Adela, her pain and sorrow.

The next chapter will present some of the light that was missing from the German holidays in camp. We will meet people at work, German civilians and forced laborers, who personified the meaning of kindness and goodwill toward all.

10

Human Relations with the Factory Workforce and French Political Prisoners

The German Civilian Workers

The factory was directed by German civilians, including engineers, foremen, technical supervisors, mechanics, and office workers. The supervisors were somewhat older men or those who had a disability. We addressed them all as Herr Meister.

The German workers, having contact with the inmates through the work, usually developed feelings of sympathy for us. Although it was forbidden, on pain of death, for them to establish contact with Jewish prisoners, German civilian workers asked us questions when the opportunity arose, and slowly a network of human relationships developed. There followed occasional acts of kindness by workers who empathized with the young Hungarian girls under their command. At the risk of their own safety, civilian workers provided the Jewish women occasional words of consolation, an extra crust of bread, or an apple during unobserved moments: gestures so rare that they were gratefully recalled by survivors, years after liberation.

One German engineer, while adjusting Erzsike's machine, put a small paper bag in the drawer and hinted that it was for her. Erzsike looked and saw a small jam sandwich inside. As she tried to thank him, the elderly man averted his eyes and moved to adjust the next machine. When I stopped by while I was sweeping, Erzsike was all smiles and, after looking carefully around, she handed me the brown bag. I could not believe our luck. Right away we started the bargaining process with our treasure. I told Erzsike that, because she received the present, she should have it. Besides, I said, Erzsike worked harder than I did. As usual, we eventually agreed to share. Fearful of being searched on the way back to camp, we decided to finish the sandwich in the factory. Erzsike, hiding behind her machine, divided it exactly in half, down to the smallest crumbs. Turning our backs while leaning toward the machine, we gobbled up the sandwich pieces. The indescribable taste of our midnight snack could be understood only by starving teenagers. Touched by the German civilian worker's gesture and kindness, Erzsike, after many attempts, finally succeeded in catching his eye. It was important to Erzsike that the man understood her gratitude.

It seems that the same German worker with the jam sandwich helped other girls too. When, after a while, he was not seen around, Helen, who worked on a machine similar to Erzsike's, asked about him. We all regretted not knowing his whereabouts, and the inmates were sorry for his absence.

The civilian German supervisors had a kinder attitude toward us, in general. They were more interested in getting things done than in harassing people. We can understand the German workers a bit better by taking into account the fact that many of them were against fascism and were considered communist sympathizers. According to police files, some were under surveillance. Many of those under scrutiny lived nearby, in Spinnereistrasse, and had been workers at the former spinning mill, which Junkers took over and occupied.[1]

The German population assumed that we were criminals who had been brought to Germany for punishment. One German worker told Elisabeth Stein Székely that they thought we were prostitutes. Those who worked with us for awhile realized who we really were, but new employees always came. One day, as I was sweeping around the machines, a German worker whom I had not seen before asked me why I had been arrested. "You look too young to be a prostitute," he said. An inmate who worked at a nearby machine translated the question. She also provided the answer, saying that we had done nothing against the law, that we were just Jews who had been kidnapped from our homes and taken prisoner by official decree. I do not know what the worker believed, but he left us with no comment.

A young German technician who was missing one hand told Anna Klein Weiss and another inmate assigned to clean the office that he would leave bread for them. Concerned with the rules set by the SS, the technician requested that the girls eat it in the room and, if they were still caught, to say that they stole the bread and not that he had given it to them. Luckily, no problems arose.[2] In mentioning acts of compassion, I would like to pay homage to all those workers who followed the light of their own consciences and helped us, the hostages, in our stressful hours of need.

Dr. Rachel Spielmann, a former Markkleeberg Jewish inmate, in her letter to Irma Clajus in 1975, mentioned that a German foreman called Pastor secretly slipped food to the girls who worked at the polishing machines. It was risky for him because there were signs all over the factory warning that "communication with the prisoners" was "strictly forbidden."[3] Ms. Janek, a German civilian worker, also testified that she had provided stockings to the prisoners who worked with her.[4]

Helen, our fellow prisoner whom Erzsike got to know when she inquired about the engineer with the jam sandwich, became our good friend. She also had a sister, Zsuzsa, and they were both near to our age. Zsuzsa, who was the older, worked in quality control and used to come to see Helen from time to time. A pretty girl with blue eyes and curly black hair, Zsuzsa was full of life. She always had a joke to tell, and we used to smile at one another as we passed by. During lunch hour, we exchanged a few words also. Zsuzsa told us that they came from southern Hungary, where they had been the only two children at home and that, just like Erzsike and me, they had remained alone in Auschwitz. Very close as sisters, they tried to be both mother and father to each other. We identified with them and felt that they could be our friends, with equal potential to provide mutual support. We looked forward to seeing them and to discussing our ways of coping and getting along as sisters alone together. From Zsuzsa we enjoyed learning the gossip of the factory that she knew so well.

Life in the camp was a constant challenge, and one day I noticed Helen crying by her machine. Scared even to pronounce the words, she whispered that Zsuzsa had a high temperature and she was in the *Revier.* A feeling of profound sadness descended on us. We tried to comfort Helen by saying that Erzsike also had been in the *Revier* and that she did recover and come out. The following days, I cleaned around Helen's machine more than usual, looking for some consoling words to say. At lunch hour, we rushed to be with her. As the days passed, Helen grew more distressed. Girls from the quality control section who worked with Zsuzsa also came to visit her. Even Zsuzsa's inspector, a German civilian woman, appeared one day and left a piece of chocolate by Helen's machine. It was the first time in ten days that Helen mustered a faint smile. She could not wait for the end of the shift to rush and give Zsuzsa the present. We also visited Zsuzsa at the *Revier.* She made an effort to smile and to smooth her hair to give the illusion that all was well with her. Yet we saw that her face was ashen and her small body was even thinner. Pneumonia and TB were taking their toll on her. Without medication and better nutrition, Helen's love and her friends' concern could not unlock the chains of Zsuzsa's double prisons. I tried not to cry on leaving the *Revier,* but I noticed an escaping tear running down Erzsike's face. A few days later, on a Monday evening, Helen's machine was attended by another inmate. Later we learned that Zsuzsa and four others had been transported out of the camp. The sisters' separation touched us deeply, and we had to struggle against its demoralizing effects on us. We held hands tighter when returning to the camp after work that day. Helen, meantime, was also admitted to the *Revier* with a temperature and a generally run-down condition. She did get better, however, and thanks to the efforts of sympathetic women, she was among the ten weak girls who were reassigned to work in the kitchen.

Meeting Helen a few weeks later, we were pleased to see how the power of hope, a medicine so useful for survival, worked for her. She held on to the fragile possibility that Zsuzsa had been taken to a hospital and that they would meet at home. We now know how our hopes and illusions lacked happy endings. No one from Zsuzsa's transports, just like those of my mother's group who were sent to the other side in Auschwitz-Birkenau, remained alive. We stayed friends with Helen; but without Zsuzsa, our ties weakened and we lost contact during the Death March. We trust that Helen survived and built a new family after the war.

It seems that Erzsike, being so young and working at the big machine, awakened some sense of pity in some. A few weeks after the episode of the jam sandwich, a German foreman on the night shift threw an apple into the box of raw materials by Erzsike's machine. The foreman knew that Erzsike would pick it up, which she did, giving a thankful glance to the hurriedly disappearing civilian worker. Receiving the apple renewed our faith in miracles. We decided to take it to the camp and share it with our friends whose comradeship was so important and comforting for us. Just like Elza Reich Szamosi we planned to call the girls from our town. Erzsike hid the apple in her overall pants, secured with elastic at the ankle. Shortly after reaching our room, however, a curfew was declared and we were not allowed to leave our barracks. Sitting on our beds, worrying about the expected searches, we decided to have the apple ourselves. Then Vera entered the room and we knew what to do. Erzsike borrowed a knife next door and we cut the apple into three parts. Giving one to Vera calmed our conscience. Vera, a bit older then we were and who was coughing so much through the night, smiled at us thankfully.

The curfew lifted later in the evening, but we were not sorry for sharing the apple with a suffering roommate. Our good feeling of kindness grew even more because, in a few days, Vera was admitted to the *Revier.* Today I may have forgotten the everyday hunger and cold, but the memory of the foreman's gesture and Vera's heartwarming smile left a mark in my soul.

Other civilian workers in the factory also expressed their sentiments by helping the inmates. Regina Farkas Pincsefski and her friend worked in the stockroom. There was a woman who, although she could not provide food, always gave an encouraging smile. Another worker called Meisel used to bring cheese and would leave a little by each girl in the room.

A well-built elderly German foreman worked in the Westhalle with Elisabeth Stein Székely. After he went home for a visit every two weeks, he brought back with him little presents for the girls on the assembly line. Food was rationed, and the German civilian population did not have much at that stage of the war; but still he managed to bring some vitamin C, a bit of candy, and needles with thread—a real treasure for inmates.

Civilian workers, even if they were supporters of Nazism, felt sorry for us. There was an office secretary, a heavy woman who wore a swastika—

the official emblem of the Nazi party and the Third Reich—on her chest. She also had a son serving in the SS. Yet seeing young Klára Frenkel Deutsch shivering in the cold winter, she gave her an undergarment to help keep her warm. Klára wore it, even though she feared it would be found during inspection. Agnes Glück Rabinovics, who worked on an automatic machine, had a short, elderly, gray-haired German foreman. He deliberately left half of his meal next to Agnes's machine. The next time he did the same by another girl. Luckily, they were not caught.

With political changes, the attitude and the goodwill of some of the foremen improved even more. One of the civilian workers complained to Rachel Janovics Mittelman that they themselves were supervised, forced to work, and did not receive enough food.

Tereza Frankl also had a German civilian engineer supervisor. He was short and elderly, with glasses that slid down to the edge of his nose. Like all the engineers, he wore a blue cloak. He used to bring some little thing such as a piece of bread or a bar of soap and put it in the closet next to Tereza. He did this for the other girls, too, who worked with him in the Middlehalle.

Not all the German workers acted with goodwill toward the prisoners. Some could not understand the problem of hunger that beset us. Foremen also often shouted their instructions in a crude and colloquial German, mostly incomprehensible to the inmates. A German supervisor threatened to report a woman called Márta, whose machine was next to Elisabeth Stein Székely's, because she made too many mistakes. Márta, a bit older, knew little German and could not understand the instructions. She was terrified when the foreman mentioned the name "*Oberscharführer.*" She was sobbing bitterly, when an engineer who was more decent came over and calmly explained how to work the machine properly. He even knew a few words in Hungarian. After that, the malevolent supervisor, even though he tried, could find no more mistakes.

Elisabeth Stein Székely remembered a short, heavy, dark-skinned German foreman who walked around provocatively in the Westhalle eating all kinds of goodies while the inmates were starving. There was also a skinny German master who seemed to be suffering from tuberculosis, Elisabeth recalled. He was mean, shouting at the inmates and frequently giving their numbers to the *Aufseherin* for punishment.[5]

As in any group of people, there were some who were better and some who were worse among the German civilian workers. Erzsébet Frank had two German foremen. One was terrible; he threatened to accuse her with the crime of sabotage if she did not work faster. He was not only dissatisfied with Erzsébet's work, but he was certain that Hitler would win the war.[6] The other foreman, called Johanes Walter, was a bit older and was a decent person. Whenever he went home for the weekend, he always returned with some presents for the girls.

A civilian factory supervisor contended before the court that the workers' behavior with the prisoners was dictated from above. Possibly it was, to some degree; but conscientious men and women found ways to act with a bit of humanity. The Germans being cruel to us was the expected norm; those who acted with a bit of empathy were the heroes in our hearts and minds.

The apparent closeness of the end of the war encouraged many of the German foremen to be more tolerant. They did not show it openly, but they were more willing to transfer a prisoner who had difficulties working at a large automatic machine to an easier job. The SS guards and the *Aufseherins* were just the opposite. When things in the war were not going well, they harassed us even more.

Compassionate German civilian foremen tried to help the girls in any way they could. An old German worker, who supervised the machine of Agnes Kivovits Vesely, when he saw Agnes being so tired in the middle of the night, turned off the machine, just leaving the light on, and told Agnes to sit down and take a nap. The lighted machine gave the impression that it was in use.

Language and looks were important advantages for somc inmates. Many girls were still pretty, even in their run-down condition. Some felt that the men who helped them were influenced to some degree by their looks. The foreign workers warned some girls, including Rachel Janovics Mittelman, to be careful and not to go to the basement or the cellar alone with a certain German engineer.

The German civilian workers usually avoided confrontation with Knittel and the women guards. Yet when they noticed injustice, they reacted. A German civilian foreman came to the aid of Iren Lebovits Ehrenreich, whose machine was broken. Iren was much concerned, because a week had passed and the machine was still out of order. One day, two high-ranking SS officers arrived. In addition to their highly polished black boots, they wore wide armbands on their sleeves. Iren's machine was right by the door as the officers entered. To Iren's alarm, they asked her why she was not working. The foreman hurried to inform the officers that the machine was broken, but that it would be fixed the next day. The SS nodded and continued their tour of the factory. When I interviewed Iren in Israel at the age of ninety-one, she fondly remembered and still blessed with gratitude the foreman who saved her from that dangerous situation. Iren's case illuminates the tremendous fear we had of the SS soldiers. When they stopped by her machine, Iren already saw herself guilty, even though she had done nothing wrong. By the camp rules, it would not really have mattered that she was innocent.

Foreign Workers

There were two kinds of foreign workers. War prisoners were housed in fenced quarters near the camp, in the so-called Russian barracks. Many of them worked outside in the fields under harsh conditions. Among them were Russians and Ukrainians who were forced to come.[7] In the second category were the so-called "free-willing" who worked with us in the factory. Some were volunteers and others had been forced to come from the German-occupied territories. One young Belgian boy told Barbara Klein Stark that the Germans picked him up at school and he could not even let his parents know. Some forced laborers from Belgium or Holland were college students belonging to resistance movements. One of them was Freg, who brought us the raw materials and who talked to Veronica Lorant Berk.

The forced laborers in the factory were French, Dutch, Belgian, Italian, Polish, and Yugoslavian nationals. They were young and, except for a small minority, unmarried. Freedom of movement was allowed to them, but they had to report for work daily and they were under surveillance.[8] They were given some wages. The forced laborers had radios and were allowed to receive letters and packages from home.

The foreigners worked as technicians, setting and attending the machines. Among them were foremen who supervised the production and others who worked on the machines. When Erzsike left after the night shift, a man from Holland took over her place. Ilana Sajovits Breiner's neighbor on the next machine was a huge Polish guy. Ilana was afraid of him at first, but she relaxed when she found out that he was only eighteen.

The foreign workers who themselves suffered under the Germans were generally sympathetic to the Jewish prisoners. They did not have much food either, but they felt sorry for us and shared some of their portions. Agata Trattner Klein, who was one of the welders, always remembered how a Dutch technician, before Christmas, surreptitiously placed half an apple and a piece of bread in the drawers by the machines of the girls who worked with him. He hinted with a wink to Agata that the others should also check their drawers.

Although some forced laborers were nice, others, like one Ukrainian woman, could be very mean. Sarah Ehrmann Sterba received a small piece of an apple from a German civilian worker. The Ukrainian woman jumped up, grabbed the apple, and threw it into the acid solution.

Members of the *Electrocommando*

The girls who worked mainly with forced laborers belonged to the *Electrocommando.* To be chosen for the task, they were required to speak German and have a higher education. Gabriella Braver Kosinka wanted to be selected but was concerned that she had not yet completed her studies. Her friend laughed and said, "They will not ask for your diploma!" Everyone could claim to be whatever she wanted; there was no proof available.

The *Electrocommando* foreman wanted professionals, but Knittel believed that intelligent inmates could learn. The final selection was based on a mixture of education and experience. When Eva Czitter volunteered for the job, she was asked where she learned electrical work. Eva quickly answered that her father had an electric-supply store where she had helped many hours a day. Her father actually had an outerwear clothing store. Eva, who spoke German well, realized that there was no way for them to check. Her friend Eda, who did not know German, followed everything Eva said with "*Ich auch*" (I am too).

The ten-member *electro* crew had a separate room next to the *Härterai.* Roberto, an Italian forced laborer, was the foreman. Among the professional electricians was a German civilian worker named Heinz Guenter who had a medical condition that prevented him from serving in the army. He was especially kind to Gabriella. He brought her food when he could and spoke to her and the other girls who worked with him in the camp, despite the warnings. Heinz Guenter also offered Gabriella a hiding place with his mother during the evacuation of the camp. Other members of the *Electrocommando* were an Italian electrician named Enrico and a Polish forced laborer, Josef Lubera.[9]

The *Electrocommando* was responsible for the electricity in the plant. When the lightbulbs burned out in a machine or anyplace in the factory, Roberto was called. He sent an inmate who checked with her probe lamp to see if she needed to change the lightbulb. The inmates from the *Electrocommando* also knew how to turn off the electricity on the machines. Sometimes they helped their friends who wanted to rest a bit by turning a machine off for half an hour. The real electricians handled the more serious electrical projects.

It was forbidden to talk, but workers in a small group tended to become friends and tried to help one another on the personal level. Girls like Gabriella Braver Kosinka, who knew German and Czech, had an advantage. Polish forced laborer Joseph Lubera brought Gabriella cigarettes, which she exchanged with the *Lagerälteste* Bella Spitz for food.

Enrico, the Italian forced laborer in the *Electrocommando,* mistakenly attached an electric cable on the wrong place. Not knowing enough German to explain, he was accused by the factory foreman of sabotage, which was punishable by death. The foreman was ready to call Wiegand, the SS commander of the camp. Gabriella had studied Latin in school and so understood some Italian. She interceded for him, explaining that Enrico simply did not understand the instructions. To make a stronger case for him, Gabriella explained that he had a wife and three children at home in Italy. The German engineer listened and slowly accepted the explanation. Enrico transferred the cable to the place it was intended. Enrico's friend Roberto was so grateful that he brought a package with bread and smoked meat for Gabriella and the other inmates in the *Electrocommando.* Roberto, a good-looking young man, had a German girlfriend from Markkleeberg whose husband was in the army. She supplied him with the food he brought for the inmates in the *Electrocommando.*

Language skills such as Gabriella's were a great advantage. Zsofia Gottlieb Török impressed an engineer with her educated German. He was a slim man who suffered probably from some sickness that disqualified him for the army. He asked Zsofia how she knew German so well. "I studied in school and I learned from my parents," she answered. When she told him that she spoke French too, he was delighted. It was a chance for him to practice the French he had learned while studying in Paris. Zsofia also knew English; but because that was the language of the enemy, she was afraid to mention it. The engineer, wearing his white coat with the buttons in the back, stopped a few times for short conversations. While talking to Zsofia, he noticed how hard her work was on a machine that she had to move by hand to save electricity. Zsofia was tired, and her hands were full of blisters from the hot oil and splinters that went flying when the machine cut steel bars. Zsofia would squeeze the pus from the wounds that became infected, but she would not go to the *Revier.* She still carries a mark of discoloration on her hand. Along with the physical pain, she also had the pressure of meeting the daily quota. The engineer knew all that; and one day, which was probably his last in the factory, he surprised Zsofia. A foreman came and told her that she had been transferred to the quality-control section. There she could sit and check the finished pieces according to the given measurements. Zsofia looked for him everywhere to thank him, but she never saw the civilian engineer again.

The Time of Spring

We were hungry and tired, but still the spirit of youth and romance lurked in the corners of our hearts. Next to Erzsike's machine was a divider where forced laborers worked. The closest person to her over the barrier was a young boy from Holland. Erzsike nicknamed him "Peter," because she thought it sounded like an international name. Peter had a handsome, sympathetic face and used to wave a warm hello. Once he even patted Erzsike's hair through the divider when no one was looking. He also spoke some encouraging words in German; and by sign language, he used to signal that the war would be over one day and we all would go home. Erzsike, enjoying her flowers of youth, felt so good to be receiving the attention. She answered Peter with a word or two that she knew in German. The friendship continued for awhile. Erzsike used to tell me, "Peter waved again!" Peter probably would have given her some food as appreciation, but he did not have much himself. So one day he surprised Erzsike with a ring he had made of red copper that seemed almost like gold. It looked like a signet ring without the initials, because Peter did not know Erzsike's name.

Peter gave the tenderly prepared, sweet ring to Erzsike as a school pal would, a token of first love and affection. Erzsike, still a child, was so proud; she started to imagine how our father and grandfather would be smiling to see the gift. Although a bit concerned about being searched, Erzsike wore the ring and Peter smiled back. It was a bit of platonic love asserting itself even in the harshest conditions. Erzsike continued to wear the ring even when an older worker who never peeked through the divider replaced the blue-eyed boy from Holland. Peter was probably transferred to another place of work, but during the Death March we saw him again. Erzsike sentimentally brought the ring back home to Abaújszántó. It was

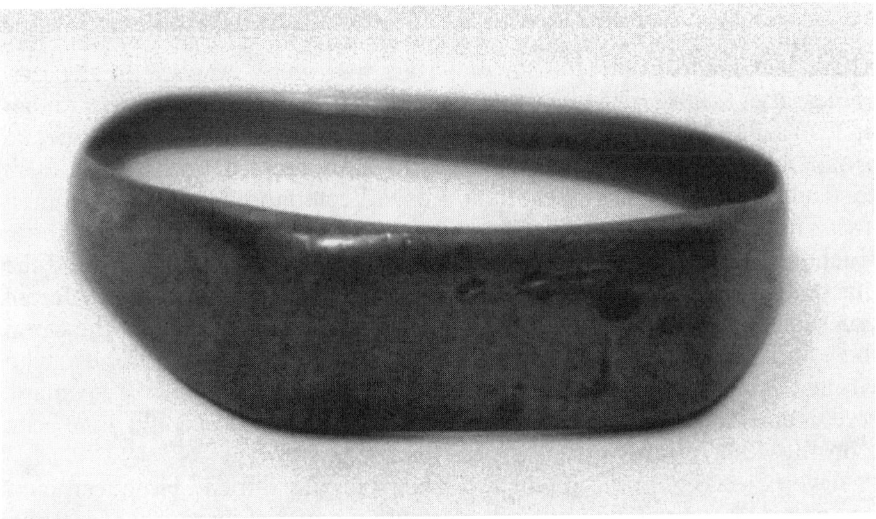

Erzsike's ring was similar to the above that was also made in the Junkers factory in Markkleeberg. Private collection.

among our treasures from the past that we lost crossing the border of Hungary.

A real romance and fairy tale was shared by a pretty girl called Agi from our neighboring city of Kosice. Agi's machine in the Westhalle was not far from Erzsike's. Agi came to the girls' attention when they noticed her exchanging glances with a Belgian forced laborer. The handsome boy supplied raw material for the machines. Gossip spread at enormous speed amid the monotone of the automatic machines. There was no escape; ladies' room conversations were livelier, and spying girls watched every move of the blond boy and his visits around Agi. Even my services were recruited by resourceful girls like our friend Klára Spitz Snitzler. Sweeping the floor around them a bit more often, I reported the Belgian's visits and the couple's romantic looks. While I observed only their silent messages, Klára already had better sources of information and could interpret the couple's language of love, based on her imagination and sentiments. The affair continued almost until the final days, providing entertainment and diversion from the air raids and the sounds of the war around us. It seems that the love story did have a happy ending, as is described in chapter 11. The survivors I interviewed remembered the episode and how they romanticized the details. Their voices were still playful at the age of eighty, as they relived their youthful emotions.

Craftsmanship and Resourcefulness

Girls who had never held a screwdriver in their hands worked with electricity and made jewelry from materials that were supplied to the machines. Eva Czitter was one of those skillful inmates. She had time on her hands as members of the *Electrocommando* were sitting in their special room waiting to be called for service. To draw their attention away from food and hunger, Eva and her friend Eda collected tools such as a hammer, a saw, and a file. They also had easy access to the sharpening and polishing machine. Eva looked for nails and screws that were available around the machines. Then they began to cut, chisel, and shape these into different types of jewelry. Eva made charms and Eda made rings. Back in the camp they bartered their creations for bread. Magda Polatsek Fischer, who worked in the supply room, wondered why these girls needed so many screws and nails. Somehow she never realized that her job could have been a profitable position.

Jewelry making involved the risk of severe punishment. However, hunger, survival instinct, and artistic satisfaction equaled their fear of retribution. Eva, who escaped from the camp before the Death March, even carried some of the jewelry home.

There were other enterprising girls who made ornaments such as pins or pendants to exchange for food. Many of the women who bartered for the jewelry, sacrificing their daily rations, were those who wanted to repay a kindness done for them by one of the workers in the factory. Even with all the risks involved, inmates managed to obtain or create a kind of handiwork to express gratitude. This was evident in the testimony of Mrs. Holl, a civilian worker mentioned above, who still treasures the jewelry she received from the prisoners.[10]

Although some entrepreneurial girls prepared rings for commercial purposes, Tereza Frankl made a ring for herself just to exercise her artistic creativity. She never thought of bartering it. She made a hole in a piece of copper that she had worked on the machine, and she chiseled it all around. Tereza was unafraid because the German civilian supervisor appreciated her as a good worker. Tereza guarded the ring carefully even after the war. Making rings was quite widespread in the factory.

The Sweepers' Treasure

As a sweeper in the factory, I had access to the garbage, an important source of "property." I emptied my pail of the debris collected around the machines into a larger container. When the container was full, I had to take it to another room for disposal and to pick up an empty one. I noticed that the other sweepers emptied their containers frequently, before they were full. Being tired and hungry, I never thought to wonder why the girls were so eager to take out the garbage. Interviewing Lea Kaff Brown, who was also a sweeper, I was astonished to learn of the opportunities I had missed and of how Lea was able to use the resources connected with our jobs in inventive ways. Although she rarely found food in the garbage pail, Lea retrieved cigarette butts that the German civilian workers and forced laborers discarded. Collecting these, the enterprising girl took out the tobacco and, with her language skills, was able to barter it for food. Lea also gave some of the cigarette butts to a German civilian worker who transported the rubbish away. When the man returned the empty container, there was always a potato, an apple, or a piece of bread that he had put in for Lea in return. Once he even brought her a piece of soap; another time, some St. John's bread. Lea had reason to wait eagerly for her container each time! The worker, meanwhile, used the tobacco to make himself new cigarettes. Lea also traded tobacco to Bella, who gave her extra soup in return.

Even though it was a harmless operation, Lea eventually got in trouble. Someone noticed that an inmate who worked in the kitchen smoked. He told Knittel, who confronted the girl about where she had gotten the cigarette. She said that a sweeper named Lea had given it to her in exchange for potatoes. Knittel found Lea and asked her about the cigarettes. Lea confessed that she had taken it from the garbage. In the evening, after *Appel,* Knittel called Lea to his office. Lea's two sisters were terrified for her and waited fretfully. Inside his office, Knittel again asked more details about the cigarettes. Then she was placed in punishment standing in front of Knittel's office. The girl who worked in the kitchen stayed two days in the bunker.[11]

The Welders

Erzsébet Frank, the poet, was inspired by a group of twelve girls who were given a special task of attending to the welding machines in the factory. The welders lived in barracks three, room twenty-two. Erzsébet was in the same barracks and admired how the women, who previously did not know each other, got along so well. She documented their story in a ballad called "The Welders." The poem starts like a fairy tale, with "Once upon a time."[12]

Once upon a time in Germany, at Markkleeberg city, Leipzig vicinity,
In a pleasant block of number three, room twenty-two,
Quietly, in exemplary order, the welders lived.
They all loved one another, which was remarkable in camp.
Together they were the twelve welders, in complete harmony.

Their room was neat, the pride of the block.
Beds were two tiers, curtains of eyelet embroidery.[13]
The eyelets were not embellished,
As thread for stitching, couldn't be obtained.
The welders worked eight hours; their clothes were clean.
They washed themselves properly; their hair was neat;
They received pullovers and had stockings on their feet;
They enjoyed the weekly baths, their overalls were clean.

Just like a fairy-tale, it was scarcely believable,
How the twelve welders lived in our block.
They got "Zulag," ate it with gusto.
At food distribution they didn't fight.
Half of them worked the morning shift every day;
They marched to the iron factory with tranquil placidity.

Efficiently they worked, with good skills,
Then, at ten past two, the new shift arrived:
Adri, Lili, Magda, Herta, and Rózsika;
The sixth member was Maderas Rózsika.[14]

In the other group were three pairs of siblings:
Two Lerners, two Zuckers, and two Trattner sisters.
While Adri was not Lili's sister,
They, like Siamese twins, walked to the W.C.
Herta was Magda's bread partner.
Unluckily, they both liked the one with the stripes.
I have never known the secret of their lives;
Who the Fleming favored, Alizka or Herta?

Twelve welders whose lives were like a dream,
Twelve monograms upon a dozen red plates.
No one in the factory could help but know
That at 2:15, six welders would be rushing in.
They were the fresh news daily in the factory.
No wonder that their arrival was so eagerly awaited.
The girls appeared promptly every day except Sundays.
Their report about the menu was the "editorial,"
In how many portions was the bread divided, and what was spread on it?

The "talk of the town," of course, was
Whether, we would have rutabaga that day.
They told us of ongoing scandals in the camp,
What was the mood of Lucifer or the *Oberscharführer*.
They usually reported correctly
The number of coal portions Lucifer confiscated in the blocks.
Twelve little welders, here I thank you,
For the way you always tell us everything.
May you keep on living in order and serenity,
The twelve of you in room twenty-two.

Epilogue

Twelve little welders, I am angry at you:
You refused to watch my blanket.
I have witnesses who saw
That exactly when you didn't look,
My blanket was "organized" away.

With the slogan, "better late than never," With sincere friendship and in good comradeship,

Erzsébet Frank.

The poem would have been lost if not for Elizabeth Zucker Mermel. She carried it during the Death March and through the long journey home which was not an easy task. I had the pleasure of connecting Frank and Zucker. It was great satisfaction for Erzsébet to see her work again and to know that it was appreciated. The paper had deteriorated and faded during the Death March and through the following years. Fortunately, Elizabeth Zucker Mermel remembered and reconstructed the words, which Erzsébet Frank checked and approved.

In Markkleeberg, when the welders read the poem, each one of the twelve girls placed on Erzsébet Frank's bed a part of her daily portion of bread as appreciation and gratitude. Erzsébet divided it between herself and her roommates. When I talked to Erzsébet Frank in 2003, she was beyond her eighties, but she emphasized how she could never forget the twelve small pieces of bread waiting in her room.

The poem sheds light on the life of the camp and the emotional world of the prisoners in minute detail. Erzsébet Frank wondered, in the poem, which of the two pretty girls was favored by the Flemish foreign worker. Adi, or Adrienne Blau, was the wife of a physician; Lili was a nurse. They were good friends both prior to and after the war. The Flemish worker who liked Adi and Lilli also brought news of the world to the factory. So did other forced laborers, which made our lives a bit more endurable. They were happy to tell us about Germany's defeat on the front, which they knew about from radio and newspapers. The workers from Holland and Belgium received printed material from home that passed the censor. The inmates, regardless of the hazards of penalty, brought the papers to the camp and tried to analyze the contents. Ten of the welders remained together through the Death March and all the way to Budapest.

Arming Our Enemy

Airpower in World War II played a vital role in deciding the outcome of the conflict. We worked in the factory that produced airplane parts for the German air force, which was responsible for military operations in the air. Initially, Erzsike and I were happy just to be inside, out of the cold and wind. The effort we had to invest to learn our tasks while we were so hungry demanded all our concentration. Then, after a while, girls started to talk about how we were producing weapons for the enemy and contributing to the success of the German war effort. We felt powerless, and to placate the little conscience we still had, we told ourselves that the war was coming to an end, so the airplanes for which we were making parts would never fly or be used against us. The foreign workers may have had stronger feelings about manufacturing ammunition to be used against their brothers and their country. For the Jewish prisoner in general, it was not a national question. We *had* no country, as the Hungarians "like the Germans," were our enemies too.

Any damaged goods that were produced were not made deliberately to hurt the German war effort. A forced laborer told Zsofia Gottlieb Török to place correct parts among the rejects. That way they could slow the production. But there was no movement or spirit of sabotage among the prisoners in our camp. Any attempt at sabotage on the part of a Jewish prisoner would have been unthinkable. Even a large number of rejects and mistakes in production cannot be taken as proof of intent to interfere with production. The girls knew that sabotage would destroy the foundation under us. By sabotage, we would risk not only our lives but the lives of our fellow inmates.

A Sign

On a sunny day in March 1945, workers repainted the glass of the factory windows. They covered it with black paint from the outside as a protection from air raids. While they were working, suddenly we noticed the communist symbol of a sickle and hammer painted in the window. The image was visible for a few minutes and then it was covered with black paint. We stood astonished and interpreted the sign to mean that the war would soon be over.

Seeing an African

In Hungary, especially in the provinces, inmates had never met a person of color. We had seen an advertisement of a dark-skinned boy pouring black coffee, but we did not think it was realistic. In cities like Kosice, in elite and exclusive nightclubs, there were bands of colored musicians, but few of the inmates had ever visited there.

One day as we were working in the factory, a tall, very dark-skinned young man entered with buckets of water, which he poured in Ilana Sajovits Breiner's machine. I was sweeping close by and saw that everyone was staring at him with amazement. Ilana, who knew many languages, talked to him in English, but the lad did not answer. Then she tried French and, astonishingly, the young man smiled a big beautiful smile. He was so happy to tell her that he was from Africa. He wanted to speak some more, but an *Aufseherin* came around and the conversation ended. As he walked away with another warm smile and a wink of his eye, the collective gaze of the girls followed behind him. I hurried to tell the news to Erzsike and the other girls by the machines. We were all fascinated by the larger world and the people in it, while we were locked in our small corner. The German foreman was impressed that Ilana knew French. The tall black youth, however, never returned.

Various Acts of Kindness

Zsofia Gottlieb Török, who was fortunate to speak both German and French, had two foreign foremen who brought her the news. Kurt and Paul also gave her a pair of scissors, a package of thread, and a sewing needle, all of which they deposited in the basket of nails and screws by her machine.

Gabriella Klein Heimlich and other inmates once worked together with Ukrainian forced laborers shoveling coal. One day they all had a surprise. The wagon with coal arrived, and the girls noticed a small note in Hungarian saying "look for the bottom." When they dug for the bottom of the wagon, they found it was full of potatoes. It seems that Hungarian Jewish prisoners, probably men, worked with potatoes, and they wanted to send some to our camp. Gabriella and the other girls were touched by that message of solidarity. The Ukrainian workers, who were also hungry, shared the potatoes and agreed to cook some for the inmates. The women were happy to have the potatoes and the encouraging message of friendship. The SS guard who spoke Hungarian simply told them to be careful. Sharing in the good spirits, he looked the other way while the girls filled their overalls with potatoes. The loud bombing in Leipzig that we could hear in the distance may have had some influence on the guard's lenient attitude.

French Women Political Prisoners

Those who openly sabotaged factory work in Markkleeberg were the French political prisoners. They were a rebellious group who refused to aid the German war industry. Their history of arrest began on August 15, 1944, when a group of French political prisoners was deported from Paris to Germany. Men and women were then separated; the men were transferred to Buchenwald and the women taken to Ravensbrück in East Germany. From there, 500 women were transported to Heeresmuna Torgau. They stayed there until October 1944 when one group was sent back to Ravensbrück while nearly 250 French, with a few Belgian and Dutch women, were transferred to BMW Abteroda. In the factory of BMW Abteroda, the group was accused of sabotage. By the order of the Buchenwald commandant, they were sent in two groups to Markkleeberg as punishment (*strafverlegt*).[15]

The first transport of 125 French political prisoners arrived in Markkleeberg on Monday, February 12, 1945. The news spread quickly in the camp. Girls who worked outdoors in the yard hurried to inform others that there were newcomers dressed in civilian clothing, with long hair and high turbans. The women looked quite good, wearing nail polish and heavy makeup. They also had coats, gloves, and handbags, the inmates reported excitedly.[16]

The newcomers stood a long time waiting until the inmates from the storage room prepared their clothing. Then they carried it to the showers, where they met the French women for the first time. The Jewish inmates, graduates of Auschwitz, cautioned the French prisoners to hide their jewelry and valuables in their shoes. It was good advice, because the *Aufseherins* stripped them of all the clothing, documents, and jewelry that the Frenchwomen did not conceal. They received some underwear and the same dark gray overalls that we had.

We were shocked to see the Frenchwomen coming out bald after the shower. This time the *Aufseherins* did the shaving and not the prisoners as in Auschwitz. The Frenchwomen smiled bravely and winked that it would soon all be over. They were then housed in a separate barracks and each one received a blanket and a dish for food, as we had. Like soldiers they marched to the *Appel* that night.

The second transport of 125 French women being punished arrived two weeks later on February 26, 1945. They were given overalls, but, for some reason, their hair was not cut.

Some of the women from the French transports were communists; others belonged to the underground. Nelly Winkler Rochlitz, whose younger sister Rozsa was a patient in the *Revier,* met there a wounded political prisoner named Raymonde Garin. Raymonde was kind and intelligent and spoke German well. She received packages from the Red Cross, which she shared with the rest of the sick girls in the *Revier.* She was especially nice to Rozsa, who suffered from TB. Garin had been born on June 19, 1920. Raymonde was arrested with some other French resisters and deported to Germany on August 15, 1944. They were in Ravensbrück, Torgau, and BMW Abteroda. There Raymonde had a serious work accident on December 30, 1944. In February 24, 1945, on the order of Ernst John, commandant of Buchenwald, she was added to the transport of 124 French women to Junkers, Markkleeberg. During the evacuation, her French friends and inmates carried Raymonde Garin in a small carriage. She survived the Death March and the war.[17]

Dr. Marguerite Dupré, whose maiden name was Mimeur, was a nurse who helped wounded soldiers belonging to the French resistance. I met her later by the dedication of a memorial in Markkleeberg. During interrogation, a captive had mentioned her name, so she was arrested and taken to Germany. After the war, Marguerite Dupré became a physician.

Having official status as political prisoners, the Frenchwomen were treated somewhat better than the Jews. They were spared from Auschwitz and the selections, which meant that older women such as Fernande Prévost, born in 1893, were among them. Unfortunately, Fernande passed away during the Death March.[18] French girls were permitted to stay with their mothers, regardless of age. Thus Jacquile "Marie" Fleury, who was involved in the dedication of the memorial at Markkleeberg, had been arrested with and stayed in the camp together with her mother. The French prisoners were entitled to stay in touch with their families, and they received packages from home with the help of the Red Cross.

We Jews, by contrast, were taken with our family units, and most of us were wiped out totally. We had no one left back at home, which made for important emotional and psychological differences between Jewish and non-Jewish prisoners. Those of us who were in the camp remained alone or with one or two sisters and, rarely, a mother. We didn't know the fate of our menfolk.

In Markkleeberg, the Frenchwomen were given training in the small factory. A few girls were allotted to each machine. On the machine where Nelly Winkler Rochlitz worked, two Frenchwomen were assigned. They indicated with their body language that they were not interested to learn or to do any work. Nelly, who did not know French, showed the girls by pantomime that the Nazis would cut their throats, but they did not care. Eventually, the Frenchwomen sabotaged the machines by breaking the drillers on them. They were then assigned to work in the fields outside of the camp.[19]

There was a significant attitude difference between Jewish and non-Jewish prisoners regarding interference with production. Unlike us, they had the support of the Red Cross. The French knew they belonged to a viable nation that was fighting the Nazis, so sabotage had both a psychological and national value for them. Usually, a French woman prisoner had been individually involved in an act of resistance before becoming a political prisoner.

Singing as they worked, some of the Frenchwomen worked at road construction, labored in the quarry, or performed other outdoor jobs. It was March, the frozen land warmed a bit and the sunshine glittered in the grimy puddles of our camp's roads. The work became easier outside. We sometimes wished to change places with the Frenchwomen, especially on those days when we worked at night and ran to the shelters during the day. We did not know that the Frenchwomen also had to clean up after the bombing outside the camp. They were "even picking up the death," as they told Ilana Sajovits Breiner.

The French prisoners spent less time being captives than we did. They took the camp less seriously and had a lighter attitude. Those who belonged to the resistance seemed to have a special language among them. Every night before going to sleep, they stood up and sang the "*Marseillaise,*" the French national anthem.

Working in the fields outside the camp, the Frenchwomen could hide some onions or carrots in their kerchiefs and overalls, which they traded for bread and margarine. You did not have to speak, Lilly Waldman recalled, just show the merchandise. Like good business ladies, the Frenchwomen checked carefully that the bread was not too thin. The margarine they purchased for an onion, the Frenchwomen used as a cream on their faces; looks were as important to them as food. Although we generally kept separate, the French ventured to our barracks for trading.

Lucifer, who liked to search the prisoners in hopes of finding some hidden jewelry for her own use, checked the French girls carefully. She took away what they collected from the fields and punished them. Yet it did not deter the women; they continued bartering because hunger was stronger than fear.

The *Blockälteste* of the French political prisoners was a Dutch woman who wore a red beret on her head. First, the *Aufseherin* took away her hat, but she made another one. Finally, they let her wear it. She was in touch with the Dutch technician who worked with Elisabeth Stein Székely, and he asked Elisabeth to give a newspaper to the *Blockälteste* of the French girls. Elisabeth hid the paper in her shoe.

The Frenchwomen somehow managed to look chic even in their prison clothing. To cover their bald heads, they unraveled part of their mattresses and, from the threads, they knitted turbans and hats. For knitting needles they just used some sticks they found. Despite regulations, they wore turbans or kerchiefs that they fashioned in different ways. They stood separately during the *Appels* in the camp. Girls who worked outdoors, of course, had more occasions to meet them. Those who knew French, including Ilana Sajovits Breiner, could find opportunities to talk with them. The Frenchwomen were friendly, relaxed, and often smiling. They showed us the "V" sign for victory.

The French culture and language were new for us. Barbara Klein Stark recalled how we were impressed with their constant exclamations of "*Oo la la!*" Erzsike and I, who had never heard French before, were amused during a Sunday air raid that the Frenchwomen danced to a chant of "*Oo la la.*" The women, who had looked so good when they arrived, soon became skeletal living on our diet, however. One day we noticed how they collected the dandelions that grew in an area next to our barracks. They selected the smaller leaves because the larger ones were too bitter, then washed and ate them as a salad. We looked at them with curiosity and astonishment; our diet at home did not include green salads. To eat a tomato would have been a daring adventure to us. Later, in the Death March, girls used greens, but they cooked them first. Among the Frenchwomen were some who spoke Hungarian. They asked Elisabeth Stein Székely for old Hungarian recipes they could use after the war.

The Frenchwomen and we had a similar present, but a different future. In the camp, we shared a common fate: The Germans were our mutual enemies and we both dreamed of victory and of going home. For the French, their homes, neighbors, and country were waiting for them. Our homecoming was muted, with only sad reality to greet us. We will meet the Frenchwomen again during the Death March when, under stress, some anti-Semitism surfaced.

Before saying goodbye to the Junkers' factory and its workers, we will observe a bit more the actions of German civilian employees at the small plant closer to the center of the city. The relationships there were more direct and personal, which can be seen amid events leading to the camp's final days.

11

Smaller Factories, the Final Days, and Evacuation of the Camp

Zwenkau

In 1944, as the bombing of Germany increased, most of Junkers' manufacturing was distributed into smaller, unknown factories near the major Junkers' production sites. In Zwenkau, not far from Markkleeberg, a brewery was taken over and established as a transfer division of Junkers' engine production plant.

Fifty prisoners from Markkleeberg were selected to work in Zwenkau. Among them were Lilly Waldman and her sister Erzsébet. Each morning, they traveled about half an hour in the train's last compartment to Zwenkau. The women received winter coats, kerchiefs, and gloves, but they still had to wear the old Dutch wooden shoes. Their wake-up call was at three o'clock in the morning, which was especially hard in the darkness, cold, and snow of winter.

The inmates traveled by train with German civilians. It was wrenching for Lilly Waldman and the other prisoners to see the civil population living their lives in freedom. The factory was quite a distance from the train station in Zwenkau. As they walked at dawn, some of the homes they passed already showed lighted windows. The prisoners could see people having breakfast in their warm kitchens or dining rooms. Meanwhile, Lilly and the others trudged in the knee-deep snow that stuck to the soles of their wooden shoes. Struggling to keep her balance, Lilly noticed a window in which hung the same curtains as they had at home. She looked at her sister with disbelief, and they both had similar longings and memories. They said that next time they would not look; but they could scarcely wait each morning to pass by.

One of the two guards who escorted them was Joseph, whom Lilly remembered as a short man. He was quite decent and let them walk at the tempo they were able to manage. The guards stayed in the factory, but they left the prisoners alone. The plant in Zwenkau was not organized for slave labor, and both the treatment and the food were better. The girls liked to work there, except that they were so tired that they needed to visit the bathroom frequently just to close their eyes for a few minutes.

Lilly had a German foreman who limped and who lived in Leipzig. He talked to them freely. Also there was Vim, a short Dutch technician, who left food for the girls as he passed by. Lilly worked on a chiseling and polishing machine that was large and intimidating. She especially dreaded the big wheel that needed particular attention to start and stop. Lilly was afraid that it would separate from the machine and that she would not be able to control it. One morning, her fears actualized. Lilly pushed the wrong button and the wheel collapsed, shutting up the whole machine. She was terrified, sure that they would kill or severely punish her. Luckily, a Polish foreman saw Lilly's desperation and hurriedly replaced the wheel without submitting an official report. The SS did not find out about it, said Lilly in our interview, still shaken even then from the thought of possible consequences.

Talking to Lilly Waldman, I realized that two of my relatives—the Linder sisters, Lenke and Hajnal—were in Markkleeberg. They were my mother's first cousins from Sátoraljaújhely.[1] We had met them visiting grandmother there. We were proud to be their cousins because people always said how beautiful they were. In Markkleeberg, the sisters were good friends and partners in the five-person line on *Appel* with Lilly Waldman, her sister, and a relative. They all worked together in Zwenkau. It would have been so good to know in Markkleeberg that we had relatives in the camp. In a crowd of 1,300 women, if they were not in our barracks or workplace, it was hard to identify people with short hair in prison uniform and especially when last names were rarely used. The Linder sisters survived the war but passed away young.

The inmates continued their daily travel to Zwenkau even when bombing damaged the railroads around February 1945. Later, when the plant received a direct hit, the girls were reassigned back to the factory in Markkleeberg.

In addition to securing production sites in smaller, mostly unknown locations, Junkers also had plans to build underground facilities. One of them was in a former mine in Heilbronn. Among the slave laborers working there was my future husband, Meier Stessel.

Until I researched the history of the camp in Markkleeberg, I did not realize that we had a shared connection to Junkers. Meier worked mostly on the night shift, digging and hollowing out the mine for the foundation. It was extremely hard labor, and he was very distressed. In addition to the tough job, he had to breathe the salty mineral air. After three months, the wiry eighteen-year-old felt that he had reached the limit of his endurance. When a boy from his hometown, Alfred Eidinger, was selected for a transport, Meier agreed to take his place. Alfred remained together with his cousin and friends. Meier left with the group of one hundred considered unfit for work. Switching places was a dangerous move. Meier, so desperate to leave the night shift at the mine, took the risk. Luckily, he and the group were not taken back to Auschwitz but to Dachau where eventually Meier was liberated by the American forces. Alfred Eidinger also survived together with his cousin and friends. Junkers' plans for a subterrarrean production facility in Helbronn were not realized.

The Former Chocolate Factory

A group of specially selected girls was assigned to work in the former chocolate factory in Markkleeberg. As enticing as the name sounds, airplane parts were manufactured by Junkers there, too. The site was about a twenty-minute walk from the camp. To get to the factory, one had to pass through a populated section of the town. For public relations purposes, the Nazis gave the inmates coats to wear over their overalls. At the front of the line marched a German soldier with a bayonet; at the back, another soldier; and on the sides were *Aufseherins*. The unarmed women guards stayed with the prisoners all day in the factory.

The area was very pretty, with Gothic-style apartment houses and white gardenias on the windowsills. The street started to fill with the early morning passersby, offering the prisoners a fleeting contact with the universe of the living. People dressed nicely; they were free, conducting their normal lives. Cruelty and degradation was not their share, thought Nelly Winkler Rochlitz, one of the daily marchers from the camp.

When it was not raining, there were even more people in the street. Some walked silently by; others, survivors noticed, stole glances at them from the windows of their apartments. There were also those who turned around, whistled, and shouted "dirty Jews!" Hearing them, the girls looked for consolation to the distance, where houses destroyed by the bombing could be seen.[2] The majority of citizens watched the prisoners with indifference as they were led by the armed guards and showed no sign of pity. They were already used to marches like that. Yet, after the war, very few admitted to knowing or even hearing about slave laborers.

The building of the former chocolate factory was a four-story baroque-style structure. Above the gate, high in the middle of the arch was a life-size elephant statue. In big golden letters that could be seen from a distance was written "RIGVET," the factory name.

The factory looked like a castle surrounded by trees. It had four floors up and three flights down. A lighted sign above it advertised coffee, tea, and chocolate. The girls who first went there believed they would be in heaven; imagining that they were tasting the chocolate already. When they

The former chocolate and Junkers' factory, as it looked in 2000. Survivors from left to right: Hava Hartmann Kleinberg, Naomi Cohen Levi, the author, Zahava Szász Stessel, and Kathy Zelmanovitz Goldstein.

entered, however, they realized that they were still slave laborers in a Junkers factory, producing engine parts for a futuristic pilotless airplane.[3]

As they walked up the four flights, Frau Elizabeth Anders, the manager of the plant, was waiting for them. She greeted the girls with a speech saying that they were special to be chosen for that factory. She hoped they would be good, conscientious workers who followed instructions and gained appreciation. The girls laughed at the word *appreciation* and waited for the end of that high-level talk.

Shortly the learning session began. The group descended two floors down to the basement. There was a big board where Frau Anders wrote down technical terms. The women had to study both theory and practice. Frau Anders also introduced the different parts, scales, and variable screws that belonged to the work. It was impossible for the women to remember all those complicated technical terms when they barely knew a few everyday words in German. Girls who had been working there since the first transport from Bergen-Belsen, such as our friend Elza Reich Szamosi, warned the newcomers that the discipline was strict and the work hard.

The next day was another study session. The women did not remember the words they had been taught the previous day, which made Frau Anders angry. Lea Keri Lesem was fearful that if she did not know the names and the uses of the different tools, she would be accused of sabotage. Lee Katz Yoskovitz also recalled it being very scary. To help the situation, translator and inmate Adel Hamer joined the group. She explained the theory of the work and interpreted Frau Anders's words. The women were then assigned to the machines, but, for a few hours each day, they continued to study the names of the parts they used. Eventually, the girls began to like the sessions, mostly because they could sit down.

Hitler Youth (*G. Hitler-Jugend*)

Boys sixteen to eighteen belonging to *Hitler-Jugend* also worked at the machines. They were members of the organization set up by Adolf Hitler in 1933 for educating and training male youths aged ten and older in Nazi principles. By 1936, it had become a state agency that all young "Aryan" Germans were expected to join. The youths lived a Spartan life of dedication, fellowship, and Nazi conformity, with little parental guidance. Late in the war they were used as frontline solders and also worked in arms production.

Hitler-Jugends in the factory answered the roll call like soldiers; each was given soup and vitamins. After that, they took their places by the machines. The work began with the sounds of filing, grading, hammering, grinding, and polishing. After completing his shift, one *Hitler-Jugend* of about seventeen years had to show Nelly Winkler Rochlitz how to work on the machine. The boy was not pleased with the assignment; he started to talk fast: "*So machen, so machen,*" and then hurried away. Nelly had no idea what to do. She was petrified that if she broke something it would cost her life. She stood anxiously by the machine until the main engineer, sitting by his table behind the glass window that surrounded the area, noticed her. He came over and asked why she did not work. Nelly, who spoke German, explained that the young man did not really show her the work and she was afraid to touch the machine already in motion. The German engineer called back the youngster from the *Hitler-Jugends* group just as he was leaving for the day. The boy returned, and the engineer gave him two slaps on his face. The *Hitler-Jugend* threw an angry look toward Nelly, but then explained to her slowly what to do. Other new workers who had difficulties with the machines were aided by inmates already in the plant.

Inmates worked on an assembly line, cutting heavy iron bars, filing, polishing, and measuring the parts to the thousandth milligram of accuracy. The work required attention and endurance. Veins quickly swelled on the hands of the fragile Jewish women. Lea Keri Lesem was assigned to a drilling machine with wheels, screws, drillers, knives, files, and graders. The work needed special alertness. With a slight oversight the fine driller could easily break, and the danger of being accused of sabotage was always looming. A bit of haste could also bring about an accident and bodily injury.

In addition to hunger, Nelly Winkler Rochlitz was faced suddenly with another concern one day. She accidentally broke the drill on her machine. The Meister, or main production manager, not known for his goodwill, grew angry, scolded, and threatened the anxious Nelly. He changed the broken part, and Nelly attended the machine with much apprehension. She knew that her fate now depended on the action of the German civilian. Would he send a note, as was his custom, to Knittel? Nelly would only find out that evening at the camp. Until then, she shuddered through the day, all the way back to the camp, and during the long *Appel.* Fortunately, the Meister had not acted on his threat. He knew that Nelly was punished anyway by the long day of terrifying thoughts.

Besides completing delicate work requiring endurance and concentration, the tired, hungry girls had to fulfill a daily quota. Although the survivors I spoke with did not recall anyone being punished, the women worked under constant supervision to their full capacity.

Mistakes in production became a problem for those who took over the machines from the *Hitler-Jugends.* The boys left their damaged work on the table, and the foremen blamed the Jewish women for the bad job. It was upsetting and stressful for the inmates, recalled Lee Katz Yoskovitz. Finally, they got the courage to request that the work by the *Hitler-Jugends* be taken away at the completion of the boys' shift. Thus, it would be clear who had made the mistakes. The foreman agreed, and eventually most of the *Hitler-Jugends* stopped working there because their work was unsatisfactory.

Some girls, like Elza Reich Szamosi, who occasionally made a mistake in production, placed the defective part at the end of the pile, hoping that the foreman who came to check would not notice. Others, such as Lee Katz Yoskovitz, put the parts with the mistakes in their sleeves and discarded them on the way home. In any case, girls worried when their parts did not come out right.

At 5:45, the work stopped. The women cleaned the machines and the floor around them, organized in five-person lines, and started back to the camp. The street was again crowded with well-dressed people, including children. They looked indifferently at the inmates being led on the road. The stores were open, and the windows displayed enticing delicacies such as salami, smoked meat, and sweets that tormented the starving prisoners. The girls smelled the bread, cakes, and other foods, licking their lips and swallowing deeply. They watched enviously as customers exited with new purchases. The girls wondered if they would ever be able to shop freely once again.

On one of the storefronts, Nelly Winkler Rochlitz noticed a sign with the name of Winkler. She looked at it each time she passed by. What would the owner say, knowing that his name was the same as hers, Nelly wondered. Still absorbed in their thoughts and dreams, the prisoners reached the camp. Passing the gate, they met another group of inmates who had just finished their work in construction outside. Girls who were not fit for factory jobs were usually sent there. Waiting to return their shovels, axes, and wheelbarrows, the girls looked at those coming from the factory with tired and envious gazes.

The Supervising Civilian German Staff

There was a large room on the fourth floor in the small factory where all the work was done. Frau Elizabeth Anders, the factory manager, was always there, walking from one row to the next and keeping an eye on every girl. One never knew when she would suddenly appear. Under the mask of a forced smile, Frau Anders was basically a mean woman who made sure that the inmates stood twelve hours at the machines with a thirty-minute break. She was right there with more work when one was caught up—she did not want anyone to have a chance to sit down. Even when she was not next to you, Elza Reich Szamosi recalled, she saw everything from her desk. If a girl leaned a bit on the machine, Frau Anders was right there reminding her to stand up straight.

Frau Anders's helper was Fräulein Elza, whose last name was either Teichgraber or Teichgerefer. She was an "old maid," and girls had no praise for her, either. She was there to please Frau Anders. Another woman forelady was named Agnes; she did not care so much and left the girls alone. Besides the women, there were six men supervisors. The Meister and the main engineer appeared from time to time, adding to the tense atmosphere.[4]

On the night shift, the inmates usually worked with three foremen, without Frau Anders and the engineer, which made the work more pleasant. Toward March, the air raids increased at night. That brought some relief. The time in the shelter shortened the number of hours by the machines; but it was also hard for the tired, undernourished women to run up and down the four flights of stairs.

Among the foremen was a friendly old German civilian who used to sing or yodel in the manner of Swiss and Tyrolean mountaineers. Girls called him the "yodeling foreman." When the inmates were low in spirit due to the actions of supervisors or an *Aufseherin,* he whispered that the end was near. At first the women mistrusted his friendliness. They thought that he was either teasing or testing their reactions. Regardless of the girls' response, however, the old man continued to tell them quietly about the development of the war. He also said how much he hated Hitler and his ideas; but the girls, experienced in German lies and deceptions, just could not believe him. There were other good-natured German civilian workers too. One gave Lea Keri Lesem a small mirror and a comb: a luxury beyond belief.

Despite the tight supervision, love found its way amid the machines in the small factory too. Hans, a young foreign technical assistant, fell in love with a pretty slave laborer. He used every opportunity to be in the area close to her machine, whispering the latest news of the war.[5] As with many unfinished stories during the war, details and progress of the romance were lost. The women I interviewed could not remember the name of the lovely girl, but they all recalled her camaraderie in dispersing Hans's news faithfully, giving everyone information about the war—and hope.

The Ladies' Room

There was a fancy bathroom on the first floor, and on the door was written in large letters, "For Women from Abroad." The girls were surprised by the mild expression. They had by now been called dogs, stupid cows, and many other derogatory names. The bathroom itself was a pleasant surprise too—it had full-length mirrors, sinks, and a clock. The flush toilets were behind doors that could be closed. At the beginning, if an inmate needed the bathroom, she locked her machine and left. Later, rigid rules were set; but enforcement depended on the harshness of the *Aufseherin* on duty. One named Anni allowed only mid-morning and mid-afternoon breaks to use the toilet. Anni was in love with the head engineer, and, to the girls' chagrin, she arranged to be at the factory daily.[6]

One day, Nelly Winkler Rochlitz had urgently needed to go to the bathroom during work. Anni decided that it was not time for a break yet and told Nelly she should wait another hour. Nelly was unable to concentrate on her work and told Frau Anders the reason. To help Nelly, who was a favorite of hers, and to avoid confrontation with the SS, Frau Anders took a box of nails and told Anni that she needed Nelly to help her. The two then went to the first floor and Nelly used the bathroom. Frau Anders encouraged her to take her time and waited patiently for her. The grateful Nelly contemplated Frau Anders's dual character and the contradictions of camp life.

Hardships and Accidents

The same Frau Anders who was so helpful to Nelly did not hesitate to place inmates on a dangerously defective machine. During a daytime shift, Erzsébet Friedmann remembered, above the different noises, someone screaming, "Oh, my god!" An eighteen-year-old girl, Hermina Schwarz, whom everyone knew by her friendly smile, had been seriously injured. Part of her face was cut away by the machine. Hermina, who had been very pretty, was taken to the hospital in Leipzig, according to the *Aufseherin* who escorted her there. The women were shocked by the accident and believed that it would be better for her if she died rather than to live so disfigured. Miraculously, both of Hermina's eyes were saved, and she survived. Erzsébet Friedmann met her in Budapest after the war. Hermina had been through a series of surgeries and looked quite good. Hermina met her Dutch husband, Philip Schelder, at the hospital in Leipzig. He had converted to Judaism, and the young couple was on their way to Amsterdam to the husband's well-to-do family when she met Erzsébet Friedmann.[7]

The same machine that injured Hermina Schwarz also wounded Jolán Flesch. It was a complicated device where the worker pushed a paddle by foot while holding by hand the steel bar to be cut in several places. If something went wrong, instead of cutting the metal, the machine could sever the finger of the worker. The job was difficult and required careful coordination. Jolán was too hungry and tired for such concentrated work. As she moved, the machine cut off three fingers from her left hand. The girls were very upset and scared that it would also happen to them, especially at that time when the air raids were so frequent and they had to hurry to turn off the machines and run to the shelter. Jolan Flesch, born August 23, 1910, in Hernádszurdok, was bleeding profusely. She also was taken to the hospital in Leipzig. The girls felt very sympathetic, and some were predicting the worst; but Jolán did survive, according to Nelly Winkler Rochlitz, who met her after the war.

The machine that caused all the injuries was defective. Another young girl, whose name Nelly could not recall, was also injured after Frau Anders insisted she use the machine. Erzsébet Friedmann and Nelly both believed that she assigned girls whom she did not like to that machine to punish them.[8] Nelly noticed Frau Anders and Fräulein Elza Teichgraber exchanging glimpses when the accidents occurred. We do not really know what happened, but there was certainly no responsibility or protection for the Jewish slave laborers. We were in the hands and at the whims of those dealing with us. A malicious civilian work organizer could harm us just as easily as the SS could.

Air Raid

The work in the factory stopped only when there was a work alarm. Many times, the girls heard the siren outside, the buzzing of the airplanes, and even the sound of bombings; but they had to wait for the special alarm. The German workforce went down to the basement of the factory during air raids. There they had especially built shelters with beds and accommodations. The Jewish prisoners were led to the shelters on the street.

When the work alarm sounded, the girls shut off the machines and lined up in five-person rows to be counted. By the time they reached the first floor, the sky was filled with enemy planes. Outside on the street, frightened residents rushed to shelters with babies and baby carriages. Nelly and the other girls were pleased to know that they were not the only victims. Sometimes disregarding safety, the girls observed with interest the enemy in distress. Usually the sound of a large explosion made the group run quickly to the shelter. As the planes passed by, the alarm sounded and the women's slavery and imprisonment continued unabated.

The air raids provided a bit of a break from the tiring work by the machines. They were especially welcomed around three o'clock, when all were ready for a rest after standing all day. The raids were no longer fun in the final days of March 1945, when the bombs were aimed directly at the factory. One time, the inmates had scarcely reached the shelter when they heard the sound of a tremendous explosion. The bombs missed their target and fell in the forest nearby. There they hit fleeing German families, killing some people. Back in the factory, the yodeling foreman told the girls that liberation was only a few days away.

The Yodeling Foreman

The old German civilian worker whom the girls mistrusted at first turned out to be a genuine antifascist German citizen who suffered from Hitler's agenda. As the inmates got to know him, they appreciated his singing and his encouraging words. The war will be over soon, he said, and he hoped to visit Hungary for its tasty salami and Tokay wine. Taking out his notebook, he wrote down the addresses of the girls. He also showed them a family photograph in which a smiling wife, two handsome boys, and a fifteen-year-old blonde girl looked relaxed in a peacetime setting. The girl, by 1945, was a young widow, and he had not heard from his boys in two years. Wiping a fugitive tear, he soon returned to yodeling his favorite tunes. The girls were touched by the old man's tenderness, and they were sympathetic to his family's adversities.

During our interview, Nelly Winkler Rochlitz remembered the yodeling foreman. She wanted so much to know what had happened to him and his family. Nelly still regretted not being able to say goodbye or to thank the old man for lifting their spirits. I myself realized fully only during this research that the German population also suffered from Hitler and his followers' distorted minds and aspirations. I had been nursing my physical and emotional scars all those years, and just the word *German* was enough to ignite my anguish, fear, and abhorrence. I did not even need to see a German face—or maybe I already had the face etched in mind: That of Mengele robbing me of my mother and grandmother and threatening to separate me from my sister. There were also the other terrifying SS guards in their high boots who carved permanent lesions in my heart.

The Final Days

In the winter of 1945, the circle of the front lines in the east and the west closed around the original borders of the German Reich. The last fighting activities were carried out on German soil in March and April. Marching columns of GIs advanced through Thüringen into the territory of middle Germany. The Red Army crossed the Oder River. In the east, the battle for Berlin began.[9]

The atmosphere in the small factory was very tense. The German staff left for a meeting and to listen to a special radio announcement, leaving the workplace unsupervised. The women used their freedom to joke around and discuss the war situation.[10]

Back in the camp, the alarms increased in March and April of 1945; the Allies were bombing the railroad close to the barracks. We were tired after the night shift, and Erzsike and I only wanted to sleep, but hearing the siren and reluctant to risk punishment, we jumped out of bed. We did not need to dress because we slept in our clothing. We only had to put on the wooden shoes and run to the shelter. On the way, we noticed how many women continued to sleep regardless of the danger and punishment. They knew that the *Aufseherins* would not stay behind to check on those who remained in the barracks. They were running, those brave tormentors of ours, toward the shelter while holding hands, scared for their lives.

The frequency and intensity of the bombings heightened our anticipation. The sound of the airplanes and the explosions made us hopeful. The thought of freedom, however, played its game with us. At the beginning, we were not afraid and lightheartedly looked at the worrying guards and *Aufseherins.* Then, at some point, we started to realize our danger and that we might not survive for the liberation that was so close. One Saturday night toward the end, we were terribly afraid, locked in our barracks, when an air attack started and the blast of the shells could be heard moving nearer and nearer. Even the ground was shaking beneath us. The bombs were so close that we could feel the change in air pressure in our beds. We had never heard such a loud noise, and it made our ears hurt. We tried to keep calm all night; no one cried. In the morning, we had to go to work as usual.

Although they did not look for us during air raids in the final days, the *Aufseherins* still came to torture us. As soon as we fell asleep after the night shift, Lucifer would chase us out with all kinds of excuses about room searches and room changes. Those who were a bit slow were attacked with her rubber nightstick. We remember a girl named Ica bleeding from the head after Lucifer hit her. Erzsike was pulling me desperately, as everyone ran screaming out of Lucifer's reach.

Once, at the beginning of April 1945, bombs fell right next to our barracks. It was daytime, and after the earlier experience at night, we all wanted to be in the shelter. This was lucky, because our barracks received almost a direct hit and the windows broke from the pressure. Had it been at night with everyone inside, the casualties would have been high. In the *Revier,* the sick usually stayed with the doctors and the nurses; but that time, the air pressure broke the doors. Sick girls, among them Nelly's sister, Rozsa, came crying to the shelter wrapped in blankets. We were so traumatized by the bombings that, when we heard planes above us in Israel after the war, we were disproportionately distressed.

The Last Sunday in the Camp

That last Sunday afternoon in April 8, 1945, was maybe the first time that they left us alone. Outside it was nice and sunny. We cleaned our overalls with water that we brought to our room from the washroom. Spring, with its sunny brightness, cleared our thoughts and lightened a bit our minds. We were energized by the hope that change was coming and that we would be going home. The word *home* had all the charm of family, peace, and shelter for us. Just to go home was our entire hope and constant thought.

On Monday April 9, 1945, the main engineer in the small factory was nervous and depressed. He lit one cigarette after another. Finally he walked away, retreating back to his room. The yodeling foreman came with the news that Frau Anders's home in Leipzig had been hit during an air attack. The women felt humbly that God had His ways. The German civilian staff gathered around to hear about the latest broadcast. As the girls looked out the windows, they saw large red posters falling from the sky. Civilians went out in the deserted streets to pick up the posters.

There was almost no work by that time. The engineer came out of his room and noticed a girl marking on a sheet that depicted an airplane diagram. He tore it up, saying there would be no need for it. An *Aufseherin* who was new at escorting the girls told them that the radio had announced the advancement of Allied troops toward Leipzig. She showed them a photo of her widowed mother and said she would be happy to have her freedom to choose what to do with her life. Elza Reich Szamosi and other girls were still afraid because one of the forced laborers told them he overheard the guards saying that the SS would rather blow up the factory than leave it for the enemy. Elza was relieved at the end of the day to leave the place and be back at the camp.

From that point on, there was no work in the factory at all. Frau Anders, red-eyed and crying, ripped the airplane model diagrams from the walls near the machines. She burned them as well as other documents. Then the staff left for a meeting and the inmates were alone. Nelly looked out the window, which was open, and noticed that the streets were deserted, but that in the yards small fires were burning. She called to the other girls, who looked and saw being piled in the nearest fires photos of *Aufseherins* and soldiers in Nazi uniform, SS membership cards, letters, and copies of Hitler's book, *Mein Kampf.* The girls were scared that, at the last minute, they might be eliminated too.

Nelly was concerned for Rozsa who was still in the *Revier,* and Hajnal her older sister who worked in the large factory. The German staff returned and, even before the end of the work day, the girls lined up and the group left with the *Aufseherins* and the guards as usual.

In the Large Factory

On our way to the large factory on April 9, 1945, we enjoyed the mild spring breeze. At work, one of the forced laborers also overheard some conversation that implied the Germans would rather blow up the factory than let it fall into enemy hands. I just wanted to be close to Erzsike's machine. In the evening, we were relieved to get out. From a distance, we heard sirens and, as we came to the block, there was the sound of a large explosion. We just hoped that it would mean that the war would be over soon.

On April 11, 1945, Buchenwald was liberated by the 6th Armored Division of the U.S. Army, and the Allied forces stood at the gates of Leipzig. We could feel the tension at work and in the barracks. The camp lost its calm appearance and its daily routine. Yet, up to the last minute, the Germans did not reveal their plans. Knittel gave a speech telling us that we should not believe rumors. When the end of the war came, he would be the first to let us know, he said. We did not have to worry: Markkleeberg was better than the other camps where we were before, and he, Knittel claimed, was always good to us—but he knew that we wanted to go back to our homes. It was strange to hear him speaking so softly and praising himself. We knew how mean he was, but there was always the hope that he might change for the better toward the end.

On April 12, the German civilian workers at the large factory where there was still a little work were pale and nervous. Erzsébet Frank's foreman, however, who was never satisfied, still looked for mistakes. It was amazing how many of the Germans carried on with their tenacity and iron determination as if nothing had changed, despite the fact that the Allies were almost at the gates.

At the quality control section, the girls continued to check the work, but the *Aufseherins* stopped walking between the lines to supervise. Later in the day, the sound of war grew stronger, and everyone stopped working. I stood by Erzsike's machine with my broom. Then, suddenly, Knittel appeared. He walked around smiling, hiding the truth, so good at keeping up appearances. Everyone was waiting for the coming events. We were also hungry because the night before we had not received our bread portions. The German foremen and engineers were confused, but Knittel acted as if nothing was happening and continued his tour from hall to hall. We were concerned that maybe the Germans would take our lives before they left the camp. The more optimistic girls reasoned that they would not do it; our moods alternated between fear and hopefulness.

The girls who worked in the cloth storage area found the place turned over by the *Aufseherins,* who were looking for unmarked civilian clothing to make their escape. An SS soldier showed Vera Deutsch De Vit, who worked in the laundry, that under his uniform he wore civilian clothing. They were all ready to escape.

The engineers in the factory were cleaning out their desks and packing. Erzsike hugged me warmly. We were still afraid to believe it, but maybe the end to our ordeal was coming. We would be going home, we thought, to see our parents and grandparents. Again we would know how to live without hunger, cold, fear, and humiliation. We tried to believe that the Germans would not have time to transfer us to another camp and would not kill us at that late stage of the war. The Americans were already in Leipzig. If not now, then by the morning we would be free, said the French foreman. Everything seemed to be going the way we had hoped. Then Ilona Eisler Glatstein, who was marking the days, reminded us that tomorrow would be Friday the thirteenth.

That night we could not sleep because of the heavy bombing. Trembling, we stayed locked inside the barracks. Bombing that aimed at the camp and the factory achieved a direct hit on the small red-roofed one- or two-family homes just over the fence from the camp. Ironically, those were my "dream houses" that reminded me of our own home. Seeing the houses burning, I had a strange feeling of fear mixed with some sense of justice. Meanwhile, the sound of war died out and all was quiet. We did not know what was happening and grew anxious that the lull in fighting would give the Germans time to lead us away. Then, gradually, the buzz of airplanes and bombing changed into the resonance of cannons and artillery. The sounds grew louder as they came closer.

On Friday, April 13, 1945, the guns were so close that we felt the shaking of the earth after each "boom" of cannon fire. We knew that the American forces were nearby. The girls who cleaned the offices at the SS headquarters told us that Knittel had been consulting with someone on the telephone all morning. Fearing they would be held responsible for their criminal acts, members of the SS tried to find a way out. Orders for the destruction of the camp and then counterorders—that the staff should demonstrate good behavior and innocence—alternated with one another.

The prisoners, meanwhile, were given some choices to make also. Those who worked inside the camp, such as Irene Keisler Schnur, the hairdresser, were told by a Dutch forced laborer that the wire had been cut and she could escape with her sister to the forests nearby. Irene decided not to take the chance and stayed with the group.

Gabriella Braver Kosinka received an offer from Hans Guenter, a civilian with whom she worked. Hans was living with his mother, and he offered to hide Gabriella in the attic. Gabriella thanked him, but she opted for the security of the group and the company of her cousin Rozsi Bauer.

Gabriella had also been told that the electric wire fence would be cut for those who wanted to escape. Yet she decided to stay with her cousin, who was reluctant to take the risk of the unknown.

One Minute of Liberation

Later in the morning of April 13, 1945, a hastily built platform was set up next to the swimming pool, opposite the *Appelplatz,* and all members of the camp were ordered for an *Appel.* The prisoners lined up block after block. Shortly Knittel appeared together with his staff and four civilian members of the Junkers' management. Then Knittel spoke; he emphasized each word:

> Today is Friday—but for you it is Sunday, because you will be free this day. The American Army is at the gates to conquer the city. I will leave with my soldiers, as we are needed to join the fight for the motherland at the other front. You will continue to work at the factory, and eventually the Red Cross will take over the camp. I say goodbye and please forgive me if sometimes I was too strict; but in a crowd it had to be this way. I was guarding you like I was your father. I wish that God will lead you all home.

Zsuzsanna Csanyi, the translator, repeated Knittel's words in Hungarian. One of the inmates from Sátoraljaújhely greeted Knittel and the Junkers' representatives. I was afraid even to smile to show my feelings of happiness that I did not yet know how to handle. I looked at Erzsike and started to cry. Some girls were screaming and dancing from excitement. The French prisoners sang the "*Marseillaise.*"

Meanwhile, additional officers from the factory arrived. The manager thanked us for the work we had done and for our efforts that allowed the production to continue until the end. He promised that our food supply would improve. "The *Oberscharführer* will leave the camp, and the SS connection will stop." We would all be Junkers workers, the director asserted.

If not for other impending developments, this would be the happy ending that we so wished for to our story. Unfortunately, it did not turn out that way. We would be passing more minefields and drifting on the highways and byways of Germany as our hardship, punctuated by occasional miracles, continued.

Junkers' manager had not yet finished his speech when the SS guard we called Tischler ran up with a broad smile and presented a telegram to Knittel. Interrupting the Junkers' executive, Knittel announced that, according to instructions from Berlin, he had to evacuate the camp, including the prisoners. Then he read us the detailed evacuation order. We would be transferred to another camp ten kilometers away. There they would merge us with other prisoners. No one should dare to hide, because the Gestapo, notorious for its brutal methods and operations, was on its way. They would check every corner and shoot anyone they found. We had to leave in an organized manner, and no one could remain in the camp.

Inmates doubted the sincerity of Knittel's speech. To prepare for the evacuation required time and consultation with the SS headquarters. They believed that Knittel knew already that we had to evacuate the camp, and that the whole speech had been staged as another of the German tricks with which we were so familiar in our camp existence.

"Evacuation" turned out to be the euphemism for the Death March, initiated at the order of SS *Reichführer* Heinrich Himmler. He sought to transfer the prisoners, still a useful workforce, deeper into Germany and away from the Russian front. To prevent witnesses of the crimes committed from speaking out, the SS was also determined not to allow concentration camp prisoners to fall into enemy hands. Shortly before the German government collapsed in the spring of 1945, camps were evacuated and inmates moved to larger centers. The Death Marches can be considered as the last organized criminal acts of the Nazi reign.

The sub-camps received different information every day on how they must transport the inmates to Czechoslovakia, according to Dr. Seidel, a researcher and senior executive at the Buchenwald memorial. The order was probably given from Buchenwald before it was occupied by the American Army. We do not know the purpose of Knittel's speech about us continuing to work in the factory. It is possible that, after Buchenwald's liberation, Knittel had no clear direction. Apart from occasional contact with higher echelons of the SS command, the SS men in charge of the actual transports were completely on their own, writes Yehuda Bauer.[11] In any case, it was a sad turn of events. Freedom had seemed so close, and it was so sweet and engaging. That genuine initial joy of liberty never came back to us. When we *were* eventually free, we in no way felt the hope and elation that we had during those few short minutes of "liberation."

Evacuation of the Camp

In Markkleeberg, when the end was so close and our hopes so high, the Germans prepared an additional station on the road to death. All of us who survived the selections in Auschwitz-Birkenau, who suffered anguish in additional camps and worked as slave laborers, had now to endure a forced wandering. It was one more unfathomable event at the time, as fate toyed with our lives.

The *Appel* ended and we had to get ready for the road. Knittel forbade us to take our blankets, because we would have to walk quickly and the blanket would be heavy for us to carry. We could take one coat each from the storage room. They could not give us food for the road because the supply had not arrived, but we would receive a meal in the camp of destination.

The soup stood unguarded in the containers when we returned to our barracks in great confusion. Girls started to open it, and soon the cry of those who were burned by the hot soup was heard. Laju, our *Blockälteste,* arrived and began to divide the lunch. Luckily, we still received a bit, but those in line behind us reached an empty container. During the bread distribution we were less fortunate. There was no arrangement and each girl grabbed as much as she could. We were unable to even get near it. Then we heard that the cellar with the rutabagas was open. The hungry crowd attacked the carefully guarded storage place. Everyone was running to get a rutabaga. Erzsike pulled me with her, but we could not hold hands in the fighting and pushing crowd. She let go of my hand, and I worried as she disappeared among the multitude. Finally I saw her—tousled, disheveled, and empty-handed. Klára Spitz Snitzler, our friend, succeeded in getting two of the round-shaped rutabagas. She quickly passed one to me. Starving, after the little bit of soup and no bread, we took turns biting into the raw round rutabaga. Then we noticed Ilona Eisler Glatstein and her sister looking so hungry and sad on the day that should have been our liberation, so we let them have some bites of ours.

Returning our blankets, we were supposed to receive coats from storage. Everyone wanted the few that were without red marks on the back. As the confusion and disorder grew, many received no coat at all. Erzsike and I were among them. Suddenly we heard terrifying screams. An inmate had been forgotten, locked in the punishment cell. Women rushed to alert the guards, who came half an hour later. When the petrified girl was finally released, she fainted from anxiety.

Before leaving our barracks on that Friday evening, we sang "Shalom Eleihem, Malahei Hashalom" with Rebbetzin Erzsébet Friedmann and the other girls. Greeting the Sabbath raised our moral and emotional security a bit. We also said goodbye to the room that had witnessed our sufferings. My eyes drifted over Vera's bed, remembering her coughing throughout those icy winter nights. I had some premonition that our fates were intertwined in some way. Vera, meanwhile, stayed in the *Revier* with her deteriorating condition. Erzsike, standing next to me, was absorbed in her own thoughts and tribulations. Outside, on the *Appelplatz,* the SS personnel were assembling with their backpacks and blankets.

In the *Revier,* those who were able to walk left. Sick girls collected their strength and stood on *Appel.* It was heartbreaking for the relatives of those who were too sick to join. Rozsa, the youngest of the Winkler sisters, suffered from pneumonia and TB. When the evacuation came, Rozsa could not get out of bed; but her sisters, Nelly and Hajnal, were determined not to leave her. Ready to share her fate, they both lay down next to Rozsa, saying that they were sick, too. Knittel came to inspect and told them to leave, but Nelly and Hajnal refused. They stayed even when the guards, with their German shepherds, looked for deserters. Knittel returned; but busy with his own exit strategy, he only told the girls to join the marchers and then left them alone. Looking around, Nelly and Hajnal found a small carriage. The SS had prepared it to carry their belongings, but then decided to use the large one and make the inmates pull it. Nelly took the small carriage and a straw mattress from the *Revier,* and they placed their sick sister on it to take with them on the road. There was also Raymonde Garin, the Frenchwoman mentioned earlier, who could not walk. Her friends from among the other French prisoners took her on a small carriage, as well. Then they all stood on line with the carriage at roll call. The remaining sick girls in the *Revier,* Vera among them, were placed on a large carriage, which Rachel Janovics Mittelman and other inmates took turns pulling.

Between five and six in the evening we were expected to leave the camp. We met Elza briefly as we gathered for *Appel.* We were all anxious, acting mechanically, and doing what was necessary to follow the events unfolding before us. The rest of our friends and others from our town we could not see because they were standing with their own blocks.

Even the weather was against us that spiteful day, with a steady rain falling as we stood for hours until it became completely dark. The SS did not want to expose us to the eyes of the populace. Late in the evening, toward night, the sign was given. The camp's inmates, some of the *Aufseherins,* the soldiers, Knittel, and his wife all were there to start the Death March. We formed a marching column of inmates, five in a line. On two sides were soldiers and a few *Aufseherins* who came with us. The guards had guns on their shoulders and revolvers or pistols on their belts. They carried backpacks, as well. A long stream of humanity started to wend its way out of the camp. A few inmates, among them our friend Hava Hartmann Kleinberg, were selected to pull the carriage with the belongings of Knittel and other staff members. At some point, Knittel and his wife were also sitting on the carriage that the girls pushed.

Frightened and hungry, we found ourselves on the way to the unknown again. Erzsike and I were each clutching a red bowl and a cup, our only luggage on the road. The bowl would be our protection against rainstorms and bombing raids on the way. It would also be instrumental in our freedom later in the march. We looked back to the camp, still lit up by the projectors and the searchlights. There were the barracks, the infirmary, the *Appelplatz*—all left deserted as we marched into the dark.

Walking silently and fearfully with Erzsike always close to me, I was wondering about our unknown destination and our future. Leaving the camp, we had the allure of freedom and hope alternating with our deepest fears. What if, instead of liberation, death was waiting for us at the end of the road?

The night continued to be ghostly and eerie, as darkness reigned all around. The soldiers' flashlights lighted just a bit of the road. I wanted to see the sky, but there was only blackness above. The sky had been my point of orientation that remained constant, even when everything else in my life changed. In April 1944, at the ghetto Kosice, still shocked by our upheaval and exile, I had looked and wondered that the sky was still the same calm expanse, with its endless hue of blue. Only our world had been severed from its foundations.

The streets of Markkleeberg were deserted as we passed by, our long lines extending through a few streets. There was quiet in the town, but later explosion sounds pierced the air. The town was in complete blackout for fear of air attacks. We heard only the uneven sounds of hundreds of wooden shoes on the road.

While we marched, we each held our treasures. Erzsébet Frank had close to her heart the manuscript that she would one day publish at home. I was carrying the drawing that Gizella, the artist, made of Erzsike at work. It was important to me, who always valued pictures and mementos. Erzsébet Zucker Mermel safeguarded the poem about the welders. She did not even know why it was so precious to her. Sometimes we do things with a subconscious awareness of a mission.

Olga Rosenberg, who said her morning prayer on our way to the factory, again recited the appropriate Friday evening prayer. Women joined her with low voices. We who marched a few lines behind heard only a bit of the melody, while the words were lost in the dark.

As we walked, on two sides of us were the guards with guns and German shepherds. The back of the line was also watched. "Everyone who steps aside will be shot," we were told. Afraid of the explosions, the soldiers urged us to go even faster: *"Schneller! Schneller!"* Those guards who were *Volksdeutsche,* volunteers in the SS army from Hungarian territories, now used their Hungarian language to spur us. They also talked among themselves in Hungarian, which they had never done in our presence before. We walked and walked, bumping into one another in the chilling wet night.

Leipzig

The girls continued taking turns to be the horses for the large carriage with our tormentors' belongings. The *Aufseherins* had all left by the time we got to Leipzig. Márta Maget Leitmann, the former *Blockälteste,* was also one of the women who pulled the carriage. When she slowed a bit, the guard was right behind urging her to hurry. Knittel's words of, "Faster, faster!" alarmed the silent crowd. The rain descended on us heavily as we walked toward Leipzig. We were led by side paths through forests, and we walked at night so as not to see or be seen. Our exhaustion and the uncertainty before us were almost too much to bear. I felt Erzsike's hand weakening and slipping out of mine. I took her arm and held it tightly as we continued on. We passed through a dense forest, while the guards in front and at the sides showed us the way with flashlights. We had seen no sights of Leipzig as we were led around it.

We continued on in a deserted area, only the sound of our march breaking the silence of the night. From a distance, lights shone at nearby homes. We were thinking about the lucky people who still lived in freedom and slept in their own beds.

Taucha

As far as the city of Taucha, we walked in side streets among small towns where residents seemingly slept behind closed blinds. They did not show any signs of waking up even with the noise of hundreds of footfalls. Maybe they were used to the sounds of inmates being led at night through their streets and under their windows.

Erzsike and I had to relieve ourselves but were afraid that in the dark we might not find our way back. We did not realize that leaving, which we could not even consider, might have been a good thing. At daybreak, we ran together with some other girls under a clump of nearby trees. We had time to catch up with the long line of marchers even though the guards were chasing them relentlessly. We continued walking that cold, dreary morning into Taucha and through yet more narrow streets.

The rain kept falling that Saturday, the second day of the march. We were hungry, wet, and uninformed of where and why we were hurrying. The guards occasionally smashed their clubs down on us. After the city, we cut through a small forest and reached the highway. The guards and their German shepherds chased us further and further. Startled, Erzsike once squeezed my hand as she felt the teeth of one of the dogs on her leg when she stepped aside a bit. We walked and walked, and eventually I began to stumble as my legs refused to obey; but Erzsike was holding onto me and I knew I had to go on.

We advanced on the main road without seeing any signs of the war. In the distance were a few private homes, and as we passed by, a man pushed something into Erzsike's hand. The guard was right there, but he did not notice and the man disappeared. Erzsike was excited, but I did not know why. As we continued to walk, the guard stepped away, and my sister slipped a little thing into my palm. Still afraid, she told me not to look. So I only felt something hard and small in a wrapper. Another passerby gave half a slice of bread to Margit Lang Stein. She shared it quickly with her friend, Márta Weisz Paren from our town. Each had one bite. By the time the guard noticed the commotion, the bread was gone. He scolded the German civilian for dealing with us. We reached a small farm, and I was still afraid to open the little gift the civilian had given to Erzsike. Exhausted, we finally got to sit in the grass with the rain pouring on us. Looking around carefully, I opened the present. It was a small, square piece of a chocolate. We were so touched that tears and rain ran together on our faces. We shared the gift, each having a bite, while we thought of the guarding spirits of our parents. We believed it was their way to send us regards. Although soaking wet, we had one minute of heaven in our march.

The women on the farm where we had stopped distanced themselves and waited for the group to leave. Soon the whistle was blown for a roll call. We had to stand again according to blocks as in Markkleeberg. Knittel, his wife, and the soldiers from the camp were with us. Knittel counted and discovered that, among others, the functionalists Erzsébet Iczkovits, the work organizer; her daughter Agnes; Zsuzsanna Csanyi, the translator; and Hanni, the nurse from the *Revier* were missing. Knittel declared that all would be shot when found.

As we resumed our march, we passed through more forest. Those who had any left ate their raw rutabaga. Erzsike and I had nothing, and we did not know whether we would get a meal at all. The sun finally came out, but our clothing still did not dry. We wanted to rest so much, but we had to run instead. Erzsike pulled me fearfully to prevent the guards from hitting us between the lines as if we were horses in a race. At the back of the column, other guards struck those who lagged behind.

Walking toward the mountains, the carriage with the belongings of the Knittels and the SS personnel became lighter because many of the SS had left the March. They then placed the luggage in a smaller cart, which the girls pulled until reaching Terezin.[12] Inmates who could not walk were placed in the large carriage, which was pulled by the Frenchwomen, who were in better physical condition, and some of the stronger girls.

We marched all day and met only military vehicles. Then, as we turned onto a new road, we noticed people on bicycles. They were not surprised to see us; they probably had met other transports. In Leipzig and the surrounding area, there had been many foreign workers in munitions factories. A civilian on a bicycle gave a sandwich to a woman in the line before us. Not having eaten for two days, she could hardly believe her luck. As she held the treasure in her hand, the guard jumped in and took it from her.

He threw the bread over the other side of the road and gave the stunned girl a huge box on her ear. The guards were vicious until the final hours.

As we continued on, the roads became empty again. At first we thought it was only because we were on side ways; then we realized that the area was deserted. The stronger girls took turns drawing the carriage with the sick: two girls in front, three in the back, and two who pulled from the sides. On the carriage were young girls from the *Revier* suffering from pneumonia, without medication, in the cold rain and the freezing night. Piri, beaten in the quarry by Lófogú, was there too. Seriously ill, the thirty-year-old woman looked as if she were a seventy-year-old near death.

We were so down, Erzsike and I, yet we could not miss seeing Vera, our former roommate, on the carriage. Vera, about eighteen, was once a very pretty girl. She was born in Budapest, and her parents sent her to stay with grandparents in the countryside, where it was thought to be safer during air attacks. Vera was there only a short time when she was caught with the deportees. Separated from her grandmother at Auschwitz, Vera was alone, knowing no one. Eventually, she found a friend but one who was rejected for the transport to Markkleeberg. The signs of TB that Vera suffered from started to be evident already during her early weeks in Markkleeberg. Coughing at night, Vera was still able to work daytime in the small factory. We liked this pleasant, quiet, and humble girl and were pleased to share our apple with her in the camp. Vera was always worrying about her mother and what had happened to her. Now, on the carriage, Vera seemed pale and disoriented. When we said "hello," she smiled and seemed happy to see us.

We left Vera and we were chased further with blows from heavy sticks. The guards on both sides of the columns, tired and angry, hovered like angels of death, beating and threatening to shoot anyone who staggered or lagged behind. I changed places with Erzsike, who was at the side of the row, and made her walk inside the column to protect her from the dogs, clubs, and rifle butts. Those who stepped out or were accidentally pushed to the side were beaten and forced back into the line. So we were rushed to keep up with the march. I was always afraid that Erzsike's hand might slip away from mine. We were no longer able to divert our attention by the thoughts of relief, recreation, or reflection on the past that used to give us some escape from the present. There was no more singing or reciting poetry. It took great effort and concentration just to keep on with the march. Our fear and anxiety temporarily stilled even the pain from the rubbing of our badly fitting clogs. We had to hurry if we did not want beatings. "*Los . . . schnell!*"—these words were always behind us.

When we turned onto the main road, we could hear bombs and explosions all around. The sky was red, and we felt sure that the front was nearby. We could not move forward because of the crowd of fleeing German citizens blocking the way. On army vehicles, women and children rode with baby carriages, suitcases, and bundles. These were followed by lines of refugees in cars, on bicycles, and all kinds of transportation to escape. Elegant women, men, and soldiers were all squeezed together. Many of those on foot pulled small wagons. A fireman told Knittel that we could not continue because of the congestion on the road and the enemy armies that came from two sides.

We sat down in the dusty road and observed the escapees. Our pleasure did not last long, however, when suddenly there was an air attack. The low-flying planes circled above us and we quickly lay down and hid our faces. The cars stopped on the road, as Germans ran for their lives or hid under the cars. As we peeked from the corners of our eyes, we saw nervous soldiers aiming their machine guns. Their action was followed by smoke and a pillar of fire rising up. Tens of airplanes shone in the sun above us; their motors buzzed and zoomed, while the thunder of explosions made the earth tremble under us. Then it was quiet. The air raid and, shortly after, the bottleneck of refugees were over, and the guards chased us further down the road. Shaken still from the fighting in the sky and on land, our guards unmercifully resumed their own war games, hitting and herding us toward death.

After the first fright of the air raid, Elza, who stayed with her block, came to check on us. She, as many others, was contemplating leaving the march, because she thought it likely that we would be killed on the road anyway. Elza, as brave and resourceful as she was, however, felt safer staying with the group. She was afraid of the unknown and of being at the mercy of the horde and the SS on the roads. We agreed with Elza, but still feared the guards and the pain of walking. Elza returned to her line, and the soldiers started to chase us again with their rubber whips, quickly followed by the screaming of the girls who were hurt.

We staggered on, hungry and tired. Most of us had no bread, and we looked with envy at the women with whole loaves that they had stolen at the camp before distribution. Elza called them "bread millionaires." We could have complained to Knittel, but no one wanted to do that. Some women commented, however, that the girls with the bread were from Máramaros, synonymous with aggressive and arrogant behavior according to Jews who lived in the original Hungarian territories.[13] Whether full or hungry, Jews from Máramaros or from Budapest, French or Nazi, all could be the victims of the next bombing raid.

We marched at the side of the main road while cars went speeding by on the highway. Knittel, by this time, rode his bicycle at the front of the line. Our destination, as we found out later, was Terezin (Theresienstadt in German), close to Prague. Yet we were told to hurry because it was late in the day, and we had to reach the new camp before nightfall. There food, beds, and shelter would be waiting, according to the guards. They continued to lure us with deception.

The Camp in Markkleeberg as We Left

Some escaped and did not go on the Death March at all. Carmen Braun and two of her friends dared to walk through the open gate that was unguarded as the whole camp stood on *Appel,* ready for the march. The second day as they were hiding in the forest, they met an SS guard from the camp who threatened to escort them back. The girls cried and pleaded for their lives. Finally, the SS, who himself was in the run, graciously agreed to leave them alone. Luckily, the next person they met was a forced laborer from the factory. He told them that they could return because the SS had left the camp. The girls were liberated by the American army on April 18, 1945.[14]

Despite the warning that anyone found hiding in the barracks would be shot, a number of girls took the risk. One of them was Agi from Kosice who was in love with the blond Belgian forced laborer in the factory. It probably meant so much to her that she was ready to risk her life. When we all went to *Appel,* Agi climbed to the top bed on the third level, covered herself with a mattress, and stayed there. The guards, occupied with their own affairs, had no time to do a thorough search of the camp. Agi remained safely in the barracks until the transport left and the Belgian boy appeared.[15] The two left, and Gitta Susitzky Hönig, heard that they were married after the war. So there was a happy ending after all.

Besides taking refuge in the barracks, forty prisoners escaped to the nearby forest when it was learned that the company locksmith, Willy Goertler, cut the wire in the fence.[16] Another twenty girls who knew about the opening in the fence also left the camp and hid in the forest. The inmates had some bread and stayed hidden until a passing German man alerted them that the Americans were in the camp and that some of the former prisoners had returned. The girls did not go back to the camp but instead joined a transport to Czechoslovakia.

Gizella Hollander and her daughter Vera Hollander Slyomovics went on the Death March, but the mother, Gizella, was unable to continue. They succeeded in leaving the lines near Leipzig and returned to the camp in Markkleeberg. When the American army entered, they were liberated. Gizella, who spoke German well, obtained the following letter from the Junkers factory, confirming that they had worked for them seven months.[17]

Dr. Spielmann, another escapee near Leipzig, described in her memoirs how she and another inmate succeeded in running away during an air raid under cover of night. Eventually they returned to the camp where they

JUNKERS FLUGZEUG- UND MOTORENWERKE AKTIENGESELLSCHAFT

MOTORENBAU ZWEIGWERK MARKKLEEBERG

WERKLEITUNG

MARKKLEEBERG I 27.April 1945
FERNRUF: SAMMEL-NR. LEIPZIG 39 41 81
Eth/Do.

Arbeitsbescheinigung

Durch das SS-Konzentrationslager Buchenwald wurde am 2.10.1944 aus dem SS-Konzentrationslager Auschwitz

Gizella H o l l ä n d e r, geb. 24.6.1905,

unserem Werk zur Arbeitsleistung zugewiesen. Sie ist von uns mit dem Tage der Besatzung durch die amerikanischen Truppen entlassen worden.

Diese Bescheinigung wird ausgestellt zum Zwecke des Rücktransportes in ihre Heimat.

JUNKERS FLUGZEUG UND MOTORENWERKE AG
MOTORENBAU ZWEIGWERK MARKKLEEBERG

Certification

By the SS-Konzentrationslager Buchenwald Gizella HOLLÄNDER, born the 24.6.1905, from the SS-Konzentrationslager Auschwitz has been assigned to our factory the 2nd of October 1944 to work there. She was dismissed on the 18th of April 1945, date of the occupation by the american troups.

This certification is drawn up for the return to her country.

Certificate from the Junkers factory to Gizella Hollander.

found other inmates. Markkleeberg was not yet liberated, but the SS had left the camp. Those who escaped the Death March and returned to the camp were treated well. Junkers sent food, and the survivors were provided with new clothing. They were allowed to walk freely in Markkleeberg, which none of them had ever seen in daytime. They stayed until the end of July because travel to Hungary was not organized until then.

Dr. Spielmann and her friend spent some time visiting a café nearby in Wolfswinkel. Café Wolfswinkel was owned by an elderly couple who were very nice to them. They provided them with food and, even more importantly, with food ration cards. A woman named Ilse came to visit them after liberation. She told them that, from her window, she could see the camp and felt very sorry for the inmates. Dr. Spielmann returned to Markkleeberg in 1965 and looked for Ilse but could not locate her. She had probably passed away by then.[18]

Perils of Leaving the March

Making a decision to escape the march was not easy. Unless one was forced to stop because of physical exhaustion or foot problems, it was a brave step to take. Many of us could not speak German, and we were all afraid of the hostile world around us. There was also the danger that the soldiers would shoot after us. Those who decided to leave hid behind gates in the dark, waiting for the rest of the marchers to pass by, then hurried in the opposite direction to meet the American army. Girls who were caught by the guards were beaten and forced back to the march. Sometimes German civilians who noticed girls slipping away from the march called for the guards—either out of hatred or because they were afraid of what would happen if their neighborhood was accused of harboring fugitives.

Later, as many of the guards themselves disappeared and the inmates became more hungry and desperate, it was easier to leave. Even then, however, a girl would not dare to escape alone. She needed the support of others and someone who spoke German.

Women who planned to leave the march looked for companions who had, in addition to the language skills, resourcefulness and daring. Children like me and Erzsike or girls in frail physical condition were undesirable teammates for such an undertaking.

Wurzen

Toward the evening, after marching all day and eager to reach a camp, we noticed the outline of a city. We walked faster, observing for the first time a German metropolis in daylight. Up until then, we had been led in populated areas only early in the morning or late at night. By the road sign, we knew that we were in Wurzen, which was full of military personnel.

We were herded with blows from heavy sticks to walk faster. As we turned into the first street in Wurzen, Anna from our barracks collapsed. The physician nearby looked at her with resignation. Poor Anna (or Annus, as those who knew her from home called her endearingly) was the wife of a well-to-do merchant from a respected family; but in the camp, she became "crazy Anna." As she lay at the side of the road, her struggle was visible in the tortured expression of her distorted face. Anna's torn overalls were hanging on her skeletal figure, and she ceaselessly scratched the painfully open wounds on her body, where lice had carved deep into her flesh. Anna, with no family or close friends in camp, found that others avoided her after she became infested with lice.

Recovering a bit, Anna sat up but was still unable to walk. The guard we called Bacskai or Birgel came over and, with no hesitation, shot her. Anna's body was left on the side of the road. Bacskai was a *Volksdeutsche* from Bácska in the Yugoslavian part of Hungary.[19] Elisabeth Stein Szekely, who witnessed the shooting, recognized him after liberation among the prisoners in Terezin. Besides Anna, there were between thirty and fifty other women shot by the SS guards, according to Sara Breiner, because they were unable to keep up with the march. Sara gave testimony to the justice department investigating Nazi crimes in Germany. Others who witnessed and testified to the killings were Piroska Winkler, Dora Kluska, and Rosalia Lazar.[20]

We were shaken and scared of who would be the next Anna. I did not see the shooting myself, but we all heard the shot. I watched Erzsike anxiously and was scared by her appearance. My little thirteen-year-old sister was dragging her sore, blistered feet in half-broken wooden shoes, her face ashen, with circles around her eyes. I was frightened. I did not know that I myself was in even worse physical condition, and that I looked just as bad as my sister. My shoe was also held together by only a few remaining nails. It might have been easier to throw it away and walk barefoot if not for the fact that we were in high elevations where the snow still remained in some places. At the camp, we were managing to keep ourselves a few steps ahead of Anna, but on the march, we were almost like her. The hunger, the fatigue, and the increasing lice infestation were plaguing our souls and bodies.

In Wurzen, many of the houses were ruined. Maybe this was the result of the large air attack we had heard on the road. Next to us on the street, people pulled a carriage with bloody human body parts—hands, legs, a torso, and more. As other girls started screaming, I had a quick look at the terrible sight; I warned Erzsike to turn away, but it was too late. We both were exposed to the massacre of war that we had not seen until then. We walked silently for a while, scared and terribly distressed. With my brief glimpse, I did not really see much, but other girls were quick to provide gruesome details.

We did not observe much of the city, even though we would have been pleased to see the destruction. Weary, hungry, and broken in spirit, we dragged ourselves along, knowing that there was no other way. If we stopped, either the rubber truncheons or the bullets would be aimed at us. Our only hope was that we would soon reach a camp, as the guards made us believe, and that there we would rest for the night.

It was dark and cold that Saturday night when we arrived at a huge bridge. We had walked since Friday evening when we left Markkleeberg. The guards directed us to go down under the arch of the bridge to a cemented area. We had to stand in lines of five, each according to her block. Knittel counted, wrote it down, and then counted us again. He grew agitated and angry; it seemed that many more were missing. Then he warned again that if anyone was found leaving the march she would be shot.

After the roll call, the guards left. It grew completely dark, and we realized that we would have to spend the night on the cold cement without food or blankets. Knittel said, "You will sleep here, as the earth will be your bed and the sky your cover." We understood what he meant. Guards walked on top of the bridge and laughed at our misery. Knittel and his wife spent the night at a hotel. The guards stayed some distance away; they did not want us to see their supper. They also slept on the ground, but had blankets and raincoats. We received no food and shivered as the coldness of the night enveloped us. We were very hungry, and we still could not believe that we must spend the night under that bridge. How was it possible? Maybe we misunderstood?

Despair soon overcame us all. Lying on the cold cement, we pressed our bodies together closely. April in Germany is cold and snowy; the cement was like a sheet of ice. We had never felt so cold even in the middle of winter in the camp. My teeth were chattering as we fell into a light sleep; but the oblivion of sleep did not last long. We heard noise and noticed, among the stars, the brilliant lights of thousands of rockets—called Stalin candles—sparkling with satanic glow. Next, the menacing noise intensified as planes shrieked by above us with their deadly cargoes. It was chilling to watch the sky as armies of the night played out their games of war. Next to us, we suddenly heard the sound of cannon fire and the steady rumbling noise of the traveling tanks. The stars brilliantly glittered above, while the thunder of war with its lightning rockets seemed to come closer and closer. A terrible fear overcame us.

The lights and the bombing seemed even more like lightning and thunder as the rockets came closer. I reminded Erzsike how, at home, when we were afraid in the storm at night, mother came, hugged us, and closed the curtains so we could fall asleep peacefully. Here we could not shut out the fright. Our teeth chattered as we cuddled together on the ice-cold cement, while the river's dark flow of rising water beat ominously against the walls of the bridge.

From the distance came a rumbling sound, like sacks of potatoes rolling down a chute. The ground shook as explosions followed, one after another. The dogfights also continued over our heads in the skies. I saw one plane get hit and go down in flames. In the darkness, a strong, blinding searchlight projected on us from time to time. We would have liked to hide from it and regretted that the guards were not with us. We looked on fearfully at the city that seemed to be in flames, as cars raced one after another across the top of the bridge. We were like a thousand eyes blinking together and a thousand hearts beating in one rhythm as we listened fearfully, on one side and the other, to the sounds in the distance. There was no one among us who could avoid thinking the worst. We wished that Elza, Klári, or some of our friends were with us; but they had to stay with the women of their barracks.

Finally, the fighting quieted down and the air raid siren stopped. We still heard a bomb explode from time to time, but both the rocket attacks and the cannon shooting were over. Intermittent explosions continued in the city for awhile, as the flames rose and black smoke temporarily darkened the stars. The sound of airplane motors had receded, and a disquieting darkness reigned all around. Once the smoke cleared, we perceived only the blinking of stars in the endless sky, as if they were lanterns for us travelers who might never reach our destination.

We eventually fell asleep, but all of us were beset with bad dreams. While I was afraid of the danger of the night, a mother next to us had a nightmare that civilians were being placed among the two fighting forces—a customary practice during wartime. Then she dreamed that they machine-gunned and killed part of the crowd, while young women were given as bounty to the militia. She feared that we would be the victims she dreamed about, between the two fighting armies, with her daughter and other young girls being the prey of the soldiers.

At daybreak, the sky filled with its rainbow of colors. As we looked around, suddenly noises came from the bridge. We were scared that an army might be coming toward us. Then someone said, "Look, they are coming from a *lager!*" A group of girls was crossing the bridge, line after line, with shaven heads and SS escorts. As they came closer, they told us that they were Hungarians. They had walked for the last five days and they did not know where they were being led, either.

The girls on the bridge were one of the many groups of marching prisoners after the dissolution of the camps. After the end of March 1945, the columns of haggard concentration camp prisoners grew and grew. They came from all possible directions. In inadequate footwear, they shuffled through the streets of the more and more constricted areas of the German Reich.

It was hard to collect ourselves that morning. We were all wet again, this time from the dew that fell during the night. I shared with Erzsike a small piece of rutabaga that Berta gave us. Berta and her sister used to be our partners on the five-person line on the way to the factory. With changing shifts we saw each other mostly on Sundays, but we felt that special closeness from both being teenaged sisters without our mothers. Berta, bright and resourceful, was the older and Viola was three years her junior. They were pleasant, pretty girls who had good voices and liked to sing as we walked to the factory. With them I even dared to intone, letting my voice be heard. During the march, they walked a few lines ahead of us. The sisters also felt kinship with us and shared a bit of their rutabaga, which was a real sacrifice. We were grateful, even though afterward we suffered stomachache and diarrhea; but this could also have been because of the cold cement we sat and slept on. Erzsike and I were hugging each other to get a bit of warmth from our bodies. The cold was so strong that a small bottle of water that one of the Frenchwomen had been lucky enough to fill along the side of the road the day before had turned to ice during the night.

As we entered the city of Wurzen, everyone was still sleeping. We could not believe that silence after the battle at night. The army, the cars, the dead had all disappeared. Here and there was a policeman. Sometimes a face peeked out from behind a curtain, then pulled back quickly. This was only the beginning of the long march ahead of us, during which sudden air raids would bring death for some and liberation to others.

12

The Death March

Air Attacks

ALLIED BOMBING THAT NEVER CAME TO DESTROY THE RAILROADS LEADing into Auschwitz reached us during the Death March. It was a new type of danger we had to face.

Early in the morning on Sunday, April 15, 1945, the third day of our march, walking on the highway we arrived at a small sleeping town near Wurzen. No one was in the street. We continued to a nearby field when, suddenly, we were attacked from the air. It was not the kind of heavy bombing from aircraft high in the sky that we had experienced in Markkleeberg. From a distance, we saw a group of light planes that began to descend with a growing roar and almost landed on our heads. They then turned in a wide angle and rose into the sky again, except for one that started to shoot. The guards ordered us to lie on the ground. The red dishes on our heads were our protective helmets. As planes descended lower again, we could even see the pilots. They were shooting at us with machine guns at close range. The attack lasted only a few minutes, but it left dozens of wounded victims.[1]

The first bullets fell on the inmates who hauled the carriages in front. Ten women were pulling and pushing the carriage with the sick. Mili or Ilona Aron from Sajomagyaros, born March 26, 1923, pushed the carriage on the right side. Formerly from the *Esscommando,* Ilona was hit and died.[2] There were many others; a girl called Rozsi from Hust lost her legs and perished. Another girl who was walking at the side of the line also died. Her sister survived.[3] The guards buried the dead whose names remained unknown. Gabriella Braver Kosinka remembered that Knittel even said a prayer over their graves.

While the women were attending the wounded, we heard someone crying disconsolately. I could not see her face, but the girls said that one of two sisters was killed. When we had a chance to come closer, I was shocked to learn that it was Berta who had died, with her sister, Viola, sobbing and hugging Berta's body with words of endearment. It was heartrending. The sisters, only a little bit earlier, had shared with us their piece of rutabaga. I was afraid to look at Erzsike. Even now, I shiver when I write about it. We tried to come closer to console Viola, the younger of the sisters, but we were forced to stay on line. The guards took the young girl together with Berta's body as she continued to weep and hold on to her sister. The unfortunate, sweet teenage girl grew confused and inconsolable. Elza Reich Szamosi, who was at the end of the line, told us that the guards were talking to Viola in Hungarian, but she would not listen. Knittel also came, and he let some women talk to her, but nothing helped. She only hugged Berta's body tighter. Knittel ordered everyone to return to their places in the lines. As we started to walk, we soon heard a shot behind us.[4]

It was tragic that the Allies did not use preventive measures to avoid bombing the prisoners in the Death Marches. Leaflets dropped might have also increased the readiness of the German citizens to help the marchers. Allied assistance to the Red Cross might have brought food and protection to the unfortunate prisoners on trains and on foot in the last days and weeks of the war, but no concerted effort was made to come to the rescue of the Death Marchers. Intelligence information collected could have perhaps avoided the tragedy of bombing of Nazi victims. The Death Marches were not known to the Jewish organizations, except under the general term "evacuation of the camps." Among the mass of British and American intelligence reports, there is an occasional, fleeting mention that the Germans were evacuating the internment camps.[5] Leading inmates on a Death March was part of the Nazi terror, and people were not aware of their true meaning.

We did not know what happened to all the wounded girls in our march after the air attack. In my research, I have learned that some of the injured were taken to a nearby inn; among them was Márta Fellmann, who was hit by a bullet. As she was standing, Márta suddenly felt a searing pain in her thigh and fell to the ground. She was bleeding profusely, and everyone around her was screaming. The guard pulled her to the side of the road and covered her with a blanket as she drifted in and out of consciousness. Márta was lying by the roadside when the guards insisted we continue the march. As we passed her, Márta noticed Magda Schön Hilf, from her hometown, passing by. The wounded Márta Fellmann collected her strength and called out Magda's name, and Magda turned back. They were both crying. Márta asked Magda to tell Márta's husband Andor, if he returned from the forced labor battalion in Russia, what had happened to her. In a few minutes, Magda was gone with the march.

The German medic who attended a few of the injured could treat them only with tissue paper on their wounds. A while later, a German doctor and two nurses arrived. Márta and some other seriously injured girls were taken to a nearby home. The owner said they could not stay there because of the lice the injured girls had. Then they took them to an inn, and, as they were waiting, a man who spoke Hungarian came in. He looked at Márta's wound and said that she would be able to go home in six weeks. The Hungarian, who was in the SS, gave Márta his mother's address in Budapest and asked Márta to call his mother and tell her that he would not be able to go home, but that he was alive. He was afraid to return home because of the identifying tattoo under his arm showing that he was in the SS. He left and soon came back with an ambulance. The whole group of about five girls was taken to a hospital. A girl by the name of Rozsi, whose sister was injured, also went with them.

In the hospital, an elderly German doctor treated the injured, and he was good to Márta. After liberation by the Russians, Márta Fellmann stayed on for six months in the hospital. Rozsi's sister died, and Rozsi left after five weeks. While in the hospital, she slept with Márta in the same bed because Rozsi was afraid of the Russian soldiers. We will see later the perils girls faced from the liberating Russian army. Márta recovered and returned home in February 1946. Unfortunately, her husband had not survived. Márta remarried and in 2005 at ninety-one, was quite well except for the three big holes in her thigh that pained her throughout her life. For German restitution, Dr. Jozsa Adler, who was the physician in Markkleeberg, gave her a letter confirming that Márta was injured by the bombing. Márta could not give the message to the Hungarian SS man's mother in Budapest because he had put the written address in a paper in Márta's pocket. When Márta was in the hospital, still dazed, she was given new clothing, and the address was taken away with the old clothes. Márta was sorry, but there was nothing she could do.[6]

We continued the march and, by the time we were about five or six kilometers past Wurzen, even the guards were tired. As we sat down to rest, we noticed some green plants growing in the ground. It was rape or colza, which we pulled out to eat. The stem was sweet, the leaves similar to those of the cauliflower, and the flower sweet like honey. One cannot eat much of it without risking diarrhea, however. Knittel and the soldiers did not say anything as we collected it. The sun was shining, but we tried to sleep a bit, even if only for a few minutes, to get strength and to keep from thinking about our hunger.

We continued although we could hardly walk. We were fewer by about three dozen who had escaped at night, according to Erzsébet Frank.[7] The Germans did not insist on counting this time. They only wanted the lines to be orderly, yelling "*Anschliessen! Anschliessen!*" or close the space between the lines. Forests were on both sides as we walked, and small groups of girls went to relieve themselves among the trees. The soldiers let them go; many did not return. As we left the forest, no one was around, and it felt as if a curtain had closed between the region of the fights and that quiet, deserted area.

We passed again by a forest and we could see, from a distance, moving figures among the trees. Coming closer, we learned that they were Polish women coming from Zeitz. They had walked for five days; very tired and sad, they had no food either. The guards did not let us talk to them further and urged us to hurry.

As we marched, we ate a bit of the colza we had picked. The guards urged us to hurry, assuring us again that the camp we were heading for was not far. We no longer believed or cared what they said, but we noticed some lights in the distance. We collected our strength and advanced toward the light. As we walked, we passed by a large ditch by the side of the road. The ditch seemed to be full of dead people in striped uniforms. Suddenly the "dead" started to move. "We thought that you were German soldiers, in your uniforms," the men said. "We have been walking for a week without any destination. The war is coming closer." By then, our guards noticed that we were speaking with the group and chased us ahead.

Late in the evening, we were permitted to sit down, but the stones on the highway were very cold. Erzsike and I hugged each other, which did not help; we still shivered in the chilly April night. After a short rest, the guards started to hit anyone they reached as they chased us further. We walked fearfully into the night. In the morning, with the light, we were scared a little less.

Oschatz

After a night walk, we reached a big ugly town where all the houses were the same. They looked like a child's drawing with their bent roofs and identical windows. Knittel walked with his wife at the front of the march. Her legs were swollen and she looked tired. She was the only German woman with us.

There was no one around, and no smoke came from the chimneys. The guards chased us onward, but we did not mind; we were scared being in that weird city with crooked roofs. We walked carefully, and Erzsike's arm quivered in mine, fearing that some terror from the long shadows might jump on us in those deserted streets. As we advanced to the center of the city, there were taller buildings, and we saw people coming out of their apartments. Their mean looks followed our transport. We observed them with apprehension—it seemed like a city of the damned. It took some time to leave because of the barricades, which only let us pass two by two. The sun gradually warmed us up, and we felt a bit more secure. There were some green meadows in the distance and we hoped the guards would let us rest there. Not far away we noticed a few similar buildings—maybe that was the promised *lager?* As we came closer, however, we noticed houses with SS soldiers. We lost all hope of ever finding the camp.

Hungarian Gendarmerie and SS Officers

Passing between two lines of trees, we reached a section of villas and summer homes on the outskirts of Oschatz. People, many well dressed, enjoyed the sunny morning. We looked at them with suffering eyes, but they turned from us with disgust. Farther among the trees, we met Hungarian gendarmerie. They were still wearing the hats with the rooster feathers. The girls were surprised and said, "Oh my God, you are Hungarians!" The gendarmerie turned their heads; they were not ready to talk to us. Then we realized how senseless it was even to try to speak to those members of the cruelest of Hungarian police forces. They had been the terror of the Jews in the rural areas such as our own town of Abaújszántó. Any time they wished, they came in to search our homes. They entered with daggers in their hands, cursing and using vulgar language with no consideration for children or respectable elderly people. Their surprise visits were our nightmares before the Germans entered Hungary. As we met them in Germany, they continued to wear on their faces the same old cruelty. Their silence arose either from new cowardice or from old hatred. We stared at them as they disappeared through the gate of a big house.

The Killing of the Sick and Infirm

As the strength of the marchers waned, women were less and less able to pull and push the carriage with the sick, especially up into the hills. One cart was taken to a forest near Oschatz where the girls pulling the carriage, including Rachel Janovics Mittelman, had to dig graves. Miriam Liberman Kirsenbaum also saw how they took the sick down from the carriage. When the girls finished digging, the guards made the sick girls sit on the side of the ditch and ordered the others to continue the march. Shortly afterward, they heard shots, as the SS guards killed the sick. Klára Fischer Neuman remembered hearing the shots as we were in the forest near Oschatz. Later she met two sisters from Halm; Klára didn't remember their names. The girls were worried about their third sister whom they had to leave on the carriage with the sick. Klára met the girls after the war, and they told her that the sister never came home.[8] By the Germans' method of confusion, while they eliminated one carriage, they continued the others. A carriage with the sick even reached Terezin, Márta Maget Leitmann recalled.

It was difficult to pull and push the carriages, so the relatives of the sick helped. There were at least fifteen girls pulling and pushing, among them Rose Hoffmann Davis and Irene Keisler Schnur, whose sister was among the sick. One carriage was at the front of the march, another in the back, and the third was in the middle of the line.

One thousand and five hundred women in Markkleeberg were sent on the forced march without sufficient clothing, shoes, or food supply. Already in fragile health, we had to sleep outdoors at night in the still wintry April weather. As we marched along in the ever-narrowing corridor between the Eastern and the Western fronts, many of the marchers died of exhaustion or starvation, or they were shot for being unable to continue.[9] Rose Hoffmann Davis saw a woman shot by a tall SS guard with a rifle. When we heard the shot, Erzsike squeezed my arm, but we were afraid to look back because they might shoot us too. Since there are no records, very few of the deaths can be confirmed, so the number is difficult to determine. Once-beautiful young girls just lay down on the side of the road and died. The route we passed through cities, towns, and villages was soaked in blood.

No longer in an official capacity as a *Lagerälteste,* Bella Spitz used her knowledge of German and her acquaintance with the guards to help the inmates. When Alex, a nasty SS soldier, picked up his gun to shoot one of the young girls we called Black Nusi, who was too tired to walk, Bella Spitz ran to him and pleaded for the girl's life. Finally, Alex put down his gun.

Women, weak and ailing, were left on the road to die while the march passed by. Some of those who died were buried, usually at the roadside, in the forest, or occasionally by the side of a barn. About fifty were interred along the way, Márta Maget Leitmann recalled. Among those who died was the second physician from the *Revier,* Dr. Szerén Elias, who was so helpful when Lucy gave birth. Dr. Elias, born in Ujpest, was thirty-five years old and had no family with her in the camp. She was a lovely person and well liked by the inmates. Márta Maget Leitmann, the former *Blockalteste,* and other women wanted to help, but Dr. Elias was unable to walk. Márta was with her, holding her hand as she died. Dr. Elias was buried at the roadside.

The Second Air Attack and Its Casualties

Low-flying planes continually machine-gunned the escape route. They attacked us for the second time when we were in the forest. The Germans ran to the woods for protection during air raids, and thus the forests also became a target. As the Allied planes came lower to shoot us, the German guards hid among the marchers. We were so tired that we had no strength to enjoy seeing them so afraid.

One plane dove down and sprayed machine gun fire into the crowd. The bullets flew all around us, falling among the trees, into the ditches, and bouncing into the puddles of water and the trenches. We watched with anxiety the routes of the bullets. We heard the shooting sounds of *tra-tra-*

tra or *plop-plop-lop*. How could it be that the Allied pilots saw us and yet continued to shoot? We were wondering how the American army could have done that to us. Maybe they thought that we were German soldiers in retreat? We wanted to hide in the nearby pond.

Meanwhile, as she was lying on her stomach, Zsofia Gottlieb Török felt something hit her and thought she had been shot. Luckily, it was only an iron splinter from an exploding bomb. She was able to pull it out, but she suffered from the wound all the way home.

As soon as we were organized to walk, there was a siren again and the sound of bombs dropping from above. We all ran for shelter. Nearby was a small tavern, a type of roadside inn with a barn where everyone who was close enough was herded in by the guards. Erzsike pulled me down to the ground because there was no room left in the barn. In a short while, as all stayed tightly packed in the barn, someone started to scream "Fire!" The panic was great; all attempted to escape, and a number of women were crushed to death trying to get out. The air attack also took its toll of victims. The dead were buried on the field, but we do not know what happened to the wounded girls. They were left on the side of the road and we were forced to move on. I was so terrified and weary by that time that only my survival instinct and holding onto Erzsike kept me alive; yet the scene of leaving those injured and suffering girls forlorn, with the fear of death in their eyes, touched me deeply. I asked about them from the survivors I interviewed, but no one knew their fate.

The Winkler Sisters' Odyssey

After the air raid, Nelly Winkler Rochlitz and her sister Hajnal continued to pull their sister Rozsa on the carriage. It was about ten days into the march when they reached a hill close to Freital. The descent from the hill was very steep; they could not keep the wheels of the carriage from sliding and rolling too fast down the steep descent. The rain, mixed with big pieces of sleet grew heavier; and, in desperation, the girls turned in the gate of a nearby home, leaving the march.

The owner of the house came out, and Nelly pleaded with him to let them stay under a roof until the rain was over. The German agreed, but then he went upstairs and called the police. The girls were arrested and taken together with their carriage to the local jail. The policeman ordered food for them and let them stay overnight. This was their first meal and first night's sleep in ten days. They would not have minded remaining in jail and waiting for the advancing American army. In the morning, they asked the police sergeant to let them stay, have pity on the sick girls, but he said that it would cost him his job. A policeman escorted them out of the town and directed them to follow a group of marchers. The girls did not want to join a march again, so instead they walked to the next town, where they were arrested anew. Their overalls with the red "X" on the back made them obvious targets. They were taken back to the same police station. The sergeant told them that if they were arrested again, he would turn them over to the Gestapo. Nelly said that they would steal something in order to stay in jail. The policeman said he could not do it. The next day they were chased out of prison and out of town again. As they walked, they all changed their overalls for civilian clothing that they took off someone's laundry line.

After walking awhile and pulling the carriage with Rozsa, they saw a camp where foreigners stayed, and they asked for shelter as non-Jewish Hungarian refugees. The doctor sent Rozsa to the hospital, but Nelly and Hajnal could not stay. They did not want to leave their sister, but the guards threatened them with their guns. Rozsa, scared that the guards might really harm her sisters, begged them to leave for their own safety. Pleased that at least the sick Rozsa would have hospital care, the sisters walked away.

The Frenchwomen in the March

During one of our rest times, we sat down in a small grove. To our surprise, a carriage arrived with large containers of warm soup, which had been sent by the townspeople. Before it was divided up for the group, a few of the Frenchwomen went to Knittel and told him that they were Christians from pure blood and that it was not fair that they should receive equal portions with the Jews. Knittel did not act on their request for larger portions.[10]

Another incident with the Frenchwomen was again induced by extreme stress. The weather was cloudy, and the rain was pouring all through the night. Wet, hungry, and tired, we arrived at a village. The SS demanded that a farmer let us into his barn. They still wore their uniforms, so the village people were afraid and let us use the upper floor of the barn, which was filled with hay for the animals. To reach the huge attic, we had to climb a ladder. The French girls were the first to go, and when the last of them reached the top, they pulled in the ladder and closed the door. The Jewish women were out in the pouring rain. The SS soldiers, meanwhile, had disappeared; they probably found shelter in one of the homes. The Jewish inmates screamed and asked for the ladder. One of the French girls stood at the entrance and said the attic was not strong enough for all the prisoners. They wanted to stay by themselves. The Jewish girls then decided to look for another ladder, which they found by one of the local homes. As they were climbing up, the French girls started to scream, "*Sale Juif! Sale Juif!*" (Dirty Jews!). "It was hard to understand that these were the girls from the anti-Nazi movement who suffered with us almost three months in the camp," writes Miriam Porat in her book.[11] Erzsike and I were among the last to climb up. The attic was large enough for everyone to sleep on the hay. The incident involved a small number of the French girls, and one cannot judge or condemn the whole group; yet, for historical accuracy, the matter merits mention. Many of the Frenchwomen left the march early, some did not even start because French forced laborers and POWs helped them to escape, according to Márta Maget Leitmann.

As noted before, the French girls were very resourceful. Gabriella Braver Kosinka marveled at how, during the air attacks, they took off their underwear and raised it to signal to the planes that we were not the enemy. The French also had somehow made a white flag that they raised. Some Jewish women too put their white underwear on a tree branch to signal the airplanes, Irene Keisler Schnur remembered.

Daily Challenges

Rainstorms

Rainstorms beset us all along the way. We walked in lines of five in the cold pouring rain mixed with snow. Erzsike hugged me from time to time to get a bit warmer. We thought that nothing could be worse than the night under the bridge at Wurzen. Yet as the downpour of cold driving rain continued and the dark night was lit by flames of a burning city, we realized the danger to our lives. Cries of *"Jaj Istenem, segits meg!"* (Oh my God, help me!) were heard in the crowd.

I was worrying about one of Erzsike's wooden clogs deteriorating and if she might have to walk barefoot if the shoe broke. Even with shoes, our feet hurt terribly; it was even harder to walk in the mud. We pulled each other along to keep up with the rest. We could not give up, could not lose heart, and could not even cry. We passed through a small town in the rain, covering our heads with our food bowls. The bowls were not too clean anymore, and dirty water poured down on our faces. Erzsike noticed how the passersby were laughing at us.

After resting a bit, we then had to get up and walk in the dark through new places. The rule of marching according to one's block slowly changed. Everyone walked however she could. We were fewer and fewer because many slipped away in the forest. We thought that those who were brave enough to leave were saved further torture; but we will see in the following chapter the many difficulties they faced.

In the morning, we reached a town where we stopped by a big barn. Our icy wet clothing stuck to us heavily. Erzsike's foot was very swollen by this time. There was no bandage or anything to wrap around it. As we sat there miserably, our friend Hava Hartmann Kleinberg came to tell us that she and her sister might leave the march because they were convinced we would die on the way anyhow. The Germans had nowhere to take us and, with the war closing in, they were likely just to shoot us like they had done with the sick on the carriage. We listened to Hava, and with the discipline lessened, we knew that it would be less difficult to slip away, but we were still afraid to leave the group. In any case, we would be scared to be alone in that unfamiliar and hostile German world. Our strength was also waning, and we were barely able to move, lacking the vigor to run away. There was also the question of where we could go. Without a good knowledge of the German language and of survival skills, we had little likelihood of succeeding. Those who planned to escape formed a support group of relatives and friends. We were weak and young and had no talent to offer; we would only be a burden on the group. Elza also continued with the march, which encouraged us. Erzsike pushed herself with great difficulty into her shoes and we went on again.

Toward the evening, we reached the edge of a city. We all had but one wish: to lie down somewhere. The ditch at the side of the road seemed an inviting, sheltering place. We were so tired that we just fell into the trench and slept. Then suddenly another storm developed and the ditches quickly filled with water. Many of the sleeping girls were unaware of the rain, and their bodies were carried by the rising water inside the trenches. Dreadfully, some drowned, as Elena Salamon Kaufman and Miriam Liberman Kirsenbaum recalled. Erzsike woke me up in time. We climbed out, as next to us, a mother pulled her reluctant daughter by the hair from the muddy water. The young girl just wanted to sleep. The march continued, and we stayed in line, even though we could hardly hold up our heads. The guards drove us further: *"Immer weiter."* We wrung out the water from our overalls, and that provided some temporary relief.

The heavy rain continued as we marched through the darkest and longest night of the march. It was so black that we could not see each other. After hours of walking, we were led again to a forest. Women started to call each other's names, which created mass confusion. One girl could not find her sister. The others helped to look for her and started to scream. The guards, not able to stop the commotion, shot into the air. Further back on the line in complete darkness, we did not know what was happening. All of us became terrified that the Germans were killing us in the forest. Religious women recited the prayer that people say when they fear death: "*Shema Yisrael Adonai Eloheinu Adonai Ehad!*" (Hear, O Israel, the Lord our God, the Lord is one!) Meanwhile, the girl who had lost her sister found her not far away; she just could not see her in the dark. The shooting stopped, and we felt we had gained back our lives for awhile longer.

We continued to march like an army of robots animated by the instinct to survive. We walked steadfastly, avoiding the guards' whips, the German shepherds, and the poised German guns. Occasionally we marched on the highways. Most of the time, however, many of the main thoroughfares were clogged with military traffic. The Germans kept us from populated areas, and we were led across back roads, through deep forests, country lanes, and rolling hills, often walking at night. We rarely saw the sights and localities we passed.

Later the terrain of gentle rolling hills changed, and our columns passed through towns and by small roadside inns. In April, the tender little green buds were already breaking through on the trees and bushes that we passed by. From a distance, we saw cities and villages while our thirst and hunger mellowed into a dull persistent ache.

Sleep

Marching all night and part of the day, we slept as we walked and bumped into one another. In the middle of the five-person lines was the one who slept, and the others just pulled her along. Sometimes all five in the line walked hand in hand and slept. We dozed when sitting at the side of the road to rest. Girls, still in a dream, said that when we got up we would have our freedom. We really did not care anymore about being free; we only wished to sleep, eat, and be in a dry place where there was no marching and no cannon fire or bombardment. Trudging along the hidden side roads and empty highways with so little rest, we learned not only to sleep, but even to dream as we walked. One bright, nippy evening, with a beautiful array of stars, I noticed a little house with lighted windows in the distance. It enticed my imagination and filled me with longing. Suddenly, I was home again by our light-brown tile stove. As my mother set the table for supper, my father entered, wearing his friendly smile. I was still admiring his expression when a sudden bump into a stone on the road brought me back to throbbing reality.

Hunger

The food supply usually depended on the commandant in charge.[12] He could organize a few containers of potatoes or rutabagas, but not every day. We were already hungry when we started, and we received no official provisions during the march. The guards had their own supply of food that they had brought with them. They could receive supplies in the places we passed.

After a week of starvation, we dared to ask for food from the civilians who came out of their homes to look at us. Our faces reflected suffering and despair as we passed the villages. Sometimes an individual passed a potato or a piece of bread into the extended hands. Erzsike and I were usually afraid to step out of the line to ask for food. Once we walked on a sidewalk close to a house where the window on the first floor was open. I was walking at the side closest to the house at that time, and I simply extended my hand. To my surprise, a whole loaf of bread was pushed out the window into my palm. I was shaking with excitement as Erzsike came to my side. Then suddenly a woman behind me grabbed the bread and ran away with it. We stood there stunned, hungry, and very hurt. We told Elza about our luck and our misfortune. She calmed us down and said that at least we were not beaten by the guards. It took some time to overcome my feelings of invasion of privacy and personal insult. I should have learned by that time the rules governing the multitude of starving prisoners.

Not being provided with regular provisions on the road, women resorted to boldness and danger to obtain some nourishment. Sometimes girls ran into private yards as we were passing by in the dark, and they seized what they could grab in the pantry or around the house. Some took eggs from chicken coops and ate them raw. From the barns, they snatched the food that was prepared for the animals. Then they ran to catch up with the march. Two girls from Kosice who walked in line behind us ventured into a barn where a cow was chewing a piece of rutabaga. They were so terribly hungry that one girl scratched the back of the cow to interrupt his meal, while the other quickly took away the rutabaga the cow was gnawing. They returned, munching the rutabaga and telling us about their adventure. In the struggle for existence, each person was left to her own resources and ability in the march, just as in normal life. Only our situation was the hardest imaginable. We could not sell our skills, and we had nothing to trade. We could search the fields, hoping for some farm produce, but they were almost bare at that time of the year. Thus, it was given to those who dared and had imagination to find ways of quieting their hunger.

After walking all night, we arrived at a large area separated by trees from the road. We stopped to rest, but hunger did not let us sleep. Klára Spitz Snitzler and some other girls collected weeds and nettle. The guards did not mind. The nettle with wide leaves stung less than that with smaller ones. Klára found a large can and two pieces of brick. She kindled a small fire with a few dry branches and the still-burning cigarette that Knittel had discarded. The nettle did not sting after being cooked. Erzsike pulled at me to join them. Our hands were red and burned like fire as we collected the nettles from the fields. I quickly developed blisters on my hands and feet. Klára gave us the fire after they finished with it. We just had to run to the brook nearby for water. We used our dish for food and cooked a delicious soup for ourselves. We even gave a little bit to Márta Weisz Paran, from our hometown, who was passing by. Years later, in the gathering of Abaújszántó survivors in Israel, Márta told everyone about that warm drink she received from us during the Death March.

In the meadow, we found yellow flowers that we remembered from home and were not afraid to eat raw with the grass. We also had some type of celery root that we found. We ate it, but at the end we were sick even from the smell of it. Some starving girls looked for snails, others climbed up and grabbed eggs from birds' nests in the trees. The women who were more resourceful, daring, and willing to take chances had a bit more food. As the prisoners grew hungrier, they often took more risks; the guards reacted by not only threatening to shoot, but also by actually firing their guns. Girls licked milk containers that stood by the side of the road and had a little milk residue. The guards warned them not to do it, and a girl who could not run fast enough was shot, Jolka Goldstein Grodan recalled. We were chased onward, and Jolka does not know what happened to the wounded girl. In a group of hundreds of women, only those close by were aware of many of the things that happened.

The SS forbade begging for food at the houses, but the starving women could not listen. They usually stopped at a nearby home as the march was passing by. They had a standard story that they told: they were coming from Leipzig and begging for food. People usually gave something, and then the girls ran to catch up with the march, which was possible because the line was so long. The guards who noticed them started to hit them with heavy sticks. If they caught the girls running to civilian places, the guards also began to shoot. On one occasion, a bullet hit Edit Welisch on the shoulder as she came out of a bakery. Edit was born on March 20, 1927, in Kaposvár. She collapsed while still clutching a loaf of bread. Edit's mother, Ilonka Wellisch, cast herself down by the side of her bleeding child. Sobbing, she helped her to get up and supported her walking, because Knittel would not allow Edit to sit on the carriage with the sick. He also prevented anyone to bandage her wound. The physician, Dr. Jozsa Adler, had to just stand there helplessly.[13] Ilonka Wellisch reached Terezin, according to the list, but we do not know what happened to her daughter Edit.

In their testimony for the Justice Department investigating Nazi crimes in Germany, witnesses confirmed that several unknown women were shot by the guards from Markkleeberg. They were hit while stepping out of the line and asking for or looking for food. The guards belonged to Knittel's group, but it is not known who actually did the killing because we usually did not know the SS personnel by name.[14]

Erzsike and I heard the shooting and the girls discussing the episode. That made us even more frightened to ask for food. The rest of the women in the march also listened to the sound and knew about the shooting. Yet, we were so hungry that some still risked going to homes pleading for food.

Our thirst was also tormenting when we walked on the highways. At one point, when we passed by a factory where women drank the dark liquid flowing from the machines, Knittel warned that they might die from that poisonous water. Still many continued to drink it. Another time, the guards were dividing soup, while the hungry crowd attacked the container and the soup poured to the ground. Some of the inmates threw themselves flat on the ground to lick up the residues of the soup.

The march stopped one night in the forest. It was cold, and we were so hungry that we could not even sleep. Early in the morning, the guards were not around, so the girls raided an agricultural field where potatoes had been sown. In minutes, all the potatoes were taken from the ground. Because the soil was dry, it was easy to dig out by hand the newly planted potatoes. Like an army of locusts, the inmates passed over the field. After that, there would be no crop for the farmer the next year. By the time Erzsike and I dared to join, not many potatoes were left. Erzsike found one piece, which she wiped carefully, and, holding it in her shaking hand, she urged me to eat it. Our argument ended as usual: we divided it carefully, leaving a tiny piece for each of us. Although we were happy at finding the potatoes, Rebbetzin Friedmann reminded us all that it was forbidden to pillage the sown seeds in the land, even if they belonged to the enemy.[15] When the owner of the field came and discovered what had happened, he started to scream. The SS apologized and we were quickly led away.

It was in brilliant sunshine that we continued through clean provincial towns. There were houses, neat little gardens, and cobblestone roads. The guards told the people that we were Jews and they should not give us any food. We were walking in a daze, and people were staring at us from the windows. Suddenly on the road I saw a half-rotten apple. As I bent to pick it up, another hungry girl, whom I knew as Judith, was faster than me and grabbed it from the ground. Actually, it was the core of the apple that someone had already eaten and thrown away. Even the core was half decayed and stepped on, probably many times. I watched with hunger mixed with a bit of disgust as Judith quickly pushed the apple core into her mouth and consumed the whole thing. When she finished, she looked at me, ashamed, and moved back to stay two lines behind me. Later on, she came to me with tears in her eyes and said that she was sorry and that she felt sick after eating that dirt. The same thing could have happened to me, too, only I would have wanted to share it with Erzsike. Hunger reigned over our whole existence.

The SS took a special pleasure in throwing the food they obtained among the starving inmates. They were amused to see how we trampled each other and the precious provisions in our attempts to keep from starving to death. One day near Meissen, as we were resting, the guards appeared with hot boiled potatoes in barrel containers. These were donated by one of the townspeople on Knittel's request. Erzsike and I were standing further down in the valley waiting for instructions. Meanwhile, the Germans decided that the prisoners were too unruly, and they poured out the boiling potatoes, leaving each girl to grab as she could. To my misfortune, the boiling potatoes rolled down in the valley right next to me. The crowds of famished, fighting, and pushing women ran from all directions to catch a piece, knocking me down on the steaming mass of potatoes. By the time I was able to free myself from the weight of the falling women, I suffered third-degree burns on my shin of the right leg. The burn was very painful, but it was above the ankle, in a place that did not prevent me from walking. With no treatment, the sore became infected badly. After liberation, not knowing enough German, I could not explain what happened, and I was treated as if I had a gunshot wound. The burn on my leg beset me for years to come. Because it did not heal and became suspicious I had to take tests and special treatments, which finally led to its healing. I still carry a deep scar on my right leg as a tangible reminder of both German brutality and our great hunger. Blanka Weisz Seidner still remembers how girls licked up the spilled potatoes off the ground, much to the guards' amusement. Visiting Erzsike once when she cooked potatoes for her children, she suddenly turned to me and said, "You know, many times when the potatoes boil I picture the women trampling over you. I could never forget."

Losing Track of Time

Days slipped by while we roamed about aimlessly near the Elbe River. We were driven through fields, meadows, woods, and villages with unfamiliar names. Kathy Zelmanovitz Goldstein recalled that endless road with sufferings when we were interviewed by a reporter in our visit to Markkleeberg in 2000.[16] The worst times were at night when the cold went through to the bones. The guards chased us further and further with no rest. Night followed day, and we forgot the count as we walked and walked. The SS did not let us rest in any one place more than a few hours. The soldiers were almost as tired as we were, but they had to lead us to be locked up again somewhere in another camp. At one point we were so exhausted and depressed that one of the women who knew German told Knittel, "Please shoot us." Knittel answered calmly that there was no order for that yet, Elena Salamon Kaufman recalled. The SS guards had an additional concern: They did not want to be drafted to fight for the protection of the fatherland against the Allied forces.

We did not speak because our spirits were so low; also we wanted to save our strength. As we marched, the silence was broken only by the urging of the SS words or beatings with the gun handles. It is hard to know what gave us strength. Maybe it was our will to live for each other and for the hope of coming home.

Our march could have been different if not for the prevailing political situation. We were caught in a stalemate in the advance of the two invading armies. The D-Day landing on June 6, 1944, along the coast of Normandy began the steady advance of the American armies toward the east, while Soviet forces moved toward Berlin from the west. The Americans were to conquer the area where we marched, but the Russians also aimed for it. Finally on April 25, 1945, Americans and Russians met on the Elbe River at Torgau, dividing the territory and cutting the German Reich in half.

Reactions of the German Population

In the final stage, the terror poured openly onto the streets, pathways, and meadows. The systematically organized killing over the years now stepped from behind the barbed wire into the public view. The SS and their accomplices did not shy from committing acts of brutality before the eyes of the civilian population, making men, women, and even children witnesses to their crimes. The kilometer-long trails of misery dragged themselves through villages and towns as tens of thousands of concentration camp inmates were struggling along various paths and roads between the Allied fronts. The prisoners broke down, half-starved and their strength gone, in front of the German populace. The SS men following the columns shot those who were left behind and rolled the dead into the ditches or had them buried in hastily dug pits.

What could the German population have felt seeing the marches? "I saw a procession of thin, staggering figures with greenish faces," said Wendelgard von Staden. "They shuffled along in wooden clogs, their jackets and pants hanging loosely. SS guards wearing gray army uniforms, with chin straps unfastened and machine guns over their shoulders, walked alongside."[17] "It was a shocking sight," additional citizens recalled. "I saw those of short hairs, with faces sunken and eyes framed deep in black," an eyewitness described. "It was a procession of ghosts, a batch of persons who were driven on along the edge of the road. They staggered, shuffled along. Their looks were apathetic, downcast. After them, lay corpses that were covered with coats or rags," others remembered.[18]

Dragging themselves forward along the route of the march, the marchers were, in the view of bystanders, "like visitors from the realm of the dead. Some were deathly ill, staggering, even crawling. They looked so bad that it was impossible to say their ages. A few stepped out of the column and plucked a bit of sparse grass and stuck it in their mouths, probably to still their thirst. With their last strength many moved forward supported and helped by their comrades in sufferings."[19]

The general reaction of the population to our march was usually hostile. The German people probably were afraid. They chased us away from their towns, feeling that they had nothing to do with us and our mistreatment.

Local police were all against us. In one town on the outskirts of Dresden, we did not even know that the guards were not with us, when suddenly the local German civilian police appeared. They were shouting and firing in the air. Some women ran back to call the guards, who were at some distance from us. The soldiers returned and led us away from the place.

The German population found the marchers a liability and did not want the conquering army to find them around their towns and cities and to hold them responsible. Local police usually arrested survivors who left the march.

Hitler Youth (*Hitler-Jugend)* attacked us too. They came in daytime as we rested in a forest, and the guards were not around. We heard screaming, as boys fifteen or sixteen years old appeared at the end of the line. They came with big sticks, hammers, stones, and guns. The angry youngsters threatened to kill us if we did not leave. The boys said that if the Allies found us in their town, they would be blamed for our mistreatment, Gabriella Braver Kosinka recalled. A few women ran again to look for the guards, whom they found not far away. The guards returned and forced the Hitler Youth to leave.

In a few places, the citizens did demonstrate compassion. They put down pails of water at the sides of the road, but the guards poured them out. The SS told the people that we were Jews, and it was forbidden to give us food. A pair of shoes fell next to Rose Hoffmann Davis—someone had thrown them from a terrace. How useful they would have been to girls walking barefoot; but the guards threw the shoes away. Crossing highways where German civilians passed by, someone occasionally threw a sandwich. The SS would beat up the inmate who happened to catch it.

Our Fate

Day followed day, as our strength and hopes waned. What will be our fate, we wondered: starvation, death at the roadside, or bullets? Will we get up after the next rest or will we be left by the road? I held on to Erzsike's hand or a piece of her clothing even when we slept. My will to struggle on and survive was connected with the hope of our future together.

One day, after marching all night, I just felt that my legs were folding under me. I could not walk anymore. I told Erzsike that we should look for the carriage at the end of the line where I could ride. We sat down at the roadside and with the final row of the marching columns we rejoined the line. The carriage with the sick was right behind us, and I was ready to beg for space on it. We left the lines and were on our way when we noticed the guards taking over the carriage. They told the inmates who had been pulling to take a rest. We realized that if I sat on the carriage, Erzsike would not be able to be next to me. I do not know how, but it seems that people have a reserve beyond the normal strength for emergency situations. I turned back, carried by the wings of horror, and hurried to keep up with the marchers. The distance between the carriage and our line grew larger and larger until, after one corner, it disappeared. Later, in one of our rests, we saw the carriage empty, ready to be filled again. I am still shaken from the thought of what could have happened. How easily, with the difference of a few seconds in timing, I would have been a traveler on the doomed carrier of the sick.

We rested only a little while before we had to carry on. Luckily, I felt better, but I was worried for Erzsike who had begun to complain. The guards hit and kicked us to keep in line. We passed villages in a never-ending march on infinite roads as the war raged around us. Night followed morning, and we walked still without knowing our final destination. It was possible to escape, but the fear of the German population, the war, and the unknown prevented many of the girls from deciding to leave. We heard gunfire and the sounds of war in the background. There were bodies on the road, girls whispered. We hurried further even though we had already walked twenty-seven kilometers that day. We listened to cries from the girls as the carriage with the sick became full again. The guards emptied it this time by leaving the sick at the roadside as we passed by a burning city.[20]

Meissen

It is hard to trace the exact line of the march. We were led in circles to avoid main and military roads. Sometimes we passed the same place twice. In certain sections, we had to run because we were told that the American army was close by. The exact route of the march we do not know; but there were certain cities like Leipzig, Taucha, Wurzen, Oschatz, Meissen, Radeburg, Freital, Dresden, and Teplitz that the survivors remember.[21]

We arrived at Meissen in the middle of the night and slept on the street. It was raining, and we were wet and cold. Ibolya Wollner Kaufman recalled that, in the morning, we heard the ringing bell of the streetcar as it tried to pass on the tracks where we were sleeping. We woke up quickly and stayed in line. The weather luckily brightened to a sunny day with good visibility, and we could see a wide body of water, which we learned was the Elbe River. There were yachts and sailing boats with people on them: How lucky they were!

Crossing a long bridge and looking back, I could see the line of marchers was still a large group. I remember vividly that day by the Elbe River, because it gave me a certain feeling of freedom. The immense view from the bridge, the natural world, and the extended horizon brightened my outlook and my hope for the future. From the height, we could see the other part of the city of Meissen, known for its fine porcelain. As the Duna did in Budapest, here the Elbe cut the city in two.

The bridge over the Elbe River, near Meissen, visited by the author in 2001.

The mountains, the villas, and the colorful roof tiles on a church reminded us of Buda. In the afternoon, we saw a busy city. The people stopped and looked at us. Some tossed carrots and raw potatoes to us. We gazed at the elegant people walking around. The SS soldiers were uncomfortable; maybe they were ashamed before the residents. They raised their sticks and chased us further. Ending our ruminations, we started to run in our broken-down clogs. We left the beautiful city of Meissen behind us. On the road were signs of destruction: huge heaps of ruins, giant holes in the asphalt, burned-down apartment houses, and broken cables that hung down on the roads. In the evening, we crossed a smaller bridge as the sirens sounded. The area was flooded by strong beams of light that gave off the brightness of daylight. The aerial fight lasted an hour, with deafening bombing and huge explosions. As the attack ended, women next to us prayed that miraculously none of us had been wounded. Knittel promised that, after Meissen, we would receive food, but it did not happen.

Hanka and Others Left to Die

Hanka was the sweet Polish girl who was our roommate at the beginning of our stay in Markkleeberg. Her calming voice and beautiful singing still resound in my mind. On the road, Hanka became totally exhausted. When the march stopped temporarily, she was taken from the carriage of the sick, where she had been a few days. The guards put her down on the ground. People, among them Bella the former *Lagerälteste,* came to talk to her in German, but Hanka did not recognize anyone at that point. Bella wiped a tear from her eye as she left. Poor Hanka was beyond all help.

The news about a girl who was dying at the side of the road spread among us. As usual, Erzsike and I tried to keep a distance from fearful sights and sorrowful happenings; but when we heard the name Hanka, we rushed to the scene. By that time, ordered by Knittel, two girls were in the process of taking off Hanka's overall top with the number. The sight touched me terribly. Hanka, who had so conscientiously folded her clothing every night, lay almost naked, dying at the roadside. Erzsébet Friedmann, the wife of a rabbi, said "*El Male Rahamin,*" a Hebrew prayer recited in honor of the dead.[22]

Erzsike and I joined the others in silent devotion. We were forced to start moving again, while Hanka was left dead by the road. The guards gave their usual treatment of striking us to go faster. Hanka's death touched everyone. Many of us looked as terrible as Hanka—ill, undernourished, dressed in rags—the shadows of once healthy, vibrant girls and women.

Not much farther there was a forest where we rested. Toward night, we had to organize in lines to march farther. Three sick girls were left behind again at the side of the forest. They looked terrified as they lay on the ground. We said goodbye without words. A few raindrops in the air were falling. We felt as if they were tears of those far away, who loved and grieved for us unfortunate outcasts of the universe.

Marching Through the Ruins

Radeburg

In the morning, radiant sunshine glowed on our colorless faces. Only the shadow of the guards and their blows dimmed a bit the sun's rays. They urged us, Erzsike and me and those lagging behind, to hurry and follow the others in the sad procession.

We reached Radeburg, where we passed through the heavily bombed main street. Tall high-rises had their floors pressed together like sandwiches of stone. In one house, the piano and the living room furniture were visible. Farther on, we saw masonry fragments, twisted metal, and other rubble that remained in a factory that had been leveled. We had not seen destruction of that magnitude before in all our meandering. We rested outside the city and then walked part of the day. At night, in a village, small groups escaped by hiding behind the gateposts of private homes. The rest of the marchers continued toward Dresden, passing a small town where the people came out from their houses to stare at us. Some marchers extended their hands and received a little food—mostly the strong or the forceful ones. For the weak and frail, not much was available.

Dresden

Dresden, the capital of Saxony, one of the states of Germany, was once called "Florence on the Elbe." Although we had heard back in Markkleeberg about the huge bombing of Dresden by the Allies, we were still not prepared for the sight. Large areas had become islands of destruction. It was impossible to see where a house had been, what a street was. There were only piles of stone. The buildings looked as if they had been cut by a huge hammer into pieces of stone. Only a few walls were standing here and there, the tops cut in zigzags. It became impossible to walk, and we had to climb or crawl. We were the only ones in sight who were walking at that time, and the SS, screaming and cursing, led us through the destroyed city. Bodies were not visible, but the smell of decaying flesh filled the air.

Our march was as tragic as the ruins around us. We walked all afternoon and then a steady rain started. The SS were terribly nervous and made great efforts to keep us in line. They had a hard time because girls got lost among the rubble. Eventually we left that monstrous place and reached organized, clean villages that had not been touched by the bombardments. It seems that we circled Dresden and exited to one of the suburbs. The streetcars were running and people strolled through the town. The windows were full of geraniums reminding us of home. It was hard to imagine that an hour's walk from there, Dresden lay in such ruins. Again groups of three or four girls hid to escape behind gates as we passed by.

Erzsike and I Left Behind

At the beginning of our forced march, the discipline was strong. Urged on by the guards and their rifle blows, we walked in orderly lines, five to a row, keeping up a steady pace. Later on, following several air attacks and after walking about twelve days, the guards relaxed their vigilance. Some of them would also have left if they could.

In the afternoon when we were on a road through a forest next to one of the peaceful suburbs of Dresden, there was suddenly an air attack. We dove hurriedly into the ditches at the side of the road. There we lay, Erzsike and I, covering our heads with our red food bowls. We were so terribly tired and weak at that point that soon we both fell asleep. When we woke up and climbed out of the ditch, we discovered that the rest of the marchers had already gone. Maybe they thought we were dead and so left us behind.

We looked with great apprehension down the narrow, winding road, seeing far in the distance the end of the marching columns disappearing as we watched. Although Erzsike and I would never have dared to leave, the march left us. As we stood there, panic-stricken, two other lost inmates—a mother and her teenage daughter—appeared. First, we wanted to catch up with the group, and then we realized the distance and our run-down condition would make that improbable, if not impossible. We listened to the mother and stayed where we were. Indicative of our state of mind, we did not find out the last name of our new friends. Last names had held little significance in the camp. We knew only that they were from Mako, Hungary. Checking the transport list, I have found the names of Szerén Grosz, born in Mako on January 15, 1910, and her daughter Zsuzsa Grosz, born November 28, 1926; they were possibly our partners in liberation.

Resigned to our fate, we noticed a small wooden shed that was probably a hunter's cabin. It was open and we entered, making it our home. While in the camp and through the march, we were hesitant to act independently; now that we were on our own, we had to find the courage to care for ourselves. Looking around the cabin, we found some dry beans and a small bag of flour. We started to eat rapidly, which was quite hard with the dry beans. Then Mrs. Grosz stopped us and said we must find some water or we would all be sick. We went out to look and soon located a small brook nearby. We filled up our soup bowls, drank the refreshing spring water, and filled them again to bring back to our cabin. Then we put the beans in to soak. Outside we also collected some green weeds to mix with the flour. It satisfied our hunger a bit. Next we returned to the brook to wash ourselves and tried to scratch the red sign from the back of our overalls. The "X" faded a bit, but it was still visible. We returned to the cabin where we found blankets, which we put on the floor. The one bed we gave to Mrs. Grosz. After that, we lay down, listened to the howls of the animals who might have been as scared as we were, then quickly fell asleep.

In the morning, after a whole night's sleep, we ventured from our cabin, the four of us together, and started to walk toward the town. It was a bright spring morning, and we saw a little girl in the garden of a one-family home playing with her doll. Erzsike, who still had one or two of her favorite dolls at home, admired the beautiful porcelain face of the doll, on which were eyes that could open and close. Erzsike smiled warmly at the little girl, who was about eight or nine years old. She smiled back and told us her name was Ilse. Then we all marveled her toys as she proudly displayed the doll's carriage and the rest of her dolly's belongings. Erzsike became Ilse's most attentive audience. She forgot for a minute how hungry she was, and she genuinely enjoyed the first steps on our freedom road with the memory of being a child again. Mrs. Grosz volunteered to make a dress for the doll, so Ilse's grandmother provided a piece of cloth, needle, and thread. In minutes, a beautiful outfit was created. Ilse's eyes sparkled and we were all invited inside the house for a meal. Ilse's mother and grandparents were waiting for us. The grandmother set the table with matching plates and cups, which had a forget-me-not flower design, and a pink tablecloth. We almost choked with emotion and memories. While the potatoes cooked, we were served fresh rolls and delicious butter. We ate slowly, politely, not wanting to display the aching hunger we felt. As she served us each a nice portion of mashed potatoes, our host apologized that they were out of salami or other meats. Ilse and her mother had been staying with the grandparents since they fled their bombed home in Dresden. Ilse's father was missing in the army and, from what we understood, they did not know his fate. We expressed our regret, and then they asked about us.

We described to them a bit of Auschwitz and the camp in Markkleeberg. We did not know then that it was not safe to say that we were Jews, but they would have known it anyway by our marked overalls. As they listened, our hosts surprised us by saying that they thought all those in camp had been criminals or prostitutes. They now knew that we were two children and a mother with her daughter, and we could only be victims.

Erzsike continued to play a bit more with Ilse, practicing the few words she knew in German. The family was sympathetic; they were suffering from the war too. We felt that their compassion was genuine. They let us into their home and said they would have permitted us to stay, sleeping even on the floor, if they were not afraid that the neighbors might report them. They prepared some additional rolls with butter to take with us. We were careful not to leave any untidiness on the table after us. Finally, we all bid good-bye, left the house, and reentered our world of runaway homeless fugitives.

Back in our little cabin, which luckily continued to be unoccupied—probably because of the closeness of the front—we rehearsed with Erzsike the few German words we knew. Grandmother had forced us to take German lessons with a private tutor; Erzsike learned some German in middle school too. German was the language of the intellectuals; besides that, grandmother had a German family background. I did not really like to memorize those words that I had no chance to practice in Hungary. On Saturdays, grandmother listened to what I had learned, and she herself taught us some German proverbs. One of them—"*Morgen Morgen nur nicht haite, zagen ale fole laite*" (Tomorrow, tomorrow, not today, lazy people say)—I have never forgotten in words or in practice.

We quickly learned to beg for food. Like all the beggars, we first asked by extending our hands. Erzsike, with her good language skills and a bit of what we still remembered from school and grandma's teaching, taught us to say, "*Genäige Frau, bitte schön geben Sie mir ein bisschen essen.*" We did not have to try hard; our tears came fast with the words because we were really hungry and very scared. As I think back, I wonder how we could have done it; but when there seems no other way, a person is able to do many things to stay alive.

Mrs. Grosz and Zsuzsa composed their own sentences for pleading, and the next day we went together to town. We canvassed each apartment separately and met in front of the buildings. Toward the evening, we walked back together, the four of us to our cabin in the forest. We got along very well together. It was good to have the company of a mother, with her wisdom and assurance.

My Encounter with a Member of the Hungarian SS

After a few days of asking for food in town, I had a scary experience with a Hungarian anti-Semite. As I finished soliciting the apartments on the first floor, I waited on the street in front of the building for Erzsike, who was asking people on the second floor. Standing there by the gate, a man about thirty years old, in civilian clothing, confronted me. Speaking Hungarian, he said, "What are you doing here, you hated miserable Jew? You are a fugitive, aren't you? I am going to report you. You deserve to be punished and die, just like the others of your kind who were already eliminated!"

Looking at him, I met his wolflike eyes, which were burning with hate and were hurling sparks of fire toward me. Probably a *Volksdeutscher* and a former camp guard, he could recognize inmates just by seeing them. The man continued his curses and, suddenly, with the strength and the fury of an angry beast, he slapped my face so hard I fell to the ground. When I arose, nursing my bleeding gums, the hateful man had disappeared. He probably would have hit me more if people in the street had not been staring and if the Russian army were not so close. I was still in shock when Erzsike arrived. She held my hand and we returned hurriedly to the forest and no longer dared to walk in the city. The following days, hiding in the hunter's cabin, I pondered the incident. The physical pain eased, but the mental anguish continued to torture me. In the camps, despite the prevailing cruelty and hardship, no one had assaulted me. The Germans' shouting and threats were frightening, but with my poor knowledge of German, I grasped only the curses' general meaning. I accepted them as part of the camp's monstrous world, which was void of positive emotion and allowed for no compassion. The incident with my Hungarian abuser was different. His physical and mental assault was direct and personal. He had harassed me in a civilian environment, and I was the sole target of his rage. His language, familiar and common to both of us, was sharp in tone, cruel in meaning, and suffused with inferences and connotations. I was deeply hurt and humiliated. The bodily pain was gone, but his unjust and repulsive words and curses struck deep into my soul. The incident remained with me as an unhealed wound.

Dazed by hunger, we finally ventured forth again under the cover of darkness to homes at the city's edge. The barking of angry dogs made me hold tightly to Erzsike. We learned that it was better to say that we were Hungarian workers and not Jews. We turned our overalls inside out so that the markings did not show. Fortunately, the end of the war was only a few days away, and we were liberated by Russian soldiers. My second meeting with the Hungarian SS, I will describe in chapter 13, under the heading of "Revenge."

The Marchers Cross the Czech Border

The marchers that left us behind continued toward Terezin in Czechoslovakia (called Theresienstadt in German). The women walked through beautiful clean villages that showed no traces of the war, Elza Reich Szamosi remembered. The stores were open, and life continued as usual. The civilians observed the marchers' sad procession. The group stopped, and Knittel's wife divided some kind of white powder to each one on line. The girls realized that it was flour, and they consumed it rapidly.

Our friend Hava Hartmann Kleinberg was planning to leave the march, but she did not dare for a long time. Hearing the guards saying that, following the forest, they would be in Czechoslovakia, she decided that the time was right. A group was quickly organized and included Hava's sister Miriam, Márta Weisz Paran (another friend of ours from Abaújszántó), Márta Groszman Pollack from the nearby town of Erdöbénye, and Jolka Goldstein Grodan, who had attended middle school in Abaújszántó. They asked Margit Lang Stein, also a good friend from the area, to come too; but Margit decided to stay, and she reached Terezin with the marchers. Two other girls, Lili and Viola, heard the girls talking about leaving and asked if they could join them. Together there were seven who escaped when the marchers left the forest.

The sun was shining brilliantly as the marchers advanced. They looked at the snow on top of the mountains near the Czech border. The highway turned left, and there were two checkpoints; on one side were German and on the other Czech guards. The Czech soldiers had grayish-red uniforms and red hats. The golden buttons on their uniform were shining in the sun. The Czech soldiers stood at attention as they greeted the marchers. The border guards who escorted the group with the SS now left. The girls became apprehensive of what was to come. As they continued, they saw only Czech soldiers on the road.

The group slept in the forest. The townspeople close to Teplitz brought food in big dishes on carriages. Everyone received cooked sweet noodles and potato soup, Elza remembered. In the next picturesque town, people stood in line to throw bread, fruits, and even salami. Close to Terezin, the Czech population continued to put food on the road where the marchers walked. They were not allowed to speak, but a few told the marchers who spoke Czech that the camp they were going to had a typhus epidemic. They advised them to escape, but the girls had nowhere to go. They were aware also that the supervision was tight at that point, so close to the new camp. The girls were anxious to know what would be waiting for them: Would they work? Would there be a selection again, forcing family members to separate? Or would it be the long-awaited freedom and liberation?

13
Liberation

Different Shades of Freedom

In Markkleeberg, we were always dreaming of the day of freedom. We had images of greeting the liberating army and of seeing the defeat and the punishment of our oppressors. This was not a question of revenge but a need to feel some satisfaction that our humiliation and physical suffering would be accounted for. The cousin of a dying girl, wanting to instill hope and courage, told her to be brave a bit longer and soon she would see the victory over our tormentors. Those were our fantasies; things turned out to be much different.

The end of the German enslavement reached the inmates in a variety of forms. The earliest freedom came to those who did not go on the march, but hid in or around the camp. Escaping or going with the march was one of the few choices we could make. The desire to remain with family members or friends was an important factor in the decision. Inmates who freed themselves from the forced march faced other types of perils, and their experiences will shed light on the prevailing atmosphere in the last days of Hitler's reign.

Diverse Groups Roaming the Highways

Toward the end of the war, the area around Leipzig was full of municipal factories that led their volunteers, forced workers, and slave laborers on marches. The roads were full of foreigners, including inmates who had escaped the march. In addition, there were American POW soldiers roving the cities of Saxony through which our marching group were led.

The foreign workers from the factory in Markkleeberg were also forced to leave. We met them on the way, quite early in the march. Klára Fischer Neuman recognized the Dutch technical assistant who worked on her machine. He threw her a whole loaf of bread. Luckily the guards were not around, and Klára quickly shared the treasure with her sister and friends. Erzsike and I also noticed someone waving; we believed it was Peter, the boy in the factory who made Erzsike the ring. Erzsike followed the group with her eyes until they turned and disappeared at the corner. Much later, when we were walking on our own in the forest near Dresden, we again saw a group of forced laborers. "Doesn't that boy look like Peter?" Erzsike asked.

Although some of the foreign workers, such as those from the Ukraine, were hostile to the escaping prisoners, most of them helped. Sara Salamon Israel, who had recited by heart the prayer for the memory of the dead on Yom Kippur, left the march with her cousin Regina Farkas Pincsefski and a friend named Rachel. Taking advantage of the confusion after the bomb attack near Oschatz, they went into a yard where the owner asked what they were doing there. The girls started to cry and say that they lost the transport during the bombing and were very hungry. The man called his wife, who cooked potatoes and gave them something to drink. When they finished, the girls were asked to leave. Sara and her friends did not know where to go. They had no coats, and the red "X" on the back of the overalls marked them for everyone to see. While they walked, a boy came by wearing a "P" sign, indicating that he was a Polish political prisoner. They talked to him in Czech, and somehow they all understood one another. The boy said that he had a Czech girlfriend and that he would bring some food. He really came with his girlfriend as he promised, and they brought cooked eggs and bread while they themselves did not have much.

The girls continued to walk to the next town when they saw a farmer on his way to the fields. They asked for work and promised to do whatever was needed on the farm. Believing that they were Hungarian volunteer workers, the farmer told them to get on the carriage, and he took them to the fields. Ability to work was always a means of survival, whether in the camps or in the outside world. At night, when they returned, the farmer gave them a small room where they could sleep. They stayed with the farmer about two weeks. Milking the cow was a real challenge. None of them had ever done it before; their reward was a glass of fresh milk. The girls were careful not to reveal that they were Jewish, although Sara said her evening prayer, "Keriyat Shema," as she had every night, even after the hardest days in the camp. The prayer reaffirms the tenets of the Jewish faith and dealt with the dangers of night and the fears of the worshipper. Sara was scolded by her cousin Regina, who feared that someone might be listening.

They stayed and worked till the Russians entered the area. The conquering Russian soldiers were drunk and rowdy, motivating Sara and her friends to put chairs and other furniture against the door of their room. At night, soldiers knocked and then departed, leaving the petrified girls fearful of the arrival of their long-awaited liberation. They left the place and arrived home safely.

The Civilian Population

The official, government-sponsored hatred of the German people toward the Jews showed signs of weakening a bit during private interactions with the former prisoners. Refugees from the bombing of Dresden, or those whose husbands or sons were fighting on the front, had a bit more compassion. They gave the former inmates food, let them take baths, and even took the chance of providing a night's stay. In the morning, however, they always asked them to leave. Citizens were afraid of the guards that might be looking for the escapees and the neighbors who might talk. Other civilians who found the women on their property not only chased them away, but they even called the police. Some of the women who knew German well tried to tell their true stories. Although some were sympathetic, others made among the first Holocaust denials, asserting that no such thing could have occurred. They maintained that the women were criminals and thus became prisoners.[1] The very nature of the Holocaust, the massiveness of it, and our persistent instinct to disbelieve—despite all available evidence—leaves us open to the revisionists' vicious acts of imagination.

"Liberators"

Most Russian soldiers were honest, good men who had suffered much from the Germans, but some behaved rowdily following victory, thus creating the general impression that Russian soldiers were wild, drunk, and dangerous to women. At the beginning, the Germans were their targets, and then slowly every woman felt in danger of rape by the Russian soldiers. Some caught their victims in daytime in the middle of busy cities, raping them in full daylight. These drunken, lawless Russian soldiers were a great danger for female survivors on the road. They did not distinguish among defeated German civilians and Jewish victims in their rush to enjoy the fruits of victory: they just wanted *Barisnya* (women). Almost every survivor who was liberated in territories under Russian control had some story to tell.

Language skills could sometimes help a woman. Russian soldiers would move to molest a girl or woman, but they often left her alone if someone knew a bit of the language and spoke in her behalf. To save themselves, girls sometimes pretended they were sick or had syphilis so the soldiers would not touch them. Others put on kerchiefs in such a way as to look like old women. Most Markkleeberg survivors will tell stories of their comrades' sufferings and death at the hands of the Russians, but they are reluctant to talk about their own possible sexual abuse by Russian soldiers.

The following is only one of those many sad events caused by the criminal behavior of Russian soldiers that was recalled by the victim herself. Two sisters among a group of twelve girls who escaped the Death March from Markkleeberg were on their way home after liberation when they stopped for the night in a school where German soldiers had previously been housed. It was full of lice, so a few girls, including the sisters, went instead into the abandoned house of the supervisor of the school. Russian soldiers arrived in the middle of the night, and most of them went to the school, but one came to the house. He knocked at the door, and the girls, not knowing about the Russian soldiers' reputation, opened it. The soldier entered and, at gunpoint, forced the older of the two sisters, whom I will call Helen (not her real name), to go with him. Unable to speak Russian, the girls were stunned and terrified, not knowing if they would ever see the unfortunate victim again. Tall and extremely pretty, Helen came from a religious home. The Russian soldier took her, with the gun to her back, to a nearby barn. There he threw her on top of the straw. Helen was forced to undress while the soldier pointed the gun at her. There was no way out for the terrified victim. Only thanks to Helen's immeasurable luck, or maybe the strength of the prayer she was reciting, the Russian soldier found himself impotent. He tried a few times, but could not perform. Angry and frustrated, he gestured at Helen to leave. When Helen returned to the room, her sister and the rest of the girls could hardly grasp the miracle that had just happened. Those women who stayed in the school fared much worse. In the morning, there were two corpses lying in the yard. One victim, who was shot when she attempted to escape, was still dressed. The other unfortunate Markkleeberg survivor was thrown outside naked and dead. It was a terrible beginning to Markkleeberg prisoners' long-awaited liberation. Survivors knew the ill-fated girls but did not want to profane their memory and good reputation by revealing their names. Rape or sexual activity outside of marriage was considered shameful in those days, even in the case when the girl was a victim.

Jewish Russian Soldiers

One ray of sunshine among the Russian army for us survivors who wandered the highways and byways of Germany was the occasional presence of a Jew among the Russian soldiers. Many of us had memorable experiences, which I will relate later, with our Russian co-religious brothers. Our good friend Klára Spitz Snitzler and others whom we knew from home were also helped by a Jewish Russian soldier. Klára, who came to talk to us a few times about escaping, finally left the march near Freital. With her were Agnes Glück Rabinovics and Olga Deutsch from Encs, Klára's hometown, as well as Ilona Roth and Eva Rosenberg Eichler from of Abaújszántó. With Agnes were her aunt and cousin, so all together there were seven of them.

After leaving the march, Klára and the group went into a summer house where they found a stove, water, and a storage bin with potatoes. Eva, the only one who knew how to cook, put the potatoes on the fire; but the girls were so tired and hungry they ended up eating raw potatoes and fell asleep. Later, following liberation at Freital, Klára and the group met a Russian Jewish soldier. He and the other Jews in the Russian army were our real heroes. They were among the first to help the survivors who were struggling to find their way out of the abyss of Germany. Klára's Jewish soldier brought them food and clothing and advised the girls to leave the area to avoid the danger of drunken soldiers. He even helped the group to find places on the train to Prague. Klára arrived in Budapest and then home, where no one was waiting for her. She was the sole survivor of her family.

Irena Lebovits Ehrenreich and her friends left the march in a group of ten. They wandered from town to town around Dresden, begging for food. In some places, the residents even let them wash themselves. Eventually their luck ran out, and they were arrested. As foreigners without identification, they were added to a group of marchers. Contemplating their escape, the girls suddenly noticed their German guards had put on civilian clothing and were telling the marchers that they were all free. As they looked for transportation, they met Russian soldiers who were gathering people to work in Russia. This was the sad fate of many liberated inmates: They were seized and taken to labor camps in Siberia and returned home only after months or even a year of hard work. Irena spoke Czech and showed them the number on her arm. Luckily the soldiers accepted that they were Jewish prisoners and let them go. Slowly the trains started to run, and the girls reached Budapest. There Irena met her younger brother, who was waiting for them. Survivors were registered on the way, and the list of names was sent by telegraph to the Joint authorities in Bethlen Square, Budapest, thus, the brother knew of their arrival. Their happiness was great but short-lived: Jolán, Irena's sister, died in childbirth, and her brother fell in Israel during the war of independence.

Rozsa Winkler

After her sisters Nelly Winkler Rochlitz and Hajnal were forced to leave the camp in Freital, Rozsa Winkler was taken to the hospital. The German staff in the hospital realized that she was Jewish, and they refused to treat her. The critically ill Rozsa was taken back to the camp. There she was alone, cast off without her devoted sisters to care for her. A little sunshine reached her after liberation. Then Rozsa and other sick inmates from Markkleeberg were taken back to the hospital. With Rozsa was Erzsébet Holzer from Kisbaromlak, who was wounded by bombing during the Death March. Later, Erzsébet 's brother came to take her home with him. Unfortunately, Erzsébet died on the road. Before they left, Rozsa gave the brother a letter addressed to the Jewish community in Vac, Hungary. In that letter, Rozsa explained how, in the hospital, they were screaming and cursing that there was not enough room even for Germans, so why would they treat the Jews? The letter reached Nelly and her sister at home in Vac. Back in the hospital at Freital, sadly not much could be done at that stage for a girl suffering from advanced tuberculosis. Rozsa Winkler died on Sunday, July 22, 1945. She was nineteen years old.

Andor Winkler, Rozsa's brother, had arrived home in Vac on a Friday afternoon from the camp at Madhausen. On Sunday, he left to look for his sister in Germany, taking with him the money the family could gather; but on the train, Russian soldiers robbed the travelers. Andor finally reached Freital and the hospital after many difficulties, only to learn that his youngest sister had passed away and was buried a day before in Christuskirche, the local Catholic cemetery in Freital. There were no other Jews then in Freital, and the heartbroken brother had no one to talk to. Having no money or resources, Andor could place only a small wooden sign to mark her grave. In chapter 15, I will describe my trip to the cemetery and the search for Rozsa's grave.

The Escape of the Welders

Elizabeth Zucker Mermel was one of the girls that Erzsébet Frank wrote about in her poem "The Welders," printed in chapter 10. In the march, the welders were beset with foot problems and hunger. They were waiting for a chance to escape, but it was not easy for ten girls to leave together. When the marchers were led among the ruins at Dresden, it was hard for the guards to keep an eye on everyone. Behind one of the still-standing walls, a welder gave a prearranged signal, and the ten girls disappeared.[2] They watched attentively as the marchers passed them by, then spent the night in that destroyed city surrounded by an eerie silence. At dawn, they left and wandered around a small town nearby. German civilians were quite generous with food, some even let them sleep in the barns, but they wanted no further connection. The girls had trouble finding a place to sleep.

In a few days, the Russians entered, and the owner of a tavern invited them to stay there. He put fresh straw on the floor in one of the large rooms. The girls believed that by inviting them in, he wanted to protect them from the Russian soldiers. They did not know then that the owner had hidden his daughter in the basement to guard her. The welders were resting and arranging their little belongings when they heard a noise and two Russian soldiers came in. Like many of their comrades, the soldiers were checking around the town for women or property, like watches, that they especially liked to take with them. They found the girls and asked two to go with them to have a "good time." Seeing that friendly persuasion did not work, one took out his gun. While he was raising the rifle in his hand, he was pulling at one of the girls and saying, "I will kill you if you don't follow me!" The situation was so real that the second soldier asked his friend whether he really meant to kill her. The first one answered that he had no bullet in his gun; he just wanted to scare her. One of the Trattner sisters spoke Czech and understood the soldiers' conversation. She told the group to hold on.

The girls pulled back their friend forcibly and joined hands together. The soldiers, quite intoxicated, cursed and threatened; but the women stood strong, saying that they could kill them all but none would go. The standoff and the tension continued for some time. While the drunken soldiers contemplated their next move, a new group entered. They too were looking around German residences. These soldiers also carried guns, but they seemed more reasonable. One of them paid attention as the Trattner sisters explained that they were camp survivors and also had suffered under the Germans. He even sat down, listened to their stories and looked at the numbers on the girls' arms. Elizabeth Zucker Mermel, who related these events to me, believed that the soldier was either Jewish or very open-minded. The first two menacing soldiers stayed for a while, still angry and with ominous expressions; but seeing that the others listened to the girls, they slowly left the place. The sympathetic Russian soldier continued to ask questions until his comrade gave a sign, and they all left. The girls burst out in tears from the stress and trauma of the night. Dawn was breaking, and they decided to leave the place as soon as they could. They were gathering their little possessions when the innkeeper's daughter came out from her hiding place, smiling. The welders were very hurt to discover they had been cheated again by a German who used them to shield his daughter.

Outside, the ten former welders found an abandoned truck with a box of red flags in it. They took a few flags and, in an empty house, they located a sewing machine. Elizabeth Zucker Mermel and another girl who knew how to sew made everyone a blouse. They also found clothing in the closets and changed their overalls, which they left there. The girls continued to help one another, and it was important for them not to separate because they knew that together they were stronger. In one of the train stations, two of the welders found their brothers who joined them. That gave them a bit more confidence against the Russian soldiers. They reached Bratislava, and then Budapest, where the Joint authorities helped them. Elizabeth and her sister learned that their older brother had also survived and that he was waiting for them at home.

The Liberation of Those Who Worked in Zwenkau

Just like the welders, Lilly Waldman left the march with five girls who worked together and had been on one line in *Appel*s at Zwenkau. With Lilly were her sister Erzsébet, her sister-in-law Jolán Waldman, and my two cousins, the Linder sisters Lenke and Hajnal, whom we did not even know were with us in Markkleeberg. That group of five was always together. During the Death March, Erzsébet was unable to walk. She sat down at the side of the road with the other four standing next to her. The guard came, urging them to move and threatening them. Nothing helped, and the girls would not leave Erzsébet. The rest of the marchers moved away from the group a bit as the guard took out his gun to solve the problem. Before he pulled the trigger, however, another guard came and said to him, "Leave them alone!" He himself hinted to the girls that they should leave the march. Erzsébet collected her strength and staggered away with her friends while their incredible luck still held. We will never know what motivated that guard's action to save Erzsébet. People's goodwill surfaced in many circumstances. Maybe the mutual suffering during the march or the guard's owns uncertain future influenced his actions. With the usual delays and tribulations, the five finally arrived in Budapest together. As of today, only Lilly Waldman, who is eighty-seven-years old, and her sister Erzsébet remain alive from the original five. When I talked to Lilly, she had just finished a conversation with her nephew, the son of Jolán Waldman, who was among the five with her in the Death March from Markkleeberg. Jolán's son calls each Friday from Australia to wish his Aunt Lilly "*Shabbat Shalom*" (a peaceful Sabbath).

Theresienstadt (Terezin)

The marchers arrived in Terezin on the morning of April 29, 1945. They had walked for sixteen days, going between 30 and 40 kilometers (18 to 25 miles) a day with almost no food—about 360 kilometers (224 miles) in total. They marched in darkness and on forest roads, under the constant blows of the guards. Countless marchers died of exhaustion and starvation on the way, and many escaped at various places in the region of the Elbe River.

On March 15, 1945, there were 1,539 prisoners in Markkleeberg.[3] The number who reached Terezin was 685, according to the list of arrivals.[4] We can add to those a few hundred who left the march. The rest of the original 1,539 marchers perished, but there is no documentation of their deaths. The camp in Terezin was under Red Cross supervision when the marchers arrived. They saw Swiss flags and a huge Red Cross sign. At the gate was a checkpoint. There, speaking Czech, stood a young Jewish man in a raincoat. There were no SS to be seen.[5]

The fourteen French women in the march who remained from their original group of 250 were separated as the marchers arrived. They wanted to come with the rest, but only Jews were admitted. The Jewish women were sorry to leave them. Knittel, his wife, and the five remaining guards also wanted to enter the gates of Terezin, but the Czech officer told them *"Abtreten! Abtreten!"* (withdraw). The camp was under the protection of the Red Cross. Knittel left, confused and disappointed, followed by his wife and the guards.[6]

Knittel's displeasure brings up the question of his motivations for why he wanted to lead us to Terezin in the first place. When we started the Death March, Buchenwald was already in the hands of the American army. Knittel made contingency plans and even gave us a farewell speech, saying that he and his staff would leave, but we would continue to work with the factory management under better conditions. Then suddenly a message arrived and everything changed. On March 12, 1945, a day before we started our Death March, Himmler drafted a document entitled "A Contract for Humanity," which promised that concentration camps would not be blown up.[7] The Germans had agreed to the entrance and supervision of the International Red Cross in Terezin. They were also willing to bring the majority of those left in concentration camps to Terezin. This was actually a token concession on the part of the Nazis, when millions of Jews had already been killed. Knittel, like other commandants, could either let us stay in the camp or leave us on the road. Although we have no documentation, we just know that, at the gate of Terezin, Knittel kept explaining that he had saved and brought us to Terezin, Frida Roth Kaller recalled. At the end of the war, German commandants hoped to gain favor by saying that they saved Jews.

The Jewish man at the gate politely organized the inmates into five-person rows and counted them. The girls were elated, their eyes dazzled. Could it be true, they wondered, that justice had triumphed? Would food, clothing, and sweet freedom be waiting for them?[8]

Markkleeberg Guards Return with Some Escaping Prisoners

Whatever Knittel's intentions were, the former Markkleeberg guards still wanted to lock up the inmates in Terezin. Ten kilometers from the camp, they met four Markkleeberg prisoners—Blanka Weisz Seidner, her sister Edit, and two of their friends. The girls had left the march after Dresden and had many adventures on the road. The guards were on their way back to Germany after having left the marchers at Terezin. Seeing the girls, they grew angry and shouted, "Because of you, we have to return now!" The inmates had a few potatoes, which the guards noticed and took away. Blanka and the other girls were terribly scared, wondering what would happen to them. At the gate of Terezin, the Markkleeberg guards handed them over and waited as the four prisoners fearfully entered the camp.

Inside the Camp at Terezin

Terezin is a sleepy little Czech town located about forty miles north of Prague. It held a fortress that Maria Theresa had built for her soldiers. In World War II, this former army barracks site was transformed into a Jewish ghetto. Nazi transports from Terezin to the east began on January 9, 1942, and continued through October 1944. Destinations included, among others, Auschwitz-Birkenau.

Set up as a model camp, Terezin/Theresienstadt was inspected (and approved) by the International Red Cross in a Nazi public relations sham. For the Red Cross officials' visit, the Nazis painted the buildings, installed flower boxes, and temporarily improved the diet. The sick prisoners were transported to death camps, and the healthiest inmates were put forward to impress the Red Cross. Theresienstadt, in truth, was rife with disease, overcrowding, and starvation. The most famous Red Cross inspection was in June 1944, at the request of the Danish government. After the visit, the Red Cross issued a favorable report.

The next International Red Cross delegation, headed by Paul Dunant, visited the Theresienstadt ghetto on April 6, 1945. The delegation was accompanied by Adolf Eichmann and other SS officers. The Red Cross reported that Theresienstadt held 17,556 prisoners.

The first 2,000 inmates evacuated from other camps reached Theresienstadt on April 20, 1945. Within the following two weeks, more than 14,000 prisoners arrived from Dachau, Buchenwald, and Flossenbürg, among other camps. A typhus epidemic soon followed.

When the marchers entered Terezin, they did not see any Germans inside the camp.[9] The strength that carried them all that way reached its final limits as they began to feel safer. Some could hardly walk the last few steps. Around eleven o'clock on the morning that they arrived, the group was taken to an underground bunker, which had been a former prison. The place was damp, dark, and dirty. Markkleeberg prisoners stayed in quarantine there before being placed in a regular block. Only the doctors and the food deliverers could enter. The next day was a brighter one. In the morning, a man brought fresh bread and hot black coffee with sugar. He filled up everyone's cup and then asked who wanted more. The girls had to remind themselves that their happiness was real. There was no wake-up call, and they received food without having to stand first on *Appel* and without any slap on the face or box on the ear! After breakfast, Dr. Brown, the main physician, continued to arrange admissions to the hospital. Hundreds of girls were ready to go, but only ten were admitted because the hospital was so crowded.[10]

They were soon able to exchange their overalls for civilian clothing. Following the quarantine, the women from Markkleeberg were transferred to a block called Yäger, or Yäger Kaszárnya, as Hungarian women called it. When they walked outside, they were surprised by the immensity of the camp and the crowds of people there, Elza Reich Szamosi recalled. Transports continued to arrive until the last day of the German reign.

Liberation at Terezin

On May 2, 1945, two days after the marchers from Markkleeberg arrived, the International Red Cross took over the camp at Terezin, and the rest of the SS men fled the area. The first Russian soldier appeared on May 8th. Inmates ran toward him, but the soldier retreated, afraid of the prevailing typhus epidemic. That same day, the German armies surrendered to the Allies.

Outside the camp, former prisoners watched the procession of disarmed German POWs. Some had their hair cut in stripes and on their backs was a large red "SS," Elisabeth Stein Székely recalled. Their former elegant, well-fitting uniforms were ragged, with torn pieces hanging down; they had no hats and some had rags on their feet. As they walked past the open gates of Terezin with their heads bowed down, some of the inmates cursed and spit on them from a distance.[11] Inmates like Elisabeth Stein Székely recognized a former guard of Markkleeberg among the prisoners, the one we knew as Bacskai. He was a *Volksdeutsche* from Bacska in the former Hungarian-Yugoslav territories. In the documents of the Center of Federal Justice Bureau for the Clarification of Nazi Crimes, there is one mentioned as Josef from Bacska.[12] Elisabeth asked a boy next to her, who spoke Russian, to alert the guard that Bacskai shot a woman during the Death March. The Russian soldier looked at Bacskai and wrote down the details. There is no further information available on whether he received punishment that might provide a bit of comfort and sense of justice to his victim's family.

My Liberation

The day Erzsike and I were long dreaming of came so plainly and simply. We were still staying in the small cabin in the forest. That particular morning, in the first week of May 1945, nature provided a beautiful sunny spring day. We hoped that people, influenced by the weather, would be in good spirits and generous. Early in the morning, all four of us were ready. The sounds of explosions had much increased during the last two days. This worried us a bit; but hunger was stronger than fear. We had just begun to walk on a side road when Mrs. Grosz called out, "Don't look!" It was too late; by then, we all had seen the bodies of soldiers lying dead on the walkway by the side of the road. Some of them may have been alive still, but we were afraid and turned back quickly to the safety of our little cabin. We sat down, shaken by the sight and by the powerful effect of the gunfire, explosions, and other sounds of war that we had heard.

Then it was quiet. We tried to sleep to forget our hunger, but we could not. Suddenly we heard voices outside our usually quiet location. We stepped out, and there were two Russian soldiers on horses. They waved and said something that we interpreted to mean that the war was over. Electrified by the good news, we collected our few belongings and left the cabin with the idea of going home. As we walked on the main road next to beautiful villas, we noticed that the door to one of them was open. We ventured inside and found a table with bread, sugar, and several kinds of homemade jam set out. It seems that the owners had left in quite a hurry. The closets were full of clothing. We hurriedly exchanged our overalls and shoes for civilian clothes. Gazing at the mirror, we were frightened to see skeletal creatures with big, hollow, scary eyes looking back at us.

We noticed all kinds of valuable crystal and art in that obviously wealthy household. We could have searched for money and jewelry, as other resourceful survivors had done. The Kaufman sisters, for instance, had found a bundle of gold in one of the homes. From that treasure, Nelly Winkler Rochlitz recalled, they rented a truck that took five girls to a distant city to catch a train. We could not think yet about material possessions; food was still the most valued asset for us. We took with us only our new clothes, the old overalls, and some provisions for the road. Outside we found a small two-wheeled handcart. We returned to the villa then and brought out additional food and clothing. We could have taken even more, but Mrs. Grosz noticed Russian soldiers in the backyard, so we left hurriedly. Taking turns pulling the handcart, which was quite heavy, we decided to discard our overalls. I was a little hesitant, but the others convinced me that food and getting home were our most important considerations. We left the overalls by the side of a tree in a park that we passed. I always have with me, however, the memory of that last look at my discarded garment and the numbers on it that were my identity in those months in Markkleeberg and throughout the long march.

We walked in the direction of Dresden—Saxony's capital in eastern Germany—hoping to find transportation. From its fishing village origin, Dresden evolved into a city of half a million people. Situated at two banks of the Elbe River, Dresden was well known after World War II as a city that was demolished by Allied firebombing. In Markkleeberg in February 1945, we had heard clearly the combined bomber fleets of Britain and the United States. Although the houses were reduced to piles of stone, the roads in Dresden were clear by that time, and we walked by tidy streets with street signs clearly posted at the corners. The dead and dying were not visible in that neatly organized destruction. In fact, there was no movement in the eerie city as we continued on our way. Being ignorant of directions, we walked for a week, only to return to our starting point. Tired and hungry, we were sitting on the corner of a roadside when we heard the sound of an automobile. Shortly, a group of five or six Russian soldiers surrounded us. As our liberators, we were pleased to see them; but instead of the sympathy and guidance we hoped for, they looked at us with the eyes of men hungry for women. We stood there with growing apprehension, when one of the soldiers quietly said something in Yiddish. Knowing only Hungarian, we were unable to respond. Feeling frightened and vulnerable, while the rest of the soldiers stood back waiting, my sister and I, as if prompted by a secret cue, heard ourselves pronouncing "*Shema Y'Israel!*" (Hear, O Israel)! Shema is the first prayer taught to a Jewish child, and it captures and expresses the beliefs and goals of the Jewish religion. The soldier's face lit up with a smile of understanding. He spoke to his comrades, who made room for us in the van, and we left our cart behind. Mrs. Grosz and Zsuzsa, our fellow inmates, who possessed no Jewish education, stood in awe at the miracle of the Hebrew words. In a short while, we reached an army post where, following a sumptuous meal and food for the road, our soldier protector brought us to a refugee collection center. There the camp supervisor confirmed that transports would be forming to go toward Prague and Hungary. At parting, our soldier hugged each of us, while we dried our eyes and sealed within our memories one of the more profound moments of our return to humanity and faith.[13]

From the collection center, where I again met my Hungarian SS attacker (more on this later), we proceeded by train to Prague. When we arrived, they disconnected the engine and attached it to another one carrying Russian soldiers. We sat and waited all night, with no information about the schedule or the return of the engine. In the morning, those who had food with them continued to wait. Being hungry, we joined a group that was going to a guesthouse in the city. It had been organized for refugees by the Joint. As we registered, we noticed a list of survivors who had previously passed through. Reading the register, our hearts started to race with excitement. The name of our father, Sándor Szász, was before us! Erzsike and I looked at each other and thought that the gates of heaven opened for us, not realizing that his name was a very common one in Hungary. We stayed a few more days, visiting the city's Jewish sights. Anxious to go home, we said good-bye to Mrs. Grosz and Zsuzsa, who had met friends and decided to stay longer.

At the railway station, only a few crowded trains were running. They were without any schedule because all the connections had been severed by the bombing that destroyed the tracks. Many of the bridges were also blown up. On the provisionary passageways, the waiting was long to accommodate the wide tide of survivors flowing across Europe. There was no mail service. We left Prague and walked for days along railroad tracks that helped us to get from one town to the next. If we found a train, it traveled only a short distance, and then we had to disembark and wait days to continue again. A minimum food supply was provided by Jewish agencies or local individuals. We were sleeping on highways or in railroad stations, waiting for the next train. Dangerous travel on top of freight cars was less fearful to us than the drunken Russian soldiers who were canvassing the stations and the trains, looking for women. Luckily they passed us by. After weeks on the road, driven by the wheels of hope, we reached Bratislava. From there, with additional delays and miracles, we finally arrived in Budapest.

New Challenges

The girls in Terezin ventured outside the camp and helped themselves from the supply of food in nearby abandoned homes. After so many months of endless deprivation, the food was too tempting to resist, which caused many to overindulge during the first hours of freedom. Survivors suffered acute abdominal cramps and, in many cases, even death. Initially, our digestive systems could not tolerate even simple substances such as butter. Women who found sugar and mixed it with butter consumed it, only to get severe diarrhea or even die. It was a common sight to see the wooden boxes in which the bodies were carried away, Sarah Mayer Fisher recalled.

Typhus

The girls were warned during the march about the typhus epidemic in Terezin. They had no choice but to go with the group, however. Some of them did contract typhus in the camp. People with weakened immune systems were the most vulnerable. Barracks called Hanover and Hamburger were set aside for those suffering from the disease. Despite the medicine and the good nutrition, hundreds died every day.[14] We know from the official list that Margit Krausz from Szatmárnémeti, born on January 27, 1927 in Sátoraljaújhely, died in Terezin on June 29, 1945. Margit had been with us in Markkleeberg. The cause of her death could have been typhus, but it was not stated in the record.[15] Hanna Kahan, who fortunately survived, stayed three weeks in the hospital in Terezin suffering from typhus.[16]

Pillaging

The food supply in the camp was not adequate for all those housed there, but in a small town near Terezin called Litomůřice, there was an army storage depot. The girls could go there and fill up bags with food—or even chocolate and cigarettes. They brought the supplies back to the camp and shared them with their friends.[17] It was unfortunate, however, that the women often met Russian soldiers. They were lucky if soldiers snatched away only the bundles of food and let them go. The Jewish guards in Terezin warned the girls not to leave the camp because of the danger from the Russian soldiers. They were also advised that it was still not safe to say that they were Jewish.

Not all the Russian soldiers lived up to their bad reputation, of course; many had goodwill and empathy toward the survivors. Former *Blockälteste* Márta Maget Leitmann and her friends who spoke Czech complained to a Russian soldier that they had no shoes. The soldier took them to one of the German homes. The residents, including children, were inside as the soldiers told the survivors to take whatever they wished. The girls felt uncomfortable, but took some shoes. Then they saw two handbags in the closet that they wanted for carrying their few possessions. They picked up one and then the second, when a young girl of maybe ten started to cry that it was hers. The girls felt so badly that they left the handbags and even took off the shoes, which angered the Russian soldier. The girls remembered how the Hungarian gendarmerie used to come to their homes and pick whatever they wanted to take with them. Regardless of how much the Germans pained and humiliated them, the women were unable to hurt that innocent little girl. The Russian soldier scolded them as they were walking again, almost barefoot, in their old broken shoes. Despite expressing his anger, the soldier was touched and mentioned the affair to his supervisor. The next day, two truckloads of shoes were brought into the camp and divided in an orderly fashion to fit the survivors who needed them.

As soon as girls obtained some goods, they were ready to barter. Ilana

Sajovits Breiner's friend found a jar of honey that she exchanged for a dress for Ilana, whose clothes had been pilfered when she took them off for the night. Due to the increasing typhus epidemic, the girls eventually were not allowed to leave the camp without written permission, Kathy Zelmanovitz Goldstein recalled. The girls were eventually organized in Terezin and left in transports. They had to register, and those from Czechoslovakia were scheduled for the earliest departures.

Wishing for Revenge

Women who were hiding in or around the Markkleeberg camp during liberation were told that Lucifer had been arrested after an inmate recognized her. It could have been possible, because Lucifer—Helena Pöschel—was a native of Markkleeberg. Yet it was probably only wishful thinking on the part of former prisoners. It was reported that Lucifer had escaped with the American forces.[18] We wanted to believe any rumor about her, because it was unbearable to think that our tormentors all escaped punishment.

My Own Chance for Revenge

The Hungarian SS who had assaulted me in a suburb of Dresden met me again. It was in the International Displaced Persons' Camp, where our Jewish Russian soldier had left us. Many Hungarian refugees were there. Those identified as Nazi collaborators were turned over by the camp police to Russian authorities or were judged locally and executed after a quick trial.

One day, as I was checking on the transports to Hungary, I noticed the Hungarian SS with the small wolflike eyes. Those eyes, the focal point of my recurring nightmares, were blunt and expressionless this time. It took a moment before I collected myself and then ran to discuss it with Erzsike and Mrs. Grosz. They knew how I had been hurt both emotionally and physically, and they encouraged me to report him. I contacted the camp guard, a former Jewish prisoner who was very interested in my story and was sympathetic. He asked a few questions about the details, and then we went to look for the SS man in the camp. I spotted him talking to people in front of one of the living quarters. The guard called him in for questioning.

Insisting on speaking only German, the accused denied knowing Hungarian or ever living in the area of Dresden. Yet I had no doubt of his identity. His eyes and expressions were stamped permanently on my heart. The inquiry continued. He may not have had the SS tattoo, but with his strong accent, the man finally admitted to being Hungarian; and he was detained for further investigation. Aware of the speedy judgment against and execution of Nazis and their collaborators by the police in those early days following the war's end, I was tormented by the responsibility of identifying my abuser. I went over the details with Erzsike many times. The next day, after a sleepless night of indecision on whether to uphold or drop the accusation, I learned that documents had confirmed and the man had confessed to staying in the suburbs of Dresden during April 1945. My case against him had become stronger.

As we were waiting for the head of camp security to arrive, the man who had so cruelly assaulted me and threatened my death, "as every Jew deserved," stood meekly next to me. Then he started to speak and apologize. His mother, wife, and two small children were waiting for him at home, he explained tearfully. If I were to testify against him, he would never see them again. "Please do not condemn me to death," he pleaded.

I moved away without an answer. Looking out of the window, I continued to agonize about my old pain and my new predicament. The man's language, my mother tongue—those soft, quiet, kind Hungarian words—brought back memories. My parents used that vocabulary as they had communicated and conveyed to me the values of decency, politeness, and fairness. Ideas of hatred and thoughts of revenge were as foreign to me as the road that had led me to be a child prisoner in Auschwitz and an outcast in the towns and forests of Germany. Captivated by the Hungarian language, and a hostage of my nonviolent upbringing, I yielded to the man's plea. After withdrawing my complaint, I was angrier with myself than the camp police were annoyed with me. I felt my shameful, cowardly decision was evidence of a meek, confused teenager.

Today I still occasionally see the man's haunting "wolf eyes" in my dreams. Yet I do not know whether my decision would be different now than it was then. The feeling of pity and compassion that I was familiar with is easier to bear and lighter to carry than the burden of revenge and retribution. I am not sorry.

The next chapter will describe our return to Hungary and encounters with more of our non-Jewish countrymen. Although no one was ever that mean to me again, facing the no-longer-deniable reality at home, we knew that we would never truly be freed and liberated.

14

Life of a Survivor

Homecoming

WHILE IN THE CAMP, WE WERE IN A KIND OF TWILIGHT ZONE: THE changes in our lives were so severe, so out of the ordinary, that we could not accept them as reality. We tried not to think, and we did not ask questions because we knew we were not ready to hear or to know the answers. Comforting thoughts that the war would soon be over and we could return to the homes we knew before were the goals that nourished us and contributed to our survival. The belief that if we just got home we would find everyone safe resounded in survivors' testimonies.[1] We hoped that if we just stayed alive, the Germans would be defeated; hatred and genocide would never plague mankind again. With the appearance of the first Russian soldier near our cabin, we thought only of the way home. How could we have known that the news waiting for us would be harder to bear than anything we endured in the camps?

With the small cart we found, we started our journey on foot. Later, after arduous travel and fueled by hopes that our father Sándor Szász—whose name we saw on a list of survivors—would be waiting, we arrived in Budapest. There, to our great delight, Aunt Hanni, my mother's sister, greeted us. She did not know anything about father. Hanni, or Hannus as mother called her as an endearment, was the lady from Kosice who had brought mother the documents to help us escape before the ghetto was established, but my mother did not act on the offer. Hanni was shocked at the terrible shape we were in. She took us to the hospital, where it was discovered that I was suffering from TB, so Hanni made arrangements for me to enter the tuberculosis ward of the Landes Institute in Budapest.[2] I was a patient there from July 31 to October 1, 1945. Before entering the Landes Institute, however, I insisted on going home with Erzsike to Abaújszántó first. Nothing, not even the illness of TB, could have stopped me.

"Coming home": The words convey such a warm feeling of love and safe haven. Having read the name of my father on the survival list, we were almost expecting him to be at the train station; but it was raining and the place was empty when we arrived. We waited awhile, looking at and inhaling the scenery that was so familiar to us. When the weather cleared a little, we started to walk home. It was early in the afternoon and all was quiet in the sleepy little town. We walked quickly and, in ten minutes, we found ourselves before grandfather's meat shop and our father's clothing store. Both still stood in front of our home—a location we had visited so many times in imagination when we were in the camps. The shades on the stores were down, which told us that father had not arrived yet. Maybe our mother and grandparents would be home. With rising excitement, we hurried into the yard, when a stranger came toward us asking what we were looking for. We told him we were looking for the Szász family. "Nobody by that name lives here," called out an annoyed woman from grandmother's terrace. We wanted to go to our apartment, which was further back in the long yard, but the man said, "I wouldn't recommend going there. The people have a big dog." Holding hands, we left the yard and found ourselves on the street under the big tree where my mother used to sit reading those enchanting tales while waiting for customers to come to the store.

Our presence was quickly noted in town. Each returnee posed a threat to the townspeople and their newly acquired Jewish possessions. Bárdos Bácsi (Uncle Bárdos), one of the Jewish community members, arrived shortly while we were standing there trembling, not knowing which way to turn. Bárdos Bácsi, a friend of my father, smiled, hugged us, and took us to the home of the rabbi, which had been vacated for the homeless returnees. A few girls greeted us warmly with that comradely spirit we knew from the camps. That night we slept on the floor, and the next morning Bárdos Bácsi arranged that the current tenants would empty a room for us in our old apartment. When we expressed concern about the "big dog," they assured us that it was only a small puppy that would not harm anyone.

Finally "home," we sat down in our empty room. Lonely and disheartened, we both started to sing our mother's song about a street in a village where geraniums embellished the windows, and they saluted their neighbors on the opposite side. When a window failed to open, there was a void—someone was missing from that lane. With tears in our eyes, we repeated the short song with its beautiful longing melody:

> Little windows open, one following the other;
> Geraniums wave to their opposite side.
> Only one window stares with blind eyes,
> As all seems so empty; someone is missing from that street.[3]

The song reflects the peaceful life of a country town, yet there was also the pain of loss. The town was the same; the street was still there, the windows were unchanged; only our parents, grandparents, and the geraniums were missing.

Camp survivors had to face the tragic truth after liberation. Many did not return home at all. Erzsike and I had a slow awakening after the camps, but still we could not accept being orphans, having no one. We were guided by the power of the memory of our parents and the possibility of recovering their world. In Budapest, like the rest of the survivors, we had received some money at the office of the Joint in Bethlen Square. It was not much, but for us it was the first currency of our own. Instead of buying clothes or even the food that we needed, we went to the town hall in Abaújszántó and paid off the taxes on our home. We felt so good, imagining in our minds' eyes how our parents would be pleased and proud of us. We remembered the struggle they had had with the payments in the last few years of economic hardship. We also looked for Boriska, our former maid, but she left town and no one knew her whereabouts.

Our days filled with anticipation as survivors struggled home. We waited for the arrival of the train day after day. Then slowly, following many discouraging visits to the train station, we started to realize that our mother and grandparents would not be coming back. A slow, dull pain took up permanent residence in our hearts. Unlike Mother and Grandmother, we had not seen Father going down the road of the condemned, and for him I have never given up hope. Even today, although in my heart I feel that my father probably perished at Auschwitz, without concrete evidence, I cherish even the sketchiest information about him. I will probably never know for sure. As in the camps, I still keep my protective delusion so as not to face the certainty of his terrible death.

Jewish Property

Like Erzsike and I, many other returnees, after all their difficulties, arrived in their town or city only to find that strangers occupied their homes and that their personal belongings were held by townspeople. Each of us has painful memories of seeing our precious things used by others. Some were able to reclaim part of their property with the aid of the police, but the majority had no strength or spirit to fight for things. When I saw my mother's suit being worn by a woman on the street, I collected my strength and dared to ask for it back. Mother's elegant black costume had much sentimental value for us, and I remembered the times she had prayed in the synagogue wearing her favorite holiday outfit. The woman in my mother's suit, a local resident, angrily rebuked me for stopping her in the street and said I was an audacious, impudent teenager with no manners and shame. "I bought the suit legitimately at an auction conducted by the government, and you have no right to it!" she said, using the law an excuse as she walked provocatively away. I was lucky she did not ask her son, who was with her, to beat me up. I stood there helpless and dumbfounded; the only thing I could do was to cry, which I did.

The Sanatorium

After being home awhile, I returned to Budapest and entered the tuberculosis ward of the Landes Institute. Erzsike was very concerned to be so far from me; we had never been separated before. Aunt Hanni promised to visit me, but the borders with Czechoslovakia where Kosice was located were closed, and Hanni was unable to come. Erzsike, with great effort, saved some bread by depriving herself, and she sent me a few packages. Hungary, being on the losing side in the war, had a very pronounced food shortage. Budapest was a bombed-out, hungry city. Food was rationed, and our meals in the sanatorium consisted mostly of beans.

After being in the sanatorium a week or two, I was sitting forlorn and down-spirited in the courtyard among other TB sufferers and waiting for Erzsike's letter, when a visitor arrived. It was Aunt Rózsi or "Rózsi Néni," the wife of my father's first cousin, József Reinitz. Looking for surviving relatives, Rózsi located me from the patient lists of nearby hospitals. We knew Rózsi from home. She and Józsi Bácsi (uncle) came to see us whenever they visited their family in nearby Encs. At our last meeting, around 1942, we preadolescent girls found Rózsi, our elegant guest from Budapest, very interesting. Mother, a naturally pretty lady with dark brown hair smoothed and gathered into a knot at the back of her head, wore very little makeup. Rózsi insisted on introducing her to the latest in cosmetic innovations. When she completed her makeover, the transformation was so pronounced that everyone stared at Mother. I still could see my mother's blushing and her awkwardness as she tried to avert attention from herself.

Rózsi, a pleasant woman about the same age as Mother, hugged me at the sanatorium with tears in her eyes. She had lost most of her family and had never had children, but luckily her husband survived. They continued to occupy their old spacious apartment on 19 Veselényi Utca, in the center of Budapest. After her first visit, Rózsi came every Friday, bringing homemade cake or cookies and some fruit that she had been able to obtain for Sabbath. One day, Józsi Bácsi also accompanied her and told me about the time he stayed with our family before I was born. He was a tailor's apprentice in Abaújszántó and attended trade school there. During the three to four years of working to receive his license, he enjoyed free room and board at Grandmother's home. In Budapest, Józsi became the owner of a successful tailoring workshop and employed several workers.

In her visits, Rózsi talked a bit about the past and our possible future, always emphasizing the importance of learning. She was anxious to check my medical reports and the many X-rays that were taken. One day, she told me with shining eyes that the latest tests had come out very well and that I would be released shortly. I was delighted to be going back to Abaújszántó, but Rózsi Néni had another idea. She invited both of us to stay with them and attend high school in Budapest. I was touched by the kindness and the offer. I knew that it was the sensible thing to do, but emotionally we were not yet ready to pick up the pieces of our broken lives. I left for Abaújszántó with the promise that we would be thinking about her offer. Later, we bid both Rózsi Néni and Józsi Bácsi good-bye as we were on our way toward a new life in Palestine or Israel. Schooling was far from our minds. As the distance grew between us and Budapest, however, my desire for knowledge became clearer and stronger. I did not know then that it would take a whole lifetime to catch up what I missed by not returning to school at that time. I wrote to Rózsi Néni from Israel, but my letter came back with the comment that the family had been relocated. The Russians needed spacious apartments in good locations for their Communist members, and they moved many people to the countryside. To my great regret, we lost contact. In my first return to Budapest, I went to look for them at their former address. I asked around, but no one really wanted to recall the past or volunteer information, especially with a new tenant occupying the Reinitz apartment.

The Search for a New Life

Mikéfe

After I was released from the hospital and moved back to Abaújszántó, we still could hardly focus on much beyond pure survival. Not knowing what we would do, we were happy when, during one of those disappointing waits at the train station, a visitor came looking for us. Zeev Shahar, an amiable young man, had come as an emissary from Palestine. Zeev was also a distant relative of ours, and he knew that some of his family had lived in Abaújszántó. Even though we had no idea about Palestine and we had no Zionist training, we decided to join a group in Mikéfe, near Budapest, that Zeev recommended.

It was a darkening and windy fall day in 1945 when we left our hometown once more. Our suitcase and knapsacks were ready, waiting in the small room that was our home since we returned from Germany. We had already said farewell to our town and good-bye to the few remaining friends. The kinship that once tied us together slowly started to fall apart. We did not belong to them or to the town any more. Realizing that our parents would never be there again, Abaújszántó lost its former importance to us.

Prior to starting on our way toward the railway station, we looked at our garden in the back of the yard, with the sour cherry trees, branches of red currants, and the old walnut tree that gave us so much pleasure and many childhood memories. We left our room without making any arrangement for its future use. We could not deal with giving it away. Saying good-bye, we were, in a way, parting with the past. Mourning our parents and grandparents, whose memories we took with us, remained a lifelong process. The pain of that loss kept them with us forever.

The travel to Budapest was a journey from the past on the road to the future and the unknown. Erzsike and I were moving from what previously had been our whole lives—both the pleasant and the sad segments—to survive. Thirty years later, I was back again, searching for familiar faces and links to that past. I needed that reconnection, but leaving Abaújszántó in 1945 was an emotional relief and a necessity.

After the war, Mikéfe, an agricultural school in Budapest, offered a *Hachshara,* or preparation, usually in agriculture, to those planning to settle in Palestine. We arrived, as many of the orphaned did, alone, with but a few belongings. We were greeted with warmth and vigor by a group of young people. Zeev Shahar, our mentor, introduced us; then we were on our own.

The young teenagers who came to Mikéfe, mostly orphaned and each with a different background, arrived with their war traumas behind them. In Mikéfe they found a sanctuary. Among ourselves, we could laugh again and relieve a bit the responsibility of the adult world that was suddenly placed on our shoulders. We were all equal in the group, with none of the priorities or constraints of the class system so prevalent in Hungary. We did not need papers or credentials, and we made fun of all those documents that were important before the war and then became valueless. It was a bit of relief from the restraints of the old world. We did not speak of the past; and slowly we regained and developed our individuality, each of us valued and appreciated by the group on his or her own merits and personality. We relished having common goals and mutual aspirations. We gave ourselves wholeheartedly to building a new life and a new future together.

In Mikéfe, we also discovered boys for short romances. Some of the more outgoing girls and boys went "steady," and we watched them, sharing their happiness and disappointments. The danger of Russian soldiers that we knew from the time of liberation in Germany loomed still in Hungary. We blocked the door to our room with chairs and other heavy objects.

The time we spent in Mikéfe was filled with adjustments and anticipation. The forward-looking atmosphere in general and the company and comfort of members of the group provided us with a great psychological lift. It filled us with the strength and hopes to overcome, as well as possible, our war experiences. I could not imagine how we may possibly have lived in adoptive homes, as some of our friends and other orphans who came directly to America did. Being in the group, nobody replaced our parents; they remained fully in our memories, secured in our hearts. To stay with adoptive families would have been much more painful. Talking to teenage survivors who were accepted by families in the United States or who lived with relatives, I learned that they, with a few exceptions, did have difficulty adjusting and a hard time gaining independence.

Zahava and Hava

As we were working toward becoming new persons building a country of our own, we also picked up Hebrew first names for ourselves. Based on my Hebrew name, I became Zahava, and Erzsike turned into Hava. Havicsku is what we called her as an endearment, and I was called Zahavicsku by those close to me.[4]

Sometimes I think of the girl Katalin that I left behind in Hungary with my childhood and Holocaust memories. A shy, sheltered, small-town teenager, Katalin was taken from her warm, loving home, with her younger sister, Erzsike. The only grandchildren of doting grandparents, they were cruelly thrown into a sea of people fighting to stay alive. Katalin was terrified, always in fear of separation from her sister. She was terribly cold and hungry, working twelve-hour shifts as a slave laborer. In the Death March, she limped with an injured foot in those terrible wooden shoes. Suffering from TB, she slept by the roadside in pouring rain and blowing wind in thin overalls. How did she, how did we, do it? Was I really there among the inmates in Markkleeberg? I will be looking for Katalin again in my return visits to Abaújszántó. Katalin will be there in the school, in the synagogue, or playing with her best friends. I will be with her, standing in front of our dilapidated house, searching for familiar views and faces; my lights and shadows of the past.

Life, with all its challenges and strivings, has brought me some recompense. I have my husband, my children, and my profession; but for my parents and grandparents, there are no amends. Their lives shortened, the opportunity to see their children and grandchildren creating life circles of their own was stolen from them. That is my biggest sorrow. When I write, I want to touch people's hearts with the injustice that happened to them.

Leaving Hungary

Finally the news arrived that it was time to depart Mikéfe and begin the road toward Palestine. We left Hungary with no regrets; we had nothing there anymore. We each collected some sentimental items, such as Mother's candelabras, grandfather's Kiddush cup, a painting of me as a little girl done by a local artist, the drawing made of Erzsike in the factory at Markkleeberg, the ring, and a few other mementoes that filled a small suitcase. The travel was organized by an underground movement, the

Bricha (the flight), which helped surviving Jews escape from Eastern to Western Europe and then to Palestine. We had to steal over the border, under cover of night, through forests and mountain paths. We traveled by truck until we reached the Slovakian border, where we had to continue on foot. The truck was to meet us with our belongings on the other side, but it never arrived. We were pained to lose those few small but precious things we possessed. Today, when I see the "antique road shows," with people my age bringing out belongings from their grandparents, I feel my loss anew. The paintings, ceremonial artwork, and other sentimental and valuable collections of the generations in my family all went into the hands of people who hated us. I have not a single item from the past, and my children are thus robbed of their heirlooms.

Indersdorf

From Slovakia, we continued by train to Bratislava and Vienna. Then we were taken by military trucks to the American occupation zones in Bavaria and on to a cloister in Indersdorf. The Children's Center in Kloster Indersdorf was established by the United Nations Relief and Rehabilitation Administration (UNRRA) and the Joint to shelter and rehabilitate non-German children left homeless after the war. The cloister maintained a population of 350 young people where UNRRA provided services, with assistance from a local order of Catholic nuns.

We arrived at Kloster Indersdorf at the beginning of March 1946 and joined a group called *Mahapeha* (Revolution). We all spoke Hungarian. Our destination was Palestine. We learned Hebrew and general studies taught by educators (*madrichim*) from Eretz-Yisrael who joined our group.[5] In the evenings we took long beautiful walks in the greenery around the fields. We kept busy watching sports tournaments and cheering the players, members of our group.

The Voyage on the *Lanegev*

Finally the news arrived that we would be leaving for Palestine. We again crossed borders, this time to France. On the illegal boat called the *Lanegev* (to the Negev), we started our travel. The plan was that a small vessel could avoid the British blockade and we would land at one of the ports close to the Negev. Almost as soon as the journey began, the travelers all became seasick. It was the beginning of January, and the sea was turbulent most of the time. All passengers stayed in their hastily constructed three-level berths. It was scary being rocked and thrown like seaweed in the endless ocean. The storm lifted and lowered the tiny vessel with its six hundred fearful passengers. The fact that no one was hurt, with the baggage flying all around, was another miracle in our ordeal. The boys kept it a secret that they were taking turns, day and night, collecting the water that entered the boat. Passing the days in the poorly lit semidarkness below deck, we listened to one another's aspirations and visions of hope. Being shy and reserved, I never told my friend that the boy she was so highly praising and planning to meet in the kibbutz was also the hero of my dreams.

Early in February 1947, on the twenty-third day of torturous travel, we reached the shores of Palestine. Two or three battleships of the English Royal Navy followed and surrounded us. Each was ten times the size of our little boat. One of the vessels gave a push to the engine room of our boat and the engines stopped working immediately. After that, the *Lanegev* was tied to the British warship. To force the powerless ferry to surrender, heavy combat ensued. The travelers, all of them survivors looking for shores of haven and hope, were not ready to give up without a fight. In an embodiment of the accumulated pain of our former inability to express our defiance, the refugees stood and hurled canned food toward their captors. The shots the British fired just made us more desperate. Erzsike and I joined the fighting unit until we ran out of cans, and then the British soldiers boarded our boat. Far behind me was that quiet, law-abiding, small-town Jewish girl. We did not heed the orders to evacuate, thus they carried us forcibly, one by one, onto their large ship. Later we learned that, during the battle, the British soldiers had used live ammunition in firing on us, killing one and injuring a few others. From the deck of the British ship, we watched Haifa, the city in lights, slipping away in the distance. Singing "Hatikvah," the national anthem of Israel, we waited again for the next chapter in our uncertain existence.

Cyprus

The imprisonment in Cyprus—with the barbed wires, watchtowers, barracks, and other hardships—would have been more agonizing if not for the zeal of the group and the optimism of our youth. The steady rains of February hammering the top of our tin barracks sounded to us like a musical orchestra. Living twenty-five or thirty boys and girls in round, barrel-shaped barracks, each of us had a designated place. Food was supplied from a common kitchen and planned activities were made known in weekly pamphlets published by the different Zionist organizations.[6] We passed our days studying Hebrew, and those who wished could learn knitting or embroidery. We also did combat exercises with wooden sticks. We were eager to participate to learn the skill of fighting back. We also had folk dancing and singing. Some teens composed a song with the lyrics, "It is not so terrible to stay in Cyprus, which is the door to Israel." This way, we passed six months until August 1947 when, in honor of the queen's birthday, the British allowed 500 children to enter Palestine.

Israel

On arrival, the British transferred us to another type of jail in Atlit. There we stayed three weeks in quarantine. Then on August 17th, we were taken to Kibbutz Heftziba.

In the beginning, we worked only half a day and we studied in the afternoons. Then the kibbutz needed additional labor, and our group was assigned to full-time work. We were so disappointed and, with a courage that forever amazes me, I contacted the Jewish agency, and a meeting in Haifa was set up for us. We voiced our desire to study and were transferred on November 20th to Ajanot, an agricultural middle school not far from Tel Aviv. By then, Erzsike and I were strong enough to separate from the Indersdorf group and were ready to direct our own destinies. As other young adult survivors, we had been able to recover our capacities and resume the path our lives might have taken before the Holocaust. During Israel's war of independence in 1948, we stayed in Ajanot. We were trained to handle guns then, but luckily we never had to use them. Shortly after my graduation from Ajanot, I met Meier. We married on March 2, 1949.

Meier and Zahava Szász Stessel in 1950.

Erzsike and her husband Baruch Ginsburg in 1953.

Erzsike studied at the Rambam Hospital in Haifa and became a registered nurse. She married Baruch Ginsburg, a *Sabra* (a person born in Israel), and they made their home in Haifa.

Their son Amir was born in 1954. All this time, I was still very close to Erzsike, living only a few houses away. Not having children, however,

Meier and I decided to travel and spend some time in the United States. In 1957, I left Erzsike and Israel for a few months—which extended into a lifetime. Missing that sweet, close connection and the warm sisterly love, I questioned time and again the soundness of that decision.

Learning About the Gas Chamber

When I was in Auschwitz, I had seen the smoke and sparks, yet I did not *really* know about the full horror of the crematorium and the gas chambers. I only found out the details twenty years later when I was talking courses at Brooklyn College and one of my American schoolmates told me about the lunchtime screening of a film on the Holocaust. I had to wait around for my afternoon classes anyway, so we agreed to meet. I was tired and looked forward to sitting comfortably in the dark auditorium, maybe even catching a little nap. Then the showing of *Night and Fog* (*Bei Nacht und Nebel,* in German) began. *Nacht und Nebel* was the code name for a decree under which those deported were never to return. Directed by Alain Resnais and written by Holocaust survivor Jean Cayrol, this 1955 French production combines documentary footage and stills to produce a film of unsurpassed power. Unprepared, I sat there breathless and motionless, viewing the execution chamber of my mother and the other people who were so precious to me. I do not know how I endured watching until the end, shocked as I was. As I stumbled out into the sunshine afterward, I could not meet the eyes of my friend or the other viewers. I do not think I ever want to see that film again, or any other graphic description of that most painful blow to my heart. After all these years, I still have not completely comprehended the truth about the murder of those I dearly loved. Although I knew it in my mind and intellect, I never fully fathomed in my heart the presence of my mother in that execution chamber with the false shower that sprayed poisonous gas at them: my gentle mother, my little grandmother, and my amiable grandfather.

Although I could not handle the facts of the gas chamber, my granddaughter Keshet, when she was twelve years old, picked up the topic and expressed herself in the following poem.

The Flames at Auschwitz

You leap and dance and tower high
Destroying all that's in your path.
Your stretched out limbs consume the sky
And crackle with your heated wrath.
Through night and day you glint with roar
Greeting each man with fear and terror.
No tears will make your hate subside

No cries have, or will, lessen your pride.
With young and old you do your duty.
Stronger with your victims' blood.
Nothing, it seems, can harm your beauty,
Reaching to infinity and beyond.
And every day I watch you flicker,
Waiting to cause more strife.
The reason I never will decipher
Or know how one flame can erase a life.
—Keshet Shenkar

Being a Survivor

The Sense of Loss

There was no ecstasy, no joy at our liberation. Freedom brought new sorrows. We had lost our families; our homes were occupied by people who still hated us; and our money, businesses, and possessions were all gone. The memories survivors carry are part of our post-Holocaust identities. Our parents vanished, and we are their only trace. We lived during times when the laws of our country were both unlawful and inhumane. Instead of protecting, they led us to Auschwitz.

The life of each of us changed forever when the Holocaust marked our existence. My life path would have taken me to a wholly different course. I would probably have remained in Hungary. My mother would have helped me to provide my children with our traditions. Being so young during the war, I could transfer only a little of our culture, of the sense of extended family, and of the strong family values that are missing from life today.

Marriages

The decision to marry was solely our own, without any consideration of ancestry or lineage that was so significant before the war. The importance of dowry, which was so crucial in pre-Holocaust Hungary and which kept many girls from being able to marry, diminished. Without the question of economics, marriages became quicker and easier. It was sufficient that the boy was the best friend of the girl's brother, or if two people were from the same town. There were many girls who felt they lost the most important years of their youth with the outbreak of the war and with the men away years in forced-labor battalions. They looked for immediate matrimony and family, and many married widowers who had lost their wives and children in Auschwitz. A 28-year-old girl marrying a 40-year-old widower was very common. Some girls, however, were reluctant to marry widowers whom they knew from home if they had children from the previous marriage. Without documents, it was hard to arrange a civil ceremony in those first months after the war. A married man had to prove that his wife had died. The rabbis often conducted religious ceremonies, and then they waited for the official government papers.

Older girls usually married among their Hungarian peers, sharing their common culture and adhering to the traditional values. Younger ones, like we were, acclimated ourselves more easily to new circumstances. Erzsike married an Israeli, and they raised their three children in the new culture that Erzsike easily absorbed. My husband Meier is from Transylvania, a former Hungarian territory that today belongs to Romania. He is from a religious family and did not share the same secular Hungarian culture in which I grew up, but we were young and both survivors.

While new marriages were created, the Holocaust sometimes shattered previous commitments. Magda Schön Hilf returned home only to find out that her fiancé had married someone else. The intended bridegroom returned early and was lonely. Believing that Magda would never come back, he married a non-Jewish girl to have a partner and a home. When Magda arrived, there was heartbreak for the two of them. Her former fiancé was ready to seek a divorce, but the disappointed Magda refused the offer. At home, her neighbor had faithfully guarded and returned the small package that Magda left for safekeeping during deportation; it contained love letters and a few photographs of the formerly happy couple. Ironically, it was the only thing Magda was able to recover from their home. She thanked the kind neighbor, and then, when she was alone, she tore the letters and the photos into hundreds of tiny pieces.[7]

Jewish Functionaries after the War

Erzsébet Iczkovits, the work organizer, left the women with many painful memories. Looking for information and interviewing former Markkleeberg prisoners, I was pleased to locate the address of Erzsebet's daughter, Agnes Iczkovits Lanyi. Agnes was with her mother in Markkleeberg. Dealing directly with the commandant and other German staff, I knew that Agnes could provide details that others did not have about the camp. I called her in the summer of 2002 and heard both tension and hostility in her voice. I gave my name and telephone number and said gently that if she was busy, I could call back, that I wanted to ask just a few questions about her recollections from Markkleeberg. She said, "Call me back at night," so I did. When she answered the phone and heard my voice, as I said, "Agi, . . ." she slammed the telephone down in my ear. I was stunned and felt again what it was like to be mistreated in the camp by Jewish inmates. Some of them, like Agnes's mother, were unkind people with power in their hands. I could not stop crying after Agnes's treatment of me, and I was depressed for days. Agnes did not have to be so mean; she could have told me that she simply did not want to talk about that time. I would have understood and left her alone. Among the hundred survivors I interviewed, Agnes was the only one who behaved in such a crude and uncivilized manner. The others were all polite, pleasant women who were pleased to talk about our camp experiences.

Differences in Survivors

Treating survivors as a unified group ignores important personality differences and pre-Holocaust backgrounds. Level of education, age, economic standing, religious observance, and gender all contributed to the way survivors responded to their situation. Women who lost children had a harder time coping emotionally after the war. We who were younger adjusted more easily to new challenges. Nevertheless, like all survivors who had been liberated from death and from the fear of death in the camps, we still had to struggle to get on with our lives. Staying busy with daily chores and future plans gave us, I think, less time to feel sorry for ourselves. Yet, even though we show toughness and might smile while telling our Holocaust stories, all survivors need a few words of encouragement and a hug for comfort. The compassion we never received in the camp and the pity we did not want after the war left us with a burden of some sorrow and regret.

Bound by Silence

The first few years after liberation, Erzsike and I did not talk about the camp. The war and its humiliations we hid inside us. Survivor couples, like me and my husband, also did not mention the war between each other. Later on, when we had to fill out papers for German compensation, we brought up the names of the camps, but we did not go into details.

Survivors were reluctant to speak or identify themselves also because of the stigma attached. When Erzsike became engaged, her future mother-in-law was concerned about whether she would be able to bear children. I myself was not a good example, because I had been married four years already, and I did not have a child. The mother-in-law's concern was understandable in light of the prevailing ideas about and attitudes toward survivors, who aroused ambivalent feelings of astonishment, pity, and apprehension.

Survivors wanted neither pity nor prying questions. There was always that probing query—"What did you do to survive?"—implying that one would do, or had to have done, something appalling. Other inquirers wanted to know whether all the awful things they had heard of in camps happened to us, too. In my job as a librarian, a co-worker once gave me the compliment, "You are too nice to be a Holocaust survivor!" She believed that only the aggressive and ruthless stayed alive in the camps; that the fine, sensitive people perished.[8] A pro-Arab speaker announced that everyone who lived through the Holocaust, including many in Israel, were cruel and brutal people; otherwise they could not have remained alive. I, who was not tattooed, could hide behind the mask of a regular person. My concealment worked for awhile, but the epitaphs of my parents and grandparents became heavier in my heart. Slowly I started to write.

Forever Searching

There are survivors who have never stopped searching for their lost family members. Advertisements saying "Have you seen my brother, my sister?" continue to appear in Holocaust publications.[9] I myself, in some ways, am still looking for my father. Not knowing his fate or his whereabouts has haunted me all the years after liberation. The search for my father or some proof of his fate took me back to Hungary time and again. On one trip back, I met Ilonka Kohn Friedenberg in Miskolc. Born in Abaújszántó, Ilonka was so fond of my father, Sándor Szász, she was convinced that only her economic situation prevented her from marrying him. "The dowry was very important in those days," she painfully recalled. When I first saw her, Ilonka started to cry. "Poor Sándor, he was there when we arrived in Auschwitz. In a striped prison uniform, he was digging with a shovel among other men. Hardly raising his head, he called 'Ilonka, have you seen someone of my family?' 'No Sándor,' I answered. As he tried to say something else, the SS appeared and the group moved." I tape-recorded Ilonka's story several times. She repeated it on my return visits until she passed away in 1992.

An earlier message from my father reached us when we were in Auschwitz, downhearted and depressed. We lost hope in the future and of ever seeing our parents. Life without them was not worth living, we concluded. In resignation, we decided to touch the fence's electric wire. As we walked toward the fence, a boy in prison uniform passed by. He looked at Erzsike and handed her a small round bread and an onion. "Take it, your father has sent it to you." The boy seemed to recognize my sister by a photograph father showed him. We returned safely to our barracks, hiding the bread in hand. After that, our spirits never fell so low again to produce suicidal thoughts. No one from my town except Ilonka had seen my father. I have searched for him relentlessly over the past sixty years. Only recently I received a Red Cross note stating that, even with the newly released documents, my father's name could not be found. Somehow, I feel that he did not survive the selection in Auschwitz. Yet, I cannot accept the terrible thought that the fate of my beloved, idealistic father was choking to death from lack of air in that devilish room created by demonic minds.

Health Issues

Survivors, in seeking to rebuild their lives, scattered all over the world. Most rehabilitated their lives, but for those with permanent disabilities, life after the camps was harder and more challenging. Tuberculosis was one affliction that many of us suffered in the camps and after liberation. Since my release from the tuberculosis ward of the Landes Institute in Budapest, I have had many chest X-rays that were negative, so slowly, I began to feel liberated from the disease. It was hard later when I realized that TB, just like the emotional enormity of the Holocaust, would never leave me. The tuberculosis germs invaded my fallopian tubes and long prevented me from having children. Following treatment with streptomycin, and after suffering two miscarriages, I was exceptionally lucky that finally I had my first baby after ten years of marriage. I called her Miriam, my mother's name. A year later, we had our second daughter, whom we named Yonit after my husband's mother.

TB was the AIDS of my generation. Even today, many of the survivors shun the subject. Just like me, they seldom mentioned TB in interviews with Survivors of the Shoah Foundation and Yad Vashem. Some explained that they were treated for pneumonia, but it was mostly TB. I am bringing up the subject for historical accuracy and out of empathy for all those women, my fellow inmates from Markkleeberg, who also suffered from TB and its heartrending consequences.

Infertility in general was a tragic outcome of the camp. Although I was lucky, several of my camp mates were less fortunate. Many women of childbearing age found that their menses had been interrupted not only for months, but for years after the camps. There were also those whose period was never regulated again. There is not enough research, but it is known that a large number of survivors were unable to have children. Many also delivered a first child who was underdeveloped and died at birth. We speak about the six million victims, but there are also the other millions of children who were never born and the inmates who were saved but whose lives suffered irreparably. In addition to not knowing the meaning of motherhood, they could never reproduce their family's DNA, the genetic code of life carried from generation to generation. In their case, the Germans succeeded fully with their "final solution."

Face to Face with Holocaust Denial

Immediately after the war, Erzsike and I just wanted to be away from the camps and away from memories of Hungary that caused us so much hurt.

When my fate led me to the United States, I made great efforts to Americanize. I had no Hungarian friends, and I was pleased with my English-speaking neighbors and co-workers. In New York, a city with so many immigrants, I did not feel I was an outsider. I kept busy studying and working; the events of the Holocaust I mentally pushed away, far back in my past. Then a confrontation jolted me out of my complacency. I was tending the information desk as a librarian at the New York Public Library on Fifth Avenue and 42nd Street in Manhattan. It was a snowy Thursday evening in January 1983, and a number of readers quietly occupied the large reading room. A tall husky man with a big mustache approached my table and, with an annoyed countenance, he muttered, "All those stories about the concentration camps!" His voice echoed hundreds of others who had expressed in print the same idea. "Show me one person who was really there!" he said. The stillness of the reading room resounded with his words.

Keeping silent about the time I was in the camps was different than for someone to tell me that there were no camps at all. Facing the speaker, I heard myself uttering the words, "You are looking at one, sir!" The man did not reply. He was not interested in discovering the truth. I watched as he turned and left the reading room. It took me some time to collect myself. Then I was no longer in doubt. I was not ashamed anymore, nor did I need to shield the world from the brutality of which man is capable. I knew suddenly that it was incumbent on me to tell what my parents and the other victims could never tell on their own behalf.[10] Shortly after that, I began writing the history of my town's Jewish community.

Inheriting the Holocaust

The Nazis who imprisoned me affected not only my life, but also the lives of my children and grandchildren. I would like to protect and save them from the emotional turmoil of their family's wounds, but I cannot. They became victims of the Holocaust before they were even born.

Very few of us talked about the camps to our children. We were reluctant to tell them what happened, as if we were the ones who had to be ashamed. Most of us answered specific questions only. We wished our kids to grow up without the burden of the Holocaust. They should feel as free as their friends and other children. There were also some of the second generation who did not want to hear about the camps. All the terrible things, they assumed. The daughter of one survivor asked her mother cautiously whether she had been raped in the camp. Some took courses on the Holocaust, but they could not talk about it with their parents. Many sons and daughters of survivors avoided asking questions, believing that it would be painful to the parents to talk about that time.

I was unable to speak about the camps to my daughters directly. European parents with our upbringing do not want our children to see us as weak or as victims. We sought to give them the security of having parents who were strong and would protect them. How could we talk about being so vulnerable, humiliated as we were in the camps? Whether Jews or Nazis, no one talked for a while, neither parents nor children. Then I started to write and publish some articles that my children read. Even then, they hardly asked questions. It seemed that, indirectly, it was their story too.

Israeli children had an even more difficult time dealing with the Holocaust. I am guarding a beautiful essay written by Amir, Erzsike's son, in the sixth grade. In this composition, he vehemently protested and asserted that his mother was not a coward, that she was not led like a sheep to slaughter. He was combating the prevailing atmosphere in Israel, which softened only after the Eichmann trial. Amir, who resembles my father, told me recently that he had spent Yom Kippur afternoon reading a book on the Holocaust. I was touched by Amir having my father's looks and the burden of a victim. On the lighter side, his action symbolized a connection to the world of his grandparents, whom he never met. Amir is a handsome, confident Israeli *Sabra;* not too many are aware of this sensitivity in his character.

Our behavior in the camp was an expression of the teachings we received at home. When I speak about the humanity and friendship among us, I am describing the influence of my parents and the society they created. Their absence affected my life and my actions. I did not go through a normal adolescence myself, and it was harder for me to deal with my teenage daughters; maybe I could have been more tolerant with their quest for independence.

Grateful for a Kind Word

Hungarian-born Piroska Kornagel, married to a professor living in Leipzig, was surprised to see the memorial tablet at the site of the former camp in Markkleeberg. Ms. Kornagel, who is not Jewish, inquired at the City Hall, where she was provided information about the camp. Ms. Kornagel was touched by the story of Erzsike and I, and she wrote an article, which appeared in a Hungarian Israeli newspaper. Ms. Kornagel called her account "*Szász Kati golgotája*" (The Golgotha of Szász Kati). Kati, or Katalin, Szász was my maiden name. About ten survivors of Markkleeberg who read the article responded that they were prisoners in the same camp. Ms. Kornagel forwarded the letters to Dr. Bernd Klose, the mayor of Markkleeberg. Dr. Klose wrote each one a letter and enclosed a beautiful calendar showing different sites of the city. The survivors, among them ninety-one-year-old Irena Lebovits Ehrenreich, told me excitedly how much the attention and the appreciation meant to them.[11]

A Delayed Need to Transfer Memories

It is a disquieting thought that the times my parents and grandparents lived through, as well as their tragedy, may be lost with us. Unlike the anguish in the camp, which I could suppress in my mind, I could not forget the times with my parents and grandparents. With all the pain and reservation I have, I am proud that our children are the heirs of the ethical and moral values that had guided many previous generations. We know that our lives are limited; but books, letters, and stories told by parents to their children and grandchildren make it possible to preserve memory for a while longer.

As grandparents, we are conscious of that small link in the chain of generations between something gone and something yet to be that we represent. When we celebrate the birth of each new grandchild, memories of the past and the feeling that we need to leave a record of family and roots become stronger. Although we did not speak about the war to our children out of an idea that we needed to protect them, with the grandchildren it is easier. Both the distance in time from the events and the immediacy of our relations lessen the tension. We are eager to provide answers to questions that the third generation wants to know and that the second could never ask.

When I visited Israel some years ago, my ten-year-old grandson Dovi heard that I had written a book about my hometown in Hungary. He was very proud and told his teacher during a class discussion. It was around the Holocaust Memorial Day, and the teacher asked Dovi to bring his grandmother in to talk about the book. I was a little anxious, but what would a grandmother not do to please her oldest grandson? Dovi was excited as he solemnly held my hand and led me to his class. It was a small intimate setting, all of us sitting in a circle. I do not think that any of the other students were descendants of camp survivors. The teacher introduced the subject of the Holocaust. Then I told them how sad it was when we were deported from our homes. I also spoke of returning with my sister, when only memories were waiting for us. I said that later, visiting the town again, I was sorry to leave behind all those traces of people and community that were part of my life. I decided to take them with me by writing down their history. Now the book can travel, even to Israel where many of the survivors live. Dovi listened with the rest of the children, and I was pleased for the opportunity to communicate with him.

During the question-and-answer period that followed, the boys wanted to hear about some action and "juicy stuff." They said, "Tell us how it was with the SS; did they beat you up hard?" Their query was echoed by two other voices, "Yeah, tell us what happened!" Preparing my answer, I noticed Dovi's concerned expression and his flashing eyes. It is not easy to have one's grandmother on display. Luckily, the ringing of the school bell saved the situation. As the children dispersed and Dovi came to escort me to the door, I felt his arm still trembling. He did not say much, and I wished I could give him a better way to be proud of me.

The discontinuity of cultural heritage is ever present in the life of survivors. Our children lack the chain of their family's communal and traditional history. Many grew up without hearing family stories or seeing photographs of their parents' or grandparents' childhood.

Back at the end of the war, facing our sad reality, the majority did not want to know. Today, things are different. I am pleased that our experience did not rob our children of their ability to prepare themselves for useful and creative lives. Looking at my children and grandchildren, I slowly feel the joy of liberation and the full meaning of survival.

Religion

The Holocaust experience affected survivors in different ways. Some remained religious, while others lost their faith. Those who were a bit older in the camps adhered more closely to their pre-Holocaust level of practice. In general, survivors remained close to their upbringings. At the beginning, many left the religion; but gradually they returned and practiced, especially at the holidays. Our basic childhood education was the factor that most strongly defined our religiosity.

As for me, although we had been orthodox at home, the group we joined after the war belonged to Dror Habonim, a Zionist socialist pioneer youth movement. Although the members possessed different religious backgrounds, as a group we did not practice religion. The first holiday after we arrived in Israel and Kibbutz Heftziba was Rosh Hashanah. Although there were no synagogue services, we did not work and the day had a holiday ambiance. Yom Kippur meant a day of rest with festival meals, we were told. We had a sumptuous supper before the night of Yom Kippur, and then the group dispersed. Some took a walk, others sat around listening to music. I returned to my room. The lack of inspiration and the spiritual bareness of that important holiday evening left me sad and dispirited. I sat down by the window, watching the dim lights of the emerging stars on the horizon. It did not take much imagination to carry me back home for Kol Nidre night in Abaújszántó. The candles were lit in the newly polished silver candelabras on top of the shimmering tablecloth. Wearing her white lace kerchief and small round embroidered apron, my little grandmother Roza (or Rachel) stood blessing us, one by one. I felt her trembling hands touch my head, while large tears dropped from her eyes. Merging our tears—hers imagined, mine real—I started to pray. Some were Hebrew words I knew, the rest were in Hungarian. Collecting my strength and regaining my tranquility, I wiped my eyes and went back to the recreation area to join the others.

The next morning, at the invitation of friends, I entered the dining room for breakfast. Even though I had made the decision not to eat that day, I took my seat at the table. Moving some plates here and there, I slowly got up and walked away. To conceal my action and be faithful to the group's ideas, at lunch I was back among the diners pretending again to eat. I stayed away from Erzsike, who did not know my secret. I have never dared to ask how she spent mealtimes on that Yom Kippur day in 1947.

Holocaust experiences defy meaning. As I was thinking and writing about my time in the camps, I began to realize that a special hand directed my fate and Erzsike's. I became fully aware of all the terrible possibilities that could have, but did not, happen. I felt a growing gratitude to God for guiding our destiny. I have pain for my mother's terrible end, but found consolation that at least my sister remained with me. I am grateful for the grace that the two of us passed all those "selections" and escaped the perils on the road. Being among the last ones to leave Bergen-Belsen for work in Markkleeberg was extraordinary good luck, and falling asleep during the Death March saved us. The more I am aware of the uncertain roads we passed, the more my faith is strengthened in God. I remain a practicing Jew also because of the strong connection with my parents. I did not want to lose their memory and the religious faith that tied us together. Other survivors, too, adhered to their religion keeping the memories and traditions from home. Many other survivors, however, questioned their religion. There were also those who became so disheartened when no one was waiting for them at home after the war that they stopped fasting on Yom Kippur, even though, in Markkleeberg, they had made the greatest efforts not to eat on that holy day.

In general, we all relaxed a bit in our religious practices after the war. There are survivors whose children married out of the faith and who raise their offspring as non-Jewish. One Markkleeberg survivor who prefers not to have her name mentioned finds consolation in the fact that her grandchildren will no longer suffer "the fate of the Jews." Seeing the resurgence of anti-Semitism, my heart goes out in concern, too, for the safety of my children and grandchildren. I would do anything to protect them. In desperate thoughts sometimes, I question whether it would be better if they were relieved of their "Jewish burden." What a painful heritage and yoke I am giving them, I think. Then I quickly return to my roots and to who I am: Judaism is my belief, my tradition—I would never leave it. It could not be my escape; I was born Jewish and this is my destiny. Jewish faith is what I received and that is what I can bestow on my children. I am happy that they have remained Jewish. There is no complete certainty in life. People can suffer from anti-Semitism, but there are many other afflictions: fatal diseases, accidents, natural disasters, or other calamities. Fate works in its own strange ways.

Family Connections

This special bond of survivors extends even more strongly between family members. Erzsike and I grew to be protectors of one another. As the years passed, our relationship deepened. Even as dependence on one another relaxed a bit, our friendship still contained the key to our emotional and collective memories. Erzsike is my representative from that world I lost in the Holocaust. She is the only other one who called my parents "mother" and "father." Erzsike knows and remembers all those childhood places and events that fashioned both of our lives. We understand each other because our basic view of the world is from the same source, from a similar childhood experience. With her, I can still discover new details about the family and the life that is forever gone. Although we live on different continents, we visit and call each other regularly. Our children know that unusually strong ties bind us. Erzsike's children come to see us in New York, and my younger daughter, Yonit, who lives in Israel, has Erzsike as her second mother and advisor.

Erzsike and I still feel responsibility to assist one another in stressful situations. During my second visit to Markkleeberg, my granddaughter Ella had a car accident in Israel. Erzsike stayed at her side in the same hospital where she had worked as a nurse for twenty-five years; she was a great help to Ella. Knowing how stressed I was and what the visit to Markkleeberg meant to me, Erzsike decided not to inform me unless the situation worsened. Thank God there was no need: Ella felt better, she recovered, and I completed my trip to Germany.

Besides Erzsike, I keep in contact with the few cousins who survived. Each possesses a segment of our fractured lives and memories. The sadness of loss comes with the passing of each relative. Olga Kogel, who died at the age of ninety in Israel, was eighteen years my senior. Her mother was the oldest among my mother's sisters. Olga used to describe to me my mother's life as a single girl and later as a young married woman. I listened to her with awe as her words opened a window to my mother's world and her persona that I knew so little about. As with many Auschwitz survivors, Olga had no children. Erzsike helped her, especially after her husband passed away. Olga was gradually losing her eyesight and finally became completely blind. I admired Olga as a courageous woman who, despite her handicap, did not like to ask for help. She kept her independence almost until the end. After each visit, she was the last one I called before boarding the plane back to New York.

Olga's much younger sister, Edit Adler, was together with her in the camp. Edit is a highly intelligent, good-humored, and pretty lady who, at eighty-six, still interprets the news in her own way. It is good to call her and receive answers to my questions about our shared memories. Edit has a happy family, with two children, as well as grandchildren and great-grandchildren. The loss of our parents at such a young age was a trauma with lasting effects. In Israel, Erzsike found Olga to be a mother figure, while here, I adopted a lady from my hometown. Her name was Teresa Keiszer Pick, and I met her while writing the history of Abaújszántó. Teresa, who was close to my mother's age, had a sister in Budapest; but in New York, after her husband's death, she was alone, having had no children. When I first saw her, she was already a widow, firmly independent, and supporting herself, as she had done all her adult life. I derived much pleasure from talking to Teresa about the old times and about my parents, whom she knew so well, and other people from our town. We were mentally transported back to Hungary many times as our conversations lasted long into the evenings. Teresa was always invited and was happy to come to my house. Slowly she started to trust me and to share her concerns. Eventually I became her official correspondent and translator because her English was poor. When she called me from a doctor's or a government office, or even from a store, to translate something, I left whatever I was doing, no matter how important it was, to help her. My husband and children all knew about Teresa and my devotion to her. When Teresa passed away at the age of ninety-two, I felt a genuine regret, but also a satisfaction that I had helped someone who knew my parents in our old world.

Photographs

The destruction of photographs was an irreparable loss to many families. When a photograph is recovered, like a survivor, it has a story of its own.

An American cousin in New Jersey presented me with a photograph of my mother's family. It was taken about 1939 in Satoraljaujhely, Hungary, when my uncle Meny Markovitz visited Hungary before the United States entered the Second World War. It is a picture of my mother's mother, brothers, and sisters. They are standing or sitting there, smiling at the camera, not knowing that the killing factory in Auschwitz is being prepared for them.

Aunt Hanni carried with her into hiding my father's photograph, and she gave it back to us when we met in Budapest. It was the picture my father

The author's mother with her brothers and sisters in 1939. From left to right, standing: Anna, Mariska (mother), Herman, Sam, Bernad, Malvin. Sitting: Frida, Rozsi, Grandmother Regina and Hanni.

had taken for the emigration papers that Aunt Hanni was preparing for the family in hopes that we could go to the United States. Father was to be the first to visit, and we would follow him. The application was not accepted, but at least I can show my children a photo of the grandparents they lost.

Visiting My Hometown

It was hard to return to Hungary alone after thirty years away. My first visit was in July 1976. The town of Abaújszántó, where I knew every gate and every corner, still contained the structures, the houses, and the stores; but it was empty of Jewish inhabitants. Overwhelmed by the physical manifestations of the vanishing past, I started to walk. In my world of imagination, the owners of the Jewish stores that still lined the main street were moving comfortably about. Other friends and neighbors also appeared in front of their homes. One of them was Márta Krausz, my friend and schoolmate, whom we met with her sister in Bergen-Belsen. Márta was playing hopscotch in her front yard and called me to join her. Her voice rang out excitedly, as if she had not been away and her shrunken little body had not been among those awaiting burial in Bergen-Belsen.

As I continued to search amid the former landmarks and remembrances, I reached our house, whose silhouette is etched with permanent markers in my heart. At the entrance of their stores stood, in my mind's eye, my father and grandfather. They were just closing up at the end of the day. In the yard behind, my little grandmother waited with her warm and trusting smile as she called mother to let her know that I had arrived. A few moments later, as I looked up at our kitchen window, my mother's tall slender figure came into view. She, like the rest of my family, seemed so natural, so tranquil, as if they had not been among the condemned in Auschwitz. I returned a few times, touching the gate and the front wall. Even from the train station, I ran back for a final look at the house and the physical setting of my memories.

My journeys to Abaújszántó always included a tour of the cemetery. A short walking distance from town, the cemetery is located within a beautiful landscape of vineyards and fruit orchards at the foot of the distant mountains. When I visited there the first time, I was astounded by the power of the overwhelming stillness and moved by the weight of history around me.[12]

As children, we were not taken for visits to the cemetery; I did not know about family members buried there. My astonishment was great when I noticed my maiden name Szász. It was on one of the graves pointed out to me by the caretaker. Slowly the shape of a pitcher, known as the sign of the tribe of Levi, was revealed. Recalling our childhood pride in being a Levite, my ties to the unknown soul buried there began to form. Gradually, the full name of Szász Mór grew visible, and I realized that the grave of my great-grandfather was before me. A feeling of wonderment and overwhelming awe captured me. The elegantly simple gravestone, erected in 1915, was a statement, a written message that reached me at that moment in time. It was inspiring to read the poetic praise of the old man whose passing "touched the hearts." The tender words warmed me in that chilly and lonely return. Other sentences carved in the stone mentioned his "good name," which was the esteemed attribute of the kind man being eulogized; he was a person of good name, which he had acquired during his eighty-four years on earth. The words on the epitaph were expressed in an acrostic pattern, each line beginning with a letter, eventually forming the name of Moshe, the son of Natan.

With the gravestone of Moshe or Mor, the memories of my studious little grandmother and my mustached and smiling, pipe-smoking, patriotic grandfather came to my mind. Their values of honesty and respect for the

The author by the grave of her great-grandfather, Moshe, Mor Szász, in Abaújszántó.

law remained their guide in Auschwitz as they entered dutifully into that final chamber of no return.

Looking again at the delicate carving of the slim-lined pitcher, placed in the frame of a Magen David at the top of the tombstone, my heart overflowed with thanks and humility. I had the honor, and mine was the destiny, of reconnecting the broken chain. "You see," I wished to say to the good old man, whose love and respect were transferred to me, "not everything was lost. A bit of your spirit and heritage has been given the grace to be carried onward. Your grave, as the remnant of a world scattered by the hurricane of hate, will be preserved."

I continued to visit Hungary and Abaújszántó, as if some invisible force were drawing me back to the place where I was once so happy with my family. Maybe it was my way of mourning, which I could not do before. My husband Meier accompanied me twice, when he could take time out of his work. When he saw me so downhearted, he stood there and reminded me that we were together. Finding each other so distant from our birthplaces, we wondered about the mysteries of existence and felt that every bad thing has some kernel of good in it. Thus, if not for the Holocaust, Meier and I would probably never have known each other.

In subsequent trips, escorted by our children and grandchildren, I found many changes in my dream town. The Jewish stores gradually were converted to apartments, and most of the houses were altered or had disappeared. The synagogue, famous for its majesty and devotion-inspiring beauty in the center of the town, was now a lumber depository. My imagination could summon fewer sights and people from the past as the town began to wear an unfamiliar face. With the vanishing past, the cobblestone roads were no longer there on my last visit in 2001. Our house, with leaking roof, collapsing walls, trampled gardens, and dead branches on the lilac trees, was in desperate need of repair. The stores were empty, and the apartments were occupied by Gypsies. My daughter Yonit picked up a few of the fallen stones to take with her to Israel, as she wiped a tear from her eyes.

After each trip back to Abaújszántó, I am so happy and relieved to get home to New York. Then, after a while, like one who is allowed a previously denied food and cannot satisfy her craving, I am ready for the next journey. I wish to be back, at least once more, yearning and grateful for anything that can spark a memory.

With my final journey I hope to take with me two of my grandchildren who have not yet been to Abaújszántó. Together we will search the last remaining traces of their ancestors' vanished world.

Compensations

Compensation by the Germans

Psychologists call it the trauma of reparation. Survivors had to go through painful processes of meeting deadlines, filling out long application forms, and finding witnesses. The questions they had to answer in detail after so many years were very stressful. In some cases, we were required to supply the very documents that the Germans and the Hungarians had taken from us.

Women from Markkleeberg offered to testify for one another, and many discovered their former camp mates that way. If claiming health problems or medical conditions as a result of the Holocaust, survivors had to bring documentation from their doctors. Then, to validate it, we were required to go in front of physicians assigned by the German government! The evaluation and judgment of these German doctors decided the degree of disability and the merit of each claim. The aim of the compensation bureau, of course, was to lessen the extent of the claimed damage to lower the payment. The office of reparation denied many claims, contending that the survivor's disease was not connected with the camps but developed from natural causes. When I was called for an examination and judgment of my request for health benefits, the German physician involved was unfriendly and intimidating. He spoke to me sternly in official German. I was petrified and confused. The language and the tone brought back all my dormant fear and reignited my nightmares. The doctor reminded me of the SS. His probing questions, loud voice, and harsh expression left me terrified, as I had been in the camps. My body responded with stomach problems and weight loss that persisted for months after that visit.

The German foundation "Remembrance, Responsibility, and the Future" was established in 2000 to compensate former slave and forced laborers through a German–U.S. agreement to end Holocaust-related lawsuits against German companies.[13] Average payment of the foundation "Remembrance, Responsibility, and the Future" to former slave laborers was £7,660 ($6,907). The amount is comparable to the cost many elderly patients incur during a two-day stay in an American hospital. The families of slave laborers who had already died received no reparation.

The compensations, although small, helped survivors, the majority of whom were middle or lower class. The pension still provides a degree of freedom and independence for elderly survivors, and it relieves them from reliance on their children, who are not always able to assist.

Hungarian Reparation

The payment from Hungary for the death of parents, siblings, and spouses was equally troubling. The hurt was so deep that survivors did not want to turn to the government with requests for money. By not filling out applications, they meant to demonstrate their pain and resentment to their former countrymen. The amount of compensation at first was insultingly small, so that survivors—even those in great need—returned the payment notification. The Hungarian government also placed a condition on the compensation that the money had to be spent in Hungary. The second time, with the amount increased and restrictions removed, people were urged to apply. Some Markkleeberg survivors felt good being able to donate part of the payment to wounded Israeli soldiers.

My family belonged to generations of Hungarian patriots, and I grew up as one of them. It made the wound of my insult from Hungary even greater and deeper. The Germans detested Jews in general, but with Hungarians, the hatred was personal. Hungarians were my fellow citizens; I was one of them, a co-patriot with the same cultural affinity, education, language, and loyalty. When the anti-Jewish laws started to take effect in Hungary, I was in about the third grade. It was painful when I realized that I was not a "true Hungarian," as I thought. I remember sitting in my grandfather's store by the large bay window, observing and envying those townspeople walking around who were free from fear and persecution. I did not understand: I was a loyal young girl who was singing the songs of Hungarian nationalist poets even in the camps. After filing for Hungarian compensation and then tearing up the forms a few times, I realized that the application was an opportunity to document the loss of my parents and to grant some official recognition to their deaths.

Return to Auschwitz

Visiting Auschwitz with my daughter Miriam and a professional guide in June 1992, I wanted to be just a tourist. I let the guide, who spoke English well, explain the place and its statistics. Respecting my feelings, and herself overwhelmed by the place, Miriam walked silently next to me. Later, as we moved from Auschwitz to Auschwitz-Birkenau, I was overcome by the memories and walked as one who was possessed: I hurried from one barracks to another, looking around each very carefully. By then the guide realized I must be a survivor. He came with me to the ruins of the gas chambers and the crematoria, while Miriam sat down, lamenting, close to the place where the trains had arrived.

Toward the end, I almost collapsed, but a force beyond me was driving me onward. I was once again that scared prisoner, but I felt I had just gained my freedom and could walk to the once-forbidden places. I returned again and again, not to the crematorium, but to the place of arrival

The author with her daughter Miriam Shenkar at the gate of Auschwitz in June 1992.

where I had been still together with my parents and grandparents. I felt satisfaction, as if I was showing them that I did come back, I did not forget. All the years have not separated us. It was like visiting their grave, yet I still could not accept that they were in a grave. I remembered them as I had left them, healthy and alive.

I found the painful spot where my mother, grandmother, and I were separated. The old wound opened again. My mother (Anyuka, in Hungarian) was a young woman and could have remained with us. The pain of "why and what if," although accompanying me all my life, had lessened a bit over the years. I realized how horrible it would have been if I had seen my mother beaten by the SS, suffering through the selection processes, humiliated, made to kneel on the bricks, and driven along in the Death March.

Unlike my birthplace, where I have dreams and memories to revisit, I do not ever want to see Auschwitz again. Not that its sight is ever far away from my thoughts. Wherever I go, whatever I start, the way somehow leads back to Auschwitz, a place of pain and hope. Auschwitz is where my life both ended and began anew. I hope today that the memory of Auschwitz, where my parents and the other victims found no escape, will be a deterrent for individuals and for mankind. Auschwitz will be there, the last checkpoint before language of hate fuels new factories of death; before man lets his evil inclination cloud his mind and actions. Then perhaps the death of Auschwitz victims will not be completely in vain. My mother, representing kindness on earth as she walked arm in arm with grandmother on that road of no return, may be the guardian to save our world from destruction. That is my deepest trust and bitter consolation.

15
Return to Markkleeberg

EARLY IN JUNE 1998, AN INVITATION FOR THE UNVEILING OF A MEMORIAL plaque at the site of the former camp arrived from Markkleeberg. My initial eagerness to go quickly changed to apprehension. All those alarming memories started to surface, yet I knew I had to be there. I wanted to revisit not only the place but also that fourteen-year-old girl that I had been when I survived the events there. Nervously I called the office of the mayor in Markkleeberg and, speaking English, asked for directions. They transferred me to an old gentleman who, in flowery language, told me, "Frau Dr. Stessel, we consider you our most distinguished guest, coming all the way from the United States. A delegation will be waiting for your arrival."

I panicked and rushed to the city to buy a new suitcase befitting the occasion. On my way, I heard a tourist speaking German. The pure German dialect brought back the fearful memories associated with the language I had heard in the camp. How would I handle my trip, I wondered—wouldn't it be too much stress? There was still time to cancel. At home, my husband looked at my worried face and declared, "You are not going!" I might have even listened to him, but I knew I had to be there to see the town outside of our camp, our prison. I yearned to walk free in the former camp, to come in and go out at the gate. I also wanted to show them—the people of Markkleeberg—who those prisoners were: those whom they had seen dressed in rags, barefoot in wooden shoes, led around town by armed guards. The knowledge that Erzsike was also invited gave me a bit more courage and confidence.

On June 10, 1998, when I flew on Lufthansa Airline, the announcements were in English and German, even though most of the travelers understood both. I sat by the window looking out and isolating myself from the rest of the passengers until the loudspeaker's repeated announcement attracted my attention. We were informed that a suitcase had been checked in but the passenger owning it had failed to board the plane. The luggage had to be located and retrieved before we could take off. We sat and waited for further instructions. Having no control over these events, I again was reminded of the camp. There, too, forces beyond us governed our plans and our schedules. The unusual delay, I thought, might be happening because of me: Maybe I was not supposed to be there going back to Germany. I felt like Jonah the prophet, whose presence almost caused the boat to sink. I continued to wrestle with this thought until it was announced that all was clear, bringing an end to my foreboding reverie.

Our plane arrived three hours late, and my fashionable new suitcase was left behind. It did not really matter because only two people from the delegation stayed to wait for me. They were Ms. Evelin Müler, a lovely lady I later would get to know better, and Mr. Andreas Höhn, a historian, both representatives of the city. Mr. Höhn greeted me in English, which he spoke well. Seeing their friendly welcoming smiles and eagerness to help, the veneer of the German monster in my mind started to peel. I was surprised to find myself at ease and letting down my guard. Before settling into my hotel at Markkleeberg, we had a short tour of Leipzig. It was wonderful to see the big city that was so often mentioned in the camp.

Mr. Andreas Höhn, an intelligent young man who has written books on local history, drove me around scenic Markkleeberg and gave me a short glimpse of the sights that had previously only been sketched by my imagination. We stopped by the apartment houses where we had seen lights coming on during morning and evening *Appels.* From their balconies, citizens had been able to observe the camp. I was told that the area had not changed much and that some older people were still living who had been there in the 1940s. The apartments were opposite and on higher ground than the camp. The view of the camp was still visible when we looked down. I could see the flat stone barracks, which serve today as textile and other businesses. The factory after the war became again the spinning plant as it was before. In 1990 it closed, and around 1995 it was demolished to make place for a new housing project. At the time of my visit, it was an empty place where the factory stood. The barracks were rented to local business enterprises.

The next day, Erzsike, Hava Hartmann Kleinberg, and her daughter Dr. Rika Zissin, a physician, arrived from Israel. I was so happy to be with them. We felt triumphant just by being in town. Together again, comrades against the German world around us, we felt anew that sense of belonging we had in the camps. Basking in the warmth of friendship helped us regain our emotional strength.

Three survivors from among the French Resistance women also arrived and greeted us warmly. They were Jaqueline Fleury, Dr. Marguerite Dupré, and Schola Mocige, who came with her husband Henri. They were very friendly and stayed in the same hotel. As in the camp, we had a bit of a language problem; luckily, Mr. Henri Mocige spoke some English.

In the evening, an elaborate dinner was given where we met the mayor, Dr. Bernd Klose, Mrs. Klose, and other invited guests. All were friendly, cordial, and genuinely interested in our story. To my surprise, I did not feel the fury and resentment inside me. Unlike in Hungary, here I heard the words, "We are sorry" several times. It sounded genuine; even so, the blame was placed on Nazism and the SS.

The Idea of a Memorial

In the spring of 1945, both participants and bystanders to the horror of the concentration camps cautiously slipped from view. To the outside world, they have remained invisible ever since. The former camp in Markkleeberg was private property. In August 1945, the question arose about utilization of the barracks that had been erected by Junkers. Rather than tearing them down, it was decided to rent them to different concerns.[1] The thought of saving one of the barracks was cast aside since the land was private property. In altering the remains of the camp, local residents and officials contributed to the destruction of the memory of all that transpired there.

In 1971, Ms. Irma Clajus, a teacher and a former non-Jewish inmate of Ravensbrück, was walking in the Wolfswinkel section of Markkleeberg and noticed a few barracks not far from the railway track. She sensed that they were the remnants of a former forced-labor camp. Since she had been living in town only since 1952, after the war, she wanted to know details about the camp. Attempting to research its history, Ms. Clajus could only get a little information from the town's older residents. Many did not know about the factory and the camp, while those involved were reluctant to speak. After reading the document "Buchenwald, Warning and Obligations," she understood that there had been a concentration camp in Markkleeberg.[2] Consequently, she found the record of an ex-Buchenwald prisoner, Bruno Eisert, which had been prepared at the request of the Buchenwald Committee in 1968. Mr. Eisert had interviewed a few people who provided some concrete information about the camp in Markkleeberg.[3]

In 1974, Ms. Clajus did additional research, which confirmed the details in Mr. Eisert's report. She visited the camp in 1974, and there were columns made of cement and barbed wires still standing. The watchtowers were removed, but the pillars at the entrance and part of the wires around the blocks remained.[4] Ms. Clajus suggested marking the site "where so many women suffered unspeakably, by a memorial tablet." Based on the facts known at that time, the first memorial, a bronze plaque, was dedicated.

Hava Hartmann Kleinberg had an idea early in 1985 to place a sculpture at the former *Appelplatz* in the camp. A resourceful lady, Hava even knew a sculptor who would accept the assignment. She talked to her sister Miriam, who liked the idea; so the sisters went together to the German consulate for advice, and they were given the address of Buchenwald

Memorial Museum. From Buchenwald, Hava's letter was transferred to Markkleeberg, and she was informed that there was already a memorial tablet, which she could see if she visited the area.

Ms. Kleinberg continued the correspondence and, eventually, in 1996 the city of Markkleeberg invited her and her daughter Dr. Rika Zissin for a visit (her sister Miriam Hartmann Carmi had passed away). When they arrived, the memorial tablet was not only in poor condition, but Mrs. Kleinberg noticed that it was inaccurate. She knew there had been far more than the 600 prisoners mentioned on the plaque.

Former French inmate Jaqueline Fleury also visited the camp. She was concerned that the women of the French Resistance who were brought to the camp in February 1945 were not mentioned. Following a correspondence with Dr. Bernd Klose, mayor of Markkleeberg, it was decided that a new memorial, with more accurate information, would be erected. The dedication of the second memorial tablet took place on June 13, 1998. Rika, the daughter of Hava Hartmann Kleinberg, held an Israeli flag as we sang "*Am Yisrael Chai*" (The People of Israel Live). In a very emotional state, I presented the following speech in English. It was translated, sentence-by-sentence, by a friendly college student, A. Schonfeld, whose only problem was that he had to wear a tie for the occasion.

My Speech at the Dedication

I am number 50226, and my sister, who is here in the audience, is number 50225 on the list of Hungarian Jewish women, slave laborers arriving from Bergen-Belsen to the camp at Junkers-Markkleeberg on December 8, 1944. Being here today after years of striving to distance myself is an overwhelming experience.

My return was not easy. Similar to many survivors, I hesitated to come, to renew memories and deal with issues that I worked so hard to suppress. Yet I am here with you, respected audience, and I am pleased. I can see the world outside my former prison. Here are the small houses, close to the camp, that always reminded me of my home back in Abaújszántó, Hungary. I can now observe the daytime view of the homes that I once saw only by night from the lights of distant windows, as we marched from Markkleeberg to Theresienstadt in April 1945.

By being here, I pay tribute to my fellow inmates in Markkleeberg with whom I dreamed of freedom and a better world. Many perished, leaving no grave site for remembrance. I returned also because I yearned to reinforce my belief that it was wrong to take my parents, grandparents, my sister, and me so far from our home, from our town, to Auschwitz. How unjust it was to make my sister and me orphans and slave-laborers at the ages of thirteen and fourteen.

As we stood there on that clear day in May 1944 in Auschwitz, asking what had happened to our parents, we were told, "Look at the sparks of fire from the smoking chimney. There is your old world, your family, your loved ones, who are now being burned." More terrible then the words was the fact that it was true; our nightmare was our reality. We continued in that dreadful world in Markkleeberg, standing barefoot in wooden shoes on the frozen snow and ice, motionless for hours, while our tormentors celebrated the holiday in December 1944. Our nightmarish reality extended throughout the forced Death March in April 1945.

Amidst all the evil, there were also acts of kindness, minutes of good feelings, creating a kind of a flower in the frost of icy existence. Such a bouquet of flowers was the love my sister Erzsike—or Hava—and I shared. We each wanted, for instance, that the other one should have the small ration of bread we received. We saved it until someone stole both of our portions. The memory of our sisterly devotion today outlives the remembrance of the crudest treatment we received.

Another flower in the frost was the kindness of a worker in the factory of Markkleeberg who gave my sister a jam sandwich. We never saw that good man again, but I hope my words of thanks may yet reach him.

The facts that we were young during the Holocaust and we had a warm family upbringing helped us to continue with our lives. My sister chose to be a nurse and was in charge of the emergency room in a large hospital in Israel. I myself became a librarian and served at the information desk of the New York Public Library, at Fifth Avenue, as well as a freelance writer.

The loss of my family and home has never been forgotten. I feel echoes of the camps each time I say good-bye, and the Holocaust enters every important decision of my life. My twelve-year-old granddaughter writes poems evoking the flames of Auschwitz for a school assignment. I know that even her daughter will carry the scars. Yet, I am not as bitter as I could be. I feel, somehow, that the Holocaust experience exists to prevent the world from ever going so far again in mistreating a human being.

I thank you for your kind attention. I offer my gratitude to those who organized the memorial and made this event possible.

It was important for me to speak in that place where we were nameless numbers and our cries of suffering could not be expressed. The speech was published in the local newspaper, the *Markkleeberger Stadtnachrichten,* in July 1998.[5]

I felt no hatred toward the people I met. I was inspired by the kind expressions of the audience, listening and voicing their comments. They were nice to me and I regarded them as fellow human beings. They did not remind me of the mean *Aufseherins* or the SS guards. I expressed that feeling to a reporter during my visit.[6]

My concern was only with the text of the monument, which lists Wolfswinkel, the section of town where the camp was located, and leaves out the name Markkleeberg. For us, Markkleeberg, not Wolfswinkel, was the place we knew and the name under which the records, including the documents in Buchenwald, are listed.

Zahava Szász Stessel, left, and Erzsike Hava Szász Ginsburg at the dedication of the memorial in Markkleeberg, 1998.

As the voices of those who were in the camp are getting fainter, what we write and say will matter. I am pleased, therefore, that this book will preserve both the name and the history of the Markkleeberg concentration camp.

The area was private property, thus a small stand was built in front of a former barracks, and the memorial tablet was fastened to the stand, rather than to a building.

Text of the Memorial in the Original German

"0m 31, August 1944 bis zum 13.4.1945 befand sich hier im Wolfswinkel
ein Aussenlager des Konzentrationslagers Buchenwald, in dem
mehr als 1000 Ungarische Jüdinnen und
250 französische Widerstandskämpferinnen inhaftiert waren.
Diese Häftligsfrauen wurden verpflichtet,
Zwangsarbeit zu leisten und
Begannen hier unter unmenschlichen Bedingungen ihrer Todesmarch.
Wir ehren das Andenken dieser Frauen, die Opfer des Nazismus sind."

Text of the Memorial in English

From August 31, 1944, until April 13, 1945, here at Wolfswinkel
was a sub-camp of the concentration camp Buchenwald,

in which more than 1,000 Hungarian Jewish women and
250 captured women of the French Resistance were imprisoned.
These inmates were obligated
to forced labor and
began here, under inhuman conditions, their Death March.
We honor the memory of these women who are victims of Nazism.

Visiting the Camp

After the dedication, we took a quick tour with the mayor and members of the audience through the site of the former camp. Except for a few barracks that were being used as commercial establishments, nothing really remained.

The firm Junkers Flugzeug und Motorenwerke A.G., Dessau, transferred into a Soviet Shareholding Company in September 1945. Some former designers for Junkers allegedly reached Cairo to help President Nasser develop his own aircraft to carry high-explosive rocket warheads.[7] In July 1951, the West German government took over the remaining Junkers assets. The main office was transferred in 1958 from Dessau to Munich. In February 1965, Messerschmitt became the new owner, and Junkers Flugzeug and Motorenwerke A.G. was dissolved.[8]

Once the physical traces of the events of the past were gone, only our memories of them lingered on. Entering the site, we reached the central location where the water basin, although neglected, remained. While the others were wondering about the function of the "swimming pool," my mind filled with the former *Appelplatz* next to the pool. I was back in time with the masses, standing in roll call or shuffling about in ill-fitting shoes. I also recalled the high flagpole that flew the Nazi flag, and I could point out its exact location to the touring group. As we walked further, looking for the barracks, it was a challenge to determine the old sites in the new setting.

In the afternoon, during a musical interlude in the Westphalschen Haus, as the vocalist was performing, I gazed out the window into the distance, and I was suddenly back in the camp. I had no difficulty locating my barracks, number six, or hearing the voices of my fellow prisoners. Their singing, which delivered hope for us, fused with the current musical presentation, as ties of past and present merged in my mind. The gentle breeze from the leaves of nearby trees carried memories and brought messages to me from the barracks and the girls. I knew that their story had to be told. I expressed that determination to the inquiring reporter in 2001.[9]

The Town Beyond the Gates

The horror of the concentration camp made it seem like a separate universe. Yet that place of torment and killing was never completely sealed off from the ordinary world. It cast a shadow across the surrounding landscape and over the gardens and rooftops of the neighboring homes and streets. In the physical space, there existed two distinct worlds, but the boundaries separating these worlds were never impermeable. Some of the guards and *Aufseherin*s lived in town and, although it was forbidden for them to discuss the camp, we can assume that little pieces of information were leaked. Everybody in Markkleeberg really knew that the camp existed. Some also heard that it was "pretty bad" there.

After the war, silence prevailed among the Germans and the survivors. It was difficult to obtain information on Germany when East and West grappled with their nation's past and its indignity. The history of the camp was ignored by both the local historians and the municipal politicians. The Americans were in Markkleeberg only about two months, then they left, and according to the Yalta agreement, Saxony belonged to the Russian zone of occupation. Most people had little exposure to living Jews and, unlike in West Germany, the subject of the Holocaust was rarely dealt with. The population in Markkleeberg claimed that they did not know about the camp or the kind of people who were there.

Angyal Fischer Weisz and her husband visited Markkleeberg around 1986. She recognized the railroad nearby, but the campsite had changed. As they asked around, the people in the neighborhood asserted that there was never a camp there. The older generation and former workers of Junkers who are still alive do not want to speak today. They are afraid to remember and make themselves public.

Prior to our departure in 1998, we wanted to take another look at the camp, and we called for a taxi. The driver had no knowledge of the camp or the memorial, which is not surprising because it is too small and insignificant to be considered a public site in the town. We provided him the address and other details about it.

Yearly Memorials

In 1999, an exhibition about the camp opened in Markkleeberg on January 27: the anniversary date of Auschwitz's liberation and the official Holocaust Memorial Day in Germany. With a little material based on our testimonies and some archival documents, they made a nice presentation. I was pleased, seeing my mother's photograph at the display.

Besides the exhibition, every year on January 27 there is a special Holocaust memorial event in Markkleeberg. The program typically includes an address by Dr. Bernd Klose, the Oberbürgermeister, and invited speakers and musical presentations by high school students.

I usually send photos and information about the commemoration to Markkleeberg survivors and have received many positive responses. We all find hope in remembering. Seeing Markkleeberg residents with the bouquets around the memorial touches our hearts with optimism and recognition that people are kind, after all.

Repeat Journeys

On my second visit to Markkleeberg in 2000, I was joined by survivors Kathy Zelmanovitz Goldstein, who came with me from New York, and Hava Hartmann Kleinberg from Israel. Naomi Cohen Levi was there from Israel, also, to see her former hometown. She lived in Markkleeberg before the war, then survived with her mother by hiding in Leipzig. Naomi, or Trude as she was called in German, amazed us with her recollections. For her, "Rigvet," which we knew as the small "chocolate factory," was a place to spend a happy hour with her mother. They used to go there to buy chocolate on sale at special times of the week. Looking at the building as we passed by, her eyes were shining with good memories. Naomi also pointed out some of the former Jewish sections of the town. Strangely, among them was Gautzschen, the area close to the Junkers factory. It was a special pleasure for us to see Markkleeberg through the eyes and memories of one who had been a local Jewish teenager there.

Visiting a School

Responding to a request by the mayor's office, we agreed to visit the Rudolf-Hildebrand High School. I prepared a short introduction, and the three of us were ready for questions. The session went well; the students were lovely and had many questions. Looking at my book on Abaújszántó, they wanted to know details of the history and my feelings about my hometown. Answering them gave me the opportunity to tell a bit about my family, as well. The students who were struggling with their English were sympathetic to our language problems in the camp. They wanted to know how we managed to get along without speaking German. Their inquiries were addressed directly to one of the three of us. We were impressed by how the young girls and boys were quiet as they listened with attention. They even stayed a bit longer after the ringing of the bell. As we were leaving, we received flowers and noticed photos on the wall that were part of an exhibition about the camp. The photographs and the flowers spoke to me with their silent, nonverbal communication, and I noticed my mother looking at us from one of the photos.

My third visit was in August 2001 with Hava Hartmann Kleinberg.[10] We came by invitation of the museum of Buchenwald to participate in the

With students at Rudolf Hildebrand High School. On the walls is an exhibition of photos about the camp.

opening of the exhibition called "The Forgotten Women of Buchenwald," which had been prepared by Dr. Irmgard Seidel from the Buchenwald Memorial Museum. Erzsike and I contributed photographs and testimony. Buchenwald, which is known as a camp for men, had twenty-six sub-camps for women. In these camps, 26,000 women were imprisoned from thirty nationalities that were under German occupation. The exhibition contains the biographies and photographs of twenty-four women from different camps, and it includes our testimonies. The introduction states "that the women attest the will that the Nazis couldn't destroy." Eighteen of the survivors who contributed their biographies were present at the opening.[11] This exhibition is traveling today to different cities. The Paris Musées published a hardcover catalog containing photographs and biographies.[12] It makes me feel good that people care. Knowing what happened to us, communities may learn how incredibly short and fast the road is to Auschwitz.

The Search for Rozsa's Grave

From Buchenwald, we proceeded to visit Markkleeberg, where we were provided with a guide, Mr. Andreas Höhn, from the mayor's office. Mr.

Höhn, a local historian we knew from our previous visits, came with us to retrace our Death March route. Reaching Freital, we looked for Rozsa Winkler's grave. I had the address of the cemetery from Nelly Winkler Rochlitz, Rozsa's sister, with whom I had talked in New York before departing for Germany. Nelly was very excited and extremely grateful. As mentioned in chapter 13, her brother Andor Winkler arrived the day after Rozsa was buried in the Christuskirche Cemetery at Freital.

With the address in hand, Mr. Höhn located the cemetery; but to our regret and chagrin, we could not find the graves of Rozsa or any of the other Markkleeberg victims who were buried there. In the cemetery record, Rozsa Winkler is listed, but we were told that, after a certain number of years, if no one claimed the grave and paid for the upkeep, the place is given to someone else to be buried above, according to the cemetery law. We could only recite a prayer for the soul of Rozsa and the other victims from the camp in their unmarked graves. It was sad and disappointing for Nelly when I gave her the somber news that even the remnants of her beloved sister can no longer be located.[13]

I left Markkleeberg with the hope that my next and final return will be with this book, and that its letters will fill the silence of the cemetery and make the remaining barracks and the *Appelplatz* in the camp speak. I hope

The author's visit to Christuskirche Cemetery in Freital, Germany, August 2001.

the volume will document for history not only the dreadful occurrences, but also the human spirit that survived in the camp and after. Today, Markkleeberg is populated mostly by people born after 1945. Having historical distance, I trust that they will be able to observe the events and judge the ensuing tragedy of their country's actions.

Lingering Memories

Knowing that the seed of hatred cannot be easily removed, I was hardly surprised when Dr. Bernd Klose, Der Oberbürgermeister of Markkleeberg, informed me in his letter of October 23, 2006 that the memorial tablet was vandalized and broken. It was encouraging, however, that the police investigated the matter and the city repaired the monument.

Exhibiting further goodwill was expressed by Dr. Bernd Klose, in his letter of January 8, 2008, addressed to the author:

> The city of Markkleeberg would like to honor your outstanding merit and work about the history of the camp. We would like to award you the honorary citizenship of our city and want to ask for your entry in our golden book. Describing the everyday hardship of Hungarian Jewish women and French resistance fighters in the camp will help in creating a lasting memory of them. By depicting the martyrdom of these women they will not fall into oblivion and we can hopefully teach future generations that such terrible crimes can never happen again.
>
> Signed: Dr. Bernd Klose, Der Oberbürgermeister.

Past and Present

Shortly after my September 2001 journey from Markkleeberg to New York, the attack of 9/11 took place. My city lost its naïveté as it met with the forces of terror that pass the boundaries of men's intellectual capacity or imagination. Just as in the Holocaust, nothing was considered by the aggressors to be sacred, inhuman, or immoral. The realm of concentration camps that seemed like another planet descended to our earth, our city. Evil showed how evil it can be, as people were trapped inside a nightmare trying to find their way out of it. When the towers collapsed to dust, what was once inconceivable became real and scary. "We have a new apocalyptic legend," wrote Jonathan Mark, "a death camp that descended on New York; klieg lights suddenly glaring through a pale, smoky night haze; noses sensing a stench that couldn't quite be placed; soldiers rolling by on lorries; the sense of soils piled upon soils beneath ash and palsied metal. . . . the soot and death that falls as gently as snow."[14] Something sinister arose with the towers' collapse, an eerie silence—akin to the gas chamber after the dropping of the Zyklon-B—hovered over Ground Zero. The Germans opened the gates for man's murderous instinct that had been kept in check by rules of civilization. Auschwitz was the road map to 9/11, ushering in the age of terror.

The yearly 9/11 memorials are hard for us survivors. The cries of anguish over the loss of all those victims are our cries. They speak to us and for us. We commiserate with them, with some added bittersweet memories of those early days of survival. For me, there are the images of orphaned teenagers, destroyed Jewish communities, and thousands of victims with no families and homes and having no one really care or set a day of mourning.

Years passed when landsmen's organizations had their small commemorations followed by the different world gatherings and memorials of Holocaust survivors. The latest was the UN resolution, unanimously accepted, to set the date of January 27th, the anniversary of the liberation of Auschwitz, as an international memorial to the Holocaust. "Remembrance and beyond" was the theme of the First Annual International Day of commemoration. It was held at the United Nations on January 27, 2006, the 61st anniversary of the liberation of the death camp at Auschwitz-Birkenau.

After years of silence, the decision of the United Nations was a momentous step for us survivors. We were pleased that representatives of the world finally took official notice of the atrocities against the Jewish people. I attended the first commemoration; people were eager to participate in that historic event. The General Assembly Hall filled beyond capacity with nearly two thousand people. The organizers were surprised by the size of the crowd and had to turn many people away. We wondered whether the feeling of vulnerability after 9/11 was one of the factors in the change of position by the United Nations. The international community may have belatedly realized that what happened to us could be the fate of any group.

The prevailing hatred of Jews and the Jewish state throughout Europe and the Arab world, despite the mounting global terror, is a painful irony, especially for us survivors. Erzsike's life was in serious danger and her home almost destroyed under Hezbollah's deadly barrages in July 2006. One of the rockets fell near her apartment in Haifa. We were terrified and trembling while waiting for the next attack, as the European countries called Israel's defense of its citizenry, including many Holocaust survivors, an overreaction and a crime against humanity. Those nations are still infected with the same pitiless hatred that robbed our homes and had the Jewish population slain sixty years before. They do not recognize that the emergence of radical Islam, a successor to Nazism with the likelihood of achieving nuclear capabilities, could put the whole world on its terror map.

Extremists do not differentiate among their victims. More than eighty different nationalities counted their dead on 9/11. They were European, Asian, African, women, men; old and young, from all walks of life, of diverse religions and economic levels. Most shocking, by eyewitness accounts, was the scene of people holding hands as they jumped from the burning towers. To prevent similar sights and assaults, the international community must block the path of this new hurricane of terror. As we extended our arms in adversity, let us join together to safeguard our liberty and civilization.

Our world is one and fear is one, thus the longing for life without terror unites us as human beings. In my family, the olive branch is carried by our younger daughter Yonit, whose name means "dove" in Hebrew. She inherited that name and its symbol of peace from her grandmother who died in Auschwitz. The love and yearning for peace that survived the Holocaust will triumph, I hope, replacing the horror of the terrorist hate; and in the end it may make the difference. My greatest wish and deepest prayer is, "Oh, God, please keep away that *other planet* we knew so well in the camps, from our children and all the children on earth!"

Amen.

The following is a song of unity for love, expressing our universal humanity, that I have heard in my mother tongue.

> Let's love each other, folks;
> Life sails, anyhow, swiftly away.
> Every minute counts.
> Let's love each other, folks.
> The heart is the greatest treasure;
> There is no nicer word than love.
> Through all around the world
> Let's love each other, folks.[15]

Appendix A

Markkleeberg Prisoners' List

Alphabetical Listing, Based On The Transport Lists Of Women In The Camp Of Markkleeberg, Including Jews And French Political Prisoners.

All the prisoners listed are Hungarians, except 250 of French nationality. They can be identified by their old and new numbers that are beyond fifty thousand; for example: Arbelin Henrette, Old # 52004, New # 50302; or Aubree Jacqueline, Old # 52005, New # 50303. The ages of the women ranged from thirteen to forty-nine. The date of birth is not always accurate as the registering Jewish women listed the older ones as younger and the young ones older, in order to have them "fit for work" rather than the gas chamber. The youngest listed on the transport list were fifteen-year-olds.

Among the professions for the girls and women, many were registered as seamstresses and tailors but there were also hairdressers, teachers, pharmacists, nurses, clerks, photographers, students, and workers. Professions given were not always exact. Expecting better treatment, inmates declared the types of skills they thought would be desirable.

Some of the names are not accurate. Believing that they could stay together, women changed their names.

The transport list is available at The International Tracing Service, Bad Arolsen and the Archives of Buchenwald Memorial Museum.

Last Name	First Name	Birth Date	Place of Birth	Profession	Old Number	New Number
Abraham	Iren	25.04.1925	Felsöbügate			50001
Abraham	Regina	01.04.1925	Kovacsrot		30845	49001
Abrahomovics	Roza	12.02.1928	Alsokalocsa		30844	49003
Abrahomovics	Rozalia	07.10.1925	Bilke		30661	49002
Ada	Eva	05.04.1922	Budapest	Pianistin		50002
Adam	Eva	18.02.1923	Marosvasarhely		37867	49500

Last Name	First Name	Birth Date	Place of Birth	Profession	Old Number	New Number
Adelsber	Zsuzsanna	12.06.1926	Sümeg			50003
Adler	Jozsa	17.08.1908	Bazin	Aerztin	30974	49004
Adler	Sali	25.12.1923	Dombo	Schneiderin		50004
Adler	Terez	07.06.1908	Mezökövesd			50005
Alexander	Elisabeth	17.04.1910	Satoraljaujhely	Pflegerin	30841	49005
Almasi	Bella	18.02.1911	Gyergyoszarhegy	Srickerin	37868	49501
Almasi	Edit	15.10.1924	Szentlöeino	Schneiderin		50006
Alt	Lenke	17.05.1925	Ujpest	Schneiderin	37869	49502
Altmann	Rozsi	20.02.1912	Satoraljaujhely		35768	49799
Alweisz	Etelka	02.11.1915	Budapest			50007
Ambrus	Klara	06.09.1919	Matetelke	Pflegerin	30842	49006
Angels	Gabrielle	14.06.1907			31940	50301
Apfelbaum	Lili	05.09.1926	Vac		37870	49503
Arbelin	Henriette	02.07.1905			52004	50302
Aron	Ilona	26.03.1923	Sajomagyaros		30662	49006
Asztalos	Rozsi	10.02.1925	Izaszacsa	Bürnstenbinderin	37871	49504
Aubree	Jacqueline	17.06.1914			52005	50303
Ausch	Eva	29.01.1922	Gyöngyös	Bürokraft	30523	49008
Ausch	Vera	16.01.1924	Gyöngyös	Kürnschner	30524	49009
Bachusz	Erzsebet	29.07.1925	Kolosvar		35769	49800
Bachusz	Szidi	11.06.1920	Kolozsvar		35770	49801
Balp	Madeleine	22.11.1899			52006	50304
Barany	Katalin	18.01.1930	Buzsak			50008
Barany	Viola	26.06.1924	Pozsony		37872	49505
Bard	Rosa	16.11.1914	Budapest	Elektrikerin		50009
Barna	Anna	02.05.1920	Budapest	Ingenieur		50011
Bauer	Rozsi	23.07.1923	Kassa	Schneiderin	35771	49802
Beck	Judit	04.12.1924	Tölna	Schneiderin		50010
Beck	Lili	13.02.1927	Janki		30853	49010
Beck	Rossi	10.11.1927	Tolna	Schneiderin		50012
Bekö	Helena	14.06.1924	Ilonkaujfalu		30666	49013
Benkö	Zsuzsanna	26.06.1925	Solt	Weberin	30851	49014
Berg	Erzsebet	13.07.1920	Dercske			50013
Berg	Rozsi	15.11.1914	Osorna			50014
Berger	Anna	22.09.1923	Szarvas		37873	49506
Berger	Berta	10.03.1921	Nagykomjad	Schneiderin	30532	49015
Berger	Francoise	06.01.1912			52009	50305
Berger	Ilona	12.06.1925	Fehergyarmat	Schneiderin	30527	49016
Berger	Iren	24.03.1921	Nagymursaly		37874	49507
Berger	Terez	25.08.1916	Osorna	Schneiderin		50015
Berkovics	Erzsebet	15.09.1909	Budapest		30667	49018
Berkovics	Gabriella	06.10.1926	Satoraljaujhely		30854	49017
Berkovics	Jolan	24.06.1921	Vac		37875	49508
Berkovics	Livia	26.06.1923	Satoraljaujhely		30854	49017
Bernet	RenceBlanc	25.12.1914			52011	50306
Bernier	Rosine	07.10.1924			52012	50307
Bernstein	Helena	07.06.1916	Hasfalva	Schneiderin	30847	49011
Bernstein	Lenke	11.05.1915	Harsfava	Schneiderin	31020	49020
Bernstein	Rozsa	05.05.1918	Harsfalva	Schneiderin	30846	49012

Last Name	First Name	Birth Date	Place of Birth	Profession	Old Number	New Number
Biber	Lili	17.07.1922	Dacsokeszi		30531	49021
Biber	Magda	13.07.1924	Ipolysag		30530	49022
Bienestock	Edit	07.03.1924	Papa	Schneiderin	37876	49509
Bienenstock	Zsuzsanna	07.02.1926	Papa	Schneiderin	37877	49510
Biener	Aranka	08.04.1017	Felsözolca		35772	49803
Bihari	Margit	26.07.1905	Budapest			50016
Bihari	Margit	09.02.1926	Beregujfalu			50017
Biller	Fany	25.07.1908	Bara	Schneiderin	30525	49023
Bineth	Hedvig	28.09.1925	Borsodsztmarton	Köchin	30852	49024
Biresak	Frida	17.11.1909	Budapeat	Pflegerin		50018
Birnbaum	Magda	09.08.1918	Gat		30855	4925
Biro	Erzsebet	22.10.1910	New York		37878	49511
Blau	Adrienne	28.10.1923	Satoraljaujhely		30978	49026
Blau	Aranka	30.09.1924	Vasarosnameny		35773	49804
Blau	Eva	04.04.1929	Mateszalka		30979	49027
Blau	Magda	30.06.1927	Nagymagyar	Schneiderin		50019
Blau	Margit	14.11.1919	Papa	Schneiderin	37879	49512
Bleyer	Eva	30.06.1924	Szolnok			50020
Blum	Anna	14.03.1924	Nagyecsed		30668	49028
Blum	Irena	15.04.1925	Nyideros		39080	49029
Bois	Lucienne	29.12.1914			52015	50308
Boros	Klara	06.06.1924	Budapest			50021
Bourghon	Amelia	30111908			52019	50309
Braun	Barbara	25.11.1915	Mezökövesd			50022
Braun	Berta	25.02.1926	Vasarosnameny		35774	49805
Braun	Carmen	19.04.1922	Budapest			50023
Braun	Edith	05.02.1911	Kassa		30856	49030
Braun	Eva	10.10.1924	Keszthely	Schneiderin		50024
Braun	Ilona	13.04.1916	Nagyatad		37880	49513
Braun	Juliska	28.03.1911	Komarom		30526	49031
Braun	Szidi	29.03.1910	Fertöszentmiklos			50025
Braun	Vera	01.02.1927	Budapest		30848	49032
Braun	Zsuzsanna	20.06.1927	Mateszalka		30669	49033
Braunstein	Ibolya	27.05.1927	Gyümölcsenes		35775	49806
Braunzweig	Mili	09.09.1921	Teke		30663	49035
Braubzweig	Rozsa	24.12.1924	Teke		30664	49034
Braver	Gabriella	29.12.1926	Ungvar		35776	49807
Breitner	Aranka	27.09.1908	Poosaj			50026
Breuer	Roza	22.06.1924	Sold		30850	49036
Breyer	Katalin	09.12.1924	Mezökövesd	Schneiderin		50027
Brezecka	Maria	02.02.1924			52021	50311
Brochay	Rolande	07.02.1918			52020	50310
Brociner	Margit	22.10.1919	Szendrö		30665	49037
Brunner	Iren	20.06,1918	Levelek			50028
Brunner	Anna	12.05.1924	Aroktö	Schneiderin	30528	49038
Brunner	Edith	12.09.1923	Aroktö	Schneiderin	30529	49039
Brunwasser	Magda	16.10,1926	Raho			50029
Burnichon	Jeanne	12.10.1906			52024	50312
Carancho	Suzanne	29.09.1922			52050	50318

Last Name	First Name	Birth Date	Place of Birth	Profession	Old Number	New Number
Casimir	Therese	15.08.1901			52028	50313
CateronLaufrey	Claudine	28.09.1908			52029	50314
Champrenault	Yvette	25.07.1918			52032	50315
Chasseigne	Francoise	12.02.1925			52035	50316
Chasseigne	Lucienne	06.03.1905			32036	50317
Chatre	Josephine	31.01.1913			52037	50319
Clair	RolandeMa	09.01.1924			52039	50320
Come	Denise	13.10.1905			52040	50321
Couttenier	Jeanne	16.02.1910			52044	50322
Creff	ReneeMari	14.05.1903			52045	50323
Croise	Marie	11.06.1911			520465	50324
Csanyi	Zsuzsanna	21.05.1922	Gyöngyös	Bürokraft	30670	49041
Csendes	Marianne	30.01.1927	Baja			50030
Czeisler	Erzsebet	26.12.1926	Szakacsi		30858	49042
Czeisler	Gabriella	18.05.1925	Sarospatak		30857	49043
Czeisler	Ilona	20.01.1916	Miskolc		30533	49040
Czeisler	Jolan	11.04.1907	Miskolc		30534	49044
Czigler	Rozsa	16.02.1906	Hatvan		30859	49045
Czikk	Ella	10.07.1907	Dunaszerdahely	Schneiderin	37881	49514
Czikk	Margit	28.06.1914	Debrecen	Schneiderin	37882	49515
Czitrom	Izabella	30.11.1916	Harasztkerek		37883	49516
Czorn	Gabriella	17.07.1924	Sarspatak	Schneiderin	30981	49046
Dambuyant	Marinette	15.09.1907			52048	50325
Danten	Lucette	20.05.1923			520495	50326
Danzinger	Irena	17.10.1924	Nagykallo		30674	49047
Darvas	Gabriella	09.12.1922	Pecs	Landwirtin	37885	49518
Darvas	Stefania	20.09.1905	Pecs		37886	49519
Daszkal	Maria	10.12.1911	Rusokava		30863	49048
Daszkalovits	Rozsi	29.08.1926	Taracköz		35777	49808
David	Berta	16.12.1925	Marcslaka	Schneiderin	30671	49049
David	Maria	26.10.1922	Kolozanagyida		30672	49050
David	Miriam	10.02.1922	Szekelyudvarhely	Strickerin	37887	49520
Davidovics	Erzsebet	15.08.1921	Nagyszölös		35778	49809
Davidovits	Blanka	07.10.1920	Marosvasarhely	Weberin	37888	49521
Davidovits	Helen	04.06.1926	Dombo			50032
De Giraud	Louise	25.071914			52093	50349
De Rrugne	Andree	14.03.1912			52223	50409
Deballe	Alfreda	23.03.1910			52051	50327
Dervarits	Matild	28.04.1913	Zalaegerszed	Stenotipistin	37889	49522
Deutch	Agnes	30.09.1923	Budapest	Schneiderin		50033
Deutch	Bella	27.02.1927	Vac	Schneiderin		50035
Deutch	Eva	24.10.1929	Peröcseny		30536	49052
Deutch	Eva	25.07.1923	Budapest	Modistin	37890	49523
Deutch	Hedwig	18.07.1904	Nagytapolcsany		30860	49053
Deutch	Helen	14.01.1904	Lebeny	Erzieherin	30538	49054
Deutch	Helen	13.10.1922	Vac	Schneiderin		50035
Deutch	Ibolya	18.10.1918	Mezöszakall		37891	49524
Deutch	Ilona	10.09.1913	Szak		30539	49055
Deutch	Jolan	05.05.1922	Nagybwrezna	Schneiderin	37892	49525

Last Name	First Name	Birth Date	Place of Birth	Profession	Old Number	New Number
Deutch	Klara	10.04.1925	Tolmas	Schneiderin		50036
Deutch	Lenke	11.05.1918	Papa	Schneiderin	37893	49526
Deutch	Márta	04.09.1923	Minaj		35779	49810
Deutch	Olga	07.11.1921	Damak		37894	49527
Deutch	Olga	02.11.1921	Kassa		35780	49811
Deutch	Szeren	12.01.1924	Vac	Schneiderin		50037
Deutch	Vera	22.04.1923	Satoraljaujhely		30975	49056
Devai	Adela	07.09.1922	Edeleny		30673	49051
Devaquez	Anne-Cecil	29.04.1901			52055	50328
Diamant	Anna	20.04.1920	Kisnemedi		37895	49528
Diamant	Rozsi	20.04.1920	Kisnemedi		37896	49529
Dittler	Frida	27.01.1902	Zolyom		37897	49530
Doktorczyk	Hela	15.05.1919	Litzmannstadt			50038
Dominjon	Genevieve	01.05.1912			52058	50329
Dondana	Mauguerittt	28.06.1912			52059	50330
Donisa	Odette	29.03.1916			52060	50331
Donjon	Andree	24.07.1914			52061	50332
Doros	Ilona	22.15.1908	Ajnacskö		37898	49531
Drigeard-Curat	Antioinette	02.09.1905			52063	50333
Droth	Lil	11.02.1922	Vatta		30862	49058
Droth	Margit	06.06.1912	Vatta		30861	49057
Dub	Olga	13.06.1914	Mezökaszony	Schneiderin		50039
Dub	Regina	22.05.1908	Mezökaszony			50040
Dub	Rozsi	11.12.1928	Feies			50041
Duche	Fernande	23.11.1929			52065	50334
Duche	Liliane	18.01.1928			52066	50335
Dufayet	Raymonde	11.05.1913			52067	50336
Düm	Elza	15.03.1921	Ujfeherto		30535	49059
Dumontiev	Suzanne	02.03.1921			52068	50337
Duerte	Jacqueline	15.05.1914			52069	50338
Dzitter	Eva	22.07.1924	Budapest	Kürcschnerin		50031
Eckstein	Judith	18.12.1924	Kassa	Zeichnerin	35781	49812
Ehrenthal	Margit	12.02.1916	Nagymagyar	Schneiderin		50042
Ehrenthal	Valeria	26.10.1927	Nagymagyar	Schneiderin		50043
Ehrmann	Eva	15.09.1924	Kirlyhelmec		35782	49813
Ehrmann	Szeren	13.06.1921	Eperjes		35783	49814
Einhorn	Bendke	26.01.1926	Dombo	Schneiderin		50046
Einhorn	Helen	19.07.1923	Dombo	Schneiderin		50045
Einhorn	Gizi	05.07.1924	Dombo	Schneiderin		50044
Eisdörfer	Lili	28.05.1923	Szukszava	Schneiderin	30676	49060
Eisenberger	Nelly	26041909	Nagyszölös	Köchin	30678	49060
Eisenberger	Olga	04.10.1920	Nagyszölös	Köchin	30677	49062
Eisikovics	Sara	08.03.1917	Alsoapsa		35784	49815
Eisler	Ilona	01.11.1923	Demend		30865	49063
Eisner	Edith	25.11.1923	Demend		30866	49064
Eisner	Klara	01.11.1926	Szügye		30867	49065
Elfer	Erzsebet	11.03.1918	Vac		37899	49532
Elias	Szeren	08.06.1909	Ujpest	Arztin	35785	49816
Engel	Judith	24.07.1929	Nagymagyar		30541	49066

Last Name	First Name	Birth Date	Place of Birth	Profession	Old Number	New Number
Engel	Katalin	19.07.1928	Budapest			50047
Engel	Sara	15.01.1922	Ujfeherto		30540	49067
Engelhardt	Aranka	09.01.1905	Esztergom		30864	49068
Engelsberg	Rossa	23.05.1925	Jaszeberny	Schneiderin		50048
Engelstein	Fanny	13.07.1924	Petrova		35786	49817
Engländer	Magda	24.01.1924	Borsod		35787	49818
Erdös	Katalin	23.10.1919	Obecse	Turnlehrerin	37900	49533
Ernst	Piroska	23.01.1926	Udvard	Schneiderin	30675	49069
Evesard	Julienne	04.10.1902			52071	50339
Faber	Erzsebet	26.06.1907	Ipolysag	Rechtswalt	30870	49070
Farkas	Berta	02.06.1922	Hericse		37901	49534
Farkas	Gizella	28.05.1924	Avasujfalu		30693	49071
Farkas	Gizella	05.04.1926	Rozsaly		30869	49072
Farkas	Hajnal	24.10.1909	Kalifalva			50049
Farkas	Iren	24.03.1919	Szatmarnemeti		37902	49535
Farkas	Magda	01.07.1927	Nagyszöllös		30985	49073
Farkas	Regina	04.07.1924	Szeklence		35788	49819
Farkas	Roza	15.10.1922	Nagyszölös	Schneiderin	30521	49074
Farkas	Sali	15.08.1912	Yisko	Schneiderin		50050
Faure	Marie-Louise	07.04.1909			52075	50340
Fayot	Germaine	13.01.1921			52076	50341
Feher	Edith	07.10.1925	Papa		37903	49536
Feher	Rozsa	26.10,1926	Szombathely		37904	49537
Fehervary	Magda	20.02.1918	Petroszeny		37905	49538
Feldbauer	Ilona	01.06.1923	Udvard		30680	49076
Feldmann	Cecilia	21.08.1922	Vac	Schneiderin	37906	49539
Feldmann	Gizella	02.02.1927	Vac	Schneiderin	37907	49540
Feldmann	Ilona	17.12.1908	Szerenos		30695	49078
Felmann	Márta	30.11.1914	Vinna		30926	49079
Fenyö	Anna	11.03.1927	Satoraljaujhely		30983	49080
Fenyö	Piroska	18.06.1906	Paci		30984	49081
Ferber	Sarolta	21.02.1918	Huszt	Schneiderin	35789	49820
Ferencz	Irena	11.10.1911	Tunyog		30692	49082
Feuereisen	Hajnal	29091817	Lelesz		30545	49083
Feuerstein	Lilli	11.04.1926	Lelesz		30544	49084
Finger	Magda	27.08.1924	Lelesz		30546	49085
Fischer	Iren	25.10.1924	Munkacs		35790	49821
Fischer	Olga	24.12.1924	Ujpest		37908	49541
Fischer	Erzsebet	18.05.1910	Szentistvanbaksa		30805	49086
Fischer	Ilona	17.05.1927	Sajopetri			50051
Fischer	Katalin	09.02.1920	Kaposvar		37910	49543
Fischer	Klara	01.07.1922	Tornyospalca		35791	49822
Fischer	Sara	24.01.1922	Nagyatad		37911	49544
Fischer	Szeren	28.05.1924	Fehergyarmat	Schneiderin	30543	49087
Fischer	Vera	01.05.1916	Pecs		37912	49545
Fischer	Zsuzsanna	29.03.1924	Nagyatad		37913	49546
Fischer	Zsuzsanna	18.11.1923	Tornyospalca	Schneiderin	35792	49823
Fischler	Edit	29.01.1919	Gyulafehervar	Arbeiterin	35793	49824
Fischmann	Livia	16.09.1928	Ujfeherto		30551	49088

Last Name	First Name	Birth Date	Place of Birth	Profession	Old Number	New Number
Fischmann	Margit	23.07.1923	Ujfeherto	Schneiderin	30552	49089
Fixel	Debora	18.07.1922	Szaszregen		30561	49090
Fixler	Anna	22.01.1921	Kassa	Kometikerin	35794	49825
Flesch	Agnes	02.11.1923	Hernadpetri	Schneiderin	37914	49547
Flesch	Jolan	23.08.1910	Hernadszurdok	Schneiderin	37925	49548
Flesch	Margit	01.07.1924	Tapioszele	Arbeiterin		50052
Floch	Judit	15.04.1928	Siogard	Schülerin		50053
Flohr	Edith	26.01.1910	Miskolc	Weberin	30557	49091
Fodor	Margit	10.11.1915	Papa	Schneiderin	37916	49549
Fogel	Fani	15.04.1922	Tecsö		35795	49826
Fogel	Helen	15.01.1924			35796	49827
Fonque	Raymonde	05.12.1907			52079	50342
Franchet	Odette	18.02.1921			52081	50343
Francom	Antoinette	19.11.1897			52082	50344
Frank	Erzsebet	05.05.1918	Mezökeresztes	Kosmetikerin	30559	49092
Frank	Katalin	23.09.1920	Budapest	Lehrerin	30558	49093
Fränkel	Borbala	03.09.1923	Gyöngyös		30550	49097
Fränkel	Eva	12.02.1921	Budapest	Pflegerin	30694	49098
Fränkel	Gizella	07.07.1924	Ujfeherto	Schneiderin	30690	49099
Fränkel	Helena	12.03.1925	Ujfeherto		30691	49100
Fränkel	Ilona	02.02.1922	Jaszfenyszaru	Schneiderin		50054
Fränkel	Lili	24.04.1924	Gyöngyös		30871	49101
Fränkel	Rossi	21.04.1915	Jaszfenyszaru	Schneiderin		50055
Fränkel	Roza	17.081923	Guta	Schneiderin	30542	49102
Franfurt	Ilona	28.02.1924	Abaujszanto		37917	49550
Frankl	Edith	09.08.1928	Bankeszi		30683	49094
Frankl	Erzsebet	14.04.1926	Totmagyar		30682	49095
Frankl	Terez	07.08.1925	Totmagyar	Schneiderin	30681	49096
Freikind	Piroska	25.03.1906	Possaj			50056
Frenkel	Edit	05.10.1925	Vasarosnameny	Näherin	35797	49828
Frenkel	Klara	22.04.1927	Vasarosnameny		35798	49829
Frenkel	Magda	17.12.1924	Kapolcsapati		35799	49830
Freund	Alice	14.07.1918	Budapest	Schneiderin	37919	49552
Freund	Helen	19.07.1926	Szatmarnemeti		35800	49831
Freund	Magda	03.11.1927	Tany		30553	49103
Fried	Josefa	23.08.1924	Dombo	Strickerin		50057
Fried	Rosa	23.01.1927	Ersekujvar	Arbeiterin		50058
Friedman	Adel	06.09.1920	Bodrogkeresztur		35801	49832
Friedman	Aranka	04.10.1929	Tiszabarcel		30843	49104
Friedman	Arany	29.03.1927	Ungvar		35802	49833
Friedman	Bella	16.11.1925	Sarospatak		30986	49105
Friedman	Doris	25.03.1908	Hardfalva	Schneiderin		50059
Friedman	Edit	01.10.1922	Bodrogkeresztur		35803	49834
Friedman	Elvira	11.06.1924	Rozsaly		30547	49106
Friedman	Erzsebet	04.03.1910	Baja			50061
Friedman	Eta	03.09.1917	Bodrogkeresztur		35804	49835
Friedman	Eva	06.09.1926	Szatmarnemeti		37920	49553
Friedman	Fany	18.11.1927	Harsfalva	Modistin	30560	49107
Friedman	Gyöngyi	16.03.1922	Beregillosva			50062

Last Name	First Name	Birth Date	Place of Birth	Profession	Old Number	New Number
Friedman	Jolan	19.05.1925	Zeteny		35805	49836
Friedman	Judit	26.07.1926	Budapest			50063
Friedman	Katalina	05.05.1924	Mateszalka	Bürokraft	30687	49108
Friedman	Kato	26.09.1925	Nagyvarad	Strickerin	37918	49551
Friedman	Klara	09.01.1916	Bodrogkeresztur		35806	49837
Friedman	Livia	27.01.1924	Bodrogkeresztur		35807	49838
Friedman	Margit	31.08.1922	Rozsaly		30548	49109
Friedman	Margit	26.01.1920	Tab		37921	49554
Friedman	Margit	18.01.1925	Helyöcsaba		35808	49839
Friedman	Maria	16.12.1915	Tiszadob			50060
Friedman	Oecillia	15.08.1922	Halmi			50064
Friedman	Olga	30.05.1924	Halmi	Friseurin		50065
Friedman	Piroska	02.08.1925	Vasaronameny		35809	49840
Friedman	Rozsi	19.12.1918	Bodrogkeresztur		35810	49841
Fritsch	Ella	20.04.1924	Marosvasarhely	Student	37922	49555
Fromentin	Jeanne	18.04.1895			52085	50345
Frommer	Terez	23.02.1926	Harsfalva	Schneiderin		50066
Fruchter	Judit	17.08.1924	Borsa		35811	49842
Frühzeitig	Sara	02.11.1910	Tolcsva		30549	49110
Fuchs	Blanka	02.06.1925	Nagymagyar		30555	49111
Fuchs	Judit	26.10.1929	Marosvasarhely	Schneiderin	37923	49556
Fuchs	Rozalia	12.04.1926	Nagymagyar		30556	49112
Fuchs	Szerena	03.09.1920	Poprad	Schneiderin	30873	49113
Fülep	Agnes	27.03.1929	Mateszalka		30685	49114
Fülep	Anna	08.06.1927	Mateszalka	Schneiderin	30689	49115
Fülep	Erzsebet	17.06.1923	Mateszalka	Schneiderin	30679	49116
Fülep	Olga	03.02.1926	Mateszalka	Schneiderin	30688	49117
Fülep	Roza	28.09.1905	Mateszalka		30684	49118
Fulmann	Roza	31.07.1924	Szabatin		30868	49077
Füredi	Magda	17.02.1922	Ujpest	Arbeiterin		50067
Fürst	Erzsebet	17.01.1913	Kiskunhalas			50068
Galand	Xenia	06.10.1916			52086	50346
Ganz	Kornelia	10.09.1910	Miskolc		30565	49119
Garfinkel	Gizella	30.03.1915	Budapest		37924	49557
Garini	Raymonde	19.06.1920			52089	0
Gati	Judit	08.03.1928	Szekesfehervar		37925	49558
Gedaljovits	Dori	15.08.1918	Irkoc	Schneiderin	30880	49120
Gedaljovits	Eva	28.06.1922	Szekelyhid		35812	49843
Gedaljovits	Iboly	28.10.1924	Szekelyhid	Schneiderin	35813	49844
Gedaljovits	Pepi	11.01.1921	Irkoc		30563	49121
Gelb	Dora	25.02.1925	Ilonaujfalu		30701	49122
Gelbermann	Manya	17.03.1925	Huszt		35814	49845
Gelbermann	Rozsi	11.05.1926	Huszt		35815	49846
Gelbmann	Roza	16.10.1910	Gyergycsalmas		37926	49559
Genuth	Rozsi	19.04.1922	Közepviso		35816	49847
Genuth	Sari	14.05.1921	Közepviso		35817	49848
Gergely	Magda	03.03.1925	Miskoc	Schneiderin	35818	49849
Gerler	Helen	20.08.1915	Budfalva	Schneiderin		50069
Gerö	Iren	10.06.1927	Kecskemet			50070

Last Name	First Name	Birth Date	Place of Birth	Profession	Old Number	New Number
Gerö	Klara	13.07.1921	Sarospatak	Bürokraft	30987	49123
Gerö	Maria	25.01.1924	Sarospatak		30988	49124
Gertsch	Sari	19.05.1920	Magyarmegye	Strickerin	37927	49560
Gilles	Lucienne	13.12.1908			52092	50348
Glanzmann	Ella	06.06.1915	Gymes		37928	49561
Glück	Agnes	30.08.1928	Miskolc		37929	49562
Glück	Aranka	01.04.1920	Mateszalka	Schneiderin	30698	49125
Glück	Erzsebet	23.09.1923	Mori		35819	49850
Glück	Eva	14.03.1925	Ujpest	Schneiderin	37930	49563
Glück	Gizella	16.03.1913	Mateszalka	Schneiderin	30697	49126
Glück	Margit	17.05.1922	Mateszalka	Schneiderin	30699	49127
'Glück	Rebekka	25.06.1924	Szilagycseh	Schneiderin	30564	49128
Glück	Valeria	18.05.1928	Szatmarcseke	Schneiderin	30710	49129
Godart	Genevieve	05.04.1929			52094	50350
Godinger	Ida	04.04.1926	Harsfalva	Schneiderin		50071
Godinger	Regina	28.01.1928	Harsfalva	Schneiderin		50072
Godinger	Sara	30.03.1925	Felsöbisztra	Schneiderin	30881	49130
Gold	Eta	12.04.1923	Romoli		30569	249132
Gold	Gabriella	13.08.1927	Püspökladany	Schneiderin		50073
Gold	Helen	04.07.1917	Romoli		30569	149132
Goldberger	Helena	27.09.1917	Nagyrakoc		30878	49133
Goldberger	Lenke	08.06.1925	Beregkövesd		30696	49134
Goldberger	Magda	07.05.1927	Tiszaujlak		35820	49851
Goldberger	Szeren	15.12.1925	Foroencs			50074
Goldenfeld	Aranka	10.12.1922	Kissarmas		37931	49564
Goldkranc	Chaja	05.05.1919	Litzmannstadt			50075
Goldner	Maria	12.04.1922	Kassa	Schneiderin	35821	49852
Goldner	Rozsi	30.10.1908	Tokod		37932	49565
Goldner	Terez	31.03.1923	Dulfalva		35822	49853
Goldstein	Eva	17.03.1923	Tiszavec	Kindergärtnerin	37933	49566
Goldstein	Eva	15.11.1925	Deaki		37934	49567
Goldstein	Golda	16.12.1910	Budfalva			50076
Goldstein	Jolan	15.03.1917	Göncz		30711	49135
Gottdiener	Anna	09.08.1925	Kotaj		30700	49136
Gottesmann	Agnes	31.10.1922	Sarospatak	Bürokraft	30566	49137
Gottlieb	Anna	13.02.1905	Prügy	Schneiderin	30702	49138
Gottlieb	Erzsebet	30.06.1909	Prügy	Schneiderin	30703	49139
Gottlieb	Margit	03.10.1929	Orkuta		37935	49568
Gottlieb	Zsofia	22.05.1924	Kaposvar	Schneiderin	30706	49140
Graf	Ilona	09.02.1919	Kassa	Schneiderin	37936	49569
Graf	Valeria	17.07.1921	Kassa	Schneiderin	37937	49570
Granier	Juliette	18.10.1922			42099	50351
Grasz	Amalia	14.11.1912	Budapest	Beamtin		50077
Greiner	Ibolya	13.08.1928	Nagymagyar		30707	49141
Griesz	Erzsebet	22.08.1922	Nagybaracska	Arbeiterin		50078
Griffel	Eszter	13.09.1905	Alsoviso		30876	49142
Grof	Erzsebet	03.11.1908	Balassagyarmat		30793	49143
Grof	Erzsebet	26.02.1926	Nolland	Schneiderin		50079
Gross	Agnes	05.05.1923	Szikszo		35823	49854

Last Name	First Name	Birth Date	Place of Birth	Profession	Old Number	New Number
Gross	Berta	15.06.1923	Magyaregregy		37939	49572
Gross	Eszter	01.10.1926	Magyaregregy		37940	49573
Gross	Eva	13.02.1929	Kapos		37941	49574
Gross	Irma	26.03.1925	Magyaregregy	Schneiderin	37942	49575
Gross	Lili	28.09.1922	Celöcze	Schneiderin	37943	49576
Gross	Márta	15.07.1926	Kiralyhelmec		35824	49855
Gross	Szeren	27.07.1924	Magyaregregy	Schneiderin	37944	49577
Gross	Szeren	12.12.1917	Nagyszeben		35825	49856
Grossmann	Ella	06.06.1910	Miskolc		30715	49148
Grossmann	Eva	20.06.1926	Miskolc		30712	49149
Grossmann	Márta	05.04.1924	Erdöbenye		37938	49571
Grosz	Anna	11.06.1925	Tokaj		30713	49145
Grosz	Denee	09.08.1916	Kadas	Schneiderin		50082
Grosz	Erzsebet	26.05.1913	Komarom		30568	49146
Grosz	Helena	26.12.1926	Raholya		30875	49144
Grosz	Ibolya	21.04,1927	Szeged			50080
Grosz	Ilona	08.01.1911	Komarom		30567	49147
Grosz	Katalin	22.02.1918	Budapest	Schneiderin		50081
Grosz	Szeren	15.01.1910	Mako	Schneiderin		50083
Grosz	Zsuzsa	28.11.1926	Kareag	Schneiderin		50084
Groszmann	Erzsebet	30.10.1926	Szatmarökörito		37945	49578
Groszmann	Olga	03.03.1928	Szatmarökörito		37946	49579
Grün	Iren	19.01.1920	Marosvasarhely		37947	49580
Grün	Jolan	05.09.1920	Palotailva		35828	49859
Grünbaum	Edit	28.08.1925	Tapolca	Schneiderin		50085
Grünbaum	Ilona	21.04.1919	Apc		35826	49857
Grünbaum	Jolan	24.03.1920	Budapest	Pflegerin		50086
Grünberg	Erzsebet	13.04.1918	Tasnad		35829	49860
Grünberg	Lenke	14.03.1929	Keneszpatak			50087
Grünberg	Rossi	28.08.1927	Keneszpatak			50088
Grünberger	Berta	09.05.1918	Kassa		35830	49861
Grünberger	Erzsebet	21.08.1921	Keszthely		35831	49862
Grünberger	Ilona	24.01.1917	Hernadnemeti		37948	49581
Grünberger	Jolan	07.07.1915	Budapest		30562	49150
Grünberger	Magda	21.05.1928	Satoraljaujhely		35827	49858
Grünberger	Sari	07.04.1925	Dombo	Schneiderin		50089
Grundman	Antonia	01.03.1906			52102	50352
Grünfeld	Juliana	16.06.1924	Gyöngyös	Schneiderin	30877	49151
Grünfeld	Rossi	22.08.1914	Magyarregon	Arbeiterin		50090
Grünfeld	Roza	21.08.1925	Budapest		30989	49152
Grünspann	Piroska	31.05.1928	Kassa		37949	49582
Grünwald	Margit	31.12.1908	Köszeg		37950	49583
Grünwald	Zsofia	02.01.1917	Taos	Beamtin		50091
Guena	Lea	12.03.1904			52104	50353
Guillon	Marie	11.05.1903			52106	50354
Guth	Anna	29.08.1922	Barcs		37951	49584
Guttmann	Aranka	12.03.1924	Hernadvecse		30879	49153
Guttmann	Eva	24.10.1923	Dombovar		30708	49154
Guttmann	Irena	30.09.1925	Nyiregyhaza		30705	49155

Last Name	First Name	Birth Date	Place of Birth	Profession	Old Number	New Number
Guttmann	Magda	11.01.1923	Nyiregyhaza		30704	49156
Guttmann	Regina	12.12.1919	Nyiregyhaza	Schneiderin	30709	49157
Gymes	Agnes	18.06.1925	Miskolc	Lehrerin	30714	49158
Hager	Erzsebet	11.12.1920	Debrecen		35832	49863
Hager	Hanna	20.01.1924	Felsöviso		35833	49864
Hajdu	Magda	31.05.1911	Ujvidek	Bürokraft	35834	49865
Halasz	Boris	25.01.1909	Marosvasarhaly		35835	49866
Halpern	Helen	01.03.1925	Munkacs	Arbeiterin		50093
Halpern	Maria	07.01.1924	Munkacs	Arbeiterin		50092
Hamer	Adel	12.10.1919	Budapest	Färberin		50094
Hartmann	Eva	17.07.1927	Abaujszanto		37952	49585
Hartmann	Magda	08.05.1926	Abaujszanto		37953	49786
Hazai	Flora	22.02.1920	Satoraljaujhely		30882	49159
Heisler	Eva	03.03.1926	Budapest		30747	49160
Heisler	Helen	25.08.1925	Halmi		37954	49587
Heisler	Klara	08.09.1917	Kiskörös		30885	49161
Heisler	Roza	07.12.1911	Alsorepa		30717	49162
Heller	Erna	02.12.1924	Gyimesbükk	Ärztl.assisst	37955	49588
Heller	Eta	02.09.1928	Yirdercs		50990	49163
Heller	Iren	08.09.1912	Egri		35836	49867
Helmer	Elma	28.02.1907	Mezösamson		37956	49589
Henke	Helene	29.05.1910			52109	50355
Hercz	Zsuzsa	24.11.1919	Zsibo		37957	49590
Herkovics	Erzsebet	22.06.1923	Bikszad	Schneiderin	30571	49166
Hermelstein	Magda	25.05.1922	Nagyszölös		30744	49286
Hersko	Helen	10.10.1914	Nagykaroly		30716	49164
Herskovics	Blis	03.11.1910	Munkacs		30572	49165
Herskovics	Eta	13.05.1920	Nyirbator		37959	49592
Herskovics	Ibolya	24.06.1924	Margita		37960	49593
Herskovics	Iren	18.11.1921	Szilagyperecseny		37961	49594
Herskovics	Lenke	02.05.1916	Somogycsurgo		37958	49591
Herskovics	Margit	06.03.1907	Budapest	Schneiderin	37962	49595
Herskovics	Maria	06.06.1923	Dobruska	Schneiderin	37963	49596
Herskovics	Sara	15.02.1922	Sziagyperecseny	Schneiderin	37964	49597
Herskovics	Berta	10.08.1925	Rovkolostor			50095
Herskovics	Eszter	25.08.1927	Rovkolostor			50096
Herskovics	Etel	11.06.1921	Hersenyfalva	Schneiderin		50097
Herskovics	Helen	10.05.1928	Rovkolostor			50098
Herskovics	Lenke	24.03.1920	Hersenyfalva	Schneiderin		50099
Herz	Magda	15.01.1924	Fehergyarmat		35837	49868
Hettler	Anna	25.06.1908	Tarnaszadany			50100
Heulin	YvonneRen	22.05.1901			52110	50356
Hicker	Margit	13.10.1920	Pestujhely	Arbeiterin		50101
Hilf	Ilona	06.10.1904	Nagysarkany		30884	49167
Hirsch	Agnes	23.08.1927	Nagyatad		37965	49598
Hirsch	Bella	22.09.1908	Mezöpand		37966	49599
Hirsch	Ilona	23.05.1927	Szentmihaly		30885	49168
Hirsch	Lili	22.03.1915	Esztergom		30886	49169
Hirsch	Maria	30.11.1926	Kacko			50102

Last Name	First Name	Birth Date	Place of Birth	Profession	Old Number	New Number
Hirsch	Rozsi	23.12.1914	Petele		37967	49600
Hochfelder	Anna	19.12.1919	Ujpest		37968	49601
Hochfelder	Zsuzsanna	15.10.1927	Zakany	Schneiderin	37969	49602
Hoffer	Katalin	13.03.1913	Tapioszele	Schneiderin		50103
Hoffer	Klara	24.04.1904	Sarkad		35828	49869
Hoffman	Margit	19.09.1918	Papa		37970	49603
Hoffman	Rozsi	25.08.1924	Papa		37971	40604
Holländer	Zsuzsa	22.05.1927	Sarkad			10105
Holländer	Gizella	22.061909	Bustyahaza		30718	49170
Holländer	Vera	20.3.1925	Busthahaza		30719	49171
Holzer	Margit	34.09.190	Zalasztbalasz			50104
Holzer	Erzsebet	04.07.1920	Kisbaromlak		30721	49172
Holzer	Margit	08.10.1921	Kisbaromlak		30720	49173
Holzer	Margit	27.01.1910	Papa		37972	49605
Hutterer	Margit	21.10.1925	Vac		37973	49606
Iczkovits	Agnes	11.08.1922	Sarospatak	Pflegerin	30888	49174
Iczkovits	Erzsebet	29.07.1910	Nyitrazsambokret	Pflegerin	30887	49175
Indig	Erzsebet	08.02.1922	Marmarossziget	Näherin	35839	49870
Indig	Sara	14.06.1918	Marmarossziget		35840	49871
Infeld	Rana	14.02.1910	Ozarkow	Schreiderin		50106
Inberg	Piri	21.07.1919	Budfalva	Schreiderin		50107
Inberg	Rossi	21.08.1912	Budfalva	Schreiderin		50108
Ipar-Span	Elvira	30.05.1924	Nagymagyar		30640	49176
Ipar-Span	Livia	14.08.1925	Nagymagyar		30641	49178
Ipar-Span	Emma	01.11.1926	Nagymagyar		30642	49177S
Izrael	Eszter	04111927	Alör			50109
Izrael	Margit	01.05.1925	Alör			501010
Izrael	Piroska	16.07.1915	Nagykaroly	Schneidrin		50111
zrael	Sara	11.11.1926	Mezöband		37974	49607
Izsak	Edit	13.03.1926	Kaposvar	Schneiderin		50112
Izsak	Ilona	29.12.1924	Tarbolc		37975	49608
Izsak	Juci	29.06.1928	Tarbolc		37976	49609
Izsak	Klara	17.04.1911	Maramarossziget		38166	49610
Jäger	Erzsebet	08.01.1921	Szatmatnemeti	Bürokraft	37980	49614
Jäger	Lili	26.08.1922	Szatmarnameti		37981	49615
Jäger	Sara	01.01.1922	Dulfalva		35844	49875
Jakobovics	Magda	11.09.1923	Ujpest	Schneiderin	37977	49611
Jakobovics	Faidla	20.12.1926	Skernivice	Schneiderin		50113
Janicka	Jaina	21.01.1913			52116	50357
Jakabovits	Helena	13.11.1919	Szara		30889	49180
Jakabovits	Margit	20.10.1923	Szendrö		30574	49181
Janovics	Edit	03.07.1923	Ujpest	Schneiderin	37978	49612
Janovics	Erzsebet	20.05.1927	Szolnocska		35841	49872
Janovics	Ibolya	30.10.1923	Szolnocska		35842	49873
Janovics	Rozsi	26.09.1922	Boly		25843	49874
Jaszinger	Jolan	24.04.1912	Debrecen			50115
Javor	Aranka	10.05.1906	Szöreg		37979	49613
Jeanne	Genevieve	29.10.1919			52119	50358
Jellinek	Anna	02.12.1918	Verge		30890	49876

Last Name	First Name	Birth Date	Place of Birth	Profession	Old Number	New Number
Jeudon	Aline	23.01.1923			52120	50114
Joel	Etelka	28.03.1919	Magyarlaos		35845	496876
Jonas	Matild	26.09.1917	Katolatszed			50114
Jozefovics	Olga	24.05.1926	Marosvasarhely		37982	49616
Jurovics	Julia	19.04.1916	Marmarossziget		37846	49877
Jurovics	Rozsi	19.08.1922	Marmarossziget		35847	49878
Juskovits	Ilona	06.06.1916	Ungvar	Arbeiterin		50116
Kaff	Flora	06.04.1916	Bonyhad	Schneiderin	37983	49617
Kaff	Julia	05.01.1922	Bonyhad	Schneiderin	37984	49618
Kaff	Lea	15.09.1918	Bonyhard	Schneiderin	37985	49619
Kahan	Hanna	05.06.1923	Otvösfalva		35848	49879
Kahan	Márta	06.04.1925	Gyöngyös		30907	49183
Kahan	Regina	18.01.1926	Tecsö		35848	49880
Kail	Ibolya	07.08.1926	Miskolc	Arbeiterin	30580	49184
Kaller	Frida	04.04.1921	Olahozertiz		35850	49881
Kallus	Márta	27.11.1926	Nagygeres	Laborantin	35851	49882
Kalman	Roza	08,04,1907	Sebsisztgvölgy	Arbeiteri.	30729	49185
Kalmanovits	Katalin	11.12.1920	Bagota	Schneiderin		50117
Kalmanovitz	Magda	26.12.1927	Tokaj	Schneiderin	30905	49186
Kalmar	Katalin	01.09.1926	Ipolynyek	Schneiderin	30579	49187
Kardos	Barbara	22.09.1920	Kaposvar	Schneiderin		50118
Karpelesz	Anna	03.05.1917	Palotaolva		30578	49188
Kartschmaroff	Erzsebet	04.06.1922	Szombathely		30898	49189
Katz	Edith	21.04.1923	Nagyboske		30583	49190
Katz	Elza	14.12.1918	Marosvasarhely		37986	49620
Katz	Erzsebet	16.01.1911	Marosvasarhely	Strickerin	37987	49621
Katz	Etel	12.12.1920	Olahosertiz		35852	49883
Katz	Ibolya	26.05.1923	Brasso	Schneiderin	30897	49191
Katz	Ilona	21.03.1912	Satoraljaujhely		30896	49192
Katz	Jolan	31.08.1923	Mariapoos		30582	49193
Katz	Lili	06.07.1925	Dombo			50119
Katz	Roza	15.06.1908	Satoraljaujhely		30893	49194
Katz	Roza	29.07.1926	Nagyboosko		30584	49195
Katz	Rozsi	22.09.1922	Dombrad		37988	49622
Katz	Tobi	25.10.1924	Dombo	Schneiderin		50120
Kaufman	Iren	24.04.1924	Kisar		35855	49884
Kaufman	Magda	15.03.1926	Kisar		35854	49885
Keil	Maria	20.02.1924	Eustyahaza		30581	49196
Keisler	Iren	10.08.1926	Nyiregyhaza	Friseuse	37989	49623
Keisler	Klara	15.07.1928	Nyiregyhaza	Schneiderin	37990	49624
Kelemen	Gizella	01.06.1919	Magyarszntbenedek		37991	49625
Kelemen	Ibolya	07.06.1922	Magyarszntbenedek		37992	49626
Kelemen	Johanna	21.04.1913	Podrolycska	Pflegerin	30892	49197
Kelemen	Piroska	20.05.1918	Magyarszntbenedek		37993	49627
Kelemen	Rozalia	10.05.1924	Magyarszntbenedek		37994	49628
Keli	Rozsa	03.01.1914	Alsopatak	Scneiderin		50121
Keller	Ibolya	08.08.1920	Satoraljaujhely		35855	49886
Kellner	Frida	11.11.1909	Hercegszabad	Pflegerin	37995	49629
Kemeny	Anna	05.10.1905	Nezsider			50122

Last Name	First Name	Birth Date	Place of Birth	Profession	Old Number	New Number
Kerebel	Simone	08.04.1923			52122	50360
Keri	Márta	10.08.1920	Gardony	Schneiderin	37996	49630
Keri	Zsuzsanna	18.02.1927	Csepel	Schneiderin	37997	49631
Kern	Dudi	03.08.1918	Rigacs	Schneiderin	37998	49632
Kertesz	Alice	29.06.1926	Pecs	Schneiderin	37999	49633
Kertesz	Anna	26.10.1926	Tamasi			50123
Kertesz	Katalin	02.02.1908	Nagykanizsa	Schneiderin	38000	49634
Kertesz	Klara	25.06.1919	Barcs		38001	49635
Kertesz	Zsuzsa	17.12.1924	Tamasi			50124
Kivovits	Agnes	19.12.1928	Satoraljaujhely		30904	49198
Klang	Magda	27.01.1921	Hatvan		30906	49199
Klein	Agnes	02.08.1925	Sarospatak		30959	49200
Klein	Agnes	29.04.1927	Satoraljaujhely		30995	49201
Klein	Agnes	03.08.1916	Ersekujvar			50125
Klein	Anna	25.12.1928	Nagyhalasz	Schneiderin	38002	49636
Klein	Borbala	01.03.1921	Nagygeres	Schneiderin	35856	49887
Klein	Edit	06.09.1925	Kiralyhelmec		35857	49888
Klein	Edith	18.06.1928	Rod		35858	49889
Klein	Edith	18.04.1926	Satoraljaujhely	Schneiderin	35859	49890
Klein	Erzsebet	31.01.1911	Tolcsva		30734	49202
Klein	Erzsi	08.04.1899	Sergelyes			50126
Klein	Eszter	23.04.1927	Szilagyballa	Schneiderin	38003	39637
Klein	Eva	13.06.1927	Budapest		30900	49203
Klein	Eva	01.01.1927	Seregelyes			50127
Klein	Eva	17.08.1929	Debrecen			50128
Klein	Franciska	19.02.1910	Eger		30902	49204
Klein	Gabriella	29.03.1924	Nagyhalasz		38004	49638
Klein	Gizella	15.03.1910	Tolcsva	Lehrerin	30997	49205
Klein	Gizella	02.02.1910	Ilka	Schneiderin	30727	49806
Klein	Gizella	18.03.1911	Miskolc		30593	49207
Klein	Hedvig	05.03.1926	Margita		38005	49639
Klein	Hermin	26.08.1920	Nyiregyhaza		30585	49208
Klein	Ibolya	25.04.1918	Satoraljaujhely	Schneiderin	30994	49209
Klein	Ilona	25.03.1926	Büdszentmihaly		308006	49640
Klein	Karolin	18.02.1907	Kiskunfelegyhaza	Schneiderin		51029
Klein	Katalin	02.09.1922	Miskolc	Schneiderin	30899	49210
Klein	Klara	31.01.1921	Gyulahaza		30591	49211
Klein	Klara	20.05.1923	Soroksar	Gläserin		50130
Klein	Livil	16.07.1928	Budapest		30751	49212
Klein	Livia	24.03.1929	Satoraljaujhely		35860	49891
Klein	Margit	15.02.1923	Nyirbelteg		30590	49213
Klein	Maria	10.01.1926	Ersekujvar	Schülerin		50131
Klein	Roza	11.04.1913	Bikcse		30737	49214
Klein	Roza	14.03.1915	Nyirbeose		30589	49215
Klein	Roza	09.08.1917	Fehergyarmat	Schneiderin	30736	49216
Klein	Roza	07.08.1920	Halmi		30725	49217
Klein	Sara	30.09.1926	Sivopuszta		30726	49218
Klein	Sari	26.12.1907	Tunyog		30724	49219
Klein	Szerena	27.12.1912	Kiskunfelegyhaza	Schneiderin		50132

Last Name	First Name	Birth Date	Place of Birth	Profession	Old Number	New Number
Klein	Szerena	06.06.1924	Szatmarcseke		30728	49220
Klein	Terez	03.08.1908	Szeklence	Schneiderin	30996	49221
Klein	Zsuzsa	23.10.1928	Marmarossziget			50133
Klein	Zsuzsa	08.02.1920	Encs	Schneiderin	38007	49641
Klein	Zsuzsa	16.04.1921	Budapest	Arbeiterin		50134
Kleinmann	Helena	21.02.1924	Nagyabranka		30901	49222
Kleinmann	Maria	04.10.1925	Harsfalva	Schneiderin	30722	49223
Klepner	Boriska	10.09.1920	Vac	Näherin	38009	49643
Klepner	Boris	03.01.1926	Meggyesgombas		38008	49642
Klepner	Fanni	12.11.1924	Meggyesgombas		38010	49644
Kleszozowska	Zofia	13.11.1914			52124	50361
Knoblowits	Helena	24.11.1919	Szörnyeg	Scneiderin	30733	49224
Kohn	Brucha	18.08.1925	Litzmannstadt	Schneiderin		50136
Kohn	Edit	28.11.1923	Ujpest		38011	49645
Kohn	Edit	16.12.1925	Budapest	Kürcshnerin		50137
Kohn	Erzsebet	01.09.1920	Trencseny		38012	49646
Kohn	Erzsebet	19.09.1912	Nyiregyhaza			50138
Kohn	Eta	17.09.1922	Nagyigmand		30575	49225
Kohn	Eva	23.06.1917	Feketepatak		35861	49892
Kohn	Hedi	20.04.1920	Zenta		35862	49893
Kohn	Ibolya	28.03.1923	Acs	Schneiderin	30732	49226
Kohn	Ilona	19.12.1906	Zanyugrocz		38013	49647
Kohn	Magda	08.09.1915	Korompa		30592	49227
Kohn	Magda	06.12.1926	Györ	Schneiderin	38014	49648
Kohn	Malka	06.03.1923	Litzmannstadt	Schneiderin		50139
Kohn	Margit	21.04.1916	Pocsaj			50130
Kohn	Roza	07.03.1912	Magyarkeresztur	Schneiderin	30891	49228
Kohn	Rozsi	03.12.1908	Felsöoroszi		38015	49649
Kohn	Vera	08.03.1925	Kolozsvar	Schneiderin	30577	49229
Kollmann	Edit	15.05.1926	Vac		308016	49650
Kollmann	Ella	28.12.1927	Vac	Schneiderin	38017	49651
Kollmann	Eszter	06.10.1915	Vac		38018	49652
Kollmann	Sari	10.02.1922	Vac	Schneiderin	38019	49653
Kopp	Ella	20.11.1905	Erdötelek		30735	49230
Korenitzer	Alice	02.02.1923	Szerenos		30998	49231
Kornstein	Lidia	25.10.1918	Fegyvernek		28020	49654
Korsch	Anna	02.10.1916	Beregszasz	Pflegerin	25863	49894
Kosa	Agnes	05.05.1920	Sarospatak	Chemistin	30730	49232
Koszteliz	Szidi	12.11.1907	Buzsaj			50141
Kövesi	Julianna	26.02.1924	Esztergom		30992	49234
Kövesi	Magda	03.03.1922	Szeged	Schneiderin	30993	49235
Kövesi	Margit	18.02.1905	Esztergom	Schneiderin	30991	49236
Kozner	Karolina	30.12.1910	Marmarossziget		30999	49233
Krämer	Hermin	13.05.1907	Gat		38023	49657
Krämer	Klara	13.06.1923	Bodrogszerdahely		30903	49237
Krausz	Alica	23.01.1926	Edeleny		30723	49238
Krausz	Aranka	11.02.1913	Debrecen			50142
Krausz	Erzsebet	18.04.1914	Salföld			50143
Krausz	Eva	23.03.1923	Satoraljaujhely		35864	49895

Last Name	First Name	Birth Date	Place of Birth	Profession	Old Number	New Number
Krausz	Ilona	15.02.1922	Satoraljaujhely	Schneiderin	35865	49896
Krausz	Iren	17.01.1919	Budapest		38021	49655
Krausz	Magda	23.09.1918	Papa	Schneiderin	38022	49656
Krausz	Margit	10.10.1925	Bana		30576	49239
Krausz	Margit	27.01.1921	Szatmarnemeti	Schneiderin	35866	49897
Krausz	Rozsi	15.01.1920	Kiralyhelmec		35867	49898
Kreiszman	Lenke	03.03.1920	Bilke	Schneiderin		50144
Krischer	Olga	25.03.1922	Hernadvecse	Schneiderin	35868	49899
Kupferstein	Eva	09.05.1924	Ujfeherto		30588	49240
Kupferstein	Klara	10.10.1919	Ujfeherto		30586	49241
Kupferstein	Margit	27.02.1917	Ujfeherto		30587	49242
Kurländer	Magda	23.02.1025	Budapest		38024	49658
Kurmann	Gabi	30.04.1916	Budapest		38025	49659
Kurmann	Piroska	23.01.1920	Budapest		38026	49660
Lachmann	Fanni	10.12.1915	Lecfalva	Schneiderin		50145
Laissac	Suzanne	21.04.1911			51125	50362
Lallemand	Madeleine	01.04.1914			52126	50363
Lambert	Georgette	24.09.1924			52129	50364
Ländler	Agnes	05.11.1927	Galocas		38035	49669
Landstein	Elisabeth	02.08.1926	Totmegyer		30739	49243
Landstein	Erzsebet	15.10.1923	Totmegyer	Schneiderin	30740	49244
Landstein	Sara	26.04.1925	Izsnyete	Schneiderin	30441	49245
Lang	Elisabeth	21.02.1922	Izsnyete	Schneiderin	31007	49246
Lang	Margit	17.08.1923	Göncz		38027	49661
Lansner	Helen	21.06.1925	Kolozsvar	Schneiderin		50146
Laquere	Maryanne	17.09.1918			52130	50365
Latourette	Margueritte	23.12.1921			52131	50366
Lauber	Erna	12.12.1926	Bethlen		35869	49900
Lauber	Magda	07.02.1922	Szaszregen	Schneiderin	30596	49247
Laudais	Yvette	26.11.1922			52132	50367
Laufer	Rozsa	22.04.1907	Kerkeskapolna		38028	49662
Lautmann	Erna	06.04.1925	Csenger		38029	49663
Lax	Edit	02.08.1923	Marosvasarhely		38033	49667
Lax	Eva	22.04.1928	Marosvasarhely		38034	49668
Lazar	Anna	21.04.1926	Ermihalyfalva		35872	49903
Lazar	Cecil	02.08.1906	Almasmal		30633	49248
Lazar	Erzsebet	13.09.1925	Ermihajfalva		35870	49901
Lazar	Ilona	06.01.1908	Szatmarnemeti	Köchin	35871	49902
Lazar	Jolan	08.06.1906	Tunyog		30743	49249
Lazar	Judit	09.08.1926	Kolozsvar	Student	38030	49664
Lazar	Rozsi	22.10.1926	Beszterce			50147
Lazarovics	Gizi	21.02.1926	Bilke	Schneiderin	38031	49665
Lazarovics	Helen	15.02.1925	Bilke	Schneiderin	38032	49666
Le Gallie	Germaine	02.02,1923			52087	50347
Le Lay	Augustine	20.11.1925			52134	50368
Leb	Ilona	26.11.1922	Marosbogat	Schneiderin		50148
Leb	Margit	30.10.1923	Marosbogat	Schneiderin		50149
Lebovics	Etel	15.11.1922	Nagyrakocs		35873	49904
Lebovics	Etel	17.07.1925	Alsoapsa		35874	49905

Last Name	First Name	Birth Date	Place of Birth	Profession	Old Number	New Number
Lebovics	Lili	08.02.1910	Brasso		38036	49670
Lebovics	Malvin	08.08.1925	Bilke	Schneiderin		50150
Lebovics	Margit	12.10.1922	Alsoapsa		35875	49906
Lebovics	Margit	20.09.1924	Marmarossziget	Arbeiterin		50151
Lebovics	Pepi	03.09.1924	Dombo	Schneiderin		50152
Lebovics	Piri	20.05.1923	Harsfalva	Schneiderin		50153
Lebovics	Rezsi	23.04.1914	Nagyszölös		35876	49907
Lebovics	Rozsi	01.03.1924	Alsoapsa		35877	49908
Lebovics	Szeren	28.05.1924	Bilke	Schneiderin		50154
Lebovitz	Iren	27.07.1913	Abaujcsecs		30597	49250
Lebovitz	Jolan	16.04.1916	Ipolykslenye	Schneiderin	30598	49251
Lebovitz	Rozsi	22.04.1923	Herinoze		31006	49252
Leclezio	Suzanne	13.09.1898			52136	50369
Lecourtios	Lucienne	14.12.1923			52137	50370
Lefkovics	Aranka	08.02.1924	Vac		38037	49671
Lefkovics	Lea	18.02.1922	Vac		38038	59672
Lefkovits	Elisabeth	12.04.1926	Tunyog	Schneiderin	30742	49253
Lefkowitz	Maria	28.07.1907	Satoraljaujhely	Köchin	31002	49254
Leichtag	Irena	31.03.1922	Erdötarosa		30910	49255
Leichtag	Maria	11.07.1924	Demony		30911	49256
Lemee	Marie	23.08.1898			52138	50371
Lengyel	Edith	12.10.1921	Budapest		30594	49258
Lengyel	Márta	29.06.1913	Hont		30599	49259
Lengyel	Vera	10.08.1927	Budapest	Schneiderin		50155
Lengyel	Zsuzsanna	20.09.1921	Satoraljaujhely		31005	49260
Lenkei	Klara	10.07.1908	Kaptalantoti		38039	49673
Lerner	Alice	01.01.1921	Satoraljaujhely		31004	49261
Lerner	Lili	29.11.1924	Satoraljaujhely		31003	49257
Lesidanner	Emilienne	11.11.1913			52140	50372
Leyel	Marquerite	29.10.1923			52141	50373
Lichtblau	Valeria	06.01.1923	Vac		38040	49674
Lichtig	Etel	26.05.1911	Felsöhidegpatak			50156
Lichtman	Jolan	05.09.1920	Batiz		35878	49909
Lichtmann	Judit	24.04.1930	Debrecen			50157
Lieber	Dora	14.05.1920	Sajolad	Bäckerin		50158
Lieber	Magda	31.12.1921	Sarospatak	Friseurin		50159
Liebermann	Maria	09.05.1928	Strajna	Stickerin	30912	49262
Linden	Hajnal	28.05.1922	Satoraljaujhely		35879	49910
Linden	Lenke	03.09.1920	Satoraljaujhely	Schneiderin	35880	49911
Lipsitz	Adel	22.04.1920	Bilke		38041	49675
Lipsitz	Fanni	11.01.1918	Bilke	Schneiderin	38042	49676
Lipsitz	Roza	08.04.1922	Bilke	Schneiderin	38043	49677
Löbel	Hedy	18.02.1924	Gyergyotölgyes		35881	49912
Löbel	Magda	05.09.1920	Nagybeoskerek		35882	49913
Lorant	Aranka	23.10.1907	Tolcsva		31000	49265
Lorant	Vera	08.05.1926	Miskolc		31001	49266
Lorbeer	Edit	28.01.1924	Püspökladany			50160
Lorbeer	Gabriella	29.12.1924	Püspökladany			50161
Lorbeer	Margit	02.09.1918	Püspökladany			50122

Last Name	First Name	Birth Date	Place of Birth	Profession	Old Number	New Number
Lorbeer	Margit	08.04.1922	Püspökladany	Schneiderin		50163
Lörinch	Izabella	02.04.1927	Okany			50164
Lörincs	Edit	30.12.1924	Toti		38044	49678
Lörincs	Ibolya	15.09.1922	Toti		38045	49679
Lörincs	Margit	19.05.1916	Toti		38046	49680
Lörincz	Margit	08.06.1921	Bihar			50165
Loustaunau	Adeline	17.06.1892			52142	50374
Loustaunau	Germaine	02.12.1890			52144	50376
Löw	Gizella	18.07.1925	Vac		38047	49681
Löwinger	Frida	16.01.1921	Vac		38048	49682
Löwy	Hilda	01.01.1923	Nagytarna			50166
Löwy	Ilonka	08.12.1914	Alsotapard		38049	49683
Löwy	Judit	10.12.1925	Kapuvar	Schneiderin		50167
Löwy	Karolin	15.05.1926	Nagytarna			50168
Löwy	Livia	23.09.1921	Vamespercs	Schneiderin	38050	49684
Löwy	Margit	23.01.1920	Martonvasar		30738	49267
Löwy	Margit	01.12.1904	Wien			50169
Löwy	Rozsi	25.05.1915	Barcs	Schneiderin	38051	49685
Lucas	Jaqueline	03.08.1909			52143	50375
Luria	Hedvig	11.01.1913	Budapest	Musiklehrerin	30595	49268
Macher	Ida	22.08.1908		Schneiderin		50170
Maget	Márta	12.06.1923	Osontosfalva	Modistin	31008	49269
Majzlik	Gizella	17.07.1912	Sztrajna		30919	49283
Majzlik	Hanna	21.10.1916	Sztrajna		30920	49284
Majzlik	Margit	26.10.1925	Sztrajna	Schneiderin	30921	49285
Malek	Helena	31.01.1925	Aninasza	Schneiderin	35883	49914
Malek	Renee	10.05.1922	Bikszad		35884	49915
Mandel	Erzsebet	19.01.1910	Maroshidas		38052	49686
Mandel	Regina	05.11.1909	Miskolc		38053	49687
Mandl	Gertrud	31.05.1925	Tata	Schneiderin		50173
Mann	Ibolya	17.07.1924	Helyöcsaba		30977	49270
Mantner	Edit	28.08.1926	Iregszenoze			50171
Marcepoil	Lolita	28.02.1912			52148	50377
Mark	Lea	15.07.1906	Temesvar		38054	49688
Markovics	Dora	16.02.1924	Domokos		35885	49916
Markovics	Ilona	16.01.1920	Mezökiralyfalva		38055	49689
Markovics	Ilona	08.08.1920	Avasfelsöfalu			50174
Markovics	Klara	24.08.1925	Halmi	Schuhmacherin		50175
Markovics	Lili	16.12.1922	Domokos		35886	49917
Markovits	Etelka	03.12.1922	Nagyalmas		30604	49272
Markstein	Agnes	23.07.1923	Ipolysag		30602	49273
Markstein	Gizella	09.03.1908	Ipolysag	Schneiderin	30601	49274
Markstein	Jozse	28.03.1915	Vaghoszufalu		38056	49690
Markus	Magda	11.07.1915	Szaszregen		30603	49275
Marozaly	Terezia	20.02.1922	Jaszapati		30913	49271
Marton	Edith	13.10.1921	Esztergom	Schneiderin	30914	49276
Marton	Jolan	26.01.1915	Zalaegerszeg		38057	49691
Marton	Julia	09.07.1925	Ipolysag	Schneiderin	30600	49277
Marton	Rozsi	13.10.1922	Erdogyoszlo		38058	49692

Last Name	First Name	Birth Date	Place of Birth	Profession	Old Number	New Number
Marx	Jeanne	06.12.1902			52155	50378
Mauskopf	Cecil	19.03.1922	Nagyabranka	Schneiderin	30749	49278
Mauskopf	Frida	03.03.1924	Olahcsertiz		30923	49279
Mauskopf	Gizella	29.11.1925	Kisabrakka		30750	49280
Mauskopf	Helena	02.03.1922	Olacsertiz		30922	49281
Mauskopf	Malvine	14.04.1923	Kenezpatak		30924	49282
Mauwen	Gustave	01.01.1908			52158	50379
Mayer	Julia	02.06.1907	Apostag		38059	49693
Mayer	Sara	21.07.1922	Papa		38060	49694
Mechlovics	Kornelia	10.08.1923	Szatmarnemeti		35887	49918
Mehes	Erzsebet	18.12.1913	Somogycsurgo		38061	49695
Meizner	Hermin	08.08.1923	Budapest	Schneiderin		50172
Mendelovits	Dora	15.05.1924	Visooroszi		35888	49919
Mendelovits	Etel	20.06.1920	Visooroszi		35889	49920
Mendelsohn	Sari	20.08.1923	Alapret	Schneiderin		50176
Menetrier	Cecile	20.08.1917			52160	50380
Mieu	Jeanne	26.04.1903			52163	50381
Milhe	Anne-Rose	31.12.1897			52164	50322
Miller	Katalin	18.061925	Magyarhegymeg	Schneiderin	30605	49295
Miquel	Denise	18.03.1921			52167	50383
Miselbach	Ella	02.05.1913	Sashalos			50177
Moldovan	Iren	03.06.1919	Batiz		35891	49922
Moldovan	Helen	12.01.1907	Okörmezö		35890	49921
Morcau	Lucie	02.09.904			52172	50384
Moskovics	Erzsebet	15.06.1922	Alsozsolca		325892	49923
Moskovics	Margit	02.10.1921	Beregkövesd	Arbeiterin		50178
Moskovitz	Dora	21.05.1922	Irkoc	Schneiderin	30915	49287
Moskovitz	Eva	18.03.1026	Sarospatak		30748	49288
Moskovitz	Gizella	25.08.1925	Irkoc	Schneiderin	30917	49289
Moskovitz	Ilona	16.02.1910			38062	0
Moskovitz	Irena	06.08.1926	Saszlekence		30745	49290
Moskovitz	Piroska	24.02.1907	Beregszasz		30925	49291
Moskovitz	Regina	20.08.1919	Irkoc	Schneiderin	30916	49292
Moskovitz	Sara	21.11.1921	Irkoc	Schneiderin	30918	49293
Mozes	Piri	14.05.1916	Nagysomkut		38063	49696
Mühlbauer	Jolan	23.06.1920	Galambos		30746	49294
Müller	Fanni	26.08.1918	Dombo	Schneiderin		50179
Müller	Helen	15.11.1924	Karinfalva	Schneiderin		50180
Müller	Rozsi	12.01.1922	Alsokalinfalva	Schneiderin		50181
Müller	Rozsi	04.04.1923	Dombo			50182
Müller	Zsuzsa	27.06.1927	Tolna	Schneiderin		50183
Nadas	Ilona	22.11.1910	Budapest	Schneiderin		50184
Nadaud	Marguerite	06.02.1914			52177	50385
Nasch	Erzsebet	15.09.1912	Szentdemeter		39064	49697
Neu	Irena	23.01.1916	Udvard		30752	49296
Neulat	Marguerite	14.09.1920			52179	50386
Neumann	Bella	19.10.1915	Abaujszanto		30607	49297
Neumann	Fani	24.03.1924	Alsokalinfalva			50185
Neumann	Frida	13.051927	Halmi			50186

Last Name	First Name	Birth Date	Place of Birth	Profession	Old Number	New Number
Neumann	Ilona	31.10.1919	Rimaszombat	Weberin	30606	49298
Neumann	Margit	17.04.1922	Nagytapolcsany		35893	49924
Neumann	Vera	24.05.1927	Mezocsat		30608	49299
Neumark	Ibolya	16.03.1923	Debrecen	Arbeiterin		50187
Noch	Margit	14.01.1926	Udvard		30751	49300
Noy	Agnes	0912.1924	Keszthely	Schneiderin		50188
Nussbacher	Lia	12.05.1919	Naszod		38065	49698
Ott	Katalin	05.10.1911	Somogycsurgo			50189
Ozitrom	Magda	05.031928	Marosvasarhely		37884	49517
Pairiot	Marcelle	17.03.1926			51185	50387
Pajzs	Agnes	09,12,1924	Budapest	Sprachlehrerin		50190
Palfi	Edit	19.01.1925	Marosvasarhely		38066	49699
Palos	Rozsi	25.05.1915	Sarbogard		38067	49700
Papa	Márta	27.01.1920	Vac		35894	49925
'Papa	Renee	04.03.1918	Vac		35895	49926
Payen	Marie-Loui	19.08.1899			52186	50388
Pejot	France	17.10.1914			52187	50389
Perl	Cecilia	06.05.1911	Soltvadkert			50191
Perl	Renee	02.08.1923	Alsoegrogy		30753	49301
Perl	Terez	06.09.1927	Alsoegrogy		30754	49302
Perlstein	Viola	02.02.1926				50192
Perquis	MariJoseph	05.03.1915			52188	50390
Petit	Jacqueline	05.03.1987			52189	50391
Picard	Jeanne-Lou	25.08.1899			52191	50392
Piorik	Lea	21.10.1923	Budapest		38068	49701
Pinet	Suzanne	13.01.1913			52192	50393
Polatsek	Magda	27.05.1926	Karcag		38069	49702
Polejaeff	Nina	30.09.1905			52193	50394
Pollack	Eszter	18.06.1921	Nagyszölös		30785	49303
Pollack	Josefine	28.08.1920	Nagyszölös		30757	49304
Pollack	Erzsebet	19.11.1920		Schneiderin		50193
Pollack	Eszter	18.08.1926				50194
Pollack	Rozsi	29.08.1924	Kolozsvar	Klemptnerin		50195
Politzer	Maria	18.03.1927	Papa		38070	49703
Ponson	Marie-Loui	13.13.1907			52194	50425
Porteres	Jeanne	16.07.1893			52195	50395
Preisler	Aranka	16.02.1926	Budapest	Zahntechnikerin		50196
Preisler	Magda	12.02.1915	Debrecen	Arbeiterin		50197
Pressburger	Margit	06.10.1917	Bicske		30756	49305
Pressburger	Roza	30.11.1915	Bicske		30755	49306
Prieur	Madeleine	07.11.1906			52197	50397
Provost	Fernande	08.06.1893			52196	50396
Py	Marie	15.10.1925			52198	50398
Raab	Agnes	18.05.1928	Gyöngyös		30933	49307
Raab	Etelka	16.08.1923	Kiskomarom		30611	49308
Raab	Irene	12.08.1920			30764	0
Raab	Katalin	12.11.1926	Gyöngyös		30931	49309
Raab	Maria	01.01.1915	Szombathely		30610	49310
Raab	Szeren	24.01.1912	Nagyszölös		30932	49311

Last Name	First Name	Birth Date	Place of Birth	Profession	Old Number	New Number
Räder	Ilona	31.07.1912	Budapest		38071	49704
Rault	Jeanne-Madeleine	09.11.1916			52203	50399
Reboure	Marcelle	17.12.1920			52202	50401
Regeni	Eta	16.10.1916	Budapest		38072	49705
Regnier	MariaMadl	19.11.1916			52203	50402
Reich	Elza	15.12.1925	Abaujker		38073	49706
Reichhardt	Mili	29.08.1922	Viragosberek		30773	49312
Reinfeld	Judith	19.09.1926	Budapest		30976	49313
Reinitz	Ilona	11.03.1911	Damak		30614	49314
Reinitz	Terez	15.10.1915	Nyiresvasar			50198
Reisz	Agnes	31.08.1928	Dombovar		38074	49707
Reisz	Katalin	29.06.1916	Nagyatad		38075	49708
Renner	Helen	31.01.1912	Vac	Weberin	38076	49709
Renner	Sara	03.02.1921	Vac		38077	49710
Revai	Dora	06.08.1923	Tab			50199
Revai	Rozsi	28.01.1906	Gyaludpuszta			50200
Revesz	Katalin	08.07.1917	Marosvasarhely		38078	49711
Revesz	Margit	30.05.1907	Zubony		30782	49315
Rheinfeld	Elvira	03.12.1920	Lörinozi	Schneiderin		50201
Rheinfeld	Erna	20.04.1913	Lörinozi	Schneiderin		50202
Rheinfeld	Ibolya	25.12.1924	Lörinozi	Schneiderin		50203
Riesel	Edit	24.08.1923	Nagyszeben		35896	49927
Riesner	Rozsa	09.12.1919	Szikszo		31009	49316
Riesz	Eva	05.06.1927	Jaszfesnyszaru	Schneiderin		50204
Riesz	Ibolya	13.01.1928	Jaszfenyszaru	Schneiderin		50205
Ripkovits	Jolan	18.02.1906	Satoraljaujhely		30909	49263
Ripkovits	Vera	28.01.1925	Kassa		30908	49264
Rischko	Jekaterina	—1907				0
Robert	Marie-Anet	02,05,1907			52201	50400
Rocher	Genevieve	26.02.1910			52206	50403
Roder	Anna	02.08.1926	Ozera			50206
Romana	Maud	08.10.1926			52208	50404
Röna	Erzsebet	28.02.1912	Budapest	Arbeiterin		50207
Roquier	Marie	28.07.1911			52209	50405
Rosenbaum	Iboly	10.07.1923	Dobra		35897	49920
Rosenbaum	Manic	06.03.1918	Kiralyfüszallas	Lehrerin	30930	49317
Rosenbaum	Szorena	17.08.1927	Kiralyfüszallas	Schneiderin	30767	49318
Rosenberg	Agnes	25.11.1927	Ungvar	Pflegerin	35898	49929
Rosenberg	Aranka	19.07.1919	Miskolc	Strickerin	30621	49319
Rosenberg	Edith	21.07.1916	Edeleny	Friseuse	30613	49320
Rosenberg	Erzsebet	03.03.1926	Keresztvar	Schneiderin	30762	49321
Rosenberg	Eva	26.05.1924	?	?	30928	49322
Rosenberg	Eva	31.03.1925	Nagyberezha	Köchin	38079	49712
Rosenberg	Eva	29.05.1928	Abaujszanto		38080	49713
Rosenberg	Hajnal	16.06.1925	Zagon	Schneiderin	30929	49323
Rosenberg	Helen	24.04.1910	Nyirbege		35899	49930
Rosenberg	Ilona	22.10.1923	Satoraljaujhely		30761	49324
Rosenberg	Ilona	03.05.1921	Munkacs	Schneiderin	30763	49325
Rosenberg	Ilona	18.09.1914	Veszprom	Schneiderin		50208

Last Name	First Name	Birth Date	Place of Birth	Profession	Old Number	New Number
Rosenberg	Laura	02.05.1923				50209
Rosenberg	Lenke	24.06.1923	Karancs		38081	49714
Rosenberg	Magda	24.06.1923	Petres		37071	49326
Rosenberg	Olga	18.12.1904	Zubogy	Schneiderin	30620	49327
Rosenblatt	Sarolta	14.05.1925	Teke		30766	49328
Rosendorn	Agnes	12.02.1926	Dombovar	Schneiderin		50210
Rosendorn	Elvira	29.05.1910	Dombovar			50211
Rosenfeld	Anna	17.09.1923	Edeleny		30609	49329
Rosenfeld	Berta	16.10.1915	Ratosnya		30623	49330
Rosenfeld	Elisabeth	05.11.1922	Bely		30537	49331
Rosenfeld	Elza	21.101909	Deva		38082	49715
Rosenfeld	Klara	24.09.1924	Margits		38083	49716
Rosenfeld	Lotte	12.09.1908	Körösmezö		30622	49332
Rosenfeld	Magda	10.02.1925	Ratosnagya		30624	49333
Rosenfeld	Márta	20.01.1925	Nograd		30927	49334
Rosenfeld	Sari	12.07.1926		Schneiderin		50212
Rosenfeld	Szerena	22.02.1922	Nagysajo		30774	49335
Rosenthal	Eliz	26.01.1926	Miskolc		30627	49336
Rosenthal	Eva	24.07.1928	Nyiragybarany	Arbeiterin		50213
Rosenthal	Frida	19.04.1928	Fehergyarmat		30765	49337
Rosenthal	Magda	09.03.1921	Keresztpüspök		30625	49338
Rosenthal	Maria	12.12.1919	Szombathely		30626	49339
Rosenthal	Márta	23.03.1924	Ujpest		38084	49717
Rosenthal	Sara	24.01.1925	Retteg		35900	49931
Rosenzweig	Rozsi	21.10.1911	Dunabogdany		38085	49718
Rosner	Aranka	26.05.1927	Vac		38086	49719
Rosner	Fanny	03.04.1908	Szolyva		30768	49340
Rosner	Hedvig	05.07.1927	Marmarossziget		30615	49341
Rosner	Helena	12.02.1914	Alsosarad		30784	49342
Rosner	Huguette	02.05.1920			52210	50406
Rosner	Judith	09.12.1027	Marmarossziget		30785	49343
Rosner	Lili	29.12.1925	Vac		38087	49720
Rosmann	Anna	05.03.1917	Erdöszentgyörgy		38088	49721
Rosmann	Julia	21.02.1919	Erdöszentgyörgy		38089	49722
Roth	Berta	21.02.1921	Nagyvarad	Stickerin	35901	49932
Roth	Edith	07.05.1926	Kassa		38090	49723
Roth	Ella	10.06.1927	Tiszabercel		30777	49346
Roth	Erzsebet	08.04.1920	Tiszabercel		30776	49347
Roth	Erzsebet	14.07.1924	Tiszabercel		30774	49348
Roth	Eszter	03.04.1915	Udvard		30780	49349
Roth	Gizella	14.07.1925	Nagykallo		30760	49344
Roth	Klara	05.06.1924	Szegilangy		30778	49350
Roth	Livia	31.08.1919	Csetnek		30781	49351
Roth	Magda	22.03.1926	Szegyiland		30779	49352
Roth	Olga	03.01.1925	Tiszabarcel		40775	49353
Roth	Piroska	24.08.1928	Egregy	Stickerin	35902	49933
Roth	Rozsa	25.12.1925	Nagykallo		30759	49345
Roth	Rozsi	24.01.1924	Hanfihunyad	Stickerin	35903	49934
Rothschild	Lucretia	23.03.1921	Felsöviso		35904	49935

Last Name	First Name	Birth Date	Place of Birth	Profession	Old Number	New Number
Rotbaum	Jolan	31.12.1915	Kisvarda		38091	49724
Rottberger	Irma	22.05.1922	Bidapest		38092	49725
Rottberger	Márta	05.07.1922	Vac	Modistin	38093	49726
Rottenstein	Helena	15.12.1926	Nagytorna		30770	49354
Rottenstein	Lenke	15.04.1923	Nagytorna		30769	49355
Rozenberg	Frida	21.04.1925	Nagyberezna		38094	49727
Rozenberg	Rozsi	27.09.1914	Karancs	Käsemacher	38095	49728
Ruallem	Charlotte	18.12.1907			52216	50407
Rubin	Erzsebet	28.11.1920	Csolto		30783	49356
Rubin	Klara	13.04.1924	Encs		38096	49729
Rubinstein	Eszter	18.05.1914	Komarom		30612	49357
Ruhig	Erzsebet	03.11.1906	Bela		30618	49358
Ruhig	Magda	26.09.1927	Vamosmikola		30617	49359
Ruhig	Szeren	10.07.905	Bela	Bürokraft	30616	49360
Ruhl	Ilona	17.01.1922	Des		38097	49730
Rundberg	Berta	22.12.1920	Litzmannstadt			50215
Ruttner	Fanny	12.11.1926	Tecsö		35905	49936
Rüwel	Lili	17.07.1920	Marosvasarhely	Pflegerin	30619	49361
Sajovics	Erzsi	14.05.1924	Micske		35906	49937
Sajovics	Eva	10.03.1926	Micske		35907	49938
Sajovits	Ilona	04.12.1919	Kiskalota	Schneiderin	30635	49362
Sajovits	Sara	22.01.1922	Kiskalota	Schneiderin	30634	49363
Salamon	Etel	19.05.1915		Schneiderin		50216
Salamon	Irena	22.05.1926	Balassagyarmat		30792	49364
Salamon	Rossa	12.10.1904	Mako	Schneiderin		50217
Salamon	Sara	22.09.1924	Velete		31012	49365
Salamon	Sara	30.10.1925	Szentmate	Schneiderin	30797	49366
Salamonovits	Ilona	23.07,1928	Sjopetri			50218
Saleur	Raymonde	26.04.1919			52218	50408
Salomon	Eta	12.11.1926	Nagysikarlo	Schneiderin	35907	49939
Salomon	Eva	05.08.1925	Kisbozinta	Schneiderin	35909	49940
Salomon	Helen	22.03.1924	Domokos	Schneiderin	35910	49941
Salomon	Ilona	29.06.1906	Nagyvarad	Lehrerin	38098	49731
Salomon	Iren	02.04.1922	Kisgeres		35911	49942
Salomon	Olga	14.10.1929	Marosvasarhely		38099	49732
Salomon	Szidonia	13.04.1924	Szamosborhid	Schneiderin	35912	49943
Samuel	Seren	16.12.1924	Domokos		35915	49944
Sas	Edit	17.05.1924	Kassa	Uhrmacher	35914	49945
Schattin	Edith	14.05.1925	Sarospatak		30951	49392
Scheer	Erzsebet	24.11.1921	Kamocse			50228
Scheer	Ilona	24.11.1921	Kamocse			50229
Scheer	Klara	19.05.1926	Keke		35934	49965
Scheer	Lili	21.03.1921	Ujfeherto		30651	49393
Scheer	Magda	22.01.1925	Keke		35935	49966
Scheiner	Berta	01.01.1921				50230
Scheiner	Eszter	28.02.1923	Nagyboczko	Zahntechnikerin		50231
Scheiner	Iren	28.09.1926	Nagyboczko	Friseurin		40232
Scheiner	Rozsi	16.04.1924	Nagyboczko	Friseurin		50233
Scherfer	Maria	26.02.1906	Racalmas		38113	49746

Last Name	First Name	Birth Date	Place of Birth	Profession	Old Number	New Number
Schindler	Rezsin	07.12.1924	Malmos	Schneiderin	30941	49394
Schlanger	Sara	10.06.1910	Zombor		35936	49967
Schlesinger	Ilona	03.05.1925	Kecskemet	Lehrerin		50234
Schlesinger	Klara	13.09.1920	Pecs		38114	49747
Schlesinger	Lenke	11.09.1923	Kecskemet	Arbeiterin		50235
Schlesinger	Olga	02.02.1920	Sasd		38115	49748
Schlesinger	Rozsi	18.01.1922	Kecskemet	Schneiderin		50236
Schlosser	Regina	18.01.1920				0
Schmidek	Ilona	26.01.1923	Peröcseny		40942	49395
Schön	Magda	19.12.1921	Kiskövesd		35937	49968
Schönberger	Alice	25.08.1925	Budapest			50237
Schönberger	Erna	18.07.1927	Bonyhad	Schneiderin		50238
Schönfeld	Elza	26.10.1914	Sajoszentpeter		30628	49396
Schönfeld	Irena	15.12.1911	Zalabaksa		30936	49397
Schreiber	Anna	23.08.1925	Kondoros	Schneiderin		50239
Schück	Livia	25.12.1924	Ipolysag		30645	49400
Schulek	Erzsebet	08.05.1910	Losonc	Schneiderin	30639	49398
Schuler	Marcelle	05.02.1928			52224	50410
Cshulzbeck	Magda	10,06.1920	Jaszpati			50240
Schulzinger	Zelma	15.08.1915	Beszterce	Schneiderin	30794	49399
Shüttler	Ilona	30.07.1907	Somogycsurgo	Schneiderin	38116	49749
Schvarcs	Boriska	08.09.1902	Vaja		38121	49754
Schvarcs	Edit	17.07.1928	Sasd		38117	49750
Schvarcs	Ilona	25.02.1915	Legenymihaly		38118	49751
Schvarcs	Julianna	18.11.1924	Nyirbator		38120	49753
Schvarcs	Rozsi	25.07.1914	Felsösegesd		38119	49752
Schwarz	Aranka	27.11.1909	Henye	Schneiderin	30790	49401
Schwarz	Blanka	03.05.1925	Sarospatak		31015	49402
Schwarz	Edit	18.10.1918	Wien	Schneiderin	30647	49403
Schwarz	Elza	29.09.1921	Mako			50241
Schwarz	Erzsebet	12.07.1894	Berettyoszeplak	Strickerin	30945	49403
Schwarz	Erzsebet	29.09.1921	Pusztamoneszter	Schneiderin		50242
Schwarz	Erzsebet	13.12.1923	Budapest	Schneiderin		50243
Schwarz	Frida	30.05.1907	Losonc		30638	49405
Schwarz	Hermina	08.05.1926	Szamosujvar	Arbeiterin		50244
Schwarz	Ibolya	13.04.1911	Törökszentmiklos			50245
Schwarz	Ilona	03.06.1927	Komando		30947	49406
Schwarz	Ilona	25.07.1907				50246
Schwarz	Ilona	27.06.1927	Szamosujvar	Arbeiterin		50247
Schwarz	Irena	24.02.1909	Ujfeherto		30801	49407
Schwarz	Johanna	21.04.1927	Szaszlekanoe		30796	49408
Schwarz	Katalin	28.02.1923	Szamosujvar	Arbeiterin		50248
Schwarz	Katalin	24.06.1924	Debrecen			50249
Schwarz	Katalina	10.05.1925	Hatvan		30937	49409
Schwarz	Lenke	27.02.1923	Sarospatak		31014	49410
Schwarz	Magda	04.02.1924	Beregszasz	Lehrerin	30686	49075
Schwarz	Magda	04.04.1926	Miskolc	Schneiderin	30940	49411
Schwarz	Margit	23.12.1923	Komando	Modistin	30946	49412
Schwarz	Regina	24.12.1922	Szamosujvar	Arbeiterin		50250

Last Name	First Name	Birth Date	Place of Birth	Profession	Old Number	New Number
Schwarz	Roza	25.07.1922	Miskolc		30939	49413
Schwarz	Roza	28.05.1926	Pozsony	Schneiderin	30789	49414
Schwarz	Rozsi	06.08.1922	Barak			50251
Schwarz	Zsuszanna	24.10.1924	Udvard	Schneiderin	30788	49415
Schwarzberg	Magda	03.11.1926	Kassa		30949	49416
Schweiger	Erzsebet	12.11.1910	Satoraljaujhely		30952	49417
Schwimmer	Hajnal	18.12.1929	Nagybereg		38122	49755
Sebestyen	Rachel	19.10.1920	Parajd		38100	49733
Seelfreund	Ella	08.06.1925	Nagyhalasz		38101	49734
Seelfreund	Iren	11.12.1926	Nagyhalasz		38102	49735
Segal	Gizella	04.08.1927	Gyergyoszarhegy		30636	49367
Segal	Regina	03.10.1914	Satoraljaujhely		30953	49369
Segal	Roza	05.01.1928	Gyergyoszarhegy		30637	49368
Seidenfeld	Aranka	24.12.1923	Bodrogkeresztur		35915	49946
Seidenfeld	Edit	06.07.1926	Bodrogkeresztur		35916	49947
Seidenfeld	Emma	26.02.1925	Bodrogkeresztur		35917	49948
Seidenfeld	Rozsi	01.12.1925	Rako		35918	49949
Seidler	Rozsi	11.11.1918	Marosvasarhely	Pflegerin	38103	49736
Seidner	Olga	31.10.1920	Ujvidek		35919	49950
Serbu	Teresia	06.01.1924	Gyergyotölgyes	Schneiderin	30650	49370
Silber	Szerena	02.03.1907	Satoraljaujhely	Schneiderin	31010	49371
Silberstein	Gitta	25.03.1927	Zenta		38104	49737
Silberstein	Iren	09.12.1922	Hidalmas		35920	49951
Silberstein	Lenke	10.02.1915	Hidalmas		35921	49952
Silberstein	Szeren	26.06.1921	Hidalmas		35922	49953
Simon	Klara	08.10.1920	Balaszembogar	Schneiderin		50219
Singer	Aranka	17.07.1906	Nagybicske			50220
Singer	Helena	25.07.1926	Ilosva	Schneiderin	30948	49372
Singer	Ilona	10.02.1913	Haromfa	Schneiderin	38105	49738
Singer	Julia	22.09.1910	Rutka	Schneiderin		50221
Sonnenschein	Magda	13.08.1924	Fony	Schneiderin		50222
Spierer	Ilonka	12.12.1924	Marosvasarhely		30944	49373
Spitz	Anna	26.10.1926	Sarospatak		30799	49374
Spitz	Bella	26.11.1914	Kassa		30800	49375
Spitz	Herta	16.03.1923	Pozsony	Kozmetikerin	30787	49376
Spitz	Ilona	06.04.1917	Verböc	Arbeiterin		50223
Spitz	Katalin	07.01.1926	Sarospatak		30895	49377
Spitz	Klara	29.07.1926	Forroencs		38106	49739
Spitzer	Ilona	30.07.1920	Miskolc	Schneiderin	30649	49378
Spitzer	Margit	12.04.1925	Barcs		38107	49740
Spitzer	Roza	26.03.1921	Kozepbögye	Schneiderin	30798	49379
Spitzer	Rozsi	03.04.1924	Huszt		35923	49954
Spitzer	Terez	04.03.1914	Vasvar	Strickerin		50224
Stark	Agnes	25.05.1924	Szevata	Flechterin	38123	49756
Stark	Erzsi	10.02.1917	Szevata		38124	49757
Stark	Margit	28.02.1913	Paszto		30935	49418
Stark	Márta	06.07.1910	Marosvasarhely	Flechterin	38125	49758
Stauber	Goldi	25.02.1925	Petrova		35938	49969
Stauber	Piri	20.05.1924	Petrova		35939	49970

Last Name	First Name	Birth Date	Place of Birth	Profession	Old Number	New Number
Stauber	Tobi	15.05.1925	Petrova	Schneiderin	35940	49971
Stechler	Ilona	21.03.1918	Kassa	Arbeiterin	35941	49972
Stein	Elizabeth	25.02.1923	?		31013	49419
Stein	Jolan	10.07.1919	Szekelyudvarhely	Näherin	38126	39759
Stein	Szerena	05.11.1921	Poznus		30795	49420
Steiner	Erzsebet	30.06.1908	Kassa		30522	49421
Steiner	Julia	19.04.1925	Budapest		38127	49760
Steiner	Julia	16.10.1922	Budapest	Arbeiterin		50252
Steiner	Katalina	31.10.1910	Esztergom	Schneiderin	30938	49422
Steiner	Margit	14.12.1919	Udvard	Schneiderin	30791	49423
Steiner	Roza	24.08.1921	Udvard		30632	49424
Steiner	Bözsi	20.10.1910	Budapest	Schneiderin	38128	49761
Steinlauf	Ilona	29.04.1925	Vac		38129	49762
Steinmetz	Eszter	16.12.1918	Nagyhalasz	Schneiderin	30786	49425
Stern	Bella	15.08.1928	Harsfalva		30802	49426
Stern	Erzsebet	16.11.1911	Komarom	Professorin	30648	49427
Stern	Frida	21.01.1909	Harsfalva			50253
Stern	Irma	23.04.1903	Alacapaszt	Schneiderin	38130	49763
Stern	Rozsi	21.05.1909	Harsfalva	Schneiderin		50254
Stern	Rozsi	21.02.1911				50255
Stern	Terez	05.11.1914	Gyöngyös		30943	49428
Sternberg	Irena	28.05.1914	Tarcal		30944	49429
Sternberg	Lucy	03.01.1925	Szeged		30643	49430
Stieglitz	Eta	03.03.1927	Saszlekence	Schneiderin	30553	49431
Strausz	Olga	19.07.1922	Mako		35942	49973
Strausz	Szidi	03.07.1920	Kolozsvar		35943	49974
Susitzky	Margit	26.03.1921	Moson	Schneiderin	30646	49380
Süssmann	Magda	27.09.1912	Pohorela		35924	49955
Szabo	Ilonka	23.08.1023	Halmi		35925	49956
Szabo	Klara	26.05.1920	Halmi		35926	49957
Szabo	Lenke	26.06.1918	Halmi		35927	49958
Szabo	Lola	26.02.1924	Szaszregen		30630	49381
Szabo	Malvina	17.09.1920	Ratosnya		30631	49382
Szabo	Piroska	25.08.1925	Szaszregen		30629	49383
Szabo	Roza	22.10.1901	Nagybocsko	Köchin	30950	49384
Szakacs	Irena	18.04.1924	Budapest		30803	49390
Szalai	Edit	21.03.1931	Marosvasarhely		38108	49741
Szalavics	Hermina	25.07.1908	Manya	Strickerin	35928	49959
Samet	Cecilia	05.11.1925	Bodrogkeresztur		35929	49960
Samet	Etel	09.08.1927	Bodrogkeresztur		35930	49961
Samet	Helen	28.08.1919	Bodrogkeresztur		35931	49962
Samet	Margit	06.07.1925	Kivarda		35932	49963
Samet	Szeren	18.11.1922	Bodrogkeresztur		35933	49964
Szarvas	Klara	20.09.1921	Szamosdara		30804	49386
Szasz	Erzsebet	24.11.1924	Abaujszanto	Arbeiterin		50225
Szasz	Ilona	01.05.1904	Budapest	Schneiderin	30956	49387
Szasz	Ilona	13.04.1908	Tolcsva	Pflegerin	30954	49388
Szasz	Katalin	19.02.1926	Abaujszanto	Arbeiterin		50226
Szasz	Szuszanna	19.04.1926	Tokaj	Pflegerin	30955	49387

Last Name	First Name	Birth Date	Place of Birth	Profession	Old Number	New Number
Szauer	Agota	21.03.1920	Györ		31011	49385
Szebenyi	Iren	18.04.1918	Mohacs		38109	49742
Szebenyi	Judit	04.08.1911	Almaspuszta	Gärtner	38110	49743
Szekely	Anna	20.05.1925	Kecskemet	Lehrerin		50227
Szekely	Eva	04.01.1921	Szeged		30644	49391
Szepne	Katalin	14.12.1906	Obecse		38111	49744
Szirtes	Anna	20.05.1900	Budapest	Bürokraft	38112	49745
Szokoly	Anna	20.05.1925		Lehrerin		50227
Tabak	Cili	05.10.1926	Dombo			50256
Tabak	Eta	17.09.1922	Dombo			50257
Tabak	Margit	03.01.1928	Dombo			50258
Tabak	Regina	03.04.1925	Dombo	Schneiderin		50259
Tanneur	Jeanne	28.01.1911			52227	50411
Taub	Borbala	04.08.1920	Bodrogkeresztur		35944	49975
Taub	Erzsebet	15.12.1922	Sonogyszob		38131	49764
Taub	Gizella	26.10.1914	Nyirlugos		35945	49976
Taub	Ilona	12.04.1922	Bodrogkeresztur		35946	49977
Taub	Iren	05.11.1914	Ladamoc		35847	49978
Taurau	Therese	22.02.1908			52228	50412
Teichmann	Aranka	21.12.1918	Kisvarda	Sprachlehrerin	38132	49765
Teichmann	Eta	15.04.1921	Kisvarda		38133	49766
Teichmann	Vera	15.09.1920	Kisvarda		38134	49767
Teichmann	Jolan	10.07.1912	Gava		30872	49432
Teszler	Eszter	12.06.1924	Hidalmas		35950	49981
Teszler	Hedi	07.07.1922	Alsoapsa		35948	49979
Teszler	Margit	25.03.1922	Bacsova		35949	49980
Thaler	Roza	12.10.1923	Teke		30806	49433
Thoreau	MarieLouis	26.06.1897			52232	50413
Tierce	Suzanne	10.04.1914			52233	50414
Tiles	Raymonde	25.08.1916			52234	50415
Tischler	Berta	25.12.1908	Erpatak		30982	49434
Torner	Piroska	06.08.1929	Marmarossziget		38135	49768
Toutin	Berangere	22.06.1910			52236	50416
Trattner	Agnes	22.04.1926	Magyarsas		30957	49435
Trattner	Aranka	08.01.1925	Magyarsas		30958	49436
Traub	Jolan	29.04.1912	Budapest		30652	49437
Traub	Julia	20.04.1923	Marosvasarhely		35951	49982
Troztler	Lola	20.11.1911	Bercs		38136	49769
Ujvari	Erzsebet	14.09.1920	Sztropko		30808	49438
Ungar	Lenke	27.02.1922	Fehergyarmat	Lehrerin	30807	49439
Unsdorfer	Edit	25.05.1921	Szatmarcseke		30811	49440
Unsdorfer	Irena	21.05.1923	Szatmarcseke		30810	49441
Unsdorfer	Margit	14.12.1924	Szatmarcseke		30809	49442
Vajda	Agnes	22.10.1913	Mohacs	Pflegerin	38137	49770
Vajda	Erzsebet	13.08.1919	Nagymagyar		30660	49443
Varadi	Erzsebet	20.09.1906	Papa		30658	49444
Varbire	Zsuzsa	10.10.1917	Baja	Strickerin		50261
Vasen	Márta	12.07.1910	Wien	Schneiderin		50262
Vegh	Fani	28.03.1922	Alsoapsa		35952	49983

Last Name	First Name	Birth Date	Place of Birth	Profession	Old Number	New Number
Vegh	Sara	17.08.1924	Alsoapsa		35953	49984
Venyige	Erzsebet	22.12.1927	Nagyhalasz	Schneiderin	38138	49771
Veullien	Odette	18.05.1922			52239	50417
Vidal	Suzanne	19.02.1913			52240	50418
Villechenon	Lucienne	22.08.196			52241	50419
Vivol	Yvonne	06.05.1924			52242	50420
Wachsmann	Zseni	10.07.1922	Magyarlapos		30813	49445
Wachtenheim	Rozsi	07.12.1924	Harsfalva	Schneiderin		50263
Wagner	Anna	24.02.1920	Ersekujvar	Schneiderin		50264
Waldhauser	Edit	07.04.1927	Keszthely			50265
Waldmann	Jolan	02.04.1915	Sajoszentpeter	Näherin	35954	49985
Waldmann	Lili	28.07.1919	Keszthely		35955	49986
Wartenberg	Eva	30.01.1923	Alsovarad	Schneiderin	35956	49446
Weisz	Rozsi	12.07.1920	Kantorjanos		35962	49993
Weicz	Etelka	13.12.1923	Beszterce	Schneiderin	30962	49447
Weil	Erzsebet	23.10.1908	Miskolc	Schneiderin	30971	49448
Wein	Ilona	24.12.1925	Lizmannstadt	Schneiderin		50266
Weinberger	Erzsebet	03.08.1924	Ladazoc		30815	49449
Weinberger	Erzsebet	17.02.1924	Kassa	Modistin	38139	49772
Weinberger	Frida	06.12.1922	Harsfalva	Schneiderin		50267
Weinberger	Gitta	16.03.1926	Zenta		38140	49773
Weinberger	Ibolya	05.11.1916	Legenye		30965	49450
Weinberger	Irena	21.11.1908	Ungvzr	Schneiderin	30874	49451
Weinberger	Irena	01.01.1916	Fehergyarmat	Schneiderin	30831	49452
Weinberger	Julia	03.09.1922	Kolozsvar		35956	49987
Weinberger	Lea	02.02.1925	Zenta		38141	49774
Weinberger	Roza	26.08.1925	Galambos	Schneiderin	30832	49453
Weinberger	Sara	04.01.1922	Tibava	Schneiderin	30835	49454
Weiner	Erzsebet	27.11,1923	Budapest		38142	49775
Weiner	Frici	15.06.1918	Maroshejviz		38143	49776
Weingarten	Leoni	28.08.1919	Majdan	Schneiderin		50268
Weinstein	Ilona	09.04.1921	Buly	Schneiderin	35957	49988
Weiser	Regina	20.01.1917	Harzsin	Schneiderin	30830	49467
Weisz	Anna	15.01.1914	Somogyszob		38144	49777
Weisz	Anna	24.01.1926	Ujpest	Arbeiterin		50269
Weisz	Berta	20.08.1926	Kanyahaza			50270
Weisz	Blanka	06.07.1924	Tiszalok			50271
Weisz	Carolta	10.10.1912	Bacska		30917	49469
Weisz	Edit	07.12.1925	Tiszalok			50272
Weisz	Erzsebet	28.04.1911	Bacska	Pflegerin	30816	49470
Weisz	Eszter	05.05.1928	Tokaj		30829	49455
Weisz	Etel	17.10.1913	Alsoarad	Schneiderin	30836	49456
Weisz	Etel	15.07.1912	Rababogyoszlo		38145	49778
Weisz	Etel	06.05.1908	Kialocfalva	Schneiderin		50273
Weisz	Eva	09.12.1920	Losonc			50274
Weisz	Fany	08.09.1924	Szatmar		30833	49457
Weisz	Frida	05.03.1914	Nyirbogard		30894	49458
Weisz	Gizella	22.03.1925	Szürajna	Schneiderin	30961	49459
Weisz	Helen	10.10.1915	Kalna			50275

Last Name	First Name	Birth Date	Place of Birth	Profession	Old Number	New Number
Weisz	Ibolya	07.05.1925	Szekelyvaja		30655	49471
Weisz	Ida	22.11.1922	Szatmar	Schneiderin	30834	49460
Weisz	Ilona	06.01.1922	Mako		35958	49989
Weisz	Iren	14.01.1922	Torna		38146	49779
Weisz	Iren	28.05.1921	Mezökaszony	Strckerin		50276
Weisz	Irena	02.12.1909	Fehergyarmat		30837	49461
Weisz	Jenny	30.07.1921	Podmuc		30814	49472
Weisz	Jolan	26.12.1919	Tungyog		31017	49462
Weisz	Jolan	04.09.1919	Nyirbogard		30657	49463
Weisz	Julia	07.03.1914	Mezökövesd			50277
Weisz	Juliana	07.08.1925	Baracska		30960	49991
Weisz	Katalin	27.05.1922	Ujpest	Arbeiterin		50278
Weisz	Lenke	24.01.1923	Ilonakujfalu	Schneiderin	30838	49464
Weisz	Lenke	04.06.1918	Paszto		35959	49990
Weisz	Lili	12.12.1924	Tiszaujlak		35960	49991
Weisz	Lousza	06.10.1923	Ujpest	Arbeiterin		50282
Weisz	Magdolna	21.06.1925	Osorna	Schneiderin		50279
Weisz	Malvina	02.04.1926	Nagymagyar		30659	49474
Weisz	Margit	24.06.1919	Szücsi		30963	49465
Weisz	Margit	25.07.1917	Mezökaszony	Strickerin		50280
Weisz	Maria	13.01.1911	Zenta		38147	49780
Weisz	Maria	20.03.1928	Marosvasarhely		38148	49781
Weisz	Marta	05.03.1923	Olahosertiz		38149	49782
Weisz	Paula	22.06.1922	Halmi		35961	49992
Weisz	Piroska	14.04.1925	Harsfalva	Schneiderin	30812	49466
Weisz	Piroska	19.09.1923	Szekelyvaja		30654	49475
Weisz	Piroska	05.12.1919	Veghosszufalu		38150	49783
Weisz	Rosa	12.11.1917	Tunyog		31016	49468
Weisz	Szeren	01.09.1921	Nagyberezna		38151	49784
Weisz	Terez	05.02.1915	Nagyszölös		38152	49785
Weisz	Tilda	10.03.1926	Kanyahaza			50281
Weisz	Zseni	25.06.1916	Bilke		38153	49786
Weisz	Zsuzsa	17.10.1927	Labod		38154	49787
Weiszberg	Judit	25.01.1924	Marmaros		35963	49994
Weiszhaus	Aranka	13.07.1926	Misk		30820	49476
Weiszhaus	Blanka	25.04.1925	Misk		30821	49477
Weiszhaus	Edith	13.05.1925	Rozsaly		30818	49479
Weiszhaus	Hedvig	26.08.1926	Rozsaly		30819	49478
Wellisch	Edit	20.03.1927	Kaposvar	Kürschnerin		50283
Wellisch	Ilona	22.02.1906	Kaposvar	Kürschnerin		50284
Wetzler	Aranka	16.09.1922	Losonc	Schneiderin		50285
Wieder	Roza	11.01.1925	Mojnes		38155	49788
Wiedor	Irena	09.01.1914	Csikszereda		30969	49480
Wiedor	Sara	20.05.1922	Alsoviso		30970	49481
Wiegner	Erzsebet	28.02.1922	Magyaro		30967	49482
Wiegner	Ibolya	10.05.1915	Magyaro		30968	49483
Wiegner	Klara	26.11.1917	Magyaro		30966	49484
Wiener	Lenke	21.03.1921	Gyöngyös		30964	49485
Wilhelm	Adela	28.10.1924	Udvard	Schneiderin	30824	49486

Last Name	First Name	Birth Date	Place of Birth	Profession	Old Number	New Number
Wilhelm	Anna	21.10.1906	Udvard		30826	49487
Wilhelm	Gabriella	27.03.1925	Komarom	Schneiderin	30653	49488
Wilhelm	Irma	24.09.1920	Udvard	Schneiderin	30825	49489
Wikinson	Jeanne	23.01.1915			52244	50421
Winkler	Anna	14.05.1918	Levolek			50286
Winkler	Ella	04.06.1923	Levolek			50287
Winkler	Emma	07.10.1927	Hapkor			50288
Winkler	Erzsebet	07.11.1923	Kaloshelyen			50289
Winkler	Hajnal	24.03.1919	Vac	Näherin	38156	49789
Winkler	Ibolya	13.03.1922	Vac		38157	49790
Winkler	Lili	21.11.1920	Vac	Näherin	38150	49791
Winkler	Magda	29.01.1912	Kaloshelyen			50290
Winkler	Marta	19.12.1920	Levelek			50291
Winkler	Nelli	20.08.1923	vac		38159	49792
Winkler	Olga	14.12.1920	Kaloshelyen			50292
Winkler	Piroska	26.06.1918	Nagyhalasz			50293
Winkler	Rozsa	15.01.1926	Vac		38160	49793
Winter	Anita	02.09.1918			52245	50422
Wirt	Magda	14.09.1926	Dunaföldvar		38164	49797
Witteles	Magda	19.03.1926	Bustyahaza		30827	49490
Witteles	Zseni	17.02.1918	Bustyahaza		30828	49491
Wittmann	Magda	30.03.1919	Dunaföldvar			50294
Wittmann	Rozsi	27.11.1915	Papa		38165	49798
Wohlstein	Katalin	08.02.1925	Pecs		38161	49794
Wolf	Piroska	16.04.1922	Pinohely	Schneiderin		50295
Wollak	Gertrud	18.04.1926	Neisol	Schneiderin		50296
Wollner	Edith	22.08.1923	Udvard		30823	49492
Wollner	Ibolya	30.03.1925	Udvard	Schneiderin	30822	49493
Xanthoppulos	Jole	20.07.1912			52247	50423
Zelikovics	Ida	16.01.1925	Visko	Schneiderin		50297
Zelikovics	Zali	16.01.1925	Visko	Schneiderin		50298
Zelikovics	Szeren	08.01.1926	Olahcsertiz		35964	49995
Zelmanovits	Katalin	18.11.1924	Tiszaujlak		30839	49494
Ziegler	Yvone	01.06.1902			52248	50424
Zielinska	Nacha	04.02.1912	Litzmannstadt	Schneiderin		50299
Zimmermann	Alice	15.11.1922	Miskolc	Schneiderin	30840	49495
Zimmermann	Margit	26.02.1924	Agosernyö		35965	49496
Zimmermann	Szeren	28.04.1921	Agosernyö		35966	49497
Zinner	Szeren	06.03.1908	Ujpest		38162	49795
Zizovits	Blanka	04.10.1922	Tiszavinna	Arbeiterin		50300
Zoldan	Iren	28.11.1910	Losonc	Professorin	35967	49998
Zsilla	Katalin	10.12.1923	Budapest	Schneiderin	38163	49796
Zubek	Eva	10.10.1927	Baraska	Schneiderin	30973	49496
Zucker	Alice	01.11.1925	Satoraljaujhely		31019	49497
Zucker	Erzsebet	12.06.1924	Satoraljaujhely		31018	49498
Zwass	Fanny	19.11.1915	Satoraljaujhely	Schneiderin	30972	49499

The following is a sample of the original transport list showing the fourth transport in which the author and her sister arrived.

Waffen- SS
KL Buchenwald
Arb.Lager Markkleeberg

Waff...
Konzentrationsl...
— Verwal. —
12. DEZ 1944

Markkleeberg, am 9.12.1944

An die

Verwaltung
des KL Buchenwald

Weimar-Buchenwald

Obiges Kommando bestätigt die Ankunft der 300 weibl.Häftlinge aus dem A.-Lager Bergen-Belsen. Der Transport ist am 8.12. um 17.^{00} hier eingetroffen. Arbeitseinsatzführer- Hptstruf.Schwartz wurde heute telegrafisch benachrichtigt.

Die Namenslisten werden in den nächsten Tagen hier abgesandt. Nach Erhalt derselben bitten wir um Bekanntgabe der neuen Häftlingsnummern.

Der Kommandoführer
Oberscharführer

Politische Abteilung.

Weimar-Buchenwald, 17. Dez. 1944.

0 11587

Neuzugänge vom 17. Dezember 1944.

300 weibl. Häftlinge von KL. Bergen-Belsen nach Akdo Junkers-Markleeberg.
(eingetroffen am 8. Dez. 1944)

Politische Ungarinnen-Jüdinnen.

1.	50001	Abraham	Iren	ld 25. 4.25	Felsöbogata	
2.	50002	Ada	Eva	ld 5. 4.22	Budapest	Pianistin
3.	50003	Adelsber	Zsuzsanna	ld 12. 6.26	Sümeg	
4.	50004	Adler	Sali	ld 25.12.23	Dombo	Schneiderin
5.	50005	Adler	Teres	vh 7.6.08	Mezökövesd	
6.	50006	Almasi	Edit	ld 15.10.24	Szentlörinc	Schneiderin
7.	50007	Alweiss	Etelka	vh 2.11.15	Budapest	
8.	50008	Barany	Katalin	ld 18. 1.30	Buzsak	
9.	50009	Bard	Rosa	vh 16.11.14	Budapest	Elektrikerin
10.	50010	Beck	Juiit	ld 4.12.24	Tolna	Schneiderin
11.	50011	Barna	Anna	ld. 2. 5.20	Budapest	Ingenieur
12.	50012	Beck	Rozsi	ld 10.11.27	Tolna	Schneiderin
13.	50013	Berg	Erzsebet	ld 13. 7.20	Derecske	
14.	50014	Berg	Rozsi	ld 15.11.14	Csorna	
15.	50015	Berger	Teres	ld 25. 8.16	Csorna	Schneiderin
16.	50016	Bihari	Margit	vh 26. 7.05	Budapest	
17.	50017	Bihari	Margit	ld 9. 2.26	Beregujfalu	
18.	50018	Biresak	Frida	vh 17.11.09	Budapest	Pflegerin
19.	50019	Blau	Magda	ld 30. 6.27	Nagymagyar	Schneiderin
20.	50020	Bleyer	Eva	ld 30. 6.24	Szolnok	
21.	50021	Boros	Klara	vh 6. 6.24	Budapest	
22.	50022	Braun	Barbara	ld 25.11.15	Mezökövesd	
23.	50023	Braun	Carmen	ld 19. 4.22	Budapest	
24.	50024	Braun	Eva	ld 10.10.24	Keszthely	Schneiderin
25.	50025	Braun	Szidi	vh 29. 3.10	Fertöszentmiklos	
26.	50026	Breitner	Aranka	vh 27. 9.08	Pocsaj	
27.	50027	Breyer	Katalin	9.12.22 ld	Mezökövesd	Schneiderin
28.	50028	Brummer	Iren	vh 20. 6.18	Levelek	
29.	50029	Brannwasser	Magda	ld 16.10.26	Baho	
30.	50030	Csendes	Marianne	ld 30. 1.27	Baja	
31.	50031	Szitter	Eva	vh 22. 7.24	Budapest	Kürschnerin
32.	50032	Davidovits	Helen	ld 4. 6.26	Dombo	
33.	50033	Deutsch	Agnes	ld 30. 9.23	Budapest	Schneiderin
34.	50034	Deutsch	Bella	ld 27. 2.27	Vac	Schneiderin
35.	50035	Deutsch	Helen	ld 13.10.22	Vac	Schneiderin
36.	50036	Deutsch	Klara	ld 10. 4.25	Tolnas	Schneiderin
37.	50037	Deutsch	Iseren	ld 12. 1.24	Vac	Schneiderin
38.	50038	Doktorczyk	Hela	ld 15. 5.19	Litzmannstadt	
39.	50039	Dub	Olga	vh 13. 6.14	Mezökaszony	Schneiderin
40.	50040	Dub	Regina	vh 22. 5.08	Mezökaszony	
41.	50041	Dub	Rozsi	ld 11.12.28	Feies	
42.	50042	Ehrenthal	Margit	ld 12. 2.16	Nagymagyar	Schneiderin
43.	50043	Ehrenthal	Valeria	ld 26.10.27	Nagymagyar	Schneiderin
44.	50044	Einhorn	Gizi	ld 5. 7.24	Dombo	Schneiderin
45.	50045	Einhorn	Helen	ld 19. 7.23	Dombo	Schneiderin
46.	50046	Einhorn	Bendike	ld 26. 1.26	Dombo	Schneiderin
47.	50047	Engel	Katalin	ld 19. 7.28	Budapest	
48.	50048	Engelsberg	Rossa	ld 23. 5.25	Jaszbereny	Schneiderin
49.	50049	Farkas	Hajnal	ld 24.10.09	Kalinfalva	
50.	50050	Farkas	Zali	vh 15. 8.12	Ylako	Schneiderin

51.	50051	Fischer	Ilona	ld	17. 5.27	Sajopetri	
52.	50052	Flesch	Margit	ld	1. 7.24	Tapioszele	Arbeiterin
53.	50053	Floch	Judit	ld	15. 4.28	Sioagard	Schülerin
54.	50054	Fränkel	Ilona	ld	2. 2.22	Jaszfenyszaru	Schneiderin
55.	50055	Fränkel	Rosai	vh	21. 4.15	Jaszfenyszaru	Schneiderin
56.	50056	Freikind	Piroska	vh	25. 3.06	Pocsaj	-
57.	50057	Fried	Josefa	ld	23. 8.24	Dombo	Strickerin
58.	50058	Fried	Rosa	ld	23. 1.27	Erzsekujvar	Arbeiterin
59.	50059	Friedmann	Boris	vh	21. 3.08	Harsfalva	Schneiderin
60.	50060	Friedmann	Maria	ld	16.12.15	Tiszadob	-
61.	50061	Friedmann	Erzsebet	vh	4. 3.10	Baja	
62.	50062	Friedmann	Gyöngyi	ld	16. 3.22	Beregillosva	
63.	50063	Friedmann	Judit	ld	26. 7.26	Budapest	
64.	50064	Friedmann	Cecilia	ld	15. 8.22	Halmi	
65.	50065	Friedmann	Olga	ld	30. 5.24	Halmi	Friseurin
66.	50066	Frommer	Teres	ld	2[illegible]. 2.26	Harsfalva	Schneiderin
67.	50067	Füredi	Magda	ld	17. 2.22	Ujpest	Arbeiterin
68.	50068	Fürst	Erzsebet	ld	17. 1.13	Kiskunhalas	-
69.	50069	Gerler	Helen	ld	20. 8.15	Budfalva	Schneiderin
70.	50070	Gerö	Iren	ld	10. 6.27	Kecskemet	
71.	50071	Godinger	Ida	ld.	4. 4.26	Harsfalva	Schneiderin
72.	50072	Godinger	Regina	ld	28. 1.28	Harsfalva	Schneiderin
73.	50073	Gold	Gabriella	ld	13. 8.27	Püspökladany	Schneiderin
74.	50074	Goldberger	Szeren	ld	15.12.25	Ferones	-
75.	50075	Goldkranc	Chaja	vh	5. 5.19	Litzmannstadt	Schneiderin
76.	50076	Goldstein	Golda	vh	16.12.10	Budfalva	
77.	50077	Grass	Amalia	ld	14.11.12	Budapest	Beamtin
78.	50078	Griesz	Erzsebet	ld	22. 8.22	Nagybaracska	Arbeiterin
79.	50079	Gref	Erzsebet	ld	26. 2.26	Hollad	Schneiderin
80.	50080	Gross	Ibolya	ld	21. 4.27	Szeged	-
81.	50081	Gross	Katalin	vh	22. 2.18	Budapest	Schneiderin
82.	50082	Gross	[illegible]	ld	9. 8.16	Nadas	Scheniderin
83.	50083	Gross	Szeren	vh	15. 1.10	Mako	Schneiderin
84.	50084	Gross	Zsuzsa	ld	28.11.26	Karcag	Schneiderin
85.	50085	Grünbaum	Edit	ld	28. 8.25	Tapolca	Schneiderin
86.	50086	Grünbaum	Jolan	ld	24. 3.20	Budapest	Pflegerin
87.	50087	Grünberg	Lenke	ld	14. 3.29	Kenesspatak	-
88.	50088	Grünberg	Rossi	ld	28. 8.27	Kenesspatak	-
89.	50089	Grünberger	Sari	ld	7. 4.25	Dombo	Schneiderin
90.	50090	Grünfeld	Rossi	vh	22. 8.14	Magyarregen	Arbeiterin
91.	50091	Grünwald	Zsefia	ld	2. 1.17	Tass	Beamtin
92.	50092	Halpern	Maria	ld	7. 1.24	Munkacs	Arbeiterin
93.	50093	Halpern	Helen	ld	1. 3.25	Munkacs	Arbeiterin
94.	50094	Hamer	Adel	vh	12.10.19	Budapest	Färberin
95.	50095	Herskovics	Berta	ld	10. 8.25	Nevkolostor	-
96.	50096	Herskovics	Eszter	ld	25. 8.27	Nevkolostor	-
97.	50097	Herskovics	Etel	ld	11. 6.21	Keresenyfalva	Schneiderin
98.	50098	Herskovics	Helen	ld	10. 5.28	Nevkolostor	
99.	50099	Herskovics	Lenke	ld	24. 3.20	Keresenyfalva	Schneiderin
100.	50100	Hettler	Anna	vh	25. 6.08	Tarnaszadany	
101.	50101	Hicker	Margit	ld	13.10.20	Pestujhely	Arbeiterin
102.	50102	Hirsch	Maria	ld	30.11.26	Kacko	
103.	50103	Hoffer	Katalin	vh	13. 3.13	Tapioszele	Schneiderin
104.	50104	Holoser	Margit	ld	24. 9.09	Zalasztbalasz	
105.	50105	Holländer	Zsuzsa	ld	22. 5.27	Sarkad	
106.	50106	Infeld	Hana	vh	14. 2.10	Ozarkow	Schneiderin
107.	50107	Ingberg	Piri	ld	21.17.19	Budfalva	Schneiderin
108.	50108	Ingberg	Rossi	ld	21. 8.12	Budfalva	Schneiderin
109.	50109	Israel	Eszter	ld	4.11.27	Alör	
110.	50110	Israel	Margit	ld	1. 5.25	Alör	

O 11569

111.50111	Izrael	Piroska	vh	16. 7.15	Nagykaroly	Schneiderin
112.50112	Izsak	Edit	ld	13. 3.26	Kaposvar	Schneiderin
113.50113	Jakobovits	Fraidla	ld	20.12.26	Skernivice	Schneiderin
114.50114	Jonas	Matild	ld	26. 9.17	Kalotaszeg	
115.50115	Jaszinger	Jolan	ld	24. 4.12	Debrecen	
116.50116	Juskovits	Ilona	ld	6. 6.16	Ungvar	Arbeiterin
117.50117	Kalmanovits	Katalin	vh	11.12.20	Bagota	Arbeiterin
118.50118	Kardos	Barbara	ld	22. 9.20	Kapuvar	Schneiderin
119.50119	Katz	Lili	ld	6. 7.25	Dombo	
120.50120	Katz	Tobi	ld	25.10.24	Dombo	Schneiderin
121.50121	Kell	Rozsa	vh	3. 1.14	Alsopatak	Schneiderin
122.50122	Kemeny	Anna	vh	5.10.05	ezsider	
123.50123	Kertesz	Anna	ld	26.10.26	Tamasi	
124.50124	Kertesz	Zsuzsa	ld	17.12.24	Tamasi	
125.50125	Klein	Agnes	ld	3. 8.26	Ersekujvar	
126.50126	Klein	Erzsi	vh	8. 4.99	Seregelyes	
127.50127	Klein	Eva	ld	1. 1.27	Seregelyes	
128.50128	Klein	Eva	ld	17. 8.29	Debrecen	
129.50129	Klein	Karolin	ld	12. 2.07	Kiskunfelegyhaza	Schneiderin
130.50130	Klein	Klara	ld	20. 5.23	Soroksar	Gläserin
131.50131	Klein	Maria	ld	10. 1.26	Ersekujvar	Schülerin
132.50132	Klein	Sari	ld	26.12.07	Kiskunfelegyhaza	Schneiderin
133.50133	Klein	Terez	ld	3. 8.08	Marmarossziget	
134.50134	Klein	Zsuzsa	vh	8. 2.20	Budapest	Arbeiterin
135.50135	Klein	Zsuzsa	ld	16. 4.21	Ersekujvar	Beamtin
136.50136	Kohn	Barucha	ld	18. 8.25	Litzmannstadt	Schneiderin
137.50137	Kohn	Edit	vh	16.12.25	Budapest	Kürschnerin
138.50138	Kohn	Erzsebet	ld	19. 9.12	Nyiregyhaza	
139.50139	Kohn	Malka	ld	6. 3.23	Litzmannstadt	Scheniderin
140.50140	Kohn	Margit	ld	21. 4.16	Poosaj	
141.50141	Kosztelitz	Szidi		12.11.07 vh	Bussaj	
142.50142	Krausz	Aranka	ld	11. 2.13	Debrecen	
143.50143	Krausz	Erzsebet	vh	18. 4.14	Balföld	
144.50144	Kreiszmann	Lenke	vh	3. 3.20	Bilke	Schneiderin
145.50145	Lachmann	Fanni	vh	10.12.15	Lecfalva	Schneiderin
146.50146	Lansner	Helen	ld	21. 6.25	Kolozsvar	Schneiderin
147.50147	Lazar	Rozsi	ld	22.10.26	Beszterce	
148.50148	Leb	Ilona	ld	26.11.22	Marosbogat	Schneiderin
149.50149	Leb	Margit	ld	30.10.23	Marosbogat	Schneiderin
150.50150	Lebovics	Malvin	ld	8. 8.25	Bilke	Schneiderin
151.50151	Lebovics	Margit	ld.	20. 9.24	Marmarossziget	Arbeiterin
152.50152	Lebovics	Pepi	ld.	3. 9.24	Dombo	Schneiderin
153.50153	Lebovics	Piri	ld	20.5/9.23	Marsfalva	Schneiderin
154.50154	Lebovics	Szeren	ld	28. 5.27	Bilke	Schneiderin
155.50155	Lengyel	Vera	ld	10. 8.27	Budapest	Schneiderin
156.50156	Lichtig	Etel	vh	26. 5.11	Felsöhidegpatak	
157.50157	Lichtmann	Judit	ld	24. 4.30	Debrecen	
158.50158	Lieber	Dora	ld	14. 5.20	Sajolad	Bäckerin
159.50159	Lieber	Magda	ld	31.12.21	Sarospatak	Friseurin
160.50160	Lorber /e	Edit	ld	28. 1.24	Püspökladany	
161.50161	Lorber/e	Gabrielle	ld	29.12.24	Püspökladany	
162.50162	Lorber /e	Margit	ld	2. 9.18	Püspökladany	
163.50163	Lorbeer	Margit	ld	8. 4.22	Püspökladany	Schneiderin
164.50164	Lörinch	Izabella	ld	2. 4.27	Okany	
165.50165	Lörincz	Margit	ld	8. 6.21	Bihar	
166.50166	Löwy	Hilda	ld	1. 1.23	Nagytarna	
167.50167	Löwy	Judit	ld	10.12.25	Kapuvar	Schneiderin
168.50168	Löwy	Karolin	ld	15. 5.26	Nagytarna	
169.50169	Löwy	Margit	vh	1.12.04	Wien	
170.50170	[illegible]acher	Ida	vh	22. 8.08	Fertöszentmiklos	Schneiderin

17.Dezember 1944.

171.	50171	Mautner	Edit	ld	28. 8.26	Iregszemcse	
172.	50172	Meixner	Hermin	ld	8. 8.23	Budapest	Schneiderin
173.	50173	Mandl	Gertrud	ld	31. 5.25	Tata	Schneiderin
174.	50174	Markovics	Ilona	ld	8. 8.20	Avasfelsöfalu	
175.	50175	Markovics	Klara	ld	24. 8.25	Halmi	Schuhmacherin
176.	50176	Mendelsohn	Sari		20. 8.23 ld	Alapret	Schneiderin
177.	50177	Miselbach	Ella	vh	2. 5.13	Szabalcs	
178.	50178	Moskovics	Margit	ld	2.10.21	Boregkövesd	Arbeiterin
179.	50179	Müller	Fanni	ld	26. 8.18	Dombo	Schneiderin
180.	50180	Müller	Helen	ld	15.11.24	Karinfalva	Schneiderin
181.	50181	Müller	Hessi	ld	12. 1.22	Alsokalinfalva	Schneiderin
182.	50182	Müller	Rozsi	ld	4. 4.23	Dombo	
183.	50183	Müller	Zsuzsa	ld	27. 6.27	Tolna	Schneiderin
184.	50184	Nadas	Ilona	vh	22.11.10	Budapest	Schneiderin
185.	50185	Neumann	Fanni	ld	24. 3.24	Alsokalinfalva	
186.	50186	Neumann	Frida	ld	13. 3.27	Halmi	
187.	50187	Neumark	Ibolya	vh	16. 3.23	Debrecen	Arbeiterin
188.	50188	Ney	Agnes	ld	4. 6.25	Keszthely	Schneiderin
189.	50189	Ott	Katalin	vh	5.10.11	Somogyesurgo	
190.	50190	Pajes	Agnes	ld	9.12.24	Budapest	Sprachlehrerin
191.	50191	Peri	Cecilia	vh	6. 3.11	Soltvadkert	
192.	50192	Perlstein	Vilma	ld	2. 2.26	Szilagy Somlyo	
193.	50193	Pollak	Erzsebet	ld	19.11.20	[illegible]	Schneiderin
194.	50194	Pollak	Eszter	ld	18. 8.26	[illegible]	
195.	50195	Pollak	Rozsi	vh	29. 8.24	Kolozsvar	Klempnerin
196.	50196	Preisler	Aranka	ld	16. 2.26	Budapest	Zahntechnikerin
197.	50197	Preisler	Magda	vh	12. 2.15	Debrecen	Arbeiterin
198.	50198	Rainitz	Teres	ld	15.10.15	Nyiresasarj	
199.	50199	Revai	Dora	ld	6. 6.23	Tab	
200.	50200	Revai	Rozsi	vh	28. 1.06	Gyalndpuszta	
201.	50201	Rheinfeld	Elvira	ld	3.12.20	Lörincsi	Schneiderin
202.	50202	Rheinfeld	Erna	ld	20. 4.13	Lörincsi	Schneiderin
203.	50203	Rheinfeld	Ibolya	ld	25.12.24	Lörincsi	Schneiderin
204.	50204	Riess	Eva	ld	3. 6.27	Jaszfenyszaru	Schneiderin
205.	50205	Reiss	Ibolya	ld	13. 1.26	Jaszfenyszaru	Schneiderin
206.	50206	Roder	Anna	ld	2. 8.26	Ozora	
207.	50207	Roma	Erzsebet	vh	28. 2.12	Budapest	Arbeiterin
208.	50208	Rosenberg	Ilona	ld	3. 3.21	Veszprem	Schneiderin
209.	50209	Rosenberg	Laura	vh	18. 9.14	Kecskemet	
210.	50210	Rosendorn	Agnes	ld	12. 2.26	Dombovar	Schneiderin
211.	50211	Rosendorn	Elvira	vh	29. 3.10	Dombovar	
212.	50212	Rosenfeld	Sari	ld	12. 7.26	Szeged	Schneiderin
213.	50213	Rosenthal	Eva	ld	24. 7.28	Nyirabrany	Arbeiterin
214.	50214	Rosenzweig	Hanna	ld	23.11.25	Litzmannstadt	Schneiderin
215.	50215	Sandberg	Berta	ld	22.12.20	Litzmannstadt	
216.	50216	Salamon	Etel	vh	19. 5.15	Nagybocsko	Schneiderin
217.	50217	Salamon	Rossa	vh	12.10.04	Mako	Schneiderin
218.	50218	Salamonovits	Ilona	ld	23. 7.28	Sajopetri	
219.	50219	Simon	Klara	ld	8.10.20	Balatonboglar	Schneiderin
220.	50220	Singer	Aranka	vh	17. 7.06	Nagybicsko	
221.	50221	Singer	Julia	vh	22. 9.10	Stenotypistin	Rutka
222.	50222	Sonnenschein	Magda	ld	13. 8.24	Ponyod	Schniedrin
223.	50223	Spitz	Ilona	ld	6. 4.17	Verböc	Arbeiterin
224.	50224	Spitzer	Teres	vh	4. 3.14	Vasvar	Strickerin
225.	50225	Szasz	Erzsebet	ld	24.11.24	Abaujszanto	Arbeiterin
226.	50226	Szasz	Katalin	ld	19. 2.26	Abaujszanto	Arbeiterin
227.	50227	Szekely	Anna	ld	20. 5.25	Kecskemet	Lehrerin
228.	50228	Scheer	Erzsebet	ld	24.11.21	Kemecse	
229.	50229	Scheer	Ilona	ld	10. 1.24	Kemecse	
230.	50230	Scheiner	Berta	ld	1. 1.21	Nagybocsko	

0 11570

231. 50231	Scheiner	Eszter	ld	28. 2.23	Nagybocsko	Zahntechnikerin
232. 50232	Scheiner	Iren	ld	28. 9.26	Nagybocsko	Friseurin
233. 50233	Scheiner	Rozsi	ld	14. 6.24	Nagybocsko	Friseurin
234. 50234	Schlesinger	Ilona	ld	3. 5.25	Kecskemet	Lehrerin
235. 50235	Schlesinger	Lenke	ld	11. 9.23	Kecskemet	Arbeiterin
236. 50236	Schlesinger	Rozsi	ld	18. 1.22	Kecskemet	Schneiderin
237. 50237	Schönberger	Alice	ld	25. 8.25	Budapest	-
238. 50238	Schönberger	Erna	ld	18. 7.27	Bonyhad	Schneiderin
239. 50239	Schreiber	Anna	ld	23. 8.25	Kenderes	Schneiderin
240. 50240	Schulsbeck	Magda	ld	10. 6.20	Jaszapati	-
241. 50241	Schwarz	Elsa	ld	29. 9.21	Mako	
242. 50242	Schwarz	Erzsebet	ld	29. 9.21	Pusztamonostor	Schneiderin
243. 50243	Schwarz	Erzsebet	vh	13.12.23	Budapest	Schneiderin
244. 50244	Schwarz	Hermina	ld	8. 5.26	Szamosujvar	Arbeiterin
245. 50245	Schwarz	Ibolya	ld	13. 4.11	Törökszentmiklos	-
246. 50246	Schwarz	Ilona	vh	25. 7.07	[illegible]	
247. 50247	Schwarz	Ilona	ld	27. 6.27	Szamosujvar	Arbeiterin
248. 50248	Schwarz	Katalin	ld	28. 2.23	Szamosujvar	Arbeiterin
249. 50249	Schwarz	Katalin	ld	24. 6.24	Debrecen	-
250. 50250	Schwarz	Regina	ld	24.12.22	Szamosujvar	Arbeiterin
251. 50251	Schwarz	Rozsi	ld	6. 8.22	[illegible]	
252. 50252	Steiner	Julia	vh	16.10.22	Budapest	Arbeiterin
253. 50253	Stern	Frida	vh	21. 1.09	Karcfalva	
254. 50254	Stern	Rozsi	ld	21. [illegible]	Karcfalva	Schneiderin
255. 50255	Stern	Rozsi	ld	21. 2.11	[illegible]	-
256. 50256	Tabak	Edit	ld	5.10.26	Dombo	
257. 50257	Tabak	Eta	ld	17. 9.22	Dombo	
258. 50258	Tabak	Margit	ld	[illegible] 1.28	Dombo	
259. 50259	Tabak	Regina	ld	[illegible] 4.25	Dombo	Schneiderin
260. 50260	[illegible]	Margit	vh	19.11.11	Pincehely	Schneiderin
261. 50261	Varhire	Zsuzsa	vh	10.10.17	Baja	Strickerin
262. 50262	Vasas	Marta	ld	12. 7.10	[illegible]	Schneiderin
263. 50263	Wachtenheim	Rozsi	ld	7.12.24	Karcfalva	Schneiderin
264. 50264	Wagner	Anna	ld	24. 2.20	Ersekujvar	Schneiderin
265. 50265	Waldhauser	Edit	ld	7. 4.27	Keszthely	-
266. 50266	Wein	[illegible]	ld	24.12.25	Litzmannstadt	Schneiderin
267. 50267	Weinberger	Frida	ld	6.12.22	Karcfalva	Schneiderin
268. 50268	Weingarten	Rozsi	ld	28. 8.19	Hajdan	Schneiderin
269. 50269	Weiss	Anna	ld	24. 1.26	Ujpest	Arbeiterin
270. 50270	Weiss	Berta	ld	20. 8.26	[illegible]	-
271. 50271	Weiss	Blanka	ld	6. 7.24	Miskolc	-
272. 50272	Weiss	Edit	ld	7.12.25	Miskolc	
273. 50273	Weiss	Etel	vh	6. 3.08	Kislecsfalva	Schneiderin
274. 50274	Weiss	Eva	ld	9.12.20	Losonc	
275. 50275	Weiss	Helen	ld	10.10.15	Kalna	-
276. 50276	Weiss	Iren	ld	28. 5.21	Mezökaszony	Strickerin
277. 50277	Weiss	Julia	vh	7. 3.14	Mezökövesd	
278. 50278	Weiss	Katalin	ld	27. 5.22	Ujpest	Arbeiterin
279. 50279	Weiss	Magdolna	ld	21. 6.25	Csorna	Schneiderin
280. 50280	Weiss	Margit	ld	25. 7.17	Mezökaszony	Strickerin
281. 50281	Weiss	Hilda	ld	10. 3.28	[illegible]	-
282. 50282	Weiss	Zsuzsa	ld	6.10.23	Ujpest	Arbeiterin
283. 50283	Wellisch	Edit	ld	20. 3.27	Kaposvar	Kürschnerin
284. 50284	Wellisch	Ilona	ld	22. 2.08	Kaposvar	Kürschnerin
285. 50285	Wetzler	Aranka	ld	16. 9.22	Losonc	Schneiderin
286. 50286	Winkler	Anna	ld	14. 5.18	Levelek	-
287. 50287	Winkler	Ella	vh	4. 6.23	Levelek	
288. 50288	Winkler	Emma	ld	7.10.27	Napkor	
289. 50289	Winkler	Erzsebet	ld	7.11.23	Kalocsemlyen	
290. 50290	Winkler	Magda	ld	29. 1.22	Kalocsemlyen	

17.Dezember 1944.

291.	50291	Winkler	Marta	ld 19.12.20	Levelek	
292.	50292	Winkler	Olga	ld 14.12.20	Kaloszenlyen	
293.	50293	Winkler	Piroska	vh 26. 6.18	Nagykalasz	
294.	50294	Wittmann	Magda	vh 30. 3.19	Dunaföldvar	
295.	50295	Wolf	Piroska	ld 16. 4.22	Pincehely	Schneiderin
296.	50296	Wollak	Gertrud	ld 18. 4.26	Neisol	Schneiderin
297.	50297	Zelikovics	Ida	ld 16. 1.25	Visko	Schneiderin
298.	50298	Zelikovics	Zali	ld 16. 1.25	Visko	Schneiderin
299.	50299	Zielinska	Nacha	vh 4. 2.12	Litzmannstadt	Schneiderin
300.	50300	Zisovits	Blanka	ld 14.10.22	Tiszavinna	Arbeiterin

Listenstärke : 300 Häftlinge.

[signature]

SS - Unterscharführer

0 11572

Appendix B

List of Arrivals at Theresianstadt

In April 1945 about 4,500 women, whose last address before deportation was Hungary and its annexed territories, were driven to Theresianstadt. They came from different camps, Markkleeberg one of them. When they arrived they requested to register, but some were too sick to give information about themselves. Thus, names may be missing from the list.[1]

Women changed their dates of birth to make themselves younger or older in order to receive *zulage,* an additional portion of food. The majority however, did give their real age.[2]

The list of inmates arriving Terezin at the end of the war is available: (1) In the archives of Buchenwald, Germany, (2) The Central State archive in Prague, Czechoslovakia, and (3) Theresienstadt Martyrs Remembrance Association, Givat Haim-Ihud, Israel.

Markkleeberg inmates reaching Thereseianstadt after the Death March on April 29, 1945:

Last Name	First Name	Date of Birth	Residence	Place of Birth
Abelsberg	Zsuzsi	12.6.1929	Dombovar	Sümeg
Abraham	Iren	14.4.1925	Felsöbogad	Felsöbogad
Admowicz	Rana	14.2.1910	Lodz	Ozorkow
Alexander	Isa / Elisa	17.4.1917	Satoraljaujhely	Satoraljaujhely
Almasi	Edit	15.10.1924	Toalmas	Szentlörincz
Alt	Lenke	17.5.1925	Ujpest	Ujpest
Altmann	Roza	20.2.1912	Satoraljaujhely	Satoraljaujhely
Apfelbaum	Lili	5.9.1926	Vac	Vac
Aron	Lilly	26.3.1925	Teke	Sajomagyaros
Asztalos	Rozsi	8.4.1925	Kdenvar	Izasocsor
Bachus	Sidonie	11.6.1920	Cluj	Cluj
Bachus	Erzsebet	29.7.1927	Cluj	Cluj
Barany	Katalin	18.1.1930	Buzsak	Buzsak
Barany	Viola	25.6.1924	Tornoc	Bratislava

Last Name	First Name	Date of Birth	Residence	Place of Birth
Barta	Rosa	2.4.1915	Jaszfenyszaru	Jaszfenyszaru
Beck	Rozsa	10.11.1927	Tolna	Tolna
Beck	Judith	4.12.1924	Tolna	Tolna
Beck	Lilly	13.2.1929	Fehergyarmat	Jank
Berger	Ilona	12.6.1925	Fehergyarmat	Fehergyarmat
Berger	Rozsi	15,11,1914	Csorna	Csoma
Berger	Anna	22.9.1923	Nagyatad	Szarvas
Berger	Therese	25.8.1916	Csorna	Csorna
Bergerová	Berta	10.1.1921	Velke Komiaty	Velke Komiaty
Berko	Helena	14.6.1924	Ilonak Ujfalu	Ilonak Ujfalu
Berkovitsch	Lena	28.6.1925	Satoraljaujhely	Satoraljaujhely
Berkovits	Gabriela	6.10.1930	Satoraljaujhely	Satoraljaujhely
Bernstein	Helena	21.6.1912	Harsfalva	Holobino
Bernstein	Lenke	11.5.1917	Harsfalva	Harsfalva
Bernstein	Regine	13.5.1920	Harsfalva	Harsfalva
Bienenstock	Edith	7.3.1924	Papa	Papa
Bienenstock	Susane	1.7.1926	Papa	Papa
Biener	Aranka	8.4.1917	Magyarlados	Felsöszöcs
Bimbaumová	Magda	10.10.1919	Kosice	Gat
Biro	Erzsi	22.10.1910	Zalaegerszeg	New York
Blau	Magda	30.6.1929	Nagymagyar	Nagymagyar
Blau	Eva	4.4.1929	Mateszalka	Mateszalka
Blau	Margit	14.11.1928	Papa	Papa
Belier	Rosa	1.11.1911	Aszod	Eger
Blum	Irene	15.4.1924	Nyiderzs	Nyiderzs
Braun	Ilona	13.4.1912	Nagyatad	Nagyatad
Braun	Julia	28.3.1911	Komarom	Komarom
Braunová	Edita	5.2.1921	Kosice	Warszawa
Braunstein	Ibolya	27.5.1929	Gyumölcsenes	Gyumölcsenes
Bronner	Anna	12.5.1928	Mezöcsat	Mezöcsat
Bronner	Edith	16.9.1926	Mezöcsat	Mezöcsat
Brummer	Irene	20.7.1918	Nyirbator	Levelek
Czeisler	Ilona	20.1.1916	Miskolc	Miskolc
Czeisler	Jolan	11.4.1909	Miskolc	Miskolc
Czigler	Rosaile	15.2.1904	Hatvan	Hatvan
Czitrom	Magda	5.3.1928	Tirgu Mures	Tirgu Mures
Czorn	Gabriela	17.7.1924	Sarospatek	Sarospatek
Danzinger	Iren	17.10.1924	Nagykallo	Nagykallo
Darvas	Gabriela	9.12.1922	Homokszentgyor	Pecs
David	Berta	17.11.1926	Alsorepa	Maroszlako
David	Miriam	10.2.1930	SzekelyUdvarhel	SzekelyUdvarhel
Davidovicz	Blanka	7.10.1921	Tirgu Mures	Tirgu Mures
Davidovits	Erzsebet	15.9.1921	Oetvösfalva	Nagyszölös
Davidowitz	Helena	4.6.1928	Dombo	Dombo
Deutsch	Jolan	5.5.1022	Vel.Bereznyj	Vel.Bereznyj
Deutsch	Vera	31.3.1927	Szeged	Szeged
Deutsch	Vera	22.4.1923	Satoraljaujhely	Satoraljaujhely
Deutsch	Szeren	12.1.1924	Balassagyarmat	Vac
Deutsch	Lenke	11.3.1928	Papa	Papa

Last Name	First Name	Date of Birth	Residence	Place of Birth
Deutsch	Helene	13.10.1922	Balassagyarmat	Vac
Deutsch	Bella	27.2.1927	Balassagyarmat	Vac
Deutsch	Agnes	30.9.1923	Tapioszele	Budapest
Deutsch	Márta	4.9.1922	Satoraljaujhely	Minaj
Devai	Margit	7.12.1922	Rudabanya	Edeleny
Diaman	Anna	20.4.1920	Kisnemeti	Kisnemeti
Diamant	Rozsi	20.4.1920	Kisnemeti	Kisnemeti
Dittler	Frieda	27.1.1902	Ujpest	Zvolen
Donath	Frida	30.5.1905	Lucenec	Lucene
Doros	Helena	22.5.1908	Ujpest	Ojnacskö/Gomo
Dorvas	Stefanio	20.9.1896	Homokszentgyor	Pecs
Dub	Rosa	11.9.1929	Tecsö	Tecsö
Düm	Elsa	10.30.1920	Ujfeherto	Ujfeherto
Ehrenthal	Margit	12.2.1916	Nagymagyar	Nagymagyar
Einhorn	Gisella	5.7.1928	Dombo	Dombo
Einhorn	Lenke	31.10.1928	Dombo	Dombo
Einhorn	Helena	19.7.1923	Dombo	Dombo
Eisdorfer	Lilli	28.5.1928	Suskova	Suskova/Svalava
Eisler	Etelka	25.11.1921	Demend	Demend
Eisler	Ilona	1.11.1924	Demend	Demend
Eisner	Klari	1.1.1926	Fehergyarmat	Fehergyarmat
Elfer	Elizabeth	11.3.1918	Vac	Vac
Engel	Katalin	13.7.1931	Budapest	Budapest
Engel	Sara	15.1.1922	Ujfeherto	Ujfeherto
Engelstein	Fanny	13.6.1924	Marmarospetrov	Marmarospetrov
Ernst	Piri	27.1.1927	Udvard	Udvard
Faber	Elisabeth	26.11.1907	KralovskyChlme	Ipolysag
Farkas	Hajnal	15.10.1909	Wisck	Alsokalinfalva
Farkas	Rozsi	15.10.1923	Sevljus	Sevljus
Farkas	Gizi	28.5.1924	Csenger	Avasivaros
Farkas	Gizella	5.4.1926	Fehergyarmat	Rozsaly
Farkas	Zali	15.8.1912	Visk	Visk
Farkas	Berta	2.6.1922	Lipcse	Heringse
Feldmann	Helene	17.12.1908	Gönc	Szerencs
Fenyo	Anna	11.3.1929	Satoraljaujhely	Paczen
Fenyo	Piroska	18.6.1906	Satoraljaujhely	Satoraljaujhely
Ferenz	Irene	20.7.1911	Tunyog	Tunyog
Feuereisen	Lili	11.4.1929	KralovskyChlmec	Lelesz
Feuereisen	Magda	27.8.1925	KralovskyChlmec	Lelesz
Feuerisen	Hajnal	29.9.921	KralovskyChlmec	Lelesz
Feuerstein	Iren	28.10.1924	Munkacevo	Munkacevo
Fischer	Angyal	11.5.1912	Gyekenyes	Gyekenyes
Fischer	Charlotte	25.11.1921	Nagytat	Nagytat
Fischer	Ilona	10.10.1928	Sapi Petrij	Sapi Petrij
Fischer	Katharine	9.2.1920	Nagytat	Kaposvar
Fischer	Seren	28.5.1924	Fehergyarmat	Fehergyarmat
Fischer	Serene	8.6.1899	Ujpest	Ujpest
Fischer	Suzanna	29.3.1924	Nagytat	Nagytat
Fischmann	Lina	16.9.1929	Ujfeherto	Ujfeherto

Last Name	First Name	Date of Birth	Residence	Place of Birth
Fischmann	Margit	23.7.1923	Ujfeherto	Ujfeherto
Fixel	Debora	18.6.1922	Szaszregen	Szaszregen
Flach	Judith	15.4.1928	Siogard	Siogard
Flesch	Jolan	23.6.1910	Aszalo	Hernadszurdok
Flohr	Edith	26.1.1910	Miskolc	Miskolc
Fodor	Margit	10.11.1910	Papa	Papa
Frank	Elisabeth	5.5.1917	Miskolc	Mezökeresztes
Frank	Katharina	23.9.1921	Miskolc	Budapest
Frankel	Helene	10,3,1924	Ujfeherto	Ujfeherto
Frankel	Foriska	3.11.1923	Gyöngyös	Gyöngyös
Frankel	Giselle	7.7.1923	Ujfeherto	Ujfeherto
Frankel	Edith	3.8.1929	Bankesi	Bankesi
Frankel	Alice	16.6.1929	Slov.Meder	Slov.Meder
Frankel	Therese	7.8.1925	Slov.Meder	Slov.Meder
Frankl	Eva	2.2.1921	Budapest	Budapest
Frankl	Helene	2.2.1922	Jaszfenyszaru	Jaszfenyszaru
Fried	Josefa	23.8.1924	Budapest	Dombo
Friedmann	Margarete	31.8.1926	Rozsaly	Rozsaly
Friedmann	Margit	26.1.1920	Tötibyhormegye	Tötibyhormegye
Friedmann	Jolan	18.5.1928	Seteny	Seteny
Friedmann	Maria	16.12.1915	Tiszadob	Tiszadob
Friedmann	Elvira	11.6.1924	Rozsaly	Rozsaly
Friedmann	Lili	27.1.1926	Bodrogkeresztur	Bodrogkeresztur
Friedmann	Rosa	17.12.1919	Bodrogkeresztur	Bodrogkeresztur
Friedmann	Judit	26.7.1930	Dombovar	Dombovar
Friedmann	Etel	3.9.1917	Bodrogkeresztur	Bodrogkeresztur
Friedmann	Boris	21.3.1908	Budapest	Harsfalva
Friedmann	Klara	9.1.1929	Bodrogkeresztur	Bodrogkeresztur
Friedmann	Aranka	29.6.1929	Szeteny	Szeteny
Friedmann	Aranka	4.10.1927	Tiszabercel	Tiszabercel
Friedmann	Adele	21.9.1921	Bodrogkeresztur	Bodrogkeresztur
Friedmann	Edit	1.9.1924	Bodrogkeresztur	Bodrogkeresztur
Frommer	Therese	19.2.1929	Harsvolvo	Harsvolvo
Fuchs	Judit	28.10.1929	Tirgu Mures	Tirgu Mures
Fuchs	Rozsi	31.7.1924	Nagymagyar	Nagymagyar
Fuchs	Blanka	2.7.1929	Nagymagyar	Nagymagyar
Fuchs	Szeren	30.9.1923	Kosice	Poprad Oekros
Fülep	Agnes	27.3.1929	Mateszalka	Mateszalka
Fulmann	Rozsi	31.7.1924	Szabatin	Szabatin
Fülöp	Rosa	28.9.1898	Mateszalka	Mateszalka
Fürst	Babi Blanka	2.5.1914	Nagyatad	Somogycsurgo
Garfunkel	Gisela	30.3.1915	Siklos	Budapest
Gaty	Judith	8.3.1928	Szekesfehervar	Szekesfehervar
Gedajlovics	Dora	15.8.1920	Fecsi	Irhoc
Gedajlovics	Josefine	11.1.1931	Irhoc	Irhoc
Gelb	Dora	25.2.1926	Ilonkaujfalu	Ilonkaujfalu
Geller	Helene	20.9.1915	Budfalva	Budfalva
Gerö	Irena	10.6.1927	Kecskemet	Kecskemet
Glück	Valeria	18.5.1928	Szatmarcseke	Szatmarcseke

Last Name	First Name	Date of Birth	Residence	Place of Birth
Glück	Aurelie	1.4.1922	Mateszalka	Mateszalka
Glück	Margit	17.5.1924	Mateszalka	Mateszalka
Glück	Erzsebeth	27.11.1923	Hort	Hort
Glück	Gisella	16.3.1915	Mateszalka	Mateszalka
Glückova	Irena	11.11.1908	Kosice	Uzhorod
Goddiner	Anna	9.8.1925	Gebe	Kotali
Godinger	Ida	4.4.1928	Harsfalva	Harsfalva
Godinger	Regina	28.1.1930	Harsfalva	Harsfalva
Goldberger	Lenke	8.6.1928	Berekövösd	Berekövösd
Goldberger	Serena	13.12.1925	Foroencs	Foroencs
Goldberger	Helene	27.9.1917	Nagyrakocs	Nagyrakocs
Goldenfeld	Aranka	10.12.1927	Cluj	Kisarmas
Golkranz	Chaja	5.5.1910	Lodz	Lodz
Goldstein	Jolan	15.3.1917	Gönc	Gönc
Goldstein	Rozsi	21.8.1912	Kokovölt	Bodfalu
Gottesmann	Agnes	31.10.1922	Sarospatak	Sarospatak
Gottlieb	Erzsi	29.6.1909	Taktaprugy	Prugy
Gottlieb	Anna	13.2.1905	Prugy	Prugy
Greiner	Ibolya	13.8.1928	Huta	Nagymagyar
Griffel	Eszter	13.9.1901	Ratosnya	Also Viso
Gross	Márta	15.7.1928	Krachlumec	Krachlumec
Grosz	Susane	28.11.1927	Karcag	Karcag
Grosz	Anna	15.6.1925	Tokaj	Tokaj
Grosz	Elisabeth	30.10.1926	Komarom	Komarom
Grosz	Eva	20.7.1926	Gelenes	Nyirpapos
Grosz	Ilona	8.1.1911	Komarom	Komarom
Groszmann	Elisabaeth	3.10.1926	Budapest	Szatmarokorirto
Groszmann	Eva	20.7.1926	Gönc	Miskolc
Groszmann	Olga	3.3.1929	Debrecen	Szatmarokorirto
Grün	Jolan	15.6.1917	Tirgu Mures	Palotailva
Grünbaum	Edit	28.811925	Keszthely	Tapolcsa
Grünberger	Rozsi	28.8.1929	Keneszpata	Keneszpata
Grünberger	Charlotte	7.4.1925	Dombo	Dombo
Grünberger	Ilona	24.1.1917	Tirgu Mures	Hernadnemeti
Grünberger	Jolan	7.6.1911	Tiszabogdany	Kozeppapsa
Grünberger	Magdolna	21.5.1918	Satoraljaujhely	Satoraljaujhely
Grünspanova	Piroska	31.5.1928	Kosice	Kosice
Guttmann	Eva	24.10.1923	Szaszregen	Dombo
Guttmann	Irene	30.9.1925	Osta	Nyiregyhaza
Guttmann	Regine	12.12.1924	Szaszregen	Nyiregyhaza
Guttmann	Magda	1.11.1923	Osta	Nyiregyhaza
Guttmann	Aranka	12.3.1924	Hernadvecse	Hernadvecse
Gyamant	Edit	31.12.1927	Toti Bihov	Toti
Gyemant	Ibolya	15.9.1922	Toti Bihov	Toti
Heisler	Rozsi	7.12.1911	Olsorepa	Olsorepa
Heisler	Helena	25.8.1925	Halmi	Halmi
Heller	Erna	2.12.1924	Tirgu Mures	Gyemesbukk
Heller	Erena	8.9.1912	Szatmarnemeti	Egri
Hercz	Magda	15.1.1924	Temesvar	Fehergyarmat

Last Name	First Name	Date of Birth	Residence	Place of Birth
Hersckovits	Ester	25.8.1929	Kalma	Revkolostor
Herschovitc	Elisabeth	3.11.1920	Munkacevo	Munkacevo
Hersko	Helen	10.10.1917	Nagykaroly	Nagykaroly
Herskovics	Etel	6.11.1921	Oszemere	Bercsenye Falva
Herskovics	Lenke	24.3.1920	Oszemere	Bercsenye Falva
Herskovits	Irene	20.11.1920	Margitta	St. Peredzeny
Herskovits	Margarete	6.3.1913	Budapest	Budapest
Herskovits	Mariska	8.7.1923	Doboruska	Doboruska
Herskovits	Helene	10.5.1930	Kalna	Revkolostor
Herskovits	Iboja	10.5.1929	Margitta	Margitta
Herskovits	Berta	10.8.1927	Kalna	Revkolostor
Herskovits	Sara	15.2.1925	Margitta	Szilagy Perncry
Herskovits	Etel	13.1.1920	Ujpest	Nyirbator
Hilf	Helena	6.10.1908	KralovskyChlmec	Nagytarkany
Hirsch	Bella	22.9.1908	Tirgu Mures	Mezyponyt
Hirsch	Ilona	23.5.1928	St.Michaly	St.Michaly
Hirsch	Maria	30.11.1926	Kacko	Kacko
Hirsch	Lilli	22.3.1915	Esztergom	Esztergom
Hoffmann	Margit	18.9.1929	Papa	Papa
Hoffmann	Rozsi	25.8.1928	Papa	Papa
Hochfelder	Anna	19.12.1919	Budapest	Budapest
Hochfelder	Franziska	15.10.1927	Zakany	Zakany
Hutterer	Margit	24.10.1925	Vac	Vac
Ilkovicz	Margit	25.3.1923	Bacsava	Bacsava
Indig	Erzsebet	8.2.1922	Marmarossziget	Marmarossziget
Indig	Sari	14.6.1918	Marmarossziget	Marmarossziget
Israel	Margit	1.5.1925	Alör	Alör
Israel	Sara	11.11.1926	Mazöband	Mazöband
Israel	Eszter	4.11.1928	Alör	Alör
Izsak	Laura	5.2.1921	Balavasan	Kiskend
Janduich	Rosa	26.9.1922	Boly	Boly
Jankovits	Helene	13.11.1919	Füzösmezö	Füzösmezö
Janovits	Ibolya	30.10.1923	Szolnocska	Szolnocska
Janovits	Erzsi	20.5.1928	Szolnocska	Szolnocska
Jassinger	Jolan	24.4.1912	Debrecen	Debrecen
Javor	Aranka	10.5.1900	Budapest	Szöreg
Jurovits	Rozsi	19.8.1924	Marmarossziget	Marmarossziget
Jurovitsch	Julia	19.4.1918	Marmarossziget	Marmarossziget
Juckoviczova	Ilona	6.9.1916	Uzhorod	Uzhorod
Kaff	Lea	15.9.1928	Bonyhad	Bonyhad
Kaff	Flora	6.4.1917	Binyhad	Binyhad
Kaff	Judith	15.9.1828	Bonyhad	Bonyhad
Kahan	Hanna	6.2.1923	Taktoharkany	Ötvösfalva
Kahan	Márta	6.4.1925	Gyöngyös	Gyöngyös
Kaller	Frida	26.4.1921	Ollaczertes	Ollaczertes
Kardos	Borbala	22.9.1920	Kapuvar	Kapuvar
Karischmaroff	Elisabath	21.7.1921	Budapest	Szombathely
Karpeles	Anna	3.5.1917	Polotailva	Polatailva
Katz	Ilona	21.3.1917	Satoraljaujhely	Satoraljaujhely

Last Name	First Name	Date of Birth	Residence	Place of Birth
Katz	Tobi	25.10.1924	Dombo	Dombo
Katz	Jolan	30.8.1923	Mariapocs	Mariapocs
Katz	Rozsi	22.11.1922	Dombrad	Dombrad
Katz	Rosa	29.7.1926	Nagyrucska	Nagyrucska
Katz	Ibolya	26.3.1923	Kezdyszentlelek	Braso
Katz	Rosa	26.6.1913	Satoraljaujhely	Satoraljaujhely
Katz	Etelka	12.12.1923	Ollaczertes	Ollaczertes
Katz	Edith	21.4.1923	Nagyricska	Nagyricska
Keisler	Iren	10.8.1926	Nyiregyhaza	Nyiregyhaza
Keisler	Klara	15.7.1928	Nyiregyhaza	Nyiregyhaza
Keller	Ilona	9.8.1920	Satoraljaujhely	
Kemeny	Anna	5.10.1905	Kiskunfelegyhaza	Nezsidek
Kertesz	Alice	29.6.1928	Berzence	Pecs
Kertesz	Katherina	2.2.1908	Berzence	Nagykanizsa
Kivovits	Agnes	19.12.1929	Nagykovesd	Satoralaujhely
Klein	Margit	15.3.1923	Ujfeherto	Nyirbator
Klein	Sari	25.12.1909	Kiskunfelegyhaza	Kiskunfelegyhaza
Klein	Karoline	18.11.1907	Kiskunfelegyhaza	Kiskunfelegyhaza
Klein	Sara	17.10.1927	Tunyog	Tunyog
Klein	Terez	31.8.1908	Marmarossziget	Marmarossziget
Klein	Roza	15.3.1920	Ujfeherto	Nyirbeltek
Klein	Livia	16.7.1929	Bicske	Budapest
Klein	Lilli	24.3.1929	Satoraljaujhely	Satoraljaujhely
Klein	Klara	31.1.1921	Ujfeherto	Gyulahaza
Klein	Seren	6.7.1924	Szeklence	Szeklence
Klein	Gisella	2.12.904	Ujfeherto	Ilk
Klein	Eva	17.8.1929	Debrecen	Debrecen
Klein	Edith	18.6.1929	Rad	Rad
Klein	Rozsi	9.8.1917	Fehergyarmat	Fehergyarmat
Klein	Edith	18.4.1926	Satoraljaujhely	Satoraljaujhely
Klein	Edith	28.9.1906	Krachlumec	Krachlumec
Klein	Agnes	29.4.1927	Satoraljaujhely	Satoraljaujhely
Klein	Hermine	26.8.1920	Ujfeherto	Ujfeherto
Kleinmann	Mimi	4.10.1925	Harsfalva	Harsfalva
Kleinman	Helene	21.12.1928	Nagyabrany	Nagyabrany
Klempner	Bruis	2.11.1926	Megyesgombas	Megyesgombas
Klempner	Fanni	12.11.1924	Megyesgombas	Megyesgombas
Kohn	Eta	17.9.1922	Nagyigmand	Nagyigmand
Kohn	Margarete	21.4.1916	Pocsaj	Pocsaj
Kohn	Magda	8.11.1915	Lucenec	Krompach
Kohn	Ilona	19.12.1901	Budapest	Zajugrov
Kohn	Erzsebeth	9.10.1910	Nyiregyhaza	Nyiregyhaza
Kohn	Rozsa	8.3.1912	Baracska	Magyarkeresztur
Kohn	Edit	28.11.1924	Budapest	Budapest
Kohn	Erzsebeth	1.9.1920	Ujpest	Trencin
Kolman	Ester	6.10.1913	Vac	Vac
Kolman	Edith	14.5.1929	Vac	Vac
Korach	Anna	2.10.1910	Berehovo	Berehovo
Kornitzer	Alice	2.7.1923	Tolicsva	Szerencs

Last Name	First Name	Date of Birth	Residence	Place of Birth
Kosa	Agnes	5.5.1920	Sarospatak	Sarospatak
Kostolitz	Sidonia	22.11.1907	Buzsak	Buzsak
Kövesi	Julia	26.2.1929	Esztergom	Esztergom
Kövesi	Magda	3.7.1922	Esztergom	Szeged
Kövesi	Margit	18.2.1900	Esztergom	Esztergom
Kramer	Hermine	15.3.1907	Budapest	Budapest
Krammer	Klara	13.7.1923	Streda/Bodrogom	Streda/Bodrogom
Krausz	Rozsi	15.1.20	Satoraljaujhely	Satoraljaujhely
Krausz	Margit	27.1.1927	Satoraljaujhely	Szatmarnemeti[3]
Krausz	Margarete	10.10.1928	Bana	Bana
Krausz	Ilona	15.4.1928	Satoraljaujhely	
Krausz	Alice	23.1.1926	Edeleny	Edeleny
Krausz	Eva	18.2.1929	Satoraljaujhely	Satoraljaujhely
Kreisman	Lenke	3.2.1920	Bilke	
Krelan	Jozsefin	25.7.1922	Dzialoszyce	Bilke
Kremer	Margarete	18.1.1928	Bodrogkeresztur	
Krischer	Olga	25.3.1922	Hernadvecse	Hernadvecse
Kuhn	Rozsi	3.12.1908	Tirgu Mures	Felsöoroszi
Kupferstein	Eva	9.5.1925	Ujfeherto	Ujfeherto
Kupferstein	Klari	7.12.1920	Ujfeherto	Ujfeherto
Kupferstein	Margit	27.2.1917	Ujfeherto	Ujfeherto
Kurlender	Magda	23.2.1925	Budapest	Budapest
Kyri	Susane	18.2.1928?		Cseper
Kyri	Márta	11.8.1920	Szigedvar	Gardony
Laendler	Agnes	5.11.1927	Cluj	Galocas
Landstein	Lilli	2.7.1929	Totmagyar	Totmagyar
Landstein	Elisabeth	15.10.1923	Totmagyar	Isznyete
Landstein	Charlotte	26.4.1925	Totmagyar	Isznyete
Lang	Margarete	17.8.1923	Gönc	Gönc
Lang	Elisabeth	21.1.1922	Abaujvar	Abaujvar
Lauber	Magda	7.2.1922	Szaszregen	Holtmaros
Lauber	Erna	12.12.1930	Bethlen	Bethlen
Lautmann	Erna	6.4.1929	Csenger	Csenger
Lazar	Judith	9.8.1927	Cluj	Cluj
Lazar	Rozsi	22.10.1926	Kovarad	Besterice
Lazar	Gizela	25.10.1914	Nyirvasvari	Nyirlugos
Lazar	Jolan	8.7.1906	Szaszregen	Kisbudakon
Leb	Ilona	26.11.1925	Rodaszinye	Marosbogato
Leb	Margit	30.10.1927	Rodaszinye	Marosbogato
Lebovics	Szeren	28.4.1929	Bilke	Bilke
Lebovicz	Piri	20.5.1923	Harsfalva	Harsfalva
Lebovitc	Rosa	22.4.1923	Herincse	Herincse b.Chust
Lebovitc	Malvine	8.8.1926	Bilke	Bilke
Lebovits	Lilly	8.2.1910	Szekelyudvarhely	Kronstad
Lebovits	Pepi	3.9.1924	Dombo	Dombo
Lefkovics	Lilli	12.4.1926	Tunyog	Tunyog
Lefkovits	Aranka	8.2.1924	Vac	Vac
Lefkovits	Lea	18.2.1922	Vac	Vac
Lefkowicz	Maria	28.4.1907	Satoraljaujhely	Satoraljaujhely

Last Name	First Name	Date of Birth	Residence	Place of Birth
Leichtag	Irene	31.3.1922	Domony	Ordötarsa
Leichtag	Margit	11.6.1924	Domony	Domony
Leiner	Elisabeth	30.6.1908	Kosice	Kosice
Liebermann	Mancy	9.5.1930	Szolyva	Strojno
Lichtblau	Valerie	1.6.1923	Vac	Vac
Lichtig	Eta	26.5.1911	Uzhorod	Vysni Studeny
Lichtmann	Jolan	5.9.1920	Szatmarnemeti	Batiz
Lichtmann	Judith	14.4.1930	Debrecen	Debrecen
Löbl	Gedwig	18.2.1926	Tirgu Mures	Gyergyöfoldes
Lorand	Vera	8.5.1928	Tolcsva	Miskolc
Lorand	Aurelie	23.10.1904	Tolcsva	Tolcsva
Lorber	Edit	28.1.1924	Püspökladany	Püspökladany
Lorber	Margit	8.4.1922	Püspökladany	Püspökladany
Lorber	Gabriella	29.12.1923	Püspökladany	Püspökladany
Lorber	Margit	2.9.1918	Püspökladany	Püspökladany
Lörincz	Margit	19.5.1912	Margitta	Szilagycseh
Löw	Gizella	18.7.1925	Vac	Vac
Löwy	Livia	23.9.1921	Soroksar	Vamospercs
Löwy	Helene	8.12.1914	Barcs	alsotapaszt
Löwy	Rosa	25.5.1925	Barcs	Barcs
Maget	Márta	12.6.1923	Kosice	Kostany
Macher	Ida	22.7.1908	Kapavar	Felsöszentmiklos
Markovits	Dora	15.2.1928	Domokos	Domokos
Markovits	Ilona	16.1.1920	Mezökiralyfalva	Mezökiralyfalva
Markovits	Lilly	16.12.1922	Domokos	Domokos
Markowits	Etel	3.12.1922	Bereknagyalmas	Bereknagyalmas
Marton	Rozsi	13.10.1928	Margita	Erbogyoszlo
Mauskopf	Frieda	3.3.1927	Irsava	Volosko
Mauskopf	Gizi	29.11.1927	Irsava	Kisbaranko
Mauskopf	Helene	2.5.1926	Irsava	Volosko
Mauskopf	Malvine	14.4.1926	Irsava	Kanyispatak
Mautner	Edith	28.8.1924	Iregszemcse	Iregszemcse
Mayer	Sari	21.7.1928	Papa	Papa
Mayer	Julie	26.1.1907	Budapest	Apastag
Mehes	Erzsebet	18.12.1913	BarcsDraeropuszta	Csurgo
Mechlowits	Cornelia	18.6.1923	Szatmarnemeti	Szatmarnemeti
Meizlik	Gizi	17.7.1912	Strojo	Strojo
Meizlik	Hani	21.8.1918	Strojo	Strojo
Meizlik	Margit	26.10.1928	Strojo	Strojo
Mendelovitc	Rozsa	15.5.1924	Viso Orosi	Viso Orosi
Mendelsohn	Sali	20.8.1926	Alparet	Alparet
Mermelstein	Magda	1.1.1929	Nagyszölös	Nagyszölös
Mojzler	Eva	23.3.1926	Miskolc	Budapest
Moldovan	Irene	3.6.1919	Szatmarnemeti	Batiz
Molnar	Ibolya	25.4.1918	Satoraljaujhely	Satoraljaujhely
Moskovits	Margit	12.10.1921	Vaja	Bereg-kövesd
Moskovits	Piroska	24.2.1904	Berehovo	Brehovo
Moskovits	Sari	21.11.1921	Tiaczevo	Volchovce
Moskovits	Eva	19.3.1928	Sarospatak	Sarospatak

Last Name	First Name	Date of Birth	Residence	Place of Birth
Moskovits	Iren	6.8.1926	Szaszlekentze	Szaszlekentze
Moskovitz	Erzsebet	15.7.1922	Jaszarokszallas	Felsöszolcza
Mozes	Piri	14.5.1916	Nagysomkut	Nagysomkut
Müller	Katharina	18.6.1925	Losonu	Magyarhegymeg
Müller	Rosa	12.1.1924	Alsokalinfolvo	Alsokalinfolvo
Müller	Helene	15.11.1928	Alsokalinfolvo	Alsokalinfolvo
Müller	Szerena	30.3.1928	Majdan	Vysni Bystra
Neu	Irene	23.1.1919	Udvard	Udvard
Neuman	Frida	13.5.1932	Halmi	Halmi
Neumann	Fanny	12,1,1927	Alsokalinfolvo	Alsokalinfolvo
Neumann	Ilona	31.10.1919	Rimaszombat	Rimaszombat
Nussbacher	Lea	12.5.1919	Tirgu Mures	Nassa
Perl	Rene	2.8.1923	Alsoegred	Alsoegred
Perl	Therese	6.9.1928	Alsoegred	Alsoegred
Politzer	Maria	18.5.1929	Papa	Papa
Pollak	Esti	18.8.1926	Cluj	Maramaros
Preisler	Magda	12.2.1915	Debrecen	Debrecen
Preisler	Aranka	16.2.1926	Vac	Budapest
Preisz	Agnes	31.8.1925	Pecsvarad	Dombovar
Pressburger	Rozsi	17.9.1930	Bicske	Bicske
Pressburger	Margit	6.10.1920	Bicske	Bicske
Raab	Agnes	18.5.1928	Gyöngyös	Gyöngyös
Raab	Katharina	12.11.1926	Gyöngyös	Gyöngyös
Rabin	Elizabeth	28.11.1920	Kosice	Csolto
Regeni	Etel	16.10.1925	Tirgu Mures	Budapest
Reich	Elza	1512.1925	Abaujszanto	Abaujker
Reinfeld	Elvira	3.12.1920	Dombovar	Lörinczi
Reinfeld	Erna	20.4.1913	Dombovar	Lörinczi
Reinfeld	Ibolya	25.12.1914	Dombovar	Lörinczi
Reinitz	Ilona	12.3.1911	Damak	Damak
Revesz	Katalin	8.7.1917	Tirgu Mures	Tirgu Mures
Riesz	Eva	5.6.1927	Jaszfenyszo	Jaszfenyszo
Riesz	Ibolya	13.1.1929	Jaszfenyszo	Jaszfenyszo
Roab	Marion	1.1.1915	Komarom	Komarom
Roab	Ethel	26.8.1923	Komarom	Komarom
Rosenbaum	Manci	1.9.1928	Solocsin	Solocsin
Rosenberg	Ilona	25.8.1912	Budszentmihaly	Budszentmihaly
Rosenberg	Olga	18.12.1904	Cluj	Zutor
Rosenberg	Magda	15.6.1923	Berland	Petres
Rosenberg	Helene	16.12.1929	Csenger	Nyirgebe
Rosenberg	Helene	2.10.1923	Csalökzaranyos	Mukacevo
Rosenberg	Edit	9.7.1919	Edeleny	Edeleny
Rosenberg	Ilona	3.5.1921	Keszthely	Veszprem
Rosenberg	Hajnal	29.5.1928	Bata	Zagon
Rosenberg	Eva	30.1.1921	Bita	Kereszvar
Rosenblatt	Sarolta	14.5.1925	Teke	Teke
Rosenfeld	Elisabeth	5.11.1922	Bely	Bely
Rosenfeld	Magda	20.10.1925	Ratesnya	Ratesnya
Rosenfeld	Szeren	22.2.1922	Nagy Sajo	Nagy Sajo

Last Name	First Name	Date of Birth	Residence	Place of Birth
Rosenfeld	Else	21.10.1909	Tirgu Mures	Deva
Rosenfeld	Charlotte	12.9.1908	Cluj	Korosmezo
Rosenfeld	Berta	16.10.1915	Ratosnya	Ratosnya
Rosenfeld	Anna	17.9.1923	Edeleny	Edeleny
Rosenthal	Frieda	19.4.1928	Fehegyarmat	Fehegyarmat
Rosenthal	Alis	25.1.1928	Miskolc	Miskolc
Rosenzweig	Rosa	21.10.1911	Ujpest	Dunabogdany
Rosner	Lilly	29.12.1926	Nagyigmand	Vac
Rosner	Aranka	26.5.1929	Nagyigmand	Vac
Roth	Olga	3.1.1925	Tiszaberczel	Tiszaberczel
Roth	Magda	22.3.1926	Tiszaberczel	Tiszaberczel
Roth	Klara	5.5.1928	Tiszaberczel	Tiszaberczel
Roth	Ella	10.6.1927	Tiszaberczel	Tiszaberczel
Roth	Elisabeth	8.4.1920	Tiszaberczel	Tiszaberczel
Roth	Elisabeth	14.7.1924	Tiszaberczel	Tiszaberczel
Rothberg	Eva	22.5.1928	Hortyszger	Budapest
Rotschild	Etta	12.4.1923	Szaszregen	Romoly
Rotschild	Lukretia	28.3.1922	Felsoviso	Felsoviso
Rotschild	Helene	4.7.1917	Szaszregen	Szaszregen
Rottberger	Eva	22.5.1922	Budapest	Budapest
Rottenstein	Helene	15.2.1930	Nagy Torno	Nagy Torno
Rottenstein	Lenke	15.4.1924	Nagy Torno	Nagy Torno
Rubin	Klara	13.4.1928	Szikszo	Szikszo
Rubinstein	Eszter	18.5.1926	Komarom	Komarom
Ruder	Anna	2.8.1927	Ozora	Ozora
Rundberg	Berta	20.12.1920	Lodz	Lodz
Ruttner	Fanny	12.11.1926	Tecso	Tecso
Sajovits	Eva	2.12.1929	Micske	Micske
Sajovits	Ilona	4.12.1921	Cluj	Kyskaldta
Sajovits	Sara	22.1.1924	Cluj	Kyskaldta
Sajovits	Elisabeth	24.6.1926	Micske	Micske
Salamon	Rosa	12.10.1895	Mako	Mako
Salamon	Ilona	29.6.1910	Tirgu Mures	Nagyvarad
Salamon	Irene	28.7.1928	Nagyecsed	Nagyecsed
Salamon	Olga	14.10.1929	Tirgu Mures	Tirgu Mures
Salamonovits	Ilona	29.7.1930	Sajopetry	Sajopetry
Seelfreund	Irene	18.12.1928	Nagyhalasz	Nagyhalasz
Seelfreund	Ella	8.6.1927	Nagyhalasz	Nagyhalasz
Segal	Gisella	4.8.1927	Györgyö	Gyergyuszarhegy
Segal	Rozsi	5.1.1928	Györgyö	Gyergyuszarhegy
Seidenfeld	Emma	14.2.1926	Bodrogkeresztur	Bodrogkeresztur
Seidenfeld	Edith	6.7.1929	Bodrogkeresztur	Bodrogkeresztur
Seidenfeld	Aranka	24.12.1923	Bodrogkeresztur	Bodrogkeresztur
Seligokovits	Seren	8.1.1929	Alacsertes	Alacsertes
Selikovic	Ida	31.1.1925	Visk	Visk
Selikovic	Saly	31.1.1925	Visk	Visk
Serbu	Therese	6.1.1924	Gyergyosztmiklos	Gyergyovolges
Serfer	Maria	26.2.1906	Dunafoldvar	Ragolmas
Schattin	Edith	14.12.1925	Sarospatak	Sarospatak

Last Name	First Name	Date of Birth	Residence	Place of Birth
Scheer	Magda	22.2.1926	Demecser	Kek
Scheer	Klara	25.7.1929	Demecser	Kek
Scheer	Helena	10.1.1924	Kemecse	Kemecse
Scheer	Elisabeth	24.12.1921	Kemecse	Kemecse
Scheiner	Rozsi	14.6.1924	Szaploncza	Nagybocsko
Scheiner	Berta	1.1.1921	Szaploncza	Nagybocsko
Scher	Lilly	22.5.1921	Ujfeherto	Ujfeherto
Schindler	Rezi	8.12.1928	Strojno	Strojno
Schönberger	Erna	18.7.1927	Bonyhard	Bonyhard
Schück	Livia	25.12.1924	Ipolyszog	Ipolyszog
Schulek	Elisabeth	8.10.1910	Lucenec	Lucenec
Schulsinger	Selma	15.8.1928	Szaszregen	Bystritz
Schüttler	Ilona	30.7.1907	Csingo	Csingo
Schvarts	Julianna	18.11.1922	Budapest	Nyirbator
Schvarts	Irene	24.2.1010	Ujfeherto	Ujfeherto
Schvartz	Zuze	24.10.1924	Udvar	Udvar
Schwarcz	Johanna	21.6.1928	Szaszlekencze	Szaszlekencze
Schwartz	Margit	23.12.1923	Sapsisztentgyorgy	Komando
Schwartz	Aranka	27.10.1910	Udvard	Menyhe
Schwartz	Edith	8.10.1918	Komarno	Wien
Schwartz	Elisabeth	12.7.1922	Sapsisztentgyorgy	Beretoszaplok
Schwartz	Helena	29.6.1929	Szamosujvar	Szamosujvar
Schwartz	Ilona	3.6.1927	Sapsisztentgyorgy	Komando
Schwarz	Hermina	8.6.1927	Szamosujvar	Szamosujvar
Schwarz	Katharina	10.6.1925	Hatvan	Hatvan
Schwarz	Katharina	24.6.1924	Szamoaujvar	Szamoaujvar
Schwarz	Magda	4.2.1928	Miskolc	Beregszasz
Schwarz	Regina	24.12.1922	Szamosujvar	Szamosujvar
Schwarz	Rosalia	29.5.1928	Udvard	Bratislava
Schwarz	Rosalia	6.8.1922	Felsö Barakony	Felsö Barakony
Scweiger	Erzsebet	12.11.1910	Satoraljaujhely	Satoraljaujhely
Schwimmer	Hajnal	8.12.1929	Nagybereg	Nagybereg
Silber	Szeren	2.3.1907	Satoraljaujhely	Satoraljaujhely
Silberstein	Lenke	10.2.1918	Hidalmas	Hidalmas
Silberstein	Gitta	25.3.1927	Vac	Zenta
Silberstein	Irene	9.12.1927	Hidalmas	Hidalmas
Silberstein	Szerena	12.7.1924	Hidalmas	Hidalmas
Simon	Klara	9.10.1920	Heviz	Balatonboglar
Simon	Cecilia	2.8.1906	Cluj	Almasmalon
Singer	Helene	25.7.1930	Irsava	Irsava
Singer	Helene	10.2.1913	Zakany	Haromfa
Singer	Aureile	17.7.1906	Neusatz	Nagybicse
Solomon	Helene	25.3.1927	Domokos	Domokos
Solomon	Sari	30.10.1925	Szaszlekence	St. Mate
Span	Elvira	30.5.1928	Nagymagyar	Nagymagyar
Span	Erna	1.11.1930	Nagymagyar	Nagymagyar
Span	Livia	14.8.1922	Nagymagyar	Nagymagyar
Spirer	Ilonka	12.12.1924	Czikzereda	Nyaradgalfalva
Spitz	Anna Judit	26.5.1928	Sarospatak	Sarospatak

Last Name	First Name	Date of Birth	Residence	Place of Birth
Spitz	Bella	26.11.1906	Sarospatak	Kosice
Spitz	Herta	16.3.1923	Komarno	Bratislava
Spitz	Katalin	7.1.1926	Sarospatak	Sarospatak
Spitzer	Rozsa	26.3.1921	Koszeb Borge	Koszeb Borge
Stauber	Piri	5.5.1920	Petrova	Petrova
Stein	Livia	25.11.1923	Vasarosnameny	Budapest
Stein	Szeren	5.11.1926	Posmus	Posmus
Stein	Jolan	10.7.1919	Szekelyudvarhely	Szekelyudvarhely
Steiner	Katharina	31.10.1910	Esztergom	Esztergom
Steiner	Rozsi	20.10.1910	Budapest	Budapest
Steiner	Rozsa	24.2.1921	Cluj	Alsojaro
Stern	Ilona	21.4.1919	Ape	Ape
Stern	Irma	4.4.1903	Barzs	Alsotapaszd
Stern	Frieda	21.1.1909	Harsfalva	Harsfalva
Stern	Bella	15.8.1928	Harsfalva	Harsfalva
Stern	Rozsi	1.3.1912	Marmarossziget	Barcanfalva
Stiglitz	Etta	3.3.1928	Szaszlekence	Szaszlekence
Strausz	Szidonie	30.6.1920	Mako	Cluj
Szabo	Malvine	17.9.1921	Ratosnya	Ratosnya
Szabo	Rozsa	22.10.1901	Szaszregen	Nagybocsko
Szabo	Regina	15.7.1920	Irhocz	Irhocz
Szabo	Piri	25.8.1925	Szaszregen	Szaszregen
Szabo	Lola	26.2.1924	Szaszregen	Szaszregen
Szabo	Gisela	15.6.1930	Irhocz	Irhocz
Szabo	Dora	1.5.1928	Irhocz	Irhocz
Szalay	Edith	21.3.1930	Tirgu Mures	Tirgu Mures
Szameth	Cacilie	5.11.1925	Bodrogkeresztur	Bodrogkeresztur
Szameth	Helene	28.8.1919	Bodrogkeresztur	Bodrogkeresztur
Szameth	Szerene	18.11.1923	Bodrogkeresztur	Bodrogkeresztur
Szameth	Ethel	9.8.1927	Bodrogkeresztur	Bodrogkeresztur
Szasz	Suse	10.4.1929	Tokay	Tokay
Szasz	Ilona	23.4.1905	Tokay	Tokay
Szasz	Ilona	1.5.1904	Budapest	Budapest
Szegal	Regina	3.10.1914	Satorajaujhely	Satorajaujhely
Szekely	Anna	20.5.1925	Kecskemet	Kecskemet
Szep	Katharina	14.12.1900	Budapest	Obecse
Taub	Irene	3.11.1912	Bodrogkeresztur	Ladmocz
Taub	Borbala	4.6.1920	Bdrogkeresztur	Bdrogkeresztur
Taub	Elisabeth	15.11.1922	Somogyszob	Somogyszob
Taub	Helene	12.4.1922	Bodrogkeresztur	Bodrogkeresztur
Terner	Piroska	6.8.1929	Marmarossziget	Marmarossziget
Tischler	Erzsebet	18.5.1910	Balkany	Szentistvanbaksa
Tischler	Erzsebet	12.12.1912	Ujfeherto	
Tischler	Eszter	12.6.1925	Hidalmas	Hidalmas
Tobag	Cilli	5.10.1927	Dombo	Dombo
Tobag	Eta	7.9.1924	Dombo	Dombo
Tobag	Regina	3.4.1929	Dombo	Dombo
Tobag	Margit	1.1.1931	Dombo	Dombo
Traub	Jolan	29.4.1912	Komarno	Budapest

Last Name	First Name	Date of Birth	Residence	Place of Birth
Ungar	Margarete	19.11.1911	Dombovar	?
Vachtenhejm	Rozsa	7.12.1924	Harsfalva	Harsfalva
Vamos	Agnes	2.8.1925	Srospatak	Srospatak
Varadi	Elisabeth	20.9.1908	Komarno	Papa
Vasen	Márta	12.7.1910	Sopron	Wien
Vidder	Sara	25.5.1921	Borgo	
Vogel	Helene	15.5.1924	Kistecsu	Kistecen
Vogel	Fanny	15.4.1922	Kistecen	Kistecen
Wachsman	Jenni	16.7.1922	Bystrica	Magyarlapos
Wartenberg	Eva	30.1.1923	Bistritz	Bistric
Weil	Elisabeth	23.10.1908	Hatvan	Miskolc
Wein	Bluma	24.12.1924	Lodz	Lodz
Weinberger	Iren	1.1.1916	Fehergyarmat	Szatmaicshe
Weinberger	Ibolya	3.11.1916	Legenye	Legenye
Weinberger	Elisabeth	17.2.1924	Kosice	Kosice
Weinberger	Bozsi	3.8.1926	Ladamuc	Ladamuc
Weiner	Futzi	15.6.1918	Tirgu Mures	Marosheviz
Weinstein	Ilona	9.4.1926	KralovskyChlmec	KralovskyChlmec
Weisberg	Judka	25.7.1925	Borzsa Maramuz	Borzsa Maramuz
Weiser	Regina	10.9.1917	Male Zaluzice	Hazin
Weiss	Gizi	22.3.1928	Skolyva	Strojno
Weisz	Zsuzsanna	6.10.1923	Ujpest	Ujpest
Weisz	Maria	13.1.1911	Berzence	Szenta
Weisz	Paula	20.6.1925	Halmi	Halmi
Weisz	Piroska	19.9.1923	Szekelyvalya	Szekelyvalya
Weisz	Rosa	12.6.1928	Kantorjanosi	Kantorjanosi
Weisz	Rosa	19.10.1917	Tunyog	Tunyog
Weisz	Sarolta	10.9.1912	Bacska	Bacska
Weisz	Serena	1.8.1921	Kosice	Nagyberezno
Weisz	Susanne	17.10.1927	Labod	Labod
Weisz	Tinda	10.5.1928	Kanyahaza	Kanyahaza
Weisz	Anna	24.1.1926	Ujpest	Ujpest
Weisz	Maria	4.3.1928	Tirgu Mures	Tirgu Mures
Weisz	Terez	5.2.1915	Nagyszölös	Nagyszölös
Weisz	Irene	28.5.1921	Mezököszöny	Mezököszöny
Weisz	Anna	15.1.1911	Somogyszob	Somogyszob
Weisz	Eszter	5.5.1927	Kotaj	Kotaj
Weisz	Margit	15.6.1919	Gyöngyös	Szucsi
Weisz	Fany	6.2.1924	Nagyecsed	Nagyecsed
Weisz	Berta	20.8.1926	Kanyahaza	Kanyahaza
Weisz	Ida	22.10.1922	Nagyecsed	Nagyecsed
Weisz	Helene	25.10.1918	Kalma	Kalma
Weisz	Ibolya	7.4.1925	Szekelyfalva	Szekelyfalva
Weisz	Erzsebet	29.4.1914	Bacska	Bacska
Weisz	Iren	2.12.1908	Mateszalka	Fehergyarmat
Weisz	Jenny	30.7.1925	Pozmus	Pozmus
Weisz	Jolan	4.9.1919	Fehergyarmat	Fehergyarmat
Weisz	Jolan	26.12.1919	Tunyog	Tunyog
Weisz	Julianne	8.8.1925	Baracska	Baracska

Last Name	First Name	Date of Birth	Residence	Place of Birth
Weisz	Kato	27.5.1922	Ujpest	Ujpest
Weisz	Lenke	4.6.1918	Paszto	Paszto
Weisz	Lenke	24.1.1923	Illonakujfalu	Illonakujfalu
Weisz	Malvin	2.4.1929	Nagymagyar	Nagymagyar
Weisz	Margit	26.7.1917	Mezököszöny	Mezököszöny
Welc	Etel	15.12.1923	Alsosarad	Alsosarad
Welisch	Ilona	22.2.1908	Domlovai	Kaposvar
Wiegner	Klara	26.11.1923	Csikszerda	Magyaro
Wiegner	Elisabeth	28.4.1925	Csikszerda	Magyaro
Wiegner	Ibolya	10.5.1920	Csikszerda	Magyaro
Wiener	Lenke	21.3.1921	Gyöngyös	Gyöngyös
Willheim	Anna	18.10.1903	Udvard	Udvard
Willheim	Adela	28.10.1925	Udvard	Udvard
Winkler	Emma	17.10.1930	Biri Ottotanya	Napkor
Winkler	Magda	29.1.1922	Nagykallo	Kallosemjen
Winkler	Anna	14.4.1918	Nagykallo	Levelek
Winkler	Elisabeth	7.11.1923	Nagykallo	Kallosemjen
Winkler	Lili	21.12.1924	Vac	Vac
Winkler	Ibolya	23.4.1928	Vac	Vac
Winkler	Olga	14.12.1920	Nagykallo	Kallosemjen
Winkler	Piroska	18.5.1918	Kemecse	Nagyhalasz
Winkler	Ella	1.6.1923	Nyirecsaholy	Levelek
Wohlstein	Golda	16.12.1910	Budfalva	Budfalva
Wohlstein	Katharina	8.2.1923	Budapest	Pecs
Wolf	Piroska	16.4.1922	Pinczehely	Pinczehely
Zeisler	Gabriela	18.5.1925	Saroapatak	Saroapatak
Zeisler	Erzsebet	28.12.1929	Szasfe	Szakaczi
Zelmanovits	Kato	18.11.1924	Nagyszölös	Tiszaujlak
Zimmermann	Margit	26.2.1924	Cierna	Cierna
Zimermann	Szeren	28.4.1921	Cierna	Cierna
Zinner	Szeren	6.3.1908	Ujpest	Ujpest
Zisszovitz	Blanka	14.10.1922	Tiszaszirma	Tiszaszirma
Zubek	Eva	10.10.1927	Baracska	Baracska
Zwass	Fanni	29.11.1920	Satoraljaujhely	Satoraljaujhely

[1]Written communication from Theresienstadt Martyrs Remembrance Association, Givat Haim-Ihud, Israel, January 27, 2001.

[2]Rose Hoffmann Davis interview.

[3]Margit Krausz died in Thereseianstadt on 29.6.1945

Appendix C

The Songs in Their Original Text

The following songs were translated into English by the author and included in the narrative.

SONG NUMBER ONE - FROM THE INTRODUCTION:

Múlnak a napok a hetek és honapok;
És még mi már olyan rég a lágerban vagyunk.
Azóta dolgosztunk már mi sokat.
Bejártuk mi már az összes lágerokat,
Elöször Auschwitz azután meg Krakow,
Most Lepzigban vagyunk;
És holnap ki tudja hol leszünk.
Csak ez az egy bátorit:
Hogy nem lesz ez mindég igy.
Egyszer csak mindennek vége lesz,
Az Isten is megsegit.

SONG NUMBER TWO - FROM CHAPTER TWO:

Büszke a Zsidó mert sárga a csillag rajta
Nem busul az nem is olyan fajta,
Huzza az igát egy szebb jövöre várva.

Eljön az idö mikor nem lesz sárga csillag
Akik adták majd csak észbe kapnak
Akik adták ráfognak majd jönni
Hogy a zsidok nélkül nem lehet meglenni

SONG NUMBER THREE - FROM CHAPTER THREE:

Markkleebergbe minden nap hajnal felé mentünk az appelplatz felé.
Es ottan álltunk órákig kezünk lábunk átfázik
Sorakozz ötösével, élén a Blockeltestével

Es a stuben átszámol, Isten öriz ha hiányzol
Löknek jobbra és balra, álljál mindjárt vigyázba
Es ha esik vagy ha fuj, te Zsidó vagy hát ne busulj
Minden elmulik egyszer, minden a végére ér,
Minden December uj Májust igér

SONG NUMBER FOUR - FROM CHAPTER THREE:

Három kislány fen a gáton, elmereng egy rosz lapáton;
Héj nehéz tolni eszt a teli taligát!
Huzzad és vonjad a teli talicskát,
Még ha meguntad is huzzad az igát!
Mert aki eszt elrendelte annak a jó Isten verje,
Hey, vas szögekkel ki a ronda pofáját.

(This was sung to the popular tune of a Hungarian song called "Zöld a kukorica, Kati")

SONG NUMBER FIVE - FROM CHAPTER FOUR:

Drága Lenkém mit kivánjak néked
Valami kedveset, szépet amiböl megérzed
Hogy milyen tiszta szivből szeretlek téged
Szerettem volna hogy otthon legyél
Es ne abstant levest hanem kindlit egyél
De ami késik az nem mulik
Es minden láger élet egyszer csak elmullik.
Hanem mostan te nekünk igéretet teszel
Hogy mához egy évre boldog menyaszony leszel
Is ha esküvődre nem is fogsz meghivni
Szeretettel fogol ránk visza gondolni.

SONG NUMBER SIX - FROM CHAPTER FIVE:
Reggel füttyre ébredünk, jön a blockeltesterünk
Kiabálja minekünk, "alles brics shön machen."
Asztán jön a Zahlappel, sorba állni, aber schnell
Nem kapni ott semi mást csak egy hátbavágást.
Asztán jön a melozás meg a sok sok pofozás
De ez nekünk mit sem tesz mert tudjuk hogy vége lesz.

SONG NUMBER SEVEN - FROM CHAPTER FIVE:

Leipzig mellett van egy kicsi láger,
Ahol furcsa dolgok történnek
Ami othon csak a vicc lapokban jelenhetik
Néha néha meg

Répafaszung volt az egyik este
Amitöl egy lány nagyon rosszul lett.
Szaladtunk is majd kétségbeesve
Hivtuk az Oberscharführert.

A szakramentumát!
Nem kaptok több répát
Es nem fogtok többet freszolni.
Hát kihallott már egy ilyen esetet
Es a nő ijedtébe szûlt egy kis gyereket

(This song was composed to the tune of the Hungarian hit song [*slager*] "Jóska lelkem nézz a fényes égre, hogyha levelem majd megkapod. Gondolj csak az otthoni vidékre és megtalàlod azt a csillagot . . .," which has the same melody as the German wartime song "Pannikam.")

SONG NUMBER EIGHT - FROM CHAPTER SIX:

Mindenki aki a Junkers gyárba jár
Huszon egy, huszon kettö, huszon három
A melót én már alig várom
Aufseherin, csak az az én kérésem
Hogy kilenc napot dolgoztason egy héten
Sok a meló kevés kaja
Senkinek sincs gyomor baja
Este hatkor indulunk mi a gyárba.

SONG NUMBER NINE - FROM CHAPTER SIX:

Mindenki aki a Junkers gyárba jár
Tudja nagyon jól hogy az öreg mit csinál.
Félûnk is tőle, jaj nagyon
Be kel öszintén vallanom.
Markkleeberg egy gyár,
De reméljûk nem halál gyár.

SONG NUMBER TEN - FROM CHAPTER SEVEN:

1944 Mitte November im Markkleeberg
Fünfundzwanzig Jahre Mitte November
Heiratete unser Herr Oberscharführer.
Wir haben heute einer Feiertag,
Und beten zu Gott, da§ er ihn mal,
Da§ der ihn weiter mal.

Er ist unser Führer,
Liebt selten den Scherz;
Aber zu seinen Häftlingen

Hat er doch ein gutes Herz.
Erlebe er in Glücklichkeit.
Sehr viel Freunde und mit G'sundheit,
Die Goldene Hochzeit,
Die Goldene Hochzeit.

Wir feiern von Herzen,
Und stehn hier alle Post
Und bitten Sie bescheiden, heben sie die Kost.
Erleben Sie in Glücklichkeit,
Viel freunde mit G'sundheit
Die Goldene Hochzeit,
Die Goldene Hochzeit.

Wir sagen jetzt alles
Was uns am Herzen lag:
Weineger Zählappell und je öfter Zulage.
Erleben Sie in Glücklichkeit,
Sehr viel freunde mit G'sundheit
Die Diamant-Hochzeit,
Die Diamant-Hochzeit.

SONG NUMBER ELEVEN - FROM CHAPTER SEVEN:

Lesz majd ujra othonunk haza megyünk még
Hatos barrack Isten véled!
Áso, kapa, répa leves elfelejtünk még
Mikor haza felé visz a végzet.
Edes anyánk édes apánk, testvéreink és férjeink
Szép lesz ujra az othonunk, mert élni, élni akarunk.

SONG NUMBER TWELVE - FROM CHAPTER NINE:

Jo anyácskám jaj de szép a térkép
Nem volt ily szép játekom soha
Menyi szin és mennyi ország
Ugy vágyom oda
Am de régen nem mutattad nékem
Hol jár apa Muszka határ szélen
Edesanya át fogja őt forron
Menyországbol nincs térkép szegénykém.

VERSE NUMBER THIRTEEN - FROM CHAPTER NINE:

Israel nincs elveszve még
Táplál minket a reménység,
A Jó Isten amit megigért
Aszt a földet visza adja még.

VERSE NUMBER FOURTEEN - FROM CHAPTER NINE:

Hivnak engem mesze földről balzsamos hegyek
Vége lesz a bujdosásnak, már haza megyek
Otthon, otthon szép hazámban lelkem ujra él
Am Yisrael chai, Am Yisrael chai
Ad bli vidai, ad bli vidai, ad bli vidai

SONG NUMBER FIFTEEN - FROM CHAPTER TEN:

SWEISSEROK

Egyszer volt hol nem volt, volt Németországban
Markkleeberg városában, Lipcse szomszédságában.
A szép hármas blokkban a huszonkettesben
Élt példás rendben és csendben ott tizenkettesben.
Egymást mind szerették, lágerben ez nagy szo
Egyetértésben élt a tizenkét sweisseló.

Szobájuk szép rendes, blokkunkban a példa
A priccsük mind kettes, függönyük madeira.
A lyukak kivágva, kivarrva nem voltak,
Mert himzö pamuthoz jutni már nem tudtak.
Nyolc órát dolgoztak, tiszta volt ruhájuk.
Rendesen mosdottak, szép volt frizurájuk.
Pulóvert is kaptak, lábukon harisnya
Hetenként fürödtek, overáljuk tiszta.

Egyszer volt hol nem volt, ez el is hihető
Igy élt a blokkunkban tizenkét heggesztő.
Zulágot is kaptak, jó étvággyal ettek
A faszung osztásnál ők nem verekedtek.
A fele mindennap reggeli Siktában
Szép csendesen és rendben ment be a vasgyárba.

Szeréyen dolgoztak, nem volt egy megváltás
Ha két óra tizkor bejött a felváltás:
Adri, Lili, Magda, Herta és Rózsika;
Hatodik volt köztük madérás Rózsika.
A másik csoportban volt három testvérpár
Két Lerner, két Zukker meg volt a két Trattner lány.
Adri a Lilinek nem volt bár testvére,
Mint Sziámi ikrek jártak a WC-re.
Herta volt Magdának kenyérben partnere.
De sajnos pechére a csikosat szerette.
Nem ismertem soha, életüknek titkát;
Kit kedvelt a Flamand Alizkát vagy Hertát?

The handwriting of the poem "The Welders" by Erzsebet Frank. The illustrator, whose name is not known, drew the girls with overalls, glasses, and short hair.

Tizenkét heggesztö élete egy álom,
Tizenkét monogram tucat vöröstálon.
Nem is volt a gyárban olyan ki nem tudta,
Hogy negyed háromkor fut be hat sweisserka
Ez volt a friss ujság mindennap a gyárban
Csoda-e mindenki oly nehezen várta.
Megjelent minden nap pontosan délután,
Kivéve vasárnap, tiz két óra után
A vezércikk mindég a fassung volt benne
Hányban van a kenyér, mivel lesz megkenve?

Ezután ez volt a legnagyobb téma.
Nincs e véletlenûl mára marharépa?
Arról is meséltek volt e láger botrány,
Milyen kedvében volt Lucifer, Oberschár?
Leadták ők aszt is legtöbbször pontosan
Lucifer hány kokszot kobzott el a blokkban!
Tizenkét Sweisserka itt köszönöm Néktek,
Hogy Ti nekünk mindig mindent elmeséltek.
Éljetek tovább is szép csendben és rendben
A huszonkettesben: igy tizenkettesben!
EPILÓGUS
Tizenkét Sweisserka haragszom Reátok,
Hogy a pokrócomat el nem vállaltátok
Tanuim vannak rá, sajnos akik látták
Hogy pokrocom pont akkor elorganizálták.

Spät oder doch; jelszoval
Öszinte barátsággal,
Igaz bajtársiasággal.
Frank Erzsébet
Markleeberg 1945 február havában.

SONG NUMBER SIXTEEN - FROM CHAPTER FOURTEEN:

Kisablakok nyilnak egymás után sorban
Muskátli integet át a tulso sorba
Bezárult szemekkel csak egy ablak bámul
Mégis üres minden, hiányzik valaki ebböl az utcábol.

(I sang this song as a lullaby to my children and grandchildren.)

VERSE NUMBER SEVENTEEN - FROM CHAPTER FIFTEEN:

Szeressük egymást gyerekek;
Az élet úgy is tova szál
Es minden percért kár.
Szerssük egymást gyerekek.

A sziv a legszebb kincs;
Ennel szebb szó hogy szeretet
A nagyvilágon nincs
Szeressük egymást gyerekek

Appendix D

Photographs

The author's daughter, Yonit Stessel Levy.

Gitta Nelly

Gitta (Susitzky) Hönig left and her friend Nelly (Wexler) Goral, in 1942.

Sarah (Salamon) Israel with her grandson Moshe Gal, an officer in the Israeli army.

The author's daughter, Miriam Stessel Shenkar.

Gabriella (Braver) Kosinka 1943.

Elza (Reich) Szamosi, 1941.

Nelly Hajnal Rozsa

The Winkler Sisters in 1943. From left to right: Nelly, Hajnal, Rozsa.

Zahava Szász Stessel in Indersdorf, Germany, 1946.

Meier Stessel in 1946.

Amir Ginsburg, Erzsike's son.

The author's grandson, Israel Dov Levy.

The author's granddaughter, Ella Tzofia Levy, in 2006.

The author's granddaughter, Yarin Rachel Levy.

The author's granddaughter, Keshet Shenkar.

The author's grandson, Joshua Shenkar.

Rakefet Shenkar, the author’s granddaughter.

Notes

Introduction

1. Klára Heskovitz Kohen interview. (See Bibliography for complete information on this and other interviews.)

2. Hillel Klein, "The Survivors Search for Meaning and Identity," in *The Nazi Concentration Camps: Proceedings of the Fourth Yad Vashem International Historical Conference, Jerusalem, January 1980* (Jerusalem: Yad Vashem, 1984).

3. Nechama Tec, *Resilience and Courage: Women, Men, and the Holocaust* (New Haven, CT: Yale University Press, 2003), 354.

4. Rochelle G. Saidel, *The Jewish Women of Ravensbrück Concentration Camp* (Madison: University of Wisconsin Press, 2004), 165.

5. See Appendix A: Markkleeberg prisoners' list.

6.For the original Hungarian text, see Appendix C, song number one, from the "Introduction." Klára Roth Oren passed away in the summer of 2006.

Chapter 1. Establishment of the Camp

1. Andreas Höhn, "Wer kann sich an Jacob Suhl erinnern?" [Who can remember Jacob Suhl?], *Leipziger Volkszeitung,* January 26, 2001. It is possible that the Jews who owned the homes were not living in Markkleeberg; they only owned the property. See also Ingeborg Weinberger interview.

2. Heinrich Koppenberg, who in 1939 was the general manager of Junkers, constructed the JU-88, the Stuka dive bomber. Christopher Simpson, ed., *War Crimes of the Deutsche Bank and the Dresdner Bank* (New York: Holmes & Meier, 2002), 375. The Stuka was a German two-seated dive-bomber, a combat plane, used by the Luftwaffe in World War II.

3. Zentrale Stelle der Landesjusrizverwaltungen, Ludwigsburg (Center of Federal Justice, Bureau for the Clarification of Nazi Crimes, hereinafter called "Center"), 110 AR 326/99, written communication of March 2, 1999, p. 21.

4. Christa Naumann, "Das Arbeitsteilige Zusammenwirken von SS und Deutschen Rüstungskonzernen 1942–1945, Dargestelt am Beispil der Aussenkommandoes des Konzentrationslagers Buchenwald" (PhD diss., Humboldt-Universitët zu Berlin, 1969), 127.

5. Klaus Hesse, "KL Buchenwald Aussenlager Markkleeberg Am Wolfswinkel—Eine Dokumentation" [KL Buchenwald's sub-camp Markkleeberg at Wolfswinkel—a documentation] (unpublished manuscript available at Staadtverwaltung [city archive], Markkleeberg, May 1998), 6.

6. Wearing black uniforms and special insignia, the corps was divided into the General SS (*Allgemeine-SS*), the Gestapo that dealt with police matters, and the Armed SS (*Waffen-*

SS), the elite fighting force of the SS, which included the concentration camp guards. In 1946, at the Nürnberg (Nuremberg) trials, the SS was declared a criminal organization for its persecution and extermination of Jews, its brutality and murder of inmates in concentration camps, its exploitation of slave labor, and its mistreatment of POWs.

7. Simpson, *War Crimes,* 12.

8. Dieter Vaupel, "Hessisch Lichtenau Sub-Camp of the Buchenwald Concentration Camp, 1944–45." In *Studies on the Holocaust in Hungary,* ed. Randolph L. Braham, East European Monographs, no. 301 (New York: Columbia University Press, 1990), 194.

9. The original is at the Staadtverwaltung, Markkleeberg.

10. Hesse, "KL Buchenwald," 3.

11. A letter by Max Arnhold dated September 15, 1943, with signatures by Wolfswinkel residents. The original is at the Staadtverwaltung, Markkleeberg.

12. Albert Speer, *Inside the Third Reich: Memories* (New York: Macmillan, 1970), 370.

13. Jack G. Morrison, *Ravensbrück: Everyday Life in a Women's Concentration Camp 1939–45* (Princeton, NJ: Markus Wiener Publishers, 2000), 180.

14. Gordon J. Horwitz, *In the Shadow of Death: Living Outside the Gates of Mauthausen* (New York: Free Press, 1990), 10.

15. Arno J. Mayer, *Why Did the Heavens Not Darken? The "Final Solution" in History* (New York: Pantheon, 1988), 333.

16. Yehuda Bauer, "The Death-Marches, January–May 1945," *Modern Judaism* 3, (February 1983): 2.

17. Benjamin Ferencz, *Less Than Slaves* (Cambridge, MA: Harvard University Press, 1979), 28.

18. Ibid.

19. Simpson, *War Crimes,* 3.

20. Randolph L. Braham, ed., *Hungarian Jewish Studies* (New York: World Federation of Hungarian Jews, 1963), 1:516. In 1960, Adolf Eichmann was arrested near Buenos Aires and taken to Israel, where he was tried as a war criminal and hanged for his part in the Holocaust.

21. Vaupel, "Hessisch Lichtenau," 195.

22. Center, 23–27.

23. Erzsébet Frank, *365 Nap: Vallomás a Pokolok Tüzéből* [365 Days: testimony from hell's inferno], 3rd ed. (Budapest: Uránusz Kiado, 1999), 80.

24. Erzsébet Rab, *Es Nem Verik Félre a Harangot* [And the bells didn't toll] (Dombovár, Hungary: Anonymous, 1948), 257.

25. Center, 18–32.

26. Horwitz, *In the Shadow of Death,* 27.

27. Naumann, "Das Arbeitsteilige Zusammenwirken," 118.

28. Hesse, "KL Buchenwald," 8.

29. Peter Hayes, "State Policy and Corporate Involvement in the Holocaust," In *The Holocaust and History: The Known, the Unknown, the Disputed, and the Reexamined,* ed. Michael Berenbaum and Abraham J. Peck (Bloomington: Indiana University Press, 1998), 209.

30. Naumann, "Das Arbeitsteilige Zusammenwirken," 114–16.

31. Hayes, "State Policy and Corporate Involvement," 210.

32. International Tracing Service, Bad Arolsen (hereinafter referred to as International Tracing Service), Reference Sach-Nr. 12 462, written communication of August 29, 2002, p. 72.

33. Ibid. The author (Katalin Szász) and sister Erzsébet Szász were listed in the transports list (see Appendix A). Our records from Auschwitz and Bergen Belsen were also

found at the International Tracing Service, Reference T/D—414 099, written communication of April 12, 2007.

Chapter 2. Origins of the Prisoners

1. Abaújszántó is located at the Hungarian-Slovak border. The area is known for its Tokay wine, pressed from grapes that are produced in the volcanic soil.

2. Recalled by Anna Fülep Torontáli and others. The Hungarian poems in the book were translated by the author. See the original Hungarian text in Appendix C, song number two, from chapter 2.

3. Some people who worked in the city hall in town told my father that the Jews would be deported and killed. Somehow they knew, but we did not want to believe.

4. When we returned after deportation, the whole structure of the stable had disappeared.

5. See Zahava Stessel, *Wine and Thorns in Tokay Valley, Jewish Life in Hungary: The History of Abaújszántó* (Madison, NJ: Fairleigh Dickinson University and Associated University Presses, 1995).

6. Randolph L. Braham, *The Politics of Genocide: The Holocaust in Hungary* (New York: Columbia University Press, 1981), 1:545.

7. The plural is *Landsmanshaften* (Yiddish), which is a fraternal organization of people from the same community in the old country.

8. Braham, *Politics of Genocide,* 1:324.

9. See Zahava Stessel, "Ode to Mother: Melody of a Dismembered Childhood," *The Jewish Week* (New York), May 6, 1988, 26. See also Zahava Stessel, "Róza (Rachel) Szász" In *Pearls of Wisdom from Grandma.* Ed. Jennifer Gates Hayes, New York: Regan Books. An Imprint of Harper Collins Publishers, 1997.

10. Zahava Stessel, "Keserü vigasztalás" [Bitter comfort], *Newyorki Figyelö,* [New York Observer], February 2, 1984,12.

11. See Zahava Szász Stessel, "A Chance Encounter," In *And Life Is Changed Forever: Holocaust Childhood Remembered,* ed. Martin Ira Glassner and Robert Krell (Detroit, MI: Wayne State University Press, 2006), 139–49.

12. In 2004, my sister and I were among the survivors who received some symbolic compensation for medical experiments. Reference # MEF10293168C001 claim conference. January 26, 2004.

13. Erzsébet Markovics Dicker, born in 1903, was the oldest daughter of Frida and Samuel Markovics. Her husband was Dezsö (David) Dicker, from Gavan, where Bözsi and her family also resided. Their only son, Jozsika, died in Auschwitz.

14. I have never forgotten Márta. See my article, "The Memories of a Survivor; On Participating in the American Gathering of Jewish Holocaust Survivors in Washington," *The Jewish Press* (New York), April 8, 1983, 9. I passed Márta's house in Abaújszántó many times when I visited after the war. I have registered Márta and her sister Vera in the "Pages of Testimony" in Yad Veshem Archives, Jerusalem.

15. The 1944 borders of Hungary comprised a large extent of territory including areas of southern Slovakia, sub-Carpathian Russia (formerly part of Czechoslovakia), northern Transylvania (formerly Romania), and the Bacska region of Yugoslavia.

Chapter 3. Arrivals

1. Frank, *365 Nap,* 79.
2. "Buchenwald invoices and daily strength reports, N 52/E 20," in *Buchenwald: Mahnung und Verpflichtung* [Buchenwald, warning and obligations], ed. Wartel Bartel (Berlin: Kongress Verlag, 1960), 241.
3. We were registered in Buchenwald on December 17, 1944. International Tracing Service, 69.
4. *Stubendienst* or *Stuben* referred to a female inmate room attendant, responsible to the *Blockälteste.* For the Hungarian original, see Appendix C, song number three, from chapter 3.
5. Miriam Porat, *Lelo Shihrur* [Not liberated] (Tel Aviv: Eked, 1982), 70.
6. Battle of the Bulge. In World War II, this was the last German offensive on the Western Front, an unsuccessful attempt to divide the Allied forces and prevent an invasion of Germany. The Germans withdrew in January 1945, but both sides suffered heavy losses.
7. Rab, *És Nem Verik,* 226.
8. Recalled by Anna Fülep Torontáli and others. For the original Hungarian text, see Appendix C, song number four, from chapter 3.
9. Rab, *És Nem Verik,* 242.
10. Ibid., 252.
11. Porat, *Lelo Shihrur,* 79.
12. Irene Keisler Schnur interview.
13. Center, 23–27.
14. Rab, *És Nem Verik,* 243.
15. Frank, *365 Nap,* 79, 86.
16. Gabriella Braver Kosinka interview.

Chapter 4. Life in the Camp

1. Felicja Karay, *Death Comes in Yellow: Skarzysko-Kamienna Slave Labor Camp,* trans. Sara Kitai (Amsterdam: Harwood Academic Publishers, 1996), 241; Porat, *Lelo Shihrur,* 81.
2. The Gestapo was the German state secret police during the Nazi regime, notorious for its brutal methods and operations.
3. Gabriella Braver Kosinka interview.
4. Bruno Eisert, "Ermittlungen ûber KZ Frauen-Nebenlager Buchenwald in Markkleeberg-West" [Findings on the women's forced labor camp, a sub-camp of Buchenwald in Markkleeberg-West], (Research of Bruno Eisert, a former prisoner of Buchenwald, no. 1585. Tzwenkau, 14.6.1968, 2.) The original is at the Heinetmuseum in Markkleeberg.
5. See the poem "The Welders" by Erzsébet Frank in chapter 10.
6. Frank, *365 Nap,* 83. Translation by the author.
7. For the original Hungarian text, see Appendix C, song number five, from chapter 4.
8. Lenke Schwarz Fine interview. Her sister, Blanka Schwarz Friedman, passed away. Her testimony at Yad Vashem is in file 3/5048, dated November 13, 1988.
9. According to a recent government survey, the average woman consumes 1,850 calories a day; the average man 2,550. Annette B. Natow and Jo-Ann Heslin, *The Complete Food Counter* (New York: Pocket Books, 2006), 2.
10. Gabriella Klein Heimlich interview.
11. Frank, *365 Nap,* 84.
12. Flora Kaff Goldring interview.

13. Viktor Frankl, *Man's Search for Meaning: An Introduction to Logotherapy,* 4th ed., trans. Ilse Lasch (Boston, MA: Beacon Press, 1992), 5–6.
14. Nelly Winkler Rochlitz interview.
15. Rab, *És Nem Verik,* 256.
16. Eisert, "Ermittlungen über KZ," 3.
17. Dr. Irmgard Seidel, interview at Buchenwald Memorial.
18. Transport list of arrivals and departures of prisoners in the camp of Markkleeberg, International Tracing Service, 72.
19. Dr. Schmidt, Sachbearbeiter Grundsatzfragen, Der Oberbürgetmeister, Stadt Leipzig (Leipzig City Hall), communication #schm-26-02, January 14, 2002.
20. Ferencz, *Less Than Slaves,* 23.

Chapter 5. Prisoner Officials

1. Bella's daughters were Katalin and Anna Spitz. On the transport list, Bella is listed as having been born on November 9, 1914. According to the list from Terezin, which is usually closer to the true age, Bella was born November 26, 1906.
2. Anna Spitz Gilbert interview.
3. Rab, *És Nem Verik,* 257.
4. Ibid., 252.
5. Elisabeth Stein Szekely interview.
6. Zsuzsanna Csanyi was born on May 21, 1922, in the city of Gyöngyös in traditional Hungarian territory.
7. Porat, *Lelo Shihrur,* 69.
8. Márta Maget Leitmann passed away on December 17, 2003.
9. Frida Roth Kaller interview.
10. Vera Hollander Slyomovics interview; Frida Roth Kaller interview.
11. Porat, *Lelo Shihrur,* 69.
12. "Block" and "barracks" are used interchangeably. *Block* is the German word for barracks.
13. For the Hungarian original, see Appendix C, song number six, from chapter 5.
14. Center, 30.
15. Eisert, "Ermittlungen über KZ," 3.
16. Irene Keisler Schnur interview.
17. International Tracing Service, 71.
18. Ibid.
19. Márta Maget Leitmann interview.
20. International Tracing Service, 338.
21. Eva Ehrmann Koniesberg and Sara Ehrmann Sterba interviews.
22. Barbara Klein Stark interview.
23. Sadly, Jolan Lebovits, Irena Lebovits Ehrenreich's sister, died in childbirth after the war.
24. Lucy Sternberg was born in Szeged on January 3, 1925.
25. Eva Szekely Kulcsar, in her letter to the author of November 25, 1999.
26. For the Hungarian original, see Appendix C, song number seven, from chapter 5.
27. The word *répafaszung* in Hungarian means a meal of turnips or rutabaga. It also has a connotation of *fasz,* meaning sexual intercourse.
28. Dr. Seidel confirmed that, according to the records in Buchenwald, there were four women and two babies transferred to Bergen-Belsen on January 26, 1945.
29. Eva Szekely Kulcsar interview.

30. Sali Adler had cousins in the camp. They were Lili Katz Yoskovitz, Fanni Müler Hoffman, and Rozsi Müler.

31. Sali Adler, born December 25, 1925, in Dombo died at the beginning of 1945, according to the transport list of arrivals and departures of prisoners in the camp of Markkleeberg. International Tracing Service, 72.

32. Frank, *365 Nap,* 87.

33. International Tracing Service, 71.

34. Rachel Schwarz Moskovitz testimony, Yad Vashem file 03/11148, March 23, 1999, p. 42. Rab also mentions that we were artificially prevented from having periods. *És Nem Verik,* 244.

35. Miriam Weisz Shetel testimony, Yad Vashem file 03/11236, June 1, 1999, p. 18; Hanna Kahan testimony, Yad Vashem file 3725573, July 3, 1945, p. 2.

36. Tec, *Resilience and Courage,* 168; Marlene E. Heinemann, *Gender and Destiny: Women Writers and the Holocaust* (Westport, CT: Greenwood, 1986), 18–21; Dalia Ofer and Lenore J. Weitzman, eds., *Women in the Holocaust* (New Haven, CT: Yale University Press, 1998), 277.

37. Saidel, *Jewish Women of Ravensbrück,* 256.

38. Ilana Sajovits Breiner and Rachel Janovics Mittelman interviews.

39. Dr. Ingmard Seidel interview. Dr. Seidel is a senior executive of the Buchenwald Memorial, Gedenskstätte Buchenwald Direktion, Weimar-Buchenwald, Germany.

40. Sara Ehrmann Sterba interview.

Chapter 6. Finance and Work

1. Felicja Karay, *Hasag-Leipzig Slave Labour Camp for Women: The Struggle for Survival, Told by the Women and Their Poetry,* trans. Sara Kitai (London: Vallentine Mitchell, 2002), 16.

2. Simpson, *War Crimes of the* Deutsche *Bank,* 375.

3. Ibid., 376.

4. Ibid., 298, 375.

5. Ibid., 118.

6. Karay, *Hasag-Leipzig Slave Labour Camp,* 17.

7. Simpson, *War Crimes of the* Deutsche *Bank,* 32. Simpson quotes Jonathan Steinberg, *The Deutsche Bank and Its Gold Transaction During the Second World War* (Munich: Verlag C. H. Beck, 1999), 71–72.

8. Hesse, "KL Buchenwald," 12.

9. Christa Naumann, "Das Arbeitsteilige Zusammenwirken," 123.

10. Maurer, letter from the SS-Wirtschafts-Verwaltungshauptamtes to the commandant at Buchenwald, April 14, 1944, signed by Maurer, SS Obersturmführer. The original is at Thüringisches Haupsttaatsarchiv (THA), Weimar N54 Bu 224; Nuremberg documents, NI-382.

11. Hayes, "State Policy and Corporate Involvement," 209.

12. Buchenwald (Women) Junkers-Werke Markkleeberg, Bundesarchiv Koblens (NI-4185).

13. Hayes, "State Policy and Corporate Involvement," 210.

14. International Tracing Service, 11 and 61.

15. Landeshauptarchiv Sachsen-Anhalt Abteilung Oranienbaum, no. 1038, written communication of April 23, 2002.

16. "I give thanks unto thee, O King, who lives and endures, who has mercifully restored my soul into me; great is thy faithfulness."

17. Elisabeth Stein Székely interview.
18. The three groups were the Zucker, the Trattner, and the Lerner sisters.
19. Elisabeth Stein Székely, in her letter to the author dated March 22, 1999.
20. For the original Hungarian text, see Appendix C, song number eight, from chapter 6.
21. Karay, *Hasag-Leipzig Slave Labour Camp for Women,* 63.
22. For the original Hungarian text, see Appendix C, song number nine, from chapter 6.

Chapter 7. The Camp's Informal Structure

1. Klein, "The Survivors Search for Meaning and Identity," 546.
2. Tec, *Resilience and Courage, 354.*
3. Eugen Kogon, *The Theory and Practice of Hell,* trans. Heinz Norden (New York: Berkeley Books, 1980), 314.
4. To be with her cousin, Ilona Roth changed her name from Roth to Frankfurt, which is how she appears in the Markkleeberg transport list. Ilona survived, but her cousin Ica Frankfurter died in Bergen-Belsen, October 1944, from typhus. Interview with George Frankfurter, the brother of Ica Frankfurter.
5. Rachel Berkovics Zolf testimony, Yad Vashem file 03/3676, May 1973, p. 10.
6. Ibid., 277–78.
7. Rab, *És Nem Verik,* 287–88.
8. Frank, *365 Nap,* 83.
9. Saidel, *Jewish Women of Ravensbrück.* 54.
10. Tzvetan Todorov, *Facing the Extreme: Moral Life in the Concentration Camps,* trans. from the French by Arthur Denner and Abigail Pollak (New York: Metropolitan Books, 1996), 77.
11. For the original German text, see Appendix C, song number ten, from chapter 7.
12. Blanka Schwarz Friedman testimony, Yad Vashem file 03/5048, November 13, 1988.
13. Ester Grosz Lorber testimony, Yad Vashem file 03/5652, April 25,1990, p. 10.
14. For the original Hungarian text, see Appendix C, song number eleven, from chapter 7.
15. Eisert, "Ermittlungen über KZ," 3.

Chapter 8. The Commandant and His Staff

1. Bauer, "The Death-Marches," 12.
2. Eisert, "Ermittlungen über KZ," 3.
3. Center, 21. An *Oberscharführer* is equal to a staff sergeant in the U.S. Army.
4. Ibid.
5. Elizabeth Zucker Mermel interview. Elizabeth's German foreman provided the information.
6. Frank, *365 Nap,* 84.
7. Rachel Spielmann, her letter to Irma Clajus, November 9, 1975. The original is at the Staadtverwaltung (city archive), Markkleeberg.
8. Anna Székely Shindler, in her letter to the author dated July 20, 2003.
9. Rachel Berkovics Zolf testimony, Yad Vashem file 03/3676, May 1973, p. 10; Margit Krausz Nojld interview.
10. Gabriella Braver Kosinka interview. Gabriella worked in the repatriation office near Prague, in Brune, Czechoslovakia, organized by the American Jewish Joint Distribution

Committee (popularly known as the JDC and "The Joint"). Survivors received assistance there after the war. Women from the Markkleeberg camp who were in Terezin came to the office and told Gabriella about Knittel in Terezin.

11. Center, 23.

12. Ibid., 28, 30. The witnesses who testified used their married names only, so it is hard to identify them by the transport list.

13. Ibid., 23.

14. Rab, *És Nem Verik,* 234.

15. Ilana Sajovits Breiner interview.

16. Center, 28; Rab, *És Nem Verik,* 285.

17. Elisabeth Stein Székely, in her letter to the author of March 22, 1999.

18. Ibid.

19. Center, 23.

20. Vaupel, "Hessisch Lichtenau," 212.

21. Ibid., 213; Dr. Irmgard Seidel interview.

22. Vaupel, "Hessisch Lichtenau," 212.

23. Germaine Tillion, *Ravensbrück,* trans. Gerald Satterwhite. (New York: Anchor, 1975), 92, 93.

24. Karay, *Hasag-Leipzig Slave Labour Camp,* 41.

25. Center, 24.

26. Márta Maget Leitmann interview.

27. Gabriella Braver Kosinka interview. Gabriella who worked at the repatriation office in Brune was told about the killing by the girls from the *Electrocommando* who had been hiding in the forest. They returned after the camp was liberated by the American forces. Lilly Waldman interview.

28. Pöschel lived in Markkleeberg West, on Johannes Wangemannatstrasse, now Sebastianbachstrasse. Eisert, "Ermittlungen über KZ," 3.

29. Paul Schulze, "Protokoll über die Aussprache mit Herrn Paul Schulze, am 25.3.1957" [Testimony], Buchenwaldarchiv, # 63 26–1, p. 2.

30. Magda Schön Hilf, Márta Maget Leitmann, Veronica Lorant Berk, Margit Brociner Kish, Klära Roth Oren interviews.

31. Eisert, "Ermittlungen über KZ," 4.

32. International Tracing Service, 70.

33. Center, 24–27.

34. Bartel, *Buchenwald,* 262.

35. Porat, *Lelo Shihrur,* 86; Rab, *És Nem Verik,* 253; Frank, *365 Nap,* 83.

36. Rachel Spielmann, her letter to Irma Clajus, November 9, 1975. The original is at the Staadtverwaltung (city archive), Markkleeberg.

37. Klära Fischer Neuman, Elisabeth Stein Székely, Anna Fenyö Brown, Veronica Lorant Berk, Márta Maget Leitmann, and Lilly Waldman interviews.

Chapter 9. Cultural Activities

1. For the original Hungarian text, see Appendix C, song number twelve, from chapter 9.

2. For the original Hungarian text, see Appendix C, song number thirteen, from chapter 9.

3. For the original Hungarian text, see Appendix C, song number fourteen, from chapter 9.

4. Zsuzsanna Lengyel Urai, in her letter to the author dated February 6, 2000.

5. Rab, *És Nem Verik,* 239.
6. Zsuzsanna Lengyel Urai, in her letter to the author dated February 6. 2000.
7. Eisert, "Ermittlungen über KZ," 3.
8. Porat, *Lelo Shihrur,* 77.
9. Imre Kertész, *Sorstalanság* [Fateless] (Budapest: Magvetö, 1975), 306.
10. Center, 27.

Chapter 10. Human Relations

1. Andreas Höhn, in his letter to the author of January 8, 2003, with a copy of surveillance documents from the police file.
2. Gabriella Klein Heimlich interview.
3. Rachel Spielmann, letter to Irma Clajus, November 1975. The original is at the Staadtverwaltung, Markkleeberg.
4. Janek, "Protokoll über die Aussprache mit Frau Janek" [Mrs. Janek Testimony], 1961, Buchenwaldarchiv #63 26-2.
5. Elisabeth Stein Székely, in her letter to the author of March 22, 1999.
6. Frank, *365 Nap,* 81.
7. Andreas Höhn interview.
8. Karay, *Hasag-Leipzig Slave Labour Camp,* 65.
9. Gabriella Braver Kosinka interview.
10. Eisert, "Ermittlungen über KZ," 4.
11. Lea Kaff Brown interview.
12. For the original Hungarian text, see Appendix C, song number fifteen, from chapter 10.
13. Girls wanting to decorate their room covered the window with newspapers and made holes in the paper in a design similar to eyelet lace embroidery.
14. To differentiate between the two girls with the surnames Rózsika, the girls called the one who made the "eyelet lace" paper curtains "Maderas Rózsika."
15. Jacquile Fleury, testimony, March 12, 1994. The original is at the Staadtverwaltung, Markkleeberg.
16. Rab, *És Nem Verik,* 259.
17. Reymonde Garin, biography. The original is at the Staadtverwaltung, Markkleeberg; Nelly Winkler Rochlitz interview.
18. Marguerite Dupré, "Mort de Mademoiselle Prévost, une camarade 5700," *Voix et Visages, Association Nationale Des Anciennes Déportées et Internées De La Résistance,* no. 258 (January–February 1998), 2.
19. Rab, *És Nem Verik,* 264; Blanka Schwartz Friedman testimony, Yad Vashem file 03/5048, November 13, 1988, p. 18.

Chapter 11. Smaller Factories

1. Hajnal Linder, born May 28, 1922, and Lenke Linder, born September 3,1920, appear on the transport list. They were both born in Sátoraljaújhely.
2. Rab, *És Nem Verik,* 260.
3. Ibid., 232.
4. Ibid., 263.
5. Ibid., 270.

6. In the list of *Aufseherins* from Markkleeberg, there are two: Anny Tätsch and Anni Rehbein. See chapter 8 for the rest of the names.
7. Rab, *És Nem Verik,* 361. Hermina Schwarz was born on May 8, 1926, in Szamosujvar, Transylvania, according to the transport list.
8. Rab, *És Nem Verik,* 273—74.
9. Hesse, "KL Buchenwald," 14.
10. Rab, *És Nem Verik,* 266.
11. Bauer, "The Death-Marches," 3.
12. Rab, *És Nem Verik,* 285.
13. Ibid., 287.
14. Carmen Braun testimony, Yad Vashem file 3544300, July 12, 1945, p. 3.
15. Lilly Waldman interview; Vera Hollander Slyomovics interview.
16. Hesse, "KL Buchenwald," 8, 14; Eisert, "Ermittlungen über KZ," 3.
17. Vera Hollander Slyomovics interview.
18. Rachel Spielmann, letter to Irma Clajus, November 1975. The original is in the Staadtverwaltung, Markkleeberg.
19. Center, 23.
20. Ibid., 31.

Chapter 12. The Death March

1. Porat, *Lelo Shihrur,* 105.
2. Rab, *És Nem Verik,* 319; Renee Pearl Rutner interview; Márta Fellmann interview.
3. Renee Pearl Rutner interview.
4. Marika Kaufman also remembered the sister's agony and the shot.
5. No mention of the Death Marches was contained in the intelligence reports by Supreme Headquarters, Allied Expeditionary Force (SHAEF), or in other information sent back to London and Washington at the time. Only after the liberation of the camps did some partial information appear. Bauer, "The Death-Marches," 19.
6. Márta Fellmann interview.
7. Frank, *365 Nap,* 9.
8. Klára Fischer Neuman interview.
9. Rachel Moskovitz Schwarz testimony, Yad Vashem file 03/11148, March 23, 1999, p. 33.
10. Porat, *Lelo Shihrur,* 106.
11. Ibid., 110–11.
12. Dr. Irmgard Seidel interview.
13. Rab, *És Nem Verik,* 312.
14. Center, 31. The survivors who testified were Irena Ehrenreich, Emma Apai, Dora Kluska, and Olga Eisdorfer.
15. In conquering a city, one is not allowed to cut down the fruit-bearing trees (Deuteronomy 20:19–20). Consequently, this injunction probably applied also to sown seeds in the land.
16. Anja Kessler, "Es schien, als hätte die Strasse kein Ende" [It seemed as the road had no end], *Kleine Volkszeitung,* September 12, 2000:2.
17. Wendelgard von Staden, *Darkness Over the Valley: Growing up in Nazi Germany,* trans. Mollie Comerford Peters (New Haven, CT: Ticknor & Fields, 1981), 67–68.
18. Horwitz, *In the Shadow of Death,* 146.
19. Ibid., 149.
20. Rab, *És Nem Verik,* 312.

21. See also Center, 23–27.
22. Rab, *És Nem Verik,* 308–9.

Chapter 13. Liberation

1. Agata Trattner Klein interview.
2. Elizabeth Zucker Mermel believes that two of the welders, Herta and Magda, did not go with the rest of them.
3. International Tracing Service, 148.
4. See Appendix B.
5. Rab, *És Nem Verik,* 352; Ilana Sajovits Breiner interview.
6. Rab, *És Nem Verik,* 336.
7. Saidel, *Jewish Women of Ravensbrück,* 187. Heinrich Himmler was chief of the SS and the one who devised the system of concentration camps.
8. Frank, *365 Nap,* 97.
9. Vera Deutsch De Vit interview and Tereza Frankl interview.
10. Rab, *És Nem Verik,* 338.
11. Ibid., 347.
12. Center, 23, 482. We called him "Bacskai" or "Birger."
13. See also Zahava Stessel, "Shared Bequest," *The Jerusalem Post* (Israel), June 21, 1991, 11.
14. Rab, *És Nem Verik,* 339; Esther Lorber Grosz testimony, Yad Vashem file 03/5652, April 25, 1990, p. 23.
15. Transport lists, Appendix A; List of arrivals to Theresianstadt, Appendix B.
16. Hanna Kahan testimony, Yad Vashem file 3725573, July 3, 1945, p. 3.
17. Tereza Frankl interview; Zahava Friedmann Fruchter testimony, Yad Vashem file 03/6617, January 10, 1991, p. 23.
18. Eisert, "Ermittlungen über KZ," 3.

Chapter 14. Life of a Survivor

1. Hava Hartmann Kleinberg interview and testimony, Yad Vashem file 03/7292, p. 28; Ester Lorber Grosz testimony, Yad Vashem file 03/5652, p. 10.
2. T. B. C. Landes Institute Koranyi, XII Pihenő Str., Budapest, Szász Katalin.
3. For the original Hungarian text, see Appendix C, song number sixteen, from chapter 14.
4. Actually my name was Goldi, which in Hebrew is Zahava. Erzsike's name was Sarah, which has an unwelcome connotation in Hungarian, so the group suggested Hava, and that remained for the rest of our lives. I sometimes feel a bit of regret for not using the name Katalin that my parents so carefully selected and gave to me.
5. Eretz–Yisrael: Land of Israel, usually used in reference to the state of Israel before its establishment in 1948 (Palestine).
6. The social welfare work in the Cyprus detention camps, which held some 50,000 "illegal" immigrants who had been seized by the British government, was paid for by the American Jewish Joint Distribution Committee.
7. Magda Schön Hilf married and raised a beautiful family of physicians.
8. See Zahava Stessel, "Denying My Past," parts 1 and 2, *NAHOS* (National Association of Jewish Child Holocaust Survivors, Inc.) 5, no. 26 (January 2000); and 6, no. 1 (February 2000).

9. See *Together,* published by the American Gathering of Jewish Holocaust Survivors.

10. See Zahava Stessel, "The Memories of a Survivor; On Participating in the American Gathering of Jewish Holocaust Survivors in Washington," *The Jewish Press* (New York), April 8, 1983, 9. See also Zahava Stessel. "Hungarian Jewish Community Challenges Denial," *Martirdom and Resistance* (New York), May–June 1995, 5.

11. Piroska Kornagel, "*Szász Kati Golgotája*" [The Golgotha of Szász Kati], *Új Kelet* (Tel Aviv), January 9, 2004, 7. There are some oversights in Ms. Kornagel's heartfelt, sympathetic account. She assumed that we remained alive because we said during the selection in Auschwitz that we were older. It is a logical assumption, but in Auschwitz no one actually asked us, and we would never have taken an action that would separate us from mother and grandmother. On the contrary, we were beaten by the guards because we wanted so much to follow them. Events in the Holocaust, as has been proven many times, challenge understanding and are not subject to interpretations by accepted norms.

12. Zahava Stessel, "Traces of a Jewish Community in Rural Hungary," *The Jewish Press* (New York), March 25, 1988, 50C. See also Zahava Stessel, "Emléktábla Abaújszáator" [Memorial Tablet in Abaújszánto] *Új Kelet* (Tel Aviv), February 12, 1993, 2.

13. Among the contributors, to the German foundation "Remembrance, Responsibility, and the Future" to compensate former slave and forced laborers were the Deutsche Bank and the Dresdner Bank.

Chapter 15. Return to Markkleeberg

1. Hesse, "KL Buckenwald," 23.

2. Bartel, *Buchenwald,* 254–302.

3. Eisert, "Ermittlungen über KZ," 3.

4. Irma Clajus, "Ermittlungen über das KZ frauenslager, aussenstelle Buchunwald, Markkleeberg-West, Wolfswinkel" [Details of a former women's forced labor camp, a satellite of Buchenwald in Markkleeberg-West, Wolfswinkel], April 2, 1975. The original is at the Staadtverwaltung, Markkleeberg.

5. Zahava Stessel, "Rede von Frau Dr. Stessel (USA) anläßlich der Gedenkfeier am Gedenkstein im Equipagenweg am 13 Juni" [A speech given by Dr. Stessel at the dedication of the memorial in Equipagenweg in June 13], *Markkleeberger Stadtnachrichten,* no. 7 (July 1998): 25–26.

6. Monika Schmidt, "Überlebende besuchten Panitzscher Gedenkstätte" [Survivors visit Panitzscher Memorial], *Kleine Volkszeitung,* June 19, 1998, 1.

7. Ferencz, *Less Than Slaves,* 50.

8. Ibid.

9. Bert Endruszeit, "Zahava Stessel: 'Ich muss einfach davon erzählen'" [Zahava Stessel: I must tell the story], *Kleine Volkszeitung,* September 7, 2001, 4.

10. Hava Hartmann Kleinberg passed away on April 27, 2007. Engraved on her gravestone is the number from her arm that she had received in Auschwitz.

11. Evelin Müller, "Vergessene Frauen von Buchenwald" [The forgotten women of Buchenwald], *Markkleeberger Stadtnachrichten,* no.10 (September 2001): 1–2.

12. Aurore De Neuville, ed., *Les Femmes oubliées de Buchenwald* [The forgotten women of Buchenwald] (Paris: Musée, 2005), 39–42, 118–20. See also "Vergessene Frauen von Buchenwald" [The forgotten women of Buchenwald], *Weimar Culture Journal,* no. 5 (2001): 8.

13. According to the telephone inquiry by Ms. Evelin Müller, from Markkleeberg City Hall, to Christuskirche Cemetery in Freital on September 4, 2001, Rozsa Winkler is buried in a mass unmarked grave. Ms. Müller's note is in the author's library.

14. Jonathan Mark, "Realm of the Senses: Solace for Those Left Behind Found in a Swim, a Kiss, Memories of a Blessing," *Jewish Week* (New York), September 8, 2006, 16–17.

15. For the original Hungarian text, see Appendix C, song number seventeen, from chapter 15.

Bibliography

Published Works

Bauer, Yehuda. "The Death-Marches, January–May 1945." *Modern Judaism* 3 (February 1983).

Berenbaum, Michael, and Abraham J. Peck, eds. *The Holocaust and History: The Known, the Unknown, the Disputed, and the Reexamined.* Bloomington: Indiana University Press, 1998.

Braham, Randolph L. ed. *Hungarian Jewish Studies.* 3 vols. New York: World Federation of Hungarian Jews, 1963.

———. *The Politics of Genocide: The Holocaust in Hungary.* 2 vols. New York: Columbia University Press, 1981.

"Buchenwald invoices and daily strength reports, N 52/E 20." In *Buchenwald: Mahnung und Verpflichtung* [Buchenwald, warning and obligations], ed. Wartel Bartel. Berlin: Kongress Verlag, 1960.

De Neuville, Aurore, ed. *Les Femmes Oubliées de Buchenwald* [The forgotten women of Buchenwald]. Paris Musées, 2005.

Des Pres, Terrence. *The Survivor: An Anatomy of Life in the Death Camps.* New York: Oxford University Press, 1976.

Dupré, Marguerite. "Mort de Mademoiselle Prévost, une camarade 5700." *Voix et Visages, Association Nationale Des Anciennes Déportées et Internées De La Résistance,* no. 258 (January–February 1998).

Endruszeit, Bert. "Zahava Stessel: 'Ich muss einfach davon erzählen'" [Zahava Stessel: 'I must tell the story']. *Kleine Volkszeitung,* September 7, 2001.

Ferencz, Benjamin. *Less Than Slaves.* Cambridge, MA: Harvard University Press, 1979.

Flam, Gila. *Singing for Survival: Songs of the Lodz Getto, 1940-45.* Urbana, IL: University of Illinois Press, 1992.

Frank, Erzsébet. *365 Nap: Vallomás a Pokolok Tüzéből* [365 Days: testimony from hell's inferno]. 3rd ed. Budapest: Uránusz Kiado, 1999.

Frankl, Viktor. *Man's Search for Meaning: An Introduction to Logotherapy.* 4th ed. Trans. by Ilse Lasch. Boston, MA: Beacon Press, 1992.

Gurewitsch, Brana, ed. *Mothers, Sisters, Resisters: Oral Histories of Women Who Survived the Holocaust.* Birmingham: University of Alabama Press, 1998.

Hackett, David A., ed. *The Buchenwald Report.* Boulder, CO: Westview Press. 1999.

Hayes, Peter. "State Policy and Corporate Involvement in the Holocaust." In *The Holocaust and History: The Known the Unknown, the Disputed, and the Reexamined,* ed. Michael Berenbaum and Abraham J. Peck. Bloomington: Indiana University Press, 1998.

Heinemann, Marlene E. *Gender and Destiny: Women Writers and the Holocaust.* Westport, CT: Greenwood, 1986.

Höhn, Andreas. "Wer kann sich an Jacob Suhl erinnern?" [Who can remember Jacob Suhl?]. *Leipziger Volkszeitung,* January 26, 2001.

Horwitz, Gordon J. *In the Shadow of Death: Living Outside the Gates of Mauthausen.* New York: Free Press, 1990.

Karay, Felicja. *Death Comes in Yellow: Skarzysko-Kamienna Slave Labor Camp.* Trans. by Sara Kitai. Amersterdam: Harwood Academic Publishers, 1996.

———. *Hasag-Leipzig Slave Labour Camp for Women: The Struggle for Survival, Told by the Women and Their Poetry.* Trans. by Sara Kitai. London: Vallentine Mitchell, 2002.

Kertesz, Imre. *Sorstalanság* [Fateless]. Budapest: Magvető, 1975.

Kessler, Anja. "Es schien, als hätte die Strasse kein Ende" [It seemed as the road had no end]. *Kleine Volkszeitung,* September 12, 2000.

Klein, Hillel. "The Survivors Search for Meaning and Identity." *The Nazi Concentration Camps: Proceedings of the Fourth Yad Vashem International Historical Conference, Jerusalem, January 1980.* Jerusalem: Yad Vashem, 1984.

Kogon, Eugen. *The Theory and Practice of Hell.* Trans. by Heinz Norden. New York: Berkeley Books, 1980.

Kornagel, Piroska. "Szász Kati Golgotája" [The golgotha of Szász Kati]. *Új Kelet* (Tel Aviv), January 9, 2004.

Mark, Jonathan. "Realm of the Senses: Solace for Those Left Behind Found in a Swim, a Kiss, Memories of a Blessing." *The Jewish Week* (New York), September 8, 2006.

Mayer, Arno J. *Why Did the Heavens Not Darken?: The "Final Solution" in History.* New York: Pantheon, 1988.

Morrison, Jack G. *Ravensbrück: Everyday Life in a Women's Concentration Camp 1939–45.* Princeton, NJ: Markus Wiener, 2000.

Müller, Evelin. "Vergessene Frauen von Buchenwald" [The forgotten women of Buchenwald]. *Markkleeberger Stadtnachrichten,* no.10 (September 2001).

Natow, Annette B., and Jo-Ann Heslin. *The Complete Food Counter.* New York: Pocket Books, 2006.

Ofer, Dalia, and Lenore J. Weitzman, eds. *Women in the Holocaust.* New Haven, CT: Yale University Press, 1998.

Porat, Miriam. *Lelo Shihrur* [Not liberated]. Tel Aviv: Eked, 1982.

Rab, Erzsébet. *És Nem Verik Félre a Harangot* [And the bells didn't toll]. Dombovár, Hungary: Anonymous, 1948.

Reitlinger, Gerald. *The Final Solution: The Attempt to Exterminate the Jews of Europe.* 2nd ed. New York: Thomas Yoseloff, 1961.

Saidel, Rochelle G. *The Jewish Women of Ravensbrück Concentration Camp.* Madison: University of Wisconsin Press, 2004.

Schmidt, Monika. "Überlebende besuchten Panitzscher Gedenkstätte" [Survivors visit Panitzscher Memorial]. *Kleine Volkszeitung,* June 19, 1998.

Simpson, Christopher, ed. *War Crimes of the Deutsche Bank and the Dresdner Bank.* New York: Holmes & Meier, 2002.

Speer, Albert. *Inside the Third Reich: Memories.* New York: Macmillan, 1970.

Stessel, Zahava Szász. "Bucsuzás idején" [At time of parting]. *Newyorki Figyelö* [New York Observer], December 18, 1987.

———. "A Chance Encounter." In *And Life is Changed Forever: Holocaust Childhood Remembered,* ed. Martin Ira Glassner and Robert Krell. Detroit, MI: Wayne State University Press, 2006.

———. "Denying My Past." Parts 1 and 2. *Nahos* 5 (January 2000); 6 (February 2000).

———. "Emléktábla Abaújszánton" [Memorial Tablet in Abaújszántó] *Új kelet* (Tel Aviv). February 12, 1993, 2.

———. "Hungarian Jewish Community Challenges Denial." *Martyrdom and Resistance* (May–June 1995).

———. "Keserü vigasztalás" [Bitter comfort]. *Newyorki Figyelö* [New York Observer], February 2, 1984.

———. "The Memories of a Survivor; On Participating in the American Gathering of Jewish Holocaust Survivors in Washington." *The Jewish Press* (New York), April 8, 1983.

———. "A Noble Act Recalled." *Martyrdom* and *Resistance* (September–October, 1986).

———. "Ode to Mother: Melody of a Dismembered Childhood. *The Jewish Week* (New York), May 6, 1988.

———. "Rede von Frau Dr. Stessel (USA) anläßlich der Gedenkfeier am Gedenkstein im Equipagenweg am 13 Juni" [A speech given by Dr. Stessel at the dedication of the memorial in Equipagenweg in June 13]. *Markkleeberger Stadtnachrichten,* no. 7 (July 1998).

———. "Róza (Rachel) Szász" In *Pearls of Wisdom from Grandma.* Ed. Jennifer Gates Hayes. New York: Regan Books. An Imprint of Harper Collins Publishers, 1997.

———. "Shared Bequest." *The Jerusalem Post* (Israel), June 21, 1991.

———. "Town Meeting of Holocaust Survivors." *The Jewish Press* (New York), August 20, 1982.

———. "Traces of a Jewish Community in Rural Hungary." The *Jewish Press* (New York), March 25, 1988.

———. *Wine and Thorns in Tokay Valley, Jewish Life in Hungary: The History of Abaújszántó.* Madison, NJ: Fairleigh Dickinson University and Associated University Presses, 1995.

Száraz György. *Egy Előitelet Nyomában* [In trace of a prejudice]. Budapest: Magvető Kiado, 1976.

Tec, Nechama. *Resilience and Courage: Women, Men, and the Holocaust.* New Haven, CT: Yale University Press, 2003.

Tillion, Germaine. *Ravensbrück.* Trans. by Gerald Satterwhite. New York: Anchor, 1975.

Todorov, Tzvetan. *Facing the Extreme: Moral Life in the Concentration Camps.* Trans. from the French by Arthur Denner and Abigail Pollak. New York: Metropolitan Books, 1996.

Vaupel, Dieter. "Hessisch Lichtenau: Sub-Camp of the Buchenwald Concentration Camp, 1944–45." In *Studies on the Holocaust in Hungary,* ed. Randolph L. Braham. East European Monographs, no.301. New York: Columbia University Press, 1990.

"Vergessene Frauen von Buchenwald" [The forgotten women of Buchenwald]. *Weimar Culture Journal,* no. 5 (2001).

von Staden, Wendelgard. *Darkness Over the Valley: Growing Up in Nazi Germany.* Trans. by Mollie Comerford Peters. New Haven, CT: Ticknor & Fields, 1981.

Testimonies in Yad Vashem Archives, Jerusalem

Braun, Carmen. Yad Vashem file 3544300. July 12, 1945.

Friedman, Blanka (Schwarz). Yad Vashem file 03/5048. November 13, 1988.

Grosz, Ester (Lorbeer). Yad Vashem file 03/5652. April 25, 1990.

Fruchter, Zahava (Friedmann). Yad Vashem file 03/6617. January 10, 1991.

Kahan, Hanna. Yad Vashem file 3725573. July 3, 1945.

Kleinberg, Hava (Hartmann). Yad Vashem file 03/7292. November 23, 1993.

Moskovitz, Rachel (Schwarz). Yad Vashem file 03/11148. March 23, 1999.

Israel, Sara (Salamon). Yad Vashem file 03/9391. May 28, 1996.

Netzer, Ruth (Gottlieb). Yad Vashem file 03/5383. March, 1987.

Noiman, Sarah (Grosz). Yad Vashem file 03/5658. January 29, 1990.

Shetel, Miriam (Weisz). Yad Vashem file 03/11236. June 1, 1999.

Zolf, Rachel (Berkovics). Yad Vashem file 03/3676. May 1973; and Yad Vashem file 03/9673. December 25, 1995

Other Archival Sources

Budesarchive Koblens. "Buchenwald (Women) Junkers-Werke Markkleeberg." NI-4185.

Clajus, Irma. "Ermittlungen uber das KZ frauenslager, aussenstelle Buchunwald, in Markkleeberg-West, Wosfinkel" [Details of a former women's forced labor camp, a satellite of Buchenwald in Markkleeberg-West, Wolfswinkel]. April 2, 1975. The original is at the Staadtverwaltung (city archive), Markkleeberg.

Eisert, Bruno. "Ermittlungen ûber KZ Frauen-Nebenlager Buchenwald in Markkleeberg-West" [Findings on the women's forced labor camp, a sub-camp of Buchenwald in Markkleeberg–West]. (Research of Bruno Eisert, a former prisoner of Buchenwald, no. 1585 Tzwenkau, 14.6.1968.) The original is at the Heinetmuseum in Markkleeberg.

Fleury, Jacquile. Testimony. March 12, 1994. Original at the Staadtverwaltung, Markkleeberg.

Garin, Reymonde. Biography. The original is at the Staadtverwaltung, Markkleeberg;

Hesse, Klaus. "KL Buchenwald Aussenlager Markkleeberg Am Wolfswinkel—Eine Dokumentation" [KL Buchenwald's sub-camp Markkleeberg at Wolfswinkel—A documentation]. May 1998. (Unpublished manuscript available at Stadtverwaltung, [city archive], Markkleeberg.)

International Tracing Service, Bad Arolsen. Reference Sach-Nr. 12 462. Written communication of August 29, 2002.

Janek. "Protokoll über die Aussprache mit Frau Janek" [Mrs Janek Testimony], 1961. Buchenwaldarchiv #63 26-2.

Landeshauptarchiv Sachsen-Anhalt Abteilung Oranienbaum. No.1038. Written communication of April 23, 2002.

Maurer, Letter from the SS-Wirtschafts-Verwaltungshauptamtes to the commandant at Buchenwald, April 14, 1944, signed by Maurer, SS Obersturmführer. The original is at Thüringisches Haupsttaatsarchiv (THA), Weimar N54 Bu 224.

Naumann, Christa. "Das Arbeitsteilige Zusammenwirken von SS und Deutschen Rüstungskonzernen 1942–1945, Dargestelt am Beispil der Aussenkommandoes des Konzentrationslagers Buchenwald." PhD diss., Humboldt-Universitët zu Berlin, 1969.

Persch, Christa. "Die Aussenkommandos von Buchenwald und die Zwangsarbeitlager in Leipzig." PhD diss., Staatsexamensarbeit, Karl-Marx Universität, Leipzig, 1957.

Rabe, Christine. "Die Geschihte der Frauenaussenkommandos des Ehemaligen Konzentrationslager Buchenwald am Beispiel der Aussenkommandoes in Leipzig-Schönefeld, Leipzig-Schőnau und Markkleeberg." PhD diss., Martin-Luther Universität Halle-Wittenberg, 1981.

Ragwitz, Renate. "Die Frauenaussenkommandos des Konzentrationslagers Buchenwald." Buchenwald-heft Nr. 15/1982, Nationale Mahn–und Gedenkstätte Buchenwals, 1982.

Schmidt, Dr. "Sachbearbeiter Grundsatzfragen, Der Oberbürgetmeister, Stadt Leipzig" (Leipzig City Hall). Communication #schm-26-02, January 14, 2002.

Schulze, Paul. "Protokoll Über die Aussprache mit Herrn Paul Schulze, am 25.3.1957" [Testimony], Buchenwaldarchiv #63 26-1, p.2.

Spielmann, Rachel. Her letter to Irma Clajus, November 9, 1975. The original is at the Staadtverwaltung (city archive), Markkleeberg.

Zentrale Stelle der Landesjusrizverwaltungen, Ludwigsburg [Center of Federal Justice Bureau for the Clarification of Nazi Crimes]. 110 AR 326/99. Written communication of March 2, 1999.

Interviews

All the interviews were by the author and tape-recorded by her. The interviewees' current names are listed as well as the maiden names, in parentheses, of those who married after the war. The initial interview was either in person (IP) or by telephone (TI) and was followed by additional tape-recorded phone calls and written communications.

Apai, Emma (Winkler), New York. IP, November 22, 1999.

Balek, Piroska (Weisz), Hertzilia, Israel. TI, July 20, 2003.

Berk, Veronica (Lorant), California. TI, March 15, 2001.

Breiner, Ilana (Sajovits), Holon, Israel. TI, May 3, 2004.

Brown, Anna (Fenyö), Budapest. IP, July 7, 1999.

Brown, Lea (Kaff), New York. TI, May 10, 1999.

Csonka,Vera (Braun), Budapest. TI, January 23, 2001.

Czitter, Eva, Florida. TI, February 1, 2006.

Davis, Rose (Hoffmann), New York. IP, January 16, 2001.

De Vit, Vera (Deutsch), Mexico. TI, February 14, 2001.

Deutsch, Klára (Frenkel), Nir Galim, Israel. TI, May 12, 2003.

Ehrenreich, Irena (Lebovits), Kfar Yona, Israel. TI, August 3, 2004.

Eichler, Eva (Rosenberg), Tel Aviv, Israel. IP, June 14, 1999.

Engel, Elizabeth (Winkler), Toronto. TI, May 11, 1999

Fábián, Eva (Moskovitz), Canada. TI, November 13, 2000.

Fellmann, Márta, Toronto. TI, November 23, 2004.

Fine, Lenke (Schwarz), Jerusalem. TI, July 8, 2003.

Fischer, Magda (Polatsek), Haifa, Israel. IP, August 18, 2004.

Fisher, Sara (Mayer), New York. TI, February 14, 2001.
*Frankl, Tereza, Haifa, Israel. IP, January 22, 2004.
Friedman, Erzsébet (Bachusz), New York. TI, November 17, 1999.
Fritsch Dr. Ella, Beer–Sheva, Israel. TI, August 13, 2004.
Fülöp Berta (Herskovitz), New York. IP, December 8, 1999.
Gábori, Ibolya (Kail), Toronto. TI, December 9, 1999.
Gallo Katalin, (Frank), Budapest. TI, November 7, 2001.
Gilbert, Anna (Spitz), Toronto. TI, May 23, 2001.
*Glattstein, Ilona (Eisler), Naharia, Israel. TI, March 20, 2001.
Goldring, Flora (Kaff), New York. TI, May 6, 1999.
Goldstein, Kathy (Zelmanovitz), New York. IP, January 6, 1999.
Goldstein Olga (Salamon), Cleveland, Ohio. TI, February 22, 1999.
Grodan, Jolka (Goldstein), Montreal. TI, February 10, 1999.
Hadnagy, Teréz (Stern), Budapest. IP, July 21, 1999.
Heimlich, Gabriella (Klein), Toronto. TI, May 3, 1999.
Helfand, Rene (Daszkalovits), New York. TI, November, 10, 1999.
Hilf, Magda (Schön),Toronto. TI, February 20, 2001.
Hoffman, Fanny (Muler), New York. TI, April 21, 1999.
Höhn, Andreas, local historian, Leipzig, Germany. IP, September 4, 2001.
Hönig, Gitta (Susitzky), Holon, Israel. TI, July 16, 2003.
*Hollander, Gizella, Natanja, Israel. TI, November 17, 1998.
Israel, Sarah (Salamon), Natanja, Israel. TI, February 16, 1999.
Jackson, Esther (Salamon), New York. TI, November 11, 1999.
Kahan, Regina, Florida. TI, May 4, 1999.
Kaufman, Elena (Salamon), New York. IP, November 10, 1999.
Kaufman, Erzsebet (Weinberger), Akko, Israel. IP, June 16, 1999.
Kaufman, Ibolya (Wollner), Ramat Gan, Israel. TI, July 6, 2001.
Kaufman, Marie (Politzer), New Jersey. TI, March 16, 2001.
Kirsenbaum, Miriam (Liberman), Ganey Tikvah, Israel. IP, July 27, 1999.
Kish, Margit (Brociner), Bnai–Barak, Israel. IP, July 27, 1999.
*Klein, Agata (Trattner), Cote St. Luc, Canada. TI, February 15, 2001.
*Kleinberg, Hava (Hartmann), Kefar Saba, Israel. IP, October 16, 1998.
Kohen, Klára (Herskovitz), Petah Tikvah, Israel. IP, July 14, 1999.
Koniesberg Eva (Ehrmann), Montreal. TI, August 23, 2001.
Kormos, Erzsébet (Frank), Dusseldorf, Germany. TI, April 18, 1999.
Kosinka, Gabriella (Braver), Toronto. TI, July 19, 2000.
Krakowitz Margarete (Zimmermann), Toronto. TI, March 15, 2002.
Kulcsár, Eva (Székely), Sâo Paulo, Brazil. TI, November 3, 1999.
Lebowitz, Livia (Fischmann), Kiryat Ata, Israel. TI, July 7, 2002.
*Leitmann Márta (Maget), Kosice, Slovakia. TI, December 16, 2002.
Lesem Lea (Keri), Kefar Saba, Israel. IP, May 26, 2002.

Levy, Lenke (Deutsch), Tel Aviv. TI, May 4, 2001.
Mermel, Elizabeth (Zucker), California. TI, October 21, 1998.
Mittelman, Rachel (Janovics), Ilania, Israel. IP, October 25, 2000.
Netzer, Gila (Friedman), New York. IP, July 24, 2002.
Netzer, Ruth (Gottlieb), Nir Galim, Israel. TI, November 4, 2004.
Neumann, Klára (Fischer), Toronto. TI, May 15, 2001.
Noe, Elizabeth (Groszmann), Ontario, Canada. TI, December 8, 1999.
Nojld, Margit (Krausz), Givat Shmuel, Israel. TI, February, 11, 2004.
*Oren, Klára (Roth), Natanja, Israel. TI, July 14, 2004.
Paplanos, Edit (Frenkel), New York. TI, May 14, 2003.
Paran, Márta (Weisz), Shave Zion, Israel. IP, June 20, 2000.
Pincsefski, Regina (Farkas), Rananah, Israel. TI, February 16, 2000.
Rabinovics, Agnes (Glück), Holon, Israel. TI, March 25, 2001.
Rauch, Erzsébet (Gróf), Balatonfenyves, Hungary. TI, February 3, 2000.
Reich, Sara (Salamon), New York. IP, November 10, 1999.
Rochlitz, Nelly (Winkler), New York. IP, March 16, 1999.
*Rosenberg, Lenke (Schlesinger), North Carolina. TI, March 16, 2004.
Rosman, Penina, Rehovot, Israel. TI, February 11, 2003.
Roth, Frida (Kaller), New York. TI, February 18, 2003.
Rutner, Renee (Pearl), New York. TI, November 16, 1999.
Salamon, Alice (Korenitzer), London. TI, June 16, 1999.
Schlesinger, Sara (Salamon), New York. TI, July 25, 1999.
Schnur, Irene (Keisler), Winnipeg, Canada. TI, November 16, 1998.
Schwartz, Gitta (Weisz), Akko, Israel. IP, July 27, 1999.
Schwartz, Rachel (Preisler), Givatayim, Israel. TI, December 7, 2004.
Seidel, Dr. Irmgard, senior executive at the Buchenwald memorial. Gedenskstätte Buchenwald Direktion, Weimar-Buchenwald, Germany. IP, September 3, 2001.
Seidner, Blanka (Weisz), Petah Tikvah. IP, March 22, 2001.
Shindler, Anna (Székely), Holon, Israel. TI, June 22, 2004.
Slyomovics, Vera (Hollander), Vancouver, BC, Canada. TI, October 28, 1998.
*Snitzler, Klára (Spitz), Petah Tikvah, Israel. IP, October 16, 1998.
Stark, Barbara (Klein), Toronto. TI, August 1, 2000.
Stein, Margit (Láng), Naharia, Israel. IP, June 21, 2000.
Sterba, Sara (Ehrmann), Baltimore, Maryland. TI, March 26, 2001.
Sternhell, Edit (Seidenfeld), New York. TI, May 20, 2002.
*Szamosi, Elza (Reich), Fenwick, Ontario, Canada. TI, July 17, 1998.
*Székely, Elisabeth (Stein), Budapest. IP, July 22, 1999.
Szilás, Isabella (Lörinch), Debrecen, Hungary. TI, April 10, 2000.
Tardos, Margit (Bihari), Budapest. TI, January 18, 2000.
Török, Zsofia (Gottlieb), Kaposvár, Hungary. TI, September 7, 1999.
Torontáli, Anna (Fülep), Dunaùjvàros, Hungary. TI, January 30, 2000.
Urai, Zsuzsanna (Lengyel), Budapest. IP, July 22, 1999.
Waldman, Lilly, Great Neck, N.Y. TI, August 27, 2002.

Weinberger, Ingeborg, Baltimore, Maryland. TI, January 5, 2002.
Weiss, Anna (Klein), Toronto. TI, May 4, 1999.
Weisz, Angyal (Fischer), Dunaùjvàros, Hungary. TI, February 29, 2000.
Wesely, Agnes (Kivovits), Toronto. TI, January 14, 2003.
Yoskovitz, Lee (Katz), Florida. TI, January 12, 1999.

* Deceased

Index

Page numbers in *italics* refer to illustration pages

Abaújszántó. *See* Hungary
Adler, Edit Markovics, 312
Adler, Dr. Jozsa, 111–12, 114, 248, 258
Adler, Sali, 118–19
air raids, 141–42, 224–25, 246–49, 251–52. *See also* Death March/liberation
Ajanot, Israel, 298
Anders, Frau Elizabeth, 219, 221–23, 227
Apai, Emma Winkler, 163, 164
Aron, Ilona, 246
Atlit, Israel, 298
Aufseherins, 16, 22, 34, 35, 58, 60, 61, 63, 64, 71, 73, 74, 77, 82–84, 86–89, 93, 99, 103, 108, 111–14, 117, 118, 133, 138–40, 159, 161, 164–71, 173, 174, 187, 189, 190, 209, 211, 222, 227–29, 233, 234, 324, 327; Anni, 223; Kutyus, 117, 165–69, 193; Lucifer, 86, 99, 108, 169–70, 175, 188, 213, 226, 297; Rákoczi, 169; inconsistency by, 170; recruitment of, 165–66
Auschwitz-Birkenau, 17, 20, 27, 33, 37, 38, 47–52, 54, 57, 58, 60, 62, 70, 81, 83–85, 91, 95, 96, 101, 114, 122, 145, 147, 149, 152, 156, 157, 160, 197, 211, 217, 231, 237, 268, 281, 300, 301, 304, 311, 312, 323, 324, 317, 329, 332; medical experiments, 50–51; return to, 318–19; Rosh Hashanah in, 180–83. *See also* gas chambers

babies, 112–18
Bacskai, 282
bartering, 99–101. *See also* cigarettes
Bauer, Rozsi, 229, 248
Bauer, Yehuda, 231
Bergen-Belsen, 15, 27, 43, 49, 51–54, 56–57, 59–61, 50, 85, 89, 91, 117, 118, 149, 152, 157, 176, 219, 314; Yom Kippur in, 184.
Berk, Veronica Lorant, 200
Birgel, 165
Biro, Erzsébet (prisoner, born in New York), 57
Blau, Adrienne, 208
Blockälteste, 63, 64, 91, 94, 96, 106–8, 112–15, 129, 148, 150, 167, 181, 182, 213; Fajgi, 107; Laju/Lajcsu Friedman, 64, 76, 94, 107, 185, 232; Márta Maget Leitmann, 107, 113, 169, 175, 235, 250, 251, 254, 286; Piri (Piroska Weisz Balek), 107
bonding (emotional), 143–44
Boriska (Szász family housekeeper), 44, 128, 291
Barun, Carmen, 239
Breiner, Ilana Sajovits, 57, 128, 135, 168, 200, 212, 286–87
Breiner, Sara, 135, 163, 164
bromide, 121–22
Brown, Lea Kaff, 205
Buchenwald, 16, 20, 32, 112, 122, 170, 211, 228, 231; subcamps, *32.* See also *Forgotten Women of Buchenwald, The*
Budapest, 289, 291–94
bunker: prison cells, 172–73; punishment, 173–74

camp-families, 17, 144–47; birthdays, 147–49
camp-sisters, 17, 144–45
Carmi, Miriam Hartmann, 59, 62, 146, 323
Cayrol, Jean, 300

chocolate factory, the former, 217, *218,* 219. *See also* Junkers Flugzeug und Motorenwerke
cigarettes, 96–97, 205–6
Clajus, Irma, 15–16, 173, 322
cleanliness/grooming, 79–84, 141, 154, 192
clothing, 80–81, 83, 84, 86, 98–100, 105–6, 286–87
cold, 87–89. *See also* Death March/liberation
compensations, 316–18
concentration camps, 29, 31, 32, 126, 143–45, 192, 280, 281. *See also* forced labor/laborers; individual camps
cooking/recipes, 152–53
coping. *See* cooking/recipes, cultural activities, songs/poems.
crowding/lack of privacy, 86–88
Csanyi, Zsuzsanna, 61, 64, 106, 230, 236
cultural activities/holidays, 117, 134, 176–93, 309–10. *See also* songs/poems
cultural differences, 149–50
Cyprus, 297
Czikk, Ella, 163
Czitter, Eva, 158, 201, 204

Dachau, 217
Davis, Rose Hoffman, 182, 250, 251, 262
death/burial, 101–2
Death March/liberation, 19–20, 59, 72, 83, 96, 112, 120, 122, 140, 157, 161, 164, 165, 197, 203, 204, 207, 208, 211–14, 231–47, 272–88, 295; air raids, 246–49, 251–52
Deutsch, Klára Frenkel, 198
Deutsch, Olga, 275–76
Deutsch, Vera De Vit, 229
Deutsche Bank, 123–24
Dicker, Erzsébet, Markovics, 54
Dresden, 158, 261
Dresdner Bank, 123–24
Dressler, Dr., 172
Dunant, Paul, 281
Dupré, Marguerite Mimeur, 211, 321

Ehrenreich, Irena Lebovits, 113, 140–41, 163, 199, 276, 308
Eichler, Eva Rosenberg, 43, 59, 62, 145, 146, 276
Eichmann, Adolf, 27, 41, 281, 307
Eidinger, Alfred, 216–17
Eisdorfer, Olga, 163
Eisert, Bruno, 99, 270, 322
Electrocommandos, 201–2, 204
Elias, Dr. Szerén, 111–13, 251
Engel, Elizabeth Winkler, 152, 185
Esskomandos, 93–95, 150, 246

Falkenberg, Anneiles, 191
family ties, 147–49
Fellmann, Márta, 247, 248
Ferencz, Benjamin B., 101
Fine, Lenke Schwarz, 91, 146, 157
Fischer, Magda Polatsek, 204
Fisher, Sarah Mayer, 285
Flames at Auschwitz, The, 300–301
Flesch, Jolán, 223, 224
Fleury, Jacqueline, 212, 321, 323
food/hunger, 89–97, 100, 256–60. *See also* Death March/liberation
forced labor/laborers, 26–30; sub-camps, 32; women's work at, 31–32. *See also* concentration camps; Junkers Flugzeug und Motorenwerke
foreign workers, 200. *See also* French women prisoners; German civilian workers
Forgotten Women of Buchenwald, The, 329
Frank, Anne, 55
Frank, Erzsébet, 34, 93, 100, 119, 131, 134, 151, 154–55, 162, 206–8, 234, 238; *365 Days,* 177–78
Frankl, Tereza, 97–98, 178, 193, 198, 205
Frankl, Viktor, 96
French women prisoners, 19, 20, 210–14, 253–54, 280
Friedenberg, Ilonka Kohn, 304
Friedman, Blanka Schwarz, 91, 157
Friedman, Erzsébet, 223, 232, 265. *See also* Friedmann, Rebbetzin
Friedman, Rezső, 148
Friedmann, Rebbetzin, 185, 259

Gabori, Ibolya Kail, 128, 155, 178
Gallo, Katalin Frank, 131
Garin, Raymonde, 211, 233
gas chambers, (Auschwitz-Birkenau), 27, 300; poem about, 300–301
Geiger, Hanni Markovics, *31,* 40, 46, 289, 292, 312–13
gendarmerie/Hungarian, 250
German civilian workers, 194–200

German population, 274–76; reaction to Death March, 261–62
German war industry. *See* forced labor/laborers
ghettos, 45–47. *See also* Kosice/Kassa
Gilbert, Anne Spitz, 104
Ginsburg, Amir, 307, *404*
Ginsburg, Baruch, *299,* 299
Ginsburg, Hava. *See* Szász, Erzsébet (Erzsike)
Glatstein, Ilona Eisler, 232
Goertler, Willy, 239
Goldring, Flora Kaff, 94–95, 138–39, 186
Goldstein, Kathy Zelmanovitz, *34,* 260, 328
Goral, Nelly Wexler, *396*
Grodan, Jolka Goldstein, 114, 115, 258, 270
Gross, Miriam, 163
Grosz, Szerén, 267–69, 283, 284, 287
Grosz, Zsuzsa, 267–69, 284
Guenter, Hans, 201, 229

Hadnagy, Teréz Stern, 162, 184
Hamer, Adel, 21
handicrafts. *See* jewelry
health/illness, 51, 53–54, 104, 111–12, 119–22, 172, 285–86, 305. *See also* Landes Institute; Red Cross; *Revier*
Heftziba (Kibbutz), 298
Heimlich, Gabriella Klein, 92, 114, 210
Herskovitz, Mrs. Ethel, 17
Hess, Rudolf, 25, 160
Heydrich, Reinhard, 27
Hezbollah, 332
Hïlf, Magda Schön, 49, 145, 164–65, 247–48, 302
Himmler, Heinrich, 231, 280
Hitler, Adolf, 159, 219, 225
Hitler Youth/*Hitler-Jugend,* 219–21, 262
Höhn, Andreas, 25, 321, 329–30
Holl, Gertrud, 158
Hollander, Gizella, 239
Holocaust, 305–7; memorials, 332. *See also* 9/11, surviving
Holzer, Erzsébet, 277
homosexuality/lesbianism, 76, 174–75
Horthy, Miklos, 41
Hönig, Gitta Susitzky, 83, 135, 170, 239, *396*
Hungarian Jews/Jewish labor, 30–31, 35, 40–57; attitudes towards, 40–41; relocation, 41–42; selection of workers, 37–38. *See also* individual names
Hungary: Abaújszántó, 42–47, 61, 62, 291, 293–95, 304, 309, 312; cemetery in, 313–16; ghettos in, 45–47; homecoming, 290–91. *See also* Budapest

Iczkovits, Erzsébet (work organizer), 61, 65, 68, 70, 72, 73, 76, 105, 146, 236, 302. *See also* Lanyi, Agnes Iczkovits
IG Farben trial, 127
illicit possessions, 92–93, 97–99
Indersdorf, 296
information sources, 157–59. *See also* ladies room
Israel, Sarah Salomon, 130, 138, 184, 273, *397*

Jantzsech, Mrs., 109
jewelry, 203–5; rings, *203,* 205. *See also* bartering
Jewish functionaries, 100–107, 302–3. *See also* Iczkovits, Erzsébet
Jewish property, 291–92
John, Ernst, 211
Joint, the, 278, 284, 296
Junkers Flugzeug und Motorenwerke A.G., 19, 25–26, 28, 29, 31, 35, 62, 123–41, *125, 131, 218,* 230, 326; factory, 36, 127–41, 215–16, 223–24, 228–30; wages and profits, 126–27. *See also* chocolate factory; Zwenkau
Junkers, Hugo, 36
Jürss, Ulla, 166

Kahan, Regina, 286
Kaufman, Elena Salamon, 135
Kaufman, Ibolya Wollner, 263, 283
Kaufman, Marie Politzer, 145, 156
Keisler, Klára, 74
Kertész, Imre, 192
Kirsenbaum, Miriam Liberman, 170, 250, 255
Klein, Agata Trattner, 200
Klein, Rózsi Markovics, 40, 46
Kleinberg, Hava Hartmann, 15, *34,* 46, 59, 62, 126, 146, 255, 270, 321–23, 328
Kleinova, Lili Klein, 40, 46
Klose, Dr. Bernd, 307, 321–23, 327, 331

Kluska, Dora, 163, 242
Knittel, Alois (slave labor camp commander), 18, 35, 58–64, 71–75, 79–80, 82, 86, 87, 93, 97–99, 104–6, 108, 109, 111, 112, 114, 115, 120, 138–41, 154–56, 162–64, 172, 175, 184, 187, 189–92, 201, 205, 220, 228–31, 233, 235, 236, 238, 243, 236, 247–49, 253, 257–60, 265, 280; song for his wedding anniversary, 154–56
Knittel, Kurt, 163
Knittel, Mrs., 74, 157, 164, 233, 236, 249, 280
Kogel, Olga Markovics, 311–12
Kogon, Eugen, 144
Koppenberg, Heinrich, 123
Kornagel, Piroska, 307
Kosice/Kassa, 40–47, 280, 292
Kosinka, Gabriella Braver, 167–69, 201, 202, 229–30, 246, 262, *399*
Kramer, Josef, 52
Krausz, Vera, 54, 55, 237
Krausz, Márta, 43, 54–56, *56,* 286, 313–14
Krupp trial, 127
Kulcsar, Eva Székely, 114–16. *See also* babies

ladies room, the, 222–23
Lagerälteste, 97, 103–5, 108, 129, 146. *See also* Spitz, Bella
lager-sisters. *See* camp-sisters
Landes Institute, 280, 292–93, 303
*Lanegev,*296–97
language of death, 48
Lanyi, Agnes Iczkovits, 105, 236, 302–3
Lazar, Rosalia, 75, 242
Lebovits, Jolán, 113
Leipzig, 25, 111, 215, 321, 223, 224, 227, 234, 239, 240, 328, 232
leisure time, 77–78. *See also* songs/poems
Lesem, Lea Keri, 219, 220, 222
Levi, Naomi Cohen, 328
Levy, Ella-Tzofhia, 311
Levy, Israel-Dov, 308–9, *405*
Levy, Rachel-Yarin, 45, *407*
Levy, Yonit, 44. *See also* Stessel, Yonit
Liberation, 272–88. *See also* Terezin
Lindbergh, Charles, 123
Linder, Hajnal and Lenke, 216, 279
Lindenfeld, Laura, 109, 163
Lófogú, 66–72, 165, 277
Lörinch, Margit and Isabella, 53, 55, 70, 71
Lubera, Josef, 201

Mark, Jonathan, 331
Markkleeberg camp, 18–20, 25–39, *29,* 57, 58, 60–65, *60,* 79–102, 75, 239–41, 316; barracks, 74–78; camp hierarchy, 161–71; evacuation of, 231–34; first transport, 58–59; fourth transport, 59–60, 63; internal operation, 73–74; memorial at, 322–26; physical description, 33–35; prisoner/transport list, 20–21, 38–39, 334–70; second transport, 59; SS guards, 164–65; third transport, 59–60
Markkleeberg town, *33,* 110, 326–27, 329–30
Markovitz, Meny, 312
Mauthausen concentration camp, 41
Méhes, Erzsébet, 104–5
Mengele, Dr. Josef, 16–17, 49
menstruation, 121–22. *See also* bromide
Mermel, Elizabeth Zucker, 132, 207–8, 234, 277–79
Messerschmitt, 326
Mikéfe, 293–94
Mittelman, Rachael Janovics, 135, 158, 186, 198, 233, 250
Mocige, Henri and Schola, 321
Müler, Evelin, 321

Nazi Party/Nazism, 18, 160, 322
Neuman, Klára Fisher, 135, 250, 272
Night and Fog, 300
9/11, 331, 332

Oren, Klára Roth, 20, 122, 133, 140

Paran, Márta Weisz, 43, 59, 61, 62, 69, 145, 186, 236, 257–58, 270
Petőfi, Sándor, 178
Pick, Teresa Keiszer, 312
Pincsefski, Regina Farkas, 107, 273
Plaszow, 57
Pohl, Gen. Oswald, 30
Pollack, Márta Groszman, 270
Porat, Miriam, 73, 254
Pöschel, Helene. See *Aufseherins:* Lucifer
Prévost, Fernande, 211–12
Profits from slave-labor. *See* Junkers Flugzeug und Motorenwerke, WVHA

quarry, the, 65–71. *See also* Lófogú

Rabinovics, Agnes Glück, 46, 198, 275
Rambam hospital, Haifa, 299
Ravensbrück, 166, 211
Red Cross, 18, 212, 247, 280, 281, 304
Reinitz, József, 292–93
Reinitz, Rózsi, 292–93
Reisensohn, Johann, 165
"Remembrance, Responsibility, and the Future," 317. *See also* compensations
religion, 309–11, morning prayer, 128
resistance, 143–59. *See also* cultural activities/holidays; songs/poems
Resnais, Alain, 300
revenge, 287–88
Revier, 69, 88, 94, 106, 108, 111–5, 117, 118, 122, 147, 191, 192, 196, 197, 202, 211, 227, 232, 233, 236, 237, 251
Rochlitz, Nelly Winkler, 95, 105, 170, 211, 212, 217, 220–25, 227, 233, 252–53, 276, 283, 330, *401*
roll call, 107–11
Roosevelt, F. D., 159
Rosenberg, Judith, 43, 62
Rosenberg, Lenke Schlesinger, 148, 185
Rosenberg, Olga, 128, 234
Rosenberg, Seren, 163
Roth, Erzsébet, 122
Roth, Frida Kaller, 37, 280. *See also* selection
Roth, Ilona, 43, 145–46, 276
Rötzscher, Mrs. Erna, 109
Rudolf-Hildebrand High School, 328
Russian soldiers, 274–75; Jewish Russian soldiers, 275–76

sabotage. *See* French women prisoners
Saidel, Rochelle, 152
Sajovits, Sara, 164
Sátoraljaujhely, 44
Schelder, Philip, 223
Schiffmann, Veronika, 162–63
Schnur, Irene Keisler, 74, 109, 118, 119, 229, 230
Schulze, Paul, 169
Schwarz, Hermina, 223
sedatives. *See* bromide
Seidel, Dr. Irmgard, 16, 231, 329
Seidner, Blanka, 260, 281
Seidner, Edit, 281
selection, 55–56
Shahar, Zeev, 293–94
Shenkar, Joshua, *409*
Shenkar, Keshet, 300–301, *408*
Shenkar, Miriam Stessel. *See* Stessel, Miriam
Shenkar, Rakefet, *410*
Shindler, Anne Székely, 162, 185
Slyomovics, Vera Hollander, 239
Snitzler, Klára Spitz, 46, 59, 62, 69, 80, 92, 105, 132–34, 145, 153, 158, 159, 204, 232, 257, 275–76
songs/poems, 17, 22, 41, 62, 69, 72, 81, 82, 91, 108, 116–17, 134, 136, 140, 143, 154–55, 157, 164–65, 176–78, 185, 187, 189, 206–7, 290, 300–301, 333, 386–93; "The Welders," 206–7; Zionist, 179, 183
Spielmann, Dr. Rachel, 162, 173, 195, 239–41
Spitz, Bella, 61–64, 71, 73, 76, 97, 104, 105, 146, 170, 201, 205, 251, 265. *See also* Gilbert, Anne Spitz
SS, the, 160–75, 191, 195, 198, 199, 223, 227, 229–31, 233, 234, 236, 239, 242, 244, 248, 250, 251, 253, 258–62, 264, 266, 269–70
Stark, Barbara Klein, 49, 135, 145, 200, 212
Stein, Margit Lang, 46, 62, 145, 236, 270
Sternberg, Lucy, 114–18
Sternberg, Tibor, 115, 118
Sternberger, Gizella, 55, 234
Stessel, Meier, 216–17, 299, *299*
Stessel, Miriam, 216–17, 298, *298,* 300, 302, 305, 315, *398, 403*
Stessel, Yonit, *45,* 305, 311, 333, *395*
surviving, 289–319
Szamosi, Elza Reich, 43, 59, 61, 80. 139, 146, 219, 221–22, 227, 238, 247, 255, 257, 287, *400*
Szász, Erzsébet (Erzsike), 15, 17, 19, 24, 38, 42, 43, 49–51, 53–56, 59, 61, 62, 64, 66, 67, 69–73, 77, 79–82, 85–87, 89, 90, 92, 94, 96, 98, 100, 104, 105, 111 120, 127, 129, 133–35, 137, 139, 144, 147–49, 153, 176, 179–86, 188, 190, 192, 194–97, 200, 202–4, 213, 226, 228–30, 232–37, 242, 245, 247, 249, 251–52, 254–55, 257–60, 265–70, 272–73, 283, 287–89, 291, 292, 298–300, 305–6, 311, 321, 324, *325,* 329; in the Israeli war of 2006, 332; patient in *revier,* 193

Szász, Katalin, 15
Szász, Miriam-Mariska Markovics, 43, *43,* 47, 49, 182, 184, 291, 292; songs of, 178–79
Szász, Mór , 314
Szász, Nathan (grandfather), 42, 43, 44, 49–51, 157, 294, 300
Szász, Róza-Rachel, Reinitz (grandmother), 43, 44, 47, 48, 49, 51, 309, 314
Szász, Sándor, 42, 43, *43,* 44, 49–51, 285, 290, 291, 304
Székely, Elisabeth Stein, 37, 85, 121, 131, 152, 165, 195, 197, 198, 213, 242, 282
Szerén, 50, 51

Tac, Nechama, 16, 143
Teichgraber, Elza, 222
Terezin, 279–82; prisoners at, 371–85
365 Days: Testimony form Hell's Inferno (Frank), 177–78
Török, Zsofia Gottlieb, 202, 209, 210, 252
translators, 69–70. *See also* quarry
Transylvania, 41–42, 47, 57, 302
Treblinka, 27

United Nations, 332
Urai, Zsuzsanna Lengyel, 164, 189

Vesely, Agnes Kivovits, 199
von Staden, Wendelgard, 261
Volksdeutsche. *See* SS, the

Wagner, Franz, 165
Waldman, Erzsébet, 215, 279
Waldman, Jolán, 279
Waldman, Lilly, 35, 213, 215–16, 279
Walter, Johanes, 100
Wannsee Conference, the, 27–28
washrooms, 77
Weinberger, Ingelborg, 25
Weiss, Angyel Fischer, 181, 327
Weiss, Anna Klein, 117, 195
Weisz, Edit, 118, 281
Welisch, Edit, 258
Wellisch, Ilonka, 258
Wiegand (camp commander), 35, 158, 161, 169, 202
Wilhelm, Adela, 193
Wilhelm, Irma, 193
Winkler, Andor, 277, 330
Winkler, Hajnal, 227, 233, 252, 253, 276, *401*
Winkler, Piroska, 242
Winkler, Rozsa, 211, 227, 232–33, 252–53, 276–77, *401;* search for her grave, 329–30
Wolfswinkel. *See* Markkleeberg camp
Work accidents, 223, 224
World War II, 31–33
WVHA, 29–33, 126. *See also* Pohl, Gen. Oswald

Yaskovitz, Lee Katz, 119, 219–21

Zionism, 293, 297, 299. *See also* songs/poems
Zissin, Dr. Rika, 321, 323
Zolf, Rachel Berkovics, 150, 162
Zwenkau, 215–17